PAGES PACKED WITH ESSENTIAL INFORMATION

"Value-packed, unbeatable, accurate, and comprehensive."

—*The Los Angeles Times*

"The guides are aimed not only at young budget travelers but at the independent traveler; a sort of streetwise cookbook for traveling alone."

—*The New York Times*

"Unbeatable; good sight-seeing advice; up-to-date info on restaurants, hotels, and inns; a commitment to money-saving travel; and a wry style that brightens nearly every page."

—*The Washington Post*

THE BEST TRAVEL BARGAINS IN YOUR BUDGET

"All the dirt, dirt cheap."

—*People*

"Let's Go follows the creed that you don't have to toss your life's savings to the wind to travel—unless you want to."

—*The Salt Lake Tribune*

REAL ADVICE FOR REAL EXPERIENCES

"The writers seem to have experienced every rooster-packed bus and lunar-surfaced mattress about which they write."

—*The New York Times*

"[Let's Go's] devoted updaters really walk the walk (and thumb the ride, and trek the trail). Learn how to fish, haggle, find work—anywhere."

—*Food & Wine*

"A world-wise traveling companion—always ready with friendly advice and helpful hints, all sprinkled with a bit of wit."

—*The Philadelphia Inquirer*

A GUIDE WITH A SPIRIT AND A SOCIAL CONSCIENCE

"Lighthearted and sophisticated, informative and fun to read. [Let's Go] helps the novice traveler navigate like a knowledgeable old hand."

—*Atlanta Journal-Constitution*

"The serious mission at the book's core reveals itself in exhortations to respect the culture and the environment—and, if possible, to visit as a volunteer, a student, or a teacher rather than a tourist."

—*San Francisco Chronicle*

LET'S GO PUBLICATIONS

TRAVEL GUIDES

Australia
Austria & Switzerland
Brazil
Britain
California
Central America
Chile
China
Costa Rica
Costa Rica, Nicaragua & Panama
Eastern Europe
Ecuador
Egypt
Europe
France
Germany
Greece
Guatemala & Belize
Hawaii
India & Nepal
Ireland
Israel
Italy
Japan
Mexico
New Zealand
Peru
Puerto Rico
Southeast Asia
Spain & Portugal with Morocco
Thailand
USA
Vietnam
Western Europe
Yucatán Peninsula

ROADTRIP GUIDE

Roadtripping USA

ADVENTURE GUIDES

Alaska
Pacific Northwest
Southwest USA

CITY GUIDES

Amsterdam
Barcelona
Berlin, Prague & Budapest
Boston
Buenos Aires
Florence
London
London, Oxford, Cambridge & Edinburgh
New York City
Paris
Rome
San Francisco
Washington, DC

POCKET CITY GUIDES

Amsterdam
Berlin
Boston
Chicago
London
New York City
Paris
San Francisco
Venice
Washington, DC

LET'S GO
COSTA RICA

JULIA C. GOLDENHEIM BOOK EDITOR
EVELYN Z. HSIEH ASSOCIATE EDITOR

RESEARCHER-WRITERS
NADIA MOHAMEDI
ANNE MONTGOMERY
TYLER D. SIPPRELLE
ALISON TARWATER

REBECCA BARTLETT SMITH MAP EDITOR
PATRICK McKIERNAN MANAGING EDITOR

EDITORS
COURTNEY A. FISKE   RUSSELL FORD RENNIE
CHARLIE E. RIGGS   SARA PLANA
OLGA I. ZHULINA

HOW TO USE THIS BOOK

COVERAGE LAYOUT. The guide begins with a look at Costa Rica's capital, **San José** (p. 83), showing you how to get the most out of this oft-overlooked metropolis before you leave for more scenic destinations. From there coverage explores the **Central Valley** (p. 102), and continues counter-clockwise across the entire country. From the ecologically diverse **Northern Lowlands** (p. 145), it proceeds to the cloud forests and cowboy towns of the **Northwest** (p. 178) before surveying the gorgeous beaches and world-class surf spots on the **Nicoya Peninsula** (p. 209). It then continues south through the postcard beaches of the **Central Pacific Coast** (p. 266) before introducing Costa Rica's final frontier, the largely unexplored **Osa Peninsula** (p. 329) and crossing over to the **Caribbean Lowlands** (p. 353) on Costa Rica's Atlantic seaboard.

TRANSPORTATION INFO. Transportation is generally listed under the departure city. Connections can be tricky, so it's worth confirming them in advance when planning your trip. Parentheticals provide the trip duration, followed by frequency, then price. For more information on getting around and getting by in general, check out the **Essentials** chapter (p. 9).

COVERING THE BASICS. The first chapter, **Disocver Costa Rica** (p. 1), contains highlights from coast to coast, complete with **Suggested Itineraries** that include some of Costa Rica's most popular destinations. Take some time to peruse the **Life and Times** (p. 44) chapter, which includes summaries of the history, culture, and customs of the country. Check out the **Great Outdoors** (p. 70) chapter for all the information you need on camping, hiking, adventure tours, and exploring Costa Rica's diverse ecosystems. The **Appendix** (p. 402) has information on climate, a list of holidays, conversions, and a Spanish glossary. For study abroad, ecotourism, volunteer, and work options in Costa Rica, the **Beyond Tourism** chapter (p. 60) is all you need.

PRICE DIVERSITY. Establishments are listed in order of value from best to worst, with favorites designated by the *Let's Go* thumbs-up (🖐). Many establishments in Costa Rica accept US$ in addition to the native *colón*. We have made note of locations where both currencices are accepted (US$/¢).

PHONE CODES AND TELEPHONE NUMBERS. 506 is the area code for all of Costa Rica, but when calling within the country, it is not necessary to use this number. Phone numbers are all preceeded by the ☎ icon.

A NOTE TO OUR READERS. The information for this book was gathered by Let's Go researchers from May 2008 through August 2009. Each listing is based on one researcher's opinion, formed during his or her visit at a particular time. Those traveling at other times may have different experiences since prices, dates, hours, and conditions are always subject to change. You are urged to check the facts presented in this book beforehand to avoid inconvenience and surprises.

ABOUT LET'S GO

THE STUDENT TRAVEL GUIDE

Let's Go publishes the world's favorite student travel guides, written entirely by Harvard students. Armed with pens, notebooks, and a few changes of clothes stuffed into their backpacks, our student researchers go across continents, through time zones, and above expectations to seek out invaluable travel experiences for our readers. Because we are a completely student-run company, we have a unique perspective on how students travel, where they want to go, and what they're looking to do when they get there. If your dream is to grab a machete and forge through the jungles of Costa Rica, we can take you there. If you'd rather bask in the Riviera sun at a beachside cafe, we'll set you a table. In short, we write for readers who know that there's more to travel than tour buses. To keep up, visit our website, www.letsgo.com, where you can sign up to blog, post photos from your trips, and connect with the Let's Go community.

TRAVELING BEYOND TOURISM

We're on a mission to provide our readers with sharp, fresh coverage packed with socially responsible opportunities to go beyond tourism. Each guide's Beyond Tourism chapter shares ideas about responsible travel, study abroad, and how to give back to the places you visit while on the road. To help you gain a deeper connection with the places you travel, our fearless researchers scour the globe to give you the heads-up on both world-renowned and off-the-beaten-track opportunities. We've also opened our pages to respected writers and scholars to hear their takes on the countries and regions we cover, and asked travelers who have worked, studied, or volunteered abroad to contribute first-person accounts of their experiences.

FIFTY YEARS OF WISDOM

Let's Go has been on the road for 50 years and counting. We've grown a lot since publishing our first 20-page pamphlet to Europe in 1960, but five decades and 54 titles later our witty, candid guides are still researched and written entirely by students on shoestring budgets who know that train strikes, stolen luggage, food poisoning, and marriage proposals are all part of a day's work. This year, for our 50th anniversary, we're publishing 26 titles—including 6 brand new guides—brimming with editorial honesty, a commitment to students, and our irreverent style. Here's to the next 50!

THE LET'S GO COMMUNITY

More than just a travel guide company, Let's Go is a community that reaches from our headquarters in Cambridge, MA all across the globe. Our small staff of dedicated student editors, writers, and tech nerds comes together because of our shared passion for travel and our desire to help other travelers get the most out of their experience. We love it when our readers become part of the Let's Go community as well—when you travel, drop us a postcard (67 Mt. Auburn St., Cambridge, MA 02138, USA), send us an e-mail (feedback@letsgo.com), or sign up on our website (www.letsgo.com) to tell us about your adventures and discoveries.

For more information, updated travel coverage, and news from our researcher team, visit us online at www.letsgo.com.

CONTENTS

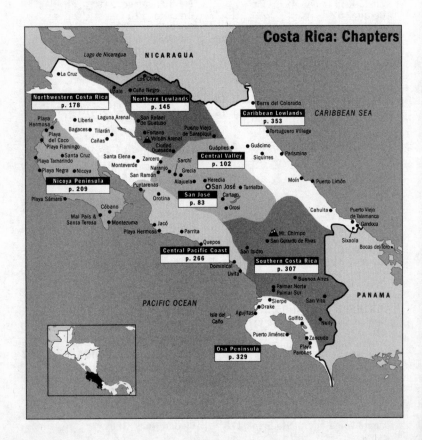

RESEARCHERS

Nadia Mohamedi   *Northwestern Costa Rica, Nicoya Peninsula*

Nadia hit the beach and didn't let anything get in her way. She strode over every bump in the road with a cool and collected attitude (and her short board, of course). She ate only the best *gallo pinto* and still had time to find the coolest hostels, bars, and hang-outs all along the Nicoya Peninsula. The fun she had and the hard work she put in shines through in her creative, energetic, and funny copy.

Anne Montgomery   *S. Costa Rica, Osa Peninsula, Central Pacific*

Hailing from Fayetteville, Arkansas, intrepid Anne navigated Costa Rica's bus system—and jungles—to bring us the low-down even in high places (like Mt. Chirripo). While she prefers crawfish pie and tira-misu, she tasted countless *casados* for the good of tourist stomachs everywhere. Anne always turned in top-notch work and kept calm, even when snakes decided to keep her company in her hostel room.

Tyler D. Sipprelle   *San José, Central Valley, Nicoya Peninsula*

Tyler hit the streets of San José and soon discovered that Costa Rican cuisine, while tasty, was not his cup of tea. Thus, he sought out all the Italian, Israeli, and sushi restau-rants within a 20 mi. radius of his hostel, and hungry budget travelers will thank him for it. Appetite sated, Tyler went through his route with a laid-back attitude and turned in insightful, interesting copy along the way.

Alison Tarwater   *Northern Lowlands, Caribbean Lowlands*

Alison jumped right into her route and managed to conquer the roads of Costa Rica in her 2WD car. She always scoped out the best budget options and found the highest-qual-ity (and lowest-cost) establishments wherever she went. Never flustered, always tough, she dealt with the trials of the road with excitement and determination, producing honest, clean copy that was all her own.

Maryam Janani   *Costa Rica*

This neurobio major from San Antonio spent much of her time in Costa Rica trying to avoid overly forward men, and the rest of it keeping her distance from, as she puts it, Costa Rica's "animal-infested rainforest." Her attention to detail made for meticulous coverage, but she still managed to have some fun—going ziplining and bungee jumping in her free time, making those of us in the office green with envy.

CONTRIBUTING WRITER

Timothy Josiah Pertz is a Special Assistant to Costa Rica's President Oscar Arias for English Communications. He graduated from Harvard in 2005 with a degree in History and Literature and was a Researcher-Writer for *Let's Go Central America* (2003) in Guatemala.

ACKNOWLEDGMENTS

TEAM COSTA RICA THANKS: Pat for making everything Sweet-O. Jessie, for her tasty treats. RWs, for living in the rain with a smile. Becca, for her patience and making CORI a navigation nation. And Pandora, for opening her music box, so we didn't have to work in *silencio*.

JULIA THANKS: Evelyn, for letting me misspell accommodations in every copybatch and showing me the wonderful world of chocolate-covered, peanut-butter-filled pretzels. Jessie, for living with the CORI stress, and for piña coladas, car rides, and peanut butter and jelly sandwiches. Pat, for the bestowment of presents and Baller Status. Becca, for hugs and knowing the things about Costa Rica that I didn't. My family for letting me stress about deadlines for six months and always calming me down.

EVELYN THANKS: Julia, for the snack drawer, elite cookies, and empathetic passive aggressive music-choice Gchats. Jessie, for defining generosity. Both, for being the best editors one could ask for. Anne, for being the hardest worker ever. Pat, for "making it rain." Becca, for making maps clear to a map noob. Annie, for dinner during that one long day. Mom, Dad, Stoofus for Hsiehmeless love. Ms. Chu and Ms. Yang for support, spice, patience, and prayer.

BECCA THANKS: Julia and Evelyn, for being awesome. Anne, Tyler, Nadia, and Alison, for your details of marriage proposals, summit attempts, *tico* rodeos, and endless edits. Derek, for putting up with us, wearing shorts, and inviting Prince to Mapland. Gretch, for the sound effects, 3:30pm giggles, and your penny jar. Elissa, for being a gcal wizard and my music soulmate. Illiana, for my camp counselor title. Prince, for keeping it real, gracing our couch, and giving us a reason to "bump that."

Book Editor
Julia C. Goldenheim
Associate Editor
Evelyn Z. Hsieh
Managing Editor
Patrick McKiernan
Map Editor
Rebecca Bartlett Smith
Typesetter
Rebecca Lieberman

LET'S GO

Publishing Director
Laura M. Gordon
Editorial Director
Dwight Livingstone Curtis
Publicity and Marketing Director
Vanessa J. Dube
Production and Design Director
Rebecca Lieberman
Cartography Director
Anthony Rotio
Website Director
Lukáš Tóth
Managing Editors
Ashley Laporte, Iya Megre,
Mary Potter, Nathaniel Rakich
Technology Project Manager
C. Alexander Tremblay
Director of IT
David Fulton-Howard
Financial Associates
Catherine Humphreville, Jun Li

President
Daniel Lee
General Manager
Jim McKellar

PRICE RANGES ❸ ❹
❶❷ COSTA RICA ❺

Our researchers list establishments in order of value from best to worst, honoring our favorites with the Let's Go thumbs-up (🖐). Because the best *value* is not always the cheapest *price*, we have incorporated a system of price ranges based on a rough expectation of what you will spend. For **accommodations,** we base our range on the cheapest price for which a single traveler can stay for one night. For **restaurants** and, we estimate the average amount one traveler will spend in one sitting. The table below tells you what you'll *typically* find in Costa Rica at the corresponding price range, but keep in mind that no system can allow for the quirks of individual establishments.

ACCOMMODATIONS	RANGE	WHAT YOU'RE *LIKELY* TO FIND
❶	Under 7300 (Under US$14)	Campgrounds, dorm rooms, and very rustic cabinas. Expect bunk beds and a communal bath. You may have to bring your own or rent towels and sheets.
❷	₡7301-13,500 (US$14-26)	Upscale hostels, small hotels, and *cabinas.* You may have a private bathroom with cold or warm water, or a sink in your room and a communal shower in the hall. Most include fans and TVs.
❸	₡13,501-26,500 (US$26-51)	A small room with a private hot-water bath or a cabina with a full kitchen. Should have decent amenities, such as phone, A/C, and TV. Breakfast may be included in the price of the room.
❹	₡26,501-41,600 (US$51-80)	Similar to a ❸, with more amenities or a more convenient location.
❺	Over ₡41,600 (Over US$80)	Large hotels, lodges, or upscale chains, usually found in heavily touristed areas. If it's a ❺ and it doesn't have the perks you want, you've paid too much.

FOOD	RANGE	WHAT YOU'RE *LIKELY* TO FIND
❶	Under ₡3150 (Under US$6)	Mostly *sodas* serving inexpensive *comida típica*, street food, or fast-food, but also university cafeterias and bakeries. Usually takeout, but sometimes limited seating is available.
❷	₡3151-5700 (US$6-11)	Some high end *sodas*, sandwiches, pizza, appetizers at a bar, or low-priced entrees. Most ethnic eateries are a ❷. Either takeout or a sit-down meal, but only slightly fashionable decor.
❸	₡5701-9900 (US$11-19)	Mid-priced entrees, seafood, and exotic pasta dishes. A bit more expensive, but chances are you're paying for a change from comida típica. More upscale ethnic eateries. Since you'll have the luxury of a waiter, tip will set you back a little extra.
❹	₡9901-13,000 (US$19-25)	A somewhat fancy restaurant. Entrees may be heartier or more elaborate, but you're really paying for decor and ambience. Few restaurants in this range have a dress code, but some may look down on T-shirts and sandals. These places tend to be in more-touristed areas.
❺	Over ₡13,000 (Over US$25)	Your meal might cost more than your room, but there's a reason—it's something fabulous, famous, or both. Expect delicious food with great service and a spectacular view. Otherwise, you're paying for nothing more than hype. Don't order a PB&J!

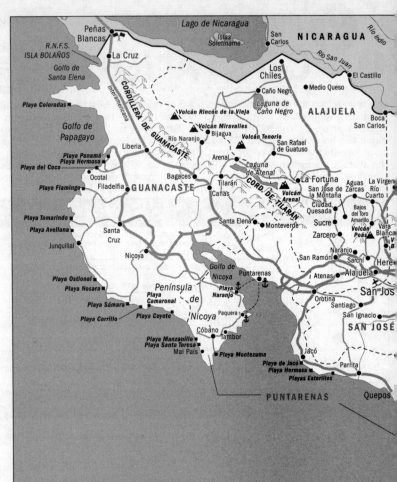

Costa Rica

DISCOVER COSTA RICA

The Spanish explorers who first arrived at this "rich coast" in 1502 named the region for the decorative gold bands worn by its native inhabitants and for the fortunes they hoped to attain there. Despite this optimistic viewpoint, later explorers found themselves unable to discover gold—or material riches of any sort—anywhere along the coast. Indeed, the country's only riches seemed to be its endless armies of mosquitoes and its unforgiving jungles, neither of which colonial settlers found in short supply. These days, however, most visitors to Costa Rica would probably attest that its initial name was not such a misnomer after all. Its well-oiled tourist industry is only too happy to recount the country's impressive statistics: though it covers only 0.03% of the world's territory, Costa Rica is home to 6% of its plant and animal species. Much of this 6% is out in full pageantry, and Costa Rica's native sons will show you the marvels of natural selection proving and amusing itself—from camouflaged vine snakes to Jesucristo lizards that "walk on water" in fantastic 50 yd. dashes. Many Costa Rican creatures come off as performers, and there is something decidedly exhibitionist about their homeland as well. The terrain seems to include all possible landforms: volcanoes, jungles, beaches, coral reefs, hidden caves, and deserted islands all lie within a day's (or even an hour's) travel of one another.

Sometimes it feels like the only thing this country can't offer is a corner that travelers haven't already found and conquered—leaving fusion bistros and high-tech canopy tours in their wake. Fortunately, rustic spots never lie too far from range, and Costa Rica's national character has remained surprisingly visible beneath the trappings of its tourist infrastructure. Though you'll find plenty of *gringos* lounging on the beaches of the Pacific, you'll find vacationing *tico* families enjoying them as well. Their *tico* friendliness only adds to the charm of the country. While Costa Rica might entice you with the convenience and flashy superlatives of its tourism industry, its more informal moments—a sudden jungle rainstorm or an unexpected roadside chat—are those that will probably end up capturing your heart.

WHEN TO GO

Dry or rainy? That's the most important thing to ask when planning a trip to Costa Rica. The rainy season is winter, which generally falls between May and November. The rest of the year, from December to April, makes up the dry season, or *verano* (summer). Asking this question is also a bit of a proxy for asking when the crowds will be most thick. Dry season is the "high season" for tourists, which in most locales translates to more tourists and higher prices. As such, the budget traveler may wish to consider a rainy season visit. Coming during this time can be particularly rewarding—only during the rainy season might you find yourself kayaking between massive mangrove roots during a thunderstorm or experiencing firsthand the dull roar of a downpour against a tin roof. Even during the rainy season, the sun generally shines for much of the day, and most afternoon rainstorms are furious but fleeting. Dry-season travel is only crucial for those in search of dark tans or for those visiting particularly isolated areas, where dirt roads and trails can be washed out for weeks during the rainy season. In addition, if holidays are an important consideration, many of the year's most exciting (and crowded) parties happen during *Semana Santa* (Holy Week during Easter) and from Christmas to the end of the year.

TOP 10 WAYS TO ENJOY LIFE IN THE TREES

In Costa Rica, where the natural landscape and wildlife reigns supreme, there is no way to avoid the trees. Why would you even want to try? From ladder cabins to ziplines, to cool off or to rev up, here are a few of *Let's Go*'s favorite arboreal indulgences.

1. The Original Canopy Tour (p. 269) still perfects what has become known throughout the country as the classic jungle adventure. Fly at high speeds through the trees on massive ziplines between 10 tree-top platforms, and test your courage (again) by rappelling back down.
2. The Rainforest Aerial Tram (p. 356) provides a more sedate ride through the canopy's "broccoli trees" in ski-lift style gondolas.
3. Living up to its name in grand style, the **Treehouse Hotel** near Fortuna (p. 161) offers surprisingly upscale rooms-on-high with wraparound balconies and luxurious double rooms.
4. Cross high above raging river rapids on **El Puente Colgante**, a massive suspension bridge at Centro Neotrópico Sarapiquis, and then descent its spiral staircase to reach crystal-clear natural swimming pools.
5. Lest we forget all the flora and fauna under the sea, the coral reef in **Cahuita** (p. 377) is the largest on the Caribbean coast and pro-

In terms of actual weather, the amount of rain that actually falls during each of these seasons depends largely on geographic location. For example, on the Pacific coast and in the highlands, the dry season can see entire weeks without rainfall. In contrast, on the Caribbean coast, nearly daily rainfall can be expected regardless of season.

Temperature is determined by altitude more than season; the highlands experience moderate highs and pleasant nights while the coastal and jungle lowlands swelter day and night. (For a temperature chart, see **Appendix**, p. 402.)

THINGS TO SEE AND DO

INTO THE WILD

With its mist-shrouded waterfalls, dewy cloud forests, fuming volcanoes, and multi-hued sands, Costa Rica feels like the living product of an overactive (and indecisive) imagination. Its magma craters seem volatile, its shores seductive, its towering trees full of mystery and their massive root mazes born of design and intent. Connecting all the elements of this living system is ecotourism, the lifeblood of Costa Rica's economy, which has managed to simultaneously preserve and profit from the country's many diverse ecosystems. Costa Rica established its national park system in 1970, and by now just over one quarter of its land has been protected by an extensive system of reserves, parks, and refuges throughout the country. These parks (and the many tourism agencies that have sprung up alongside them) cater to every whim and preference—whether you want to calmly stroll along well-maintained trails or muscle and push your way through the underbrush with a machete and a healthy supply of optimism.

Conveniently, none of the country's natural wonders lie too far from the capital city of San José. The **Monteverde Cloud Forest Reserve** (p. 185) is full of thousands of animal, plant, and insect species, which visitors encounter at varying speeds along an extensive network of trails, tree-top bridges, and ziplines. Just a short and scenic bus, boat, and taxi ride away (in that order), enjoy famous hot springs and marvel at active lava flows at **Volcán Arenal** (p. 168), or venture underground to explore 10 stalactite "galleries" at the **Cavernas de Venado** (p. 171) nearby. The slopes of nearby **Volcán Tenorio** (p. 192) are studded with hot springs, rugged craters, sparkling lakes, and surging waterfalls. Farther north, **Parque Nacional Rincón de la Vieja** offers an even more elaborate geothermic variety show, complete with sulfuric lagoons and boiling mud pits. Site of one of the Costa Rican army's first, best, and only victories, **Parque Nacional Santa Rosa** (p. 205) now hosts an enchanting cast of spider and howler monkeys in forests that border miles of secluded beach. The **Nicoya Peninsula** is a mecca for surfers and sun-worshippers, while the **Osa Peninsula** and **Parque Nacional Corcovado** (p. 350) persist in relative obscurity further south, preserving a region that National Geographic has called "the most biologically intense place on earth." Located on the Pacific coast between the two peninsulas, surf and sand meet the rainforest at **Parque Nacional Manuel Antonio** (p. 293), where visitors encounter monkeys and migrating butterflies along jungle trails that lead directly to the beach. On the Caribbean coast, mangrove swamps and fossil-filled coral caves await to the south at the **Refugio Nacional Gandoca-Manzanillo** (p. 391), while the remote **Parque Nacional Tortuguero** (p. 370) to the north draws thousands of nesting turtles each year, along with the devoted leagues of conservationists that come to study and protect them.

SUN-KISSED BY THE SEASHORE

No matter how you define beachside bliss, Costa Rica's shores can probably provide it. Postcard-perfect dreams come to life on this isthmus, where it's possible (with a short drive) to witness a Caribbean sunrise in the morning and a Pacific sunset in the evening. It seems as though every activity imaginable is available along Costa Rica's vista-blessed beaches—from surfing to sunbathing, camping to scuba diving. Depending on your mood, you can snorkel with the fish or catch one for dinner; most restaurants are happy to cook up your catch for discounted prices. **Playa Tamarindo** (p. 226) offers the perfect combination of gorgeous surfing days and wild tropical nights, while **Jacó** (p. 277) promises to be a beach bum's paradise. For a change of pace, visit the isolated beaches of **Parque Nacional Santa Rosa** (p. 205), famous for surfing and turtle-watching, or the algae-carpeted tide pools of **Playa Avellana** (p. 234). Surfing is at its best on the endless waves of **Pavones** (p. 341), while at **Brasilito** and **Conchal** (p. 220), vast broken-shell beaches make for quieter sunset strolls. Avid surfers and sunbathers flock to **Playa Hermosa** (p. 283)—not to be confused

vides opportunities for scuba diving, snorkeling, and more.

6. Climb up a tangle of roots and branches in the "Cathedral," a 200 ft. ficus tree in **Corcovado,** and ring the Tibetan prayer bell at the top before belaying back down to the underbrush (p. 350).

7. Enjoy warm Peruvian family hospitality at Playa Negra's **Kon Tiki** (p. 232), a hotel designed by its architect and owner in the grand treehouse tradition. It brings the forest to the beach with impressive surfboard racks made from logs.

8. Wander the massive bridges of one of the largest canopy walks in Central America at the **Rainmaker Conservation Project** outside of **Quepos** (www.rainmakercostarica. com). See p. 288.

9. Enjoy 50% of Costa Rica's already impressive biodiversity at the **Parque Nacional Corcovado** (p. 350), where you could discover one of the many unidentified plant and animal species.

10. Find your inner child among the trees at the **Reserva Forestal Bosque Eterno de los Niños**. Started with the support of a group of schoolchildren, the reserve strives to fight deforestation, and protect the trees of Costa Rica.

with the upscale beach of the same name on Península Nicoya—for its relaxed atmosphere, hot black sand, and exhilarating waves. Serious and casual divers alike head to **Bahía Drake** for the chance to frolic with marlins, rainbow fish, and dolphins in some of the country's clearest waters, while the bravest surfers tackle the famous **Salsa Brava** swell in **Puerto Viejo** (p. 384). **Zancudo** (p. 343) is a weekend vacation destination for many *tico* families, offering unparalleled sportfishing and five kilometers of black-sand shorelines. White-faced monkeys scamper through the coconut palms and smooth sands of **Cahuita** (p. 377), where horseback-riding tours are popular. On the nearby shores of **Manzanillo** (p. 390), the pristine waters of the Caribbean are hemmed in by rainforest and coral reefs. No trip to Costa Rica is complete without following the beaches of **Montezuma** (p. 258) to magnificent waterfalls, wildlife, and waves.

IN DEFENSE OF CULTURE

Though popular opinion might suggest that Costa Rica has neither the storied past nor the contemporary culture of other Central American countries, those visitors in search of national personality and artistic vitality will find much to enchant them here. While many travelers skip out on the less-than-charming capital, **San José** (p. 83), as quickly as possible, museums like the **Museo de Jade** (p. 95) and the **Museo Nacional** (p. 95), whose exhibits are housed in an old fortress studded with bullet holes from the 1948 revolution, make a few extra days in the big city worth it. Don't miss splendid murals, elaborate ceiling frescoes, and world-class shows at the **Teatro Nacional** (p. 95). The nearby suburb **Escazú** (p. 100) offers fine dining and classy B&Bs, while **San Pedro** features a buzzing student neighborhood packed with restaurants, bars, and clubs. Venture south during early August to witness the impressive religious pilgrimage that thousands of *ticos* make to **Cartago** (p. 130) and its **Basílica de Nuestra Señora de los Ángeles,** or visit nearby **Turrialba** (p. 140) to raft its wild rivers and explore Costa Rica's most important archaeological site at **Monumento Nacional Guayabo,** where intricate petroglyphs testify to the people who lived on the land that Columbus "discovered." Travelers interested in contemporary indigenous culture can stay with a family of artisans at the **Reserva Indígena Boruca** (p. 317), while those intrigued by expat cultural incongruity should check out nearby **San Vito** (p. 319), whose delicious restaurants and quaint shady streets were constructed by Italian immigrants after WWII. The Atlantic coast offers reggae vibes and Caribbean flair—explore **Puerto Viejo de Talamanca's** (p. 384) sprawling arts and crafts market while you sample Costa Rican staples like *gallo pinto* (rice and beans) doused in coconut milk and creole spices. For a taste of how the *sabaneros* (cowboys) party, check out the massive rodeo that fills the streets of **Liberia** (p. 201) with dancing and signature Costa Rican style bullfighting every July during the **"Expo-Feria Ganadera-Liberia."**

GOING INCOGNITO

Be warned: people have been known to disappear here—they come for a week but end up staying for years. This slice of paradise has a knack for attracting travelers and holding onto them, and idyllic outposts like **Dominical** (p. 298) and **Golfito** (p. 336) are full of expats who decided to settle here for good. If you'd like to spend more than a few weeks in Costa Rica, you'll find plenty of opportunities for study, work, and play—everything from protecting hatching turtles at **Tortuguero** (p. 366) and **Parismina** (p. 363) to taking surfing and nature photography lessons in **Jacó** (p. 277). Enroll in a summer-long Spanish classes or teach English to schoolchildren in a remote, rural village for a year. Check out **Beyond Tourism** (p. 60) for more options.

▨LET'S GO PICKS

BEST WILDLIFE: Take a boat through **Refugio Nacional de Vida Silvestre Caño Negro** (p. 175), an aquatic wonderland of mangrove labyrinths full of snakes, iguanas, and even prehistoric fish. Explore the last frontier at **Parque Nacional Corcovado** (p. 350), which protects half of the country's resident species.

BEST WILDER LIFE: Hit up the beachfiend party scene on the streets of **Jacó** (p. 277) or venture north toward the buzzing surfer clubs of **Tamarindo** (p. 226). The beaches of **Puerto Viejo de Talamanca** (p. 384) bring reggae rhythms and a Caribbean twist to the traditional Costa Rican party scene, while students rock the pulse of *la vida urbana* in **San Pedro,** near San José.

BEST PLACES TO GET HIGH: Costa Rica's mountains offer hikes to breathtaking viewpoints for every skill level. A simple, easily accessible day hike to the steaming crater atop **Volcán Poás** (p. 108) is just hours from San José. Day hikes can also be found in the trails surrounding **Volcán Arenal** (p. 168), which lead to waterfalls, hot springs, and views of the active volcano. Adventurous (and skilled) hikers can spend anywhere from three days to a week navigating the trails of **Mt. Chirripó** (p. 312). At 3820m, it is the country's tallest peak, with views to both the Pacific and Caribbean coasts.

BEST BEACH BUMMING: Where to begin? The waters of **Punta Uva** (p. 389) are perfect for swimming, and the tree-lined shores beckon those looking for a place to relax. Enjoy spectacular waterfalls, wildlife, and waves at **Montezuma** (p. 258). Don't miss the warm, powdery white sands and pristine blue waters of **Sámara** (p. 245). Short hikes through the rainforest lead to four of the most beautiful beach coves on the Pacific at **Parque Nacional Manuel Antonio** (p. 293).

BEST DIVING AND SNORKELING: Visit **Cahuita** (p. 377) to enjoy the largest coral reef on the Caribbean coast, or explore underwater wonderworlds at **Playa del Coco** (p. 209) and **Playa Hermosa** (p. 209). More remote **Sierpe** (p. 329) and **Isla de Caño** (p. 335) offer some of the best diving in Central America.

BEST SURFING: Dominical (p. 298) and **Playa Pavones** (p. 341) are essential stops on true surfers' itineraries. **Playa Negra** (p. 232) and **Playa Tamarindo** (p. 226), with their silvery waters, are also celebrated by surfers of all skill levels.

BEST PLACE TO LEND A HAND: Turtle conservation volunteers at **Tortuguero** (p. 366) work alone for six-hour night shifts to guard turtle eggs from poachers who steal them for sale on the black market. At the **Sanctuario Silvestre Wildlife Sanctuary** (p. 341), volunteers spend time nursing orphaned baby animals back to health before re-releasing them into the wild. If animals aren't your thing, reforestation efforts in many of Costa Rica's national parks are always looking for volunteers.

BEST WAYS TO LOSE AN ARM: The swamp below the **Río Tárcales Bridge,** a.k.a. **Crocodile Bridge** (p. 275), near **Parque Nacional Carara,** usually hosts 20-30 crocodiles. They have been known to prey on nearby farm animals or even the occasional hapless tourist. Adrenaline junkies can't stay away from the "Tarzan swings" at the **Monteverde Reserve** (p. 185), where the canopy tours are not for the faint of heart or limb.

BEST WAY TO GET IT BACK: The **Cartago Cathedral** (p. 130) has a room full of miniature metal body parts dedicated in gratitude to **La Negrita,** Costa Rica's patron saint, who has been given credit for curing thousands of bodily maladies.

DISCOVER

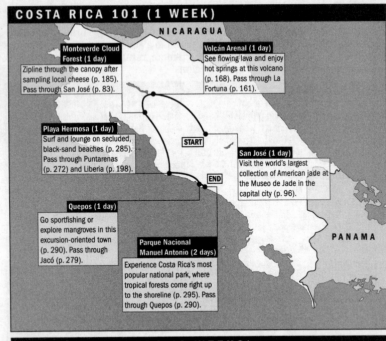

COSTA RICA 101 (1 WEEK)

NICARAGUA

Monteverde Cloud Forest (1 day)
Zipline through the canopy after sampling local cheese (p. 185). Pass through San José (p. 83).

Volcán Arenal (1 day)
See flowing lava and enjoy hot springs at this volcano (p. 168). Pass through La Fortuna (p. 161).

Playa Hermosa (1 day)
Surf and lounge on secluded, black-sand beaches (p. 285). Pass through Puntarenas (p. 272) and Liberia (p. 198).

START

END

San José (1 day)
Visit the world's largest collection of American jade at the Museo de Jade in the capital city (p. 96).

PANAMA

Quepos (1 day)
Go sportfishing or explore mangroves in this excursion-oriented town (p. 290). Pass through Jacó (p. 279).

Parque Nacional Manuel Antonio (2 days)
Experience Costa Rica's most popular national park, where tropical forests come right up to the shoreline (p. 295). Pass through Quepos (p. 290).

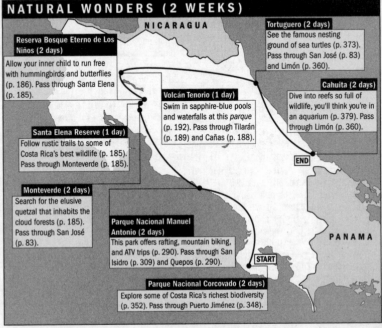

NATURAL WONDERS (2 WEEKS)

NICARAGUA

Tortuguero (2 days)
See the famous nesting ground of sea turtles (p. 373). Pass through San José (p. 83) and Limón (p. 360).

Reserva Bosque Eterno de Los Niños (2 days)
Allow your inner child to run free with hummingbirds and butterflies (p. 186). Pass through Santa Elena (p. 185).

Volcán Tenorio (1 day)
Swim in sapphire-blue pools and waterfalls at this *parque* (p. 192). Pass through Tilarán (p. 189) and Cañas (p. 188).

Cahuita (2 days)
Dive into reefs so full of wildlife, you'll think you're in an aquarium (p. 379). Pass through Limón (p. 360).

END

Santa Elena Reserve (1 day)
Follow rustic trails to some of Costa Rica's best wildlife (p. 185). Pass through Monteverde (p. 185).

Monteverde (2 days)
Search for the elusive quetzal that inhabits the cloud forests (p. 185). Pass through San José (p. 83).

Parque Nacional Manuel Antonio (2 days)
This park offers rafting, mountain biking, and ATV trips (p. 290). Pass through San Isidro (p. 309) and Quepos (p. 290).

PANAMA

START

Parque Nacional Corcovado (2 days)
Explore some of Costa Rica's richest biodiversity (p. 352). Pass through Puerto Jiménez (p. 348).

EXTREME ADVENTURE TOUR (2½ WEEKS)

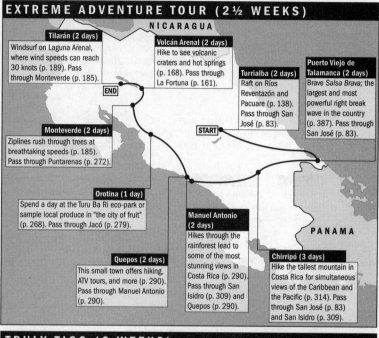

NICARAGUA

Tilarán (2 days)
Windsurf on Laguna Arenal, where wind speeds can reach 30 knots (p. 189). Pass through Monteverde (p. 185).

END

Volcán Arenal (2 days)
Hike to see volcanic craters and hot springs (p. 168). Pass through La Fortuna (p. 161).

Turrialba (2 days)
Raft on Ríos Reventazón and Pacuare (p. 138). Pass through San José (p. 83).

START

Puerto Viejo de Talamanca (2 days)
Brave *Salsa Brava;* the largest and most powerful right break wave in the country (p. 387). Pass through San José (p. 83).

Monteverde (2 days)
Ziplines rush through trees at breathtaking speeds (p. 185). Pass through Puntarenas (p. 272).

Orotina (1 day)
Spend a day at the Turu Ba Ri eco-park or sample local produce in "the city of fruit" (p. 268). Pass through Jacó (p. 279).

Manuel Antonio (2 days)
Hikes through the rainforest lead to some of the most stunning views in Costa Rica (p. 290). Pass through San Isidro (p. 309) and Quepos (p. 290).

PANAMA

Quepos (2 days)
This small town offers hiking, ATV tours, and more (p. 290). Pass through Manuel Antonio (p. 290).

Chirripó (3 days)
Hike the tallest mountain in Costa Rica for simultaneous views of the Caribbean and the Pacific (p. 314). Pass through San José (p. 83) and San Isidro (p. 309).

TRULY TICO (2 WEEKS)

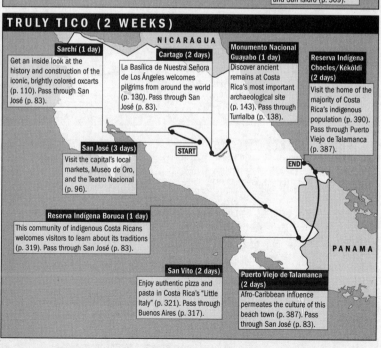

NICARAGUA

Sarchí (1 day)
Get an inside look at the history and construction of the iconic, brightly colored oxcarts (p. 110). Pass through San José (p. 83).

Cartago (2 days)
La Basílica de Nuestra Señora de Los Ángeles welcomes pilgrims from around the world (p. 130). Pass through San José (p. 83).

Monumento Nacional Guayabo (1 day)
Discover ancient remains at Costa Rica's most important archaeological site (p. 143). Pass through Turrialba (p. 138).

Reserva Indígena Chocles/Kéköldi (2 days)
Visit the home of the majority of Costa Rica's indigenous population (p. 390). Pass through Puerto Viejo de Talamanca (p. 387).

San José (3 days)
Visit the capital's local markets, Museo de Oro, and the Teatro Nacional (p. 96).

START

END

Reserva Indígena Boruca (1 day)
This community of indigenous Costa Ricans welcomes visitors to learn about its traditions (p. 319). Pass through San José (p. 83).

PANAMA

San Vito (2 days)
Enjoy authentic pizza and pasta in Costa Rica's "Little Italy" (p. 321). Pass through Buenos Aires (p. 317).

Puerto Viejo de Talamanca (2 days)
Afro-Caribbean influence permeates the culture of this beach town (p. 387). Pass through San José (p. 83).

DISCOVER

HIJO DE PLAYA (3 WEEKS)

Playa del Coco (2 days)
Snorkel, dive, or bask in the sand at one of Costa Rica's best scuba beaches (p. 213). Pass through San José (p. 83).

NICARAGUA

Puerto Viejo de Talamanca (2 days)
Watch amazing surf over coral reefs and experience Costa Rica's unique Afro-Caribbean culture (p. 384). Pass through Punta Uva (p. 389).

Potrero (1 day)
Secluded shores make for perfect sunset-watching on the beach (p. 217). Pass through Liberia (p. 191) and Santa Cruz (p. 222).

START

Cahuita (2 days)
Monkeys and beautiful surf beckon snorkelers and scuba divers to the country's largest reef (p. 377). Pass through Puerto Viejo de Talamanca (p. 384).

Brasilito / Playa Conchal (1 day)
Crushed shells give these uncluttered beaches their pink-white hue (p. 220). Pass through Potrero (p. 217).

Uvita (1 day)
A favorite spot for *tico* families and tourists looking to escape the *gringo* experience (p. 303). Pass through Dominical (p. 298).

END

Playa Tamarindo (2 days)
Surf the waves and the bars in this lively, largely expat community (p. 226). Pass through Santa Cruz (p. 222).

Jacó (2 days)
Meet other tourists at this party beach (p. 277). Pass through San José (p. 83).

Dominical (1 day)
Mountains, forests, and beaches meet in this surfer-oriented community (p. 298). Pass through Quepos (p. 288).

PANAMA

Isla del Caño (2 days)
Spend the day at one of the world's best scuba diving sites (p. 335). Pass through Neily (p. 323) and Palmar Norte (p. 318).

Playa Zancudo (1 day)
Spend the day sportfishing and sunbathing on black-sand beaches (p. 343). Pass through Golfito (p. 336).

Puerto Jiménez (2 days)
The budget traveler's delight on the otherwise expensive Osa Peninsula (p. 346). Pass through Neily (p. 323) and Golfito (p. 340).

Punta Uva (2 days)
Mango trees and brilliant sunsets highlight this Caribbean destination (p. 389). Pass through San José (p. 83).

ESSENTIALS

PLANNING YOUR TRIP

BEFORE YOU GO

Passport (p. 10). Required for all visitors. Passports must be valid for at least 30 days after date of entry. Travelers for whom a visa is required must hold passports valid for 3 months after date of entry.

Visa (p. 10). Not required for citizens of Australia, Canada, Ireland, New Zealand, US, or members of the European Union.

Work Permit (p. 11). Required for all foreigners planning to work in Costa Rica for up to a year.

Recommended Vaccinations (p. 19). Hepatitis A, Hepatitis B, Typhoid.

Vaccination/Health Certificates (p. 19). **International Certificate of Vaccination** against Yellow Fever is required of citizens from select countries. Visit the **Embassy of Costa Rica** (www.costarica-embassy.org) for information and a list of affected countries.

Other Health Concerns: Malaria pills are recommended for those heading to high-risk areas (p. 21). If your insurance (p. 23) does not cover travel, you may wish to purchase additional coverage.

EMBASSIES AND CONSULATES

COSTA RICAN CONSULAR SERVICES ABROAD

Australia: Embassy, De La Sala House, Piso 11, 30 Clarence St., Sydney, NSW 2000 (☎61 2 9261 1177; fax 9261 2953). Open M-F 10am-5pm.

Canada: Embassy, 325 Dalhousie St., Ste. 407, Ottawa, Ontario, K1N 762 (☎+1-613-562-2855). Open M-F 9am-5pm.

UK: Embassy, Flat 1, 14 Lancaster Gate, London W2 3LH (☎171 706 8844; fax 171 706 8655). Open M-Th 8am-noon and 12:30-4pm, F 8am-1pm.

US: Embassy, 2114 "S" St., NW, Washington, DC 20008 (☎+1-202-234-2945; www.costarica-embassy.org). Open M-F 9am-5pm. **Consulate:** 2112 "S" St. NW, Washington, DC 20008 (☎+1-202-328-6628; fax 202-234-6950). Open M-F 10am-1pm.

CONSULAR SERVICES IN COSTA RICA

Australia, Ireland, and New Zealand don't have embassies in Costa Rica.

Canada: Embassy (mailing address: Apdo. 351 1007, Centro Colón, San José), Office west of downtown San José in Sabina Sur, behind the Contraloría in the Oficentro Executive complex, bldg. 5 (☎2242 4400, after hours for Canadian citizens +1-613-996-8885; www.sanjose.gc.ca). Open M-Th 8am-4pm, F 7:30am-1pm.

UK: Embassy (mailing address: Apdo. 815 1007, San José), Centro Colón (11th fl.), San José, Costa Rica (☎2258 2025; fax 2233 9938; britemb@racsa.co.cr). Open M-Th 8am-noon and 12:30-4pm, F 8am-10pm.

US: Embassy (Apdo 920 1200, San José; US address: US Embassy San José, APO AA 34020), Av. Central, Pavas, Calle 120, San José (☎2519 2000, after-hours 2519 2280; http://sanjose.usembassy.gov). Open M 8-11:30am and 1-3pm, T-F 8-11:30am.

TOURIST OFFICES

The **Instituto Costarricense de Turismo (ICT),** is the official tourist bureau. It offers free maps and hints and publishes a list of tour companies and lodgings. Its pamphlets are in tourist offices throughout the country. The San José office is at Av. Central/2, C. 5, Plaza de la Cultura, next to Pre-Columbian Gold Museum. (☎2299 5800; www.visitcostarica.com. Open M-F 8am-5pm.) The **Costa Rican National Chamber of Tourism** (www.tourism.co.cr) also has information.

DOCUMENTS AND FORMALITIES

PASSPORTS

REQUIREMENTS

All visitors need valid passports to enter Costa Rica and to re-enter their home countries. Costa Rica does not allow entrance if the holder's passport expires in under three months after the date of entry; returning home with an expired passport is illegal and may result in a fine.

NEW PASSPORTS

Citizens of Australia, Canada, Ireland, New Zealand, the UK, and the US can apply for a passport at any passport office or at selected post offices and courts of law. Citizens of these countries may also get passport applications from the official website of their country's government or passport office. Any new passport or renewal applications must be filed well in advance of the departure date, though most passport offices offer rush services for a very steep fee. Note, however, that "rushed" passports still take up to two weeks to arrive.

PASSPORT MAINTENANCE

Photocopy the photo page of your passport as well as your visas, traveler's check serial numbers, and any other important documents. Carry one set of copies in a safe place, not with the originals, and leave another set at home. Consulates also recommend that you carry an expired passport or an official copy of your birth certificate separate from other documents.

If you lose your passport, immediately notify the local police and your home country's nearest embassy or consulate. To expedite its replacement, you must show ID and proof of citizenship. It also helps to know all information previously recorded in the passport. In some cases, a replacement may take weeks to process, and it may be valid only for a limited time. Any visas stamped in your old passport will be lost forever. In an emergency, ask for immediate temporary traveling papers that will permit you to re-enter your home country.

VISAS, INVITATIONS, AND WORK PERMITS

VISAS

Citizens of Australia, Ireland, New Zealand, Canada, the UK, and the US do not need visas. Visas cost US$20 and allow you to spend 30 days in Costa Rica. Visas can be purchased from the Costa Rican consulate nearest you.

Double-check entrance requirements at the nearest embassy or consulate of Costa Rica (listed under **Costa Rica Consular Services Abroad**, p. 9) for up-to-date info before departure. US citizens can also consult http://travel.state.gov.

Entering Costa Rica to study requires a special visa. For more information, see the **Beyond Tourism** chapter (p. 60).

WORK PERMITS
Admittance to a country does not include the right to work, which is authorized by a work permit. For more information, see **Beyond Tourism** (p. 60).

IDENTIFICATION
When you travel, always carry at least two forms of identification on your person, including a photo ID. A passport and a driver's license or birth certificate will usually suffice. Never carry all of your IDs; split them up in case of theft or loss and keep photocopies of all of them in your luggage and at home.

STUDENT, TEACHER, AND YOUTH IDENTIFICATION
The **International Student Identity Card (ISIC)**, the most widely accepted form of student ID, provides discounts on some sights, such as the ever-popular canopy tours, accommodations, food, and transportation; access to a 24hr. emergency help line; and insurance benefits for US cardholders (see **Insurance**, p. 20). Applicants must be full-time secondary or post-secondary school students at least 12 years old. Because of the proliferation of fake ISICs, some services (particularly airlines) require additional proof of student identity.

The **International Teacher Identity Card (ITIC)** offers teachers the same insurance coverage as the ISIC and similar discounts. To qualify, teachers must be employed and have worked a minimum of 18hr. per week for at least one school year. For those who are under 26 years old but are not students, the **International Youth Travel Card (IYTC)** offers many of the same benefits as the ISIC.

Each of these identity cards costs US$22. ISICs, ITICs, and IYTCs are valid for one year from the date of issue. To learn more about ISICs, ITICs, and IYTCs, try www.myisic.com. Many student travel agencies (p. 24) issue the cards; for a list of issuing agencies or more information, see the **International Student Travel Confederation (ISTC)** website (www.istc.org).

The **International Student Exchange Card (ISE Card)** is a similar card available to students, faculty, and children aged 12-26. The card provides discounts, medical benefits, access to a 24hr. emergency help line, and the ability to purchase student airfares. It costs US$25; call ☎+1-800-255-8000 (in North America) or 480-951-1177 (from other continents) for more info or visit www.isecard.com.

CUSTOMS
Upon entering Costa Rica, you must declare certain items from abroad and pay a duty on the value of those articles if they exceed the allowance established by Costa Rica's customs service. Goods and gifts purchased at duty-free shops abroad are not exempt from duty or sales tax. "Duty-free" means that you won't pay tax in the country of purchase. Duty-free allowances were abolished for travel between EU member states on June 30, 1999 but still exist for those arriving from outside the EU. Upon returning home, you must likewise declare all articles acquired abroad and pay a duty on the value of articles in excess of your home country's allowance. In order to expedite your return, make a list of any valuables brought from home and register them with customs before traveling abroad. It's a good idea to keep receipts for all goods acquired abroad.

MONEY

CURRENCY AND EXCHANGE

The chart below is based on August 2008 exchange rates between local currency and Australian dollars (AUS$), Canadian dollars (CDN$), European Union euro (EUR€), New Zealand dollars (NZ$), British pounds (UK£), and US dollars (US$). The unit of currency in Costa Rica is the *colón*, which is divided into 100 *céntimentos*, though coins are becoming less useful in Costa Rican currency. Paper notes circulate in the following amounts: 50, 100, 500, 1000, 2000, 5000, and 10,000. Check the currency converter on websites like www.xe.com or www.bloomberg.com for the latest rates.

CURRENCY (¢)		
AUS$ = ¢502	¢1 = AUS$0.002
CDN$ = ¢527	¢1 = CDN$0.002
EUR€ = ¢851	¢1 = EUR€0.001
NZ$ = ¢396	¢1 = NZ$0.002
UK£ = ¢1075	¢1 = UK£0.0009
US$ = ¢552	¢1 = US$0.002

As a general rule, it's cheaper to convert money in Costa Rica than at home. While currency exchange will probably be available in your arrival airport, it's wise to bring enough foreign currency to last for at least 24-72 hours.

When changing money abroad, try to go only to banks or *casas de cambio* that have at most a 5% margin between their buy and sell prices. Since you lose money with every transaction, it makes sense to convert large sums at one time (unless the currency is depreciating rapidly).

If you use traveler's checks or bills, carry some in small denominations (the equivalent of US$50 or less) for times when you are forced to exchange money at poor rates, but bring a range of denominations since charges may be applied per check cashed. Store your money in a variety of forms. Ideally, at any time you will be carrying some cash, some traveler's checks, and an ATM and/or credit card. All travelers should also consider carrying some US dollars (about US$50 worth), which are often preferred by local tellers.

TRAVELER'S CHECKS

Traveler's checks are one of the safest, most convenient means of carrying funds. American Express and Visa are the most-recognized brands. Many banks and agencies sell them for a small commission. Check issuers provide refunds if the checks are lost or stolen, and many provide additional services, such as toll-free refund hotlines abroad, emergency message services and assistance with lost credit cards or passports. Traveler's checks are accepted in more touristed areas. Ask about toll-free refund hotlines and the location of refund centers when purchasing checks, and always carry some cash.

American Express: Checks available with commission at select banks, at all AmEx offices, and online (www.americanexpress.com; US residents only). AmEx cardholders can also purchase checks by phone (☎+1-800-528-4800). Checks come in Australian, British, Canadian, European, Japanese, and US currencies, among others. AmEx offers the Travelers Cheque Card, a prepaid reloadable card. Cheques for Two can be signed by either of 2 people traveling together. For purchases or more information, contact AmEx's service centers: in Australia ☎+61 2 9271 8666, in New Zealand +64 9 367 4567, in the UK +44 1273 696 933, in the US and Canada +1-800-221-7282; elsewhere, call the US collect at +1-336-393-1111.

Visa: Checks available (generally with commission) worldwide. For the location of the nearest office, call Visa Travelers Cheque Global Refund and Assistance Center: in the UK ☎+44 0800 895 078, in the US +1-800-227-6811; elsewhere, call the UK collect at +44 2079 378 091. Checks come in British, Canadian, European, Japanese and US currencies, among others. Visa offers TravelMoney, a prepaid debit card that can be reloaded online or by phone. For more information on Visa travel services, see http://usa.visa.com/personal/using_visa/travel_with_visa.html.

CREDIT, DEBIT, AND ATM CARDS

Where they are accepted, credit cards often offer superior exchange rates—up to 5% better than the retail rate used by banks and other currency exchange establishments. Credit cards may also offer services such as insurance or emergency help and are sometimes required to reserve hotel rooms or rental cars. **MasterCard** and **Visa** are the most frequently accepted; **American Express** cards work at some ATMs and at AmEx offices and major airports.

The use of ATM cards is widespread in Costa Rica. Depending on the system that your home bank uses, you can most likely access your personal bank account from abroad. ATMs get the same exchange rate as credit cards, but there is often a limit on how much money you can withdraw per day (usually around US$500). There is typically a surcharge of US$1-5 per withdrawal.

Debit cards are as convenient as credit cards but withdraw money directly from the holder's checking account. A debit card can be used wherever its associated credit card company (usually MasterCard or Visa) is accepted. Debit cards often also function as ATM cards and can be used to withdraw cash from associated banks and ATMs throughout Costa Rica.

The two major international money networks are **MasterCard/Maestro/Cirrus** (for ATM locations ☎+1-800-424-7787 or www.mastercard.com) and **Visa/PLUS** (for ATM locations ☎+1-800-847-2911 or www.visa.com). Most ATMs charge a transaction fee that is paid to the bank that owns the ATM.

GETTING MONEY FROM HOME

If you run out of money while traveling, the easiest and cheapest solution is to have someone back home make a deposit to your bank account. Otherwise, consider one of the following options.

WIRING MONEY

It is possible to arrange a **bank money transfer,** which means asking a bank back home to wire money to a bank in Costa Rica. This is the cheapest way to transfer cash, but it's also the slowest, usually taking several days or more. Note that some banks may only release your funds in local currency, potentially sticking you with a poor exchange rate; inquire about this in advance. Many banks in Costa Rica require that you open an account before they accept a bank money transfer. Money transfer services like **Western Union** are faster and more convenient than bank transfers—but also pricier. Western Union has many locations worldwide. To find one, visit www.westernunion.com, or call in Australia ☎1800 173 833, in Canada and the US ☎+1-800-325-6000, or in the UK +44 0800 833 833. To wire money using a credit card (Discover, MasterCard, Visa), call in Canada and the US +1-800-CALL-CASH, in the UK ☎+44 0800 833 833. Money transfer services are available to **American Express** cardholders.

US STATE DEPARTMENT (US CITIZENS ONLY)

In serious emergencies only, the US State Department will forward money within hours to the nearest consular office, which will then disburse it according to instructions for a US$30 fee. If you wish to use this service, you must contact the Overseas Citizens Services division of the US State Department (☎+1-202-501-4444, from US ☎888-407-4747).

COSTS

The cost of your trip will vary considerably, depending on where you go, how you travel, and where you stay. The most significant expenses will probably be your round-trip (return) airfare to Costa Rica (see **Getting to Costa Rica: By Plane,** p. 24) and bus pass. Before you go, spend some time calculating a reasonable daily budget, so you'll know what to expect when you arrive.

STAYING ON A BUDGET

To give you a general idea, a bare-bones day in Costa Rica (camping or sleeping in hostels/guesthouses, buying food at supermarkets) would cost about US$18 (¢9300); a slightly more comfortable day (sleeping in hostels/guesthouses and the occasional budget hotel, eating one meal per day at a restaurant, going out at night) would cost US$30 (¢15,600); and, for a luxurious day, the sky's the limit. Don't forget to factor in emergency reserve funds (at least US$200) when planning how much money you'll need for your trip.

TIPS FOR SAVING MONEY

Some simple ways to save money include finding opportunities for free entertainment, splitting accommodation and food costs with trustworthy fellow travelers, and buying food in supermarkets rather than eating out. Bring a **sleepsack** (p. 15) to save on sheet charges in hostels and do your **laundry** in the sink (unless you're prohibited from doing so). Museums often have certain days when admission is free; plan accordingly. If you are eligible, consider getting an ISIC or an IYTC (p. 11); many sights and museums have reduced admission for students and youths, but often, only if you have proof of your status as a student. For getting around quickly, bikes are the most economical option. Don't forget about walking, though; you can learn a lot about a city by seeing a place on foot. Drinking at bars and clubs quickly becomes expensive. It's cheaper to buy alcohol and imbibe before going out. That said, don't go overboard. Though staying within your budget is important, don't do so at the expense of your health or a great travel experience.

TIPPING AND BARGAINING

As practices, tipping and bargaining in the developing world are quite different from what you might be accustomed; there are many unspoken rules to which tourists must adhere. Tipping is not particularly widespread in Costa Rica. Restaurant bills already include a 10% service charge as well as the 13% sales tax on all goods and services. In smaller restaurants frequented by locals, tipping is rare. Tour guides appreciate something extra; small change is appropriate for porters in hotels and restaurants. Taxi drivers do not expect to get tipped. In general, particularly good service may deserve an extra tip of 5% or so.

At outdoor markets, handicraft markets, and some handicraft shops, bargaining is expected and essential. Prices at supermarkets and most indoor stores are not negotiable. Bargaining for hotel rooms is often a good idea, but only at cheaper establishments, and more in the low season (or if the hotel isn't full).

Taxis may charge outrageous fares if they know that you are a tourist, so it is better to bargain if you know what the fare should be.

THE ART OF THE DEAL. Bargaining in Costa Rica is a given. It's up to you to get vendors and drivers down to a reasonable rate. With these tips and some finesse, you may be able to impress the most hardened hawkers:

1. **Bargaining needn't be a fierce struggle laced with barbs.** Quite the opposite; good-natured wrangling with a smile may be your best weapon.
2. **Use your poker face.** The less your face betrays your interest the better. If you touch an item, the vendor will "encourage" you to name a price or purchase it. Don't get too enthusiastic; point out flaws, and be cool.
3. **Know when to bargain.** In most cases, it's quite clear when it's appropriate to bargain. Most private transportation fares and things for sale in outdoor markets are all fair game. Don't bargain on prepared or pre-packaged foods on the street or in restaurants.
4. **Never underestimate the power of peer pressure.** Try having a friend discourage you from your purchase—if you seem reluctant, the merchant will want to drop the price to interest you again.
5. **Know when to turn away.** Feel free to refuse anyone who bargains rudely, and don't hesitate to move on if one will is unreasonable about the price.
6. **Start low.** Never feel guilty offering a ridiculously low price. Your starting price should be no more than 1/3 to ½ the asking price.

TAXES

There is a 13% sales tax in Costa Rica. In addition, restaurants add a 10% service charge on all bills. There is also a 3.39% tourism tax in addition to the sales tax on hotel rooms. Usually these charges will be included in the prices posted, but ask beforehand to be sure. Often Costa Rican restaurants will include two price columns: one with tax-inclusive prices and one without.

PACKING

Pack lightly: lay out only what you absolutely need, then take half the clothes and twice the money. The **Travelite FAQ** (www.travelite.org) is a good resource for tips on traveling light. The online **Universal Packing List** (http://upl.codeq.info) will generate a customized list of suggested items based on your trip length, the expected climate, your planned activities, and other factors. If you plan to do a lot of hiking, also consult **The Great Outdoors,** p. 70. Some frequent travelers keep a bag packed with all the essentials: passport, money belt, hat, socks, etc. Then, when they decide to leave, they know they haven't forgotten anything.

Luggage: If you plan to cover most of your trip on foot, a sturdy **internal-frame backpack** is unbeatable. (For the basics on buying a pack, see p. 76.) Unless you are staying in 1 place for a large chunk of time, a suitcase or trunk will be unwieldy. In addition to your main piece of luggage, a **daypack** (a small backpack or courier bag) is useful.

Clothing: No matter when you go, it's good to bring a warm jacket or sweater, a rain jacket (Gore-Tex® is waterproof and breathable), sturdy shoes or hiking boots, and thick socks. Flip-flops or waterproof sandals are must-haves for hostel showers. You may also want 1 outfit for going out. If you plan to visit religious or cultural sites, remember that you will need respectful dress. Costa Rica highlands get cold at night—be sure to take a sweater or fleece. For information on local dress, see **Customs and Etiquette,** p. 11.

Sleepsack: Some hostels require that you either provide your own linen or rent sheets from them. Save cash by making your own sleepsack: fold a full-size sheet in half the long way, then sew it closed along the long side and one of the short sides.

Converters and Adapters: The standard current in Costa Rica is 110V AC—the same as Canada, Mexico, and the US. The outlets take 2-pronged US plugs, so you will need to purchase an adaptor to change the shape of the plug if you are using something that requires a 3-pronged socket. If you are using equipment built for a different current, you must also purchase a converter, which can be purchased at hardware stores. For more on all things adaptable, check out http://kropla.com/electric.htm.

Toiletries: Condoms, deodorant, razors, tampons, and toothbrushes are often available, but it may be difficult to find your brand. Contact lenses are likely to be expensive and difficult to find, so bring extra pairs and solution for your entire trip. Also bring your glasses and a copy of your prescription in case you need emergency replacements.

First-Aid Kit: For a basic first-aid kit, pack bandages, a pain reliever, antibiotic cream, a thermometer, a multifunction pocketknife, tweezers, moleskin, decongestant, motion-sickness remedy, diarrhea or upset-stomach medication (Pepto Bismol® or Imodium®), an antihistamine, sunscreen, insect repellent, and burn ointment.

Other Useful Items: You should bring a **money belt** and a small **padlock.** Basic **outdoors equipment** (plastic water bottle, compass, matches, pocketknife, sunglasses, sunscreen, hat) may also be handy. Quick repairs of torn garments can be done with a needle and thread; consider bringing electrical tape for patching tears. Other things you're liable to forget include: an umbrella, **plastic bags** (for damp clothes, soap, food, shampoo, and other spillables), an **alarm clock,** safety pins, rubber bands, a flashlight, earplugs, garbage bags, and a small calculator. A **cell phone** can be a lifesaver (literally) on the road; see p. 33 for information on acquiring one that will work in Costa Rica.

Important Documents: Don't forget your passport, traveler's checks, ATM and/or credit cards, adequate ID, and photocopies of all of the aforementioned in case these documents are lost or stolen (p. 10). Also check that you have any of the following that might apply to you: a hosteling membership card (p. 35); driver's license (p. 11); travel insurance forms (p. 20), ISIC (p. 11), and/or rail and bus passes (p. 28).

SAFETY AND HEALTH

GENERAL ADVICE

In any type of crisis, the most important thing to do is **stay calm.** Your country's embassy abroad (p. 9) is usually your best resource in an emergency; registering with that embassy upon arrival in the country is a good idea.

LOCAL LAWS AND POLICE

Costa Rica is a democratic republic and maintains a strong emphasis on human rights and democracy. Law does require that foreigners carry passports, or at least a photocopy of their passport datapage and Costa Rican entry stamp, with them at all times. An aggressive program against sexual tourism exists in Costa Rica, and any sexual activity with a minor is punishable by imprisonment.

In late 2006, Costa Rica established a Tourist Police force to assist with the reporting of crimes that would normally be difficult to report due to language barriers and bureaucratic difficulties. Costa Rica has no military, but it does have a domestic police force. *Let's Go* lists the location and number of the local police station, if available, in the **Practical Information** of each town; in case of an emergency, dial ☎911, unless otherwise specified.

DRUGS AND ALCOHOL

Penalties for possession, use, and trafficking of illegal drugs in Costa Rica are strict, and convicted offenders can expect lengthy jail sentences and substantial fines. People may try to sell you everything from marijuana to cocaine (*cocaína*); use your head, and don't buy it. Your home embassy will be of minimal assistance should you get into trouble. You are subject to the laws of the country in which you travel, not those of your home country, and it is your responsibility to familiarize yourself with these laws before leaving. If you carry **prescription drugs** while you travel, have a copy of the prescriptions themselves and a note from your doctor. It is also a good idea to have the Spanish translations of all of your prescriptions. Avoid public drunkenness; in certain areas it is against the law and can jeopardize your safety while earning the disdain of locals. Costa Rica also has dry laws, prohibiting the sale of liquor on the day prior to, of, and following elections. The legal drinking age in Costa Rica is 18, and, with the exception of those days, liquor is sold every day.

SPECIFIC CONCERNS

> **TRAVEL ADVISORIES.** The following government offices provide travel information and advisories by telephone, by fax, or via the web:
> **Australian Department of Foreign Affairs and Trade:** ☎+61 2 6261 1111; www.dfat.gov.au.
> **Canadian Department of Foreign Affairs and International Trade (DFAIT):** ☎+1-800-267-8376; www.dfait-maeci.gc.ca. Call for their free booklet, *Bon Voyage...But.*
> **New Zealand Ministry of Foreign Affairs:** ☎+64 4 439 8000; www.mfat.govt.nz.
> **United Kingdom Foreign and Commonwealth Office:** ☎+44 20 7008 1500; www.fco.gov.uk.
> **US Department of State:** ☎+1-888-407-4747; http://travel.state.gov. Visit the website for the booklet, *A Safe Trip Abroad.*

NATURAL DISASTERS

FLOODS. The rainy season occurs between May and November, contributing to an average rainfall of 254cm per year; floods often occur during this time. The Caribbean coast and the areas surrounding major rivers are most prone to floods. Roads may become impassible during the rainy season, so plan ahead and ask locals about road conditions.

EARTHQUAKES. Costa Rica is located over two tectonic plates, which results in a significant number of quakes. Tremors are not unusual, but large-scale earthquakes are rare. If an earthquake occurs, be sure to stay away from anything that could fall on you. If indoors, stand in a doorway or go under a desk. If you are driving, pull over to the side of the road until the quake passes.

RIPTIDES. Riptides are a problem at many beaches, both on the Atlantic and Pacific Coasts. These strong currents occur when there is an excess of water brought to shore by waves. Rather than accumulate on the beach, the excess water creates a channel to carry itself back out to the ocean. This can create a strong current capable of pulling swimmers out to sea. To avoid riptides, check for safety advisories before swimming at any beach, and never swim alone.

TERRORISM

Terrorism is not of particular concern in Costa Rica. The country is firmly democratic and has been politically stable for many decades. There are no known terrorist groups currently in Costa Rica. For information on Costa Rica's current events, see **Costa Rica Today,** p. 49. The box below lists offices to contact and webpages to visit to get the most updated list of your home country's government's advisories about travel.

PERSONAL SAFETY

EXPLORING AND TRAVELING

To avoid unwanted attention, try to blend in as much as possible. Respecting local customs (in many cases, dressing more conservatively than you would at home) may ward off hecklers. Familiarize yourself with your surroundings before setting out and carry yourself with confidence. Check maps in shops and restaurants rather than on the street. If you're traveling solo, be sure someone at home knows your itinerary and never tell anyone you meet that you're by yourself. When walking at night, stick to busy, well-lit streets and avoid dark alleyways. If you ever feel uncomfortable, leave the area quickly and directly.

There is no way to avoid all the threatening situations you might encounter while traveling, but a good **self-defense course** will give you concrete ways to react to unwanted advances. **Impact, Prepare,** and **Model Mugging** can refer you to local self-defense courses in Australia, Canada, Switzerland, and the US. Visit the website at www.modelmugging.org for a list of nearby chapters.

If you are using a **car,** learn local driving signals and wear a seatbelt. Children under 40 lb. should ride only in specially designed car seats, available for a small fee from most car-rental agencies. Study route maps before you hit the road and, if you plan on spending a lot of time driving, consider bringing spare parts. For long drives in desolate areas, invest in a cellular phone and a roadside assistance program (p. 30). Park your vehicle in a garage or well-traveled area and use a steering-wheel locking device in larger cities. Sleeping in your car is the most dangerous way to get your rest and is also illegal in many countries. For info on the perils of **hitchhiking,** see p. 32.

POSSESSIONS AND VALUABLES

Never leave your belongings unattended; crime can occur in even the most safe-looking hostel or hotel. Bring your own padlock for hostel lockers and don't ever store valuables in a locker. Be particularly careful on **buses** and **trains;** horror stories abound about determined thieves who wait for travelers to fall asleep. Carry your bag or purse in front of you where you can see it. When traveling with others, sleep in shifts. When alone, use good judgment in selecting a train compartment: never stay in an empty one and use a lock to secure your pack to the luggage rack. Use extra caution if traveling at night or on overnight trains. Try to sleep on top bunks with your luggage stored above you (or in bed with you) and keep important documents and valuables on you at all times.

There are a few steps you can take to minimize the risk associated with traveling. First, **bring as little with you as possible.** Second, buy a few combination **padlocks** to secure your belongings in your pack or in a hostel or train-station locker. Third, **carry as little cash as possible.** Keep your traveler's checks and ATM/

credit cards in a **money belt**—not a "fanny pack"—along with your passport and ID cards. Fourth, **keep a small cash reserve separate from your primary stash.** This should be about US$50 (US dollars or euros are best) sewn into or stored in the depths of your pack, along with your traveler's check numbers, photocopies of your passport, birth certificate, and other important documents.

In large cities, **con artists** often work in groups and may involve children. Beware of certain classics: sob stories that require money, rolls of bills "found" on the street, mustard spilled (or saliva spit) onto your shoulder to distract you while they snatch your bag. **Never let your passport and your bags out of your sight.** Hostel workers will sometimes stand at bus and train-station arrival points to recruit tired, disoriented travelers to their hostel; never believe strangers who tell you that theirs is the only hostel open. Beware of **pickpockets** in city crowds, especially on public transportation. Also, be alert in public telephone booths: if you must say your calling card number, do so very quietly; if you punch it in, make sure no one can look over your shoulder.

If you will be traveling with electronic devices, such as a laptop computer or a PDA, check whether your homeowner's insurance covers loss, theft, or damage when you travel. If not, you might consider purchasing a separate low-cost insurance policy. **Safeware** (☎+1-800-800-1492; www.safeware.com) specializes in covering computers and charges US$90 for 90-day comprehensive international travel coverage up to US$4000.

PRE-DEPARTURE HEALTH

In your passport, write the names of any people you wish to be contacted in case of a **medical emergency** and any allergies or medical conditions. Matching a prescription to a foreign equivalent is not always easy or safe, so if you take **prescription drugs,** consider carrying up-to-date prescriptions or a note from your doctor stating the medication's trade name, manufacturer, chemical name, and dosage. Be sure to keep all medication with you in your carry-on luggage. For tips on packing a **first-aid kit** and other health essentials, see p. 15.

The names in Costa Rica for common drugs are: *aspirina* (aspirin), *paracetamol* (acetaminophen), and *antihistimínico* (antihistamine). Brand names like Tylenol®, Advil®, and Pepto Bismol® are also well known.

IMMUNIZATIONS AND PRECAUTIONS

Travelers over two years old should make sure that the following vaccines are up to date: MMR (for measles, mumps, and rubella); DTaP or Td (for diphtheria, tetanus, and pertussis); IPV (for polio); Hib (for *haemophilus influenzae* B); and HepB (for Hepatitis B). Adults traveling to the developing world on trips longer than four weeks should consider the following additional immunizations: Hepatitis A vaccine and/or immune globulin (IG), typhoid and cholera vaccines, particularly if traveling off the beaten path, as well as a rabies vaccine and yearly influenza vaccines. While yellow fever is only endemic to parts of South America and sub-Saharan Africa, many countries may deny entrance to travelers arriving from these zones without a certificate of vaccination. For recommendations on immunizations and prophylaxis, consult the **Centers for Disease Control and Prevention (CDC;** below) in the US or the equivalent in your home country and check with a doctor for guidance. Travelers heading to the provinces of Alajuela, Limón, Guanacaste, or Heredia should obtain malaria pills; begin taking them at least a week before departure. The CDC recommends chloroquine for Costa Rica. Insect protection measures, such as insect repellent and mosquito nets, are recommended against malaria and other insect-borne diseases like dengue fever (for which no vaccine currently exists).

INSURANCE

Travel insurance covers four basic areas: medical/health problems, property loss, trip cancellation/interruption, and emergency evacuation. Though regular insurance policies may well extend to travel-related accidents, you may consider purchasing separate travel insurance if the cost of potential trip cancellation, interruption, or emergency medical evacuation is greater than you can absorb. Prices for travel insurance purchased separately generally run about US$50 per week for full coverage, while trip cancellation/interruption may be purchased separately at a rate of US$3-5 per day, depending on length of stay.

Medical insurance (especially university policies) often covers costs incurred abroad; check with your provider. **Homeowners' insurance** (or your family's coverage) often covers theft during travel and loss of travel documents (passport, plane ticket, railpass, etc.) up to US$500.

ISIC and **ITIC** (p. 11) provide basic insurance to US cardholders, with US$100 per day of in-hospital care for up to 100 days and US$10,000 of accident-related medical reimbursement (see www.isicus.com for details). Cardholders have access to a 24hr. helpline for medical, legal, and financial emergencies overseas. **American Express** (☎+1-800-338-1670) grants cardholders automatic collision and theft car rental insurance on rentals made with the card.

USEFUL ORGANIZATIONS AND PUBLICATIONS

The American **Centers for Disease Control and Prevention** (**CDC;** ☎+1-877-FYI-TRIP; www.cdc.gov/travel) maintains an international travelers' hotline and an informative website. Consult the appropriate government agency of your home country for consular information sheets on health, entry requirements, and other issues for various countries (see the listings in the box on **Travel Advisories,** p. 18). For quick information on health and other travel warnings, call the **Overseas Citizens Services** (from overseas ☎+1-202-501-4444, from US 888-407-4747; line open M-F 8am-8pm EST), or contact a passport agency, embassy, or consulate abroad. For information on medical evacuation services and travel insurance firms, see the US government's website at http://travel.state.gov/travel/abroad_health.html or the **British Foreign and Commonwealth Office** (www.fco.gov.uk). For general health information, contact the **American Red Cross** (☎+1-202-303-4498; www.redcross.org).

STAYING HEALTHY

Common sense is the simplest prescription for good health while you travel. Drink lots of fluids to prevent dehydration and constipation and wear sturdy, broken-in shoes and clean socks. Adequate fluid intake is especially important for travelers dealing with (aptly named) traveler's diarrhea, but the contaminated water that makes this issue a widespread problem for Costa Rican travelers also makes it imperative to approach all fluid intake with care; do not drink tap water, drinks with ice, or fruit and vegetables that have not been peeled or cooked. Visitors should stay away from unpasteurized dairy products and avoid purchasing beverages from street vendors.

ONCE IN COSTA RICA

ENVIRONMENTAL HAZARDS

Heat exhaustion and dehydration: Heat exhaustion leads to nausea, excessive thirst, headaches, and dizziness. Avoid it by drinking plenty of fluids, eating salty foods (e.g., crackers), abstaining from dehydrating beverages (e.g., alcohol and caffeinated beverages), and always wearing sunscreen. Continuous heat stress can eventually lead to heatstroke, characterized by a rising temperature, severe headache, delirium and cessation of sweating. Victims should be cooled off with wet towels and taken to a doctor.

Sunburn: Always wear sunscreen (SPF 30 or higher) when spending excessive amounts of time outdoors. If you get sunburned, drink more fluids than usual and apply an aloe-based lotion. Severe sunburns can lead to sun poisoning, a condition that can cause fever, chills, nausea, and vomiting. Sun poisoning should always be treated by a doctor.

High Altitude: Allow your body a couple of days to adjust to less oxygen before exerting yourself. Note that alcohol is more potent and UV rays are stronger at high elevations.

INSECT-BORNE DISEASES

Many diseases are transmitted by insects—mainly mosquitoes, fleas, ticks, and lice. Be aware of insects in wet or forested areas, especially while hiking and camping. Wear long pants and long sleeves, tuck your pants into your socks, and use a mosquito net. Use insect repellents such as DEET and soak or spray your gear with permethrin (licensed in the US only for use on clothing). **Mosquitoes**—responsible for malaria, dengue fever, and yellow fever—can be particularly abundant in wet, swampy, or wooded areas. In Costa Rica, there is risk of malaria in Alajuela, Limón, Guanacaste, and Heredia.

Malaria: Transmitted by Anopheles mosquitoes that bite at night. The incubation period varies anywhere between 10 days and 4 weeks. Early symptoms include fever, chills, aches, and fatigue, followed by high fever and sweating, sometimes with vomiting and diarrhea. See a doctor for any flu-like sickness that occurs after travel in a high-risk area. To reduce the risk of contracting malaria, use mosquito repellent, particularly in the evenings and when visiting forested areas. Make sure you see a doctor at least 4-6 weeks before a trip to a high-risk area to get up-to-date malaria prescriptions and recommendations. A doctor may prescribe oral prophylactics, like mefloquine or doxycycline. Be aware that mefloquine can have some very serious side effects, including paranoia, psychotic behavior, and nightmares.

Dengue fever: An "urban viral infection" transmitted by Aedes mosquitos, which bite during the day (rather than at night) and favor densely populated areas. The incubation period is 3-14 days, usually 4-7 days. Early symptoms include a high fever, severe headaches, swollen lymph nodes, and muscle aches. Many patients also suffer from nausea, vomiting, and a pink rash. If you experience these symptoms, see a doctor immediately, drink plenty of liquids, and take a fever-reducing medication like Tylenol. Never take aspirin to treat dengue fever. There is no vaccine available for dengue fever. Dengue is endemic to Costa Rica, and 35,000 cases were identified in 2005.

Yellow fever: A viral disease transmitted by mosquitos; derives its name from one of its most common symptoms, the jaundice caused by liver damage. While most cases are mild, the severe ones begin with fever, headache, muscle pain, nausea, and abdominal pain before progressing to jaundice, vomiting of blood, and bloody stools. While there is no specific treatment, there is an effective vaccine that offers 10 years of protection.

Other insect-borne diseases: Lymphatic filariasis is a roundworm infestation transmitted by mosquitos. Infection causes enlargement of extremities and has no vaccine, though it can be fairly easily treated. Within Costa Rica, the risk is greatest in Limón.

Leishmaniasis, a parasite transmitted by sand flies, is an issue is some cattle-raising areas in the northwest as well as some coastal regions (Limón and Golfito). Common symptoms are fever, weakness, and swelling of the spleen, as well as skin sores weeks to months after the bite. There is a treatment but no vaccine. **CHAGAS disease (American trypanomiasis)** is another relatively common parasite transmitted by the cone nose and kissing bug, which infests mud, adobe, and thatch. The disease is particularly prevalent in Alajuela, Liberia, and Puntarenas. Its symptoms are fever, heart disease, and enlarged intestines. There is no vaccine and treatment options are limited, but risk to travelers is generally quite low.

FOOD- AND WATER-BORNE DISEASES

Prevention is the best cure: be sure that your food is properly cooked and the water you drink is clean. Watch out for food from markets or street vendors that may have been cooked in unhygienic conditions. Though Costa Rica's street markets offer an amazing selection of fresh produce—everything from Asian water apples to *zapote* (like a sweet potato with an avocado pit)—this produce should be carefully purchased and prepared: it should be obtained unpeeled, or else only consumed once cooked. Other culprits are raw shellfish, unpasteurized milk, and sauces containing raw eggs. Buy bottled water or purify your own water by bringing it to a rolling boil or treating it with **iodine tablets;** note, however, that boiling is more reliable.

Traveler's diarrhea: Results from drinking fecally contaminated water or eating uncooked and contaminated foods. Symptoms include nausea, bloating, and urgency. Try quick-energy, non-sugary foods with protein and carbohydrates to keep your strength up. Over-the-counter anti-diarrheals (e.g., Imodium®) may counteract the problem. The most dangerous side effect is dehydration; drink 8 oz. of water with ½ tsp. of sugar or honey and a pinch of salt, try uncaffeinated soft drinks, or eat salted crackers. If you develop a fever or your symptoms don't go away after 4-5 days, consult a doctor. Consult a doctor immediately for treatment of diarrhea in children.

Dysentery: Results from an intestinal infection caused by bacteria in contaminated food or water. Common symptoms include bloody diarrhea, fever, and abdominal pain and tenderness. The most common type of dysentery generally lasts a week, but it is highly contagious. Seek medical help immediately. Dysentery can be treated with the drugs norfloxacin or ciprofloxacin (commonly known as Cipro). If you are traveling in high-risk (especially rural) regions, consider obtaining a prescription before you leave home.

Cholera: An intestinal disease caused by bacteria in contaminated food. Symptoms include diarrhea, dehydration, vomiting, and muscle cramps. See a doctor immediately; if left untreated, cholera can be lethal within hours. Antibiotics are available, but the most important treatment is rehydration. No vaccine is available in the US.

Hepatitis A: A viral infection of the liver acquired through contaminated water or shellfish from contaminated water. Symptoms include fatigue, fever, loss of appetite, nausea, dark urine, jaundice, vomiting, aches and pains, and light stools. The risk is highest in rural areas and the countryside, but it is also present in urban areas. Ask your doctor about the Hepatitis A vaccine or an injection of immune globulin.

Giardiasis: Transmitted through parasites and acquired by drinking untreated water from streams or lakes. Symptoms include diarrhea, cramps, bloating, fatigue, weight loss, and nausea. If untreated, it can lead to severe dehydration. Giardiasis occurs worldwide.

Typhoid fever: Caused by the salmonella bacteria; common in villages and rural areas in Costa Rica. While mostly transmitted through contaminated food and water, it may also be acquired by direct contact with another person. Early symptoms include high fever, headaches, fatigue, appetite loss, constipation, and a rash on the abdomen or chest. Antibiotics can treat typhoid, but a vaccination (70-90% effective) is recommended.

OTHER INFECTIOUS DISEASES

The following diseases exist all over the world. Travelers should know how to recognize them and what to do if they suspect they have been infected.

Hepatitis B: A viral infection of the liver transmitted via blood or other bodily fluids. Symptoms, which may not surface until years after infection, include jaundice, appetite loss, fever, and joint pain. It is transmitted through unprotected sex and unclean needles. A 3-shot vaccination sequence, 6 months before traveling, is recommended for sexually active travelers and anyone planning to seek medical treatment abroad.

AIDS and HIV: For detailed information on **Acquired Immune Deficiency Syndrome (AIDS)** in Costa Rica, call the 24hr. National AIDS Hotline at ☎+1-800-342-2437.

Sexually transmitted infections (STIs): Gonorrhea, chlamydia, genital warts, syphilis, herpes, HPV, and other STIs are easier to catch than HIV and can be just as serious. Though condoms may protect you from some STIs, oral or even tactile contact can lead to transmission. If you think you may have contracted an STI, see a doctor immediately.

OTHER HEALTH CONCERNS

MEDICAL CARE ON THE ROAD

Costa Rica provides free, universal health care to its citizens. The quality of medical care is high in both public and private hospitals. The number of facilities may be limited outside of the more urban areas. Most doctors have received training in the US, Europe, or Canada, and a large number speak English.

If you are concerned about obtaining medical assistance while traveling, you can employ special support services. The **MedPass** from **GlobalCare, Inc.,** 6875 Shiloh Rd. East, Alpharetta, GA 30005, USA (☎+1-800-860-1111; www.globalcare.net), provides 24hr. international medical assistance, support, and medical evacuation resources. The **International Association for Medical Assistance to Travelers** (**IAMAT;** US ☎+1-716-754-4883, Canada 519-836-0102; www.iamat.org) has free membership, lists English-speaking doctors worldwide, and offers detailed information on immunization requirements and sanitation. If your regular insurance policy does not cover travel abroad, you may want to purchase additional coverage (p. 20).

Those with medical conditions (such as diabetes, allergies to antibiotics, epilepsy, or heart conditions) may want to obtain a **MedicAlert** membership (US\$40 per year), which includes, among other things, a stainless-steel ID tag and a 24hr. collect-call number. Contact the MedicAlert Foundation International, 2323 Colorado Ave., Turlock, CA 95382, USA (☎+1-888-633-4298, outside US 209-668-3333; www.medicalert.org).

WOMEN'S HEALTH

Costa Rica is considered to be one of the most sanitary countries in Central America, but women should still take caution, especially in rural areas. Women traveling in unsanitary conditions are vulnerable to urinary tract (including bladder and kidney) infections. Vaginal yeast infections may flare up in hot and humid climates. Wearing loosely-fitting trousers or a skirt and cotton underwear will help, as will over-the-counter remedies like Monostat® or Gynelotrimin®. Bring supplies from home if you are prone to infection, as they may be difficult to find on the road. And, since tampons, pads, and reliable contraceptive devices are sometimes hard to find when traveling, bring supplies with you. Abortion is illegal in Costa Rica, unless the mother's life is in danger.

GETTING TO COSTA RICA

BY PLANE

When it comes to airfare, a little effort can save you a bundle. Courier fares are the cheapest for those whose plans are flexible enough to deal with the restrictions. Tickets sold by consolidators and standby seating are also good deals, but last-minute specials, airfare wars, and charter flights often beat these fares. The key is to hunt around, be flexible, and ask about discounts. Students, seniors, and those under 26 should never pay full price for a ticket.

AIRFARES

Airfares to Costa Rica peak between December and April and from July to September; holidays, especially Christmas and Easter, are also expensive. The cheapest times to travel are between mid-September and November and between April and July. Midweek (M-Th morning) round-trip flights run US$40-50 cheaper than weekend flights but are generally more crowded and less likely to permit frequent-flier upgrades. Not fixing a return date ("open return") or arriving in and departing from different cities ("open-jaw") can be pricier than round-trip flights. Patching one-way flights together is the most expensive way to travel. Flights between cities within Costa Rica will tend to be cheaper (see **San José: Flights,** p. 83).

If Costa Rica is only one stop on a more extensive globe-hop, consider a round-the-world (RTW) ticket. Tickets usually include at least five stops and are valid for about a year; prices range US$1200-5000. Try **Northwest Airlines/KLM** (☎+1-800-225-2525; www.nwa.com) or **Star Alliance,** a consortium of 16 airlines including United Airlines (www.staralliance.com).

Fares for roundtrip flights to San José from the US or Canadian east coast cost US$450-850, US$350-750 in the low season (May-Nov.); from the US or Canadian west coast US$400-700/500-800; from the UK, UK₤500-800 in both the high and low seasons; from Australia AUS$2400-4000 for both the high and low seasons; from New Zealand NZ$2500-3200/3100-8800.

BUDGET AND STUDENT TRAVEL AGENCIES

While knowledgeable agents specializing in flights to Costa Rica can make your life easy, they may not spend time to find the lowest fare—they get paid on commission. Travelers with ISICs and IYTCs (p. 11) can get discounts from student travel agencies. Most flights from budget agencies are on major airlines, but in peak season some may put you on less-reliable chartered aircraft.

STA Travel, 5900 Wilshire Blvd., Ste. 900, Los Angeles, CA 90036, USA (24hr. reservations and info ☎+1-800-781-4040; www.statravel.com). A student and youth travel organization with over 150 offices worldwide (check their website for a listing of all their offices), including US offices in Boston, Chicago, Los Angeles, New York City, Seattle, San Francisco, and Washington, DC. Ticket booking, travel insurance, railpasses, and more.

Walk-in offices are located throughout Australia (☎+61 3 9207 5900), New Zealand (☎+64 9 309 9723), and the UK (☎+44 8701 630 026).

The Adventure Travel Company, 124 MacDougal St., New York, NY, 10021, USA (☎+1-800-467-4595; www.theadventuretravelcompany.com). Offices in Canada and the US including Champaign, New York City, San Diego, Seattle, and San Francisco.

USIT, 19-21 Aston Quay, Dublin 2, Ireland (☎+353 1 602 1906; www.usit.ie). Ireland's leading student/budget travel agency has 20 offices throughout Northern Ireland and the Republic of Ireland. Offers programs to work, study, and volunteer worldwide.

FLIGHT PLANNING ON THE INTERNET. The Internet may be the budget traveler's dream when it comes to finding and booking bargain fares, but the array of options can be overwhelming. Many airline sites offer special last-minute deals on the web. **American Airlines** (www.aa.com), **Continental** (www.continental.com), **Delta** (www.delta.com), **United Airways** (www.united.com), **US Airways** (www.usairways.com), **Taca** (www.taca.com), and **Copa** (www.copaair.com) all fly to San José; American, Continental, and Delta also fly to the smaller airport in Liberia. **STA** (www.statravel.com) and **StudentUniverse** (www.studentuniverse.com) provide quotes on student tickets, while **Orbitz** (www.orbitz.com), **Expedia** (www.expedia.com), and **Travelocity** (www.travelocity.com) offer full travel services. **Priceline** (www.priceline.com) lets you specify a price and obligates you to buy any ticket that meets or beats it; **Hotwire** (www.hotwire.com) offers bargain fares but won't reveal the airline or flight times until you buy. Other sites that compile deals include www.bestfares.com, www.flights.com, www.lowestfare.com, www.onetravel.com, and www.travelzoo.com. **SideStep** (www.sidestep.com) and **Booking Buddy** (www.bookingbuddy.com) are online tools that can help sift through multiple offers; these 2 let you enter your trip information once and search multiple sites. **Air Traveler's Handbook** (www.faqs.org/faqs/travel/air/handbook) is an indispensable resource on the Internet; it has a comprehensive listing of links to everything you need to know before you board a plane.

COMMERCIAL AIRLINES

The commercial airlines' lowest regular offer is the **APEX (Advance Purchase Excursion)** fare, which provides confirmed reservations and allows "open-jaw" tickets. Generally, reservations must be made seven to 21 days in advance, with seven- to 14-day minimum-stay and up to 90-day maximum-stay restrictions. These fares carry hefty cancellation and change penalties (fees rise in summer). Book peak-season APEX fares early. Use **Expedia** (www.expedia.com) or **Travelocity** (www.travelocity.com) to get an idea of the lowest published fares, then use the resources outlined here to try to beat those fares. Low season fares should be cheaper than the high season (Dec.-May) ones listed here.

TRAVELING FROM NORTH AMERICA

Basic round-trip fares to Costa Rica range roughly US$350-850. Standard commercial carriers like American and United will probably offer the most convenient flights, but they may not be the cheapest, unless you snag a special promotion or airfare-war ticket. You will probably find flying one of the

following "discount" airlines to be a better deal, if any of their limited departure points happens to be convenient for you.

> **Taca International.** Offers flights from most major US cities with fares starting at US$600
> (☎+1-800-400-TACA/8222; www.taca.com). Also includes Lacsa Airlines.

> **Copa.** Departs for San José from Los Angeles, Miami, New York City, and Orlando with
> fares starting at US$300 (☎+1-800-FLY-COPA/359 2672; www.copaair.com).

> **Martinair Holland.** Departs for Costa Rica from only the Miami airport, but offers the
> cheapest fares starting at US$200 (☎+1-305-704-9800 ; www.martinair.com).

TRAVELING FROM IRELAND AND THE UK
No Irish airlines provide service to Costa Rica. British Airways flies from London to a number of locations before providing connecting flights to San José.

TRAVELING FROM AUSTRALIA AND NEW ZEALAND
From Australia or New Zealand, the least expensive route is via Los Angeles or
Miami. Many airlines provide comparable flights to these destinations.

AIR COURIER FLIGHTS

Those who travel light should consider courier flights. Couriers transport
cargo on international flights by using their checked luggage space for freight.
Generally, couriers are limited to carry-ons and must deal with complex flight
restrictions. Most flights are round-trip only, with fixed-length stays (usually
one week) and a limit of one ticket per issue. Most of these flights operate only
out of major gateway cities, mostly in North America. Courier fares from the
US to Costa Rica run about US$89-280. Most flights leave from Los Angeles,
Miami, New York, or San Francisco in the US; and from Montreal, Toronto, or
Vancouver in Canada. Generally, you must be over 18 (in some cases 21). In
summer, the most popular destinations require an advance reservation of about
two weeks (you can usually book up to two months ahead). Super-discounted
fares are common for "last-minute" flights (from three to 14 days ahead).

STANDBY FLIGHTS

Traveling standby requires considerable flexibility in arrival and departure
dates. Companies dealing in standby flights sell vouchers rather than tickets,
along with the promise to get you to your destination (or near your destination) within a certain window of time (typically 1-5 days). You call in before
your specific window of time to hear your flight options and the probability
that you will be able to board each flight. You can then decide which flights
you want to try to catch, show up at the appropriate airport at the appropriate time, present your voucher, and board if space is available. Vouchers can
usually be bought for both one-way and round-trip travel. You may receive a
monetary refund only if every available flight within your date range is full; if
you opt not to take an available (but perhaps less-convenient) flight, you can
only get credit toward future travel. To check on a company's service record in
the US, contact the **Better Business Bureau** (☎+1-703-276-0100; www.bbb.org). It
is difficult to receive refunds, and clients' vouchers will not be honored when
an airline fails to receive payment in time.

TICKET CONSOLIDATORS

Ticket consolidators, or **"bucket shops,"** buy unsold tickets in bulk from commercial airlines and sell them at discounted rates. The best place to look is in the Sunday travel section of any major newspaper (such as *The New York Times*), where many bucket shops place tiny ads. Call quickly, as availability is extremely limited. Not all bucket shops are reliable, so insist on a receipt that gives full details of restrictions, refunds, and tickets, and pay by credit card (in spite of the 2-5% fee) so you can stop payment if you never receive your tickets. For more info, see www.travel-library.com/air-travel/consolidators.html.

TRAVELING FROM CANADA AND THE US

Consolidators include **Rebel** (☎+1-800-732-3588; www.rebeltours.com), **Cheap Tickets** (www.cheaptickets.com), **Flights.com** (www.flights.com), and **TravelHUB** (www.travelhub.com). *Let's Go* does not endorse any of these agencies. As always, be cautious, and research before handing out a credit-card number.

CHARTER FLIGHTS

Tour operators contract charter flights with airlines in order to fly extra loads of passengers during peak season. These flights are far from hassle free. They occur less frequently than major airlines, make refunds particularly difficult, and are almost always fully booked. Their scheduled times may change or be canceled at the last moment (as late as 48hr. before the trip, and without a full refund). In addition, check-in, boarding, and baggage claim for them are often much slower. They can, however, be much cheaper.

Discount clubs and fare brokers offer members savings on last-minute charter and tour deals. Study contracts closely; you don't want to end up with an unwanted overnight layover. **Travelers Advantage** (☎+1-800-835-8747; www.travelersadvantage.com; US$90 annual fee includes discounts and cheap flight directories) specializes in **European travel** and tour packages.

BY BOAT

Costa Rica's natural beauty and exotic beaches make it a celebrated stop for cruise lines. **Royal Caribbean Cruise Lines** (www.royalcaribbean.com) and **Princess Cruise Lines** (www.princess.com) stop by Costa Rica en route to their main destinations. Both Royal Caribbean and Prince cruise lines have multiple departure points around the world.

BORDER CROSSINGS

NICARAGUA. There is one land crossing at **Peñas Blancas/Sapoa** (p. 206), 75km north of Liberia and near Rivas, Nicaragua. There is also a crossing at **Río San Juan** near Los Chiles (p. 173), south of San Carlos, Nicaragua.

PANAMA. There are three land crossings: **Paso Canoas** (p. 327) is 18km southeast of Neily, Costa Rica, near David, Panama. **Sixaola/Guabito** (p. 392) is on the Caribbean coast about 1hr. from Puerto Viejo de Talamanca, near Changuinola, Panama. Another crossing at **Río Sereno,** east of San Vito, is rarely used.

GETTING AROUND COSTA RICA

A word of advice: ask. *Ticos* are extremely friendly, and signs in Costa Rica are very limited (nonexistent in some places), so if you have any doubts, or carrying a map isn't helping, just stop and ask. People are usually quick to help. Landmarks are the way of the wise in most of Costa Rica. Most mid-range and larger towns have streets in an orderly grid of *avenidas* (avenues) and *calles* (streets); *avenidas* typically run east-west and *calles* north-south. Usually, odd-numbered *avenidas* increase in number to the north and even-numbered to the south, while odd-numbered *calles* lie to the east of the grid's center and even-numbered *calles* to the west. The grid is usually centered on some sort of *parque central* (central park), and its axes are usually called Av. Central and C. Central. An address given as Av. 3/5, Calle 2 means the building is between Avenidas 3 and 5, on Calle 2. Locations are often specified by a certain number of *metros* from the *parque*. *Metros* here refers to portions of city blocks, not actual meters, with 100 *metros* being the equivalent of one city block; 100 *metros al norte del parque central* indicates a building one block north of the *parque*. When it comes to walking, cars have the right of way, not pedestrians, so look twice before crossing the street, even if you have a crosswalk.

BY PLANE

Domestic air travel is more expensive but more convenient than traveling by bus. While smaller airlines do offer domestic flights, it is recommended that you use the two larger airlines, **Sansa** and **NatureAir.** Sansa (US ☎+1-877-767-2672; www.flysansa.com) and the pricier, more reliable NatureAir (☎US or Canada +1-800-235-9272; www.natureair.net), have flights connecting San José with destinations throughout Costa Rica (p. 83). Both have several years of experience. Children under age 2 fly for free on Sansa (one-way trips for adults US$53-89 depending on destination; round-trips US$108-180). Children under the age of 12 get a 25% discount off the regular fare on NatureAir (one-way domestic trips for adults US$90-140; round-trips US$106-198).

BY BUS

The bus system is thorough, cheap, and reliable. From San José, you can travel almost anywhere in the country for under US$6. However, it's not always immediately clear where the buses arrive, when they leave, where tickets can be purchased, or even how much they cost. Some tickets can only be purchased on the bus, while others must be purchased at a ticket window ahead of time. Just ask around and people will know. The bus system is a maze; every destination is served by a different company, and each company is located in a different part of town. Note, however, that a seemingly microscopic, direct distance between two points on a map often translates into hours on a bumpy, windy road. You can find the most accurate bus information, including detailed schedules and maps at the **Instituto Costarricense de Turismo** (ICT; ☎299 5800, from the US 1-866-COSTARICA/267827422), along C. 5 in San José, next to El Museo de Oro (see **San José: Buses,** p. 86).

BY CAR

If you're traveling by car, you'll have a good network of highways at your disposal. A seat belt must be worn by the driver and any passengers. Keep your passport and driver's license with you at all times. Although the government has been working on paving and fixing roads, road conditions still vary and tend to be quite rough (by international standards) in some places. Potholes and bumps may make it hard to relax while driving. Watch out for open manholes along side roads, especially after rain. Also be wary of speedy drivers who want to pass you on narrow, windy roads. If they try to pass, let them.

Many places do require four-wheel-drive (4WD) vehicles, especially during the rainy season, so it's good to know where you're going and what the roads are like there before you rent your car. Car rental agencies might be able to help you with information on road conditions. Visit the **Association for Safe International Road Travel** (**ASIRT;** www.asirt.org) for information on safe road travel.

RENTING

Renting a car in Costa Rica is a great idea if you're planning on leaving the city and would prefer not to wait for a potentially crowded bus. Most tourist destinations are only a few hours away, and you will definitely enjoy the scenery and beautiful countryside as you drive. If you're staying in the city, however, it could be a hassle. Parking and traffic make it more difficult to drive than to walk or use public transportation, which isn't very expensive. Also, in urban areas, rental cars are a common target for theft.

When choosing a car, it is important to consider that cheaper cars tend to be less reliable and harder to handle on difficult terrain. Although many places can be accessed without 4WD during the dry season, road conditions can change drastically during the rainy season. If you're planning on visiting Monteverde, any place south of Golfito, the southern Nicoya Peninsula, or the Osa Peninsula, a 4WD vehicle is recommended regardless of the time of year. It's important to be careful about the type of 4WD vehicle you rent. Less-expensive 4WD vehicles tend to be more top-heavy and more dangerous when navigating particularly bumpy roads. Knowing how to drive standard cars is essential.

RENTAL AGENCIES

You can generally make reservations before you leave by calling major international offices in your home country. It's a good idea to cross-check this information with local agencies as well. The local desk numbers are included in town listings; for home-country numbers, call your toll-free directory.

To rent a car from most establishments in Costa Rica, you need to be at least 23 years old. Some agencies require renters to be 25, and most charge those 21-24 an additional insurance fee of around US$50. Small local operations rent to people under 21, but be sure to ask about insurance coverage and deductible, and always check the fine print. Rental agencies in Costa Rica include:

Adobe Rent a Car (☎2258 4242 or toll free to US and Canada +1-800-769-8422; www.adobecar.com). High season prices range from US$43 per day for a sedan to US$107 for a 4WD. 21+. Valid license, passport, and credit card required. Free road assistance and drop off and pick up at hotels near agency offices.

Budget Rent a Car (☎2436 2000; www.budget.co.cr). Prices in high season range from US$43 to US$100. Low season prices range from US$30 per day for a sedan to US$69 for a 4WD. Valid license and passport required. 21+. Major credit card with at least $750 plus the cost of rent is required with each purchase.

COSTS AND INSURANCE

Rental car prices start at around US$28 per day from national companies and US$32 from local agencies. Expect to pay more for larger cars and for 4WD. Cars with **automatic transmission** can cost up to US$12 per day more than cars with manual transmission (stick shift), and automatic transmission can be hard to find in the first place. It is often difficult to find an automatic 4WD.

Remember that if you are driving a conventional rental vehicle on an unpaved road in a rental car, you are almost never covered by insurance, so ask about this before leaving the rental agency. Be aware that cars rented on an **American Express** or **Visa/MasterCard Gold** or **Platinum** credit card in Costa Rica might not carry the automatic insurance that they would in some other countries; check with your credit-card company. Insurance plans from rental companies almost always come with an **excess** of around US$20 for conventional vehicles; excess ranges up to around US$50 for younger drivers and for 4WD. This means that the insurance bought from the rental company applies only to damages over the excess. Damages up to that amount must be covered by your existing insurance plan. Some rental companies in Costa Rica require you to buy a **Collision Damage Waiver (CDW),** which will waive the excess in the case of a collision. **Loss Damage Waivers (LDWs)** do the same in the case of theft or vandalism.

National chains often allow one-way rentals (picking up in one city and dropping off in another). There is usually a minimum hire period and sometimes an extra dropoff charge of several hundred dollars.

DRIVING PERMITS AND CAR INSURANCE

INTERNATIONAL DRIVING PERMIT (IDP)

If you plan to drive a car while in Costa Rica, you must be over 18 and have an International Driving Permit (IDP), though Costa Rica does allow travelers to drive with a valid American or Canadian license for as long as your visa lasts. Proof of entry is also required for a police officer to accept your license, so carry your passport. It may be a good idea to get an IDP anyway, in case you're in a situation (e.g., an accident in a small town) where the police do not know English. Information on the IDP is printed in 11 languages, including Spanish.

Your IDP, valid for one year, must be issued in your own country before you depart. An application for an IDP usually requires one or two photos, a current local license, an additional form of identification, and a fee. To apply, contact your home country's automobile association. Be vigilant when purchasing an IDP online or anywhere other than your home automobile association. Many vendors sell permits of questionable legitimacy for higher prices.

CAR INSURANCE

Most credit cards cover standard insurance. If you rent, lease, or borrow a car, you will need a **green card,** or **International Insurance Certificate,** to certify that you have liability insurance and that it applies abroad. Green cards can be obtained at car rental agencies, car dealers (for those leasing cars), some travel agents, and some border crossings. Rental agencies may require you to purchase theft insurance in countries that they consider to have a high risk of auto theft.

ON THE ROAD

The speed limit on the highway varies. The minimum speed is 40kph. On secondary roads the speed limit is 60km per hr. unless otherwise listed. In urban areas it is 40kph. Around school zones, hospitals, and clinics, it is 25kph.

Driving on the beaches is prohibited everywhere, except when there is no road or path that connects two towns. All passengers must wear seatbelts, and you must pull over if police ask you to do so. Never forget your personal documents and the vehicle's registration papers. Some travelers report that police may ask for a small fee instead of issuing a ticket; as tickets rarely exceed US$30, it's a good idea to just pay the ticket instead of risking getting in trouble and encouraging a bad practice. Gasoline (petrol) prices vary, but average about ¢600-650 per liter thoughout the country.

DRIVING PRECAUTIONS. When traveling in the summer or in the desert, bring lots of water (a suggested 5L of water per person per day) for drinking and for the radiator. You should always carry a spare tire and jack, jumper cables, extra oil, flares, a flashlight, and heavy blankets (in case your car breaks down at night or in the winter). If you don't know how to change a tire, learn before heading out, especially if you're planning on traveling in deserted areas. If your car breaks down, stay in your vehicle.

DANGERS

The most important rule is to be confident and stay alert. In general, roads in Costa Rica are not very wide and can be quite curvy and dangerous in the outskirts of the country, especially when leaving the Central Valley to reach the coasts. There are few road signs and many blind curves. Don't pass other cars when you don't have perfect visibility, and if someone is passing, just let them cut in line. When driving in the city, keep your doors locked and your windows shut at all times. Never leave your car parked in a poorly lit or deserted area, and never leave any visible valuables in a parked car.

CAR ASSISTANCE

If you are involved in an accident, you should usually wait until the police arrive to move your vehicle so that an officer can prepare a report. If you do not feel safe at the scene of the accident, however, drive to the nearest lit, public area and call the police from there. If a police officer attempts to retain your personal documents for no clear reason, ask him to escort you to the nearest police station. You can report an accident by calling ☎911 or 800 012 3456.

BY BOAT

Boat transportation is only necessary to enter and exit Parque Nacional Tortuguero (p. 370). However, it is a fairly common mode of transportation along the Caribbean Lowlands. Ranging from *panchas* or water taxis to larger ferries, boats are just as reliable as buses. However, boats are almost always open to the elements, with little shelter from bad weather. Public boat transport is available daily out of Limón, but it might be easier to stick to prearranged packages set up by your hotel or by tour operators.

ESSENTIALS

BY THUMB

LET'S NOT GO. *Let's Go* never recommends hitchhiking as a safe means of transportation, and none of the information here is meant to do so.

Let's Go strongly urges you to consider the risks before you choose to hitchhike. Hitching means entrusting your life to a stranger and risking assault, sexual harassment, theft, and unsafe driving. For women traveling alone (or even in pairs), hitching is just too dangerous. A man and a woman are a less dangerous combination; two men will have a harder time getting a lift, while three men will go nowhere. In Costa Rica, tourists report that hitchhiking is generally safe, but it is not too common and is discouraged on main roadways and urban areas. In rural areas, it is considered a safer, slightly more common form of transportation. Women should not hitchhike alone.

KEEPING IN TOUCH

BY EMAIL AND INTERNET

Internet service is plentiful and speedy in Costa Rica. Service is provided by Radiográfica Costarricense, a government-owned subsidiary of the ICE (Instituto Costarricense de Electricidad), and Internet cafes are scattered all over the country. Rates vary, ranging from $2-4 per hour, but in smaller cities, it may be more expensive. You can also rent computer time in ICE offices. Some hotels will have free Wi-Fi or Internet access.

Although in some places it's possible to forge a remote link with your home server, in most cases it is a slower (and more expensive) option than taking advantage of free **web-based email accounts** (e.g., www.gmail.com and www.hotmail.com). **Internet cafes** and the occasional free Internet at a public library or university are listed in the **Practical Information** sections of major cities. For lists of additional cybercafes in Costa Rica, check out www.cybercaptive.com.

Laptop users can call an Internet service provider via a modem using long-distance phone cards intended for such calls. They may also find Internet cafes that allow them to connect their laptops to the Internet. Lucky travelers with Wi-Fi-enabled computers may be able to take advantage of a number of Internet "hot spots," where they can get online for free or a small fee. Newer computers can detect these hot spots automatically; otherwise, websites like www.jiwire.com, www.wififreespot.com, and www.wi-fihotspotlist.com can help you find them. For information on insuring your laptop while traveling, see p. 18.

WARY WI-FI. Wireless hot spots make Internet access possible in public and remote places. Unfortunately, they also pose **security risks.** Hot spots are public, open networks that use unencrypted, unsecured connections. They are susceptible to hacks and "packet sniffing"—ways of stealing passwords and other private information. To prevent problems, disable ad hoc mode, turn off file-sharing and network discovery, encrypt your email, turn on your firewall, beware of phony networks, and watch for over-the-shoulder creeps.

BY TELEPHONE

CALLING HOME FROM COSTA RICA

Prepaid phone cards are a common, relatively inexpensive means of calling abroad. Each one comes with a Personal Identification Number (PIN) and a toll-free access number. You call the access number and then follow the directions for dialing your PIN. To purchase prepaid phone cards, check online for the best rates; www.callingcards.com is a good place to start. Online providers generally send your access number and PIN via email, with no actual "card" involved. You can also call home with prepaid phone cards purchased here.

PLACING INTERNATIONAL CALLS. To call Costa Rica from home or to call home from Costa Rica, dial:
1. The **international dialing prefix.** To call from **Australia,** dial 0011; **Canada** or the **US,** 011; **Ireland, New Zealand,** or the **UK,** 00.
2. The **country code** of the country you want to call. To call **Australia,** dial 61; **Canada** or the **US,** 1; **Ireland,** 353; **New Zealand,** 64; the **UK,** 44; Costa Rica, 506.
3. The **local number.**

Another option is to purchase a **calling card,** linked to a major national tele-communications service in your home country. Calls are billed collect or to your account. To call home with a calling card, contact the operator for your service provider in Costa Rica by dialing the appropriate toll-free access number (listed below in the third column).

COMPANY	TO OBTAIN A CARD:	TO CALL ABROAD:
AT&T (US)	☎+1-800-364-9292 or www.att.com	0800-011-4114
Canada Direct	☎+1-800-561-8868 or www.infocanadadirect.com	0800-015-1161
MCI (US)	☎+1-800-777-5000 or www.minutepass.com	0800-012-2222
Telecom New Zealand Direct	www.telecom.co.nz	0800 22 55 98

Collect calls through international operators can be expensive, but may be necessary in an emergency. You can call collect without possessing a company's calling card just by calling its access number and following instructions.

CALLING WITHIN COSTA RICA

The simplest way to call within the country is to use a coin-operated phone. Prepaid phone cards (available at newspaper kiosks and tobacco stores, or supermarkets), usually save time and money in the long run. Phone rates typically tend to be highest in the morning, lower in the evening, and lowest on Sunday and late at night. The numbers in Costa Rica have recently changed from seven digits to eight. All land-line phones have added a "2" to the beginning of the number, and all cell phones have added an "8."

CELLULAR PHONES

The **Instituto Costarricense de Electricidad (ICE)** is the sole provider of cell phone service in Costa Rica. Your cell phone will probably not work unless you arrange it with ICE and your home carrier before leaving. Cell phones are popular in Costa Rica, and coverage is becoming more widespread.

The international standard for cell phones is **Global System for Mobile Communication (GSM)**. To make and receive calls in Costa Rica, you will need a GSM-compatible phone and a **SIM (Subscriber Identity Module) card,** a country-specific, thumbnail-sized chip that gives you a local phone number and plugs you into the local network. Many SIM cards are prepaid, and incoming calls are frequently free. You can buy additional cards or vouchers (usually available at convenience stores) to "top up" your phone. For more information on GSM phones, check out www.telestial.com, www.orange.co.uk, www.roadpost.com, or www.planetomni.com. Companies like **Cellular Abroad** (www.cellularabroad. com) rent cell phones that work in a variety of destinations around the world.

GSM PHONES. Just having a GSM phone doesn't mean you're necessarily good to go when you travel abroad. The majority of GSM phones sold in the United States operate on a different frequency (1900) than international phones (900/1800) and will not work abroad. Tri-band phones work on all three frequencies (900/1800/1900) and will operate through most of the world. Additionally, some GSM phones are SIM-locked and will only accept SIM cards from a single carrier. You'll need a SIM-unlocked phone to use a SIM card from a local carrier when you travel.

TIME DIFFERENCES

Costa Rica is six hours behind Greenwich Mean Time (GMT) and does not observe Daylight Saving Time. Note that between early April and late October, Costa Rica is one hour further behind the other countries in the chart below.

4AM	5AM	6AM	7AM	8AM	NOON	10PM
Vancouver Seattle San Francisco Los Angeles	Denver	Chicago **Costa Rica**	New York Toronto	New Brunswick	London	Sydney* Canberra* Melbourne*

*Note that Australia observes Daylight Saving Time from October to March, the opposite of the Northern Hemisphere. Therefore, it is 14hr. ahead of Costa Rica from March to October and 16hr. ahead from October to March.

BY MAIL

SENDING MAIL HOME FROM COSTA RICA

Airmail is the best way to send mail home from Costa Rica. **Aerogrammes,** printed sheets that fold into envelopes and travel via airmail, are available at post offices. Write "airmail," *"par avion,"* or *"correo aéreo"* on the front. Most post offices will charge exorbitant fees or simply refuse to send aerogrammes with enclosures. **Surface mail** is by far the cheapest and slowest way to send mail. It takes one to two months to cross the Atlantic and one to three to cross the Pacific—good for heavy items you won't need for a while, such as souvenirs that you've acquired along the way.

SENDING MAIL TO COSTA RICA

To ensure timely delivery, mark envelopes "airmail," *"par avion,"* or *"correo aéreo."* In addition to the standard postage system whose rates are listed below, **Federal Express** (Australia ☎ +61 13 26 10, Canada and the US

+1-800-463-3339, Ireland +353 800 535 800, New Zealand +64 800 733 339, the UK +44 8456 070 809; www.fedex.com) handles express mail services from most countries to Costa Rica. Sending a postcard within Costa Rica costs ¢115, while sending letters up to 500g domestically requires ¢340. Keep in mind that mail from Costa Rica is not the fastest you'll ever come across.

There are several ways to arrange pick-up of letters sent to you while you are abroad. Mail can be sent via **Poste Restante** (General Delivery; Lista de Correos) to almost any city or town in Costa Rica with a post office, but it is not very reliable. Address **Poste Restante** letters like so:

Oscar Arias

Lista de Correo

City, Costa Rica

The mail will go to a special desk in the central post office, unless you specify a post office by street address or postal code. It's best to use the largest post office, since mail may be sent there regardless. It is safer and quicker, yet more expensive, to send mail express or registered. Bring your passport (or other photo ID) for pickup; there may be a small fee. *Let's Go* lists post offices in the **Practical Information** section for each city and most towns.

American Express's travel offices offer a free **Client Letter Service** (mail held up to 30 days and forwarded upon request) for cardholders who contact them in advance. Some offices provide these services to non-cardholders (especially AmEx Travelers Cheque holders), but call ahead to make sure. *Let's Go* lists AmEx locations for most large cities in **Practical Information** sections; for a complete list, call ☎+1-800-528-4800 or visit www.americanexpress.com/travel.

ACCOMMODATIONS

HOSTELS AND CABINAS

Many hostels are laid out dorm-style, often with large single-sex rooms and bunk beds, although private rooms that sleep from two to four are becoming more common. They sometimes have kitchens and utensils for your use, bike or moped rentals, storage areas, transportation to airports, breakfast and other meals, laundry facilities, and Internet access. However, there can be drawbacks: some hostels close during certain daytime "lockout" hours, have a curfew, don't accept reservations, impose a maximum stay, or, less frequently, require that you do chores. In Costa Rica, a dorm bed in a hostel will average around US$7-10 and a private room around US$12-18. While hostels are common, *cabinas* are most prevalent: a step up from hostels, but still simple. Basic beds, fans, and a bathroom sometimes with hot water, but sometimes only cold. The pricier *cabinas* sometimes have cable TV and A/C.

A HOSTELER'S BILL OF RIGHTS. There are certain standard features that we do not include in our hostel listings. Unless we state otherwise, you can expect that every hostel has no lockout, no curfew, free hot showers, some system of secure luggage storage, and no key deposit.

OTHER TYPES OF ACCOMMODATIONS

HOTELS AND HOSPEDAJES

WHAT TO EXPECT. Rooms in Costa Rica can cost as little as US$40 or so per night, though US$40-50 may be a better general figure. Accommodations go by many different names. *Hospedaje*, *hotel*, *pensión*, *posada*, and *casa de huéspedes* are all common terms; the differences between them are by no means consistent. Generally, *pensións* and *hospedajes* tend to cost less than hostels and hotels. Standards vary greatly, but generally speaking, for a basic room expect nothing more than a bed, a light bulb, and perhaps a fan; other amenities are a bonus. The very cheapest places may not provide towel, soap, or toilet paper. For a slight price jump you can get a room with private bath, and for a little more you might find a place with some character and charm.

AMENITIES TO LOOK FOR. In sea level areas, try to get a room with a fan (*ventilador* or *abanico*) or a window with a coastal breeze. In more upscale hotels, air-conditioning may be available. Also look for screens and mosquito netting. At higher elevations, a hot-water shower and extra blankets will be most welcome. Make safety a priority in urban areas; you can often get more comfort and security for only a couple extra dollars. In more-isolated areas, accommodations will usually be basic but friendly. If you plan on staying off the beaten path, your own mosquito net, toilet paper, towel, and flashlight are a must.

BATHROOMS. *Let's Go* quotes room prices with and without private bath. Note that "with bath" means a sink, toilet, and basic shower in the room, not an actual bathtub. Shared baths are typically the same sort of thing, just off the hall. Hot shower is a relative term in Costa Rica: "hot" can often be tepid at best. Quite frequently, the heating device will be electric coils in the shower head. Such devices work best at low water pressure. The electrical cord should be an easy reminder that water, electricity, and people do not mix well, so be sure to avoid touching the shower head or other metal objects during a shower. Toilets in Central America often do not have toilet seats. Moreover, the sewer systems generally cannot handle everything thrown in them. As a rule, do not flush used toilet paper, tampons, or other waste products. Instead, use the receptacle (usually) provided. Toilet paper always seems to be missing when you need it most; it is wise to carry some on you wherever you go.

GETTING A GOOD PRICE. Hotels in Costa Rica charge a hotel tax (16.39% cumulative sales and tourism tax); double-check if this has been included in the rate. Rooms shared with other travelers usually cost less per person. Often, a hotel will first show you the most expensive room. Ask if there's anything cheaper (*¿Hay algo más barato, por favor?*). You can sometimes bargain for a lower rate at hotels, particularly during the low season, on days when there are vacancies, or if you're staying for several days.

BED AND BREAKFASTS (B&BS)

For an alternative to impersonal hotels, B&Bs (private homes with rooms for travelers) range from acceptable to sublime. Rooms in B&Bs can cost US$40-60 for a single and US$50-90 for a double in Costa Rica. A number of websites provide listings for B&Bs; check out InnFinder (www.inncrawler.com), InnSite (www.innsite.com), BedandBreakfast.com (www.bedandbreakfast.com), or Pamela Lanier's Bed & Breakfast Guide Online (www.lanierbb.com).

HOME EXCHANGES AND HOSPITALITY CLUBS

Home exchange offers the traveler various types of homes (houses, apartments, condominiums, villas, even castles in some cases), plus the opportunity to live like a native and to cut down on accommodation fees. For more information, contact **HomeExchange.com,** P.O. Box 787, Hermosa Beach, CA 90254, USA (☎+1-310-789-3864; www.homeexchange.com), or **Intervac International Home Exchange** (☎+33 6 1612 2022; www.intervac.com).

Hospitality clubs link their members with individuals or families abroad who are willing to host travelers for free or for a small fee to promote cultural exchange and general good karma. In exchange, members usually must be willing to host travelers in their own homes; a small membership fee may also be required. **GlobalFreeloaders.com** (www.globalfreeloaders.com) and **The Hospitality Club** (www.hospitalityclub.org) are good places to start. **Servas** (www.servas. org) is an established, more formal, peace-based organization, and requires a fee and an interview to join. An Internet search will find many similar organizations, some of which cater to special interests (e.g., women, GLBT travelers, or members of certain professions). As always, use common sense when planning to stay with or host someone you do not know.

CAMPING

Camping is a popular, economical way to spend a night in Costa Rica. Many hostels offer camping rates (about US$2 per person) to camp on their property and have access to the bathrooms and kitchens. It is also common to camp on beaches or in the numerous National Parks for free, although you should always check to make sure camping is allowed at the specific site. For more information on outdoor activities, see **The Great Outdoors,** p. 70.

ORGANIZED ADVENTURE TRIPS

Organized adventure tours offer another way of exploring the wild. Activities include hiking, biking, skiing, canoeing, kayaking, rafting, climbing, photo safaris, and archaeological digs. Tourism bureaus often can suggest parks, trails, and outfitters. Organizations that specialize in camping and outdoor equipment like REI and EMS also are good sources for info. **Specialty Travel Index,** P.O Box 458, San Anselmo, CA 94979, USA, a group that connects travelers with adventure and special interest trips, can be a good place to start your planning. (US ☎+1-888-624-4030, elsewhere 415-455-1643; www.specialtytravel.com.)

SPECIFIC CONCERNS

SUSTAINABLE TRAVEL

As the number of travelers on the road rises, the detrimental effect they can have on natural environments is an increasing concern. *Let's Go* promotes the philosophy of sustainable travel with this in mind. Through a sensitivity to issues of ecology and sustainability, today's travelers can be a powerful force in preserving and restoring the places they visit.

Ecotourism, a rising trend in sustainable travel, focuses on the conservation of natural habitats—mainly, on how to use them to build up the economy without exploitation or overdevelopment. Travelers can make a difference by doing advance research, by supporting organizations and establishments that pay attention to their carbon footprint, and by patronizing establishments that strive to be environmentally friendly.

Ecotourism is alive and well in Costa Rica, and visitors are encouraged to partake in activities that sustain as opposed to harm the environment. Ecotourism opportunities are around every corner, but be careful as many companies interested solely in profits and not in their negative impact on the environment pretend to be eco-friendly in order to gain business. Be aware of the guidelines for some types of tours; boat tours are required by law to use electric motors and to move slowly through the water. When on a natural tour, be sure that your tour guide is following the laws designed to protect the surrounding wildlife. Guides are often available in national parks through MINAE, a government organization devoted to encouraging sustainable development For resources and ideas for ecotourism, see **Beyond Tourism** (p. 60).

ECOTOURISM RESOURCES. For more information on environmentally responsible tourism, contact one of the organizations below:

Conservation International, 2011 Crystal Dr., Ste. 500, Arlington, VA 22202, USA (☎+1-800-406-2306 or 703-341-2400; www.conservation.org).

Green Globe 21, Green Globe vof, Verbenalaan 1, 2111 ZL Aerdenhout, the Netherlands (☎+31 23 544 0306; www.greenglobe.com).

International Ecotourism Society, 1333 H St. NW, Ste. 300E, Washington, DC 20005, USA (☎+1-202-347-9203; www.ecotourism.org).

United Nations Environment Program (UNEP), 39-43 Quai André Citroën, 75739 Paris Cedex 15, France (☎+33 1 44 37 14 50; www.uneptie.org/pc/tourism).

RESPONSIBLE TRAVEL

Your tourist dollars can make a big impact on the destinations you visit. The choices you make during your trip can have powerful effects on local communities—for better or for worse. As one of the major industries supporting Costa Rica's economy, tourists would do well to consider their impact on the environment and community. Simple decisions such as buying local products, paying fair prices for products or services, and attempting to learn Spanish can have a positive effect on the community.

Community-based tourism aims to channel tourist money into the local economy by emphasizing tours and cultural programs that are run by members of the host community. This type of tourism also benefits the tourists themselves, as it often takes them beyond the traditional tours of the region. *The Ethical Travel Guide* (UK£13), a project of Tourism Concern (☎+44 20 7133 3330; www.tourismconcern.org.uk), is an excellent resource for information on community-based travel, with a directory of 300 establishments in 60 countries.

TRAVELING ALONE

Traveling alone can be extremely beneficial, providing a sense of independence and a greater opportunity to connect with locals. On the other hand, solo travelers are more vulnerable targets of harassment and theft. If you are traveling alone, look confident, try not to stand out as a tourist, and be especially careful in deserted or very crowded areas. Stay away from areas that are not well lit. If questioned, never admit that you are traveling alone. Maintain regular contact with someone at home who knows your itinerary, and always research your destination before traveling. For more tips, pick up *Traveling Solo* by Eleanor Berman (Globe Pequot Press; US$18), visit www.travelaloneandloveit.com, or subscribe to **Connecting: Solo Travel Network,** 689 Park Rd., Unit 6, Gibsons, BC V0N 1V7, Canada (☎+1-604-886-9099; www.cstn.org; membership US$30-48).

WOMEN TRAVELERS

Solo women inevitably face some additional safety concerns. Women can consider staying in hostels with single rooms that lock or in religious organizations with single-sex rooms. It's a good idea to stick to centrally located accommodations and to avoid solo late-night treks or metro rides.

Always carry extra cash for a phone, bus, or taxi. **Hitchhiking** is never safe for lone women or even for two women traveling together. Look as if you know where you're going and approach older women or couples if you're lost or feeling uncomfortable in your surroundings. The less you look like a tourist, the better off you'll be. Dress conservatively, especially in rural areas. Wearing a conspicuous **wedding band** sometimes helps to prevent unwanted advances.

In Costa Rica, catcalls and attention from men is common, and usually harmless. Just be a little more mindful when going out alone. Your best answer to verbal harassment is no answer at all; feigning deafness, sitting motionless, and staring straight ahead will usually work. The extremely persistent can sometimes be dissuaded by a firm, very public "Go away!". Don't hesitate to seek out a police officer or passerby if you're being harassed. Know the emergency numbers in places you visit, and consider carrying a **whistle.** A self-defense class will prepare you for a potential attack and raise your level of awareness of your surroundings (see **Personal Safety,** p. 18). It might be a good idea to talk with your doctor about health concerns that women face when traveling (p. 23).

GLBT TRAVELERS

Attitudes toward GLBT travelers can vary drastically from region to region in Costa Rica. Legally, all Costa Rican citizens are considered equal, regardless of their sexuality, and consensual homosexuality and bisexuality are not a crime. Although gay, lesbian, bisexual, and transgender communities exist and may even thrive in the largest cities, the government of Costa Rica still has a rather unfavorable outlook toward homosexuality (even if laws banning homosexuality no longer exist), and keeping a low profile about your sexuality is probably your best bet. In general, the government, media, and citizens of Costa Rica are much more open about homosexuality than they were 10 years ago, yet the traditional Roman Catholic family and the *machista* culture might still make gay and lesbian life uncomfortable. Generally, there are not too many establishments catering exclusively to gay and lesbian clientele.

However, Costa Rica is known for its tolerance and friendliness. Homosociality (camaraderie between members of the same sex, particularly men) is more common than you may be accustomed to; hand-holding between two men cannot be interpreted according to Western norms. Listed here are organizations, catalogs, and publishers offering materials addressing some specific concerns. **Out and About** (www.planetout.com) offers a newsletter addressing travel concerns and a comprehensive site, as well. The newspaper **365gay.com** has a travel section (www.365gay.com/travel/travelchannel.htm).

Gay's the Word, 66 Marchmont St., London WC1N 1AB, UK (☎+44 20 7278 7654; http://freespace.virgin.net/gays.theword). The largest gay and lesbian bookshop in the UK, with both fiction and non-fiction titles. Mail-order service available.

Giovanni's Room, 345 S. 12th St., Philadelphia, PA 19107, USA (☎+1-215-923-2960; www.queerbooks.com). An international lesbian and gay bookstore with mail-order service (carries many of the publications listed below).

International Lesbian and Gay Association (ILGA), Avenue des Villas 34, 1060 Brussels, Belgium (☎+32 2 502 2471; www.ilga.org). Provides political information, such as homosexuality laws of individual countries.

ADDITIONAL RESOURCES: GLBT

Spartacus International Gay Guide 2008 (US$33).

Damron Men's Travel Guide, Damron Road Atlas, Damron Accommodations Guide, Damron City Guide, and *Damron Women's Traveller.* Damron Travel Guides (US$18-24). For info, call ☎+1-800-462-6654 or visit www.damron.com.

The Gay Vacation Guide: The Best Trips and How to Plan Them, by Mark Chesnut. Kensington Books (US$15).

Gayellow Pages USA/Canada, by Frances Green. Gayellow Pages (US$20). It also publishes regional editions. Visit Gayellow pages online at http://gayellowpages.com.

TRAVELERS WITH DISABILITIES

Costa Rica is not particularly well-outfitted for visitors with disabilities. Handicap-accessible facilities are not always readily available. Thus, those with disabilities should inform airlines and hotels of their needs when making reservations; some time may be needed to prepare special accommodations. Call ahead to establishments to find out if they are wheelchair-accessible. Guide-dog owners should ask about the quarantine policies of each destination country.

USEFUL ORGANIZATIONS

Accessible Journeys, 35 W. Sellers Ave., Ridley Park, PA 19078, USA (☎+1-800-846-4537; www.disabilitytravel.com). Designs tours for wheelchair users and slow walkers. The site has tips and forums for all travelers.

Flying Wheels Travel, 143 W. Bridge St., Owatonna, MN 55060, USA (☎+1-507-451-5005; www.flyingwheelstravel.com). Specializes in escorted trips to Europe for people with physical disabilities; plans custom trips worldwide.

Mobility International USA (MIUSA), P.O. Box 10767, Eugene, OR 97440, USA (☎+1-541-343-1284; www.miusa.org). Provides a variety of books and other publications containing information for travelers with disabilities.

Society for Accessible Travel and Hospitality (SATH), 347 5th Ave., Ste. 610, New York, NY 10016, USA (☎+1-212-447-7284; www.sath.org). A group that publishes online travel information. Annual membership US$49, students and seniors US$29.

MINORITY TRAVELERS

A majority of the Costa Rican population is of Spanish European ancestry—around 94% identify as white or *mestizo*. The minority population consists primarily of blacks—found among the Afro-Caribbeans on the coast—and indigenous people. According to most *ticos*, Nicaraguans are the source of the increase in crime and poverty in Costa Rica. Nicaraguans tend to have darker skin than *ticos*, thus those with darker skin are more likely to face discrimination.

DIETARY CONCERNS

While adjusting to a Costa Rican diet, it's not unusual for travelers to have diarrhea and stomach aches. You can avoid indigestion by avoiding tap water, foods washed in tap water, and ice. Drink bottled water—unlike locals, travelers sometimes aren't immune to the tap water. The water in Costa Rica is generally safe in large cities and touristed areas, but check with authorities before drinking. Places you should be careful about the water are: Parque Nacional Corcovado, parts of the Osa Peninsula, and the Northern Caribbean. Veggie-eaters should watch out, as foods washed with tap water can make you sick.

In general, vegetarians and vegans shouldn't have a hard time finding meals. While there may not be exclusively vegetarian restaurants (although a growing number of vegetarian establishments are springing up), most offer rice and beans (staple foods), fresh fruits, and cooked vegetable dishes. When asking for a vegetarian dish, be sure to stress *vegetariano;* just asking for a dish *sin carne* might give you a dish with a meat other than beef.

The **The Vegetarian Resource Group's** website, at www.vrg.org/travel, has a list of organizations and websites that are geared toward helping vegetarians and vegans abroad. They also provide a restaurant guide. For more information, visit your bookstore or health food store and consult *The Vegetarian Traveler* by Bryan Geon (Warwick Publishing, $13). Vegetarians will also find resources on the web; try www.vegdining.com or www.vegetariansabroad.com to start.

Travelers who keep kosher can contact synagogues in larger cities for information on kosher restaurants. Your own synagogue or college Hillel should have access to lists of Jewish institutions across the nation. If you are strict in your observance, you may have to prepare your own food on the road. A good resource is the *Jewish Travel Guide,* edited by Michael Zaidner (Vallentine Mitchell; US$20). There are resources and a restaurant guide at http://shamash.org/kosher. Those looking for halal restaurants can visit www.zabihah.com.

OTHER RESOURCES

Let's Go tries to cover all aspects of budget travel, but we can't put everything in our guides. Listed below are books and websites that can serve as jumping-off points for your own research.

USEFUL PUBLICATIONS

The Tico Times, San José, Costa Rica (☎258 1558; www.ticotimes.net). Central America's leading English-language newspaper covers news, business, and cultural development in Costa Rica and Central America.

La Nación, San José, Costa Rica (☎247 4664; www.nacion.com). Costa Rica's leading Spanish-language newspaper.

Actualidad Económica, San José, Costa Rica (☎224 2411; www.actualidad.co.cr). Learn about economics, banking, finance, and entrepreneurship in Costa Rica.

ESSENTIALS

Costa Rica Explorer, San José, Costa Rica (☎247 4664; www.nacion.co.cr). Useful news and info for travelers. Published every 2 months.

WORLD WIDE WEB

Almost all aspects of budget travel is accessible via the web. In 10min. at the keyboard, you can make a hostel reservation, get advice on travel hot spots, or find out how much a bus from San José to Orotina costs.

Listed here are some regional and travel-related sites to start off your surfing; other websites are listed throughout the book. Because website turnover is high, use search engines (e.g., www.google.com) to strike out on your own.

> **LET'S GO ONLINE.** Plan your next trip on our newly redesigned website, **www.letsgo.com.** It features the latest travel info on your favorite destinations, as well as tons of interactive features: make your own itinerary, read blogs from our trusty researcher-writers, browse our photo library, watch exclusive videos, check out our newsletter, find travel deals, and buy new guides. We're always updating and adding new features, so check back often!

THE ART OF TRAVEL

Backpacker's Ultimate Guide: www.bugeurope.com. Tips on packing, transportation, and where to go. Also tons of country-specific travel information.

BootsnAll.com: www.bootsnall.com. Numerous resources for independent travelers, from planning your trip to reporting on it when you get back.

How to See the World: www.artoftravel.com. A compendium of great travel tips, from cheap flights to self-defense to interacting with local culture.

Travel Intelligence: www.travelintelligence.net. Travel writing by distinguished writers.

Travel Library: www.travel-library.com. Links for information and personal travelogues.

World Hum: www.worldhum.com. An independently produced collection of "travel dispatches from a shrinking planet."

INFORMATION ON COSTA RICA

CIA World Factbook: www.odci.gov/cia/publications/factbook/index.html. Tons of vital statistics on Costa Rica's geography, government, economy, and people.

Geographia: www.geographia.com. Highlights, culture, and people of Costa Rica.

TravelPage: www.travelpage.com. Links to official tourist office sites in Costa Rica.

PlanetRider: www.planetrider.com. A subjective list of links to the "best" websites covering the culture and tourist attractions of Costa Rica.

Costa Rica Guesthouse

KING SIZE BED - PRIVATE BATH - ONLY $42 A NIGHT

* Private rooms with king size bed
* Free internet & wifi access in rooms
* Free coffee & tea
* Free parking & 24hr security
* Free shuttle from bus stations
* Pool, garden & bar-restaurant access
* Friendly & bilingual staff
* Kitchen facilities & lounge area
* Airport shuttle on request
* Ensuite $42, standard $35

CALL (506) 2223-7034

BOOK ONLINE WWW.COSTA-RICA-GUESTHOUSE.COM

LIFE AND TIMES

No country in the world better embodies the adage "good things come in small packages" like Costa Rica does. Though the entire country could be placed squarely inside the US state of Maine, Costa Rica is internationally renowned for its natural wonders and unparalleled biodiversity. Images of its tropical beauty fill the fronts of postcards and the imaginations of travelers throughout the world. In the lush cloud forests and jungle lowlands of this "rich coast," the air is laced with trailing vines, and quiet evenings are punctuated by the piercing calls of howler monkeys. Its vast beaches—many of them still unspoiled—are graced by the muted hues of Caribbean sunrises, the bolder shades of Pacific sunsets, and the perfect waves that have earned this tiny nation its status as a promised land for surfers worldwide. Its beauty seems to render words inadequate.

The people and researchers of Costa Rica are as remarkable as their stunning, natural backdrops—from Quaker expats making cheese in the jungle to entomologists harvesting caterpillars from the forest ground cover. Costa Rica's ecosystems are full of as much intellectual vitality as they are with biological exuberance; there are three major Organization of Tropical Studies research stations located within the country's borders.

Some of Costa Rica's greatest wonders are fairly quiet ones. Bereft of famous ruins or relics, without any legendary poets or colonial freedom fighters to call its own, Costa Rica is often derided as a country without an interesting past or a cultural core. Anyone who spends much time here will quickly realize how inaccurate and ungenerous these claims truly are. In small towns from one ocean to another, communities thrive with a warm-hearted *manera de ser* (way of being) that speaks to an enduring cultural inheritance as striking as any of Central America's better-known historical legacies.

HISTORY

BEFORE COLUMBUS

Costa Rica's development actually follows a dynamic timeline that both mirrors and defies the typical story of Central America. Spanish explorers arrived in Costa Rica at the dawn of the 16th century and found upwards of 25,000 people from five distinct native groups. The history of the country predates their arrival by several hundred years, with the oldest archeological site in Costa Rica dating back to 1000 BC. The area that is now Costa Rica played an important historical role as a meeting place for various pre-Columbian civilizations, such as the Mesoamericans to the north and the Andeans to the South. The Spanish conquest, while often characterized as a peaceful settlement, was in fact especially destructive to the native cultures and peoples. Due to their resistance to the Spanish presence, the conquistadors believed the natives to be hostile. Due to there being five distinct native groups, the conquistadors were left without a central area to attack, and thus the native people remained for a significant amount of time. However, following Columbus's arrival in Costa Rica in 1502, new settlements and diseases drastically reduced the native population to 120,000 by 1521, to 10,000 by 1611, and to only 500 by 1675. Today, only 1% of Costa Rica's population descends from its original indigenous inhabitants.

THE COLONIAL PERIOD

When Christopher Columbus arrived in Costa Rica in 1502, he called the region La Huerta (The Garden). Despite enthusiastic tales of the land he discovered, Costa Rica was not settled until explorer Gil Gonzalez Davila set off from Panama to settle the region in 1522. The golden bands the natives wore in their ears and noses inspired him to name the region Costa Rica, or the "Rich Coast." The early settlement years were tumultuous, marked by ongoing conflict between European settlers and native residents as well as recurring attacks from British pirates along both coasts. In 1564, Juan Vásquez de Coronado finally managed to establish himself in the Central Valley and proclaimed the city of Cartago as his capital. More towns began to appear, including San José in 1736, usually in the presence of already established churches. Throughout the colonial years, powerful nobles went to "hot spot" colonies farther south on the isthmus, while less influential bureaucrats and inferior aristocracy ended up settling down in the less-developed territory of Costa Rica. Due to its status as a remote outpost within the Spanish colonial kingdom, Costa Rica had the opportunity to develop under weaker colonial influence than that of many of its neighbors. Its remote location in relation to regional centers like Honduras and Guatemala also benefited Costa Rica after liberation from Spain, allowing it to avoid the massive civil wars many countries experienced in the post-Independence era.

LIBERATION AND "EL GRANO DE ORO"

Although Central America officially gained independence from Spain on September 15, 1821, Costa Ricans didn't hear about it until a month later, when the news arrived by mule from Mexico. Predictably, liberation led to a power struggle. While Costa Rica's four largest cities (San José, Cartago, Heredia, and Alajuela) vied to govern the country from within its borders, nearby nations (Guatemala, Mexico, and Nicaragua) vied to govern it from beyond them. Costa Rica eventually became a member of the United Provinces of Central America and was one of the first to become its own country when the collective dissolved in 1838.

Much of Costa Rica's socio-economic development during the 19th century was defined by the export of coffee and bananas, two fruits that, surprisingly, were not native to the country. The coffee bean was introduced to Costa Rica in the late 18th century. Producers of the lucrative commodity were so successful that the coffee bean eventually earned the name *grano de oro* (golden bean), and these farmers became known as highly influential "coffee barons." The

AD 500
The Chorotegas tribe leaves Southern Mexcio for the Nicoya Peninsula of Costa Rica, bringing with them Aztecan calendars, games, and farming methods.

1502
Christopher Columbus arrives, naming the area he encounters La Huerta (The Garden) because of its beauty.

1561
Spain's Juan de Cavallon establishes the first successful colony in Costa Rica.

1564
Juan Vásquz de Coronado names the city of Cartago as the capital of Costa Rica.

LIFE AND TIMES

1779
Cultivation of coffee begins in Costa Rica.

Sept. 15, 1821
Costa Rica gains independence from Spain. The citizens do not find out until October when a messenger on a mule arrives from Mexico with the good news.

1870
General Tomás Guardia seizes power as the dictator of Costa Rica. He rules for 12 years.

1880
Minor Keith, a US engineer, makes the first shipment of bananas out of Costa Rica to New Orleans.

development of the coffee industry in Costa Rica was as artificial as the arrival of the coffee bean itself. Dictator Braulio Carrillo instigated its genesis in the 1830s because he could see the country needed a cash crop, and coffee—rapidly gaining in popularity in Europe—seemed like a good bet. Land was handed out for free to any farmers who would plant coffee on it. The industry's broad base and widely distributed profits gave rise to a large middle class. Since most arable land had already been divided on a small, equitable scale, the increased income didn't lead to the stratified system of land-owning elites and working peasants that characterized Costa Rica's Central American neighbors.

For 70 years, coffee was the country's only major export, obstructing the growth of even basic foodstuffs. It remained dominant until the 1870s, when Minor Keith, an American engineer building a railroad connecting San José and Puerto Limón, began to plant banana trees along the sides of the train tracks. The railway eventually went bankrupt, but the money made from banana trade allowed Keith to establish the United Fruit Company in 1899, turning Costa Rica into the world's leading banana exporter, a title it would hold until surpassed by Ecuador during the 20th century.

INVASION AND DICTATORSHIP

The only serious external threat to Costa Rican national security during the late 19th century came from William Walker, a rogue gold miner from Tennessee who wanted to annex the country as a slave-holding American state. The Costa Rican people had been asked by an enemy of Walker's, Cornelius Vanderbilt, to stop Walker's mission. The Costa Rican army invaded Guanacaste in 1856, spurring the development of a Costa Rican civilian army 9000 men strong. Fueled by a newly forged sense of territorial pride, the Costa Rican army drove Walker's forces back to Rivas, Nicaragua, where a drummer boy and precocious military strategist named Juan Santamaría set fire to Walker's troops' impromptu barracks, ending their deluded campaign and launching himself into the sparsely populated ranks of Costa Rican national heroes. Costa Ricans now celebrate the day Juan Santamaría sacrificed his life to burn the Mesón de Guerra and secure national freedom annually on April 11.

General Tomás Guardia, one of Costa Rica's only dictators, seized power soon after in 1870 in order to end the rule of the coffee barons. During Guardia's 12 years in power, his ambitious, iron-fisted policies modernized the country in important ways, though they cost Costa Ricans their civil liberties and accrued a sizable deficit. He established a base for future economic progress and implemented free, compulsory primary education for all citizens, allowing Costa Rica to attain high literacy levels early in its history. After his dictatorship, the country saw a peaceful transition back to democracy. In 1889, Costa

Rica conducted the first legitimate large-scale elections in Central American history, though women and African descendants were not allowed to vote.

DOMESTIC REFORM AND CIVIL WAR

Costa Rica underwent a rather ungraceful transition into the 20th century. These years were marked by border disputes with Panama and another dangerous flirtation with autocracy. In the 1914 elections, the people of Costa Rica were unable to give a majority vote to any candidate. As a result, congress chose Alfredo González as a compromise, but he was soon overthrown by the reactionary General Federico Tinoco. The dictatorship was unpopular and brief, however, and the decades to follow were smooth and prosperous. A powerful, and probably highly caffeinated, coffee elite continued to ensure that income taxes were low (as they still are today), though social discontent grew among laborers and radicals. Moderate president Rafael Ángel Calderón Guardia implemented important labor reforms, including health care and minimum wage for laborers, but he lost popular support soon after World War II. In 1944, he annulled the results of the election and installed a puppet president instead.

A disaffected middle class rose up against this puppet regime during the War of National Liberation in 1948 under the leadership of José Figueres Ferrer, a wealthy coffee farmer and intellectual. Widely known as "Don Pepe," Figueres appealed to a popular distrust of communism's foreign ideology and called for the renewal of Costa Rican democracy. Backed by US CIA forces looking to stop communism, Figueres defeated the government's machete-clad forces in six weeks before inaugurating the Founding Junta of the Second Republic and instituting a wide range of political reforms. In 1949, he banned the Communist party and wrote a new constitution that gave women and African descendents the right to vote. It abolished the Costa Rican military, making Costa Rica the first country ever to operate under a democratic system without an army. All that remains of the army today is the Civil Guard, a government police force composed of only 8400 members. After 18 months in power, Figueres stepped down and handed over the presidency to Otilio Ulate, the initial winner of the incendiary 1944 election. Widely admired for his actions, Figueres was elected president in 1953. Once in office, he instituted a number of leftist reforms—like nationalizing banks and unions—similar to those that had motivated civil war in the first place.

GLOBAL ROLES AND NOBEL LAURELS

Since dissolving its army in 1949, Costa Rica has enjoyed peace, political stability, and a relatively high degree of

1884
All Jesuits are expelled from Costa Rica, and other religious orders were forbidden to enter it.

June 15, 1939
The purple orchid was deemed the national flower of Costa Rica.

1949
A new Costa Rican constitution abolishes the national army and gives women and individuals of African descent the right to vote.

March 19, 1963
Volcán Irazú erupts the same day that US President John F. Kennedy visits Costa Rica to meet with Latin American presidents pledging to fight communism

Oscar Arias and the Politics of Peace

Costa Rica's political system has three claims to fame: its democracy, its military's non-existence, and its president's Nobel Prize. Not only is Costa Rica the Latin American country with the longest uninterrupted record of free elections and the first on the planet to voluntarily abolish its military, but its president, Óscar Arias Sánchez, is the first Nobel Laureate in history to be elected to such a post.

Born in 1940 to coffee plantation owners, Arias received degrees in law and economics from the University of Costa Rica, and then earned his PhD in Political Science from the University of Essex in England. After teaching at the University of Costa Rica and serving as Minister of Planning and as Secretary General of the National Liberation Party (Partido Liberación Nacional), Arias was elected President in 1986. He took office at a time of great discord. Civil wars raged in Guatemala, El Salvador, and Nicaragua, and activity by the American-funded contras in Honduras and Costa Rica threatened to drag those countries into Nicaragua's conflict.

Fighting financial and diplomatic pressure from the United States, Arias banished the CIA-funded contras and pushed for regional negotiations that included Daniel Ortega, the president of Nicaragua. On August 7, 1987, after tireless prodding from President Arias, the five Central American presidents established procedures to bring peace to the area. Esquipulas II, as the accords were known, committed the nations to free elections, national reconciliation commissions, and rejection of foreign interference in Central America. For his efforts, Oscar Arias was awarded the 1987 Nobel Prize for Peace.

Arias left office in 1990, barred from seeking a second term. Working with the Arias Foundation for Peace and Human Progress, which he founded with the monetary portion of the Nobel Prize, he traveled the world advocating for disarmament, debt relief, and equality. Then, in 2003, a controversial Supreme Court decision interpreted the constitution as allowing presidents to be reelected to non-consecutive terms. In the wake of scandals that had seen presidents jailed for corruption, Arias declared to restore credibility to the office.

The 2006 election was the closest in Costa Rica in 40 years and in Latin American history. Though polls predicted a large victory for Arias, the result, certified after a month-long hand recount, showed the former president winning by just 1.2%. His closest opponent was Ottón Solís, the candidate of the Citizen Action Party (Partido Acción Ciudadana, or PAC) and the Minister of Planning in Arias's first term. Surveys revealed that voters turned to the third-party candidate at the last minute, as a protest against the two-party system, without thinking he had a chance.

Arias vowed to help the poor. He gave up to ¢80,000 per month to families as incentive to keep their children in school. He promised to repair highways, boost education, and, controversially, approve the Dominican-Republic Central American Free Trade Agreement (DR-CAFTA).

...peace is one thing on which all Costa Ricans car agree.

The process of ratification has led to a graffiti campaign: one cannot walk far without seeing "NO TLC" (referring to Tratado de Libre Comercio, the Spanish translation of DR-CAFTA) on buildings and monuments.

But these demonstrations are extremely unlikely to lead to violence. From its president to its protesters, peace is one thing on which all Costa Ricans can agree.

Timothy Josiah Pertz *is a Special Assistant to Costa Rica's President Oscar Arias for English Communications. He graduated from Harvard in 2005 with a degree in History and Literature and was a Researcher-Writer for Let's Go Central America (2003) in Guatemala.*

A CLOSER LOOK

economic comfort, earning it the nickname "Switzerland of the Americas," a title it bears with pride. It has not, however, been unaffected by civil strife in nearby nations. Thousands of refugees (some Salvadorean, most Nicaraguan) have crossed the border each year since the late 1970s, causing unemployment, and tensions to rise.

The 1980s were a tough period for Costa Rica. In addition to the internal crisis of currency devaluation and soaring welfare and oil costs, the country faced plummeting prices in the coffee, sugar, and banana markets, as well as a nearby civil war in Nicaragua. In 1987, however, then-former president Oscar Arias earned the Nobel Peace Prize when he achieved a consensus among Central America leaders with the Plan de Paz Arias, negotiated a cease-fire agreement, and laid the groundwork for a unified Central American Parliament. In 1988, he increased his commitment to democracy by creating the Arias Foundation for Peace and Human Progress.

COSTA RICA TODAY

Today, Costa Rica is one of the most prosperous countries in Latin America. Its well-educated population maintains a strong democratic spirit and displays an admirable level of collective sensitivity to issues surrounding ecological conservation, democratic development, and commercial vitality. In 2006, following the passage of a constitutional amendment that allowed for the re-election of presidents, former president and Nobel Laureate Oscar Arias was re-elected as president in one of the closest elections in Costa Rican history. Economically, the country has experienced relatively stable growth and a slow reduction in inflation. Though unemployment, poverty, and the management of an emerging welfare state are still pressing issues, Costa Rica has consistently managed to sustain generally positive economic trends.

ECONOMY

Costa Rica has a strong agricultural history, and its economy has traditionally been based on the exportation of bananas and coffee. Today, though agriculture continues to be important to the economy, with the addition of pineapples to the export market, the economy has been greatly diversified. After economic trouble in the 1980s, the economy has begun to turn around, and Costa Rican wealth is fairly well distributed among the different social classes.

Costa Rica has always gone about using its natural resources in a fairly prudent manner. Though wood and minerals are hardly left untouched, other industries are approached with more caution. In order to protect Costa Rica's environment and its ecotourism industry, the government has banned all open-pit mining. The nation is also looking to expand its economic horizons. In 1998,

---

June 29, 1968
Volcán Arenal erupts after 450 years of dormancy. The eruption kills 95 people and wipes out the village of Tabacon.

1983
Earl Tupper, the US-born inventor and founder of Tupperware, dies in Costa Rica. Tupper immigrated to the country 30 years prior when he became disillusioned with American government and tax laws.

1987
Then-former Costa Rican president Oscar Arias wins the Nobel Peace Prize following his efforts to end the war in Nicaragua.

1996
Fresh Del Monte Co. secures a patent for its "gold" pineapple, grown in the volcanic soils of Costa Rica.

2006
Oscar Arias wins the presidential election after a neck-and-neck race with Otton Solis. The election was one of the closest races in Costa Rican history.

LIFE AND TIMES

US chip-manufacturer Intel opened two large chip-processing plants in Heredia, and recently, Hewlett-Packard began a program to extend Internet service to the more rural areas of the country, securing Costa Rica a comfortable place in the high-tech global market. In 2004, Costa Rica became an observer in the Asia-Pacific Economic Cooperation Forum and began to widely increase its trading with South East Asia.

Today, Costa Rica's export-oriented economy relies primarily on tourism, and the industry is growing. Statistics have recorded a significant increase in tourism from year to year, making it even more important. Governmental development strategies for Costa Rica have been geared increasingly toward environmental and social sustainability, as tourists mainly come to Costa Rica for two reasons: its wilderness and its reputation for convenience and safety.

ECOTOURISM

The official slogan of Costa Rica's tourist industry—"Costa Rica: No Artificial Ingredients"—reveals just how intentional the country has been about continuing its reputation as a natural and eco-friendly tourist environment. Ecotourism has made the Costa Rica famous worldwide. It remains a huge draw for foreign tourists, promoting sustainable, responsible travel to natural sites, as well as encouraging low-impact cultural and environmental exploration that will generate income for farther conservation. In fact, Costa Rica has even been awarded and honored by the Sustainable Tourism Certification program for its sustainable approach to tourism.

One of the most unique elements of Costa Rica's ecotourism industry is its opportunity for turtle-watching. Visitors come from all over the world to watch turtles come ashore to lay their eggs at night on various Pacific and Caribbean beaches. Some of the most important nesting sites for turtles in the western hemisphere are located in **Tortuguero** (see p. 366) and **Parismina,** a smaller, less-touristed town 50km south, home to a turtle conservation organization which draws hundreds of volunteers each year to protect the eggs from poachers. In addition to the turtles, Costa Rica boasts 6% of the world's biodiversity even though it covers only 0.03% of the world's surface.

Though proponents of the industry maintain that it benefits the environment and travelers alike, Costa Rican ecotourism remains a delicate endeavor. While there has been a push to move tourism toward luxury ecotourism in order to attract wealthier travelers seeking comfortable wilderness adventures, conservation groups are concerned that larger facilities will put an unreasonably heavy burden on the nation's ecosystems.

COSTA RICA IN THE WORLD

While Costa Rica has managed to avoid nearly all large-scale regional conflicts, it continues to experience some problems, including border conflicts with Nicaragua and Panama, illegal immigration, and drug trafficking. It has managed to navigate these issues through diplomacy and a commitment to international institutions, including the Organization of American States, the United Nations, and the Inter-American Human Rights Court. Economically, as a member of the **Central American Common Market (CACM),** Costa Rica subscribes to a uniform external tariff as well as a policy of internal free trade. To help combat drug trafficking, Costa Rica signed a bilateral maritime counter-drug agreement with the US, which has been in effect since late 1999.

COSTA RICA AND NICARAGUA

Two issues continue to strain Costa Rican-Nicaraguan relations: conflicts over use of the San Juan River and illegal immigration from Nicaragua. Dating back to 1858, the **Cañas-Juarez Treaty** holds that the San Juan River constitutes the border between Costa Rica and Nicaragua but belongs to Nicaragua, though Costa Rica was granted perpetual free commercial access to its waters. Negotiations continue as both countries try to reach a consensus about what constitutes "commercial use." The borders of both countries are paying the price for this tension, as the political conflict impedes investment and development.

The issue of migration between these two countries also remains an urgent one. Because Costa Rica is prosperous and economically stable, it has drawn massive numbers of illegal immigrants from Nicaragua. Many come to work because of better job opportunities, and a signifcant portion of the Costa Rican population is made up of Nicaraguans. Both the Costa Rican and the Nicaraguan government have made attempts to resolve the disputes, but their isolation and political pride have made resolution an elusive concept. In the midst of this tension, *ticos* tend to look down upon their Nicaraguan neighbors, commonly known as *nicas*. Immigrant *nicas* are accused of stealing jobs, bringing violent crime, and using up many of the country's social resources.

SOCIAL INSTITUTIONS

Costa Rica has free, compulsory education through the ninth grade. In the first six grades, there is a 99% attendance rate, which drops to 71% in the last three grades. Over the past decade, the government has made noticeable, significant strides to improve both the quality and quantity of public schools, spending about 25% of its budget on this effort.

Costa Rica's health care system is one of the best in Latin America, and is generally on a par with international standards. Its low-cost, universal health care system provides high-quality care for all its citizens and contributes to a high average life expectancy of 77 years for men and 80 years for women. Private healthcare is also available and is generally quite good.

Despite its well-developed welfare system, nearly 20% of Costa Ricans live below the poverty line. Large differences in rural and urban wages are a major contributor to poverty levels, which manifest themselves in crime and prostitution problems that tourism only exacerbates. While Costa Rica does not have much trouble with organized crime (beyond drug trafficking), some corruption and nepotism continue to be problematic aspects of political life.

DEMOGRAPHICS

Out of nearly 4.3 million inhabitants, indigenous people comprise less than 1% of the population, while individuals of African descent make up only 3% and are concentrated on the Caribbean coast. A staggering 94% of the population is of European and *mestizo* descent, making Costa Rica one of the most racially homogeneous countries in Latin America.

Most of the eight groups of *indígenas* in Costa Rica who wish to protect their traditional lifestyles and languages do so on one of the 22 reserves scattered throughout the country. Reserve boundaries are often disrespected, however, and indigenous lands are constantly threatened. Other ethnic groups, including Germans, Americans, Italians, Britons, Chinese, and other Latin Americans have immigrated to Costa Rica over the past 150 years and have established communities. The town of Monteverde, for example, was founded by Quakers and is now home to a community that supports itself with cheese production.

LANGUAGE

Spanish is the official language, though Costa Ricans speak with a characteristic *tico* twist in accent and usage. Rare in other regions of the country, English is common along the Caribbean coast, where a Caribbean Creole dialect is used. Indigenous groups maintain their traditional languages.

Costa Rica has more country-specific vocabulary than many larger nations, generally known as *tiquismo*, which comes from adding the diminutive "-ito" or "-ico" to words in order to make them more friendly. They have ventured into the realms of the phonetically implausible by turning the word *chiquito* (small) into *chiquitico*, and they use this ending so often that *"ticos"* has come to refer to Costa Ricans in general. The country's most popular phrase, *pura vida* (literally "pure life"), is extremely versatile and may be used to mean "hello," "goodbye," "awesome," or "good luck." While the phrase is not used too often in major cities, it is kept alive by rural communities, enthusiastic tourists, and a thriving souvenir industry. Some other common words include: *tuanis*, the spanglish pronunciation of the English phrase "too nice"; *mae* (dude); and *rico/a*, an adjective often used to describe excellent food.

SLANG. When people pass each other, saying *adios* is just as common as saying *hola*. Don't get confused, if you're a girl with a guy friend and a man calls him *cuñado*, which means brother-in-law. He is pretending you are his girlfriend, and your male escort merely your brother. If he calls your mother *suegra* (mother-in-law), you can be certain this cat-caller fancies you. Friends sometimes use *primito* (little cousin) as a term of endearment for each other. The word *mae* is the *tico* counterpart of man or dude, derived from *maje* (which means stupid) and spoken with a lilting tone: *¡Pura vida, mae!*

RELIGION

Costa Rica is a politically secular country with weak links between church and state. Though the constitution provides for religious freedom, **Roman Catholicism** is the official religion, practiced by almost 77% of the population. As such, only Catholic marriages receive state recognition—all others must have a civil ceremony. Semana Santa (Holy Week), a national holiday culminating on Easter Sunday, is a balance of piety and partying. Protestantism has a presence, though it has yet to gain the ubiquity it has in other Central American countries. There are small numbers of Jehovah's Witnesses, Jews, Mennonites, Quakers, and people of other denominations throughout the country.

CULTURE

FOOD AND DRINK

If it doesn't have rice and beans, it isn't *tico!* Rice and black beans infiltrate almost every meal. In one day, it's possible to have them for breakfast as *gallo pinto*, (literally, "spotted rooster"; rice and beans fried with spices and served with meat or eggs), then take a *casado* for lunch and have a hearty bowl of black bean soup for dinner. "Casado" literally means "married," and it refers to the hearty combination plates (usually rice and beans with meat, plantains, cabbage, and tomato). *Tamales*, *empanadas*, and *tortas* are also typical dishes. **Comida típica** (native dishes) in Costa Rica are usually mild and can even be bland. As if to answer this need for flavor, *lizano salsa*, a slightly sweet and spicy sauce of vegetables, has become Costa Rica's most popular condiment.

Informal restaurants called *sodas*, which serve flavorful, home-style cooking at inexpensive prices, dominate the landscape. Larger and generally more expensive *restaurantes* are slightly less common. If you're far from the city, you may find yourself at a small *soda* where they only offer you a spoon. This is because *campesinos* (rural field workers) often eat only with this utensil. Don't be embarrassed to ask for a fork and knife. Many meals come with bread or corn tortillas, both of which you can hold and eat with your hand.

Though vegetables are not a large part of the Costa Rican diet, fruits are popular snacks. Common favorites include pineapple, banana, coconut, mango, and papaya, but you can also find more exotic *tamarindos*, *guayabas*, *manzanas de agua*, *marañones* (the fruit of cashews), and *pejiballe*, a fleshy fruit from palm trees that is boiled, salted, and usually eaten with mayonnaise. Though fruit vendors abound, many *ticos* will jump out of their cars to pick fruits from roadside trees, but be careful, as eating fruit without washing it can have some uncomfortable consequences.

Taking advantage of their bounty of tropical fruit, Costa Ricans enjoy refreshing fruity beverages year-round. *Batidos*, or *frescos* (fruit shakes) are common; they combine fruits with milk or water. The most popular shakes are mango, blackberry, and pineapple. If fruit in a glass seems too tame, try *agua de pipa*, the liquid contents of green coconut with the top chopped off. There's also *horchata*, a cornmeal or ground rice drink flavored with cinnamon, and *agua dulce*, a traditional drink made with boiled water and sugar.

In terms of popularity, nothing can compete with the widespread appeal of Costa Rica's world-class coffee. *Ticos* young and old enjoy a big mug of *café* (usually mixed with milk) multiple times a day. Despite the high quality of Costa Rican blends, most *ticos* seem to prefer a sweetened brew. For a stronger cup of joe, look for restaurants and cafes that cater to tourists, or buy your own beans. Ask for *café sin leche* or *café negro* to skip the cream and sugar.

Though coffee has captured the hearts of Costa Ricans, alcohol is still putting up a fight for their livers. *Guaro*, made from sugar cane and similar-tasting to rum, is the national liquor. It mixes well with anything, though *coco loco* (*guaro* with coconut juice) is a popular choice. When it comes to lower proof options, Imperial, Pilsen, and Bavaria beers are popular among *ticos*.

The Atlantic coast has a stronger Caribbean influence than the rest of the country. Though you won't escape *gallo pinto*, you will find the national specialty served with a coconut twist. Other regional specialities include deep-fried plantains and *rondon*, a stew with the freshest catch on hand. Though turtle meat and eggs are considered a local speciality in many Caribbean towns and bars across the country—men sometimes drink the eggs straight as aphrodisiacs—they are often harvested and sold illegally, so be aware.

CUSTOMS AND ETIQUETTE

BEING COSTA RICAN. *Ticos* are very family oriented. Kids live with their parents through their college years and generally don't leave home before marriage. Close extended families are common and contribute to fairly cohesive communities, particularly in rural areas. Costa Ricans are known for their relaxed temperament, as well as their willingness to lend a hand — or even a home — in times of need. The phrase *quedar bien*, which means "stay on good terms," is one of the essential tenets of Costa Rican lifestyle values. Costa Ricans will often want to *quedar bien* by saying "yes" when they mean "no" in order to avoid conflict. This may also mean that promises made during face-to-face interactions are more symbolic than authentic; a friendly gesture is emphasized over a desire for particularly deep or intimate friendship.

PUBLIC DISPLAYS OF AFFECTION. In general, Costa Ricans are very affectionate and are often physically expressive. It isn't unusual to see couples holding hands or walking arm in arm. In public places like bars and discos, it isn't taboo for couples to hug or kiss, or even for girls to sit on their boyfriend's lap. When dancing, it is usual to dance close together, but "grinding" is frowned upon.

HOUSEGUEST MANNERS. Gratefulness is an admirable quality in houseguests, and hospitality should be received with articulated gratitude (say *"gracias,"* and say it often). Middle- and upper-class families will often have an *empleada*, a young girl or woman who lives in the house and gets paid to help with house chores. Nonetheless, hosts appreciate if guests offer to help serve others or clean after a meal is over, especially if they're doing the work.

BEING POLITE. When speaking Spanish in Costa Rica, you'll find an important distinction between the *usted*, *vos*, and *tú* forms of verbs. Use *usted*, the third person singular, or *ustedes*, the third person plural, when speaking to a stranger or someone older; it is more formal and respectful. Costa Ricans are distinct for using *usted* very broadly: with family, friends, children, and even pets. *Vos*, the second person plural, is the informal counterpart to *usted*, literally translating as "you all." It is rarely used in the city, but it is still common in the country. Using *vos* is appropriate when talking to friends. *Tú*, the second person singular alternative to *vos*, is emerging in some areas, but there are still strong feelings against its use. It is important to use *Don* or *Doña* before an older person's name; call a friend's father Don Alberto and not just Alberto.

Machismo has left a mark on Costa Rican gender relations. Out of tradition, men are very chivalrous, often assuming a protective role, though women might also find themselves subjected to unwanted male attention on the streets. It is considered good manners for men to open doors and help carry bags.

GREETINGS. The traditional kiss-on-the-cheek greeting is not as popular among Costa Ricans as it is with other Latin Americans. It tends to be reserved for more familiar greetings. To be safe when meeting someone for the first time, follow their lead. When saying "hi" to a friend, young or old, it is routine to kiss the person once on the cheek. Men greet each other with a firm handshake.

TABOOS. Although times are changing, most people in the country are Catholic, and their religious beliefs make sexual relations before marriage at least a surface-level taboo, especially among older generations. Homosexuality is a controversial topic, and although people are generally more open about their sexual orientation than in many developing nations, public displays of affection may be received with some level of public discomfort.

DRESS CODE. Costa Ricans are always very conscious about looking presentable and tidy when they go out. People often dress much more conservatively than the warm weather would call for. Men usually wear slacks, jeans, t-shirts, polo shirts, or button-down shirts. Women usually wear pants, jeans, or skirts in the city. Travelers should try not to wear shorts in the city; shorts are acceptable in more rural areas and at the beach. When in doubt, it's a good idea for visitors to present themselves in a fairly conservative manner.

TICO TIME. People in Costa Rica tend to be very laid-back—being on time is not a major point of concern. *Ticos* can be late for almost everything, which often comes as a surprise to foreigners accustomed to punctuality. While it is usual for people to be 15-30min. late for business appointments, a meeting with friends can be delayed by up to several hours.

SPORTS AND RECREATION

Among Costa Ricans, there is no question as to which sport captures the country's full attention: *futból*. *Ticos* eat, drink, sleep, and breathe *futból*, known elsewhere as **soccer.** Indeed, soccer matches are one of the few events that everyone gets to on time. Costa Rica has one major national league with a season that stretches from Aug. to May, but competition runs just as fierce on the local level, where villages battle for territorial honor and unofficial crowns on muddy fields. *Futból* is such a large part of Costa Rican life that an area cannot be legally considered a political district unless it has a soccer field—usually located in the center of town. Though travelers can easily find their way into casual pick-up matches across the countryside, the country offers tons of alternative recreational options.

Introduced in 1944, **golf** in Costa Rica is played on world-renowned courses. In the 1970s, the Cariari Country Club, between San José and the International Airport, built the first course in the country. High-ranking Garra de León Resort and Valle del Sol in the Central Valley are also challenging courses.

Bordered by two oceans, Costa Rica is home to some of the world's best **surfing,** including **Pavones** (p. 341)—location of the second largest left-hand waves in the world—and the infamous *salsa brava* (angry sauce) waves of **Puerto Viejo** (p. 384). Despite the availability of beautiful beaches and awesome waves, surfing just recently began to take off as a competitive sport in Costa Rica. The natural splendor of Costa Rica also makes adventure sports popular, especially among tourists. Everything from sportfishing to kayaking to ziplining through the rainforest can be found within Costa Rica's coasts. For more information on the wheres and hows of adventure sports, see **Great Outdoors** (p. 70).

THE ARTS

Unlike some of its other Central American neighbors, Costa Rica is not known for its artistic heritage. Typical artifacts include **statues** in gold, jade, and stone, as well as breastplates featuring stylized jaguars, crocodiles, and hook-beaked birds from the Pre-Columbian era. Some of the most famous and mysterious artifacts are the more than 300 almost perfectly spherical **Diquis stones,** called *Las Bolas* by locals, which are found in the southern territories. The stones are arranged in geometric formations that point to earth's magnetic north and are estimated to be around 1600 years old. Archaeologists still are confounded by their origin. With the arrival of Spanish colonial rulers, Costa Rica's arts and culture were dominated by European norms for centuries. In the modern era, Costa Ricans have begun to take an active interest in their pre-Columbian history and culture, and excavations have fueled this process of rediscovery.

While periodicals rule the reading market, Costa Rica does have a colorful literary history. Before the 20th century, Costa Rican literature drew largely from European models, though it also gained inspiration from folk tales and colloquial expression in a movement known as *costumbrismo*. Despite the strength of this early movement, Costa Rican literature didn't find its expressive voice until the 20th century, when it began dedicating itself to political and social criticism. **José Marín Cañas's** *Inferno verde*, a depiction of the Chaco War between Paraguay and Bolivia, bolstered anti-imperialist sentiment. **Oreamuni's** *La ruta de su evasión* explored inter-generational tensions and the subtleties of Latin American *machismo*. Writer **Fabián Dobles,** winner of the Premio Nacional, Costa Rica's highest distinction for artistic and intellectual achievement, has also gained recognition beyond the borders of the country; and **Carlos Salazar Herrera** is one of the nation's premier artists, working as a painter, poet, and professor. Costa Rica also serves as a haven for expat writers and artists from around the world, offering inspiration or simply a secluded backdrop.

Much of Costa Rica's popular culture is imported from elsewhere, and often its cultural offerings can remain frustratingly elusive to travelers hungry for authenticity. While the rule of thumb was once a simple American conditional (if it's *norteamericano*, it's cool), cultural tastes have grown more inclusive. US movies and singers have substantial fan bases across the country, but people are also drawn to music and cinema from the rest of Latin America. Mexican films like *Y tu mamá también* or *Amores perros* are favorites, while cowboys in the Northwest listen to Mexican *ranchero* bands like Los Tigres del Norte.

As for music, travelers may be treated to Latin remixes of American oldies like "Hotel California" by the Eagles or a surprisingly large portion of The Beatles's canon. While teenybopper hits have effectively conquered the radio waves, traditional salsa and merengue are often played in nightclubs. Indeed, *discotecas* make no apologies for their juxtapositions—American pop from several years ago, including selections from the Backstreet Boys and 'N Sync, often serve as preludes to Latin American beats. Reggae is popular along the Caribbean coast, where it's especially hard to escape the sounds of Jamaican reggae star Sean Paul, who specializes in ragga. Ragga is a subgenre of reggae, souped up with synthesizers, and has gained popularity in towns and clubs across the country. Its raw, edgy quality has found particular appeal among young people looking for lyrical expression and intensely danceable beats.

MEDIA

Costa Rica has seven nationally broadcast **television** channels, not counting cable and satellite options. Most channels feature an eclectic mix of sports, gaudy variety and game shows, American programs dubbed in Spanish, and Latin American *telenovelas* (soap operas). Nudity and vulgar language are almost always edited out on broadcast television, and cable has become subject to increasing censorship as well.

The two most popular Spanish-language **newspapers** are *La Nación* (www.nacion.com) and *La República* (www.larepublica.net). *La Nación* has a slightly broader circulation and is owned by the same company that puts out *Al Día* (www.aldia.co.cr), a more sensationalist paper devoted largely to sports and celebrity gossip. In English, the weekly *Tico Times* (www.ticotimes.net) offers extensive summaries of cultural events, hotels, restaurants, and news. Online newspapers, such as *A.M. Costa Rica* (www.amcostarica.com) and *Inside Costa Rica* (www.insidecostarica.com), offer Costa Rican news in English.

COSTA RICA'S FESTIVALS (2009)

DATE	NAME AND LOCATION	DESCRIPTION
First 2 weeks of January	Fiestas de Palmares (Palmares)	Fairgrounds are set up in town. Festivities include dances, concert, fireworks, food, music, horseback parades, and bullfighting.
Week of January 15	Fiestas Patronales de Santa Cruz (Guanacaste)	History and traditions are revived in honor of Santo Cristo de Esquipulas, the patron saint of Santa Cruz. Local celebrations include dances, marimba music, and rodeo.
Late February	Fiesta de los Diablitos (Rey Curre)	This festival, held annually for 3 days on the Boruca Indigenous Reserve, turns history on its head with a reenactment of the war between the native Boruca and the Spanish conquistadors in which the Boruca (who originally lost) are victorious.
March 8	Día del Boyero (Escazú)	Day of the oxcart driver, celebrated on the Colorful, hand-painted oxcarts parade down the streets of San Antonio de Escazú.
April 1-7	Semana Santa	Holy Week. Celebrated with religious processions throughout the country.
Late April, early May	Semana Universitaria (San José)	The University of Costa Rica sponsors a week-long cultural celebration in San José that includes numerous parades, concerts, dances, and, most notably, the crowning of a new beauty queen.
June 29	Día de San Pedro y San Pablo (San José)	Celebrated with religious processions in and around San José.
July 14	Fiesta de la Virgen del mar (Puntarenas)	Parades, dances, and carnivals abound at this coastal festival. The highlight of the day is a parade of elaborately decorated boats that sail through the harbor.
August 30	Día de San Ramón (San Ramón)	Over 20 statues of saints from surrounding towns are carried to San Ramón, where they are paraded in a colorful religious procession.
Week of December 8	Fiesta de los Negritos (Boruca)	A festival that includes costumed dancing and celebrations of the traditions of the indigenous Boruca people.
December 26 (daytime)	Tope Nacional, Paseo Colón (San José)	Nearly a century-old tradition, Paseo Colón in San José is shut down for a horseback parade of more than 3000 of the country's finest horses and their riders.
December 26 (nighttime)	Festival de la Luz, Paseo Colón (San José)	A light festival complete with elaborate floats and colorful lights that parade down 2 of San José's main streets. Fireworks light up the night sky.
December 27	Carnaval Nacional, Paseo Colón (San José)	An end-of-the-year celebration. Colorful floats compete for prizes; costumed revelers join the parade, complete with live bands and music.
Last week of December	Fiestas de Zapote (Zapote, a suburb southeast of San José)	A big fair is set up in Zapote to celebrate the Christmas season and the New Year. Costa Ricans from all over the country come to enjoy the live music, fireworks, food, and non-fatal Costa Rican style of bullfighting.

COSTA RICA'S OFFICIAL HOLIDAYS

DATE	NAME	DESCRIPTION
January 1	Año Nuevo	Celebrated with festivities in San José's Parque Central.
April 9-12	Maundy Thursday, Good Friday, Easter	Paid holidays celebrated with elaborate religious processions in cities throughout the country, including Tres Ríos, Cartago and San Joaquín de Flores.
April 11	Día de Juan Santamaría	Commemorates the day Costa Rica's only national hero, Juan Santamaría, burned down the filibusters' fort and helped Costa Ricans win the Battle of Rivas (1856). Celebrated with parades in Alajuela.

DATE	NAME	DESCRIPTION
May 1	Día del Trabajo	Labor Day. National paid holiday for all workers.
July 25	Día de la Anexión de Guanacaste	Celebrates the day in 1824 when the province of Guanacaste became part of Costa Rica. Civic activities take place in every school, and there are musical and folkloric festivities throughout the country, especially in Santa Cruz, Liberia, and San José.
August 2	Día de la Virgen de Los Angeles	The Day of the Virgin honors the patron saint of Costa Rica, la Negrita. People across the country make a religious pilgrimage to the Basílica de los Ángeles cathedral in Cartago.
August 15	Día de la Madre	Mother's Day
September 15	Día de la Independencia, San José	Costa Rica's independence from Spain in 1821 is celebrated with parades, marching bands, and parties throughout the country. At 6pm, runners carrying the ceremonial Freedom Torch from Guatemala arrive in San José. Lantern-lit parades and marching bands bring streets to life at night.
October 12	Día de las Culturas/ Día de la Raza	Celebrates indigenous cultures and/or Columbus's arrival.
November 2	All Souls Day	Church processions and pilgrimages to the cemeteries.
December 25	Christmas Day	Celebrated with family dinners, trips to the beach, and lots of parties.

ADDITIONAL RESOURCES

HISTORY

Costa Rica: Quest for Democracy, by John A. Booth.

The Costa Rica Reader: History, Culture, Politics, edited by Steven Palmer and Ivan Molina. A rich collection of essays on everything from the coffee industry to the plight of the indigenous people.

The Ticos: Culture and Social Change in Costa Rica, By Mavis Biesanz, Richard Biesanz, and Karen Biesanz. An in-depth examination of Costa Rican history, economy, family, education, and religion, and how they have contributed to modern *tico* culture.

FICTION

When New Flowers Bloomed: Short Stories by Women Writers from Costa Rica and Panama, edited by Enrique Jaramillo Levi. A richly imagined collection of recent fiction from Central America.

Juan Valera, by Adolfo Herrera Garcia. A 1939 novel that follows its rural peasant protagonist as he moves into an urban environment full of poverty and social discontent.

Costa Rica: A Traveler's Literary Companion, edited by Barbara Ras. A collection of 26 short stories written by 20th-century Costa Rican authors, organized by regional focus.

La Loca de Gandoca, by Anacristina Rossi. Though it's only available in Spanish, this novel offers an perspective on sustainable tourism, chronicling one conservationist's struggle to stop the construction of a hotel along an undeveloped stretch of the coast.

Jurassic Park, by Michael Crichton. Hard to list without cringing, but impossible to exclude. Though it hardly offers anything close to a perspective on contemporary Costa Rica, this page-turner is set here and features its nonexistent "Air Force" to amusing effect.

TRAVEL BOOKS

Costa Rica: The Last Country the Gods Made, by Adrian Colesberry. Essays on a variety of topics, ranging from indigenous religion to the politics of coffee.

Breakfast of Biodiversity: The Political Ecology of Rainforest Destruction, by John Vandermeer, Ivette Perfecto, and Vandana Shiva. Examines the relationships among agriculture, ecology, global warming, and economic progress in the Costa Rican ecosystem.

Green Phoenix: Restoring the Tropical Forests of Guanacaste, Costa Rica, by William Allen. The story of Costa Rican and American scientists and volunteers who set out to save northwestern Costa Rica in a large-scale tropical forest restoration project.

Monkeys are Made of Chocolate: Exotic and Unseen Costa Rica, by Jack Ewing. After moving to Costa Rica from his native Colorado, Ewing spent 30 years in the jungles of Costa Rica. This collection of essays chronicles his experiences and observations.

WEBSITES

www.visitcostarica.com. The official website of the Costa Rica Tourism Board. Includes general information on Costa Rican culture, popular destinations, and hotels, as well as maps and an extremely useful national bus schedule.

www.infocostarica.com. An excellent source of general Costa Rican information. If you can navigate through all the ads, you'll find hundreds of articles on Costa Rican attractions, art, culture, and history.

www.govisitcostarica.com. True to its name, this website encourages visitors to experience the best Costa Rica has to offer, with detailed listings of hotels, transportation options, and activities. A free monthly newsletter offers travel tips to those who sign up.

www.tourism.co.cr. Yet another compilation of various articles, tips, and pictures of Costa Rica. Small articles on everything from how to dress to partying "*tico* style."

www.entretenimiento.co.cr. This Spanish website contains detailed information on entertainment in Costa Rica, including movie times, music reviews, and information on television, theatrical, and sporting events.

LIFE AND TIMES

BEYOND TOURISM

A PHILOSOPHY FOR TRAVELERS

As a tourist, you are always a foreigner. Sure, hostel-hopping and sightseeing can be great fun, but connecting with a foreign country through studying, volunteering, or working can extend your travels beyond tourist traps. We don't like to brag, but this is what's different about a *Let's Go* traveler. Instead of feeling like a stranger in a strange land, you can understand Costa Rica like a local. Instead of being that tourist asking for directions, you can be the one who gives them (and correctly!). All the while, you get the satisfaction of leaving Costa Rica in better shape than you found it (after all, it's being nice enough to let you stay here). It's not wishful thinking—it's Beyond Tourism.

As a **volunteer** in Costa Rica, you can unleash your inner superhero with projects from protecting endangered turtles from poachers and predators on the coast to farming one of Costa Rica's biggest exports, pineapples, in a sustainable environment. This chapter is chock-full of ideas on how to get involved, whether you're looking to pitch in for a day as part of a vacation or run away from home for a whole new life in Costa Rican activism.

The powers of **studying** abroad are beyond comprehension: it can actually make you feel sorry for those poor tourists who don't get to do any homework while they're here. Most college programs combine Spanish immersion with environmental or ecological studies and field work. Homestays with Costa Rican families allow you to see the country beyond the tourist lens, and maybe even find a second home. Interested in research? Costa Rica's ecological and biological diversity make it the ideal place to find or join a research project.

Working abroad immerses you in a new culture and can bring some of the most meaningful relationships and experiences of your life. Yes, we know you're on vacation, but these aren't your normal desk jobs. (Plus, it doesn't hurt that it helps pay for more globetrotting.) Although it may be difficult to find work in Costa Rica, it is not impossible. The country is reluctant to surrender jobs to foreigners, but there are opportunities for work and internships, as well as numerous opportunities to teach English in a variety of settings.

Beyond Tourism will prove particularly appealing to backpackers traveling through Central America and spending at least three to four weeks in each country, as well as high school and college-age students interested in cultural immersion and Spanish language instruction. If you're just traveling through the country and looking for an interesting alternative to tourism, read newspapers, hotel information boards, and fliers posted on the streets in touristed areas for local opportunities. Whether you're repairing trails at a national park for a few days, rafting and hiking through the jungle, or learning Spanish from natives in a small village, you're bound to have a unique and culturally illuminating experience, not to mention plenty of stories to bring home with you.

SHARE YOUR EXPERIENCE. Have you had a particularly enjoyable volunteer, study, or work experience that you'd like to share with other travelers? Post it to our website, www.letsgo.com!

VOLUNTEERING

Feel like saving the world this week? Volunteering can be a powerful and fulfilling experience, especially when combined with the thrill of traveling in a new place. Costa Rica faces a variety of issues—ethical, structural, financial, and bureaucratic—in its ongoing quest to develop a tourist industry while preserving its cultural integrity and biological diversity. Playing another role beside that of tourist and consumer in this industry can be a unique and exciting experience. The vast majority of volunteer work in Costa Rica involves conservation efforts in the rainforests, in the mountains, and on both coasts. They almost always involve working directly with the animals and plant life that make Costa Rica so unique. There are also several opportunities to work in communities teaching English, developing the ecotourism industry, and working with orphans and immigrants.

Most people who volunteer in Costa Rica do so on a short-term basis at organizations that make use of drop-in or once-a-week volunteers. The best way to find opportunities that match your interests and schedule may be to check with local or national volunteer centers. **The International Volunteer Programs Association** (☎914 380 8322; www.volunteerinternational.org) provides an up-to-date database of hundreds of volunteer and internship opportunities around the world. As always, read up before heading out.

Those looking for longer, more intensive volunteer opportunities usually choose to go through a parent organization that takes care of logistical details and often provides a group environment and support system—for a fee. There are two main types of organizations—religious and secular—although there are rarely restrictions on participation for either. Websites like **www.volunteerabroad.com, www.servenet.org,** and **www.idealist.org** allow you to search for volunteer openings both in your country and abroad.

I HAVE TO PAY TO VOLUNTEER? Many volunteers are surprised to learn that some organizations require large fees or "donations," but don't go calling them scams just yet. While such fees may seem ridiculous at first, they often keep the organization afloat, covering airfare, room, board, and administrative expenses for the volunteers. (Other organizations must rely on private donations and government subsidies.) If you're concerned about how a program spends its fees, request an annual report or finance account. A reputable organization won't refuse to inform you of how volunteer money is spent. Pay-to-volunteer programs might be a good idea for young travelers who are looking for more support and structure (such as pre-arranged transportation and housing) or anyone who would rather not deal with the uncertainty of creating a volunteer experience from scratch.

SAVE THE ANIMALS

With an increasing number of tourists visiting every year, there is a higher demand for protection of the wildlife. Programs focus on protecting turtles from poachers or volunteering in a wildlife refuge.

Earthwatch, 3 ClockTower Pl., Ste. 100, Box 75, Maynard, MA 01754, USA (☎+1 800-776-0188 or +1 978-461-0081; www.earthwatch.org). Arranges 10- to 14-day programs in Costa Rica to promote conservation of natural resources and provide the opportunity to participate in cutting-edge scientific research. Volunteers have the opportunity to gather data on leatherback turtles, howler monkeys, and caterpillars; to work on restoring the rainforest; and to develop sustainable tourist and agricultural practices in the Gandoca-Manzanillo wildlife refuge. Fees vary; average US$2800, plus airfare.

Global Vision International (GVI) (US ☎+1 888-653-6028, UK+44 01727 250 250; www.gvi.co.uk). Conducts 5- and 10-week conservation expeditions based out of the Caño Palma Biological Station in Tortuguero. Partnered with MINAE, GVI allows volunteers to work on turtle and bird conservation and to organize tourist education programs. No previous experience is needed. After the first 5 weeks of the 10-week program, volunteers have the opportunity to become interns and continue for an additional 10 weeks free of charge. The first 2 weeks feature an intensive training program. Both the 5-week (US$2890) and 10-week (US$4690) programs include training, food, accommodations, and domestic transportation.

Talamanca Dolphin Federation (TDF), 3150 Graf St. #8, Bozeman, MT 59715, USA (US ☎+1 406-586-5084, Manzanillo 2795 9115; www.dolphinlink.org). A non-profit association of cetacean specialists and local naturalists, guides, business owners, and boat captains devoted to preserving the dolphins of Talamanca. Volunteers assist visitors at the Dolphin Education Center and Dolphin Lodge, help with the Federation's organized tours, teach local children about marine life, and perform various office-related tasks.

Volunteer Visions, Casa Roja de Dos Pisos, Playa Samara, Guanacaste, Costa Rica (US ☎+1 330-871-4511; www.volunteervisions.org). Provides affordable volunteer opportunites for adventurous individuals. Based in Costa Rica, Volunteer Visions's wildlife conservation project in the Guanacaste region of Costa Rica strives to reintroduce birds, monkeys, and other animals to the wild. Volunteers help to care for the animals and work to keep the park operating. Trips range from 2 weeks (US$650) to 12 weeks (US$1800). Fee includes 2-3 meals per day (if staying in a homestay), accommodations, orientation, and excursions.

World Endeavors, 2518 29th Ave. S., Minneapolis, MN 55406, USA (☎+1 612-729-3400; www.worldendeavors.com). Opportunities for volunteers to rescue and rehabilitate parrots, macaws, and other native tropical birds in Atenas. The organization also runs a sea turtle conservation project. Programs range from 2 weeks (US$1455) to 3 months (US$2865); includes housing, 3 meals per day with a family, and cultural activities. Placements longer than 1 month receive 2 weeks of Spanish language classes.

SAVE THE TREES

Costa Rica is one of the most environmentally diverse places on earth. Numerous organizations work to protect the national parks, tropical forests, and beaches from unsustainable farming practices and tourist practices. The following programs offer volunteer opportunities ranging from trail maintenance and reforestation to teaching sustainable farming techniques.

▨ Punta Mona Center (www.puntamona.org), located 5km south of Manzanillo. An 85-acre organic farm and educational center dedicated to sustainable agriculture. Volunteers spend their days and nights picking (and eating) 100+ varieties of tropical fruit, observing huge marine turtles nest on the beach, living in houses built completely of fallen trees, and using solar-powered, eco-friendly energy. Meals included. Internships (US$610 per month) and volunteer opportunities (US$124 per month) available.

Asociación Preservacionista de Flora y Fauna Silvestre (APREFLOFAS), P.O. Box 917 2150, Moravia, San José (☎2240 6087; www.preserveplanet.org). A non-profit volunteer organization that promotes reforestation, works to guard Costa Rica's natural resources from illegal exploitation, and provides a wealth of information on ecotourism in Costa Rica's parks. APREFLOFAS also operates a tour agency, Raccoon Tours, which finances the volunteer program and conservation efforts.

Asociación de Voluntario de Areas Protegias Silvestres (ASVO), Apdo. 11384-1000, San José (☎2258 4430; info@asvocr.com). Your link to virtually every national park in Costa Rica. Although some parks prefer that volunteers contact their conservation areas directly, you can always reach a specific park through this office. Live and work in the same conditions as the park rangers. 15-day commitment.

FARMING

Agriculture is a major part of the livelihood of Costa Rica. The export of crops is an important part of the economy, and there is a plethora of opportunities for involvement in this industry.

Finca Lomas, (☎2224 3570; www.anaircr.org). An environmentally friendly farm in the Talamancan Lowland Rainforest. Works to establish sustainable economic and environmental groups and encourage community self-sufficiency. 6-weeks. Housing US$90 per month. Food US$3 per day. Registration US$160 per person.

uVolunteer (Volunteer Costa Rica), Apartado 130-4250, San Ramon, Alajuela, Costa Rica (☎2447 6856; www.uvolunteer.org). Strives to create a sustainable, conservative method of farming that is realistic for Costa Rican farming communities. Volunteers will work on many different projects on the farm in Perez Zeledon, 3hr. south of San José and can work from 2 weeks (US$780) to 12 weeks (US$2180) on the farm.

World-Wide Opportunities on Organic Farms (WWOOF), P.O. Box 2154, Winslow, Buckingham, MK18 3WS, England, UK (www.wwoof.org). A network that connects volunteers with organic farms around the world, including Costa Rica. Promotes sustainable, organic farming by providing travelers with information on farms that will host them for free. Membership fee (US$16) to receive a book of host farms from which to choose.

YOUTH AND THE COMMUNITY

Not the rugged, outdoor activity type? There are many organizations that offer activities beyond working in national parks or rainforests. Many rural communities of Costa Rica live in poverty, with low-quality schools, health care, and resources. The programs listed below operate community service projects in some of these small villages.

Alliances Abroad, 1221 South Mopac Expressway, Ste. 100, Austin, TX, USA (☎+1 866-6ABROAD/622-7623; www.allianceabroad.com). Language classes followed by between 2 and 12 weeks of volunteer work in social services, humanitarian organizations, women's services, health care, environment, or national parks. Fees start at US$1300 for 2 weeks in the program.

Amigos de las Americas, 5618 Star Ln., Houston, TX 77057, USA (☎+1 800-231-7796; www.amigoslink.org). Sends high school and college students in groups of 2-3 to work in rural Latin American communities for up to 8 weeks. 2 years of high-school Spanish or equivalent instruction required. Costs average US$3990, airfare included.

Centro de Educación Creativo (Creative Learning Center), Apdo. 23-5655, Monteverde, Puntarenas (☎2645 5161; www.cloudforestschool.org). A private English immersion environmental education program for pre-school to grade 11 students. Volunteers who commit at least 3 months assist teachers in classrooms. Short-term (3-week min.) volunteers can work on outdoor projects but not in the classroom.

Cross-Cultural Solutions, 2 Clinton Pl., New Rochelle, NY 10801, USA (☎+1 800-380-4777 or 914-632-0022; www.crossculturalsolutions.org). Operates 2- to 12-week humanitarian programs in health care, child care, education, social development, and disability assistance. Dorm-style accommodations and all meals included. Fees start at US$2588 for 2 weeks of service.

Global Routes, 1 Short St., Northampton, MA 01060, USA (☎+1 413-585-8895; www.globalroutes.org). College and high school students teach English, promote environmental awareness, and construct health clinics, playgrounds, and schoolhouses for 1-3 months. 1-year Spanish instruction required. 17+. Fees start at US$5450.

Habitat for Humanity International (☎2296 3436 in San José; www.habitatcostarica.org). The Global Village Program builds houses for 1-3 weeks. Minimum donation US$200. US$20 per day transportation and homestay fee. Basic Spanish required.

Peace Corps (☎800-424-8580; www.peacecorps.gov). Opportunities in agriculture, social development, sustainable communities, and health care in 74 developing nations. Projects in Costa Rica focus on rural community development and the education and training of youth. 2-year min. commitment, plus 3 months training.

STUDYING

It's hard to dread the first day of school when the cities and towns of Costa Rica are your campus and exotic, *tico* restaurants are your meal plan. A growing number of students report that studying abroad is the highlight of their learning careers. If you've never studied abroad, you really don't know what you're missing—and if you have studied abroad, you do know what you're missing. Either way, let's go back to school!

VISA INFORMATION. Citizens of Canada, the UK, and the US do not need a visa for visits to Costa Rica that last less than 90 days; only a stamp, sticker, or insert in your passport specifying the purpose of your travel and the permitted duration of your stay are required. A passport valid for at least 30 days after date of entry and a pre-paid airline ticket to exit the country are required of all travelers. Carry a copy of your passport (the page with your photo on it and the page with the stamp) with you at all times. For **short-term** (one year or less) study or volunteer programs, permits are required. They require multiple forms of identification and letters from the accredited school, university, or program. For specific requirments, consult the **Embassy of Costa Rica** (www.costarica-embassy.org).

Study-abroad programs range from language and culture courses to university-level classes, often for college credit (it's legit, Mom and Dad). In order to choose a program that best fits your needs, research as much as you can before making your decision—determine costs and duration as well as what kind of students participate in the program and what sorts of accommodations are provided. In Costa Rica, you could be taking classes and writing papers at a university or studying in the rainforest—the options are endless, so figure out what works for you. Back-to-school shopping was never this much fun.

In programs that have large groups of students who speak the same language, there is a trade-off. You may feel more comfortable in the community, but you will not have the same opportunity to practice a foreign language or to befriend other international students. For accommodations, dorm life provides a better opportunity to mingle with fellow students, but there is less of a chance to experience the local scene. If you live with a family, you could potentially build lifelong friendships with natives and experience day-to-day life in more depth, but you might also get stuck sharing a room with their pet iguana. Conditions can vary greatly from family to family.

UNIVERSITIES AND STUDY PROGRAMS

Most university-level study-abroad programs are conducted in Spanish, although many programs offer classes in English as well as lower-level language courses. Savvy linguists may find it cheaper to enroll directly in a university abroad, although getting college credit may be more difficult. You can search **www.studyabroad.com** for various semester-abroad programs that meet your criteria, including your desired location and focus of study. If you're a college student, your friendly neighborhood study-abroad office is often the best place to start. The programs offered in Costa Rica are as diverse as the country itself, so shop around.

AMERICAN PROGRAMS

American Field Service (AFS), 198 Madison Ave., 8th fl., New York, NY 10016, USA (☎+1 800-237-4636; www.usa.afs.org). Offers homestay exchange programs in Costa Rica primarily for high school students and graduating seniors. Financial aid available. Regional office locations on website. Summer US$7700; winter US$7750.

American Institute for Foreign Study (AIFS), College Division, River Plaza, 9 W. Broad St., Stamford, CT 06902, USA (☎+1-800-727-2437; www.aifsabroad.com). Organizes programs for high-school and college study in universities at Veritas University in San José. Courses include Spanish language, environmental studies, and Latin American literature. Fee without airfare US$4495.

Council on International Educational Exchange (CIEE), 300 Fore St., Portland, ME 04101, USA (☎+1-207-553-4000 or 800-40-STUDY/407-8839; www.ciee.org). One of the most comprehensive resources for work, academic, and internship programs around the world, including in Costa Rica, where you can study biology and ecology in Monteverde. Summer fee US$5670. Semester fee US$11,700.

COSTA RICAN PROGRAMS

No matter what your style is, there is an opportunity for study in Costa Rica. Whether you'd prefer to live in a bustling metropolis, on a deserted beach, or in a tropical rainforest, you can find what you are looking for. Some programs specialize in Spanish and academics, while others focus more heavily on field research. For more info, go to www.westnet.com/costarica/education.html.

Cultural Experiences Abroad (US ☎+1 800-266-4441; www.gowithcea.com). Earn college credit at Veritas University, one of the most recognized private universities in Costa Rica. Offers language courses and business, ecology, and environment electives. Includes housing (homestay available), meal plan, excursions, medical insurance, internships, scholarships, and financial aid opportunities. 1-month intensive program US$2595; summer US$3695-4295; trimester US$7695.

Instituto Monteverde, Apdo. 69-5655, Monteverde, Puntarenas, Costa Rica (☎2506 645 5053; www.mvinstitute.org). This non-profit association provides educational and cultural resources for the local community. Offers programs in tropical ecology, biology, architecture, landscaping, and planning. Fee starts at US$4152.

University of Costa Rica Rainforest Adventure (☎+1 800-321-7625; www.educationabroad.com). A tropical field ecology program for English-speaking undergraduates at Costa Rica's main national university. Students take Spanish lessons and stay with Costa Rican families. Credit accepted by many US universities. US$8500.

LANGUAGE SCHOOLS

Enrolling at a language school has two major perks: a slightly less rigorous courseload and the ability to learn exactly what those kids in Puntarenas are calling you under their breath. There can be great variety in language schools—independently run, affiliated with a larger university, local, international—but one thing is constant: they rarely offer college credit. Their programs are also good for younger high-school students who might not feel comfortable with older students in a university program. Some organizations include:

A2Z Languages, 5112 N. 40th St., Ste. 101, Phoenix, AZ 85018, USA (Canada and US ☎+1 800-496-4596, worldwide 602 778 6794; www.a2zlanguages.com), offers 1-week to 4-week group or private language programs and arranges educational and cultural tours. Includes homestay, 2 meals per day, airport pickup. US$370-3500.

Academia Latinoamericana de Español S.A., Apdo. 1280-2050, San Pedro, Montes de Oca, San José, Costa Rica (☎2224 9917; www.alespanish.com). Spanish taught in small groups of no more than 6 students. Homestay program (US$150 per week). Classes start every M. US$170 per week. US$17 per hr. of private class.

AmeriSpan Study Abroad, 117 S. 17th St., Ste. 1401, Philadelphia, PA 19103, USA (Canada and US ☎800-879-6640, worldwide 215 751 1100; www.amerispan.com), offers 1-week to 6-month language immersion and study abroad programs in Alajuela, Heredia, Manuel Antonio, Monteverde, Playa Flamingo, Playa Sámara, San José, San Joaquín de Flores, and Tamarindo. Classes start every M. College credit available. US$100 registration fee. Classes start at US$260 per week, includes 4hr. daily classes with the option of private lessons, airport pickup, homestay, meals, and excursions.

Comunicare, P.O. Box 1383-2050, San José, Costa Rica (☎2281 0432; www.comunicare-cr.com). A non-profit organization offering Spanish language classes, cultural studies, Central American studies, and a number of volunteer opportunities in the community around San José. 10% discount with ISIC.

Costa Rican Language Academy, P.O. Box. 1966-2050, San José, Costa Rica (US ☎+1 866-230-6361 or Costa Rica 2280 1685; www.spanishandmore.com). 1 to 4-week language and cultural study program, custom-tailored for each individual student. Options include homestays and weekend excursions, lessons in Latin dance, Costa Rican cooking, and Spanish music and conversation classes. Fees start at US$147 for 1 week of classes, with homestay US$311.

Escuela Idiomas d'Amore, Apdo. 67-6350, Quepos, Costa Rica (☎777 1143, US +1 800-261-3203; www.escueladamore.com). Spanish immersion classes in a Pacific beach location for 2-6 weeks, between Quepos and Parque Nacional Manuel Antonio. Homestay available. 18+. Classes start at US$845 for 2 weeks. Homestay US$995.

Forester Instituto Internacional, P.O. Box 6945, 1000 San José, Costa Rica (☎2225 3155; www.fores.com). Short- and long-term Spanish language immersion programs in the nation's capital. Latin dance classes at no additional cost. Homestay available (US$130). US$20 per private lesson. Programs start at US$480 for 1 week.

School of the World, Aptd. 239-4023, Playa Jaco, Costa Rica (☎2643 2462; www.schooloftheworld.org). School in Jacó offers a 1- to 4-week "learning vacation" in Spanish, surfing, yoga, and photography. Weekends are free for travel. 18+. Fees start at US$505 for 1 week. US$275 non-refundable deposit. Group discounts available.

Languages Abroad (US ☎+1 800-219-9924, worldwide 416 925 2112; www.languagesabroad.com). Offers 1- to 12-week standard and intensive language programs for all levels in San José, Heredia, Manuel Antonio, Monteverde, and Playa Sámara. Options for homestay, private classes, tours, and excursions. 17+. Starts at US$490 for 1 week.

WORKING

Nowhere does money grow on trees (though *Let's Go*'s researchers aren't done looking), but there are still some pretty good opportunities to earn a living and travel at the same time. As with volunteering, work opportunities tend to fall into two categories. Some travelers want long-term jobs that allow them to integrate into a community, while others seek out short-term jobs to finance the next leg of their travels. **Transitions Abroad** (www.transitionsabroad.com) also offers updated online listings for work over any time span.

While Costa Rica is generally reluctant to give jobs to traveling foreigners, it's not impossible to obtain work. Making friends with locals can help expedite work permits or arrange work-for-accommodations swaps.Note that working abroad often requires a special work visa.

MORE VISA INFORMATION. Costa Rica has one of the lowest unemployment rates in Central America. As such, the country is wary of allowing foreign workers to come in and potentially raise that number. Fear not, though, because working in Costa Rica is not impossible. **Long-term** programs requiring special entry documentation often handle the documentation procedures for participants. The **Embassy of Costa Rica** (www.costarica-embassy.org) has specific application requirements for temporary (1 year or less) work permits. US citizens can take advantage of the **Center for International Business and Travel** (**CIBT;** ☎800-929-2428; www.cibt.com) and **G3 Visas and Passports** (☎888-883-8472 or 703-276-8472; www.g3visas.com), which secure visas for travel to almost every country for a fee. Double-check on entrance requirements at the nearest embassy or consulate for up-to-date information before departure. US citizens can consult http://sanjose.usembassy.gov. UK citizens can consult www.britishembassycr.com.

LONG-TERM WORK

If you're planning on spending a substantial amount of time (more than three months) working in Costa Rica, search for a job well in advance. International placement agencies are often the easiest way to find employment abroad, especially for those interested in teaching. Note that many jobs require previous experience and/or some knowledge of Spanish. Although they are often only available to college students, **internships** are a good way to ease into working abroad. Many say the interning experience is well worth it, despite low pay (if you're lucky enough to be paid at all). Be wary of advertisements for companies claiming to be able get you a job abroad for a fee—often the same listings are available online or in newspapers. Some reputable organizations include:

AmeriSpan Study and Work Abroad—Costa Rica (worldwide ☎215 751 1100; www.amerispan.com/volunteer_intern). Volunteer and internship placements in a multiple fields, from turtle preservation to social work. Spanish immersion programs available.

Intern Abroad, 7800 Point Meadows Dr., Ste. 218, Jacksonville, FL, USA (☎+1 720-570-1702; www.internabroad.com/CostaRica.cfm). Has numerous postings for recent semi-temporary and long-term job opportunities and internships.

TEACHING ENGLISH

While some elite private American schools offer competitive salaries, let's just say that teaching jobs abroad pay more in personal satisfaction and emotional fulfillment than in actual cash. Perhaps this is why volunteering as a teacher instead of getting paid is a popular option. Even then, teachers often receive some sort of a daily stipend to help with living expenses. However, even though salaries at private schools may be low compared to those in the US, a low cost of living makes teaching jobs much more profitable. In almost all cases, you must have at least a bachelor's degree to be a full-fledged teacher, although college undergraduates can often get summer positions teaching or tutoring. English instruction is probably the most readily available profession for foreigners looking to stay in Costa Rica for the long haul.

Many schools require teachers to have a **Teaching English as a Foreign Language (TEFL)** certificate. You may still be able to find a teaching job without one, but certified teachers often find higher-paying jobs. The Spanish-impaired don't have to give up their dream of teaching, either. Private schools usually hire native English speakers for English-immersion classrooms where no Spanish is spoken. Teachers in public schools will more likely work in both English and Spanish. Placement agencies or university fellowship programs are the best resources for finding teaching jobs. An alternative is to contact schools directly or to try your luck once you arrive in Costa Rica. The best time to look is several weeks before the start of the school year, which begins it late January. The following organizations can be helpful in placing teachers in Costa Rica.

International Schools Services (ISS), 15 Roszel Rd., P.O. Box 5910, Princeton, NJ 08543, USA (☎+1-609-452-0990; www.iss.edu). Hires teachers for more than 200 overseas schools, including in Costa Rica. Candidates should have teaching experience and a bachelor's degree. 2-year commitment is the norm.

Office of Overseas Schools, US Department of State, Office of Overseas Schools, Room H328, SA-1, Washington, D.C. 20522-0132, USA (☎+1 202-261-8200; www.state.gov/m/a/os). Has information on worldwide American-sponsored elementary and secondary schools and current fact sheets on American international schools.

WorldTeach, Inc., Center for International Development, Harvard University, Box 122, 79 John F. Kennedy St., Cambridge, MA 02138, USA (☎+1 800-483-2240 or 617-495-5527; www.worldteach.org). Sends students and college graduates for 1-year and 2-month summer program positions to teach English, environmental education, and other subjects in public schools. Fees range US$3990-4990; scholarships and fundraising options available.

SHORT-TERM WORK

Traveling for long periods of time can be hard on the wallet. Many travelers try their hand at odd jobs for a few weeks at a time to help pay for another month or two of touring around. Short-term work in Costa Rica, however, is extremely limited and is not offered regularly. Most opportunities can be found aiding the ongoing conservation efforts. Travelers looking for jobs in Costa Rica typically resort to asking around at local business if foreign help is needed and taking whatever positions are available. Popular means of employment include work as tour guides, Spanish-English translators, bartenders, waiters/waitresses, and other positions that require a strong understanding of the English language. Another popular option is to work several hours a day at a hostel in exchange for free or discounted room and/or board. Most often, these short-term jobs are found by word of mouth or by expressing interest to the owner of a hostel or restaurant. Due to high turnover in the tourism industry, many places are eager for help, even if it is only temporary. *Let's Go* lists temporary jobs of this nature whenever possible; look in the **Practical Information** sections of larger cities.

FURTHER READING ON BEYOND TOURISM

Alternatives to the Peace Corps: A Guide of Global Volunteer Opportunities, edited by Paul Backhurst. Food First, 2005 (US$12).

The Back Door Guide to Short-Term Job Adventures: Internships, Summer Jobs, Seasonal Work, Volunteer Vacations, and Transitions Abroad, by Michael Landes. Ten Speed Press, 2005 (US$22).

Green Volunteers: The World Guide to Voluntary Work in Nature Conservation, by Fabio Ausenda. Universe, 2007 (US$15).

How to Live Your Dream of Volunteering Overseas, by Joseph Collins, Stefano DeZerega, and Zahara Heckscher. Penguin Books, 2001 (US$20).

International Job Finder: Where the Jobs Are Worldwide, by Daniel Lauber and Kraig Rice. Planning Communications, 2002 (US$20).

Live and Work Abroad: A Guide for Modern Nomads, by Huw Francis and Michelyne Callan. Vacation Work Publications, 2001 (US$20).

Volunteer Vacations: Short-Term Adventures That Will Benefit You and Others, by Doug Cutchins, Anne Geissinger, and Bill McMillon. Chicago Review Press, 2006 (US$18).

Work Abroad: The Complete Guide to Finding a Job Overseas, edited by Clayton A. Hubbs. Transitions Abroad, 2002 (US$16).

Work Your Way Around the World, by Susan Griffith. Vacation Work Publications, 2007 (US$22).

THE GREAT OUTDOORS

While Costa Rican culture and city life have their charms, the great outdoors is undoubtedly the country's main attraction. Manifold opportunities exist for visitors looking for a quiet retreat from civilization or an unforgettable adventure in the wild. Boasting 12 distinct ecosystem zones, the forests, coasts, mountains, and countrysides of Costa Rica offer some of the most breathtaking natural spectacles in the world. Because of its unique location at the center of an isthmus straddling North and South America, the country is host to a variety of unique environments in which flora and fauna from both hemispheres can thrive. This distinctive status has created an environment where 6% of the world's biodiversity occurs in a country with only 0.1% of the world's landmass. Roughly 25% of Costa Rica's territory is protected by an extensive system of national parks, biological reserves, and wildlife refuges; no other country in the world protects a greater portion of its territory. Costa Rican landscapes also offer opportunities for a wide array of adventure sports and camping. From mountaintop vistas that afford simultaneous views of the Pacific Ocean and Caribbean Sea to cloud forests laced with ziplines for a thrilling experience and white-sand beaches perfect for surfing, Costa Rica offers something for everyone. With its combination of diverse flora, rare fauna, and exciting outdoor activities, the country lives up to its name, Costa Rica (rich coast).

PLANTS

Costa Rica's terrain is dominated by forest, and 99% of the country was once covered by trees. Though deforestation has reduced forest coverage in Costa Rica to around one-quarter of the land, over 10,000 plant species still remain, including over 1000 kinds of orchids and approximately a hundred tree species. The country's topology has crammed a wide variety of distinct ecosystems into concentrated space, offering vastly different experiences to anyone willing to travel the short distance (sometimes just a few meters) between one ecosystem and another. The floral diversity of Costa Rica's rainforests, located primarily on the Caribbean and Southern Pacific coasts, is truly astounding: more species of flora exist in the rainforests of these small regions alone than on the entire European continent. Within five acres of rainforest, it is possible to see as many as 100 species of trees, including such rare finds as the candela (candle), a unique flowering plant that is pollinated by bats instead of insects. While many rainforested regions of Costa Rica have found protection in national parks and reserves, the country's dry forests have recently fallen victim to severe deforestation. These endangered forests, located primarily on the Northern Pacific coast, bloom with some of the most colorful floral displays in the world between November and May.

THE POETICS OF ETYMOLOGY. For many visitors, one of the least-expected pleasures of exploring various Costa Rican ecosystems is discovering the wealth of playful monikers that their plants have earned. The nicknames range from (sac)religious—the "blood of Christ" fern with crimson splotches on its leaves—to more overtly risqué—the pouty red blossoms of the *labios de puta* (hooker's lips)—or simply charmingly appropriate—the broad leaves of the *sombrilla de pobre* (poor man's umbrella) offer instant coverage to hikers caught in sudden thunderstorms.

FOREIGN RELATIONS I: PLANTS AS DEPENDENTS. Many of Costa Rica's plants have adapted to their environments in innovative ways. Some of the most resourceful are the epiphytes, or organisms that grow on other plants. They obtain nutrients and moisture solely from the air and rain. Other plants have developed complex relationships with the creatures that share their ecosystems. Some orchids feature patterns invisible to the human eye that are readily discernible to insects, whose eyesight can access a broader portion of the ultraviolet spectrum. These patterns—often entailing intricate networks of lines and marks—create maps for foraging insects, showing them where to find nectar or nutrients. Many bromeliads, or flowering plants, are better known as "tank epiphytes" because their leaves hold large deposits of rainwater so that aquatic insects can reside in simulated homes far above the jungle floor.

FOREIGN RELATIONS II: PLANTS AND PEOPLE. Despite their astounding variety, many of Costa Rica's most spectacular plants are dwinding in number.Some are on the verge of extinction. In order to avoid aggravating the problem, visitors are advised to avoid taking plants as souvenirs and also to stay on marked trails in national parks. Ask rangers how to enjoy the vegetation in a respectful manner. Though the relationship is hardly symmetrical, vegetation can pose certain dangers to human visitors as well. While a few plants are predatory (think "insect-eating"), many more are simply poisonous. Avoid eating anything before you are certain that it's safe. When in doubt, don't experiment. It is also wise to exercise some caution about touching plants, as many can irritate or even harm the skin.

ANIMALS

Staggeringly, Costa Rica is home to over 200 known mammal, 850 bird, 180 amphibian, and 230 reptile known species, as well as an abundance of insects. Some of these species are extremely rare; Coco Island, the Highlands, and the Southern Pacific lowlands are home to animals that cannot be found anywhere else in the world, and there are a number of species that remain unidentified.

Among Costa Rica's mammal population are a number of descendants from South America, including four different types of **monkeys** (spider, capuchin, howler, and squirrel) as well as the more elusive big **cats** (jaguars, pumas, and ocelots). About half of mammal species are **bats.** By far the most numerous vertebrates in Costa Rica are **birds** (there are more birds in Costa Rica than in Canada and the US combined), making it a prime birdwatching location. Bring a pair of binoculars, patience, a silent travel companion, and lots of luck to spot the ever-elusive quetzals, along with toucans, macaws, hummingbirds, or even the world's most powerful bird of prey, the monkey-eating harpy eagle. Of course, many of these species are both scarce and skittish; the chances of spotting some of them are remote at best. The harpy eagle, for example, hadn't been spotted in such a long time that it was once assumed to be extinct in Costa Rica. The last sighting was in 2003. Some of Costa Rica's most impressive reptilian residents are the large numbers of **turtles** that return to their ancient nesting grounds during aggregations known as arribadas each year. With over 135 species within its borders, Costa Rica is also home to around 7.5% of the world's **snakes,** though 75% of them are non-venomous. The same can't be said for some of its more notorious **amphibians:** a two-inch **poison dart frog** has enough toxin to kill eight adult humans. Some of Costa Rica's least appreciated residents are its **insects,** whose most common ambassadors—mosquitoes and sandflies—are also its least endearing representatives. Visitors can appreciate other insects, though, such as the many kinds of **butterflies** and **dragonflies** in the air and the **leaf-cutter** and **army ants** that scurry from tree to ground.

OUR BESTIARY: AN A-Z CATALOGUE OF SELECTED COSTA RICAN CREATURES. Solitary **ANTEATERS** feed on the ground and in the trees, assuming "boxer" poses when startled by predators or visitors. **BRONZY hermits,** one of Costa Rica's 52 hummingbird species, are dextrous spider-hunters despite their small size. With a lineage dating back to prehistoric times, **American CROCODILES** grow up to 23 ft. in length and are still responsible for a few human deaths each decade. **Helicopter DAMSELFLIES** seem to defy the laws of physics with their delicate flight patterns, beating four wings in different directions at different speeds. The **EYELASH viper** has perfected the art of camouflage, with six color variations including gold and scaly hoods to cover its gleaming eyes. During the mating season of the magnificent **FRIGATEBIRDS,** males pound their bills against massively inflated red throat patches to announce the arrival of females overhead. The skin of the **GLASS frog** is transparent enough to show its stomach, intestines, beating heart, and blood vessels underneath. The showy color patterns of the **HARLEQUIN beetle** get lost against something much less exciting: the bracket fungus that grows on lowland rainforest trees. **IGUANAS** are known locally as the "chicken of the trees" because they are so widely hunted for meat. The **JESUCRISTO lizard** earned its nickname for its ability to run on water, and it can cover over 50 ft. in any single miraculous sprint. Though the **pygmy KINGFISHER** is only 5 in. long, it still manages to hunt fish and underwater insects with its long sharp beak; larger kingfishers eat snakes as well. Because oceanic pressure would crush their lungs, **LEATHERBACK turtles** have adapted to store oxygen in their muscle tissue when they dive deep to hunt for jellyfish. **Howler MONKEYS** are easier heard than seen, though they are common throughout the country and have earned a dubious reputation for their tendency to urinate on unsuspecting travelers below their perches. Male **NOROPS lizards** make themselves conspicuous in the underbrush when they shake their enormous dewlaps to put on mating shows for females. The majestic spotted pelt of the **OCELOT** has been so highly prized by hunters that the wild cat is now an endangered species. The **common POTOO** is an owl known as the *alma perdida* (lost soul) because of its mournful call, which can be heard echoing, lute-like, through the Guanacastean rainforests throughout the night. The resplendent **QUETZAL** protects its gorgeous emerald tail feathers by dropping backwards off perches when startled into flight. The **RED-LORED parrot** is known as a "seed destroyer" because it crushes spores for nutrients instead of dispersing them to promote plant growth. Two-toed **SLOTHS** only descend from the trees once a week to defecate. Many parasites find them to be convenient hosts because they move so slowly, and any given sloth, truly an ecosystem unto himself, can hold up to 900 insects in his fur at any given time. The huge bill of the **keel-billed TOUCAN** displays a magnificent blend of yellow, orange, lime green, sky blue, and cherry red. The **URRACA** is a striking sapphire-shaded songbird whose unmistakable topknot curves forward quite festively, resembling a stage accessory more than an evolutionary adaptation. The **VINE snake** earned its name from its imitative capacities, though its bite is more potent than benign facade would suggest. **Humpback WHALES** are visible off the Osa coast when they come south to calve during the winter. Sportfishers catch large **XIPHIAS GLADIUS** (a.k.a swordfish) off the coast. The **YURE** is a dove whose call is said to resemble the airy sound of someone blowing across the mouth of a bottle. The **ZORRA Mochila** is feistier than its American opossum cousins, attacking predators as opposed to "playing dead" to escape injury.

ENDANGERED AND DANGEROUS. Unfortunately, many of Costa Rica's most remarkable animals are . Over 100 animal species are endangered, while another 100 remain vulnerable. The list of these unfortunate creatures reads like a "who's who" of Costa Rican wildlife: the harpy eagle, red and green macaws, giant anteaters, manatees, Baird's tapir, the jaguar, the puma, the ocelot, several turtle species, the American crocodile, golden toads, and the boa constrictor. Visitors should be respectful of these creatures and their habitats and also conscious of the potential risks that Costa Rican wildlife can pose to human explorers. While some animals can be intimidating, none are malicious or "eager to attack" humans. Most fear humans and will flee if possible. A few things can greatly reduce the risk of any unpleasant encounters. Though Costa Rica is home to a number of venomous snakes, wearing sturdy shoes (ideally covering your ankles), staying on trails, and keeping your eyes open virtually eliminate the risk of getting bitten by one. In addition to snakes, there are a number of nasty crawling creatures including spiders, scorpions, caterpillars, and centipedes. Scorpions and spiders generally like dark places, so check shoes and toilet seats before use. Keep your bags completely closed while camping and check items before putting them on. Mosquitoes, sandflies, and similar flying insects are mostly a nuisance but can transmit dangerous diseases such as malaria and dengue fever. Long-sleeved clothes, insect repellent, and mosquito netting are all good defenses. Poison-dart frogs have the most powerful toxin in the animal kingdom, but the poison is only effective if it enters the bloodstream or mucus membranes, so steer clear of any form of physical contact. This is a good rule to follow with unknown animals in general. Think of them as pop stars—best admired from a distance.

LAND

Costa Rica contains an impressive variety of distinct landscapes within its narrow borders. The country is dominated by a massive arc of highlands that include four mountain chains, comprising of more than 60 **volcanoes**. Eight of these volcanoes are still active. From northwest to southeast, the chains are Cordillera de Guanacaste, Cordillera de Tilarán, Cordillera Central, and Cordillera de Talamanca, the last of which is non-volcanic. Generally, as one proceeds southeast along the isthmus, the mountains become higher and the *cordilleras* broader, culminating in **Mount Chirripó** (p. 312), Costa Rica's highest point (3820m). Between Cordilleras Central and Talamanca lies the high **Central Valley,** whose fertile soil is home to over half of Costa Rica's population. These mountain ranges exert a striking influence over the country's climate. On the Pacific side, west of the *cordilleras*, precipitation levels increase from north to south, with a rainy season from May to October in the north and from April to December in the south. East of the cordilleras, Costa Rica's Caribbean side experiences rainfall year-round. Temperatures vary mostly by elevation, ranging from steamy humidity in the lowlands, to warm and temperate climates in medium elevations and chilly conditions on Costa Rica's tallest peaks.

The Pacific shore is narrower, drier, and four times longer than its Caribbean counterpart. In contrast to the Caribbean, the Pacific coastline is a vast, broken series of bays, rocky peninsulas, and white-sand beaches— a product of plate tectonics. Sizable portions of these points of land, most notably the **Península de Osa** and the **Península de Nicoya,** were originally islands that were driven into the mainland by the collision of two tectonic plates.

Costa's Rica's unique topography has given rise to a striking diversity of vegetation zones. Shorelines marked by vast beaches—with sands that run from pumice-black to sparkling white to cinnamon-brown—are broken by densely tangled mangroves along the Caribbean, Nicoya, and Osa coasts. Further inland, the lower mountain slopes are covered with tropical rainforests and evergreen forests that resemble ecosystems further south in Latin America. At higher altitudes, the lush cloud forests for which Costa Rica has become famous are full of oaks, laurels, orchids, and thick canopies. At even higher elevations, conifers form a significant part of the forest landscape. Above the treeline, the vegetation resembles that of the Andean highland moors, with evergreen shrubs, berries, herbs, and mosses. The country's drier northwest has some savannas and deciduous forests.

The convergence of tectonic plates off Central America's Pacific coast makes Costa Rica prone to both earthquakes and volcanic eruptions. An earthquake of 6.7 on the Richter scale struck 89km south of San José in August 1999. Thankfully, the damage was much less severe than in 1991, when an earthquake measuring 7.4 struck Limón, leaving 27 dead, 400 wounded, and 13,000 homeless. An even larger risk stems from volcanic eruptions, as several active volcanoes line the densely populated Central Valley. Volcán Irazú's eruption in 1963 left clouds of smoke and ash showering over San José for two years. Though hurricanes tend to pass by over the country's northern borders, causing more destruction in Nicaragua and Honduras, they occasionally hit Costa Rica, as Hurricane Cesar did in 1996, causing widespread damage in the south.

NATIONAL PARKS AND RESERVES

Costa Rica's national park system began in the 1960s and has since expanded to form the base of the country's extensive **ecotourism** industry. In 1998, Costa Rica passed the unique **Biodiversity Law,** intended to encourage environmental education and regulate the use of its natural resources, protected areas, and biodiversity. It is through this law that Costa Rica now holds approximately 161 of these "protected areas." Though not all of these areas are tourist attractions, some of the more popular parks, like **Manuel Antonio** (p. 293) or **Monteverde** (p. 185) attract over 1000 visitors per day during the high season. Tourists primarily visit the 25 national parks and 58 national wildlife refuges in existence, while the 19 currently active biological reserves cater to those interested in scientific research on specific ecological systems. There are also a large number of private parks, native reserves, and wetlands. Although it attracts large crowds each year, Costa Rica's national park system still manages to maintain its conservation of each area with only minimum human impact.

Entrance fees vary by park, but are generally US$5-10. The use of a guide also varies by park; some parks require guides, others simply recommend them, and some do not have any available. Not all parks are easily accessible by foot. **MINAE** has a fairly large presence in the national park system and often offers guides, maps, and trail advice in heavily touristed parks.

CONSERVATION AND ECOTOURISM

It's easy being green in Costa Rica! Home to many of the rarest species found on the planet, Costa Rica is a heavy hitter in the world ecotourism industry. Approximately 27% of Costa Rica's landmass is considered protected and is kept that way through an intricate system of laws and conservation groups. Under the **National System of Conservation Areas (SINAC),** Costa Rica's forests and wildlife are protected from expansion and overdevelopment. The **Caribbean Conservation Corporation** and the **Neotropica Foundation** were both founded to establish conservation efforts in the country, ranging from adopting endangered animals to creating protected reserves like **Monteverde** (p. 185) and **Rara Avis** (p. 156).

International interest in conservation has led a number of research-minded pharmaceutical companies to fund forest conservation efforts.

The vast expanses of protected space in Costa Rica, and the current public focus on conservation, have lead to a boom in the ecotourism industry. Environmentally minded tourists looking for adventure and the chance to make a difference flock to Costa Rica to lend a helping hand. Most of these ecotourists end up volunteering at one of the country's national parks or reserves, through private or public organizations, for anywhere from one week to several months. Many Costa Ricans worry, however, that the massive expansion of tourism has happened too quickly, and that many less-than-environmentally minded organizations are trying to cash in by riding the ecotourism wave. Many tourist agencies are "green" in name only: they don't follow environmentally friendly tour practices or actually give their profits back to the community. Despite those eco-tourism minded individuals, Costa Rica possesses thousands of opportunities to spend time helping the earth as you travel.

ECOTOURISM RESOURCES. For more information on environmentally responsible tourism, contact one of the organizations below:

Conservation International, 1919 M St. NW, Washington, D.C. 20036, USA (☎1-800-406-2306 or 202-912-1000; www.ecotour.org).

Earthwatch, 3 Clock Tower Pl., Ste. 100, Box 75, Maynard, MA 01754, USA (☎1-800-776-0188 or 978-461-0081; www.earthwatch.org).

Ecotourism Latino (www.ecoturismolatino.com).

International Ecotourism Society, 733 15th St. NW, Washington, D.C. 20005, USA (☎1-202-347-9203; www.ecotourism.org).

National Audobon Society, 200 Trillium Ln., Albany, NY 12203, USA (☎518-869-9731; www.audobon.org).

Responsible Tourism Partnership (www.responsibletourismpartnership.org).

Tourism Concern, Stapleton House, 277-281 Holloway Rd., London N7 8HN, UK (☎+44 020 7753 3330; www.tourismconcern.org.uk).

CAMPING

Costa Rica's extensive national park system provides good hiking and camping opportunities, but not all parks offer camping facilities. Many parks have short, looping trails that can be easily completed as daytrips. To experience some of the most impressive parks to their fullest, consider camping. There are restrictions on how many people can be in a given park at the same time, and camping outside of official camping areas is not permitted. The **Ministerio del Ambiente y Energia (Ministry of Atmosphere and Energy),** commonly known as MINAE, is a government organization devoted to encouraging sustainable development in Costa Rica. MINAE has a strong presence in many of the natural sights of Costa Rica. In some cases it is required that you be accompanied by a guide; inquire at the local MINAE offices in advance to get the most out of your trip.

Outside national parks and a few private campsites, camping on beaches or on private property (usually for a small fee) is possible, but always check with locals beforehand. Some hostels allow travelers to camp outside and use their indoor facilities. Always agree upon a price before setting up camp. Camping should be avoided in populated areas; hotels are almost as cheap and safer.

The **Great Outdoor Recreation Pages** (www.gorp.com) provides excellent general information for travelers planning on camping or spending time outdoors.

LEAVE NO TRACE. Let's Go encourages travelers to embrace the "Leave No Trace" ethic, minimizing their impact on natural environments and protecting them for future generations. A camp stove is a safer way to cook than using vegetation, but if you must make a fire, keep it small and use only dead branches or brush rather than cutting vegetation. Make sure your campsite is at least 50m (150 ft.) from water supplies or bodies of water. If there are no toilet facilities, bury human waste (but not paper) at least 10cm (4 in.) deep and above the high-water line, and 50m (150 ft.) or more from any water supplies and campsites. Always pack your trash in a plastic bag and carry it with you until you reach the next trash receptacle. For more detailed information, contact the **Leave No Trace Center for Outdoor Ethics**, P.O. Box 997, Boulder, CO 80306, USA (☎ 1-800-332-4100 or 303-442-8222; www.lnt.org).

EQUIPMENT

WHAT TO BUY

Good camping equipment is both sturdy and light. North American suppliers tend to offer the most competitive prices. If you bring your own camping equipment with you into Costa Rica, make sure it is clean, as customs officials will check and disinfect used equipment upon arrival.

For lowland camping, a hammock and mosquito net are usually enough shelter, and both are readily available in Costa Rica. If using a hammock, bring along a generous length of rope to reach and get around any tree and a plastic tarp to keep you out of the rain. If you plan on camping at higher elevations, for example, en route to a peak or volcano, a sleeping bag and other cold-weather gear will be essential. Because fuel supplies are inconsistent, buy multi-fuel camping stoves. Camping supplies can be difficult to find once in Costa Rica; in general, you're much better off purchasing equipment before you arrive.

Sleeping Bags: Most sleeping bags are rated by season; "summer" means 30-40°F (around 0°C) at night; "four-season" or "winter" often mean below 0°F (-17°C). Bags are made of **down** (warm and light, but expensive, and miserable when wet) or of synthetic material (heavy, durable, and warm when wet). Prices range US$50-250 for a summer synthetic to US$200-300 for a good down winter bag. Sleeping bag pads include foam pads (US$10-30), air mattresses (US$15-50), and self-inflating mats (US$30-120). Bring a stuff sack to store your bag and keep it dry.

Tents: The best tents are free-standing (with their own frames and suspension systems), set up quickly, and only require staking in high winds. Low-profile dome tents are the best all-around. Worthy 2-person tents start at US$100, 4-person at US$160. Make sure your tent has a rain fly and seal its seams with waterproofer. Other useful accessories include a battery-operated lantern, a plastic groundcloth, and a nylon tarp.

Backpacks: Internal-frame packs mold well to your back, keep a lower center of gravity, and flex adequately to allow you to hike difficult trails. External-frame packs are more comfortable for long hikes over even terrain, as they carry weight higher and distribute it more evenly. Make sure your pack has a strong, padded hip-belt to transfer weight to your legs. There are models designed specifically for women. Any serious backpacking requires a pack of at least 65,000cc (4000 cubic in.), plus 8000cc (500 cubic in.) for sleeping bags in internal-frame packs. Sturdy backpacks cost anywhere from US$125-

420—your pack is something for which it doesn't pay to skimp. On your hunt for the perfect pack, fill up prospective models with something heavy, strap it on correctly, and walk around the store to get a sense of how the model distributes weight. Either buy a rain cover (US$10-20) or store all of your belongings in plastic bags inside your pack.

Boots: Be sure to wear hiking boots with good ankle support. They should fit snugly and comfortably over 1-2 pairs of wool socks and a pair of thin liner socks. Break in boots over several weeks before you go to spare yourself blisters.

Other Necessities: Synthetic layers, like those made of polypropylene or polyester, and a pile jacket will keep you warm even when wet. A space blanket (US$5-15) will help you retain body heat and doubles as a groundcloth. Plastic water bottles are vital; look for shatter- and leak-resistant models. Carry water-purification tablets for when you can't boil water. Although most campgrounds provide campfire sites, you may want to bring a small metal grate or grill. For those places that forbid fires or the gathering of firewood, you'll need a camp stove (start at US$50) and a propane-filled fuel bottle to operate it. Also bring a **first-aid kit, pocketknife, flashlight, insect repellent, sunscreen, compass,** and **waterproof matches** or a **lighter**.

WHERE TO BUY IT

The mail-order and online companies listed below offer lower prices than many retail stores. A visit to a local camping or outdoors store will give you a good sense of the look and weight of certain items.

Campmor, 400 Corporate Dr., P.O. Box 680, Mahwah, NJ 01430, USA (US ☎1-888-226-7667, elsewhere ☎201-335-9064; www.campmor.com).

Discount Camping, 880 Main North Rd., Pooraka, South Australia 5095, Australia (☎08 8262 3399; www.discountcamping.com.au).

Eastern Mountain Sports (EMS), 1 Vose Farm Rd., Peterborough, NH 03458, USA (☎888-463-6367; www.ems.com).

L.L. Bean, Freeport, ME 04033 (US and Canada ☎1-800-441-5713, UK ☎ +44 0800 891 297, elsewhere ☎207-552-3028; www.llbean.com).

Mountain Designs, P.O. Box 824, Nundah, Queensland 4011, Australia (☎07 3856 2344; www.mountaindesigns.com).

Recreational Equipment, Inc. (REI), Sumner, WA 98352, USA (US and Canada ☎1-800-426-4840, elsewhere 253-891-2500; www.rei.com).

Sierra Trading Post, 5025 Campstool Rd., Cheyenne, WY 82007, USA (☎1-800-713-4534; www.sierratradingpost.com).

WILDERNESS SAFETY

HIKING

Staying **warm, dry,** and **well-hydrated** is key to a happy and safe wilderness experience. For any hike, prepare yourself for an emergency by packing a first-aid kit, a reflector, a whistle, high energy food, water, rain gear, a hat, and mittens. For warmth, wear wool or insulating synthetic materials designed for the outdoors. Cotton is a bad choice— it dries slowly and doesn't provide warmth. On any hike, you should pack equipment to keep you alive should a disaster occur.

Check weather forecasts often and pay attention to the skies when hiking, as weather patterns can change suddenly. Be especially wary during the rainy season, when rivers swell and daily afternoon rains can make trails dangerous.

GREAT OUTDOORS

Always let someone (a friend, your hostel owner, a park ranger, a local hiking organization) know when and where you are hiking. Know your physical limits and don't attempt a hike beyond your ability. Park rangers and locals should know about the local conditions, so if you're unsure, ask. See **Safety and Health** (p. 16) about outdoor ailments and medical concerns.

WILDLIFE

SNAKES. Snakes usually don't attack unprovoked, and only a small number of Costa Rica's snakes are venomous. It's very unlikely you will have any close encounters. The best way to prevent snake bites is to hike with a guide, wear hiking boots and long pants, stay on trails, and keep your eyes open. Don't grab branches without looking for snakes, and keep your bags closed.

The most dangerous snake, the **fer-de-lance,** known to the locals as *terciopelo*, is named for its triangular, pointed head, and is a highly venomous pit-viper that lives in the forests and agricultural lands of Costa Rica. It grows up to two meters long and is well camouflaged with a grey-and-brown coloration and a large diamond pattern on the top of its back.

Venomous **coral snakes** have a red, black, yellow, and white coloration. It is difficult to identify coral snakes due to the large number of variations and subspecies. On average, they are 60cm long and live in a wide variety of habitats. Fortunately, they are rather shy, so you are not very likely to encounter them.

If you are bitten by a snake, don't panic. Try to figure out what the snake that bit you looks like, but avoid more bites: keep your distance and don't try to kill or capture it. Don't do anything to the bite wound; don't cut, suck, or ice it. Immobilize the bitten area and put on a bandage two to four inches above the bite, but don't cut off the blood flow (you risk losing your limb). It should be loose enough to slip a finger under the bandage. Keep the bitten limb lower than your heart. Most importantly, get to a hospital immediately.

SPIDERS. Spiders and scorpions are overall much less dangerous than people think, although some species' bites can be rather painful and may require medical attention. Bites are best avoided by checking your shoes and clothes before putting them on, by not going barefoot, and by checking under toilet seats. Make a habit of closing bags when not in use, and of keeping clothes and other belongings off the floor. Avoid reaching into dark places and crevices.

CROCODILES. The large **American crocodile** kills about one person per year in Costa Rica. Rangers and guides know the habitats of crocodiles, and uncomfortably close encounters with these creatures are easily avoided by not swimming in waters where they are known to live.

OUTDOOR AND ADVENTURE ACTIVITIES

Costa Rica is renowned for the diversity and affordability of its outdoor adventures, and many travelers come specifically to pursue these high-quality offerings. Activities run the gamut from scenic to strenuous, including sportfishing, surfing, scuba diving, snorkeling, kayaking, white-water rafting, mountain biking, and golf. (Yes, golf. Costa Rica boasts the best 18-hole courses in Central America.) While tour groups and guides are even more widespread than *típico* food, their numbers have forced them to offer more competitive prices and to conform to wildly adopted and fairly stringent safety requirements.

ATTRACTION	WHERE TO FIND IT
Hiking	Costa Rica's most famous peak, **Chirripó** (p. 312), is a difficult 3-day trek that puts you on top of the world. Hike through waterfalls at **Montezuma** (p. 258). Journey through cloud forests to the steaming crater atop **Volcán Poás** (p. 108).
Scuba diving and snorkeling	The waters of **Isla del Caño** (p. 335), off the coast of **Bahía Drake**, are said to have some of the world's most spectacular scuba diving. Swim with fish amongst the beautiful Caribbean reefs near **Cahuita** (p. 377). Calm waters and diverse marine life make **Playa Hermosa** (p. 209) the perfect place for underwater exploration.
Surfing	Surfers come from all over the world to conquer the waves at **Pavones** (p. 341) and **Playa Negra** (p. 232). **Jacó** (p. 277) promises great surf by day and wild parties by night. With consistent swells, **Mal País** is a surfer's paradise (p. 252).
Views and vistas	Enjoy sunsets from the white sands of **Punta Uva** (p. 389). Tectonic plates collide to form the ridge trails of **Monteverde** (p. 178), which offers amazing views of the entire **Central Valley**. Observe the glowing magma of **Volcán Arenal** (p. 168) from the safety of luxurious hot springs at its base. **Bocas Town, Panama** (p. 395) promises delightfully tropical views above and below the water.
Wildlife	Catch a glimpse of the rare quetzal in **Monteverde** (p. 178). Rehabilitate baby animals at the **Santuario Silvestre Wildlife Sanctuary** (p. 340), near **Golfito**. Over 50% of Costa Rica's famous biodiversity can be found in **Parque Nacional Corcovado** (p. 350). Protect and observe endangered turtles in **Tortuguero** (p. 366).
Horseback riding	Gallop through the waterfalls of **Montezuma** on a trusty steed (p. 258). Observe thick jungles and rolling hills on a horseback hike between **La Fortuna** (p. 161) and **Monteverde** (p. 178). Explore the beaches surrounding **Jacó** (p. 277).
Kayaking and rafting	With Class II-IV rapids, **Turrialba** (p. 140) provides fun for visitors at every skill level. Spend an exhilarating day in the Class IV rapids at **Puerto Viejo de Sarapiquí** (p. 152). Kayak in the Pacific Ocean near **Quepos** (p. 288).
Sportfishing	Some of the largest catches lie off the shores of **Osa Peninsula** and **Golfo Dulce** (p. 329). Spend a week on the rivers of **Barra del Colorado** (p. 373), catching fish and a glimpse of local wildlife. Troll the Pacific waters around **Quepos** (p. 288) from the deck of a yacht.
Canopy tours and ziplines	The original canopy tour at **Orotina** (p. 266) stretches between the trees high above a rainforest valley. The timid and intrepid alike can find a zipline to suit their style in **Monteverde** (p. 178). Watch smoke rise from **Volcán Arenal** from the hanging bridges of **La Fortuna** (p. 161).
Beaches	If there is one thing Costa Rica has, it's beautiful beaches. Some of the best include **Manuel Antonio** (p. 293), **Zancudo** (p. 343), **Playa Sámara** (p. 245), and **Bahía Drake** (p. 332).

GREAT OUTDOORS

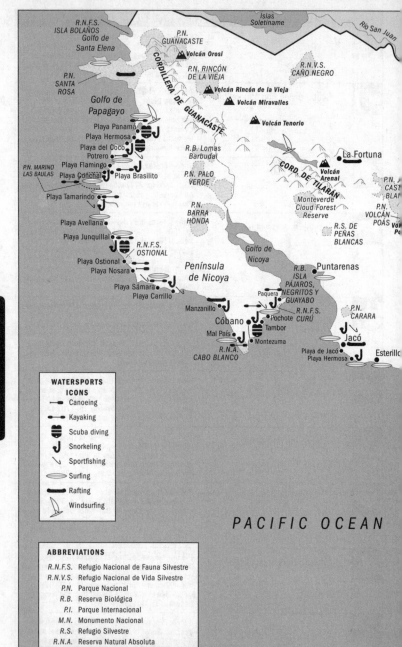

GREAT OUTDOORS

WATERSPORTS ICONS

- Canoeing
- Kayaking
- Scuba diving
- Snorkeling
- Sportfishing
- Surfing
- Rafting
- Windsurfing

ABBREVIATIONS

R.N.F.S. Refugio Nacional de Fauna Silvestre
R.N.V.S. Refugio Nacional de Vida Silvestre
   P.N. Parque Nacional
   R.B. Reserva Biológica
   P.I. Parque Internacional
   M.N. Monumento Nacional
   R.S. Refugio Silvestre
  R.N.A. Reserva Natural Absoluta

PACIFIC OCEAN

Costa Rica: Parks & Watersports

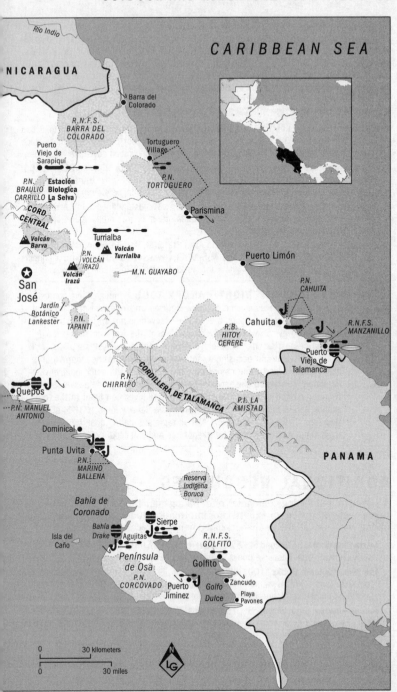

ORGANIZED ADVENTURE TRIPS

Organized adventure tours offer another way of exploring the wild. Activities include hiking, biking, skiing, canoeing, kayaking, rafting, climbing, photo safaris, and archaeological digs. Tourism bureaus can often suggest parks, trails, and outfitters. Organizations that specialize in camping and outdoor equipment like **REI** and **EMS** (p. 77) are also good sources of information. In Costa Rica, tourist agencies and hotels offer organized adventure packages, and there are many adventure tour agencies scattered throughout the country.

Bill Beard's Costa Rica (☎1-877-853-0538; www.billbeardscostarica.com). Offers tours that range from a day to a little over a week. There are over 11 different tour packages that include rafting, hiking, ziplines, and kayaking. Bill's also arranges honeymoon adventure vacations.

Costa Rica Expeditions, Av. 3, C. Central, San José, Costa Rica (☎2257 0766; www.costaricaexpeditions.com). Offers single- and multi-day tours throughout Costa Rica, including kayaking, whitewater rafting, and bungee jumping tours.

Costa Rica Ríos Aventuras (☎1-888 434 0776; www.costaricarios.com). A reputable rafting and kayaking operator, this company also offers mountain biking and canyoning for full-day and multi-day tours.

Specialty Travel Index, 305 San Anselmo Ave., Ste. 309, San Anselmo, CA 94960 (US ☎1-888-624-4030, elsewhere 415-455-1643; www.specialtytravel.com). Connects travelers to tour companies throughout the world. Search by location or activity.

CHOOSING THE RIGHT CANOPY TOUR. Though their domesticated cousins have become the rope-courses and obstacle challenges of American corporate retreats, these zipline labyrinths are anything but white-collar jungle gyms. Would-be flyers sail through the trees on swings, cords, and harnesses, getting an up-close view of canopy ecosystems along with stomach flutters and occasional motion sickness. Not every canopy tour is alike, however, and some cater to the faint of heart with safer indulgences: intricately connected suspension bridges and even gondola-style trams. Those who scoff at these low-adrenaline alternatives can head to the "old-school" establishments near **Monteverde** (see Canopy Tours, p. 186) or **Orotina** (see Canopy Tours, p. 269). Not all tours are made equal; be prepared to shell out a bit more cash for a reputable and safer tour company.

ADDITIONAL RESOURCES

A variety of publishing companies offer hiking guidebooks to meet the educational needs of novices or experts. For information about camping, hiking, and biking, write or call the publishers listed below to receive a catalog.

Sierra Club Books, 85 Second St., 2nd fl., San Francisco, CA 94105, USA (☎415-977-5500; www.sierraclub.org). Resource books on hiking and camping.

The Mountaineers Books, 1001 SW Klickitat Way, Ste. 201, Seattle, WA 98134, USA (☎1-206-223-6303; www.mountaineersbooks.org). Boasts over 600 titles on hiking, biking, mountaineering, natural history, and conservation.

Toucan Guides, 934 W Oak St., Fort Collins, CO 80521, USA (☎1-970-224-9660; http://costa-rica-guide.com). A wealth of information available concerning national parks and reserves in Costa Rica.

SAN JOSÉ

At first, Costa Rica's capital is sure to frustrate the tourists eager to experience the country's natural beauty. Modern concrete structures encroach on the city's surviving examples of colonial architecture. Smog and grime dominate the capital, while piercing car horns never stop blaring. During the summer rainy season, travelers should expect daily downpours.

Still, San José is filled with the energy of a young and bustling city. As irritating as the fast-food joints on every corner may be for someone attempting to escape civilization, the neon facades demonstrate how rapidly the city is modernizing. Internet cafes have sprung up on nearly every corner. Luxury hotels and restaurants offering international cuisine provide the discerning traveler with a plethora of culinary options. But have no fear, loyal lovers of *comida típica*—the authentic *casado* can still be found just about anywhere.

For those seeking nightlife, bars and clubs in San Pedro and El Pueblo are alive with energy and music until the wee hours of morning. San José is home to approximately 300,000 people (over 1 million including the suburbs), and most of them will show you up on the dance floor—the speed and elegance of *salsa* takes most gringos by surprise.

The transportation and economic hub of Costa Rica, San José offers a glimpse into the country's future. Surrounded by mountains and perched 1132m above sea level, San José was first settled in 1736, though it spent much of the colonial era as a tobacco-farming town. In 1823, San José replaced Cartago as the capital of Costa Rica and came into its own as the nexus of the coffee trade. As an ever-changing city, it is a worthy stop between the two coasts. Be sure to give yourself enough time; there's plenty to see here in bustling San José.

✈ INTERCITY TRANSPORTATION

FLIGHTS

International Flights: Juan Santa María International Airport (SJO), about 15km northwest of San José in Alajuela. Most cheaply accessible by bus from San José to Alajuela. Official **airport taxis** to and from San José charge ₡13,366 (US$23). The taxi driver will meet you at the airport exit to confirm a price and will then take you to the window on your left to pay the fare. **Grayline Tours** (☎2291 2222; www.graylinecostarica.com) runs an **airport shuttle** that picks up travelers across the street and upstairs from the airport exit and drops off at many mid-range and top-end hotels around town for ₡5,811 (US$10). Online booking available. Airlines include: **American** (☎2223 5426); **Continental** (☎2296 4911 or 0800 044 0005); **Copa** (☎295 7400); **Delta** (☎2257 4141 or 1-800-221-1212); **Iberia** (☎2441 2591); **Mexicana** (☎2257 6334); **Taca,** through **Sansa** (☎2221 9414); **United** (☎2220 4844 or 2441 8025). Arriving at the airport 2½hr. early is recommended for all international flights. **Sansa** (☎2666 0307; www.flysansa.com) offers the cheapest domestic flights from a terminal just to the left of the international terminal (₡39,514-56,947/US$68-98). Departures and one-way fares on Sansa: **Barra de Colorado** (1 per day M, F, Sa; ₡45,907/US$79); **Drake Bay** (2 per day, ₡56,367/US$97); **Golfito** (4 per day, ₡55,205/US$95); **Liberia**

PEREGRINA COLIMA TO HEREDÍA (11km) TO MORAVIA (5km)

San José Overview

TIBÁS

URUCA CINCO ESQUINAS SANTO TOMÁS

ROBLEDAL COPEY 5

TO JUAN SANTAMARÍA INT'L AIRPORT (15km), ALAJUELA (17km) EL-PUEBLO 32

TO GUADALUPE (5km)

Río Torres

General Cañas Hwy. Río Torres

1 SABANA NORTE

Parque Zoológico Simón Bolívar

SEE SAN JOSÉ CENTER MAP (p. 85)

Estadio de Fútbol Parque Metropolitano La Sabana

Museo de Arte Costarricense

COCA COLA AMÓN OTOYA

TO ESCAZÚ (6km) Gimnasio Nacional

27 Prospero Fernández Hwy.

Mercado Central Parque Central Parque Morazán Av. Central Parque Nacional (railroad not in use) CALIFORNIA 2

TO LA UNIVERSIDAD DE COSTA RICA & SAN PEDRO (5km), CARTAGO (25km)

LAS VEGAS

Hospital San Juan de Dios SOLEDAD

Cementerio Calvo Cementerio General LOS YOSES

Clínica Bíblica

SABANA SUR

Parque Gonzáles Víquez

CUBA

Río María Aguilar SAN CAYETANO Río Ocloro QUESADA DURÁN

SAGRADA FAMILIA

N LG

0 1 kilometer

0 1 mile

HATILLO SAN SEBASTIÁN 39 Parque de la Paz JARDINES DE CASCAJAL

TO ALAJUELITA (2km) MUSMANNI

(6 per day, ₡55,205/US$95); **Nosara** (1 per day, ₡55,205/US$95); **Palmar Sur** (3 per day, ₡50,555/US$87); **Puerto Jimenez** (6 per day, ₡55,205/US$95); **Quepos** (9 per day, ₡32,541/US$56); **Samara** (1 per day, ₡56,948/US$98); **Tamarindo** (6 per day, ₡55,205/US$95); **Tambor** (5 per day, ₡43,583/US$75); **Tortuguero** (1 per day, ₡45,907/US$79).

Tobías Bolaños Airport, in Pavas, 20min. from San José by taxi. Serves **NatureAir** (☎2229 6000, US reservations +1-800-235-9272; www.natureair.net).

Domestic Flights: Online reservations available. Departures and one-way fares for NatureAir: **Arenal** (1 per day, ₡43,001/US$74); **Bocas del Toro** (1-2 per day M, W, F, Su; ₡76,705/US$132); **Drake Bay** (2 per day, ₡63,340/US$109); **Golfito** (1 per day, ₡61,597/US$106); **Liberia** (4 per day, ₡61,597/US$106); **Limón** (1 per day M, W, F, Su; ₡47,650/US$82); **Nosara** (1-2 per day, ₡61,597/US$106); **Palmar Sur, Dominical** (1 per day, ₡55,785/$96); **Puerto Jiménez** (5 per day, ₡63,340/US$109); **Punta Islita** (1 per day, ₡63,340/US$109); **Quepos** (3 per day, ₡35,447/US$61), **Tamarindo** (3 per day, ₡61,597/US$106); **Tambor** (2 per day, ₡45,907/US$79); **Tortuguero** (1 per day, ₡50,556/US$87). When booking online, you may find cheaper deals with more restrictions.

San José Center

ACCOMMODATIONS
Casa León, **25**
Casa Ridgway, **9**
Costa Rica Backpackers Hostel, **7**
Hostel Pangea, **6**
Hotel Boston, **21**
Kabata Hostel, **5**
Toruma Youth Hostel, **14**
Tranquilo Backpackers, **4**

FOOD
La Grand Ma, **11**
Nuestra Tierra, **23**
Restaurante Grano de Oro, **22**
Rest. Vishnu Vegetariano, **10**
Shakti, **24**
Soda el Parque, **18**
Taquería la Moderna, **20**
Tin Jo, **27**

NIGHTLIFE
Av. 2 Bar/Restaurant, **15**
Bongo's, **2**
Ebony 56, **1**
El Cuartel de la Boca del Monte, **13**
Salidas Orbital 2000, **12**
Salsa 54, **8**
Twister Club, **3**

○ **GOVERNMENT BUILDINGS**
Asamblea Legislativa, **16**
Corte Suprema de Justicia, **19**
Organismo de Investigación, **17**
Tribunales de Justicia, **26**

SAN JOSÉ

BUSES

Buses to almost everywhere in the country arrive and depart from the city's stops and terminals. Many depart from around **Terminal Coca-Cola**, between Av. 1/3, C. 16/18. The schedule is available at the **Instituto Costarricense de Turismo (ICT)** at the **Museo de Oro**. Times often change, so double-check with your hostel. Fares for domestic trips are not listed and change frequently, but expect rides under 4hr. to cost ¢2000 or less, with longer trips under ¢4000. **All fares must be paid in colones, so carry small bills or change.**

Domestic Buses:

Alajuela-Airport: TUASA, Av. 2, C.12/14 (☎2442 6900). 35min.; every 10min. 4:30am-10pm, every 30min. 10-11pm.

Cahuita: Terminal Caribe, Av. 13, C. Central (☎2257 8129). 4hr.; 6, 10am, 2, 4pm.

Cariari: Terminal Caribe, Av. 13, C. Central (☎2222 0610). 2hr., 9 per day 6:30am-8:30pm.

Cartago: Empresa Lumaca, Av. 10, C. 5 (☎2537 2320). 45min., every 10min. 5:05am-midnight.

Fortuna: Auto Transportes, Av. 7/9, C. 12 (☎2255 0567). 4hr.; 6:15, 8:40, 11:30am.

Golfito: Tracopa, Av. 18/20, C. 5 (☎2221 4214). 8hr.; Su 7am, 3:30pm.

Guápiles: Empresarios Guapileños, Av. 13, C. Central. 1½hr., every hr. 5:30am-7pm.

Heredia: Transportes Unidos 400, Av. 7/9, C. 1. Other locations at Av. Central, C. 8 and Av. 5/7, C. 4. 30min., every 10min. 5am-11pm (5am-3am from Av. 7/9, C. 1).

Jacó: Transportes Morales, Terminal Coca-Cola, Av. 3, C. 16 (☎2223 1109). 2hr.; 6am, every 2hr. 7am-7pm.

Liberia: Pulmitan, Av. 5/7, C. 24 (☎2256 9552). 4½hr., 8 per day 6am-10pm.

Limón: Caribeños, Terminal Caribe, Av. 13, C. Central (☎2221 0610). 2½hr., every hr. 5am-7pm.

Monteverde: Autotransportes Tilarán, Atlántico Nte. Terminal, Av. 7/9, C.12 (☎2222 3854). 5hr., 6:30am and 2:30pm.

Playa Nosara and Garza: Tracopa-Alfaro, Av. 3/5, C. 14 (☎2222 2666). 6hr., 5:30am.

Playa Panamá: Tralapa, Av. 1/3, C. 20 (☎2221 7202). 6hr.; 3:30pm. Return 3pm.

Playa Tamarindo: Tracopa-Alfaro, Av 5, C. 14/16 (☎2222 2666). 5hr., 11:30am and 3:30pm. Tralapa, Av. 3/5, C. 20 (☎2221 7202), 4pm.

Playas del Coco: Av. 5/7, C. 24 (☎2222 1650). 5hr.; 8am, 2, 4pm. Return 4, 8am, 2pm.

Puntarenas: Empresarios Unidos de Puntarenas, Av.12, C. 16 (☎2222 8231). 2hr.; every hr. 6am-7pm; return every hr. 4-7pm.

Quepos and Manuel Antonio: Transportes Morales, Terminal Coca Cola, Av. 3, C. 16 (☎2223 5567). Direct 3hr.; 6, 9am, noon, 2:30, 6, 7:30pm. Return 4, 6, 9:30am, noon, 2:30, 5pm. Indirect 5hr.; 7, 10am, 2, 3, 4pm. Return 5, 8am, 2, 4pm. Only direct buses continue to Manuel Antonio.

Siquirres: Terminal Caribe, Av. 13, C. Central (☎2222 0610). 1hr.; 11 per day 6:30am-6pm.

Turrialba: Transtusa Av. 6, C. 13 (☎2222 4464). 1hr.; every hr. 5:15am-10pm; return 7am, 9pm.

Volcán Irazú: Av. 2, C. 1/3. 2hr.; Sa-Su 8am. Return Sa-Su 12:30pm.

Volcán Poás: TUASA, Av. 2, C. 12/14 (☎2222 5325). 2hr.; 8:30am. Return 2:30pm.

International Buses:

El Salvador: TicaBus, Av. 2/4, C. 9 (☎2221 8954; www.ticabus.com/ingles). 48hr. with 1 night in Managua; 6, 7:30am, 12:30; ¢23,244 (US$40).

Guatemala: TicaBus, Av. 26, C. 3. 60hr. with 1 night in Nicaragua and 1 night in El Salvador; 6, 7:30am, 12:30pm; ¢32,541 (US$56).

Tegucigalpa, Honduras: TicaBus, Av. 2/4, C. 9. 48hr. with 1 night in Managua; 6, 7:30am, 12:30pm; ¢20,338 (US$35).

San Pedro Sula, Honduras: TicaBus, Av. 2/4, C. 9. 48hr. with 1 night in Managua; 6, 7:30am, 12:30pm; ¢27,311 (US$47).

Nicaragua: TicaBus, Av. 26, C. 3. 8hr.; 6, 7:30am, 12:30pm; ¢8,135 (US$14).

Panamá City: TicaBus, Av. 26, C. 3 (☎2221 8954). 20hr., midnight and 11pm, US$26. Panaline, Av. 3/5, C. 16 (☎2256 8721, www.panalinecr.com). 18hr., 1pm, ¢13,365 (US$23).

☢ ORIENTATION

San José's design follows a typical Costa Rican grid: *avenidas* run east-west and *calles* run north-south. Directions in San José, as well as in other large cities, are usually given by listing the street and cross street where a destination is located. For example, a building located at Av. 2, C. 5/7 would be located on Av. 2, somewhere in the block between C. 5 and 7. **Avenida Central** (called Paseo Colón north of C. 22) is the main drag, with a shopping and eating area blocked off to traffic between C. 2 and C. 5. Just west of the city center is the frantic **Mercado Central,** bordered by Av. Central/1 and C. 6/8. Four blocks farther west of the market is **Terminal Coca-Cola,** on Av. 1, C. 16/18. Many streets are not labeled; the staff at stores rarely knows its own address, so counting blocks between destinations and relying on landmarks is necessary.

Barrio Amón, northeast of Av. 5 and C. 1, and **Barrio Otoya,** slightly east of Amón, are the most architecturally interesting neighborhoods in the city center, housing Spanish colonial buildings dating back to the 19th century. West of downtown, past C. 42, **La Sabana** contains the large **Parque Metropolitano La Sabana.** Five kilometers farther west, the quiet suburb of **Escazú** is home to gorgeous B&Bs and some of San José's most posh restaurants. Other upscale regions include **Los Yoses,** east of downtown past C. 3, and **San Pedro,** home to the University of Costa Rica and some of the city's best entertainment.

 WATCH OUT! Although San José is relatively safe, theft, prostitution, and drugs make some areas a bit risky. Problem spots include: **Terminal Coca-Cola,** south of Av. 8 between C. 2 and 14, Av. 4 to 6 between C. 4 and 12, areas north of the **Mercado Central,** and areas around the mall and C. de la Amargura in **San Pedro.** Generally, areas beyond a few blocks from San José's center pose a greater threat after dark. The city's parks and crowded streets can present the risk of pickpockets and grab-and-run thiefs, so hold on to your belongings. After sunset, the safest way to get around is by taxi, especially for women traveling alone.

☢ LOCAL TRANSPORTATION

Buses: Local buses run every 5-10min. from 5am to 10pm and travel all over San José, including to the suburbs and the airport. There are no official printed schedules and timing is generally approximate. Ask locals and drivers for info or check bus fronts. Most bus stops are marked with the destination they serve. As local destinations generally run no more than ¢300, it's best to carry small change. Major bus stops include **Escazú** (Av. 1/Central and C. 16), **Guadalupe** and **Moravia** (Av. 3, C. 3/5), and **San Pedro** (Av. 2, C. 11/13 and Av. Central, C. 9/11).

Private Buses: Grayline Tours (☎2220 2126; www.graylinecostarica.com). Offers **buses** to and from popular destinations throughout Costa Rica (one-way ¢14,527-24,987/US$25-43). Buses run once or twice daily between **San José** and **Arenal, Conchal, Golfo Papagayo, Jacó, Manuel Antonio, Monteverde, Playa Hermosa, Playa Tamarindo, Puerto Viejo de Talamanca, Rincón,** and **Sámara.** Most leave daily 7:30-10:30am. AmEx/D/MC/V.

Car Rental: Prices range from ¢11,622/US$20 (for a small manual sedan) to ¢61,015/US$105 (for a 4x4) per day. Avis and Economy tend to offer some of the lowest rates. Minimum rental age is 21, although a few companies require drivers to be at least 23 or 25. Some companies will rent to those 18-21 with double or triple the deposit. A passport, valid driver's license, and major credit card are required; International Driver's Permits are not necessary for rentals of less than 3 months. Online reservations available with the following companies:

Avis (☎2232 9922; www.avis.co.cr), at the Hotel Corobicí, north of the Parque La Sabana on C. 42, and at the airport (☎2442 1321). Minimum rental of 48hr. Minimum age 23.

Budget, Paseo Colón, C. 28/30 (☎2255 4240; www.budget.co.cr), and at the airport (☎2440 4412). Open M-Sa 7am-6pm, Su 7am-4pm; airport office open daily 6am-10pm. 21+. Offers combination packages with specific hotels. Rents to ages 18-21 for surcharge.

Economy (☎2299 2000; www.economyrentacar.com), in Sabana Nte. and at the airport (☎2442 8100). Open daily 7am-10pm, airport office open 5am-2am. Rents to ages 18-21 for surcharge.

Europcar, Paseo Colón, C. 36/38 (☎2257 1158; www.europcar.co.cr), and at the airport (☎2440 9990). Open daily 8am-6pm; airport office open daily 5am-midnight. Surcharge 5-6am and 10pm-midnight.

Hertz, Paseo Colón, C. 38 (☎2221 1818; www.hertz.com). Open M-F 7am-6pm, Sa-Su 7am-5pm. 25+.

National Car Rental, Av. 7, C. 36 and (☎ 2242 7878, toll-free from US +1 800-227-7368; www.natcar.com), at the airport (☎2440 0085). Also at the Hotel Irazu and Hotel Real Intercontinental in San José. Main office open daily 7:30am-6pm; airport 6am-10pm. 21+.

🔢 PRACTICAL INFORMATION

TOURIST AND FINANCIAL SERVICES

Tourist Offices: Instituto Costarricense de Turismo (☎2299 5800, from US or Costa Rica 1-866-COSTARICA/267-8274). Offices located at Av. Central/2, C. 5 (☎2222 1090; open M-F 9am-1pm and 2-5pm), next to El Museo del Oro, and Av. Central/1, C. 5, 2nd fl. (☎2257 8064; open M-F 8:30am-5:30pm). Free country and city maps, intracity bus schedules, and brochures. Another office in the post office (Oficina de Correos). **OTEC Viajes,** an office of **STA Travel,** Av. 1/3, C. 3 (☎2256 0633, www.otecviajes.com), can help you makes changes to your STA ticket, but cannot book new ones. ISIC card available for purchase. Open M-F 8am-6pm, Sa 9am-1pm.

Tours:

Costa Rica Expeditions, Av. 3, C. Central/2 (☎2257 0766 or 2222 0333; www.costaricaexpeditions.com), 1 block east of the post office. Tours throughout the country in collaboration with other companies. Class III and IV whitewater rafting on the Río Pacuare ₡86,584 (US$149) per person. 2-day rafting trip ₡165,614 (US$285). 10% student discount. English spoken. Open daily 8am-5pm. AmEx/D/MC/V.

Costa Rica Nature Escape, Av. Central/1, C. 5, 2nd fl. (☎2257 8064, 24hr. line 8381 7178; www.crnature.com). Student rates for all sorts of adventure, relaxation, and ecotourism packages. One-day Tortuguero tour ₡79,030 (US$136), students ₡74,380 (US$128). Class III whitewater rafting on the Río Reventazón or Río Sarapiquí ₡43,582 (US$75), students ₡40,677 (US$70). Class IV whitewater rafting on the Río Pacuare from ₡57,529 (US$99), students from ₡48,812 (US$84). Open M-F 8:30am-5:30pm. Cash only for student discounts. MC/V.

Ecole Travel, Av. Central, C. 5/7 (☎2223 2240; www.ecoletravel.com), inside Edificio Plaza de la Cultura, 2nd fl. A reputable and relatively inexpensive tour company. Tours to Tortuguero (2 days from ₡121,450/US$209, 3 days from ₡167,937/US$289) and Volcán Arenal and Monteverde (4 days from ₡188,857/US$325). Online booking available. Open M-F 8am-5pm, Sa 9am-1pm.

Ecoscape Nature Tours (☎2297 0664, US and Canada +1 866-887-2764; www.ecoscapetours.com). The Highlights Tour for travelers short on time (₡49,393/US$85). The 1-day tour involves visits to Volcán Poás and its surrounding cloud forest, La Paz, San Fernando Waterfalls, Selva Verde Rainforest Lodge, a boat ride on the Río Sarapiquí, and a drive through Braulio Carillo National Park. A 2-day tour is available as well (₡122,030/US$210, with rafting ₡139,464/US$240).

Embassies: See **Essentials,** p. 9.

Currency Exchange and Banks: There are dozens of banks all over San José; nearly all of them have Cirrus/Plus/V **24hr. ATMs,** sometimes labeled "ATH." All require photo ID to exchange currency, and most require passport and charge 1% commission to cash travelers' checks. Listed below are the main offices.

Banco Central, Av. Central/1, C. 2/4 (☎2243 3333). Open M-F 9:20am-4pm.

Banco de Costa Rica, Av. Central/2, C. 4/6 (☎2287 9000). Open M-F 8:30am-6pm.

Banco Nacional, Av. 1/3, C. 4 (☎2212 2000). Open M-F 10:45am-3:45pm. **ATM** daily 5am-10pm.

Banco de San José, Av. 3/5, C. Central (☎2295 9797). Open M-F 8am-7pm.

BANCO B.C.T., Av. Central/1, C. Central (☎2212 8000). Open M-F 8:15am-5pm.

Banco Popular, Av. 2 and C. 1 (☎2202 2020). Open M-F 8:15am-7pm, Sa 8:15-11:30am. **ATM** open daily 6am-11pm.

HSBC, Av. 1, C. Central (☎2287 1111). M-F 9am-6:30pm, Sa 9am-6pm. **24hr. ATM,** Av. 2, C. Central/2, next to KFC, across from the *parque central.*

American Express: Sabana Sur, Edeficio #1 (☎2242 8585). Passport required to cash traveler's checks. M-F 8am-6pm.

Western Union: Av. 2/4, C. 9 (☎+1 800-777-7777). International ID needed. **Currency exchange.** Open M-F 8:30am-5pm, Sa 9am-12:30pm.

Beyond Tourism: For complete listings, see p. 60.

WORK IT OUT. Crowded streets, small parks, and cars that don't stop for pedestrians make the San José center a terrible place for jogging. If you want to get some exercise, take the bus from Av. 2, C. 3 (¢140) to the huge Parque Metropolitano in La Sabana. While there, check out the new national soccer stadium, scheduled to be completed in late 2009.

LOCAL SERVICES

English-Language Bookstore: 7th Street Books, Av. Central/1, C. 7 (☎2256 8251). Sells a selection of new and used fiction and nonfiction English-language books. Foreign newspapers and maps available. New books ¢5000-10,000, used ¢900-2500. Open M-Sa 9am-6pm, Su 10am-5pm. AmEx/MC/V. **Librería Lehmann,** Av. Central, C. 1/3 (☎2522 4848). Large selection of reading and stationery supplies. Second-floor **Café Latino** is a delightful spot to read while sipping a cappuccino. Open M-F 8am-6:30pm, Sa 9am-5pm, Su 11am-4pm.

Pasajes Plazavenidos: Av. Central, C. 7/9, diagonally across from Fiesta Casino. Two levels of souvenir shops, ATMs, and fast food restaurants. Bathrooms located upstairs in the back (¢150).

Laundromat: Leavened Lavandería, Av. Central/1, C. 8 (☎2258 0621), to the left of the Gran Hotel Imperial. ¢4000-¢6000 per load. Open M-F 8am-6pm. **Sixaola,** Av. 2, C. 7/9 (☎2221 2111). ¢1000 per kg. Same-day service if in by 10am. Open M-F 8am-6pm, Sa 8am-noon. AmEx/MC/V.

Public Toilets: There are sparkling restrooms on Av. Central, C. 5, underground at the Plaza de la Cultura, next to the Museo de Oro. Some fast food restaurants along Av. Central will allow non-customers to use the *sanitarios,* but they have long lines. **Librería Lehmann** (see above), 1 block north from the Museo de Oro on Av. Central, has a free bathroom in its cafe.

EMERGENCY AND COMMUNICATIONS

Emergency: ☎911.

Police: ☎911. To report a theft, contact the **Organismo de Investigación Judicial (OIJ),** Av. 6/8, C. 15/17 (☎2295 3643). To report a theft in person, proceed east on Av. 6, then turn right onto the walkway paved with square tiles. The entrance is on the right, at the ATM. Follow the signs to the Oficina Denuncias. Ask for an English speaker if necessary. Open 24hr. During business hours, contact the **Crime Victims Assistance Office** (☎2295 3565), on the 1st floor of OIJ. Open M-F 7:30am-noon and 1-4:30pm. To report a sexual or life-threatening assault, call ☎2295 3493.

Pharmacy: Farmacia Fischel, Av. 3, C. 2 (☎2275 7659), near the center of town. Large selection of pharmaceutical and beauty products. ATM inside. Open daily 7am-8pm. AmEx/D/MC/V. Smaller location at Av. 2, C. 5. (☎2233 0231). Open M-F 7:30am-7:30pm, Sa-Su 8am-7pm.

Medical Services: Hospital San Juan de Dios,Paseo Colón, C. 14/16 (☎2257 6282), in the building where Av. Central becomes Paseo Colón, after C. 14. **Clínica Bíblica,** Av. 14/16, C. 1 (☎2522 1000). English spoken. **24hr. emergency service** and pharmacy.

Telephones: Card and coin phones are all over town, especially along Av. Central. Most phones accept ¢5 and ¢10 coins. Most *ticos* buy phone cards from street vendors. Cards charge around ¢5 per min. for local calls and ¢100 per min. for calls to the US. **Radiográphica,** Av. 5, C. Central/1 (☎2287 0087; www.racsa.co.cr). Collect calls ¢1,743 (US$3). Also has AT&T Direct, MCI, and Sprint service. Sells prepaid internet cards. Open M-F 7:30am-4:30pm, Sa 9am-1pm. Directory assistance ☎113.

PHONE HOME. The easiest way to make both domestic and international calls from a pay phone in Costa Rica is by using a **phone card.** Pick one up at the airport, pharmacy, or from a street vendor, scratch off the silver backing to find your phone card number, and follow the instructions on the back of the card. The cheapest way to reach home is to use a VoIP phone service, such as **Skype,** to place calls from either your computer or one of the many internet cafes around San José.

Internet Access: Internet cafes abound in San José. Here are 2 near the city center:

Café Digital, C. 7, Av. Central/1, 2nd fl. (☎2248 0701). New computers. Internet ¢400 per hr. Scanner, printing, and copies ¢100-200 per page. Skype and webcams available. Calls to the US ¢60 per min. Open M-Sa 8am-9pm, Su 9am-8pm.

Cybernético, on the corner of Av. Central and C. 4, 4th fl. Internet, video, faxing, scanning, and international internet calls. Internet ¢350 per hr. Copies ¢90. Open daily 7am-10pm.

Post Office: Av. 1/3, C. 2 (☎2223 9766), in the large green building. San José has no street mailboxes, so all mail must be sent from here. Open M-F 8am-6pm, Sa 7:30am-noon. Letter to the US ¢160. **Postal Code:** 1000.

🗝 ACCOMMODATIONS

San José has hundreds of accommodations for every budget, from bare-bones hostels to Holiday Inns. That said, it's best to steer clear of the cheapest lodgings; paying the relatively "pricey" ¢5000-6800 (US$10-13) for a dormitory bed is worth it for clean, comfortable lodgings, relatively hot water, and a friendly atmosphere. Avoid the city center to escape from noisy crowds. The accommodations listed below are divided into four categories by location. Staying east of the *parque central* is highly recommended, as accommodations here tend to be safe and comfortable. Hotels south of the *parque central* are generally reasonably priced but are often louder because of their proximity to bars. Though they are often the cheapest options, try to avoid places north and west of the *parque,* as these tend to be the areas with the highest concentration of prostitutes, drunken bar patrons, and criminal activities. Pleasant alternatives to staying downtown are found in **San Pedro,** a 10min. bus ride from San José, and the suburb of **Escazú,** a 20min. bus ride, which offers splurge-worthy B&Bs.

EAST OF PARQUE CENTRAL

▩ **Hostel Pangea,** Av. 7, C. 3/5 (☎2221 1992; www.hostelpangea.com). Walls with dark jungle colors, metal accents, and a location near the city center create an urban feel. Plenty of social space makes this a great place to meet travelers. Free lockers with deposit, unlimited coffee, and international calling available. The staff is extremely helpful, especially in arranging tours. Potential downsides are the wristbands guests must wear at all times and the lack of outlets in the dorm rooms. Breakfast ¢2900 (US$5). Laundry ¢5220 (US$9). Free internet and Wi-Fi. 24hr. airport transport on the hostel's shuttle (¢10,440/US$18). Reception 24hr. Dorms ¢6960; private rooms ¢17,400. Additional locations at Av. 11, C. 3/5 with fewer amenities, and a resort in Arenal. ❶

▩ **Costa Rica Backpackers Hostel,** Av. 6, C. 21/23 (☎2221 6191; www.costaricaback-packers.com). Packed with young, swim suit-clad vacationers, this inexpensive back-packer magnet adds tropical flair to what feels like a spacious college dorm. Though it's a walk from the city center, the spotless rooms, shared hot-water bathrooms, night guard, communal kitchen, flat-screen TVs with cable, tourist info, free Wi-Fi, and swimming pool will make you want to stay forever. Guests often spend their mornings laying out under the sun or swinging in hammocks near the pool while munching on breakfast. Laundry ¢3,486 (US$6). Reception 24hr. Check-out 11am. Dorms ¢7004; doubles ¢16,342. ¢2,334 key deposit. MC/V with ¢11,673 minimum. ❶

▩ **Casa Ridgway,** Av. 6/8, C. 15 (☎2233 2693; www.amigosparalapaz.org), on a quiet cul-de-sac off C.15 between Av. 6 and 8. Owned by Quakers, Casa Ridgway offers the best value for peaceful, beautifully decorated accommodations. Each room is unique and most are painted with quotes representative of the establishment's ideals. Guests have access to the communal kitchen, dining area, meeting room, and library. An active Quaker peace center is attached. Breakfast included. Public phone (☎2255 6399). Storage available. Laundry ¢2,905 (US$5). Internet. Reception 7am-10pm. Dorms ¢8171; singles ¢11,090; doubles ¢17,510. MC/V. ❷

Kabata Hostel, Av. 9/11, C. 7 (☎2255 0355; www.kabatahostel.com). Clean, quiet accommodations just blocks from some of San José's nicest parks. Shared hot-water baths, cable TV in the lobby, and free use of kitchen and dining room. Downstairs rooms have large windows and get the most sunlight. The owners are attentive to each guest's needs. Breakfast included. Free Wi-Fi. Free parking. Check-out 10am. Dorms ¢7004, group of 5 or more ¢6420; singles with shared bathroom ¢9338; doubles ¢18,676. Cash only. ❶

Tranquilo Backpackers, Av. 9/11, C. 7 (☎2223 3189 or 2222 2493; www.tranquiloback-packers.com). Bright rooms with hot showers, cable TVs, and access to a communal kitchen. Dorm rooms contain tall plain-wood bunk beds and ceiling windows. Open and sunny common room. Pancake breakfast included. Laundry ¢3000. Free internet. Reception 24hr. Dorms ¢7004; doubles ¢15,175. 2nd location in Santa Teresa/Mal País. Cash only. ❶

Casa León, Av. 6, C. 13/15 (☎2221 1651). Traveling east along Av. 2, turn right onto C. 13 and take a left to follow the train tracks; it's on the left. Casa León is a quiet and comfortable house. Internet and communal kitchen. Laundry available. Up to 6 people per dorm. Dorms ¢8171; singles ¢14,007, with private bath ¢17,510; doubles ¢17,510-23,346. Cash only. ❷

SOUTH OF PARQUE CENTRAL

Hotel Boston, Av. 8, C. Central/2 (☎2221 0563). Spacious, mint-green rooms have sturdy beds, cable TV, and clean private baths with hot water. A good choice south

DECONSTRUCTING
CASADOS

Although Costa Rica offers various cheap meals, possibly the best for your stomach is the *casado*. Wives would prepare this traditional *campesino* dish for their husbands to take to the fields. Today, the dish is enjoyed all over Costa Rica, in basic *sodas* and gourmet restaurants. Traditionally a lunch option, *casados* are also filling enough for dinner. They include a combination of the following:

Meat: The most common type used is steak, although chicken or fish are almost always available as a substitute. A *casado mexicano* features spicy steak or pulled pork. Vegetarians can ask for any *casado "sin carne."*

Rice and Beans: These Costa Rican staples—black or red beans and fried or steamed white rice—are sometimes mixed together as *gallo pinto*, or served separately. If you're lucky, your rice and beans may be spiced up with some sautéed onions or scallions.

Fried Plantains: Known as *plátano maduro* or *plátano dorado*, this delicious side is perhaps the best part of the *casado*. Sometimes served whole, sometimes served sliced, *plátano maduro* is always delicious.

Salad: Loosely interpreted, the salad can be anything—a sliced cole slaw-like concoction, or an elaborate array of local produce dressed in zesty lemon sauce.

of the city center and San José's thriving bar scene. Reception 24hr. Singles ¢5000; doubles ¢8000; triples ¢10,000. AmEx/MC/V. ❶

NORTH OF PARQUE CENTRAL

Hotel Otoya Pensión, Av. 5, C 1 (☎2221 3925 or 2221 6017). On the second floor; shares entrance with an internet cafe. The Pensión is located only a couple of blocks south of one of San José's less desirable neighborhoods. Minimal amenities include tvs and fans. Backpackers congregate in a smoky sitting area inconveniently located behind the reception desk. Microwave, fridge, and coffeemaker available for use. Laundry service available. Reception 24hr. Check-out 1pm. All rooms with shared baths. Singles ¢5000; doubles ¢8000; triples ¢10,000. Cash only. ❶

WEST OF PARQUE CENTRAL

Hotel Nuevo Alameda, Av. Central/1, C. 12 (☎2233 3551; www.hotelnuevoalameda.com). Housed in a yellow building on C. 12 near the corner of Av. Central and the *mercado central*. Clean rooms for 1-4 people with large windows, TVs, and private hot-water baths. Ask to be on the west side for a better view. Inner rooms are quieter. A volcano mural decorates the lobby. Wheelchair-accessible. Reception 24hr. Check-out noon. Singles ¢8,716 (US$15) per person. Cash only. ❷

Hotel El Descanso, Av. 4, C. 6 (☎2221 9941), entrance on C. 6. Safe, clean lodgings close to the *parque central*. Upstairs, the carved wooden doors, multicolored walls, and spacious hallways create a comfortable and private atmosphere. The downstairs common area is lacking with uncomfortable yellow couches and a small TV. Some rooms are not well-maintained. Reception 24hr. Check-out noon. Singles ¢8755; doubles ¢17,510; triples ¢26,264. Cash only. ❷

SAN PEDRO

▓ **Toruma Youth Hostel (HI),** Av. Central, C. 29/31 (☎2234 8186), between San José and San Pedro. Take the San Pedro bus (¢190) from Av. Central, C. 9/11, and get off at Kentucky Fried Chicken; it's the yellow building across the street. Run by the same brothers who own Hostel Pangea, Toruma's offers an escape from the city. Be prepared to walk 1½km or to take a taxi to get to San Pedro or San José. Has a restaurant, pool, cable TV, and computers with free high-speed internet. Shared hot-water baths. Airport shuttle ¢10,505. Dorms ¢7004; singles and doubles ¢20,427. ❶

◘ FOOD

Black beans, white rice, and chicken remain staples, though American fast food joints have found their way into the mix. Vegetarian and international cuisines are popular, offering respite from the monotony of chain-dining and *comida típica*. Authentic *tico* fare like *casados* and *gallo pinto* are sold in *sodas* throughout the city. Most have cheap lunch and dinner specials (¢1400-2200). Take advantage of the various options and consider doing a little diner-hopping.

SAN JOSÉ

The *mercado central* sells cheaper meals that you can cook in your own hostel kitchen. For a more extensive selection, head to the local supermarkets like **Más X Menos,** Av. Central, C. 11/13 (open daily 6:30am-midnight; AmEx/MC/V) and **Automercado,** at Av. 3, C. 3, on the other side of town (☎2233 5511; open M-Sa 7am-8pm, Su 8am-3pm). Most of the higher-quality, more pleasant *sodas* and restaurants are in the vicinity of Av. Central.

▨ **Restaurante Grano de Oro,** Av. 2/4, C. 30 (☎2255 3322). An international dining experience at one of San José's best hotels. The pleasant meal begins with attentive service and ends just as sweetly with a chocolate truffle. Start with an arugula, spinach, and parmesan salad (¢3300), then continue with filet mignon (¢12,100) or ravioli with spinach and goat cheese (¢6500). For an undeniably romantic setting, dine at dusk in the garden courtyard. Open daily 6am-10pm. AmEx/D/MC/V. ❸

▨ **Nuestra Tierra,** Av. 2, C. 15 (☎2258 6500). Candle-lit wooden tables decorated with newspapers from the early 1900s, *vaquero*-uniformed waiters, and meals served on palm leaves. Try the *gallo pinto* breakfast with delicious fried eggs (¢2500). For lunch or dinner, order the house cocktail (¢4900) and a steak (¢6800). There are no vegetarian options. Service is temperamental. Parking available across C. 15. Menu in Spanish and English. Open 24hr. AmEx/D/MC/V. ❸

Restaurant Tin Jo, Av. 6/8, C. 11. (☎2221 7605; www.tinjo.com). Broad selection of exotic Asian fusion cuisine, and an elegant ambience composed of an indoor fountain and warm-colored tapestries on the walls. Vegetarian-friendly menu. The food is good, but do not expect expertise in any one country's specialties. Unique desserts include fried banana tempura with vanilla or coconut ice cream (¢2200) and lemon cheesecake with blackberry sauce. The waitstaff is friendly and attentive. Start out with satay (¢2800) or sushi (¢3300-5600). Curries and pad thai ¢4200-7800. Open M-Th 11:30am-3pm and 5:30-10pm, F-Sa 11:30am-3pm and 5:30-11pm, Su 11:30am-10pm. AmEx/D/MC/V. ❷

Shakti, Av. 8, C. 13 (☎2222 4475). This haven of healthy goodness serves only vegetarian dishes and white meat, a change from the typical fare of *gallo pinto* and fried meat. Frutas Shakti offers a light mix of fruit, yogurt, and granola (¢2200). *El Vampiro* (the vampire) combines oranges, sugar beets, and carrots (¢750). The avocado sandwich is delicious and comes with salad (¢1800). In keeping with its health-minded mission, no alcohol is served. While waiting for your food, read up on the healthy and sanitary processes used to produce your meal. Various herbal supplements, breads, and cookies sold at the counter. *Especiál* (main dish, soup, salad, and drink) ¢2400. Open M-F 7:30am-7pm, Sa 7:30am-6pm. D/MC/V. ❶

Cafe Mundo (☎2233 6272). A romantic restaurant that won't break the bank. The Italian fare is served by candlelight and the outside setting overlooks a small pond (look closely for the large fish). Pastas ¢2800-5500. Chicken dishes ¢4200-5000. Desserts include crepes with strawberries, flan, and tiramisu (¢1200-2200). Open M-Th 11am-10:30pm, F 11am-11:30pm, Sa 5-11:30pm. AmEx/D/MC/V. ❶

La Grand Ma, Av. 1, C. 1/3 (☎2221 3996). Packed with locals on their lunch breaks, La Grand Ma serves a wide variety of Costa Rican comfort foods. *Casados* with chicken, beef, and fried fish (¢2250) are popular, as is the selection of *almuerzos caribeñoes*, all of which come with rice and beans (¢3150-3650). Plate of the day with drink ¢2000. Open M-F 8am-5:30pm, Sa 9am-4pm. MC/V. ❶

Restaurant Vishnu Vegetariano, Av. 1, C. Central/1 (☎2256 6063). A variety of appetizing salads available (¢2100-3000). The *ensalada de frutas*, a tropical fruit salad with granola and ice cream or yogurt, is a favorite. Veggie burger combos (¢1700) and vegetarian pizza (¢2500). Don't leave without trying the yogurt smoothie, *morir soñando* ("to die dreaming"; ¢1400). Open M-Sa 7am-9pm, Su 9am-7pm. Other locations include Av. 4, C. 1 (next to the Banco Popular), Av. 8, C. 11/13, and Av. Central, C. 14. AmEx/MC/V. ❶

Soda El Parque, Av. 4/6, C. 2 (☎2258 3681). El Parque's round-the-clock hours draw suit-clad businessmen for lunch and late-night revelers just before dawn. Everyone comes for the same reason: cheap and tasty *comida típica*. The spacious seating area with large ceiling fans provides an escape from the heat or rain. The unusually tall tables supplement the diner feel but are a bit awkward. Breakfast ¢700-3000. *Casados* ¢2500-7000. Sandwiches ¢1650-4200. Open 24hr. AmEx/MC/V. ❶

Jicaras del Campo (☎2520 1757). Take a taxi or the Escazú bus to the south side of La Sabana, 150m west from La Contrabría. Enjoy a gigantic selection of *casados* (¢2495) or go for one of the many chicken dishes (¢950). Spacious seating, arched windows, and music from a *marimba* add to the pleasant *tico* ambience. Beer ¢880. Open daily 1-10pm, buffet 1-3pm. AmEx/MC/V. ❶

Taquería La Moderna, C. 2, Av. 6/8 (☎2223 0513), near the corner of Av. 6. This tiny restaurant is easily missed—look for the line of benches with bright fruit tablecloths and a colorful mural inside. Offers incredibly cheap eats, but the portions are just as small as the prices. Tacos ¢400. Hot dogs ¢450. *Casados* ¢1500. *Empanadas* ¢350. Open M-Sa 7am-9pm, Su 8am-7:30pm. ❶

SAN PEDRO

The heart of San José's student scene, San Pedro is full of inexpensive cafes and restaurants. From San José, catch a bus to San Pedro from Av. Central, C. 9/11 (10min., every 5-10min., ¢190), pass **Mall San Pedro,** and get off when you see the outlet mall to your right. The main drag into San Pedro is **Avenida Central.** The street running perpendicular next to the outlet mall is **Calle Central.** Walk north down C. Central with the **Parque John F. Kennedy** to your left and the outlet mall behind you. The first street on your right leads to C. de la Amargura; a left on C. 3 leads to the University, and a right leads back down to Av. Central. This loop is packed with students all year.

▧ **Jazz Cafe** (☎2253 8933; www.jazzcafecostarica.com), 200m east of C. 3 on Av. Central. An upscale place with live performances every night and meals named after jazz singers and their songs. "Round Midnight" is the filet mignon (¢6300). The food is tasty, but it's the mixed drinks (¢1750-2750), like the Jazz Cocktail (a mix of rum and fruit juice), that really attract large late-night crowds. A different Costa Rican jazz or blues band performs every night. Cover ¢2500-3000. Open daily 6pm-2am. AmEx/MC/V. ❸

▧ **La Oliva Verde** (☎2280 2908), Av. Central, near OmniLife, 300m west of JFK Park. Fresh salads and wraps are made before your eyes in this Mediterranean sandwich shop. Try the Pita Oliva Verde (¢2500), with grilled vegetables, feta cheese, olives, and pesto sauce on soft pita bread. Salad ¢3375. Reduced calorie sauces and nutritional information on every meal. Fruit smoothies from ¢975. Shots of vitamins and minerals from ¢450. Open M-Sa 11am-7:30pm. AmEx/MC/V. ❶

Pizzería II Pomodoro (☎2224 0966), 25m north of JFK Park on C. Central. The aroma of garlic drifts into the street, drawing those tired of rice and beans into this welcoming Italian eatery. Generous portions of crispy thin-crust pizzas (¢2200-4200) and pastas (¢2000-3500). Beer ¢950. Wine ¢1250. Open M and W-Su 11:30am-11pm. Only pastas and salads are available between 2:30pm and 6pm. AmEx/D/MC/V. ❶

Restaurante Vegetariano (☎2224 1163), 150m north of JFK Park on C. Central. Identifiable only by a worn sign over the entrance, this small restaurant offers a surprisingly comprehensive selection of healthy vegetarian meals. Try one of the 8 different vegetable soups on the menu (from ¢1550) or go for the house special *"Plato Fuerte,"* with brown rice, salad, and avocados (¢2200). MC/V. ❶

◙ SIGHTS

▨TEATRO NACIONAL. Small but exquisite, the National Theater is a must-see. In 1897, the construction of the theater was inspired (and funded) by Costa Rican citizens clamoring for more cultural venues. Because it was originally a product of their interest and money, *ticos* take a great deal of pride in this site. The theater is graced with sculpted banisters overlaid in gold, marble floors, and frescoes. Designed by sculptor Pitro Bulgarelli, statues representing Dance, Music, and Fame adorn its facade. The lobby features Costa Rica's most famous mural, a collage of the crops that brought the country its prosperity—bananas and coffee. A grand staircase inspired by the Paris Opera ascends toward bright overhead reliefs. Performances include ballet, drama, classical music, and opera. *(Av. 2, C. 3, southwest corner of the Plaza de la Cultura. ☎2258 5135; www.teatronacional.go.cr. Open M-Sa 9am-4pm. 30min. tours available in English or Spanish on the hr., except at noon; ¢2909/US$5. Ask about performances—often 3 per week—and ticket prices at the ticket window.)*

MUSEO NACIONAL. This museum offers an overview of Costa Rican history and early Costa Rican life. The building has been transformed from a military headquarters (the Cuarto Bellarista) into the home of a collection of artifacts. Though the front is still riddled with bullet-marks from the 1948 Revolution, the interior is full of pre-Columbian art, along with exhibits on Costa Rican history, archaeology, and geology. Don't miss the view of San José from the fort's highest point or the butterfly garden on the lowest level. *(Av. Central/2, C. 17. ☎2257 1433 or 2256 4139. Open M-Sa 8:30am-5pm, Su 9am-4:30pm. ¢2325/US$4, students ¢1,162/US$2.)*

MUSEO DE ORO. Founded in 1950 by the Central Bank of Costa Rica, the Museo de Oro houses a three-part exploration of Costa Rican culture underneath the Plaza de Cultura. The museum's most impressive exhibit is its enormous collection of pre-Columbian gold from AD 500. Another exhibit houses 16th-century bills, coins, and *boletos de café* (coffee tokens), while the final hall displays temporary arts and archaeological exhibits. *(Av. Central, C. 5. ☎2243 4216. Open daily 9am-5pm. ¢5130, students ¢2850.)*

MUSEO DE JADE. Costa Rica's Social Security building is an unlikely location for, reportedly, the world's largest collection of American jade. The emerald-colored mineral was of particular importance to Costa Rica's indigenous groups, who used it for jewelry and talismans. The museum also has a small collection of tools and weapons dating back to pre-Columbian times. The exhibits have English and Spanish explanations; ask the security guards for

SAN JOSÉ

more in-depth information. *(Av. 7, C. 9/1. ☎ 2287 6034. Open M-F 8:30am-3pm, Sa 9am-1pm. ¢1162/US$2. MC/V.)*

SNEAK PEAK. The **Centro Nacional** houses the national Companies of Dance and Theater. Even if there are no performances scheduled during your visit, you will likely see the dancers, actors, or gymnasts practicing if you quietly and unobtrusively enter the building from the **Parque de España**.

MUSEO DE ARTE COSTARRICENSE. Housed in a terminal of San José's old airport, this small museum is filled with temporary modern art exhibitions and a permanent collection of Costa Rican nationalist art from the 19th and 20th centuries. Those with time on their hands can explore the walls of the Salón Dorado, carved and painted to look like gold, with the history of Costa Rica depicted across all four sides. Check out the sculpture garden behind the museum. For a better view of the stone courtyard and Parque La Sabana, go out on the terrace. *(Paseo Colón, C. 42, on the eastern edge of Parque La Sabana. ☎ 2222 7155; www.musarco.go.cr. Open M-F 9am-5pm, Sa-Su 10am-4pm. M-Sa ¢2909/US$5, students ¢1743/US$3; Su free.)*

PARQUE DE ESPAÑA AND PARQUE MORAZÁN. Complete with well-manicured lawns, benches, and a majestic dome that appears to have been taken straight from a Shakespearean play, these neighboring parks are a tranquil place to rest aching feet. Sudden downpours draw crowds of students, couples, and businessmen looking to stay dry under Morazán's dome. You might even get to see some locals practicing their juggling skills. *(Av. 3/7, C. 5/13. Free.)*

CENTRO NACIONAL DE ARTE Y CULTURA. This impressive fortress of the arts, between Parque de España and the National Library, offers cultural events in some of Costa Rica's oldest edifices—buildings that have survived earthquakes and civil unrest. Two active theaters share space with the Museo de Arte y Diseño Contemporaneo, which hosts rotating exhibits by contemporary artists in a warehouse-like space. Stop by to see if a performance is running; schedules are on the lowest level near the press office and at the airport. *(Av. 3, C. 15/17. Enter from the SE corner for the museum and the west side for performances. ☎ 2257 7202; www.mad.ac.cr. Open M-F 10:30am-5:30pm. US$2, students ¢300, free M. Performance prices vary.)*

PARQUE ZOOLÓGICO Y JARDÍN BOTÁNICO NACIONAL SIMÓN BOLIVAR. Little more than a run-down, packaged version of the natural splendor that has made Costa Rica famous, this *parque* features spectacular creatures in cramped cages. See jaguars, squirrel monkeys, agoutis, reptiles, and tapirs. Few of the displays are in English. Consider going before you set out into the country's rainforests to know what you should be aware of in the natural setting. *(Av. 11, C. 7, 300m north and 175m northwest of Parque Morazán in Barrio Amón. ☎ 2256 0012. Open daily 9am-4:30pm. ¢1500, ages 3-6 ¢1000, under 3 free.)*

CENTRO NACIONAL DE ARTE Y CULTURA. This impressive fortress of the arts, between Parque de España and the National Library, offers cultural events in some of Costa Rica's oldest edifices. These buildings that have survived everything from earthquakes to civil unrest. Two active theaters share space with the Museo de Arte y Diseño Contemporaneo, which hosts rotating exhibits by contemporary artists in a warehouse-like space. Stop by to see if a performance is running; schedules are on the lowest level near the press office and at the airport. *(Av. 3, C. 15/17. Enter from the southeast corner for the museum and the west side for performances. ☎2257 7202; www.mad.ac.cr. Open M-F 10:30am-5:30pm. Tu-Su ¢1162/US$2, students ¢300, M free. Performance prices vary.)*

GOOD TIMES, GOOD CONSCIENCE. Located 2km west of Hospital Mexico in La Uruca, San José, Parque Nacional de Diversiones is the only amusement park in the world that gives all of its profits to charity. The park started as a fair to raise funds for a Children's Hospital in 1964. Built after a polio epidemic that hit Costa Rica when the country had few youth medical facilities, the current hospital still runs on funding from the park. These days, its *diversiones* are more diverse than ever, including roller coasters, water rides, a flight simulator, and a theater. *(Free bus to the park at Av. Central/2, C. 8. ☎2242 9200; www.parquediversiones.com. Open F-Su 9am-7pm. ¢5400.)*

◧ SHOPPING

San José's size and high concentration of tourists make buying everything from basic necessities to souvenirs easier—and sometimes cheaper—than in other Costa Rican towns. You'll find the best selection of Costa Rican art, woodwork, jewelry, clothing, hammocks, and other souvenirs at a strip of vendors on Av. Central/2, C. 13/15, near the **Plaza de la Democracia.** (Most vendors open M-Sa 8am-6pm, some open Su.) Another option is **La Casona,** C. Central, Av. Central/1, where several souvenir stores are clustered under one roof. (Most stores open daily M-Sa 9:30am-6:30pm, some open Su.) Serious art collectors should check out San José's wonderful art galleries, many along Av. 1 between C. 5 and 13. **Las Arcadas,** with an entrance on C. 3 between Av. Central/2, and on Av. 2 between C. 3/5, houses clothing stores, beauty salons, an ICT office, and internet and laundry facilities in a two-story plaza. For a standard Western selection of clothing and sportswear (not to mention food courts), take a San Pedro-bound bus to **Mall San Pedro** or the **Outlet Mall.** (Both open daily 10am-8pm.)

▨ **Galería Namu,** Av. 7, C. 5/7 (☎2256 3412; www.galerianamu.com). For authentic crafts, visit the only fair-trade gallery in Costa Rica. Namu purchases works from the country's 8 indigenous groups and from folk artists. Check out the carved wood masks (from ¢70,038), colorful tiles (¢11,673), and paintings (¢81,711). Each piece comes with a page on its origins. Ships internationally. Open M-Sa 9am-6:30pm, Su 1:15-4:30pm. MC/V.

♬ ENTERTAINMENT

A number of 24hr. casinos have opened in San José, many in hotels on Av. 1 near C. 5. Movie theaters throughout San José show US releases with Spanish subtitles.

Fiesta Casino, Av. Central, C. 7/9. Tables and slots if you want to try your luck. You must be 18 or older to gamble.

Cine Variedades, Av. Central/1, C. 5 (☎2222 6108), downtown. M-Tu and Th-Su ¢1000, W ¢500. MC/V.

Sala Garbo (☎2223 1960) and **Teatro Laurence Olivier** (☎2222 1034), both on Av. 2, C. 28, 100m south of the Paseo Colón Pizza Hut. Show a varied selection of older films from Latin and North America (¢2000).

Multicines San Pedro (☎2280 0490), on the 3rd floor of San Pedro Mall. Modern theaters with digital sound (¢1800, children ¢1500). MC/V.

Salón de Patines Music, 200m west of JFK Park in San Pedro. Rollerskate (¢2000 with rental skates) and listen to pop music. Skating for kids and parents Sa-Su 10am-12:30pm. Open daily 7-10pm.

🔲 NIGHTLIFE

San Pedro pulses with life at night: the dances are *salsa* and *merengue*, and the drinks are *cervezas* and *guaro* cocktails. The scenes range from karaoke bars full of *ticos* belting Latin tunes to American sports bars packed with tourists playing pool and swapping gringo wit. **Calle de la Amargura** is always hopping and is the best place to meet young *ticos*. Most establishments have ¢1000-1500 covers (sometimes more for men), though they are somewhat negotiable and typically include drinks. Dress is casual; a t-shirt is fine in San Pedro bars, but you might want to throw on some dressier threads to go to the El Pueblo and San José clubs. It's a good idea to bring your ISIC card or passport out with you, as most clubs and bars require a valid ID for entrance.

CENTRO COMERCIAL EL PUEBLO

A 15min. ride north of San José center, El Pueblo is the place to find wild nights of dancing and drinking. The gift shops, bars, and dance clubs usually pick up after 11pm. El Pueblo is easily accessible by taxi (¢800-1200). Since the complex is saturated with tourists, petty crime is not uncommon. Beware of thieves who target drunken revelers as they exit. Likewise, be wary of cab drivers who charge too much for pick-ups inside the complex. Walk out to the road for a taxi, but be cautious.

Ebony 56 (☎2223 2195), on your right in the main parking lot. This sleek, ultra-modern club attracts a mix of travelers and locals, mostly in their 20s. Brave revelers dance on a silver stage while the rest watch from space-age couches made of leather and metal piping. Music ranges from reggae and rave to *salsa* and pop, depending on the night and mood. Th Ladies' night. Beer ¢800. Mixed drinks ¢1500. Cover ¢1000-2000. Open daily 6pm-6am.

Twister Club (☎2222 5746), toward the back and on the left of El Pueblo. Attracts a late-20s crowd that gets hot and heavy on the dance floor. Crowds form early, but house beats pumping loud enough to hear from the end of the line keep bodies moving. Gringos are welcomed and may be pleased with the American music selection. Beer ¢800. Mixed drinks ¢1000-1500. Open daily 6:30pm-3am.

Bongo's (☎2222 5746), around the corner from its sister club, Twister. A mixed-age crowd gathers to socialize and dance to house music. Bongo's offers TVs and foosball tables; more seating but less dancing than Twister. Beer ¢800. Mixed drinks ¢2000. Cover ¢1000-2000. Open daily 5pm-4am.

NEAR THE CITY CENTER

San José's center is crawling with bars and clubs, many of them hidden between *sodas* and shops. Bars and clubs often remain shuttered during the day, only to emerge at night with lit signs, loud music, and raucous laughter. Many host a wide range of ages chatting over drinks, while others blast popular Latin hits for expert dancers; most places have a little bit of both.

Salsa 54, Av. 1/3, C. 3 (☎2223 3814). A meeting place for seasoned dance veterans. The soundtrack is a hodgepodge of love songs, 60s hits, *salsa*, and reggae. Many of the dancers are experts, but don't let that stop you from joining them on the floor. Beer ¢800. Mixed drinks ¢1200-1800. Cover around ¢1500. Open M-Sa 7pm-late, Su 2-9pm.

Salidas Orbital 2000, Av. 1/3, C. 3 (☎2233 3814), above Salsa 54. A younger crowd of 20-somethings grooves to pop, tango, *salsa*, and *merengue* on 3 small stages amid a sea of plush red cocktail tables. Male and female models wearing almost nothing dance in the Model Revue. Karaoke depending on the mood. Cover ¢1500. Beer ¢800. Mixed drinks ¢1200-1800. Open F-Sa 7pm-late.

El Cuartel de la Boca del Monte, Av. 1, C. 21/23 (☎2221 0327). Restaurant by day and party spot by night. A good place for large groups—VIP area and lots of seating. Features local bands on M and occasionally on weekends. Rock on Sa. Cover ¢2000 for live music; M women no cover. Beer ¢800. Mixed drinks ¢1500. Open daily 11:30am-3pm and 6pm-3am.

SAN PEDRO

The enormous bar scene near the University in San Pedro is student-oriented and casual. People and music overflow into the streets, making the area relatively safe, though partiers should still take precautions. C. 3, north of Av. Central, known as **Calle de la Amargura,** is the heart of the college scene. There are fewer tourists, making it easier to meet outgoing *tico* students. All bars on C. de la Amargura may close early on weeknights, depending on turnout.

Caccio's. Contains a breezy outdoor patio. Beer ¢800. No cover. Open M-Sa 11am-1am.

Bar Tavarúa. A surf and skate bar that opens up a back room for dancing on crowded nights. Beer ¢650. Open M-Sa 11am-2am.

Terra U. A large student hangout often blasting reggaeton. Beer ¢650. Pitchers ¢1550 before 6:15pm, ¢2000 after. Open daily 10:30am-2am. AmEx/MC/V.

⚠ OUTDOOR ACTIVITIES

Museums and city parks aren't your style? Costa Rica is the place for you. Even from the largest city, there are plenty of opportunities for outdoor adventure.

Tropical Bungee (☎2248 2212 or 2221 4944; www.bungee.co.cr). Jumps offered at the 80m Colorado River Bridge. 1st jump ¢37,872, 2nd jump ¢17,479. Join the "addict club" by making 2 jumps in 1 day, and your third is only ¢17,479. T-shirt and video included. Leads 1-day rappelling trips (US$65). Transportation included. Discounts for groups. AmEx/D/MC/V.

Ríos Tropicales (☎2233 6455; www.riostropicales.com). Introductory and advanced kayaking and rafting trips on rivers across Costa Rica. One-day rafting on the Reventazón River ¢43,700. Two days kayaking in Tortuguero ¢262,192. Mountain biking ¢43,700. All meals included. AmEx/D/MC/V.

Aventuras Naturales, Av. 5, C. 33/35 (☎2225 3939; www.pacuarelodge.com). Offers rafting, hiking, biking, and canopy tours. One-day Pacuare River trip ¢55,351; 2-day ¢168,385. Canopy tour can be added to multiple-day Pacuare trips for ¢23,306. English spoken. Open daily 8am-8pm. AmEx/D/MC/V.

▶ DAYTRIPS FROM SAN JOSÉ

INBIOPARQUE

From San José, take a bus from Av. 7/9, C. Central to Santo Domingo (20min., ¢300); tell the driver you want to go to INBioparque. From the drop-off point, follow the sign and walk 150m west (to your left) along the main road; the complex will be on the left. To return to San José, walk back out to the main road. The bus stop is to the left (¢225). ☎ 2507 8107; www. inbio.ac.cr/inbioparque. Open Tu-F 8am-4pm, last admission 3pm; Sa-Su 8am-5pm, last admission 4pm. US$23, students US$17, children US$13. AmEx/MC/V.

If you're in San José for a few days before heading off farther afield, a visit to INBio*parque* will introduce you to the wildlife of Costa Rica. The park is great for children or those who do not have the time to explore the wonders of Costa Rica in their natural environment. The visit starts with a video on the scope of biodiversity. A large hall contains interactive displays on the geological history and evolution of life on Earth, including a sound and light show introducing Costa Rica's protected areas. Amble along the park's wheelchair-accessible trails through forest habitats, following cement paths with information about surrounding plant species like orchids, bromeliads, and guarumos. The trails also wind through a small butterfly garden and exhibitions on tarantulas, frogs, and marine animals. A restaurant with Costa Rican food and gift shop are also available. Touring the facilities on your own can take 1-2hr. Free guided tours (2hr.) are offered every hour and should be reserved to ensure availability.

MORAVIA

Moravia, northeast of San José and once engulfed by coffee plantations, now draws travelers for its artwork. For the best crafts, take a bus from San José, Av. 3, C. 3/5 (30min., ¢245), and ask the driver to drop you at La Calle de la Artesanía, running one block east of the church. You'll find a stretch of shops selling Cuban cigars, bags, hand-carved wooden sculptures, the typical oxcarts that are emblematic of Costa Rica, and more. Bargaining down the price about 15-20% is common, and discounts are offered for payments in cash.

Just off La Calle de la Artesanía past the Shell station is Hidalgo la Rueda, a family-run leather store that gives free tours of its machinery. In addition to an extensive selection of leather products, La Rueda makes custom bags and other products to order. (Enter at the souvenir shop. Take a left at the back for tours. Open M-Sa 9am-noon and 1-6pm). Before you go back, make sure to see the church, whose colorful ceiling makes it one of the most beautiful around.

The return bus (¢240) is one street west of the main road, near the *parque*.

ESCAZÚ AND SAN RAFAEL DE ESCAZÚ

Though only a short bus ride from San José, these suburbs feel like another world. Rolling hills replace the capital's grimy air, enticing increasing numbers of Americans and Europeans seeking small town serenity but big city convenience. **Escazú's** town center has a few shops and services, but the lush green hills hide some relaxing and luxurious B&Bs. **San Rafael de Escazú** (1km northeast) is a more commercial home to some very classy restaurants.

✦ ▶ ORIENTATION AND PRACTICAL INFORMATION

From San José, buses leave from Av. Central/1, C. 16 (every 15min., ¢275) and drop passengers along Calle León Cortes in San Rafael de Escazú and on Av.

SAN JOSÉ

Central at the west side of the *parque central* in Escazú. Buses return to San José from the west side of the *parque* in Escazú and every few blocks along C. León Cortes in San Rafael de Escazú. The church is on C. Central on the east side of the *parque*. C. León Cortes starts three blocks east of the *parque* in Escazú, and goes northeast to San Rafael de Escazú.

Local services include a **Banco de Costa Rica** (open M-F 10am-6pm) at the northwest corner of the *parque*, a **24hr. ATM** at the northeast corner, and the **post office,** on the northeast corner of Av. 1 and C. 1, one block east and one block north of the *parque* (open M-F 8am-5:30pm, Sa 8am-noon). **Postal Code:** 1250.

ACCOMMODATIONS

Many Escazú expats own B&Bs, hidden along winding roads outside the town center. Most guests find that cars make commuting to restaurants and stores easier, but public transportation and walking are options. San José taxi drivers may be unfamiliar with Escazú, so it's best to get directions before you leave.

- **Costa Verde Inn** (☎2228 4080; www.costaverdeinn.com), outside the Escazú town center. Follow Av. Central west until you reach a cemetery; take a left and follow signs. Escape the city for this inn, offering amenities for an excellent price. Private baths, pool, hot tub, and living room with fireplace. Airport pickup, tour service, and breakfast. Laundry priced per item. Wi-Fi US$0.10 per min. Reception 7am-10pm. Singles US$45-50; doubles US$50-60. Studios with kitchen US$75-80 per day. AmEx/DC/MC/V. ❸

- **Casa de las Tías** (☎2289 5517; www.hotels.co.cr/casatias.html). A charming B&B in San Rafael de Escazú. Victorian-style house close to town, though its tropical gardens and location make it feel secluded. Head south on Calle León Cortes, turn left after Restaurant Cerutti. It is on the right. 4 rooms and 1 junior suite with kitchenette, each with a view. Amenities include: fans, breakfast on the balcony, laundry, private hot-water bath, tours, and TV. Singles US$62; doubles US$72-82; triples US$82-92. AmEx/MC/V. ❹

- **Villa Escazú Bed and Breakfast** (☎2289 7971; www.hotels.co.cr/vescazu.html), 1km west of the Escazu Banco Nacional on Av. 2. The owner serves delicious breakfast, made with fruit and avocados picked right off the trees. Airy rooms, all with shared hot-water baths, offer lovely views of the central valley. Only English spoken. Doubles US$45-65, 2-night min. Studio apartments 5 nights US$225, 7 nights US$250. US$ only. ❸

FOOD

San Rafael de Escazú boasts some of the country's most elegant dining options. Most come at a price, but tired travelers craving exotic flavors won't regret the splurge. For those who would like to cook for themselves and remain on a budget, there is a **Palí** supermarket 100m north of the park on C. 2. (Open M-Th 8:30am-7pm, F-Sa 8:30am-8pm, Su 8:30am-6pm.)

- **Sale e Pepe** (☎2289 5750), C. León Cortes, behind Pops Ice Cream. Stop for some savory Italian food in this 2-level restaurant. Try the baked salmon (₡6500) or any of the many pizzas on the menu (from ₡2500). All meals served with crusty flatbread. Open M and W-Th noon-3pm and 6-11pm, Sa noon-midnight, Su noon-10pm. AmEx/MC/V. ❸

- **El Novillo Alegre** (☎2288 4995), 800m from San Rafael toward San José, at the bus stop in Plaza Freses. Large portions of fish, beef, chicken, and salads are served at this Argentine cowboy-themed restaurant. A meal costs around ₡9000, with wine ₡12,000. Open M-Sa noon-3pm and 6-10:30pm, Su noon-11pm. AmEx/MC/V. ❹

CENTRAL VALLEY

The Central Valley, or *Meseta Central*, makes up the heart of Costa Rica, comprising its demographic as well as geographic center. Cordoned off by the two great volcanic ranges that divide the country, this valley is home to four of the nation's five largest cities and almost two-thirds of the entire *tico* population. But the cities and coffee fields cover up the explosive truth: two of the region's towering volcanoes (Irazú and Poás) are still active and have caused the valley's residents heartache on multiple occasions. Residual volcanic ash has secured much of the region's livelihood, blessing these temperate plains and rolling hills with enough fertile soil to cultivate crops and rich coffee.

Many travelers skip over the landlocked Central Valley and rush to more-touristed vacation spots on either coast, but those with a few extra days will not regret exploring Costa Rica's interior. Even the largest cities, like San José and Alajuela, are only a short drive from more-picturesque, agricultural communities like Sarchí and Grecia, as well as national parks and pre-Columbian ruins. Visitors can experience urban conveniences while keeping massive volcanoes, butterfly gardens, and the country's wildest rafting a daytrip away.

ALAJUELA

Alajuela, 3km from the international airport and 17km northwest of San José, is perhaps the cleanest and calmest of Costa Rica's cities. Small restaurants and B&Bs anchor the city's family-oriented environment. The town is a good base for pleasant wildlife excursions. For those who simply want to stay put and soak up the scenery, Alajuela's *parque central*, which spreads out in front of a colonial red-domed cathedral, is a good place to sit and relax. As is generally the case, the area closest to the *parque central* is the safest. Tourists should avoid wandering too far afield at night. Still, Alajuela maintains a sunny character with inviting, friendly people, and is a perfect final destination before a flight out of the country.

▛ TRANSPORTATION

Buses: From the **TUASA station,** Av. Central/1, C. 8 (☎2442 6900), 350m west of the southwest corner of the *parque central,* buses go to **San José** (45min., every 5min. 4am-10pm, ¢370) and **Volcán Poás** (1hr.; M-Sa 9:15am, return 2:30pm; ¢1750 round-trip). Buses to **Sarchí** depart 200m west of the *mercado central* (1hr.; M-Sa every 25-30min. 4:55am-10:15pm, Su every 25min. 5:15am-10:15pm; ¢605).

Taxis: A ride to or from the airport should cost no more than ¢1500.

▛ ▟ ORIENTATION AND PRACTICAL INFORMATION

Arriving at the TUASA bus station, turn right onto the *avenida* at the top of the station, then walk 350m until you reach the **parque central,** boxed in by **Avenida Central/Avenida 1** and **Calle Central/Calle 2.** Look for the white **cathedral** on the far end and a white dome-like shelter over a stage. The streets of Alajuela form the standard Costa Rican grid, but street signs are rare, so it's best to count the blocks or use landmarks, as locals do.

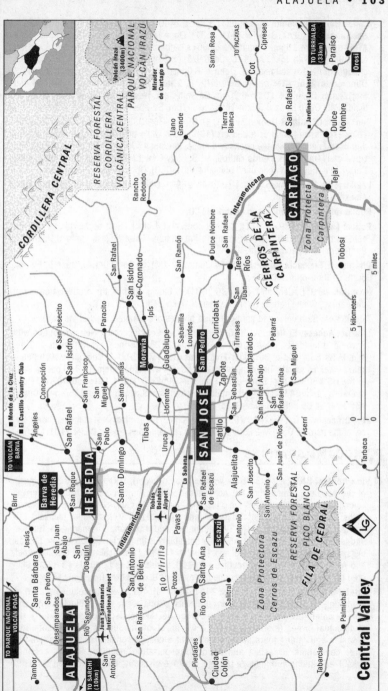

Central Valley

CENTRAL VALLEY

Banks: Banco Nacional, Av. Central/1, C. 2 (☎2440 9200). Open M-F 8:30am-3:45pm. **Scotiabank,** Av. 1/3, C. 2 (☎2441 1131). Open M-F 8:30am-6pm. Both have MC/V **ATMs** open 5am-10pm. Scotiabank changes Citibank and V traveler's checks; 1% commission. **Bac San José,** Av. 3, C. Central/1 (☎2443 4380), changes AmEx Travelers cheques for a 1% commission. Open M-F 9am-7pm, Sa 9am-1pm. There is a **BCAC/Bancrédito 24hr. ATM** on Av. Central/2, C. 2, and **24hr. ATMs** inside both Palí and MegaSuper. Open M-F 10am-6:30pm, Sa 9am-5pm. **Western Union** (☎2442 6392) is inside Palí. Open M-Sa 8:30am-1pm and 2-7pm, Su 10am-1:30pm and 2-5pm.

Bookstore: Goodlight Books, Av. 3, C. 3/5 (☎2430 4083; www.goodlightbooks.com). Enjoy *espresso* (¢400) or a dessert (¢350-500) while browsing the selection of new and used English-language books and maps. Internet ¢500 per hr. Free map of the city. Open daily 9am-6pm. **Libros Chiloé,** Av. 5, C. 2/4 (☎2242 7419), across from Hotel Cortez Azul. Buys and sells used books (¢500-3000). Open M-Sa 8:30am-6pm.

Laundry: La Batea, Av. 5/7, C.4 (☎2440 2691). Open M-F 7am-5pm, Sa 7am-4pm. AmEx/D/MC/V.

Public toilets: At the *mercado central.* ¢100.

Police: (☎2440 8889, or 911), 1 block north and 4 blocks east of the *parque*'s northeast corner, around the corner from the fire station. Some English spoken. Open M-F 9am-5pm. Emergencies 24hr.

Pharmacy: Farmacia Santa Lucia, Av. Central/2, C. 1 (☎2440 0404). Open M-F 8am-8pm, Sa 9am-6pm. MC/V.

Hospital: Av. 9, C. Central/1 (☎2436 1001), 5 blocks north of the northeast corner of the *parque*, facing Parque de las Palmeras. Open 24hr.

Telephones: Both coin- and card-operated phones are available around the *parque*.

Internet Access: El Reto, Av. 1, C. Central/1 (www.elretocr.com). New computers with Skype and headsets. Internet ¢250 per 30min., ¢350 per hr. Calls to the US ¢50 per min. M-Sa 8am-10pm, Su 10am-7pm. **Conexion,** Av. 3/5, C. 1. Computers with headsets as well as private international calling booths with fans. Internet ¢350 per hr. Calls to the US ¢60 per min. Open daily 7am-7pm. AmEx/D/MC/V. **Café Interactivo,** Av. 3, C. Central/1 (☎2431 1984), is small with older computers. Internet ¢250 per 30min., ¢350 per hr. Open M-Sa 9am-9pm.

Post Office: Av. 5, C. 1 (☎2443 2653), 2 blocks north and 1 block east of the northeast corner of the *parque.* Open M-F 8am-5:30pm, Sa 7:30am-noon. **Postal Code:** 2101. MC/V.

▄ ACCOMMODATIONS

▩ **Vida Tropical B&B** (☎2443 9576; www.vidatropical.com), 100m east and 300m north of the hospital, across from the Academia de Natación. Decorated in bright tropical colors, this comfortable B&B feels just like home. Five cozy rooms share 2 beautiful baths; 1 room at the back of the garden has a private bath. Guests enjoy pleasant 1st- and 2nd-floor sitting areas with TV, hammocks, and a balcony. The managers, Norman and Isabel, live in the building, and their hospitality is unmatched. Choose from breads, eggs, and tropical fruits for breakfast. Laundry ¢1740. Free local phone calls, internet, and Wi-Fi. Singles ¢17,400; doubles ¢26,100; triples ¢31,900; quads ¢37,700. Children under 12 free. Ask about reduced rates for extended stays. Cash only. ❸

▩ **Hotel Mi Tierra,** Av. 2, C. 3/5 (☎2441 1974 or 4022; www.hotelmitierra.net). A swimming pool, communal kitchen, and cozy sitting room with cable TV make this hotel a comfortable place to hang out. When he isn't landscaping and painting, the multilingual owner, Roberto, provides a wealth of info about the town. Personalized kayaking and rafting tours available, often at a cheaper price than those offered by large companies. Breakfast and airport transportation included. Wi-Fi in common area. Free parking and luggage storage. Package discounts for families and students.

Alajuela

⌂ ACCOMMODATIONS

El Cortez Azul, **8**
Hostel Trotamundos, **10**
Hotel 1915, **4**
Hotel Charly's Place, **6**
Hotel El Mango Verde, **13**
Hotel Mi Tierra, **15**
Hotel Pacandé, **9**
Los Volcanes, **11**
Vida Tropical B&B, **1**
Pensión Alajuela, **2**

🍎 FOOD

Café Ambrosia, **5**
Coffee Dreams Café, **12**
Cuigini Bar & Rest., **14**
Jalapeños Central, **7**
La Mansarda Bar & Rest., **16**
La Tacareña Bar & Rest., **3**

🎵 NIGHTLIFE

El Pueblo, **18**
Fiesta Casino, **17**
La Casona, **19**

Singles and doubles ₡20,300, with bath ₡23,200; triples ₡23,200/29,000; quads ₡29,000/31,900. AmEx/MC/V. ❸

Los Volcanes, Av. 3, C. Central/2 (☎2441 0525; www.hotellosvolcanes.com). Welcoming fountains and cream-colored walls accentuate the subtle sophistication of this classy accommodation. Breakfast and airport transportation included. Free Wi-Fi and local calls. Singles ₡20,300 (US$35), with hot-water bath ₡26,680 (US$46); doubles ₡26,680/34,800 (US$46/60); triples ₡34,800/42,920 (US$60/74). MC/V. ❸

Hostel Trotamundos, Av. 5, C. 2/4 (☎2430 5832; www.hosteltrotamundos.com). This backpacker hangout is family-owned and offers free internet, cable TV in all rooms, and a communal kitchen. Breakfast included. Free baggage storage and tour information. Dorms ₡6960 (US$12); singles ₡14,500 (US$25), with hot-water bath ₡20,300 (US$35); doubles ₡14,500/20,300 (US$25/35); triples ₡23,200/26,100 (US$40/45). MC/V. ❶

Hostel El Mango Verde, Av. 3, C. 2/4 (☎2441 7116; www.hostelmangoverde.com). Basic rooms surround a miniature garden courtyard and 3 open-air sitting areas with cable TV, a hammock, and video games. All rooms have fans, and services include laundry (US$5) and communal kitchen. Popular with young people and backpackers. Reservations recommended in high season. Singles US$15, with bath US$20; doubles US$25/30; triples US$10 per person. US$/₡. ❷

El Cortez Azul, Av. 5, C. 2/4 (☎2443 6145). The common area is filled with the English-speaking manager's artwork. Common kitchen, small backyard, clean rooms, 2 sitting areas with modern couches and cable TV. Services include whitewater rafting trips, tours to Volcán Poás, Volcán Arenal, the La Paz Waterfalls, and the area around Alajuela. Wi-Fi in common area. Tour info at his brother's website, www.hotelmitierra.com. Single-sex dorms ¢5800 (US$10); singles and doubles ¢14,500 (US$25), with bath ¢20,300 (US$35). AmEx/MC/V. ❶

Hotel Pacandé, Av. 5, C. 2/4 (☎2443 8481; www.hotelpacande.com). A spiral staircase at the back of this hotel leads to a brightly painted loft (with private bath) that can house up to 4 people (US$40-60/¢23,200-34,800, depending on group size). Outside common area is surrounded by flower bushes. Breakfast of fruit and coffee is served on the patio. All rooms have mirrors and towels. Free internet, local calls, and transportation from the airport. Singles and doubles ¢16,240 (US$28), with bath ¢23,200 (US$40). Their second location, Pacandé Villa, is located 2.5km north of town toward Volcan Poás. AmEx/MC/V. ❷

Hotel 1915, Av. 5/7, C. 2 (☎2441 0495 or 2440 7163; www.1915hotel.com). Formerly the home of the owner (and of her parents and grandparents before her), 1915 was recently converted into a hotel and renovated. Fancy sitting area and pleasant rooms. Breakfast (think French toast) included. All rooms have A/C; some have fridge, TV, and balcony. Café connected to reception. Free internet. Singles ¢26,100-37,770 (US$45-65); doubles ¢31,900-49,300 (US$55-85); triples ¢37,700-58,000 (US$65-100). Apartment with kitchen available just down the block ¢58,000-69,600 (US$100-120). 16% service charge with credit card. AmEx/MC/V. ❹

Hotel Charly's Place, Av. 5, C. Central/2 (☎2440 6853; www.charlysplacehotel.com). A rainbow of colors on the sheets and walls brighten up the simple dorm that has a row of bunk beds and a shared bath. Rooms have private hot-water baths and TVs. Friendly service. Breakfast with toast and fruit included. ¢300 per piece of laundry. Wi-Fi. Dorms ¢5800 (US$10); singles ¢14,500 (US$25); doubles ¢20,300 (US$35); triples ¢26,100 (US$45). AmEx/MC/V. ❶

Pensión Alajuela (☎2441 6251; www.pensionalajuela.com), 4 blocks north of the *parque*, across from the judicial court and hospital. Fans and tropical murals. Attached bamboo bar. TV and towels available. Breakfast included. Laundry ¢2000 per load. Free Wi-Fi. Internet ¢500 per 30min. Reception 24hr. Check-out noon. Singles ¢14,500 (US$25), with bath ¢17,400 (US$30), with A/C ¢23,200 (US$40); doubles ¢20,300/23,200/34,800 (US$35/40/60); triples ¢26,100/31,900/37,700 (US$45/55/65); quads ¢34,800 (US$60), with bath ¢43,500 (US$75). Reservations recommended. Weekly and monthly rates available. 6% charge for credit cards. Traveler's checks accepted. AmEx/MC/V. ❸

◪ FOOD

The largest supermarket in town is **Palí,** four blocks west and one block south of the southwest corner of the *parque.* (☎2442 6392. Open M-Th 8:30am-7pm, F-Sa 8am-8pm, Su 8:30am-6pm.) **MegaSuper,** on the south side of the *parque* at Av. Central, C. Central/2, is smaller but closer to the town center. (☎2441 1384. Open M-Th 8am-9pm, F-Sa 7am-9pm, Su 7am-8pm.) The *mercado central,* two blocks west of the *parque,* is a crowded collection of meat, cheese, fruit, and vegetable stands. (Open M-F 7am-6pm, Sa 6am-6pm.)

▨ Cuigini Bar and Restaurant, Av. Central, C. 5 (☎2440 6893). Photos of Italian celebrities line the walls of this 2nd floor restaurant. Menu mixes Southern Italian with American classics. Appetizers range from french fries (¢1150) to Sicilian shrimp (¢3560). Entrees include pasta (¢2200-6500) and the Frank Sinatra burger (¢2670). Live *troba*

3 nights per week. Extensive liquor selection from the bar. Open M-W 11:30am-10pm, F-Sa 11:30am-11pm, Su 4-10pm. Bar open until midnight or later. AmEx/MC/V. ❶

Coffee Dreams Café, Av. 1/3, C. 1 (☎2430 3970). It's not just the coffee that's a dream in this homey cafe. Dark wood tables and chairs and black-and-white photos of coffee farmers blend European style with Costa Rican authenticity. Choose from several satisfying entrees, such as the chicken lasagna, served with salad, garlic bread, *refresco natural,* and a delicious dessert (¢2500). Large selection of vegetarian dishes including salads, pies, and crepes (¢1800). Broccoli quiche ¢2500. A wide variety of coffee drinks (¢1400, without liquor ¢900) go great with the *tres leches* (¢1100) or strawberry cheesecake (¢1300). Open M-F 8am-8pm. MC/V. ❶

Jalapeños Central, Av. 3/5, C. 1 (☎2430 4027), 50m south of the post office. Mexican *ponchos* and *sombreros* decorate the walls of this popular tourist restaurant. The Columbian owner, Norman, grew up in New York City and serves delicious Tex-Mex food, including burritos (¢1750) and quesadillas (¢1800). Try the excellent *sopa Azteca* (¢2000), with cheese, guacamole, and tortillas. Taco salad ¢3250. Takeout and vegetarian options available. Open M-Sa 11:30am-9pm. AmEx/MC/V. ❶

La Mansarda Bar and Restaurant (☎2441 4390), 25m south of the southeast corner of the *parque.* A large 2nd floor restaurant whose dining area has plenty of tables with balcony seating. No Costa Rican meal is complete without *ceviche* (¢4010-5290) or steamy *sopa de mariscos* (seafood soup ¢5450). Chicken dishes ¢3200-5950. Wine ¢2000 per glass, ¢6000 per bottle. Open daily 11:30am-1am. AmEx/D/MC/V minimum ¢3000. ❷

Café Ambrosia, Av. 5, C. 2 (☎2440 3440). This simple, open-air cafe serves *típico* meals, as well as 4 types of lasagna (chicken, beef, *palmito,* and sweet corn with ham; ¢2200) and sandwiches (¢1350). Entrees come with lightly dressed salads. Coffee ¢600-850. Milkshakes ¢750. Beer ¢800-1200. Open daily 9am-6:30pm. MC. ❶

La Tacareña Bar and Restaurant, Av. 7, C. 2 (☎2441 2662). Quick service and tasty food. Burgers (¢2000) are served in the glow of a big-screen TV and posters of volcanoes and rock groups. Entrees ¢2800-4000. Personal pizzas ¢4500-7000. Beer ¢850. Open daily 11am-2am. V. ❶

🎤 🎵 NIGHTLIFE AND ENTERTAINMENT

The center of town is relatively deserted at night, and there are few nightlife options. Relax at the bar of one of the neighborhood restaurants or take a taxi (¢1300) to one of the lively, expensive bars across the street from the airport, which are packed with tourists. Though Alajuela is considered one of Costa Rica's safer cities, it is best to travel in a group or take a taxi after 9pm.

Cuigini Bar and Restaurant (☎2440 6893). Many of the waiters and patrons here speak English. Enormous selection of local and imported liquors. The restaurant upstairs serves delicious Italian-American and Southern cuisine. Don't miss the owner's special piña colada. Beer ¢700-900. Mixed drinks ¢1200-4200. Open Tu-Sa 11:30am-midnight or later, Su 4pm-midnight. AmEx/MC/V.

La Mansarda Bar and Restaurant (☎2441 4390), 25m south of the southeast corner of the *parque,* on the right. Primarily a restaurant, but the bar here sees some local action at night. Sa-Su live alternative rock music. Beer ¢700. Mixed drinks ¢1500. Open daily 11:30am-1am. AmEx/MC/V.

El Pueblo (☎2442 4270), past Fiesta Casino, on the road from the airport to Alajuela. Karaoke M-Sa 10pm, Su 4pm. Ask about the Bacardi 2-for-1 offer. Beer ¢1000. Mixed drinks ¢1500. Open M-Th and Su 9am-1am, F-Sa 9am-2:30am.

La Casona (☎2442 0066), on the road between Alajuela and the airport, across the street from El Pueblo. Popular with both tourists and locals, this spacious bar has a fountain and a big-screen TV. A large back room is sometimes used for live music and private functions. The menu includes seafood entrees (¢2600-7300) and a few Peruvian soups and ceviches (¢2500). Beer ¢1162. Mixed drinks ¢1740-2320. Open M-Th and Su 11am-midnight, F-Sa 11am-1am.

Fiesta Casino, by the airport, between Denny's and Rosti Pollo. Live music 8pm. Poker and VIP room. Beer ¢1740 (US$3). Mixed drinks ¢2900 (US$5). M Ladies' night. 18+. Open 24hr.

▶ DAYTRIPS FROM ALAJUELA

VOLCÁN POÁS

Take a taxi and arrive when the park first opens (1hr., ¢20,000 round-trip). Buses depart daily from San José's TUASA station, Av. 2, C. 12/14 (2hr., 8:30am, round-trip ¢22,250). They stop at the TUASA station in Alajuela at 9:15am (1hr., round-trip ¢1750) and arrive at Volcán Poás around 10:30am. The return bus leaves the park at 2:30pm. You may be done seeing the park before the return bus arrives; bring something to amuse yourself. Park open daily Dec.-Apr. 8am-4:30pm, May-Nov. 8am-3:30pm. ¢5800 (US$10), kids ¢11,600 (US$20).

Fifty-five kilometers northwest of San José, Parque Nacional Volcán Poás is a cloud forest accessible by trails lined with moss, orchids, and dangling bromeliads. Poás is the most-visited national park between Mexico and Panama because of its proximity to San José and Alajuela. A steam-belching crater at the top of active Volcán Poás (2574m) forms the park's main attraction. Inside the massive crater (1320m across and 300m deep) is a turquoise acid pool and *fumaroles* (vents in the earth's crust) that release bursts of volcanic steam. The cone looks like a rainbow carved into the terrain, with vibrantly colored layers of gray, white, and red earth that trace the history of the volcano's eruptions.

The **visitor center** features a small **museum** that educates guests about sustainability and eco-friendly practices. There is also a souvenir shop and a cafe with more than 20 flavors of cappuccino (¢900) and a smattering of lunch items and pastries (¢700-1000).

The most direct route to the crater is a 10min. walk up a gentle, paved path from the visitor center. **Laguna Botos,** the water-filled collapsed cone of a former volcano, is a 15min. walk beyond the crater. Look for the paved trail marked "Laguna Botos" just before the crater viewing area. It is an easy uphill walk. From there, return to the main trail or follow the more indirect Sendero Escalonia back to the parking area. Poás is most enjoyable in the morning, especially from May to November, as clouds and rain obscure the view by noon. Try to avoid visiting on Sundays, when the park is usually packed. The path to the crater is wheelchair-accessible and an ambulance is available.

FINCA DE LAS MARIPOSAS (BUTTERFLY FARM)

Call ahead (☎ 2438 0400; www.butterflyfarm.co.cr.) and the farm will provide transportation from San José or Alajuela. Otherwise, take the Guácima Abajo bus from the corner of Av. 2 and C. 8 in Alajuela (45min.; 6:45, 8:30, 9, 10:30am, 12:30, 1, 2:30pm; ¢175). Return buses run about every 30min. (11:15-11:45am and 1:15-5:15pm). Open daily 8:45am-5pm. Tours begin at 8:45, 11am, 1, 3pm, and last about 1½hr. English-language tour ¢8700 (US$15), with ISIC ¢5800 (US$10), children 4-12 ¢4350 (US$7.50). Tours with transportation from San José ¢14,500 (US$25) per person. Call to find out discounts for groups of 10 or more. AmEx/MC/V.

Southwest of Alajuela in La Guácima, the renowned Finca de las Mariposas features a pleasant, rural garden that is home to 5% of Costa Rica's butterfly species. The farm employs 300 local families who grow the butterflies. All the extra attention has dramatically increased the butterfly survival rate from its normal 2% in the wild. The tour includes a 20min. video presentation available in English, French, German, and Spanish explaining the natural history of the insect. Tours in English or Spanish can be custom-tailored for private groups depending on age and area of interest. The four-acre farm, complete with a visitors center, small cafe, and gift shop, is Latin America's oldest exporter of butterflies, selling more than 70 different species and over a quarter million pupa to zoos and insectariums worldwide. There are more species on display during the rainy season, but come early— butterflies tend to hide during afternoon showers. On some days, you can also watch as the butterfly pupas are inspected and packed for export.

ATENAS

It's hard to find tourists in the village of Atenas, 25km west of Alajuela, and locals like it that way. Atenas is a good "time out" stop on a busy itinerary—Volcán Poás and Manuel Antonio are one and three hours away, respectively, and the Butterfly Farm and Zoo-Ave are en route to the village from Alajuela.

▐ ▐ TRANSPORTATION AND PRACTICAL INFORMATION. The **bus** from San José to Atenas leaves from Terminal Coca Cola, Av. 1/3, C. 16 (every 30min.-1hr., ¢615). Return buses leave Atenas from in front of the Coopetransatenas office, 150m west of the southwest corner of the *parque* and diagonally across the street from the *mercado central*. Buses run at least every hour to Alajuela, where they drop off and pick up at the southwest corner of the lot between Av. Central/2, C. 8/10 (¢435). Printed schedules are available at the Coopetransatenas office in Atenas (☎2446 5767). Once you reach Atenas, orient yourself by the church, which is on the *parque*'s south side. The *mercado central* is located 100m west of the church. **Banco de Costa Rica** is 100m south of the southwest corner of the *parque* and has a **24hr. ATM.** (Open M-F 9am-4pm.)

▐ ACCOMMODATIONS. Ana's Place B&B ❸ is 200m east of the Acueductos y Alcatarillados (AyA) water company behind the church at the bottom of a hill on your right. A winding drive leads up to the only hotel close to the *parque central*, where rooms with big beds and quiet fans look onto a yard occupied by colorful macaws. Ana's also offers beautiful gardens with a swimming pool and gazebo, sitting area, and kitchen. (☎2446 5019. Breakfast included. High season singles US$50; doubles US$60. Low season singles US$35/45. AmEx/MC/V/ US$/¢.) **Hotel B&B Vista Atenas ❹** features the most dramatic views of the Atenas valley and surrounding mountains, but it takes a cab to get here. It has bright white rooms, a Franco-Belgian restaurant,

a cliff-side pool, and two cabins with kitchens. (☎2446 4272; www.vistaatenas.com. Singles US$65; doubles US$70; triples US$75; double cabins US$70. Tax not included. Lower weekly rates available. AmEx/MC/V/US$/¢.) **Apartamentos Atenas** ❸ offers views for low prices, but is the farthest from town. The large cabins, with kitchens, are around a pool. There is a waterfall as well. (☎2446 5792; www.apartamentosatenas.com. Breakfast US$6. English and German spoken. Singles US$35; doubles US$40; one-room triple US$50; two-room triple US$60; two-room quad US$65. Ask about special rates for longer stays. AmEx/MC/V/US$/¢.)

🍴 **FOOD. El Mejor Clima** ❶ (☎2446 3212), 200m north and 200m west of the *parque*, serves up a variety of tasty salads topped with seafood (¢1500-2200), *ceviches* (¢1100-2400), and rice dishes (¢1900-2800). Eat outside to enjoy the perfect weather that gives Atenas its motto and this restaurant its name. **Rick's Internet Café** ❷, located at the northeast corner of the *parque*, serves pizza (¢2000-4000), calzones (¢2800), and sandwiches (¢1400-3500). Sign up ahead of time for "Thursday nights at Rick's," a special meal at 8pm for ¢4000 (¢5000 at the door), that includes meat, salad, potatoes, and dessert. Work by local artists for sale. (☎2446 0810; www.ricksinternetcafe.com. Internet 30min. free with purchase, ¢500 per hr. Open M-Th 8am-6pm, F-Sa 8am-8pm, Su 10am-6pm. US$/¢.) For a quick, cheap meal, head west of the *parque*'s southwest corner for **Soda Tío Mano** ❶, a typical *soda* (*casados* ¢600) with an unusually wide variety of desserts, like *queque de melocotón* (peach cake) and strawberry cheesecake for ¢600. (☎2446 5605. Open daily 8am-9pm.)

SARCHÍ

The livelihood of this town revolves entirely around the production and sale of crafts and souvenirs. Shops selling hand-crafted furniture line the main road. Meaning "wide open jungle space" in the indigenous language of Huetar, Sarchí was inhabited by an indigenous community until 1640, and it is one of the oldest settlements in the Central Valley. This small village keeps an old tradition alive in the form of brilliantly decorated, iconic *carretas* (wooden oxcarts).

In addition to being the cradle of Costa Rican crafts, Sarchí is situated in the fertile *cantón* of Valverde Vega, between Volcán Poás and Volcán Barva. Its rolling hillsides offer lovely views of the valley and provide a beautiful backdrop for dazzling sunsets. For most travelers, Sarchí is a one-day stop for crafts and souvenir shopping, but those with time to spare will linger in the picturesque hills high above the town, descending to enjoy the peaceful, rainbow-painted park, friendly locals, and talented artisans.

🚍 TRANSPORTATION

Buses leave across from the west side of the *parque* in Sarchí Norte. Buses to Los Ángeles (6 per day 5am-6:30pm) pass by La Luisa and San Pedro, as do buses to Trojas (5:40, 10:45am, 1:30, 3:45pm; ¢155) and San Juan (9 per day 6am-5:40pm, ¢155). Buses to Naranjo (5km), Grecia, and Alajuela pass by the west side of the *parque* in Sarchí Norte and by the stop in front of the Plaza de Artesanía in Sarchí Sur every 25min. (6am-11pm; to Naranjo and Grecia ¢120; to Alajuela ¢565). Direct buses go to and from San José (1hr., every hr. 5am-10pm, ¢700). Buses run less frequently on weekends. Buses leave for Bajos del Toro Amarillo from the tourist office in Sarchí Sur (3:15pm, return 5:30am; ¢300). **Taxis** (☎2454 3205) are around the *parque* in Sarchí Norte (6am-midnight).

⚡ 🛈 ORIENTATION AND PRACTICAL INFORMATION

Sarchí is divided into Sarchí Norte and Sarchí Sur. Sarchí Norte has the town center and residential areas as well as most of the services and furniture stores. Sarchí Sur has handicrafts and oxcart vendors. The two sections are separated by a 2km road, but public buses pass by often.

Tourist Information: Information about the town can be found at newly opened **Ofiservice** (☎2454 3870), a blue and white building across the street from the Joaquín Chaverri factory and the Plaza de Artesanía. Open daily 10am-7pm. The **Revista Sarchí Guide** has good maps, as well as historical and up-to-date info about the town.

Banks: All 3 have **24hr. ATMs.**

Mutual Alajuela (☎2454 3200), at the northeast corner of the soccer field on the main road in Sarchí Norte. Open M-F 8am-5pm, Sa 8am-noon.

Banco Nacional (☎2454 4126), at the northwest corner of the soccer field on the main road in Sarchí Norte. Open M-F 8:30am-3:45pm.

Banco de Costa Rica (☎2454 1100), 50m southeast of Sarchí Norte on the main road. Exchanges US$ and AmEx traveler's checks. Open M-F 8am-4pm.

Police: Fuerza Pública (☎2454 4021), at the end of La Eva part of town. Open 24hr. Another office is next door to Ofiservice. Open M-F 8am-noon and 2-6pm.

Red Cross: (☎2454 4139, emergency 911), 50m uphill from Banco Nacional in Sarchí Norte. Office open M-F 7am-5pm, Sa 7am-noon. Emergencies 24hr.

Pharmacy: Farmacia Sarchí (☎2454 1418), next to the west corner of the *parque central* in Sarchí Norte. Open M-Sa 7:30am-8:30pm, Su 7:30am-1:30pm. MC/V. **Farmacia Santiago** (☎2454 2815), at the northwest corner of the soccer field in Sarchí Norte. Open M-Sa 7am-9pm, Su 7am-7pm. AmEx/MC/V.

Hospital: The closest **hospital** is in Grecia (☎2494 5044). See p. 113.

Internet Access: There is an **Internet Café** next to Hotel Daniel Zamora, above the liquor store (☎2454 2100). ¢350 per hr. Open M-Sa 9am-9pm, Su noon-9pm. **Ofiservice,** across from the Joaquín Chaverri factory and the Plaza de Artesanía, offers Internet service at steeper rates. US$2 per hr. Open daily 10am-7pm.

Post Office: (☎2454 4533; fax 2454 4300), 125m uphill on the main road from the *parque* in Sarchí Norte. Open M-F 8am-noon and 1-5:30pm. **Postal Code:** 4150.

🛏 ACCOMMODATIONS

Visitors to Sarchí must decide between lodging in the town center and staying in the scenic hills above the town. Accommodations close to the center are relatively utilitarian, while those outside offer fantastic views of the Central Valley but require the visitor to take taxis or buses into town.

Cabinas Paraíso Río Verde (☎2454 3003), 100m east and 100m south of the San Pedro church, about 3km from Sarchí Sur. 3 volcanoes are visible from the pool, and 1 room has a panoramic view. Paths between the attractively decorated rooms are lined with palm trees. Easily accessible by bus. Breakfast US$5. Airport transportation available. Doubles US$20-25; bungalows for 1, 2, 3, or 4 people US$45/50/60/70. ❷

Cabinas Fantasía (☎2454 2007), on C. Trojas, 1km uphill north of the San Pedro church. Among trees on a quiet hill, Cabinas Fantasía has 15 cabins with TV and private hot-water baths. Pink, 2-person cabins are simple and have a fantastic view of Grecia and Sarchí Sur. Accessible by cab or the infrequent bus to Trojas. 4-person cabins have kitchen facilities and 2 bedrooms. Cabins for 2 people US$30; 4 people US$40. ❷

Hotel Daniel Zamora (☎2454 4596; www.tiptopwebsite.com/danza), in Sarchí Norte, across the main street from the soccer field, and 25m directly up the road. 7 basic rooms with white walls, sheets, and tiled floors. Convenient to the center of town, but slightly ovepriced. Floral curtains spice up otherwise sparse rooms. Cable TV and private baths. Reception closes at 9:30pm. Singles, doubles, and triples US$40/80/120 during high season, US$35/70/105 during low season. AmEx/MC/V/US$/¢. ❸

Club Internacional Bella Vista (☎2454 4407 or 2454 1347), in the hills above Sarchí Norte, 2km north of the stadium in La Luisa. Peaceful cabins offer beautiful views of the valley at an excellent price. Amenities include spacious, private hot-water baths, TV, and free access to the pool across the street. Perfect for families; the cabins house up to 4 people. Cabins US$10-20. MC/V/US$/¢. ❶

▐ FOOD

There are three supermarkets in Sarchí Norte. **Supermercado El Pequeño Super** is 50m northeast of the *parque central* on the main road. (☎2454 4136. Open M-Sa 7am-9pm, Su 7am-6pm.) **Supermercado El Parque** is on the west side of the *parque central*. (☎2454 4588. Open daily 7am-8pm.) **Palí** is just past Super Mariscos. (Open M-F 9am-7pm, Sa 8am-7:30pm, Su 9am-3pm.)

▧ **La Finca** (☎2454 1602), downhill behind the Cooperativa de Artesanias in Sarchí Norte. Enjoy quality *comida típica* on the covered patio while looking out over a small valley. Try the *tico* chicken breast with rice, beans, potatoes, and bananas (¢3700) or stick with seafood by starting with a *ceviche* cocktail (¢1600-2500) and enjoying the 3-sauce sea bass for a main course. Open daily 8am-6pm. AmEx/MC/V/US$/¢. ❷

Super Mariscos (☎2454 4330), in Sarchí Norte, 200m northeast of the *parque central* and across from the ICE. No-frills Mariscos delights with good seafood, meat dishes, and a fish tank featuring your future meal. Ceviches ¢2300-5599. *Corvina* ¢2600-4600. Shrimp dishes ¢4900-12,100. Open Tu-Su 11am-10pm. MC/V/US$/¢. ❷

Delicias del Mar (☎2454 4213), in Sarchí Norte, across from the Cooperativa de Artesanias. If the name doesn't give away the menu at this neighborhood joint, the oceanic mural covering the walls surely will. The friendly owners, José and Ronald, specialize in seafood but serve a few chicken (¢2500) and beef (¢4600) dishes, as well. Seafood pastas ¢4500. Sea bass ¢2500-5000. Open daily 11am-10pm. MC/V/US$/¢. ❷

Las Carretas (☎2454 1633; www.rcarretas.com), in Sarchí Sur, next to the Joaquín Chaverri factory. Serves *comida típica* for breakfast and lunch (¢1000-2600), but transitions to Italian for dinner with spaghetti (¢2900-6500) and meats (¢4400-6500). Uses oxcarts as buffet tables and has a garden view. Groups of 15-20 call in advance for a US$10-13 multi-course buffet. Open daily 9am-11pm. AmEx/MC/V/US$/¢. ❸

Club Internacional Bella Vista (☎2454 1347), in Sarchí Norte, 2km north of the stadium. Appropriately named Bella Vista, this large restaurant and nightclub is perched atop a hill above the town and offers a perfect view of Sarchí, Grecia, and San José. Serves a variety of *comida típica* and more international food. Salad ¢2000. Beef tenderloin ¢4700. *Corvina* ¢4400-5200. Shrimp ¢4800. Mixed drinks ¢1500. Open M-Th and Su 11am-10pm, F-Sa 11am-11pm. MC/V/US$/¢. ❷

Restaurante El Río (☎2454 4980), in Sarchí Norte, next to the bridge over the Río Trojas. The dining room has walls of windows looking into the forest. Serves pasta, seafood, and rice dishes (¢2500-2800). Sells crafts in its *centro turístico*. Filet mignon in mushroom sauce ¢5200. Open daily from 10am to 9 or 10pm. AmEx/MC/V/US$/¢. ❷

◉ ▐ SIGHTS AND SHOPPING

COOPERATIVA DE ARTESANIAS. This group of shops has a huge selection of souvenirs, T-shirts, Café Britt products, and jewelry. Furniture is located on the lower level, as well as the ground floor. (☎ 2454 4196. *200m north of the soccer field on the main road in Sarchí Norte. Open M-F 8am-6pm, Sa-Su 9am-6pm. AmEx/D/MC/V/US$/¢.*)

PLAZA DE ARTESANÍA. A small shopping center jam-packed with arts and crafts, including leatherwork, jewelry, woodwork, textiles, ceramics, paintings, and furniture. This area caters to tourists, and although it is quite commercial, it's worth a look. Independent artists and companies have stores in the plaza. *(Located on the main street in Sarchí Sur. Most stores are open 8 or 9am to 6pm.)*

FABRICA DE CARRETAS JOAQUÍN CHAVERRI. Dating back to 1903, this is one of the biggest *carreta* factories and showrooms in the country. Woodcutters deftly shape massive cart parts while specially selected artists paint the days away in the open-air workshop. Enjoy music, coffee, fruits, and juices, and ask master craftsman **Carlos Chaverri** (the son of Joaquín) to autograph his work. (☎ 2454 4411; www.sarchicostarica.net. *22" carts US$202, shipping US$40; 32" carts US$326, shipping US$69. Also has a booth in the Plaza de Artesanía. Open daily 8am-6pm.*)

JOYERÍA MONSE'S. One of the only stores around that makes pre-Columbian replicas with fine stones. *(In the Plaza de Artesanía, Local 12. ☎ 2454 4722. Wooden necklaces US$15. Small, gold-colored earrings US$5 and up. Open daily 9am-6pm. MC/V/US$/¢.)*

KIENTZLER BOTANICAL GARDEN. If you tire of shopping, visit the serene environment at the Else Kientzler Botanical Garden. The garden is run by a German who specializes in the cultivation and sale of tropical ornamental plants. Follow the well-marked trails past orchid, fruit tree, bromeliad, and cactus collections. The gardens are exquisitely manicured, and every plant is labeled. Children will enjoy the play area and hibiscus maze. Pack a lunch and have a midday meal on top of one of the garden's elevated picnic platforms. Information packets available in English, German, and Spanish. (☎ 2242 2070; www.elsegarden.com. *1km out of Sarchí Norte on the road past the Palí supermarket. US$12, students US$6, children 5-12 US$6. Guided tours available with reservation for US$12 per hr.)*

🎵 ENTERTAINMENT

It's hard to find the locals out at night in Sarchí, but there are spots for tourists looking to have a good time. Check out a few places in the Plaza de La Artesanía in Sarchí Sur or head up into the hills to the Bella Vista Resort.

Club Internacional Bella Vista Sarchí (☎ 2454 4512), in Sarchí Norte, 2km north of the stadium in La Luisa. Large windows provide a great view of the valley. The dance floor opens up on F for karaoke and live music (7-11pm). Beer ¢800. Mixed drinks ¢1500. The pool outside has a waterslide. Pool open daily 9am-5pm. ¢1000, kids ¢700.

Disco Scratch (☎ 2454 4580), upstairs from Restaurante Helechos. A great place to see the local dance scene. Cover ¢1500; F 8-10pm ¢1000 for men, women free. Sa ladies' night, women open bar, men 1 drink included. Open F-Su 8pm-late.

Bar La Troja del Abuelo (☎ 2454 4973), at the back of the Plaza de Artesanía. Has pool tables and a TV. Popular with locals and tourists alike for drinks and conversation. The attached restaurant offers hearty fare for tourist-milking prices. Tomato cow tongue ¢4800. Steak ¢4800-5200. Beer ¢850. Mixed drinks ¢1500. Open daily 10:30am-2:30am. Upstairs bar open 6pm-2:30am. AmEx/MC/V/US$/¢.

GRECIA

Located 45km northwest of San José and 9km southeast of Sarchí, the small town of Grecia is the historical and cultural center of its *cantón*. Locals and tourists linger in the park to admire the unique red-iron church, imported from

Belgium after two wooden churches on the same spot burned down. Grecia's most-recent international claim to fame was its selection as the cleanest city in Latin America in 1989. ▓**Recycling bins** still abound today. The pleasant town, along with the nearby serpentarium, butterfly gardens, and Volcán Poás (35min. away) make Grecia a great city to visit for a day or two.

▣ ▨ TRANSPORTATION AND PRACTICAL INFORMATION

To reach Grecia, catch a **bus** from San José, between Av. 5 and C. 18 (30min., M-F 5am-10pm, ¢535). The bus terminal in town is about 400m west of the main plaza past the *mercado*. From the bus station, go up the hill and take your first right; this leads to the *parque central* and the church. The **police station** (☎2494 8750) is 400m south of the bus terminal at the corner of the cemetery, and the **Red Cross** is 100m north and 125m east of the northeast side of the church. (☎2494 3805. Open M-F 7:30am-5pm. Emergencies 24hr.)

> **⊞TIP** **USE IT, DON'T FLAUNT IT.** While the *parque central* in Grecia offers free Wi-Fi, it's not the best idea to flaunt your laptop so publicly, as theft may be an issue. Additionally, downpours begin in Costa Rica without a moment's notice. To keep your laptop safe and dry, head into one of the restaurants surrounding the park and browse the web from there.

▟ ACCOMMODATIONS

▓ **B&B Grecia** (☎2454 2573; www.bandbgrecia.com), 150m south of the southwest corner of the *parque*. Owned by a Canadian, this B&B is a rare find. Lounge in a hammock in the garden or the sitting room with cable TV. Free high-speed Internet access and Wi-Fi, coffee, spacious kitchen, and huge breakfast. Laundry US$3. Private room US$30 for 1 person, US$50 for 2; with hot tub US$40/70. US$/¢. ❸

Healthy Day Country Inn Resort and Spa (☎2444 5903 or 2494 7357; www.healthy-day-hotel.com), 1.5km from the center of town, to your left on the way to Sarchí Sur. Get back into shape or pamper yourself with mud baths and aromatherapy massages. Use of full cardio and weight gym, pool, and tennis courts is complimentary for guests. Breakfast included. Singles US$40; doubles US$48. ❸

▣ FOOD

▓ **Don Efrain Bar and Restaurant** (☎2494 0923), a 20min. walk down the road from Grecia to Sarchí. Hidden on a hill below street level just past the Healthy Day Country Inn, Don Efrain is one of Grecia's best-kept secrets, serving excellent seafood in a small dining room with bright blue-and-gold walls and a covered patio. Shrimp dishes ¢4800. *Corvina al ajillo* ¢4100. Lobster ¢12,000. Open Tu-Su 11am-11pm. MC/V/US$/¢. ❸

▓ **Café Delicias,** 50m west of the southwest corner of the *parque*. An airy, European-style cafe that serves unmatched coffee drinks (¢540-1000), sandwiches (¢1400-1900), and desserts (¢700-1250). Don't miss the frozen *café delicias* (¢980), made with cappuccino and ice cream. Free Wi-Fi. Open daily 8am-8pm. V/US$/¢. ❶

Cucina Italiana y Pizza (☎2444 5665), 100m north and 50m east of ICE, just north of the church. Fresh-baked bread accompanies meals at this authentic Italian eatery, known for its antipasto salads (¢2700) and homemade gelato (¢1000). Enjoy a hot, fresh pizza (¢4800-7000). Open Tu 4-11pm, W-Su 11:30am-11pm. MC/V/US$/¢. ❷

CENTRAL VALLEY

NARANJO

In 1838, this city was named Los Naranjos de Púas in honor of its distinctive, omnipresent orange trees, although today these have largely been replaced by coffee bushes. Few sights exist in the town center; Naranjo is a working town, producing sugar cane, beans, chile, jalapeños, coffee, and *maíz*. Visit nearby natural havens like the protected area of El Chayote, El Cerro del Espíritu Santo (which, at a height of 1353m, affords a panoramic view of the Central Valley), the Cordillera Volcánica Central, the Cordillera de Guanacaste, and Volcán Arenal. Perched in the hills, Naranjo overlooks numerous coffee mills, and *cafetales* (plantations) surround the city. Those seeking relaxation in an extremely rural setting can indulge in the plentiful *balnearios* (hot springs) like that of Las Estufas in the *poblado* of Palmitos. Those craving more adventure enjoy bungee jumping off the world-renowned 81m high Colorado bridge.

▊ TRANSPORTATION

Buses to Sarchí, Grecia, and Alajuela leave from across from the Paraíso Infantil store (about every 30min. 4:55am-10pm; Sarchí Sur ¢140, Sarchí Norte ¢250, Grecia ¢345, Alajuela ¢610). Another terminal (☎2451 3655) is located on the east side of the *mercado*, with frequent buses to San José (M-F every 15min. 4:25-8am and every 40min. 8am-8:30pm, Sa every 20-40min. 4:25am-8pm, Su every 30-60min. 5am-8pm; ¢600). Check in the blue office at the exit of the market on the right for updates. **Taxis** (☎2450 0083) are available 6am-11pm.

▊▊ ORIENTATION AND PRACTICAL INFORMATION

The ornate white-stone church faces west toward the *parque* (notice the sculpture on the northeast corner). This town operates on the standard Costa Rican grid system, with C. Central between the *parque* and the church, and Av. 0 between the church and the market. The municipal building is just north of the church. The town's *mercado* is part of the same block, just north of the municipal building. **Banco Nacional**, with a **24hr. ATM**, is across the street from the southwest corner of the *parque*. (☎2255 0620. Open M-F 8:45am-3:45pm.) **Banco de Costa Rica** is immediately north of the *parque*, with a 24hr. ATM (open M-F 8am-4pm). The nearest Western Union is located in Coopealianza, 50m west of the northwest corner of the *parque* (M-F 8am-5pm, Sa 8am-noon). The **police stations** (☎2450 0052) are located both in the market and in front of the football stadium, 200m north of the northwest corner of the *mercado*. The **Red Cross** is at the entrance of town, 200m east and 100m south of the church. (☎2451 3939 or 911. Open 24hr.) There are two **pharmacies** in town: **Montesoli**, on the south side of the church (☎2451 3517; open daily 8am-10pm) and **Nelma**, at the east side of the *mercado* (☎2450 0529; www.posadahotel. net; open M-Sa 7:30am-8:30pm, Su 7:30am-1pm). **VIP Café Internet,** next to the entrance to BCR just north of the *parque*, has fast computers with headsets and Skype. (☎2450 5379. ¢300 per hr. Open daily 8am-9pm.) **CompuExpress,** offers Internet on older computers 100m west and 75m north of the northwest corner of the *parque*. (☎2450 0109. Open M-F 8am-9pm, Sa 8am-8pm, Su 8am-noon.) The **post office** is 100m east and 50m north of the church. (☎/fax 2450 0644. Open M-F 7:30am-noon and 1-5:30pm.) **Postal Code:** 4200.

▊ ACCOMMODATIONS

Naranjo doesn't see many tourists, and thus, the accommodations are limited. However, there are a couple of accommodations outside of town.

CENTRAL VALLEY

Rancho Mirador de San Miguel (☎2450 3857), accessible by cab (¢1800) or the bus to San Ramon (¢260). Has a restaurant, small casino, single and double occupancy rooms, and 5 cabins on a hillside just outside of town. Restaurant open 5pm-late. Rooms ¢18,000; cabins ¢30,000. ❸

Cabañas Vista del Valle Plantation Inn Rosario Naranjo (☎2451 1165; www.vistadelvalle.com), on the road toward San Ramón, past the Puente Grande de Rafael Iglesias and 1km toward Naranjo. Take a right turn at the entrance to the bungee-jumping site. Arturo Sibaja keeps 10 fancy rooms here. Some of the cabins have patios with hammocks. Luxurious extras include pool and hot tub with garden views, horseback trails, and cocktail terrace. Restaurant overlooking river has no menu; order by discussing what you like to eat with the chef. Breakfast included. Reception 9am-9pm. Singles US$100-170, US$20 more for each additional person. AmEx/MC/V. ❺

🌮🎵 FOOD AND ENTERTAINMENT

Food of the mountains typically abounds with *picadillo de chayote* (a spicy vegetable stew), *pan dulce* (sweet bread), *arroz con leche* (rice pudding), and *cajetas de leche y coco* (sweet milk and coconut nougat). The market in town is quite clean; many linger to eat their purchases on the premises. In addition, **SuperCompro,** across the street north of the *mercado,* has a good selection of groceries (☎2450 0138; open M-Th 7am-8pm, F-Sa 7am-8:30pm, Su 7am-6:30pm), as does the local **Palí,** 150m east of the church (☎2451 1920; open M-Th 8am-7pm, F-Sa 8am-7:30pm, Su 8am-6pm).

Cafeteria Bandola (☎2450 0138), next to SuperCompro across the street from the *mercado.* A tiny cafe that serves Café Britt coffee (¢250-800), sandwiches (¢1300-1600), croissants (¢800-2400), and desserts (¢300-1000). Indulge with a spiked hot chocolate (¢750) or a milkshake (¢1500). Open M-Sa 10am-7:30pm. ❶

Soda y Restaurante Don Taco (☎2450 0825), 100m south and 50m east of the church. A no-frills local favorite that serves *tico* comfort food, tacos (¢650), greasy but yummy *casados* (¢2200), *chuletas* (¢2500), and shakes. Open daily 11am-3am. US$/¢. ❷

Pizza Olivera (☎2451 4824), next to Paraíso 2000, just past the *parque's* northwest corner. Pizza lovers can chow down on slices (¢850) or personal supreme pizzas with meat and veggies (¢1200). Large pizzas ¢4300-5400. Open daily 10am-11:30pm. ❶

Paraíso 2000 (☎2450 5252), on the northwest side of the *parque.* If you like karaoke, sing the night away at this local haunt. Beer ¢800. Open daily 4pm-midnight.

🏃 OUTDOOR ACTIVITIES

If you have a group of two to five people, you can go ballooning over the coffee and sugar cane mountains of Naranjo with the tour group **Serendipity.** Call in advance to find out where to be picked up. (☎2558 1000; www.serendipityadventures.com/ballooning.htm. Balloon ride US$345 per person, US$1200 for private charter.) If slow, calm ballooning doesn't get your adrenaline going, try a rapid descent off the 81m, 120-year-old Colorado bridge. **Tropical Bungee,** in business since 1991, claims to have a perfect safety record. (☎/fax 2248 2212; www.tropicalbungee.com. Reservations required. 1st jump US$65, 2nd jump US$30; includes transportation.)

SAN RAMÓN

San Ramón, 13km west of Sarchí, feels infused with the humanistic spirit that made it "the city of presidents and poets." On Sundays, families relax in the tranquil *parque* after services at the large, elegant town church, which was rebuilt after the earthquake of 1924. Placards throughout the town mark the birthplaces of great political and literary figures—among them five former presidents, and *costumbrista* poets like Lisímaco Chavarría Palma and Féliz Ángel Salas Cabezas. The town's role in the fight for democracy, education, culture, and the rights of the poor in Costa Rica is memorialized in its museum. With a population of over 10,000, San Ramón outdoes the nearby smaller towns with a plethora of affordable, comfortable accommodations and tasty restaurants.

▐ TRANSPORTATION

Buses fill up quickly in San Ramón. To get a seat, arrive at least 15 minutes early at the terminal and get in line. Be prepared to wait, however, since buses are known to be late. Buses arrive at the station northwest of the *parque;* the church is on the *parque*'s eastern side. Buses depart from the terminal 100m north and 175m west of the northwest corner of the *parque* (☎2445 7225) for Puntarenas (1hr., 12 per day 5:15am-11:30pm, ¢785) and San José via Alajuela (1hr.; M-F 13 per day 4:30am-10:15pm, Sa-Su and holidays 11 per day 4:30am-10:15pm; ¢865). Regional buses leave from the station that runs through the block northwest of the *parque* to: Fortuna (2hr.; 5:30, 9am, 12:30, 4pm; ¢1450); Naranjo (25min.; 5, 6am, every 20min. 7am-6pm, every hr. 6-10pm; ¢320); Palmares (20min.; every 15-30min. 6am-6pm, every 30min. 6-10pm; ¢170); Zarcero (1hr.; 7 per day 5:55am-5:30pm; ¢450). The main **taxi** stand is on the west side of the *parque*, but another is located in front of the market's main entrance.

▐ PRACTICAL INFORMATION

Banks: There are several additional banks on the northeast corner of the church.

> **Banco Nacional** (☎2445 7500), 100m south of the church, exchanges currency and has a 24hr. ATM. Open M-F 8:30am-3:45pm.

> **Mutual Alajuela,** 100m south of the church, has an ATM that accepts MC/V/Cirrus/Plus. Open M-F 8am-5pm, Sa 8am-noon.

> **Coopesanramon Bank** (☎2245 5525), on the south side of the church, has an ATM that accepts MC/V/Cirrus/Plus. Open M-F 8am-5pm, Sa 8-11:30am.

> **Palí,** 150m north of the northwest corner of the *parque*, has a Western Union at the Servimas counter and an ATM. Open M-Th 9:30am-1pm and 2-6:30pm, F-Sa 10am-1:30pm and 2:30-7:30pm, Su 9am-noon and 1-5pm.

Police: The **police station** is located 600m north of the northwest corner of the *parque* (☎2445 6872, emergencies 911).

Pharmacy: Farmacia Catedral, at the northwest corner of the *parque*, has a great selection and friendly service. (☎2447 4107. Open daily 8am-8pm. AmEx/MC/V/US$/¢.) The pharmacy **Botica El Pueblo** is across from the northeast corner of the church. (☎2445 7131. Open daily 8am-10pm. AmEx/MC/V/US$/¢.)

Hosptial: Hospital Carlos Luis Valverde Vega (☎2443 5388), 500m north of the *parque*. Open 24hr.

Internet Access: The area southwest of the *parque* is packed with Internet cafes.

> **Space Tech** (☎2447 9060), 25m west of the post office and tucked away at the back of a small shopping gallery, offers plenty of fast computers. ¢450 per hr. Open daily 8am-10pm.

> **Compuline** (☎2447 1834), on the corner opposite the post office to the north, has a number of computers and is open late. ¢450 per hr. Open daily 10am-1am.

> **Cybernet** (☎2447 9181), 100m east of the post office, is slightly cheaper. ¢300 per hr. Open M-F 8am-10pm, Sa 10am-8pm, Su noon-8pm.

Post Office: The **post office** is 100m south and 100m west of the *parque*. (☎2445 7606. Open M-F 8am-noon and 1-5:30pm.) **Postal Code:** 4250.

ACCOMMODATIONS

Hotel la Posada (☎2445 7359 or 2447 3131; www.posadahotel.net), 400m north and 50m west of the east side of the church. The best hotel in town, by far. The Polynesian-meets-Victorian-style reception area is full of antique *tico* furniture, rustic cooking instruments, and tropical plants. Most rooms open onto a common area, and all come with private bath, TV, full mirror, and fridge. Free Internet. Breakfast included. 24hr. reception. Night guard. Singles US$35; doubles US$50; suites US$60. ❸

Angel Valley Farm Bed & Breakfast (☎2456 4084 or 8350 7647; www.angelvalleyfarmbandb.com), located 200m north and 500m east of the church in Los Angeles. Although it's a 10min. drive from town, this cozy B&B is the most comfortable option in the area. Guests enjoy free horseback riding, mountain biking, and a sitting area with satellite TV. Thoughtful details include shower radios and fresh flowers. There are 6 rooms, some with private baths. Airport pickup US$45. Ask about discounts for longer stays. The entire house is available for weekly rent during low season. High season singles US$40, low season US$35; doubles US$60/50. US$/¢. ❸

Hotel San Ramón (☎2447 2042), 300m west and 25m south of the northwest corner of the *parque*. Modestly furnished, spacious rooms come with cable TV and baths. With many affordable rooms, the hotel is popular with large groups and tends to fill up in advance, so call ahead to make reservations. 24hr. reception. Rooms ¢8500. ❷

Gran Hotel (☎2445 6363), 100m south and 250m west of the *parque*. Offers the most affordable accommodations in town. Basic rooms overlook central courtyard. Singles US$6, with bath US$10; triples US$15. US$/¢. ❶

FOOD

The *mercado*, one block north of the *parque*, is busiest on Friday and Saturday (open M-Sa 7am-6pm). **Palí** is 150m north of the northwest corner of the *parque* and has a Western Union and an ATM inside (☎2445 6591; open M-Th 8am-7pm, F-Sa 7:30am-8pm, Su 8am-6pm). **Supermercado Perimercados** is on the northeast corner of the church (☎2445 4115; open M-Sa 7am-10pm, Su 7am-9pm). Four hundred fifty meters north of the west side of the church, **Super-Finca** sells fruits and vegetables only, but has a wider selection than either of the supermarkets. (☎2445 1071. Open M-Sa 7am-8pm.)

Café Delicias (☎2445 59455), 200m west and 100m south of the southwest corner of the *parque*. Starbucks is in big trouble. This bright little cafe serves perfectly blended coffee drinks (¢500-1000), tasty sandwiches (¢1000-2000), and scandalously sweet desserts (¢800-1250) that will keep you coming back. Try one of the exquisitely put-together *bocadillos* (¢350-800), and do not miss the unforgettable frozen *cafe delicias* (¢1100). Other locations in Alajuela and Grecia. Open daily 8am-7pm. V/US$/¢. ❶

D'Leña (☎2447 6803), 1.5km north of the church, just past the gas station on the main road. The spit turning in the front window gives away D'Leña's specialty, succulent rotisseried chicken (¢1950), but the salads (¢2000-2200) and *corvina* (¢2450) are delicious as well. Open daily 11am-1am. MC/V/US$/¢. ❷

Mi Casita (☎2447 6512), 550m north of the west side of the church. Has a plain storefront, and the menu begins with *comida típica* (*casados* ¢1300-1500), but don't be deceived; this homey restaurant is pure Italian at heart. The menu offers 15 types of pasta, from one made with carrot, zucchini, and cauliflower (¢1850) to spaghetti served with squid and shrimp (¢2500). The house specialties, veal scallopine (¢2000) and chicken milanese (¢2200), are worth having as well. Open daily 6am-6pm. ❶

El Buho (☎2445 5945), 100m south and 50m west of the church due west of the south side of the *parque central*. Popular with university students for its reasonable prices, friendly owners, and patio decorated with palm fronds. Take advantage of the diverse *bocas* menu to sample *ceviche*, *ajillo*, *chicarrones*, chicken, and a variety of other tasty dishes (¢1000-1200). *Casados* ¢1800. Plates with rice ¢2000-2500. Open M-Th 11am-11pm, F-Su 11am-midnight. V/US$/¢. ❶

Aroma's Café (☎2447 1414), 100m west and 50m south of the southwest corner of the *parque*. A cozy, chic coffee shop. Plush couches and hanging plants give this bohemian retreat a cheerful atmosphere. A wide variety of espresso drinks (¢550-1000), light snacks (¢600-1500), and desserts (¢450-1000) will tempt you to stay all afternoon. Lasagna (¢2200), salads (¢1800-200), and sandwiches (¢1700) make for heartier meals. Open M-Sa 8:30am-7pm, Su noon-7pm. MC/V/US$/¢. ❶

Soda La Paquereña (☎2447 1364), 200m west and 75m north of the *parque*. The dark wood, display of a traditional *tico* kitchen, and gourds hanging on the wall create a fitting environment for heaping platters of *comida típica*. Assorted plate ¢4500. *Casados* ¢1300. *Ceviche* ¢1200. Open daily 6:30am-6pm. MC/V. ❷

Restaurante Colinas (☎2445 7348), 50m west of the southwest corner of the *parque*. This simple, pleasant restaurant has a large, cafeteria-style kitchen in its center with plenty of seating. The menu is limited, but the large portions and appealing prices make it an attractive place to chow down on *comida típica*. *Ceviche* ¢1500. *Plato del día* ¢1800. Filet mignon ¢2800. Open daily 7am-10pm. AmEx/MC/V/US$/¢. ❷

🎵 NIGHTLIFE

The same building in San Ramón hosts two of the most popular bars in town. One hundred meters south and 100m west of the *parque*, the **Club Centro de Cultura Social** opened in 1926. Enjoy *bocas* (¢500-1000) at one of the many tables or check out photographs of San Ramón over the last century. The **Steel Disco Bar** caters to a younger crowd that likes to dance the night away to whatever beat is on that night. (☎2445 5014. Cover F-Sa ¢1000. Beer ¢750. Shots ¢800. Open M-F and Su 6pm-2am, Sa 6pm-4am.) In the parking lot of the Plaza Occidental mall, the **Berz Bar Discotheque** offers a wide variety of themed nights, from *mariachi* to techno to Hawaiian. (☎2247 6524. Cover ¢2000. Beer ¢900. Mixed drinks ¢1400. Open F-Su 8pm-2am. AmEx/MC/V/US$/¢.)

👁 SIGHTS

The largest building in San Ramón, the **Temple Parroquial de San Ramón** towers over the *parque*. The church's metal frame was designed and built in Germany in 1928, then brought to Costa Rica by ship. Work on the towering church was not completed until 1954. (Open daily. Free.) Just north of the church, the **Jose Figueres Ferrer Historic and Cultural Center** has a small biographical display about the three-time president of Costa Rica who was born in the building, his family's long-time home. Ferrer is best-remembered for abolishing the nation's army and granting suffrage to women. The center also hosts lectures, conferences, and historical and art displays. Schedules of events are available at the reception desk. (www.centrojosefigueres.org. Open M-Sa 10am-7pm. Free.)

PALMARES

Driving west on the Interamericana Hwy., a turnoff leads to the small town of Palmares. To Costa Ricans, Palmares is synonymous with a 10-day-long fiesta beginning January 14. The town starts planning its annual party, **Las Fiestas de Palmares,** during July, and the payoff is tremendous. The palm-filled park and gray stone church (made with whole slawbs of stone and a special eggshell cement) are here year-round, but there's not much more for visitors to see.

⊟ ☷ TRANSPORTATION AND PRACTICAL INFORMATION

The main road through town connects to the **Interamericana Highway** about 2km north of the town center. Facing the church, north is to your left and south to the right. The *mercado* is west of the *parque*. Return **buses** to San Ramón leave from the bus stop 100m north and 25m west of the *parque* every 15-30min. (¢170). Most of the town's services are clustered right around the *parque*.

⌁ ACCOMMODATIONS

The only hotel in Palmares is **Hotel Casa Sueca ❶**, 1.5km toward San Ramón on the main road. Reserve a room before December 15 if you want to stay during Las Fiestas. Rooms are simple, with a mirror and bath. (☎/fax 2453 3353. ¢5000, ¢7000 for larger rooms.) During Las Fiestas, it may be a better idea to stay in San Ramón (p. 116) or Grecia (p. 113) and commute to the fairgrounds.

◖ FOOD

While there is plenty of food to go around during the January fairs, there aren't many places to eat in town during the rest of the year.

> **Navcafé** (☎2452 1700; www.navcafe.com), 1km north of the town center, offers a variety of beverages and light meals. Bright couches liven up the room, while glass-covered tables filled with dried coffee beans give new meaning to the term "coffee table." Coffee ¢500-800. Salads ¢1500-2500. Sandwiches ¢2000-2400. Open daily 9am-9pm. ❶

> **Soda del Río,** 200m north of the park on the highway. Has a standard menu and gets crowded during lunch. *Casados* ¢2500. Open daily 9am-11pm. US$/¢. ❷

> **Lle's Café** (☎2453 0334). For good, cheap eats, head here, a small fast-food joint with long counters and 3 TVs. Nachos ¢1700. Hamburgers ¢800-1200. Personal pizza ¢2000. Open M-Th 9am-midnight, F-Sa 9am-2am. AmEx/MC/V/US$/¢. ❶

❀ FESTIVALS

The biggest event of the year in Palmares is its 10-day **Las Fiestas de Palmares,** which begins on January 14. The festival is welcoming, well-organized, and fun for everyone, especially young people and those looking to consume vast quantities of Costa Rican beer. The *tope*—a procession of purebred horses—kicks off the week; fairgrounds north of the town center are transformed by fireworks, roller-coaster rides, outdoor concerts, soccer games, dancing, and other sporting events. Palmares hosts its own running of the bulls and a Costa Rican-style bullfight in which the bull chases the people and ends up unharmed.

ZARCERO

Named after the aromatic *zarzaparilla* fruit found in the region, "sweet" Zarcero (pop. 4500) winds through narrow hills and scattered cheese factories. The town was erected as a city in 1918 but had been inhabited by indigenous people for centuries before its consecration. Head city of its *cantón*, Zarcero is home to a famous Gothic and Renaissance parish church, constructed in 1895 and dedicated to the archangel of San Rafael. *Zarcereños* take much pride in their divine symbol, which stands decorated with world-renowned topiary creations: bushes clipped in fantastic shapes like dancing animals and double arches. Tourists come just to see these botanical creations, but there is more to discover in the *cuna* (cradle) of organic agriculture, including three protected areas: Parque Nacional Juan Castro Blanco to the northeast, Zona Protegida Río Toro to the east, and Zona Protegida El Chayote to the southeast.

▐ TRANSPORTATION

Amid steep mountain passes, Zarcero lies on the road connecting the northern plains of Costa Rica to the capital, and as a result has very good transportation running between San José and Ciudad Quesada. Coming from San José, take a **bus** headed to Ciudad Quesada, which stops in Zarcero. (☎2256 8914. Ciudad Quesada 2hr., every hr. 5am-7:30pm, ₡1300; Zarcero 1hr., ₡730.) All buses out of Zarcero leave from the southwest corner of the *parque*. In addition to San José and Ciudad Quesada, buses run frequently to San Ramón. (☎2445 6251. 1hr., 8 per day 5:50am-5:30pm, ₡450; return buses 7 per day 7am-7pm, ₡450). **Taxis** (☎463 2161) line up in front of the pizzeria on the south side of the *parque*.

▐▌ ORIENTATION AND PRACTICAL INFORMATION

Zarcero is a linear town with all its shops on the main street. Facing the church, right is south and left is north.

Tourist Information: Available from **Luis Fernando Blando,** the owner of Cabinas La Pradera (☎2463 3959) and from the **tourism board** (☎8827 0477; www.zarcero.co.cr; info@zarcerotours.com).

Banks: All have **24hr. ATMs.**

Banco Nacional (☎2463 3190), 100m north of the *parque,* next to the Red Cross. Open M-F 8:30am-3:45pm.

Banco de Costa Rica (☎2463 3333; fax 2463 3232), 100m south of the southwest corner of the *parque,* changes AmEx and V traveler's checks. Open M-F 8am-4pm.

Coocique (☎2463 3815), 100m north of the *parque* on the main road. Open M-F 8am-5pm, Sa 8am-noon.

Police: The **police station** (☎2463 3231, emergency 911) is 75m east of the northeast corner of the park.

Red Cross: The **Red Cross** is across from Coocique (emergencies ☎2463 3131).

Pharmacy: Farmacia El Parque (☎2463 1212), on the west side of the *parque.* Open daily 7am-8pm. AmEx/MC/V. **Farmacía Zarcero** (☎2463 3855), on the south side of the *parque.* Open M-Sa 8am-8pm, Su 8am-2:30pm. V.)

Hospital: Hospital Carlos Luis Valverde Vega (☎2443 5388), 40min. away in San Ramón.

Internet access: Available at the **Internet Café** (☎2463 0020), across the street from Banco de Costa Rica. ₡400 per hr. Open M-Sa 8am-9pm, Su 10am-8pm.

Post Office: The **post office** (☎4236 3276), 100m north of the northeast corner of the *parque.* Open M-F 8am-noon and 1-5:30pm. **Postal Code:** 4350.

▐ ACCOMMODATIONS

▨ **Hotel Don Beto** (☎2463 5909; www.hoteldonbeto.com), on the north side of the church. This quaint, cozy hotel has 8 beautifully designed rooms with floral linens, paintings, and great views. They offer lunch and transportation to Bajo del Toro and Termales del Bosque, 2 nature attractions that can be hard to reach without guides or tours. Reservations are recommended. Singles US$28; doubles with bath and cable TV US$33, with twin beds, bath, and cable TV US$39. 10% discount for payment in cash. AmEx/MC/V/US$/₡.❸

Cabinas La Pradera (☎2463 3959; www.cabinaslapradera.com), 100m north and 350m east of the *salón comunal.* 4km outside of Zarcero, in the small town of Laguna. Check in at the green house west of the *guardia rural.* There are 9 cabins in a variety of configurations. The owner runs horseback riding tours to the Palmira waterfall (US$30; includes snack and

SWIMMING WITH(OUT) THE FISHES

Just because you're landlocked doesn't mean that you can't cool off by getting wet. While not quite as cheap as just standing outside in the daily summer thunderstorm, affordable swimming pools and baths can be found all over the Central Valley. Visit any of these options to swim with the locals for just a few dollars.

APAMAR, located high in the hills outside Zarcero, has indoor lap and kiddie pools overlooking a tranquil valley full of grazing horses and cows. (Follow the road south of the *parque* 500m west out of town. ☎2463 3647. Open daily 8am-3pm. ¢1000, children ¢700.)

The **Complejo Deportivo** in San Ramón offers the opportunity to shoot a few hoops and take a dip, with a basketball court and a large lap pool in the heart of downtown. (100m south and 300m west of the *parque*. ☎2345 2713. Open daily 8am-6pm. ¢1000.)

Bajo Caliente, a short distance outside San Ramón, has two pools enclosed by mosquito netting in addition to a large trampoline, indoor soccer field, and restaurant. (Follow the main road north 1.5km from the *parque central*, and bear right at the turn toward Zarcero. Turn right at the sign. ☎2445 3083. Open daily 9am-4pm. ¢1200.)

souvenir). Cabin with double bed US$25, with fireplace US$40; triple US$37; quad with kitchen US$45. ❷

🍴 FOOD

Stock up at **Super Alfaro Ruiz,** at the bottom of the hill on the main road, 400m north of the north corner of the *parque*. (☎2463 1593. Open M-Sa 7:30am-8:30pm, Su 8am-6pm. AmEx/MC/V/US$/¢.) Don't miss these prototypical Zarcero foods: *queso tierno* (soft local cheese), *natilla* (custard), and *toronjas rellenas* (stuffed grapefruits), all made in the factory at La Esperanza. For delicious bread and sweets, visit one of the local bakeries.

Fresh Mountain Cafe (☎2463 3196), across the street from the southwest corner of the *parque*. Enjoy a meal and coffee (¢400-900) while gazing out the windows at the whimsically shaped bushes on the lawn and at the local paintings and sculptures decorating the walls. Sandwiches ¢1000-2500. Tilapia ¢3000-3250. Crepes ¢2000. Open M-F 8am-8pm, Su 8am-2:30pm. ❷

Isidro's Restaurante El Higueron (☎2463 3187), a bar and restaurant that serves *típico* meals, including *casados* (¢1800) and fish plates (¢2900). As long as you don't have a heart condition, you can try their wonderfully greasy *chicharrones* (fried pork on a stick ¢3500). Open daily 10am-2am. AmEx/MC/V/US$/¢. ❷

Soda Jiffys (☎2463 2715), 100m south of the park on the main drag. Offers tasty fare in a colorful locale. Tacos and fajitas ¢2200-2300. Nachos ¢1000-1300. Open daily 10am-10pm. MC/V/US$/¢. ❶

Panadería la Marinita, 150m north of the northwest side of the garden. Offers a number of delicious breads and baked goods. Open M-Sa 5:30am-8pm, Su 6am-noon. MC/V/US$/¢. ❶

Panadería Berrocal (☎2463 3820), on the southwest side of the *parque*. Has a wide selections of donuts, *bizcochos*, and *cajetas*. Open daily 5am-8:30pm. ❶

🔭 SIGHTS

For local entertainment, people flock to the large pool and hot tub in **APAMAR,** 500m south of the *parque*, for relaxation and rehabilitation. (☎2463 3674. Open daily 8am-3pm. ¢1000, children ¢700.) The nearby **Toro Amarillo waterfall** is 120m tall, but since it is difficult to find, it's best to go in a taxi (¢6500) or with one of the tours offered by nearby hotels. There is a US$10 entrance fee. **Coopebrisas** is one of two cheese factories near Zarcero, 20min. north of town. To get there, take a taxi (¢5500 round-trip), and ask to see the production manager who can answer all of your questions and show you the cheese-making process. (☎2463 3044. Open M-Sa 7am-noon and 1-6pm, Su 7am-noon; call in advance to make sure the office will be open. Free tours; cheese about ₡2000 per kg.)

HEREDIA

Perched on a hilltop 11km north of San José, the university town of Heredia (pop. 35,000) retains the cosmopolitan air of the capital but leaves the smog and frenzy behind, creating a more relaxed vibe. Clothing shops and a student-oriented bar scene make for a modern, youthful feel, by both day and night.

Throughout the colonial era, the city lagged behind Cartago in wealth and stature, and residents even campaigned to have Costa Rica annexed by Mexico in 1821—to the rest of the country's overwhelming dissent. In the 1830s, Costa Ricans briefly chose Heredia as their capital, but reconsidered and sent the government to San José. A popular suburb for commuters working in the capital, Heredia attracts visitors with a vibrant student scene at the Universidad Nacional, as well as with its proximity to Braulio Carrillo National Park.

▐ TRANSPORTATION

Buses: Most buses load near the *parque* or the *mercado,* although a few leave from the **Parque Los Ángeles,** 2 blocks west of the *mercado,* and others from across the **Universidad Nacional** on C. 9. Most taxi drivers know when and where buses depart. Since schedules change, it can help to call and double check before departure (☎2262 1839). Some schedules are also available at **www.autobusesheredianos.com.** Small change necessary for buying tickets, which are purchased on board. From the bus stop in front of the Universidad Nacional, at Av. 1/3, C. 9, buses go to **Alajuela** (20min.; every 15min. 6am-10pm; ₡270). In front of Más X Menos, Av. 6, C. 4/6, is the stop for buses to **Armonía, La Aurora, Cahuites, Cinco Esquinas, Pasito,** and **Santa Paula** (most buses every 10-30min. 5:15am-11:30pm; ₡195). From Av. 6, C. 6/8 (bordering the *parque*), buses go to **Mercedes Sur, San Joaquín, Santa Bárbara, Santa Cecilia,** and **Santa María** (most buses every 10-15min., ₡150). From Av. 6/8, C.4, across from the west side of the *Mercado Municipal,* buses go to **Barva** and **Paso Llano** via **San José de la Montaña** (Barva 15min.; ₡140. San José de la Montaña 1hr.; 6:45am, noon, 4pm; ₡320.) Buses leave from the bus stop in front of the Universidad Nacional, Av. Central, C. 9, to **Puerto Viejo de Sarapiquí** via **Vara Blanca** (3hr.; 11am, 1:30, 3pm; ₡1550). Buses to **San José** line up on Av. 6, C. Central/3, at all hours of the day and night (30min.; every 5min. 4:50am-midnight, every hr. M-Th midnight-4am, every 30min. F-Su midnight-4:30am; with stops ₡300, direct or at night ₡365). Buses to **San José** pick up in front of the university Av Central/1, C. 9 (every 5min., ₡300-365).

Taxis: Taxis line up on the east side of the **Parque Los Angeles,** and at Av. Central/1, C. 9. ☎2262 6262. The 15min. ride from the airport is charged by the meter.

▐ ORIENTATION AND PRACTICAL INFORMATION

Heredia is organized in a grid system. From the central arteries, odd-numbered *calles* (C.) and *avenidas* (Av.) go east and north of the park, while even-numbered *calles* and *avenidas* run west and south. Few streets are labeled, so it's best to start from the *parque central.* The *parque* is boxed in by C. Central to the east, Av. Central to the north, C. 2 to the west, and Av. 2 to the south. The town's few sights are near the *parque,* and the Universidad Nacional lies five blocks east, just beyond C. 9. Two blocks southwest of the *parque*'s southwest corner is the *mercado municipal,* bordered by C. 2 and 4 and Av. 6 and 8. Diagonal to the *mercado municipal* is a newer market, *Mercado de Florencia.*

Heredia

ACCOMMODATIONS
Du Manolo Hotel, **18**
Hotel América, **11**
Hotel Colonial, **12**
Hotel Las Flores, **17**
Hotel Ramble, **14**

FOOD
Café Shalom, **13**

Fresas, **1**
Aromas de Café, **3**
Le Petit Paris, **7**
Restaurante
  Ganesha, **10**
Soda Cubito, **19**
Trigo Miel, **5**
Vishnu Vegetarian/
  Mango Verde, **2**

NIGHTLIFE
Bar Oceano, **9**
Bulevar, **6**
Miraflores Disco y
  Tropicales
  Taberna, **8**
La Choza, **4**
Speed 7, **15**
Disco Champs
  Elyse, **16**

TO BARVA (3km),
VOLCÁN BARVA (25km),
PARQUE NACIONAL BRAULIO CARRILLO (25km)

CORAZÓN DE JESÚS

SAN FRANCISCO

PIRRO

TO ALAJUELA & (10km)

TO SANTA BÁRBARA, San Joaquín, San Lorenzo

SAN FRANCISCO

Tourist Office: OTEC Viajes, Av. C/2, C.9 (☎2262 1717; www.otecviajes.com). Division of STA Travel. Open M-F 8am-6pm, Sa 8am-2pm. AmEx/DC/MC/V.

Banks: Most of Heredia's banks change cash and traveler's checks for a 1-2% commission. **Banco Coopenae,** Av. 2, C. 4/6 (open M-F 9am-5:30pm, Sa 9am-noon), and **Banco Scotiabank,** Av. 4, C. Central/2 (open M-F 8am-6pm, Sa 9am-1pm). **Scotiabank** and **Banco de Costa Rica,** Av. C, C. 5/7, have 24hr. ATMs that accept all cards (M-F 10am-6pm). **Banco Nacional,** Av. 2/4, C. 2. Banco Nacional's 24hr. ATMs only accept Plus/V cards. Open M-F 1-6pm.

Laundry: Boda's Boutique, Av. 8, C. 7 (☎2237 6273), is a wedding boutique with a *lavandería*. Run by a friendly *gringo* who relocated to Costa Rica. Wash and dry ₡1500 per kg. Open M-Sa 9:30am-5pm. **Martinizing Dry Cleaning,** Av. 1, C. 2 (☎2260 7808), will clean shirts for ₡2100, pants for ₡1800. Prices for loads of laundry negotiable. Open M-F 8am-6pm, Sa 8am-12:30pm. AmEx/DC/MC/V.

Emergency: ☎911.

Police: Av. 5/7, C. Central (☎2262 9232), 4 blocks north of the *parque*.

Pharmacy: There are a number of clinics and basic pharmacies around town, and most accept all major credit cards.

Farmacia Fishel, located at the corner of Av. 4 and C. Central (☎2261 0994). Open M-Sa 8am-8pm, Su 10am-6pm.

Farmacia Imperial, located at Av. 8, C. 8/10 (☎2260 1918). Open M-F 8am-7:30pm, Sa 8am-7pm, Su 8am-noon.

Farmacia Sucre Av. 2/4, C. 2 (☎800 327 6224). Open 24hr.

Hospital: Hospital San Vincente de Paul, Av. 6/10, C. 14 (☎2261 0091), has an adjoining pharmacy for prescriptions.

Telephones: Card and pay phones cluster around the northeast and southwest corners of the *parque*. Purchase a phone card from **Soda El Testy,** at the *parque*'s southwest corner. Open 7am-10pm. Most of the Internet cafes that have international calling booths charge ¢50 per min. for calls to the US.

Internet Access: There are many Internet cafes around town, particularly on the east side near the university. **Cosmos Internet Café,** Av. 2, C. 5/7. ¢200 per hr. Open daily 8:30am-10pm. Coupons are available for 5 free minutes of international calling in the private calling booths. **Café Internet,** Av. Central, C. 7/9 on the north side of the street, is clean and spacious, with plenty of computers. ¢200 per hr. Open 24hr. 2 smaller Internet cafes are across the street, so this is a good place to come if you need a computer. A small **Internet Café,** Av. Central/1, C. 7, next to Vishnu, has 4 computers with Skype and headsets, as well as international calling booths. Internet ¢250 per hr.

Post Office: Telégrafo Gobernación Correo, Av. Central, C. 2 (☎2260 1243), across the street from the northwest corner of the *parque*. Mail a postcard for ¢150 or less. Fax available. Open M-F 8am-5:30pm, Sa 8am-noon. **Postal Code:** 3000.

> **TIP**
>
> **SAFETY FIRST.** Heredia can be a dangerous place at night. Especially in the neighborhoods south of the *mercado*, it is best to take a taxi after 8pm, and to avoid walking alone. The areas closest to the *parque* are safest, and most are patrolled by police. Stay out of the university after dark. Avoid the area just west of the *Estadio de Fútbol*, on the west side of town.

ACCOMMODATIONS

Heredia doesn't see many tourists but maintains good, inexpensive accommodations anyway. Even places outside the city are relatively loud; barking dogs, cars blasting music, and even roosters either serenade you to sleep or keep you from it. Accommodations below have linens, towels, and soap.

Hotel Las Flores, Av. 12, C. 12/14 (☎2261 8147; www.hotel-lasflores.com). A gem among budget accommodations. Shiny marble floors, friendly owners, bright rooms with TVs, and private, high pressure, hot-water showers make the 10min. walk from the *parque* to this largely empty, but generally safe, area of town worth it. Don't miss the view on the rooftop. Singles US$14; doubles US$28; triples US$42. US$/¢. ❷

Hotel Ramble, Av. 8, C. 10/12 (☎2238 3829). Inside this cheery, quiet building with green trim, you'll find large, clean, simple rooms with private hot-water baths. A palm tree design stands out in the tile showers. All rooms US$25 per person. US$/¢. ❸

Du Manolo Hotel, Av. 12, C. 2/4 (☎2237 0476). Manolo offers 16 rooms along bright hallways. 24hr. reception. Singles and doubles US$15-20, all with private hot-water showers, satellite cable, and fans. More expensive rooms are larger. US$/¢. ❷

Hotel América, Av. 2/4, C. Central (☎2260 9292; www.hotelamericacr.com), near the *parque*. A winding staircase leads to a hallway of small rooms with fans and private hot-water showers, popular with families and large groups. The wall of the lobby features a 3-story waterfall mural. Cable TV, concierge service, laundry (priced by piece), free Internet, and a restaurant/bar downstairs. Restaurant open 11am-8:30pm, bar open 11am-midnight. Singles US$45; doubles US$55; triples US$65. AmEx/MC/V/US$/¢. ❸

CENTRAL VALLEY

Hotel Colonial, Av. 4, C. 4/6 (☎2237 5258). This central hotel has a tranquil familial atmosphere, complete with a pet dog and a worn sitting room. Owners live in the building. The bare, mid-sized rooms have shared hot-water baths and fans. 24hr. reception. Singles ¢5000; doubles ¢6000; triples ¢10,000. US$/¢. ❶

📷 FOOD

Sodas serving inexpensive burgers, basic *casados*, and ice cream line every street. Some nicer cafes surround the *parque*. A handful of American fast-food joints are just south of the Universidad near Av. 2, C. 9. Many covered butcher shops, fruit and vegetable stands, and small, inexpensive *sodas* are set up at the **Mercado Municipal** (Av. 6/8, C. 2/4), and at the newer **Mercado de Florencia,** diagonal to the *mercado* at Av. 8/10, C. Central/2. (Both open M-Sa 6am-6:30pm, Su 7am-noon.) The enormous **Más X Menos** (☎2261 0006, Av. 6, C. 4/6), carries housewares, clothing, a wide variety of foods, and some medicines. (Open M-Sa 6am-12:30am, Su 7am-10pm. AmEx/DC/MC/V.) **MegaSuper** on Av. 4, C.Central/1, down the *avenida* from Farmacia Fishel, sells a good variety of snacks and beer. (Open M-Sa 7am-9pm, Su 7am-8pm. AmEx/DC/MC/V.)

🍴 **Le Petit Paris,** Av. Central/2, C. 5 (☎2262 2564). French art prints decorate the dining room of this low-key creperie. Savory crepes (¢2500) are served with salad or rice. The French-inspired menu also includes salad Nicoise (¢2500), meat entrees (¢3000-6000), and spaghetti dishes (¢2200-2500). Beverages include wine (¢850 per glass, bottles ¢15,000-30,000), and beer (¢1250-1800). Buffet with live music F-Sa 6:30pm-11pm. Open M noon-4pm, Tu-Sa noon-11pm. AmEx/MC/V/US$/¢. ❷

🍴 **Aromas de Café y Flores,** Av. C, C. 3/5 (☎2262 6975). Adjoining a florist, this bright, airy cafe is the perfect spot to enjoy a quick lunch or dessert near the *parque central.* Photographs line the walls showing the landmarks of Heredia at different points in time. Go between noon and 3pm to take advantage of the daily special, which includes soup, salad, entree, fries, and fruit drink (¢2500). Sandwiches ¢2800, salad ¢2300, cold coffee drinks ¢2000. M-F 8am-7pm, Sa 9am-6pm, Su 9am-5pm. AmEx/MC/V/US$/¢. ❷

Fresas, Av.1, C. 7 (☎2262 5555), features the typical Costa Rican dessert, *ensalada de frutas* (fruit salad) with ice cream (¢600-1000), fruit drinks (¢675-1225) blended with milk or water, and fruit desserts (strawberries with ice cream or nutella; ¢1500-3500). The large, open dining area also serves heartier fare. Spaghetti ¢2500. *Casados* ¢2800. Open daily 8am-11pm. AmEx/DC/MC/V/US$/¢. ❷

Soda Cubito, Av. 12/14, C. 4 (☎8886 2583). A clean and pleasant *soda,* named after its owner, Cuba. Delicious *gallo pinto* with eggs (¢900), *emparededos* (¢1000-1300), *casados* (¢1400-1900), and a few Cuban dishes. Open M-Sa 7am-7pm. US$/¢. ❶

Vishnu Vegetarian/Mango Verde, Av. Central/1, C. 7 (☎2237 2526). A vegetarian chain decorated with bright colors and cheery fruit and veggie paintings, Vishnu offers a welcome break from greasy *soda* fare. The *plato del día*, with rice, entree, salad, soup, fruit drink, and dessert, is a good deal at ¢2500. Healthy veggie burgers (¢1400) and pita sandwiches (¢1400-2000) are best washed down with a *refresco natural* (¢875-1150). Open daily 8am-7pm. AmEx/MC/V/US$/¢. ❶

Café Shalom, Av. 4/6, C. 2 (☎2261 5354). Try Costa Rica's take on Israeli food in this cafe, run by a native Israeli. Large falafel and pita sandwiches, including teriyaki, honey mustard, and ham and cheese, with fries and *refresco natural* for ¢2200. Personal pizzas ¢1300. Cappuccino ¢750. Open M-Sa 10:30am-6pm. AmEx/MC/V/US$/¢. ❶

Restaurante Ganesha, Av. 2/4, C. Central (☎2260 9292). Located on the ground floor of Hotel America, the restaurant offers a extensive and eclectic Indian, Mediterranean, and Middle Eastern menu. The list of drinks is equally lengthy and ranges from strawberry lassi (¢1600) to whiskey (¢1500). For a light lunch, try the chicken shawarma (¢1750). For dinner, have the lamb kebab (¢5900). AmEx/MC/V/US$/¢. ❷

Trigo Miel, Av. Central, C. 7/9 (☎2237 9695), next to La Choza. A welcome change from dim, crowded *sodas*, Trigo Miel is a modern, spacious bakery cafe that's perfect for lunch or a coffee break, although the menu is limited to what you see on the blackboard when you walk in. Try one of their 4 varieties of lasagna while you take advantage of the free Wi-Fi. The *plato del día* includes entree, *refresco natural,* and a sweet, bite-sized dessert for ¢2500. Open M-Sa 7am-8:30pm, Su 8am-6pm. MC/V. ❶

◉ SIGHTS

Overlooking the east side of the *parque* is the weathered, gray stone **Iglesia de la Inmaculada Concepción.** The church celebrated its 200th birthday in 1997—an amazing feat considering the many earthquakes it has survived. (Open M-W and F 6am-7pm, Th 3-4:30pm. Mass Sa 4, 6pm; Su 9, 11am, 4, 6pm.) Many *ticos*, especially schoolchildren, hang out in shaded **Jardines de la Inmaculada,** church gardens dedicated to the Virgin Mary, in the northeast corner of the *parque.*

El Fortín de Heredia, north of the *parque* near the post office, is a 13m high fort built in 1876 as a sentinel tower to guard a prison long since demolished. Now a historic monument, the tower's loopholes, originally designed to maximize rifle range and minimize exposure to enemy bullets, serve as a reminder of wars past. A small park with several monuments to past Costa Rican leaders surrounds the Fortín, along with a stage where concerts are sometimes held. The **Palacio Municipal** next door will not let visitors go up because of the fort's shaky staircase, but check in the secretary's office for information on the town's history and folklore.

▣ SHOPPING

Perhaps due to its large student population, Heredia is flooded with trendy clothing boutiques and *zapaterías*, mostly concentrated along C. Central, 2, and 4, south of the *parque*. Ask about a discount, or *descuenta*, especially when purchasing more than one item, since prices are sometimes flexible. Discounts are usually not available when using a credit card.

For fresh produce, check out **La Feria,** the farmer's market that spans Av. 14 on Saturdays from 5am to 2pm. Go early for the freshest picks and best deals.

◗ NIGHTLIFE

Though most businesses shut down after 7pm, bars bustle with foreigners and *ticos* until 2am. Many students go into San José or Barva if they're looking for a night on the town, but students still flood Heredia's nightlife hotspots, especially when there is a concert going on at a club or in the *parque*. Check the postings at the university for current info.

Bulevar, Av. Central, C. 7. Full of young people watching sports and drinking beer from the bar's signature table tappers (¢800). There are tons of tables on its first- and second-floor terraces. Beer ¢750. Open daily 10:30am-2am.

La Choza, Av. Central, C. 7, diagonally across the street from Bulevar. A trendy, slightly more upscale hangout. Ask about upcoming concerts. Beer ¢800. Mixed drinks ¢1400. Cover ¢1000-1500 on concert nights. Open M-F 4pm-1am, Sa-Su 11am-1am.

Disco Champs Elysée, Av. 6, C. 9, in the Plaza Heredia complex. A disco with frequent concerts. Tu ladies' night, F reggae. Students with ID ¢1000. Open Tu-Su 7pm-2:30am.

Speed 7, in the Plaza Heredia complex. A favorite student spot with a metallic racecar theme, small dance area, and thumping music. Cover ¢1500, includes unlimited drinks for women, 2 drinks for men. Open F-Su 7:30pm-2am.

Bar Oceano, Av. 2/4, C. 4 (☎2260 7809). A popular spot for foreigners and locals alike, as it taunts the landlocked with surfboards, fishing nets, and watersports videos. During the week, the crowd is mostly *ticos* and the music is alternative rock. The weekends draw a more diverse crowd for classic rock and reggae. Beer ¢700. Open daily 11am-11pm.

Miraflores Disco y Tropicales Taberna, Av. 2, C. 2/4 (☎2237 1880). Try some karaoke at the 2nd floor "Tropical Tavern," or listen to live local music (M-F and Su). On the 3rd floor is one of the city's oldest, most popular discos, where locals merengue to Costa Rican classics played upon request. Cover ¢1500. Beer ¢800. Taberna open daily 8pm-6am; disco open F-Su 8pm-6am, though people tend to pour in after 11pm.

GUIDED TOURS

CAFÉ BRITT. Located up the hill from the **Universidad Nacional de Heredia,** half-way between Heredia and Barva, this complex offers tours in English and Spanish deconstructing the process and history of Costa Rican coffee, all given by amusing actors posing as coffee farmers. Tours conclude with a coffee-appreciation lesson and a multimedia presentation. They also lead tours to **La Guácima** butterfly farm, the **Rainforest Aerial Tram** at **Braulio Carrillo National Park,** and **Volcán Poás.** The grounds feature beautiful gardens, an extensive gift shop with free samples, and a restaurant/coffee shop featuring frozen coffee concoctions in decadent macadamia, mulatta, guayaba, and "Arenal" flavors (¢2000). This place is worth the trip even if you don't take the coffee tour. You can get 10min. of free Internet access in the gift shop. Go on foot or take a Barva bus from Heredia (¢195), and ask the driver to drop you off at the stop for Café Britt. To walk, head north on C. 12 four blocks past the city's sports complex (Av. 2/3, C. 12/16). When the road splits, bear right. Café Britt will be on your left. (☎2277 1600, international 800-GO-BRITT/462 7488; www.cafebritt.com. Tours daily Dec. 16-Apr. 30 at 9, 11am (includes buffet lunch), and 3pm; May 1-Dec. 15 at 11am. Reservations preferred. Private tours can be arranged in advance. Call for prices—they change depending on season and group size, but start at $20 for individuals, including lunch. Student discounts also available. Transportation provided from most major hotels. Open daily 8am-5pm.)

DAYTRIPS FROM HEREDIA

PARQUE NACIONAL BRAULIO CARRILLO

You can access the park from the road running north of Heredia to Sacramento, or from the San José-Puerto Limón Hwy. (Rte. 32). To reach Volcán Barva from Heredia, take a bus to Paso Llano via San José de la Montaña, departing from Av. 6/8, C. 4, on the west side of the mercado municipal (1hr.; daily 6:30am, 11:30, 3:30pm; ¢320). Try catching an early bus—the hike is much more manageable in the morning, when temperatures are still low. Check with the bus driver to make sure you're getting on a bus that goes all the way to Paso Llano; the buses that San José de la Montana will leave 15km from the park's ranger station. Ride the bus to Paso Llano (Porrosatí), where you'll be dropped off across from Chago's Bar. 3 daily buses return to Heredia from the stop outside Chago's Bar (M-F 7:50am, 1, 4:45pm; Sa 7:50am, 12:30, 5:15pm; Su 8am, 1, 5:15pm; ¢320). These buses make a long trip up a rocky road, so the exact times are slightly unpredictable. Try to arrive 20min. early for the bus. To access the Quebrada Ranger Station near the Rainforest Aerial Tram from Heredia, catch a bus to San José (¢300-365) and another to Guápiles (1½hr.; every hr. 5:30am-10pm, Sa-Su until 9pm; ¢835). Ask the driver to let you off near the ranger station. No buses make regular stops at the ranger station or tram, but flag one down when they pass by every 30min.

About 25km northeast of Heredia lies Parque Nacional Braulio Carrillo, 45,900 hectares of land named after Costa Rica's third chief of state. When Rte. 32 was constructed from San José to Puerto Limón in 1978, the park was born from conservationist efforts to save the area's biodiversity.

Despite improved access to the forest from the highway, this national park remains largely untouristed. The park's rugged landscape is accented by sweeping mountains and rippling rivers. Combining forces with the 4.5m of rain that the park sees annually, Braulio Carrillo's terrain lends itself to hundreds of rushing waterfalls and river canyons. The park is composed of two dormant volcanoes, **Volcán Cacho Negro** and **Volcán Barva**. Volcán Barva, one of the few accessible areas of the park, is an excellent, strenuous day hike destination. Although a good portion of the "trail" to the volcano is a paved road surrounded by farms and the occasional cow, a trek up the dormant volcano offers isolated forests, few crowds (you'll likely be the only hiker), amazing views, and a glimpse of Costa Rican country life. A few shrouded *lagunas* sit near the top of the volcano. Be sure to stay on the marked path, both to preserve the vegetation and because visitors have been known to go missing for days.

Apart from Volcán Barva, the trails near the northeastern corner of the park are the only areas of the forest that can be easily hiked, although rangers report that car theft and armed robberies on the trails are not uncommon. It's best to go in a group. **Let's Go does not recommend hiking these trails alone or after dark.**

VOLCÁN BARVA

From the bus stop in Paso Llano, head up the branch of the road opposite Chago's Bar. This road climbs 4km to the tiny village of Sacramento, where you can refuel at a small bar and restaurant on the left side of the road (look for the Pilsen sign). From Sacramento, it's another 4km uphill to the ranger station and entrance to the park. 1km out of town, the road turns rough and rocky, and it is difficult to find a taxi willing to make this trip. The park entrance and ranger station (☎ 2268 1038 or 2268 1039) are at the end of the road. Open daily 8am-3:30pm. Admission US$10, students ¢1000.

The 8km uphill walk to the ranger station, where the main trail to Volcán Barva begins, takes an exhausting 2-2½hr., but idyllic cow pastures, verdant tree canopies, and stunning views of the valley below, combined with the soothing, crisp air, make the journey up a worthy hike of its own. Photograph the valley below during the climb; the heavily forested summit offers a limited view. From the ranger station, the wide, 2km long main trail will bring you to the summit in about 45min., but bear off to the right onto the 1.8km **Sendero Cacho Venado** to explore a moss-covered cloud forest. Surrounding the trail are thick layers of bromeliads, robles, and huge *Gunnera insignis* plants, nicknamed **sombrillas de pobre** (poor man's umbrella) for their wide, round leaves. These plants (up to 1.5m high) are conspicuous with their bright red, heart-like centers. Cacho Venado will return you to the main trail close to the summit. Keep heading upward until you reach the point where the trail splits. The left fork, **Sendero Copey**, continues for another 2km to the **Laguna Copey**. This trail is particularly muddy and difficult during the rainy season. Head right to reach the the **Laguna Barva** and the volcano's highest point at 2900m above sea level (50m to the lagoon, 200m to the summit). Take the main trail on the way back down. If you still have the energy, follow the 900m turnoff to the **Mirador La Vara Blanca,** a scenic overlook of the area north of the volcano. On clear days (unlikely in the rainy season), you can spy the sea from this lookout. Be warned: the trail to the lookout is largely downhill, so the climb back up is inevitable. Whether you visit the lookout or not, return to the ranger station along the main trail.

The dense evergreen forest around Volcán Barva is a habitat for over 6000 species of plants (roughly half the total in Costa Rica) and 500 species of animals, including jaguars, pumas, ocelots, kinkajous, poison arrow frogs, and the bushmaster, Costa Rica's largest venomous snake. The innocuous white-

CENTRAL VALLEY

tailed deer, the quetzal ("phoenix of the forest"), and the park's three species of monkeys—howler, white-faced, and spider monkeys—are commonly sighted.

From start to finish, the hike from Paso Llano to the summit and back takes about 5½-6hr. at a moderate pace. If you take the 6:30am bus from Heredia, you will have to hike quickly to reach the top, see both lagoons, and descend the volcano to catch the 1pm bus. Since the volcano is 2.9km above sea level, rain and wind should be anticipated. It is not advisable to stray from the trails.

Although camping is prohibited elsewhere, it's allowed at the ranger station at Volcán Barva. Ask the ranger where to go and tell him when you leave. They have space for 10 tents (bring your own), potable water, and toilets, although campers should bring drinking water in March and April (US$2 per person).

CARTAGO

Cartago had its time in the limelight when it served as the nation's capital from 1563 until 1823, before the seat of power shifted to San José, 22km northwest. Its size, power, and remarkable colonial architecture have since suffered from earthquakes and volcanic eruptions, reducing the once-busy urban center to a quiet satellite of San José. Most *ticos* will tell you that it is better to pass through Cartago than to stay there, as Cartago's most famous sights—La Basílica de Nuestra Señora (The Basilica of Our Lady), Las Ruinas de la Parroquia (The Parochial Ruins), and the nearby Lankester Botanical Gardens—are easily visited on daytrips from San José or Orosí.

Cartago is not a real tourist destination these days and there is a resulting dearth of accommodations and restaurants. Use the city as a base for excursions to Volcán Irazu and Parque Nacional Tapantí, but don't plan a long stay.

TRANSPORTATION

Bus departure points are scattered around town. There are no printed schedules, but bus and taxi drivers are a good source of information for departure times and locations. Buses from Av. 1/3, C. 6, depart to: Orosi (40min.; every 30min. 7am-2pm, every 15min. 2-7pm; ¢360); from Av. 3/5, C. 6, to Paraíso for Lankester Botanical Gardens (15min., every 10min. 7am-7pm, ¢155); from Av. 6, C. 2/4, in front of the police station, to San José (☎2591 4145; 40min., every hr. daily 9:20am-10:30pm, ¢385); from Av. 6/8, C. 4, to Tierra Blanca (30min., every hr. daily 7am-7pm, ¢290); from Av. 3, C. 8/10, to Turrialba (1hr., every hr. daily 9:20am-10:30pm, ¢620). To get to Volcán Irazú, see p. 133. **Taxis** on the west side of the *parque* on Av. 1/2, C. 1.

ORIENTATION

Cartago is anchored by Avenida 1 and Calle 1, which form the southern and western edges of the *parque central*. East of the *parque* are Las Ruinas, a cathedral destroyed by an earthquake. Further to the east is La Basílica de Nuestra Señora de los Ángeles, which attracts tourists and believers alike. The *mercado central*, between Av. 4/6 and C. 1/3, is northwest of the *parque central*. Volcán Irazú soars 32km northeast of town and the Jardín Botánico Lankester is about 8km southeast. Though the city is relatively safe, don't wander too far north or west of the *mercado central*, and take taxis whenever possible at night.

PRACTICAL INFORMATION

Banks: 24hr. ATM at **Banco Proamerica** (☎2591 4848; open M-F 9am-6pm, Sa 9am-noon) accepts all cards. Change traveler's checks and cash at **Banco Popular**, Av. 1,

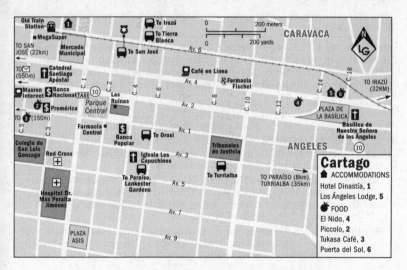

C. 2/4 (☎2591 2525; open M-F 8:15am-3:45pm, Sa 8:15-11:30am, 24hr. ATM available); **Banco Nacional** is open M-F 8:30am-3:45pm, Sa 9am-1pm.

Laundry: Friendly service and cheap prices are available at **Lavandería Fabimar,** Av. 2, C. 11 (☎2591 5357). Wash and dry ¢900 per kg. Open M-F 9am-noon and 1:30-6pm, Sa 8:30am-1pm. US$/¢ only.

Emergency: ☎911.

Police: Av. 6, C. 2/4 (☎2551 2858), in the yellow building.

Red Cross: Av. 5, C. 1/3 (☎2551 0421).

Hospitals: Hospital Dr. Max Peralta Jiménez, Av. 9, C. 1/3 (☎2055 1999).

Pharmacy: Farmacia Fischel, Av. 4, C. 8 (☎2552 1879). Has the best hours out of the city's pharmacies; open daily 8am-11pm. AmEx/DC/MC/V.

Internet access: Fast computers available at **Maxron Internet,** Av. 1/2, C. 5. ¢300 per hr. Open M-F 7:30am-9pm, Sa 9am-9pm, Su 9am-9pm. **Café en Linea** (☎2591 5371) offers Internet access (¢350 per hr.) and international calls (¢50 per min. to the US).

Post Office: The **Post Office,** Av. 2, C. 15/17 (☎2552 4595). Open M-F 7:30am-5:30pm, Sa 7:30am-noon. **Postal Code:** 7050.

ACCOMMODATIONS

San José and Orosi are better places to stay, though Cartago does have one satisfactory budget option and another, more comfortable B&B.

Los Ángeles Lodge, Av. 4, C. 14/16 (☎2551 0957), overlooking the Basílica. Rooms have private baths, and the sunny sitting area is great for watching TV or admiring the Basílica. Breakfast included, 7:30-9am. Parking ¢2000. Singles US$25-30; doubles US$40-50; triples US$60-80; quads US$80-100; quints US$100. MC/V. ❸

Hotel Dinastía, Av. 6/8, C. 3 (☎2551 7057 or 2838 7618), just north of the *mercado central.* Has 22 simple rooms with hot-water baths, TVs, and fans. Comfy sitting area with TV and sofas. Reception and guard 24hr. Singles and doubles ¢6500, with bath ¢8000; triples and quads ¢10,500/12,500. US$/¢ only. ❶

FOOD

MegaSuper, Av. 4, C. 3, has a cafeteria, a bakery, and a wide selection of snacks and essentials. (☎2551 1005. Open M-Sa 8am-9pm, Su 7am-8pm.) Other than the tiny *sodas* that come and go around here, there are mostly fast food joints and a few Chinese restaurants. Check out these cafes and restaurants instead.

> **La Puerta del Sol** (☎2551 0615), across the street from the Basílica. Offers a variety of sandwiches (¢1050-2150) and *casados* (¢2500-2700) in a large wooden dining room. Specializes in *tougue* dishes (¢4450). Open daily 8:30am-1am. AmEx/MC/V. ❷

> **El Nido,** Av. 4, C. 12/14 (☎2551 6957). A bright, little cafe and bakery that serves panini-style sandwiches (¢900) and freshly ground coffee (¢490). Open daily 6am-7pm. ¢ and small denominations of US$ accepted. ❶

> **Tukasa Café,** Av. 1, C. 7/9 (☎2552 1005). Serves a variety of international selections, including crepes (¢2000), salads (¢1400-2250), hamburgers and hot dogs (¢950-2250), and *comida típica* in an airy setting with some outdoor seating. Open M-Sa 11am-8:45pm, Su 2-8pm. AmEx/MC/V/US$/¢. ❶

> **Piccolo,** Av. 1, C. 3/5. A classy European-style cafe serving gourmet sandwiches, such as the Romano and *Canadiense de pavo* (¢2000-2500). Try the oreo milkshake (¢1550) or one of their fruit drinks. Salads ¢1500-2100. Open M-Sa 11am-8pm. MC/V. ❷

📷 SIGHTS

LA BASÍLICA DE NUESTRA SEÑORA DE LOS ÁNGELES. Costa Rica's most famous place of worship stands at the eastern edge of town. Thousands of *ticos* make an annual pilgrimage to this awe-inspiring cathedral on August 2 for *El Día de la Virgen* to worship the statue of **La Negrita,** an image of the Virgin said to have healing powers. La Negrita was declared the patron saint of Cartago in 1824, about 100 years before an earthquake destroyed the original Basílica. Construction on the Byzantine-style church visited today began in 1912.

The interior of the church is decorated with stunning stained-glass windows, intricately carved pillars, and an impressive golden altar. Back outside, walk around to the east side of the church to see the trove of offerings left for the Virgin over the years. Glass cases line the walls, displaying miniature metal body parts offered to the Virgin for the blessings that her supplicants believe cured their maladies. A shelf at the front of the room is filled with medals, miniature house models, and even graded school exams, testament to *ticos'* widespread faith in La Negrita's powers. From this room, two sets of stairs lead down to the **Cripta de la Piedra** (Crypt of the Stone), which contains the boulder where La Negrita is said to have been first sighted. *(Open daily 5:30am-8pm. Free.)*

LAS RUINAS DE LA PARROQUIA. The crumbling walls are the remains of Cartago's first parochial church. Built in 1575 and dedicated to Apostle Santiago of Spain, it stood intact until 1841, when an earthquake almost completely destroyed the structure. The cathedral was reconstructed, only to be damaged by another tremor in 1910. Today, the roofless walls enclose a pleasant garden. The lawn surrounding the ruins and the *parque central* make perfect spots for an afternoon nap. *(On Av. 1/2, C. 2/4 on the east side of the parque central.)*

📷 DAYTRIPS FROM CARTAGO

JARDÍN BOTÁNICO LANKESTER. Located 6km southeast of Cartago near the small town of Paraíso, these lush tropical gardens display the entire range of Costa Rican plant life. Several self-guided trails wind through the garden's 10 hectares of tropical premontane forest, nourishing a stunning range of flora and fauna, including heliconias, gingers, banana plants, cacti, ferns, and trees, among which flutter over 100 species of birds. The well-maintained trails are lined with informational signs, making the trip enjoyable for nature lovers as well as casual hikers. The less botanically minded might enjoy the more whimsical aspects, like the waterfalls, fish ponds with koi, and bamboo tunnel.

Founded in the 1950s by British naturalist Charles H. Lankester, the garden is now operated by the University of Costa Rica and is known best for its famed collection of orchids, the most glamorous members of the epiphyte family. The best time to see the 800 species of orchids bloom is between February and May. Brochures are available in English, Spanish, German, French, and Italian. The garden also runs field courses in tropical biology and accepts **volunteers.** *(From Cartago, take a Paraíso bus from Av. 5/7, C. 6 (15min., every 10min. 5am-10pm, ¢155) and ask the driver to let you off at Jardín Lankester. It is the stop just after the Mall Paraíso. Buses between Orosi and Cartago also stop here. Follow the road at the bus stop that forks off the main road; it's a 15min. walk. ☎ 2552 3247; fax 2552 3151. Open daily 8:30am-4:30pm. US$5, students US$3.50, under 3 free. All credit cards and traveler's checks accepted.)*

VOLCÁN IRAZÚ. With an elevation of 3432m, Volcán Irazú is Costa Rica's tallest active volcano. The name commemorates an indigenous village called Iztarú that once perched daringly on these slopes. Appropriately enough, the village name means "mountain of quakes and thunder." It first erupted in 1723 and has recorded 15 eruptions since, most recently on December 8, 1994. Its most famous eruption occurred on March 9, 1963, the day John F. Kennedy arrived in Costa Rica for an official visit. The blast severely damaged the agriculture in the Central Valley, destroyed some 300 homes, and transformed parts of the surrounding forest into a gray, dusty wasteland still visible today. Though sulfurous *fumaroles* continue to roll off a few of the volcano's five craters, Irazú is relatively inactive and is one of the few volcanoes that can be observed up close. If you're lucky—mornings in the dry season are best—you can see the Atlantic Ocean, Pacific Ocean, and Lago de Nicaragua from the summit. For the best view, walk up the hill from the small cafe and turn right onto the path upward toward the large radio tower. To see the craters, follow the cement path that begins in the parking lot next to the cafe.

The expansive **Cráter Playa Hermosa,** more a sandy field of volcanic ash than a true crater, is the first crater on the left. To the right is the **Cráter Diego de la Haya** (690m wide, 100m deep), named after the mayor of Cartago who recorded the volcano's first eruption. Straight ahead is the **Cráter Principál** (1050m wide, 300m deep), the only active crater, which boasts an enormous cauldron. The Principal Crater cradles a sulfurous iguana-green lake; the color comes from chemicals produced by volcanic gases emitted into the water.

Be sure to bring rain gear and a few extra layers of warm clothes, since temperatures range from a high of 17°C to a bone-chilling low of -3°C, and rainfall averages almost 2200mm annually. A small cafeteria, next to the main parking lot and the entrance to the craters, serves snacks, hot drinks, and souvenirs. There is no camping or lodging at the volcano. *(The best time to see Volcán Irazú is on weekends; getting there during the week is difficult without private transportation. A bus leaves San José from Av. 2, C. 1/3, across the street from the Gran Hotel Costa Rica. (2hr.; Sa-Su 8am, return 12:30pm; round-trip ¢3000.) It stops in Cartago, Av. 6/8, C. 4 (8:30-9am, round-trip ¢2000). During the week, it is easiest to arrange tours through the Orosi Tourist Info and Adventure Center (☎ 2553 1113). Take the 7am bus from Cartago to Orosi (40min.). The Orosi tour leaves at 8am and includes a visit to La Casa del Soñador, Ujarrás ruins, and a waterfall. Tours must be reserved* *by 4pm the day before (US$20, plus US$10 volcano entrance fee; 3-person min.). Park open daily 8am-3:30pm. US$10. A longer tour is also available from OTIAC that stops at other local sights.)*

OROSI

Regrettably overlooked by most travelers scurrying away to the more touristed coasts, small and welcoming with its authentic village life and natural beauty, Orosi has a great deal to offer travelers. While the peaceful streets, amiable residents, and comfortable lodgings in the town of Orosi certainly deserve a visit, the true gems here are the nearby nature reserves, waterfalls, hot springs, and rivers. Orosi's seclusion, tucked away among the coffee plantations of the Central Valley, make it well worth the trip from San José.

TRANSPORTATION

Buses to Orosi leave Cartago from Av. 1/3, C. 6 (40min.; about every 30min. M-Sa 5:30am-10pm, Su 7am-10pm; ¢360), and return to Cartago from the northeast corner of the soccer field on the main road (40min.; every 30min. M-Sa 4:45am-9:10pm, Su 5:45am-9:10pm; ¢360). **Taxis** also leave from the northeast corner of the soccer field (☎2379 3993).

ORIENTATION AND PRACTICAL INFORMATION

Despite the lack of street names, Orosi is easily navigable if you keep in mind a few landmarks and directions. **Buses** and **taxis** arrive on the main drag, which runs from north to south through town, turning east as they leave town to the south; you'll be traveling south along this road past the soccer field when you arrive from Cartago. La Iglesia de San José Orosi is on the west side of the field. Parque Nacional Tapantí is about 12km east of town on the main road.

Tourist Office: The **Orosi Tourist Info and Adventure Center** (☎2533 1113), 300m south of the southwest corner of the soccer field, offers tourist information, as well as the only mailbox in Orosi.

Tours: Many accommodations in town arrange horseback riding and tours to Parque Nacional Tapantí, Volcán Irazú, and Casa del Soñandor. Rent bikes at **Moto Tours and Rental** (☎2533 1564; www.costaricamoto.com), 100m east and 600m south, for US$1.50 per hr. Motorcycles also available.

Currency Exchange: Groceries, phone cards, fax, and photocopy service are available at **Super Anita #2,** 250m south of the southeast corner of the soccer field, where they may change US$ if you purchase something. Open M-Sa 7:30am-8pm, Su 7:30am-5pm. MC/V. Orosi's **Banco Nacional,** where you can change money and traveler's checks, is located next to Super Anita #2. Open M-F 8:30am-3:45pm. Some MC/V debit cards work in the ATM outside.

 CASH MONEY. In smaller towns such as Orosi, hold on to your smaller bills and change. Many local *sodas* and convenience stores will have trouble changing large-demonination *colónes* notes.

Police: The **police station** (☎2533 3082), is directly north of the soccer field. Open daily 6:30am-noon.

Emergency: In emergencies, call the **Red Cross** (☎2551 0421), in Paraiso.

Pharmacy: Farmacia Tabor (☎2533 3395), 150m east of the southeast corner of the soccer field, also sells phone cards. Open M-Sa 8am-noon and 2-8pm, Su 8am-noon. AmEx/MC/V/US$/¢.

Medical Services: The **medical clinic** (☎2533 3052) is right next door to the police station. Open M-Th 7am-4pm, F 7am-3pm.

Internet access: Available at **PC Orosi,** 200m south of the southwest corner of the soccer field (¢200 per 30min., ¢300 per hr.). Open daily 9am-8:30pm.

◤ ACCOMMODATIONS

▣ **Montaña Linda** (☎2533 3640; www.montanalinda.com), 200m south and 200m west of the southwest corner of the soccer field. A patchwork of tin and bamboo roofs and open-air sitting areas provide many opportunities to encounter wildlife. Guests love the shared hot-water bathrooms and kitchen with unlimited coffee (US$1). Book Spanish classes to get meals and a room included. Laundry US$4. Dorms US$7.50; singles US$12.50; doubles US$20; camping US$3 per person, with tent US$4. US$/¢. ❶

Montaña Linda Guest House (☎2533 3640; www.montanalinda.com), up the street from Montaña Linda. If you seek private baths and killer mountainside views, try the Montaña Linda guest house. Laundry US$4. Guesthouse rooms US$30. US$/¢. ❷

Orosi Lodge (☎2533 3578; www.orosilodge.com), 400m south and 100m west of the southwest corner of the soccer field. Modern rooms have fridges, coffee makers, fans, and private hot-water baths. Private balconies look out on nearby volcanoes and the hotel's interior jungle garden. The attached cafe has a small selection of pastries and snacks. Internet access available. Reception and cafe available 7am-7pm, breakfast US$5. High season doubles US$54, low season US$45; triples US$63/55; private chalet US$85/70. Tax not included in prices listed. AmEx/MC/V. ❸

Hotel Reventazon (☎2533 3838; www.hotelreventazon.com), 300m south and 25m west of the southeast corner of the soccer field. This small hotel is owned and operated by a friendly Floridian couple. Rooms include sparkling tile floors and private hot-water baths. Free Wi-Fi. 24hr. reception. Laundry ¢4000. Breakfast included at adjoining restaurant. Singles and doubles US$35-45. AmEx/MC/V/US$/¢. ❸

Cabinas Sueños de Oro (☎2533 3476 or 8822 6830 or 302 9511), 200m south of the southeast corner of the soccer field. Despite its less-than-appealing location above a butcher shop, Cabinas Sueños de Oro offers pleasant accommodations and several amenities at an affordable price. Each of the spacious rooms, with lacy curtains and hardwood floors, is equipped with a kitchenette, private hot-water bath, and cable TV. Relax on the second-floor patio. Singles, doubles, and triples US$35 per person. ❸

◖ FOOD

Bar Restaurante Coto (☎2533 3032), at the northeast corner of the soccer field, serves up heaping portions of *comida típica* on its palm-filled terrace with hanging wicker lamps. Satisfy your hunger with the mixed meat plate (¢4500), although more affordable options like sandwiches (¢1000), soups, and salads (¢1500) are also tasty. Beer ¢800-1300. Mixed drinks ¢1500. Open daily 8am-11pm. AmEx/MC/V/US$/¢. ❷

Bar Anita (☎2533 3846), a 20min. walk down the main road, across from the F.J. Orlich coffee factory (taxi ¢1000). A popular weekend trip for cheap, tasty seafood. *Ceviche* and fish dinners ¢1000-2000. *Bocas* ¢700. Some prices vary based on the market. Open M-Th 10am-9pm, F-Sa 10am-10:30pm, Su 10am-8pm. MC/V/US$/¢. ❶

Hotel Reventazón Bar and Restaurant (☎2533 3838), 300m south and 25m west of the southeast corner of the soccer field. Though the menu and prices cater to tourists, the bamboo roof and hand-painted wooden menus provide rustic charm. Bring your laptop and take advantage of the free Wi-Fi. For dessert, try the huge, fluffy crepes with ice cream and chocolate sauce (¢1585). Salads (¢1700-2260), hamburgers and sandwiches (¢960-1600), as well as beef, chicken, and fish entrees (¢2900-4900). Open M-F 10am-11:30pm, Sa-Su 8am-9:30pm; bar open later. AmEx/MC/V/US$/¢. ❷

Soda Luz, 100m north of the northwest corner of the soccer field. Serves generous portions of *comida típica* in a cheery setting with bright blue-and-white table cloths. *Gallo pinto* ¢1000. Hamburger ¢800. Open M-F 7am-4pm, F-Su 7am-9pm. ❶

Rancho San José Cabecar (☎2533 2411), 200m south of the southeast corner of the soccer field. Cowboy-themed meal, that finish on a sophisticated note with a fruit or vegetable drink (¢350). *Casados* ¢2000. Sandwiches ¢850-1200. US$/¢. ❶

👁 SIGHTS

LA IGLESIA DE SAN JOSÉ OROSI. Built in 1743, this church is not only remarkable because of its status as one of the country's oldest operational churches, but also because of its architectural fortitude—it has survived earthquakes that wiped out entire nearby villages. The church is reputed to be Costa Rica's only east-facing church. The worn, whitewashed walls, red terra-cotta tiled roof, and ornately carved wooden altar display its colonial roots and make Sunday mass (7, 9:30am, 6pm) a memorable experience. Adjoining the church, the Museo Franciscano houses a collection of Christian relics dating back to 1560, including religious paintings, several friars' robes, and wooden replicas of Christ. *(West of the soccer field. Open Tu-F 1-5pm, Sa-Su 9am-5pm. ¢3350, children ¢200.)*

BALNEARIO TERMAL OROSI. The more accessible of Orosi's two hot mineral baths, this facility has a lap pool, two small pools, and a kiddie pool all at 35°C (95°F), a drastic drop from the 60°C (140°F) water at the source. Basic showers and a restaurant are available. Have a piña colada (¢1750) at the bar. *(☎2533 2156. 300m south and 100m west of the southwest corner of the soccer field, next to Orosi Lodge. Open daily 7:30am-4pm, additional evening hours Th-F 6-10pm. US$3. US$/¢. Breakfast ¢1300-2200. Sandwiches ¢700-1400. Casados ¢2200-2300. Restaurant also accepts MC/V.)*

BALNEARIO DE AGUAS TERMALES LOS PATIOS. Slightly farther away and more scenic than Balneario Termal Orosi, Los Patios has six warm pools (41°C) and two cold pools in a country-club atmosphere, above the Orosi Valley. *(☎2553 3009. 1km south out of town along the main road. Open Tu-Su 8am-4pm. ¢1300.)*

LA CASA DEL SOÑADOR. This old-fashioned, intricately designed "Dreamer's House" is the masterpiece of late Costa Rican sculptor Macedonio Quesada, who built the bamboo and wooden *casita* in 1989. Now maintained by Quesada's sons Hermes and Miguel, as well as the handful of assistants who seem to be constantly working away downstairs carving figurines out of coffeewood (from US$9), the house is filled with nativity scenes and *campesino* figures displaying a mix of Latin-American, indigenous, and East-Asian influences. Everything in the house, from the doors to the window shutters, is carefully chiseled from sticks of bamboo. *(11km from Orosi on the road to the town of Cachí. From Orosi, cross the foot bridge over the river just east of town. Turn left and follow the main road. La Casa del Soñador is about 8km along on the right, just past the town of Cachi. A taxi from Orosi (☎2379 3993), with a visit to the nearby Ruinas de Ujarrás, ¢8500 round-trip.)*

DAM IT. To gain an understanding of how Costa Rica hopes to achieve carbon neutrality by developing renewable sources of energy, stop at **La Represa de Cachí,** a massive hydroelectric dam at the northeast end of the lake that separates Cachí from Orosi. Take a bus from Orosi to Paraíso (¢155), then get on a bus to Cachí (¢140). Or visit the dam in between visits to Las Ruinas de Ujarrás and La Casa del Soñador.

NIGHTLIFE AND ENTERTAINMENT

Orosi isn't exactly a hopping hub of nightlife, although it offers a few solid options for a fun night on the town.

Bar Restaurante El Nido (☎2533 3793), 200m north of the northeast corner of the soccer field. A favorite among locals. El Nido provides the best in bar basics—simple decor with plastic tables and chairs, but ample space for socializing and a variety of music. Beer ¢700. Mixed drinks ¢1500. Open daily 11am-2am.

Bar Zepelin, 200m east of the southeast corner of the soccer field. Also popular among locals. Zepelin features a small dancing platform complete with strobe light for the younger set to show off their moves after a few drinks. TVs broadcast music videos from the 60s to the present; ask to see the list and you can make a request. Beer ¢600. *Bocas* ¢700-900. Meat and rice dishes ¢1100-1500. Open weeknights 11am-11:30pm, weekends 11am-2am.

Orosi Tourist Info and Adventure Center (☎2533 1113), 300m south of the southwest corner of the soccer field. Offers an alternative to the bar scene in Orosi. Recently opened to serve as a cultural exchange for locals and visitors, the center offers Spanish school classrooms, a kitchen, pool tables, and TV, as well as poetry nights and concerts. An attached restaurant serves breakfast and lunch.

GUIDED TOURS

Orosi hotels work with local tour and outdoor adventure companies to arrange trips to local attractions. **Montaña Linda** (p. 135) offers whitewater rafting and guided tours of Orosi Valley, Volcán Irazú, and Monumento Nacional Guayabo. (Rafting US$65. Orosi US$5. Irazú US$20, not including park fee; 3-person min. Monumento Nacional Guayabo US$40, including park fee; 2-person min.) **Montaña Linda** offers directions, as well as other hiking directions to a swimming hole, natural hot springs, waterfall, scenic walks, and awesome panoramic views of the Orosi and Cachí Valley; check out the 3-4hr. "Yellow Church Walk." The **Orosi Lodge** (p. 135) arranges combined tours of Volcán Irazú, Mirador Orosi, and La Basílica de Nuestra Señora de los Ángeles (US$60); Parque Nacional Tapantí (US$45); Orosi Valley, a sugar cane mill, La Casa del Soñador, and the Lankester Botanical Gardens (US$40).

DAYTRIP FROM OROSI

PARQUE NACIONAL TAPANTÍ

The lengthy 12km hike from Orosi to Parque Nacional Tapantí passes by rolling coffee plantations. Head south along the main road from Orosi; the first half of the hike is fairly flat, but the road gets steeper and rockier near the park. If you're short on time or energy, you can take a cab (1-way ¢6000), and walk back down or arrange for the cab to pick you up. ☎2551 2970. Open daily 7am-5pm. US$10.

Twelve kilometers away from central Orosi, Parque Nacional Tapantí is a 61 sq. km. former wildlife refuge famous for the highest average rainfall (7m per year) in Costa Rica. The resulting 150 rivers and streams criss-cross a pristine rainforest inhabited by an enormous diversity of wildlife: 45 species of mammals, including tapirs, pacas, jaguars, and kinkajous; 260 species of birds; 32 species of reptiles and amphibians, including three types of vipers; and an average of 80-160 species of trees per hectare. The huge amounts of rainfall that Tapantí receives are used to generate hydroelectric power for most of San José's population downstream at **La Represa de Cachí.**

From the park entrance, it is 4km upward on the wide **Camino Principal** to a scenic overlook point. You are unlikely to see much wildlife on the main trail, so veer off left onto the **Arboles Caídos** (2km) trail for the best chance to see animals. **La Pava** trail branches a short way off the Camino Principal and leads to the Río Grande at two separate points. Swimming is not possible at either point, and the waterfall seen from the Catarata branch is also visible from the summit of the Camino Principal, so skip La Pava unless you have plenty of time. Before leaving the park, cool off by following the **Oropéndola** trail to the river and taking a dip. Although camping is not permitted, the park offers very basic rooms in a 15-person capacity cabin. The communal showers have lukewarm water. Bring a sleeping bag and food to cook in the kitchen. (¢1500 per person. Call ☎2551 2970 in advance to secure a bed.) Spanish- and English-language maps are available at the ranger station. Insect repellent is necessary, since the mosquitoes at the park are ravenous, particularly by the river.

TURRIALBA

Those who visit Turrialba love its down-to-earth feel and its location amid world-class rivers and stunning mountains. Nearby Ríos Reventazón and Pacuare have brought the town international fame; both are packed with Class III-V rapids and some of the world's best river runs. Whitewater rafters and kayakers of all abilities ride the waters during the rainy season; other travelers stay here on their way to Costa Rica's most significant archaeological site, Monumento Nacional Guayabo. But those uninterested in adventure tours should also consider paying Turrialba a visit; it retains a small-town feel while offering the comforts of a city. During the day, locals hang out in the attractive *parque central*, and at night they fill the restaurants and bars singing. Due to Costa Rica's economic development projects, an increasing number of rivers may soon be dammed for hydroelectric power. Adventurers should take advantage of these natural resources while they still can.

▐ TRANSPORTATION

Buses: Turrialba's bus terminal (☎2557 5050), 350m southwest of the *parque central*, on Av. 4. Tickets may be purchased at the terminal window prior to departure. Leave for **San José** (direct 1hr., indirect 2hr.; every hr. 5:15am-9pm; ¢1105) and pass through **Cartago** (1hr., ¢660). Available to **Siquirres** (2hr.; M-Th every hr. 6am-6:15pm, F-Su every hr. 6am-7pm; ¢920); **La Suiza** (30min.; M-F 5:30, 9, 11:20am, 1, 2, 2:30, 3:30, 3:50, 5, 6pm; Sa 9, 11:30am, 1, 2:30, 3:30pm, every hr. 5-10pm, Su 3:50, 4:50pm; ¢220); **Santa Cruz/Parque Nacional Volcán Turrialba** (1hr., ¢320). On weekends and in the high season you might have to buy tickets to San José a day or so in advance to grab a seat. Buses also leave from the terminal for **Monumento Nacional Guayabo**

(1hr.; M-Sa 11:15am, 3:10, 5:30pm; return 5:15, 6:30am, 12:30, 4pm; Su 9am, 3, 6pm, return 6:30am, 12:30, 4pm).

Taxis: (☎2556 7070). Line up at the corner of Av. Central and C. Central. One-way ¢7000; round-trip (includes 1hr. wait) ¢15,000.

ORIENTATION AND PRACTICAL INFORMATION

In Turrialba, 62km east of San José, *calles* run perpendicular to *avenidas*, but none of the streets run exactly north-south or east-west. With the **parque central** as a reference point, most businesses and sights aren't too tough to find.

Tourist Office: There is a tourist office located next to La Feria, but it has variable hours. Patricia or Luis at **Hotel Interamericano** (below) are also able to provide information about the town and nearby sights in English.

Banks: All banks listed have **24hr. ATMs. Banco de Costa Rica** (☎2556 0472), 2 blocks south and 2 blocks east of the park. Open M-F 9am-4pm. **Banco Nacional** (☎2556 1211), a few meters west of Banco de Costa Rica. Open M-F 8:30am-3:45pm. Long lines tend to build up at the tellers. **Banco Popular** (☎2556 6098), on Av. 4, just east of Popo's. Open M-F 8:45am-4:30pm, Sa 8:15-11:30am. **BanCredito** (☎2556 4141), next to Cafe Azul and across the street from Turribasicos. Open M-F 8am-4pm, Sa 8am-

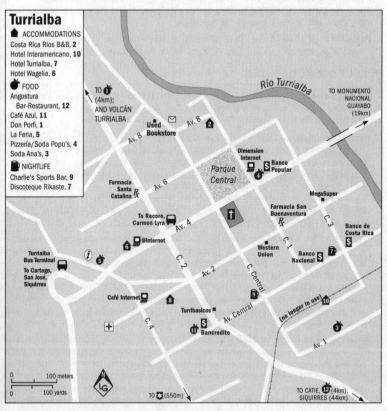

Turrialba

🏠 ACCOMMODATIONS
Costa Rica Ríos B&B, **2**
Hotel Interamericano, **10**
Hotel Turrialba, **7**
Hotel Wagelia, **6**

🍴 FOOD
Angostura
 Bar-Restaurant, **12**
Café Azul, **11**
Don Porfi, **1**
La Feria, **5**
Pizzería/Soda Popo's, **4**
Soda Ana's, **3**

🎵 NIGHTLIFE
Charlie's Sports Bar, **9**
Discoteque Rikaste, **7**

11:30pm. Western Union (☎2556 0439), 100m south and 50m east of the south corner of the *parque,* is inside of Tienda La Moda. Open M-Sa 8am-6:30pm.

Bookstore: (☎2556 1697), diagonally across from the post office, north of the *parque* on C. Central. A wide selection of second-hand books (¢2000-5000) in English, French, German, Portuguese, and Spanish are sold in this too-tiny bookstore. Owner speaks English. Hours are flexible; usually M-F 8:30-11:30am and 2:30-5:30pm.

Emergency: ☎911.

Police: (☎2556 0030 or 8265), 500m south of the town center on C. 4.

Pharmacy: Farmacia Santa Catalina (☎2556 8983), Av. 6 and C. 2. Open M-Sa 8am-8pm, Su 4pm-7pm. MC/V. **Farmacia San Buenaventura** (☎2556 0379), Av. 2 and C. 1, one block west of the *parque* on Av. 6. Open M-Sa 8am-7:30pm, Su 8:30am-1pm. AmEx/MC/V.

Hospital: (☎2558 1311). Walk up the stairs at the west end of Av. 2, or drive west on Av. 4 past the bus station and turn left into the hospital. Open 24hr.

Internet:

Eca Internet, across C. 1 from the *parque,* upstairs past Mama Mía's. Internet ¢300 per hr. Skype and webcams are available. Open M-F 8:30am-10pm, Sa-Su 9am-9pm.

@Internet (☎2556 2857), just east of Hotel Wagelia on Av. 4. Internet ¢300 per hr. Black-and-white copying ¢20. Printing ¢100-600. Open M-F 8am-10pm, Sa-Su 9am-9pm.

Cafe Internet (☎2256 4575), Av. 2 and C. 4. Modern computers, A/C. Internet ¢300 per hr.

Phone Cards: Available at **Pague aquí su Luz y Teléfono,** across the street from BanCredito. Open M-F 7:30am-5:30pm, Sa 8am-5pm.

Post Office: (☎2556 1679), 200m northwest of the north corner of the *parque,* across from the bookstore. Open M-F 8am-5:30pm. MC/V. **Postal Code:** 7150.

▊ ACCOMMODATIONS

Turrialba has a few traditional hostels, but a few budget hotels are available for comparable prices. Although most of Turrialba's hotels are pricier, they may offer a nice place to rest and will arrange trips to nearby sights.

▨ **Hotel Interamericano** (☎2556 0142; www.hotelinteramericano.com), bright coral-and-orange building 3 blocks south and 1 block east of the *parque,* just behind the row of palm trees. The owners speak English and have a wealth of info about sights, guides, and restaurants. Amenities include hot-water showers, Wi-Fi (best near the balcony), and a large sitting area with cable TV. Breakfast and laundry service (wash ¢1500 per kg, dry ¢1000 per load) available. Towels are included, but bring your own for rafting. Reception 24hr. Singles ¢6380, with bath ¢14,500; doubles ¢12,800/20,300; triples ¢19,100/31,900; quads ¢25,500/37,700. V. Traveler's checks accepted. ❶

▨ **Costa Rica Ríos Bed and Breakfast** (☎2256 6651; www.hotelturrialba.com). Renovated in a Spanish colonial style, Costa Rica Ríos primarily houses those on the week-long adventure tour (p. 143), but all are welcome. Named after surrounding rivers, the 10 airy rooms come with private hot-water baths, parking, free international calls, free self-service laundry, full breakfast, and Wi-Fi. Dinner can be requested for ¢8700. A few hang-out areas include a living room with board games, hot-tub, pool table, computer with internet, and mini-library. The rooftop deck has an amazing view of Volcán Turrialba. Reception 8am-6pm. Singles¢20,300; doubles ¢31,900; triples ¢43,500. AmEx/MC/V. ❸

Volcán Turrialba Lodge (☎2273 4335 or 0194; www.volcanturrialbalodge.com), about 1hr. from Turrialba and only a few km from the volcano's summit. Incredible views of the volcano and the valley from any of their lovely, cabin-style rooms. Perfect for those more interested in the outdoors than the town. Take advantage of the horseback, birdwatching, and hiking tours (p. 143). Common room with TV and comfortable couches. Electric heaters provided. One meal included. Homey singles, doubles, and triples, as well as a 4-bedroom cabin. ¢26,100 per person per night for any room combination. Busiest June-Oct.; reserve in advance. AmEx/MC/V. ❸

Hotel Wagelia (☎2556 1596; www.hotelwageliaturrialbacom), 1 block south of park, 1½ blocks west on Av. 2. 18 comfortable rooms surrounding a mini-garden and a bright outdoor common area. All rooms come with private hot-water baths with soap dispensers, A/C, and cable TV. A phone and safe deposit box are available. The attached restaurant-bar serves moderately priced entrees. Breakfast included. Laundry and tour service available. Wi-Fi. Check-in 2pm. Check-out noon. Singles ¢31,900; doubles ¢45,200; triples ¢48,700. AmEx/MC/V. Traveler's checks accepted. ❹

Hotel Turrialba (☎2556 6654), 100m south and 150m west of the *parque*. Murals decorate the hallways. All the rooms are simple, with wood-paneled walls, clean private hot-water baths, TVs, and ceiling and floor fans. Some rooms lack windows. Reception 24hr. Can place international calls. A/C ¢3000. Singles ¢7500; doubles ¢12,000; triples ¢15,000. AmEx/MC/V. ❷

▸ FOOD

Dining options are limited to pizza, *comida típica*, and a few less-than-authentic Chinese restaurants. For fresh produce, check out the **farmer's market** along Av. Central. (Open every F and Sa.) The local **MegaSuper** (☎2556 1242) is 100m south and 100m east of the west corner of the *parque*. (Open M-Sa 7am-9pm, Su 7am-7pm. AmEx/D/MC/V.) **Turribasicos**, on C. 2, near the corner of Av. Central/C. 2, has a pharmacy and bakery inside. (☎2556 0933. Open M-Sa 7am-9pm, Su 8am-4pm.)

▨ **Restaurante Don Porfi** (☎2556 9797), 4km outside of town on the road to Volcán Turrialba. Well worth the ¢2000 cab ride. Up the hill from Turrialba, Don Porfi is popular with locals but generally unknown to tourists. Excellent dishes include mixed seafood platters (¢3850-7000), beef tenderloin (7 varieties; ¢6200-6900), and chicken in garlic sauce (¢3600). The *batidos* are large and the service is highly professional. Try the house dessert, a fried banana crepe with ice cream (¢2000). Open M-Sa 11am-11pm, Su 11am-8pm. Reservations recommended during the high-season, especially on weekends. D/MC/V. ❸

▨ **La Feria** (☎2557 5550), 200m west of the south corner of the *parque* past Hotel Wagelia, at intersection of Av. 2 and C. 4. Run by a superb chef in a charming setting—local artists' work decorates the walls along with maps of Costa Rica and Turrialba, and soothing jazz plays in the background. Ancient Costa Rican artifacts are on display as well. Affordable gourmet fare includes filet mignon (¢5150), *casados* (¢1700), club sandwiches (¢2250), Fish La Feria (¢4850) and a wide variety of fruit drinks (¢575) and milkshakes (¢750). Plenty of veggie options, like the fantastic cream of tomato soup with toast (¢1900). Open M and W-Su 11:30am-9:30pm, Tu 11:30am-2:30pm. AmEx/MC/V. ❶

▨ **Soda Ana** (☎2557 2397), behind Hotel Interamericano on Av. 1. Though this soda has only a few tables and a very short menu, you most likely will not find a better *casado* (¢2000) in town. Rice and beans (¢2000) served F-Su. Ask one of Ana's sons to pull out their guitar from behind the counter and serenade you with classic Latin tunes. Open daily 6am-10pm. Cash only. ❶

Angostura Bar-Restaurant (☎2556 5757), 4km outside of town in the opposite direction of Don Porfi. Though not as elegant or well-established as Don Porfi, this restaurant with similar prices does dish out some nice plates. Bottles of wine ready at each table. Filet mignon (¢3800) or chicken in a cream mushroom sauce (¢4000). It can get cool in the open-air seating during the rainy season so consider bringing a light jacket. Taxi to the restaurant ¢2500-3000. Open M and W-Sa 11am-10pm. Su 11am-9pm. MC/V. ❹

Pizzería/Soda Popo's (☎2556 0064), on the east side of the *parque*. Known for its simple fare. If rafting has left you too tired to walk, you can order delivery until 11pm. Pizzas ¢2800-4000, ¢700 per slice. You may have to wait approximately 20min. for a small pizza. Burritos topped with ketchup, mustard, and mayo ¢600-850. Open daily 7am-11pm. V. ❶

NIGHTLIFE AND ENTERTAINMENT

Discoteque Rikaste (☎2556 8081), Av. Central, C. 1/3, beside Banco Nacional, 2nd floor. Dance the night away with locals and tourists on Sa. Cover depends on time and size of crowd, but may be up to ¢1500. *Ticos* come to sit in the outside area and drink beer with friends during the day. *Cervezas* ¢600. Sandwiches ¢1000-1500. *Platos fuertes* ¢1700-3000. Restaurant/bar open M-F and Su 11am-12:30am, Sa 11am-2:30am. AmEx/D/MC/V.

Charlie's Sports Bar (☎2557 6565), Av. Central, C. Central, at the back of the complex. Modern neon lighting, loud Latin music, and TVs make this new sports bar the perfect place to catch a *fútbol* game. Buffalo wings ¢3700-5900. Hamburgers and sandwiches ¢2150-4490. Mixed drinks ¢2000. Shots ¢1500. Th Ladies' night. Open M-W and Su 4pm-midnight, Th-Sa 4pm-late.

Pocho's, on the main road in La Suiza. A bus goes to La Suiza every hr. until 10pm (30min., ¢205), but you'll have to take a taxi back if you're staying out later. This popular local bar draws *ticos* and tourists alike. The energetic owner entertains customers by juggling beer bottles and a machete. Look for signs in Turrialba that advertise periodic Sa night disco parties with Costa Rica's most popular DJs. Beer ¢700. Open daily 11am-late.

> **TIP**
> **TAKE COVER!** During the rainy season, the lack of tourists means that those who brave the daily afternoon showers can often get into bars and clubs without paying a cover.

OUTDOOR ACTIVITIES AND GUIDED TOURS

Capitalizing on Turrialba's legendary rafting and kayaking opportunities, tour operators offer adventure trips for all abilities. A day on the rapids is expensive, but the experience is unforgettable, especially on the Pacuare, the most popular and beautiful of the area's rivers. If you have your own equipment or rent from one of the tour companies, your hotel should be able to arrange transportation to a nearby river. Ask about the nearby serpent farm (**Serpentario Viborana;** 10km away; ☎2538 1510), Volcán Turrialba, and the Aquiares waterfall.

Ríos Locos (☎2556 6035; www.whiteh20.com). Not one of Turrialba's largest companies, but it is one of the friendliest. 12 years of experience. These self-proclaimed Río Pacuare specialists offer rafting trips, horseback rides, and boat tours. They prefer small groups but will accommodate groups of up to 36 with advance notice. Class III-IV rafting on the Pacuare, Pejibaye, and Reventazón (half-day ¢29000, full-day ¢49,300). Photographer accompanies raft down river; photos available for negotiated price. Full day horseback tours along a jungle train line near the Peralta River (¢31,900). Can arrange a trip to Monumento Nacional Guayabo (¢23,200). Cash only.

Tico's River Adventures (☎2556 1231; www.ticoriver.com). A small local company that offers friendly service and years of experience. Specializing in rafting trips, Tico arranges day trips to the Pacuare (Class IV), Reventazón (Class II, III, or IV depending on trip), and Pascua (Class IV). Single-day trips ¢43,500 (US$75), include lunch. Special student rate of ¢34,800 (US$60) per person for groups of 10 or more. An all-inclusive 2-day Pacuare trip is also available (¢162,400/US$280 per person, includes hiking). Cash only.

Costa Rica Ríos (☎2556 9617; www.costaricarios.com), 10m north of the *parque*. Considered the most reputable rafting and kayaking operator and owns the largest fleet of water sports equipment in Central America. Offers exclusively pre-booked, all-inclusive, week-long adventure tours. Eight-day adventure (includes rafting, kayaking, canopy tour, and snorkeling) trip from ¢1,043,420 (US$1799); 8-day river-only (rafting and kayaking) trip from ¢927,420 (US$1599). The B&B provides a good place to relax after a week's worth of adventures. AmEx/MC/V.

Volcán Turrialba Lodge (☎2273 4335; www.volcanturrialbalodge.com). Offers a horseback tour to the top of Volcán Turrialba for ¢20,300 (US$35; 4-5hr. includes horse, guide, and snack). 2hr. hiking and birdwatching tours available (¢11,600/US$20). Mountain biking ¢17,400 (US$30). Rates do not include park entrance fees. AmEx/MC/V.

👁 SIGHTS

VOLCÁN TURRIALBA. The scenic road to the summit is steep and winding, and it becomes especially rocky after the town of Santa Cruz. Previously impassable by automobile, the last few kilometers have recently been repaved, so that it is now possible, though not exactly easy, to drive all the way up the volcano. The road, still bumpy and narrow, is most safely tackled in a four-wheel-drive taxi. (From Turrialba 1-2hr.; roundtrip ¢25,000, includes wait time). The Santa Cruz bus stops at the entrance to the park, 18km from the summit, ¢320.) It is best to make the trip early in the morning to avoid mid-day rains and to catch the sun rising over the valley. Bring a sweatshirt and pants, since it is often surprisingly cold at the summit.

Turrialba stands out among Costa Rica's volcanoes. Unfortunately, the path down into the crater is now closed, as the volcano is still active, but you can look down into the crater as the smoke blows away in the opposite direction. It is relatively untouched, and there is no information station or entrance fee. For a guided tour by horseback or on foot, check out **Volcán Turrialba Lodge** (p. 143).

🔲 DAYTRIP FROM TURRIALBA

MONUMENTO NACIONAL GUAYABO

Buses to the entrance leave from the Turrialba bus terminal on Av. 4. 1hr.; M-Sa 11:15am, 2:30, 5:30pm; return 5:30, 6:30, 11:30am, 4pm; Su 9am, 3, 6pm; return 6:30am, 12:30, 4pm). Taxis are available (☎2556 7070); one-way ¢7000; round-trip ¢15,000, includes 1hr. wait. ☎2559 1220. Open daily 8am-3:30pm. US$6, children under 12 US$2.

Located 19km northeast of Turrialba, Monumento Nacional Guayabo is Costa Rica's most important archaeological site and the country's only National Monument. The park covers 218 hectares, although the archaeological site is just 20 hectares, and only four of those 20 have been excavated. Much remains unknown about the civilization that built and abandoned the site, though current estimates suggest that approximately 10,000 people lived here from 1500 BC to AD 1400, with most of the construction occurring after AD 800. Some say that the Guayabo people migrated to Colombia, and, in fact, many indigenous Columbians claim to have ancestors of similar traditions. The mysterious first inhabitants left records of their sophistication: their houses were built on large *montículos* (circular foundations), and they constructed *calzadas* (long causeways), a bridge, and an aqueduct system that still works today. The remnants of these structures, at the end of an easy 1.5km trail through rainforest, are the focal point of the site, though you will pass a monolith, coffin graves, and several intricate petroglyphs on the way. Another 1km trail from the park entrance leads to a rushing stream with potable water. Both trails, especially the shorter one, are very muddy in the rainy season; be sure to bring boots and rain gear. Take a copy of the pamphlet and ask if a guide can give a tour. The ruins are interesting, but there's not much else to see. If you take a bus to the monument, you'll finish the tour long before the next bus departs. There's a campsite (US$4 per person) that has a toilet, a cold-water shower, and BBQ pits.

If you find yourself waiting for the bus, head down the road 500m to the **Guayabo Butterfly Garden** (☎8832 3586; open daily 8am-4pm; US$2). Check out the meshed enclosure filled with colorful butterflies, caterpillars, and cocoons. Also visit the neighboring restaurant **La Calzada Guayobo ❶** (☎2559 0437, open M-Tu, and Th-Su 8am-6pm). It is a bright and cheery place, decorated to seem authentically Costa Rican, with farm implements leaning against the walls and painted wagon wheels hanging from the ceiling. Go for the grilled chicken breast (¢1950) or just have the rice and beans (¢1950).

CENTRAL VALLEY

NORTHERN LOWLANDS

Though it lacks the beachside location of other tourist hot spots, Costa Rica's mountainous northern region is home to a plethora of climates and travel destinations, from mountains and rolling green pasture land to tropical rainforests and lagoons. Visitors to the lowlands will encounter a staggeringly diverse collection of wildlife, and those interested in more extreme adventure will find opportunities for windsurfing, rappelling, spelunking, and white-water rafting. Plus, while areas like Fortuna and Arenal see a huge influx of tourists every year, other parts of the lowlands are surprisingly untouristed, with a rich *campesino* culture mixed city life in towns like Ciudad Quesada and Los Chiles. A gateway to Nicaragua and both the Atlantic and Caribbean coasts, the lowlands contain some of Costa Rica's most well-conserved examples of tropical rainforests, cloud forests, and marshlands. You can hike through the pristine jungles of Tirimbina Reserve or La Selva, drift along the swampy mangroves of Refugio Nacional Caño Negro, watch the lava flow on Volcán Arenal, and climb through the winding, bat-filled tunnels of the Venado Caves. Whether in search of extreme sports or a morning of relaxing sportfishing or birdwatching, visitors to the Northern Lowlands can strike a balance between tourism opportunities and authentic rural culture in an area distinguished for the richness and diversity of its natural wonders.

CIUDAD QUESADA (SAN CARLOS)

Hovering in the sloping green hills of *Cordillera Central*, Ciudad Quesada (a.k.a. San Carlos) marks the fusion of the *campo tico* with everyday small-city life. *Campesinos* stroll along modern, freshly paved streets, and vendors hawk overflowing crates of ripe fruit beside seemingly endless clothing stores. At the center of town is the gorgeous *parque*, filled with lush trees, dotted by pink park benches, and anchored by a large concrete gazebo. Cattle is an integral part of the food and culture here. The agriculture and ranching center of the north, Ciudad Quesada pumps out much of the country's beef and milk. It also serves as a major saddlery center; locals make traditional, detailed leatherwork in the *talabarterías* (leather goods stores) around town. Northwest of San José (110km), Ciudad Quesada is also a transportation hub within the Alajuela province. Travelers connect here to nearby Fortuna and Volcán Arenal (40km), as well as to Los Chiles and Puerto Viejo de Sarapiquí.

⌐ TRANSPORTATION

The city's **bus station** (☎2460 5064), referred to as **Parada Nueva** or **El Terminal,** is northwest of town in the Plaza San Carlos mall center. A shuttle bus leaves every 15min. from the *mercado*, 100m north of the northeast corner of the *parque*, to the terminal (¢180). From the station, catch buses to: **La Fortuna**(1hr., 13 per day 6am-5:30pm, ¢600); **Los Chiles** (3hr., 14 per day 5:30am-7:30pm, ¢1935); **Puerto Viejo de Sarapiquí**(3hr., 8 per day 4:40am-6:30pm, ¢1230); **San José** (3hr., regular service 15 per day 6:05am-7:15pm, direct service express approx. every hr. 6:40am-8pm, ¢1365); **San Miguel** (1hr., 6 per day 4:50am-8pm, ¢650). **Taxis** line up on the north side of the *parque*. **Adobe Rent-A-Car** is 300m north of the northeast corner of the *parque*. (☎2460 0650; fax 2461 0202. Must be 23+ to rent. Open M-Sa 8am-8pm, Su 9am-noon.)

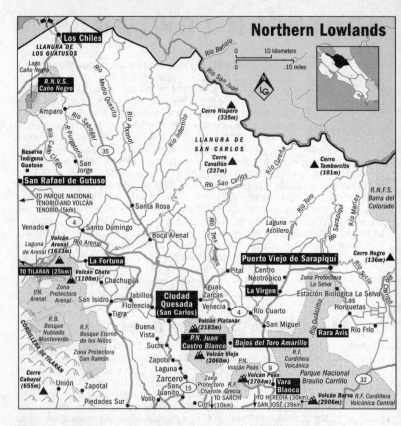

Northern Lowlands

⚡🧭 ORIENTATION AND PRACTICAL INFORMATION

Ciudad Quesada apparently has street names, but it is nearly impossible to find any. Instead, locals go by units of 100m (**cuadras,** approximately one block) up, down, right, and left, radiating out from the four corners of the *parque central.* A cream-colored **cathedral** borders the *parque* to the east. The streets go uphill to the south (*subiendo*) and downhill to the north (*bajando*).

Banks: Banco Nacional (☎2461 2000), 50m east of the *parque's* northeast corner. Exchanges currency and traveler's checks. Open M-F 8:30am-3:45pm. **Banco de Costa Rica** (☎2460 5959), 150m north of the northeast corner of the *parque,* also exchanges currency and traveler's checks. **24hr. ATM.** Bank open Tu-Sa 11am-6pm. **Cocique** (☎2401 1500), behind the cathedral. **24hr. ATM** accepts Cirrus.

Police: (☎2460 0375, emergency 911), 1.5km north of the *parque.*

Red Cross: (☎2460 0101), 200m north and 150m west of the *parque.*

Pharmacy: Farmacia Lizano (☎2460 5001), 200m north of the northeast corner of the *parque.* Open daily 7am-10pm. There are many other pharmacies on the streets radiating out from the *parque.*

Hospital: (☎2460 1176), 2.5km north of the northeast corner of the *parque*. Buses to the Hospital leave from the Mercado regularly during the day (¢200).

Internet Access: Internet Café (☎2460 7454), 100m north and 50m east of the northeast corner of the *parque*. Has the cheapest internet access in town, but the computers are a bit outdated. Internet ¢200 per 30min., ¢350 per hr. Open M-F 9am-7pm, Sa 9am-6pm. Access at **Grupo e-Café** (☎2461 2233), facing the left side of the church, runs at ¢450 per hr. Open M-Sa 9am-9pm, Su 10am-5pm.

Post Office: 300m north and 150m west of the northwest corner of the *parque*. Fax available. Open M-F 8am-5:30pm, Sa 7:30am-noon. **FedEx** available at **Aeronort** (☎2460 3711 or 3636), 300m north and 50m west of the northeast end of the *parque*. Open M-F 8am-12:30pm and 1-5pm, Sa 8:30am-12:30pm. **Postal Code:** 4400.

⌐ ACCOMMODATIONS

Ciudad Quesada is filled with small hotels, most offering simple, safe accommodations for a mainly *tico* clientele. Fortunately, the majority are clustered within walking distance of the *parque* and other key destinations in the city.

Hotel Don Goyo (☎2460 3737), 1 block south of the southwest corner of the *parque*. Quiet, cheerful ambience with rooms off a terraced back porch overlooking a calm stream. All rooms come with cable TV. Free Wi-Fi. Singles ¢8000; doubles ¢12,000; triples ¢16,000. ❷

Hotel El Parqueo (☎2460 2573), 400m north and 25m west of the northeast corner of the *parque*. While the exterior of this small hotel is unassuming, the rooms inside have cable TVs with 100+ channels, fans, and private hot-water baths. Communal fridge and microwave in the foyer. Some singles lack windows and only receive ventilation from the man-made gap near the ceilings. Free, walled-in parking lot makes this the best hotel in town for travelers with cars. Snug singles ¢8000; doubles, triples, and quads ¢6000 per person. ❷

Hotel Cristal (☎2460 0541), 75m north of the northwest corner of the *parque*. All rooms have cable TV and fans. Decor is simple, clean and pleasant. Share a cup of complimentary coffee in the small common area with the welcoming staff. Singles with shared bath ¢5000, with private bath ¢6400; doubles ¢6000/¢10000; quads ¢9000/¢18000. AmEx/MC/V. ❶

Costa Rica Treehouses Hotel (☎2475 6507; www.treehouseshotelcostarica.com), a 30min. car ride or 45min. bus ride north of the town center, toward Fortuna; ask the driver to let you off 100m north of *Cementerio de Santa Clara*. Three treehouses with 2-3 beds, A/C, hot-water baths, and balconies with panoramic views are perched in 80 acres of forest canopy in a wildlife refuge. Grounds include a river, cold water pools, and private waterfall 1.5km from the treehouses. Breakfast included. Complete the online reservation form early as accomodations may fill up two months in advance. ¢55,100 (US$95) for 2 people per cabin, extra person ¢5800 (US$10). AmEx/D/MC/V. ❺

Hotel del Norte (☎2460 5287), 100m east and 150m north of the northeast corner of the *parque*. Dark, slightly mismatched rooms have fans, plastic chairs, and small cable TVs. Despite the wallpaper that is chipping at the edges, these small rooms are clean. Ask the staff to call for laundry services (¢850 per kilo). Small singles with shared bath ¢5000; doubles with private baths ¢11,000; triples with private baths ¢15,000. AmEx/MC/V. ❶

Hotel La Central (☎2460 0301), facing the south side of the *parque*. Reasonably-sized rooms with private baths, telephones, televisions, and small desks. Free Wi-Fi. Singles ¢12,000; doubles ¢16,000; quads ¢28,000. ❷

⌐ FOOD

Lomito (steak) is what's for dinner in Ciudad Quesada. Even the humblest *soda* serves high-quality steak, and most of the restaurants around the *parque* can marinate a steak to perfection. Most of the beef and chicken served in the city comes from the ranches that surround it, making dining here fresh and cheap. Vegetarians will have a harder time eating out in Ciudad Quesada, but most *sodas* and restaurants have options with beans or cheese; just be sure to ask. **Super Granda** (☎2460 0703) supermarket, opposite the northeast corner of the *parque*, can fulfill your grocery needs. Open daily 7am-midnight. MC/V.

⊠ **Restaurant Steak House Coca Loca** (☎2460 3208), facing the west side of the *parque*. Through the swinging saloon doors, a yellow-painted bar and blue curtains create a festive mood for the hungry. Try a thick filet mignon (¢6100), or, for bold carnivores, the half-kg T-bone steak (¢6400). Meals come with an appetizer of a thick corn tortilla with refried beans, salsa, jalapeños, and pickled veggies. Open daily 11am-11pm. AmEx/D/MC/V. ❸

La Terraza (☎2460 5287 or 2461 5287), 250m north of the northeast corner of the *parque*. Polished tables, lanterns, an old iron stove, and palm trees set the mood for a relaxing dinner with a view of cloud-shrouded mountains. Locals swear by the quality of the food. Staples include your standard meats (¢2600-5000), seafood (¢2600-4000), and pasta (¢2100-3200). Mixed drinks (¢1500-2500). Open daily 11am-2am. AmEx/MC/V. ❷

Restaurante Imperio (☎2460 1453), 50m west and 100m south of southeast corner of the *parque*. A Costa Rican take on Chinese food. The house specialty is "Tacos Chinos," which consists of 4 sandwich-sized egg rolls served with sweet-and-sour sauce (¢3500). Chop Suey in special house sauce ¢2500. Vegetarian options. Entrees ¢1800-4500. MC/V. ❶

Restaurante Cristal (☎2460 0063), facing the north side of the *parque*. Popular with locals for its filling *soda*-style eats (*casados* ¢2000-2700). Great breakfast options include plates mixed and matched with ham, eggs, bacon, and beans (¢800-2000). Pick up beef nachos (¢1800) or *empanadas* (¢1700) for a picnic at the *parque*. Open daily 6am-10pm. AmEx/D/MC/V. ❶

Cachos Largo (☎2461 2358), uphill from the bus terminal. Though cattle horns hanging on walls and tall barstools scream Texas, typical Costa Rican cuisine can be found at this cowboy haven. Try the beef tenderloin (¢2500) or chicken in white wine sauce (¢2980) while you listen to the ambient country music. Entrees ¢2500-7950. Appetizers ¢800-1500. Open daily 11am-2am. AmEx/D/MC/V. ❷

Restaurante Don Goya (☎2460 3737), 1 block south of the southwest corner of the *parque*, inside hotel Don Goya. Ask for the yummy mixed fruit milkshake not listed on the menu (¢1200) to accompany the house steak (¢4750). Entrees ¢2300-7195. Side orders include old favorites: onion rings (¢1150) and mozzarella sticks (¢1650). Open daily 10am-9:30pm. ❷

Panadería Inocente Hidalgo (☎2460 1701), 100m of the northeast corner of the *parque*. This local bakery satisfies any sweet tooth. Local delicacies—*cachos* (pastry shaped like a seashell) filled with *dulce de leche* and *orejas* (a fried flat crispy bread topped with sugar, ¢375)—alongside donuts and carrot cake (¢450). Open M-Sa 5am-9pm, Su 5am-12pm. ❶

🔆 SIGHTS

EL ZOOLÓGICO LA MARINA. In 1957, a dairy farmer with a passion for wildlife started taking in abused, sick, or otherwise endangered wild animals. Doña Alba's "hobby" turned public in 1989, when it became too expensive for her to run alone. Today, Doña Alba's son and her family run El Zoológico la Marina, an impressive zoo and preserve where more than 550 animals including jaguars, elastic-nosed tapirs, toucans, crocodiles, and spider monkeys are sheltered and gradually rehabilitated. *He sido liberado* (I have been freed) signs posted on vacant cages attest to the success of the staff's efforts; about 200 animals are reintroduced into the wild each year. The park is world renowned for being the first zoo to successfully reproduce Baird's tapirs in captivity; this recognition has brought with it several international animal contributions, including African lions and ostriches. Fences are so minimal that you'll feel like you're inside the habitats—close enough to feel the heat of a full-grown jaguar's breath. There are also opportunities for volunteers to participate in feeding the animals, cleaning their habitats, and helping build new enclosures. The museum can help arrange homestays; call or email for more details. *(Take any bus heading north from the terminal toward Aguas Zarcas, Pital, Venecia, or Río Frío, and ask to be let out at the Zoológico La Marina (¢225). ☎2474 2100; www.zoocostarica.com. Open daily 8am-4pm. Adults US$8, children US$5.)*

THERMAL POOLS. The volcanic activity in the area around Ciudad Quesada, especially to the north, has created a number of natural thermal pools that make for safe, sumptuous bathing. Though there are no public pools in the vicinity of Ciudad Quesada, there are various options for accessing the privately owned pools. For a luxurious experience, walk 1km south to the beautiful **Termales del Bosque,** owned and maintained by a hotel of the same name. Follow the trail 1km from reception, where you can enjoy eight connected blue pools of different temperatures. *(☎2460 4740; www.termalesdelbosque.com. Guard 24hr. Open daily 8am-9:30pm. ¢6000)*

LEATHER. For some leather from the north and particularly cheap souvenirs, check out **Talabartería y Souvenirs La Ranita,** 150m south of the southeast corner of the *parque*(☎2460 4980; open M-F 8am-7pm, Sa 8am-4pm). **Talabartería Jesús Hidalgo,** 200m north and 25m east of the northeast corner of the *parque*, specializes in handcrafted belts and saddles. *(☎2460 2468. Open M-Sa 6am-7pm.)*

PARQUE NACIONAL JUAN CASTRO BLANCO

One of the best-kept secrets among Costa Rica's national parks is also one of its largest. This ironic oversight is partly due to the fact that **Parque Nacional Juan Castro Blanco** is so young. The 14,453-hectare park was founded on the grounds of a smaller, pre-existing conservation area in 1992. Since then, MINAE has managed to acquire only 722 hectares of the land, and they are just now establishing basics of tourist infrastructure, such as maps, marked trails, ranger offices. Unfortunately, the monetary limitations that have prevented MINAE's acquistion of the park's land have also affected the speed of trail development in the park. At this point, the rangers exist more to prevent poaching than to promote tourism. However, it is still possible to visit the park and see its pristine cloud forests, 60% of which are primary growth. Given its altitude and climate, Juan Castro Blanco is similar to heavily touristed Monteverde, but many locals favor this less-developed park for its more-authentic, small-town feel and even better opportunities for wildlife sighting. The park's forests host 80% of the country's endemic species, including sloths, white-faced monkeys, pumas, linets, wild chickens, and the ever-elusive quetzals, and MINAE officials are only beginning to document the species inhabiting this enormous park. In addition to wildlife, the park also has a stellar collection of sulfur baths, century-old abandoned mines, numerous hydroelectric projects, and four volcanoes: **Platanar, Porvenir, Viejo,** and **Cañón del Río Toro.** Visit the multi-hued lagoons of **Pozo Verde** and **El Congo** near San José de la Montaña or the majestic cold-water falls of **Catarata Río Toro, Claro, Agrio,** and **Quebrada Gata at Bajos del Toro Amarillo.** There is currently only one official pathway, extending from San José de la Montaña in the west to Bajos del Toro Amarillo in the east, but adventurous travelers can enter the park and explore as they please, if they don't mind

LOCAL LEGEND

SWIMMING OF THE BULLS

While most people go to Catarata del Toro—a plunging waterfall in a heavily forested ravine—to splurge on waterfall rappelling or hiking trips, local lore has it that the famous waterfall was once host to a more costly venture.

According to the story, the ancient peoples living in the region, in a desperate effort to appease their Gods, decided to make an offering. Forgoing the traditional blood sacrifice, they chose an even more fabulous gift: *un toro de oro* (a golden bull).

To please the Gods, the native people threw the massive, costly bull down the waterfall into the deep basin below, giving it to the Gods, but also burying it for eternity below the swirling rapids.

Today's visitors still hold on to some hope of discovering this mythical treasure; according to local legend, visitors who stand directly above the waterfall on the night of a full moon (quite a feat in itself) can see the golden bull glittering in the water below. In any case, the bull did manage to serve as the namesake for both the waterfall and the town further downstream, Bajos del Toro Amarillo—Below the Golden Bull.

the trouble of getting there and the host of potentially dangerous animals that await.

▐ TRANSPORTATION

The fact that over 95% of the park is in the hands of local *finceros* means that you can enter it from many points. Two entrances have tourist services: **San José de la Montaña** in the southwest and **Bajos del Toro Amarillo** in the east, separated by 60km of highway. Bajos del Toro Amarillo can be reached by **car** and **public transport,** but the only way to enter the park is on a trek or a 4WD vehicle.

The Bajos del Toro Amarillo entrance is served by two public transportation hubs: Sarchí in the south and Río Cuarto in the north. To reach Sarchí, take a **bus** from Av. 5, C. 18 in San José. From Sarchí, a public bus departs from in front of the Sarchí Sur Tourist Office and heads to Río Cuarto via Bajos del Toro Amarillo (1hr., 3pm, ¢800). Coming from the north, you can reach Río Cuarto by taking a bus from Puerto Viejo de Sarapiquí headed to Ciudad Quesada/San Carlos (1½hr., 10 per day, ¢765), or a bus from Ciudad Quesada/San Carlos headed for San Miguel (1hr.; 6 per day; ¢485). A bus passes through Río Cuarto on its way to Sarchí via Bajos del Toro Amarillo (1hr., 5:30pm, ¢800). If you take public transport, try to stay in the center, as other hotels tend to be 3km or more walks from town.

To get to San José de la Montaña (not to be mistaken for San José de la Montaña of Heredia) from San José, contact the rangers' office to see if one of the rangers is making the trip from El Sucre, or contact Ecological Refuge Montreal del Norte Lodge. You will need to get to El Sucre from Ciudad Quesada/San Carlos. A **taxi** from Ciudad Quesada/San Carlos to San José de la Montaña costs about ¢20,000; you'll need a 4WD to make the trip.

▐ PRACTICAL INFORMATION

Both Bajos del Toro Amarillo and San José de La Montaña are small, relatively isolated *pueblitos*. Bajos del Toro runs along one main road; the rangers' office is 2½km down a difficult gravel path that begins 200m to the north of the police station on this road. The rangers have no phone, but you can contact them by calling or sending a fax to the **police station** (☎2761 1923); they will get the message whenever they stop in town, usually every couple of days. The **rangers' office** in San José de la Montaña (☎2460 5462) is closer to town center. Although there are no official guides, the rangers are happy to point visitors in the right direction. The closest **banks** and **hospitals** from Bajos del

Toro Amarillo are in Venecia and Rio Cuarto; from San José de la Montaña, the closest are in Ciudad Quesada (p. 145). The nearest **police station** to San José de la Montaña is in El Sucre.

ACCOMMODATIONS AND FOOD

Bajos del Toro Amarillo offers a number of lodging and dining options near Juan Castro Blanco.

Cabinas Típico Toro Amarillo (☎2761 1918), in the center of town 100m north of the church. Has 2 cabins with hot-water baths. 1 has a TV. 2-person cabins ₡12,000. ❷

Centro Turístico Toro Amarillo (☎2761 1948), just north of the church. Enrique Quesada Madrigal rents 3 spacious log cabins with hot-water baths; right on the banks of Río Toro and are good options for those who want a tranquil setting with close proximity to town. Call ahead. 2-person cabins ₡10,000 each; 6-person cabin ₡26,000. ❷

Catarata del Toro (☎2200 3707, 8399 7467; www.catarata-del-toro.com), 6km north of the town of Bajos del Toro. Some more upscale accommodations, with private hot-water baths near the waterfall. Doubles US$50; triples US$65; quints US$85. ❹

Freddy Salazar's Nene's (☎2761 1933; fax 2761 1932), 500m south of the bridge at the south end of town. Offers 2 double cabins on the banks of the river with private hot-water baths and satellite TV. Doubles ₡15,000. Camp on-site ₡1000 per person. ❸

Ecological Refuge of Montereal Del Norte (☎2460 8018), in San José de la Montaña, the only option is this rustic refuge, with cabins equipped with electric lights and hot-water baths. Call in advance and tell Bernardita how many people are staying, and the lodge will prepare meals. Trout and salad ₡2400. Rooms US$30 per person. ❸

FOOD AND NIGHTLIFE

The higher altitude and lower temperatures of Bajos del Toro Amarillo make it conducive to trout farming, and you'll see many homemade signs advertising *trucha* as you enter town. **Mini Super Toro Amarillo,** across from the police station in the center of Bajos del Toro Amarillo, has a very limited selection of basic groceries. (Open daily 7am-8pm.) There is no market in San José de la Montaña, so pick up everything you need in El Sucre beforehand.

▨ Restaurante Lagos Cimarron, next to Centro Turístico Toro Amarillo. Guests are handed a fishing pole and bait, which they use to catch one of the trout in the pools in the garden. Once guests nab a fish, the chefs take over, preparing the *trucha al gusto*—be sure to try the garlic sauce. Trout ₡3300 per kg. Open M-F 8am-5pm, Sa-Su 8am-7pm. ❸

La Central (☎2761 0581), in the center of town. The starkness of the fluorescent-lit interior is warmly compensated by the friendliness of the family of owners, who serve cheap and hearty *casados* (₡1600) with a smile. Open Tu-Su 9am-9pm. ❶

Rancho Típico Toro Amarillo, next to the Cabinas of the same name, prepares excellent *trucha al gusto* (₡2000) as well as a variety of *comida típica* dishes for a mostly local crowd. Open daily 6am-6pm, though hours can vary depending on guests. ❷

Catarata del Toro serves *comida típica* from an open-air restaurant with a view of the valley. Entrees ₡1000-3000. Open daily 7am-5pm or later depending on guests. ❷

Bar el Bajo, across from El Típico Amarillo. Provides the only nightlife in town. *Bocas* ₡800-1000. Beer ₡800. Mixed drinks ₡1000-2000. Open daily 11am-midnight. ❶

GUIDED TOURS

There are currently no MINAE-licensed tour guides for Parque Juan Castro Blanco, but you can make informal arrangements with experienced locals.

NORTHERN LOWLANDS

Because most of the park is privately owned, there is no fee to enter, though if you enter private property, you may have to pay a fee to the proprietor.

In Bajas del Toro Amarillo, the main attraction is the **Catarata del Toro,** a spectacular 100m waterfall plunging down a rock wall to the heavily forested ravine below. The waterfall is accessible only through the Catarata Del Toro Hotel and Rappelling Company (p. 151), which maintains a picturesque path that leads to five *miradores*, each with a unique view of the waterfall (entrance US$10, children/students/seniors US$5; rappelling excursion US$62, students US$56; open daily 7am-5pm). The biological reserve **Bosque de Paz,** 300m down the gravel road that begins 250m south of Nene, has 22km of paths that wind through primary and secondary forest, past three waterfalls, and around a gorgeous orchid garden. (☎2761 1266, San José office ☎2234 6676; www.bosquedepaz.com. Advanced reservations necessary. Prices vary depending on the size of the group. MC/V.) Luis Guillermo Rodríguez is a knowledgeable, reputable guide who can give you tours of the area's waterfalls, the nearby cheese factory, and his own orchid garden. (☎2761 1938. 2 houses south of the church, or ask for him at Típico Toro Amarillo. Unfixed price.) In San José de la Montaña, Bernardita of the Ecological Refuge has two sons who can take you on the MINAE trail, which leads to the mines (3hr. hike, negotiable price) and to the fossilized crater of **Pozo Verde** (45min.).

PUERTO VIEJO DE SARAPIQUÍ

Puerto Viejo de Sarapiquí is rapidly becoming a top destination for nature-lovers and thrill-seekers alike. The Río Sarapiquí, which runs just 200m from the main road, has opportunities for both wildlife sightings and river rafting. Numerous adventure ranches offer mountain biking and canopy trips for those who prefer land-based action. Despite the myriad outdoor opportunities available, the influx of tourists to the former banana town have had a minimal impact on the town itself; Puerto Viejo remains very small, with one main street and only a handful of hotels and restaurants. With world-class wildlife reserves such as Tirimbina and La Estación Biológica La Selva less than 30min. from town, Puerto Viejo is an ideal base for budget travelers looking to experience the natural wonders of the region.

▐ TRANSPORTATION

Buses: All leave from the station opposite the northwest corner of the soccer field. A schedule is posted inside next to the ticket counter. To: **Ciudad Quesada** (2hr., 12 per day 4:40am-8pm, ¢1230); **Guápiles** (1hr., 11 per day 5:30am-6:30pm, ¢785); **La Virgen** (30min., every hr. 6am-6pm, ¢350); **Río Frío** (1hr., 10 per day 7am-6pm, ¢500); **San José** (10 per day 5am-5:30pm, ¢1610) via **El Tunel Zurquí** or via **Vara Blanca** (5, 7:30, 11:30am, 4:30pm). Tell the cashier at the ticket counter if you want to get off before the final stop; some express buses do not stop at intermediate destinations.

Taxis: Line up along the main street just north of the soccer field. To La Virgen ¢5000.

✴ ▐ ORIENTATION AND PRACTICAL INFORMATION

Puerto Viejo extends along one main street for about 300m. A **soccer field** bordering this street marks the town center. The **bus station** marks the northwest side of this field, while the large stucco **church** sits on the southwest corner. About 1km west of town, the main road forks south toward Guápiles and the entrance of **Estación Biológica La Selva,** and southwest toward La Virgen and the entrances of the **Centro Neotrópico Sarapiquís** and the **Serpentario.** About 150m east of the bus station, a small road to the right leads to the **Super Sarapiquí** supermarket. Two hundred and fifty meters east along the main road from the bus station, the road splits yet again, heading northwest on the left and toward the Río Sarapiquí port on the right.

Tourist Information: For the most comprehensive tourist info, talk to William Rojas of ⬛ **Oasis Nature Tours** (☎2766 6108 or 6260; www.oasisnaturetours.com), 50m west of the soccer field through a green doorway just a couple doors past the bus station. Don William arranges scenic river trips of the Río Sarapiquí all the way to Tortuguero and Nicaragua. Alex Martínez, the owner of **Posada Andrea Cristina** (see this page), is a former hunter considered by many to be the region's most knowledgeable and passionate naturalist. He is a good source for info on birdwatching and other nature tours.

Banks: Exchange travelers' checks and US dollars at the **Banco Nacional** (☎2766 6012), at the intersection of the main road and the road to the port. Open M-F 8:30am-3:45pm. **Banco Popular** is 20m east of the soccer field. Open M-F 8:45am-3pm, Sa 8:15am-11:30am. Both have **24hr. ATMs.**

Police: (☎2766 6575 or 2766 6485, emergencies 911), just off the main street along the port turnoff, next to the post office.

Pharmacy: Farmacia Alfa (☎2766 6348), 1 block east of the soccer field on the left. Open M-Sa 8am-8pm. MC/V.

Red Cross: (☎2766 6212 or 2766 6254), 250m west of the soccer field. Open 24hr.

Internet: Sarapiquí Internet (☎2766 6223), 300m west of the soccer field, past the Red Cross. Internet ₡400 per hr. Open daily 8am-8pm. Internet is available in **Mi Lindo Sarapiquí** (p. 153) for ₡400 per hr. Open daily 7am-10pm. Wi-Fi is available at **Restaurante El Surco.**

Post Office: (☎2766 6509), across from Banco Nacional at the port turn off. Open M-F 8am-noon and 1-5:30pm. **Postal Code:** 31001.

⌐ ACCOMMODATIONS

Although the area around Puerto Viejo has become a popular destination, the town itself does not have many options for travelers. Luckily, the few hotels that do exist are within walking distance of the bus station, making them convenient choices for those looking to take daytrips to the many attractions just outside of town.

⬛ **Posada Andrea Cristina** (☎2766 6265; www.andreacristina.com), 1km west of the town center. From the bus station, follow the road west toward La Virgen for about 1km; the B&B is on the right. With spacious wood bungalows scattered throughout a beautifully landscaped garden, Andrea Cristina offers a unique and peaceful lodging option for those who don't mind being a bit of a walk from town. The cabins share communal cold-water baths, but the comfy beds and tasty vegetarian-friendly breakfast make up for it. Breakfast included. Singles ₡14,500 (US$25); doubles ₡26,100 (US$45); each additional person ₡8700 (US$15). 10% discount on stays longer than 4 nights. Camp on the grounds for ₡5800 (US$10). MC/V. ❷

Mi Lindo Sarapiquí (☎2766 6281), west of the soccer field and directly opposite the bus station. This conveniently located restaurant-hotel-internet-cafe offers sunny, spacious rooms that each have a twin and double bed, ceiling and wall fans, a TV, and private hot-water baths. Laundry ₡150 per item. Singles ₡9500; doubles ₡15,000; triples ₡22,100. AmEx/D/MC/V. ❷

Cabinas Laura (☎2766 6316), 100m down the road to the port. Though its location down a short and dark pathway next to a casket store is less than ideal, this hotel has good prices for those traveling in pairs; A/C and cable TV make it even better. Singles and doubles ₡8000; doubles and triples with A/C ₡10,000-14,000. MC/V. ❷

FOOD

While many of the resorts a few kilometers outside of town serve mouth-watering cuisine, the options in town are limited. Aside from the restaurants at hotels Mi Lindo Sarapiquí and Restaurante El Surco, the only other eating spots available are *sodas* and ice cream shops.

Restaurante Mi Lindo Sarapiquí, attached to the hotel of the same name. Provides tasty *comida típica* to a busy crowd of locals. Though all of the dishes are reasonably priced, the *bocas* menu offers some particularly good deals (¢700-1500). Rice dishes ¢1600-3900. Breakfast ¢950-2500. Open daily 8am-10pm. AmEx/D/MC/V. ❶

Restaurante El Surco (☎2766 6005), in Hotel Bambú. With vaulted fan-filled ceilings under a tin roof, El Surco is the closest Sarapiquí gets to fine dining. The dishes are standard Costa Rican fare, but the atmosphere is casually elegant. *Bocas* ¢1100-1800. *Casados* ¢1850-4250. Seafood dishes ¢4800-9000. Pastas ¢1700-4000. Free Wi-Fi. Open daily 6am-10pm. AmEx/MC/V. ❷

Mister Pizza (☎2766 6138), on the east end of the soccer field. This small, fast food and pizza joint offers escape from *comida típica* in town. The pizza crust has an oddly sweet flavor, but the topping options are extensive, ranging from Hawaiian to veggie. Don't miss the combo menu (¢1400). Pizzas ¢1400-5000. Open daily 8am-10pm. ❷

OUTDOOR ACTIVITIES

Hacienda Pozo Azul (☎2438 2616; www.haciendapozoazul.com), at the bridge in La Virgen. One of the most comprehensive adventure destinations in Puerto Viejo. The sprawling ranch offers canopy tours (US$45), horseback rides (2hr., US$35), rappelling (US$28), rafting (Class II and III rapids US$50, Class IV rapids US$70), mountain biking (half-day US$45), and guided hiking treks (US$15). The ranch was originally a dairy farm, and you can still take a tour of the ranch (US$10) or camp at the on-site facilities (US$25 plus US$20 for 3 meals per person). Alternatively, stay at the pricier jungle lodge (US$60 per person).

Aventuras del Sarapiquí (☎2766 6768 or 8399 3509; www.sarapiqui.com), 15min. west of town on the bus toward La Virgen. These guys opened the first rafting company in the region nearly 20 years ago. The fun-loving group of experienced, bilingual guides leads daily Class II and III rafting trips down the Río Sarapiquí (US$50, includes fruit snack). One of the owners, Pongo, organizes the annual Sarapiquí Adventure Race (www.sarapiquiadventurerace.com), a 2-day competition in Oct. that brings participants to raft, hike, and mountain bike 60km for a charitable cause. (Entrance fee US$50 per person, equipment included.)

Aguas Bravas (☎2292 2072; www.aguas-bravas.co.cr), on the road between Puerto Viejo and La Virgen. Offers a Class II and III rafting trip (US$65) and a Class IV trip for more experienced rafters (US$85).

DAYTRIPS FROM PUERTO VIEJO

TIRIMBINA RAINFOREST PRESERVE

From Puerto Viejo, take a bus to La Virgen and ask the driver to let you off at the entrance to Tirimbina (30min., ¢320). Buses returning to Puerto Viejo stop at the Preserve approx. on the hour. A taxi from Puerto Viejo costs ¢5000. On foot from La Virgen, walk 1.6km north along the road to Puerto Viejo de Sarapiquí; the entrance to the park is on the right, 300m past the Serpentario. ☎2761 1579 or 1576; www.tirimbina.org. Self-guided tour ¢8700 (US$15), students ¢5800 (US$10); guided tour ¢12,760/9860 (US$22/17); approx. 2hr. Several tours leave each day (8, 10am, 1:30, 3pm), though it is recommended to call *in advance. Chocolate tour ₡11,600 (US$20), students ₡8700 (US$15); offered in the morning and afternoon. Reservations required.*

Although about 90% of its land remains pristinely undeveloped, without even the most basic trails, the 350-hectare Tirimbina Rainforest Preserve offers one of the most varied selections of tourism opportunities in the Sarapiquí area. Its 9km of paved trail and more extensive collection of rougher trails can be explored with or without a guide, and the views of primary forest and the Sarapiquí River afforded by the 266m **Puente Colgante** (Hanging Bridge) are some of the best around. The 4km that can be explored without a guide takes approximately 2hr. to properly hike; the other 5km requires a guide given that dangerous animals including snakes, tapirs, and even lions have been known to chow down along the path. A spiral staircase descending from El Puente Colgante, leads to an island formed by **Río Sarapiquí,** where adventurers can take a swim when the river isn't too high. A few trails cross the island, and otters and kingfishers are often spotted on the riverbanks.

For those tired of the usual wildlife-spotting, the Preserve offers several specialized tours, which must be booked in advance. The **bat tour** is a hit with those seeking a glimpse of these nocturnal rainforest residents (7:30pm), and chocoholics' mouths will water on the chocolate tour, which takes guests through a natural chocolate plantation, demonstrates traditional methods of producing chocolate, and concludes with a tasting. Insect repellent, long pants, and hiking boots are recommended for all hikes or walks. An open-air **restaurant** serves meals to guests at the lodge and will also make lunch or dinner for large groups; call the Preserve in advance to arrange a meal before or after a tour.

Though most visitors to the center stop by for only a day or two, Tirimbina also accepts volunteers and researchers for long-term stays of at least two weeks. The Preserve has lodging space for ten volunteers, most of whom help out in the general day-to-day operations of the Preserve, though Spanish speakers may also have the opportunity to help in conservation and ecology classes taught for local primary school kids. Researchers interested in studying the wildlife at Tirimbina are also welcome to stay at the Preserve. Room and board for volunteers and researchers is US$10 per night, though some financial assistance is available. Contact the Preserve for more information on current volunteer and research openings.

Tirimbina also has 12 **rooms** on the grounds available for visitors. The rooms have either a double and twin bed or three twin beds as well as private hot-water baths, Wi-Fi, and A/C. Lodging includes free access to the trails as well as breakfast in the park's restaurant. (Singles and doubles ₡34,800/US$60, students ₡29,000/US$50.)

ESTACIÓN BIOLÓGICA LA SELVA

From Puerto Viejo, take the 6:45am or 12:15pm bus headed to Río Frío (15min., ₡260) to make the 8am or 1:30pm tours. Buses to Guápiles also pass this way. Ask the driver to let you off at the Estación Biológica La Selva. From this stop, follow the dirt road on your right 1km to the station's gates; signs mark the way. To get back to Puerto Viejo, have the station call you a cab (₡3000) or wait at the bus stop on the main road for one of the buses that passes by about every 30min. (less often on Su) on their way back to Puerto Viejo. ☎ 2524 0628; www.ots.ac.cr. Private tours 2hr. Birdwatching tours begin at 5:45am, night tours 6pm; ₡18,560-22,040 (US$32-38). Make reservations online or by phone several days in advance for any of the tours.

Only 6km south of Puerto Viejo, La Selva is one of the three centers of the **Organization for Tropical Studies (OTS),** a non-profit consortium of universities and research institutions founded on the principles of investigation, education, and conservation. La Selva borders **Parque Nacional Braulio Carrillo** to the south; the park boasts

1614 hectares of primary and secondary rainforest. Hundreds of scientists and students come to La Selva each year to study the staggering number of plants and animals here, several of which the Estación has helped bring back from the edge of extinction. Though the station has an extensive collection of concrete and dirt trails, the paths can only be accessed without a guide by those staying at the lodge. The station has many guided walks and workshops to offer. Two 3½hr. walking tours leave each day (8am, 1:30pm; ¢16,240-18,560/US$28-32). Some trails are accessible to those with physical disabilities. The station also offers private tours, including a birdwatching tour, a night tour, and a workshop on rainforest photography, all of which must be arranged several days in advance.

CENTRO NEOTRÓPICO SARAPIQUÍS

Next to Tirimbina (p. 154). ☎2761 1004; fax 2761 1415; www.sarapiquis.org. Open daily 9am-5pm. The tour schedule varies; call ahead for reservations. Entry to museum, archaeological site, and botanical gardens ¢4640 (US$8). Reception open daily 6am-8:30pm. Archaeological site and gardens open 6am-4pm. Museum open 6am-6pm. Tour of museum with guide ¢8700 (US$15), archaeological site ¢5220 (US$9).

The non-profit, private Centro Neotrópico Sarapiquís is a preserve dedicated to interactive cultural, biological, and ecological awareness and conservation. The center offers **three exhibits** to tourists: a **museum** on pre-Columbian culture, an **archaeological dig** with reconstructed 15th-century pre-Columbian buildings, and a **botanical garden** featuring medicinal and edible plants. The museum is well-kept, with neat displays of masks, shamanic implements, and a film on the relationship between man and nature in pre-Columbian societies. Unfortunately, the rest of the center is not as well-organized. Much of the writing on the signs identifying the plants in the botanical gardens has been washed away by the frequent rains, and the archaeological site is quite small, with a sample home, funerary site, and replica statues constituting the majority of the exhibit. Visitors should also beware of the rock pathways in the botanical gardens and archaeological site: the stones get quite slippery when wet, making walking in the rain feel a bit like ice skating in tennis shoes.

The Center was built in a pre-Columbian village style using sustainable technologies like solar power, local natural materials, and a waste-water treatment system. The on-site ecolodge, restaurant, and bar overlook the preserve and follow the *Palenque* architectural style. Large, round huts each house eight **cabins,** all with private hot-water baths, fans, and phones. Safe deposit boxes and laundry services are also available. Eight of the 40 rooms have A/C. (High-season singles and doubles ¢60,320/US$104, triples ¢74,820/US$129; low-season ¢56,260/60, 320, US$97/104.) The center runs an extensive **education program** with over 2000 local children and hundreds of foreign volunteers, teachers, and ecologists; for information on getting involved, contact the center (see the information above). Spanish skills are helpful for most jobs, though not necessary.

RARA AVIS

This private reserve has offered some of the best ecotourism and demonstrations of sustainable development practices since 1983. Located 15km southwest of Las Horquetas de Sarapiquí and bordering Braulio Carrillo National Park and Zona Protectora La Selva, this isolated cluster of cabins and extensive trail networks is accessible only by a jerky 3hr. tractor ride. Despite the less-than-convenient transportation, most visitors agree that the trip is well worth it once they see Rara Avis's 411 hectares of rainforest, buzzing with more species of plants, birds, and butterflies than all of Europe. Tropical flowers line the pathways, and the skies twitter with 362 identified species of birds, including macaws and sunbitterns. Each guest validates founder Amos Bien's claim that developing rainforest for ecotourism rather than clearing it for cattle ranching is an economically sustainable alternative. Due to limited transportation and lodging as well as the reserve's increasing popularity, advance reservations are recommended and are absolutely necessary during the high season. Reservations should also be confirmed the night before arrival to ensure that appropriate transportation is ready. The staff recommends a minimum stay of two nights because of the difficult and lengthy transportation into the park. Check the weather before going; when it rains, there is considerably less to do.

AT A GLANCE

AREA: 411 hectares.

CLIMATE: At 700m above sea level, it is cool here year-round (25˚C/77˚F), but it often rains.

GATEWAYS: San José through Las Horquetas de Sarapiquí.

HIGHLIGHTS: Numerous trails, great green macaws, parrots, toucans, tapirs, coatimundis, anteaters, monkeys.

INFORMATION: ☎2764 1111; www.rara-avis.com.

⧉ TRANSPORTATION. Your journey to Rara Avis begins at its office in Las Horquetas de Sarapiquí. From San José, buy a ticket for the 6:30am **bus** from Terminal Caribe (Av. 13, C. Central) to Puerto Viejo de Sarapiquí (make sure you are not taking the bus to Puerto Viejo de Salamanca). Tell the driver you are getting off at the Rara Avis office in Las Horquetas; he will announce the stop (1½hr., daily 6:30am, ¢1150). You can also take the 11:30am bus to Puerto Viejo, but call the night before to make sure there will be a **tractor** running at 2pm. The bus will drop you off at a stop labeled "Rara Avis"; the office is on the right 200m down the road on the left side of the highway. You should arrive by 8:30am to store luggage and borrow a pair of rubber boots—you'll need them to hike the muddy trails. If your feet are larger than size 46 (11.5), you'll need to bring your own boots. Bring some long socks as well.

The fun begins at 9am when the open-air, **tractor-drawn cart** leaves from the office for Rara Avis 3 hr. away. The waterlogged, pot-holed road makes for a rocky ride; staying on the tractor can feel like riding a trotting horse. However, the open-air trip offers stunning views of the Caribbean lowlands and the Arenal Volcano as it makes the surroundings quickly transition from open farmland to dense rainforest. Three kilometers north of Rara Avis, the tractor makes a rest stop at **El Plástico,** a former penal colony where prisoners slept under plastic tarps (hence the name) that is now a base for students and researchers on long stints of field work. Here, passengers can take a break to use the restroom and stretch their legs. The remaining road is more difficult, and the driver may ask passengers to walk in several places. You can also choose to **hike** the remaining 3km on the Sendero Atajo trail (1-2hr.), which runs uphill through the rainforest parallel to the road. If you miss the tractor, **horses** (US $50) or a **Jeep** are available to carry you as far as El Plástico. When there is no tractor running, this service is free of charge. Either way, lunch will be waiting for you at the main lodge. The tractor returns from Rara Avis at 2pm, arriving in time to catch the last bus to San José. This schedule occasionally changes, so check with the reservations desk or the hotel manager to confirm. Buses back to San José leave Las Horquetas at 7, 8, 11am, 1:30, 3, and 5:30pm. If you wish to take an earlier bus, speak with the hotel manager to arrange for horses a day in advance, and have your heavy bags sent by tractor.

WORKING TOGETHER FOR A BETTER TOMORROW

Rara Avis Rainforest Lodge and Reserve was founded in 1983 by Amos Bien as a model of ecotourism, a movement that strives to develop the country's economy and protect its natural resources. In some rural areas of Costa Rica, residents have transformed precious rainforest areas into farmland and cattle-grazing land. By establishing rainforest lodges and tourist attractions with low impact, locals receive employment, and land is not destroyed.

Over the last two decades the amount of protected land in Costa Rica has increased dramatically, in large part due to the efforts of individuals. In Costa Rica, national parks currently comprise 13% of the country's land with another 12% of the country privately-owned and conserved (Compared to only 4% National Park land in the United States).

Not only do private, sustainable reserves protect valuable natural resources and help to alleviate rural poverty, they are also helping Costa Rica reach its goal of achieving carbon neutrality by 2020. These reserves preserve the number of trees and planting more, helping reduce the country's carbon footprint. If ecotourism succeeds in Costa Rica, it could be a great example for the rest of the world for how to preserve resources and sustain the economy at the same time.

ACCOMMODATIONS AND FOOD. Although Rara Avis offers three distinct accommodations for a range of prices, guests all hike the same trails with the same guides and eat the same delicious meals together. The only budget option, **Las Casitas ❸**, is a fantastic deal. Tucked into a forest clearing 5min. from the dining hall, spacious wooden cabins with bunk beds share a cold-water bath. Only its restaurant has electricity, however. Great views for birdwatching (US$50 per person). The more elegant two-story **Waterfall Lodge ❹** has eight large rooms, gas lamps, private hot-water baths, and wrap-around porches with hammocks in every room. (High season singles US$85; doubles $75; triples $65 per person; $60 for each additional person; low season US$80/70/60/55.) The **River-Edge ❺** cabins are also available and located a 10min. walk from the main lodge with private hot-water bath and great views of the river. (High season singles US$95; doubles US $85 per person. Low season US$90/80.) All room prices include tractor transportation to and from Rara Avis as well as trail access, naturalist guide services, and three family-style meals every day. Served in the restaurant along with an inexhaustible supply of drinking water, fresh coffee, and tea, the meals include vegetarian options, plenty of fresh produce, and typical Costa Rican specialties like *gallo pinto* and *patacones*. Homemade desserts such as *flan* and *arroz con leche* are also served. Reservations are strongly recommended, but walk-ins are occasionally possible. (☎2764 1111; www.rara-avis.com.)

HIKING AND SIGHTS. Various trails (most 1-2hr.) crisscross the property, passing under towering trees draped with dangling bromeliads, lianas, and moss-covered vines. The most popular trails are those close to the accommodations; **Sendero Nicholás** (1hr.) begins behind the restaurant and passes over several small streams before branching off into steeper hikes uphill. For a challenge, try the longer **Sendero Platanillo** (3hr.), which also starts behind the restaurant and winds through denser jungle to the magnificent Vencejo waterfall. Just above the waterfall, the river flows into a crystalline pool perfect for swimming; guests have also had good luck spotting spider monkeys here. Guides are available to lead hikes and shorter nature walks every morning (in English and Spanish), but if you prefer to hike solo, tell the manager which trail you'll be taking and how long you expect to be gone.

Numerous diversions are also available within a 200m radius of the lodge and restaurant. Located downhill from the restaurant and concealed by the tree cover lies a 50m double waterfall that cascades into a misty pool that is ideal for swimming. However, flash floods here can be very dangerous; ask the guides if conditions are safe for swimming and tell them when you are planning your dip. Alarms indicate an oncoming storm or flood. Another attraction is the peaceful **butterfly house,** a model project for sustainable rainforest development, where Rara Avis, in association with the **Worldwide Fund for Nature,** raises live butterflies for export to North American and European greenhouses and zoos. The **orchid garden** is another experiment in sustainable development; flower products are meant for export. Epiphytes, collected from fallen samples, are pollinated to produce seeds. These seeds are grown on a mesh grid suspended by pulleys. The orchids are best viewed in March when they are in full bloom.

VARA BLANCA

In between the bustling metropolis of San José and the muggy rainforests of Puerto Viejo de Sarapiquí lies the misty mountain village of Vara Blanca. Though transportation to the small town is infrequent, seeing its idyllic beauty is worth the trek, as are the surrounding attractions. Visitors can frolic at the La Paz Waterfall Gardens, with five waterfalls, a hummingbird garden, and the largest butterfly observatory in the world. Patient travelers, or those with access to a 4WD, can also explore the three hidden lagoons of nearby Cariblanco, the 120m San Fernando Waterfall in Chinchona, and the inactive Volcán Poas, as well as the numerous strawberry and coffee plantations around Vara Blanca.

▐ TRANSPORTATION

From San José, take a **bus** from **Terminal de los Caribeños,** Av. 7/9, C. 12 (☎2222 0610) toward Puerto Viejo de Sarapiquí (1.5hr.; 6:30am, 1, 5:30pm), and get off at the gas station in the center of Vara Blanca—or, if you have a more precise destination in mind, ask the bus driver if he can leave you there. From the north, catch the bus from Puerto Viejo de Sarapiquí toward San José; make sure to ask for the one that passes through Vara Blanca (2hr; 5, 7:30am, noon, 4:30pm; ¢1000). Since Vara Blanca is spread along the highway, your only option for transport once you arrive at the gas station, besides the infrequent and sometimes unreliable buses, is by **foot** (watch out for trucks), **motorcycle** (though risky when raining), or 4WD **car.** While the main road in Vara Blanca is paved, many of the smaller roads around Volcán Poas and Cariblanco are not. Watch out for the curves; one is actually a 180° turn.

▐▐ ORIENTATION AND PRACTICAL INFORMATION

Vara Blanca is organized like a "T." The main road goes east to west, the same direction that the bus from San José travels. Along this road, you will find (in order) Mi Casita, Restaurante Colbert, Restaurante Las Delicias de Tiquicia, the gas station, Cabinas El Arbollito, and then a series of lodges, including Vara Blanca Lodge. The center of the "T" is the intersection at the gas station, where the road heads north past Restaurante Vara Blanca toward Puerto Viejo. Six kilometers north along the road from Vara Blanca toward Puerto Viejo de Sarapiquí brings you to La Paz Waterfall Gardens. Another 6km toward Puerto Viejo beyond the waterfalls leads to the village of **Chinchona,** which contains the 120m San Fernando Waterfall (on the right after the ICE sign; the bus stops at a *soda* with a view of the falls). The next town is **Cariblanco,** with three hidden lagoons. The biggest one, 100m north of the gas station and 7km east of the highway, is only accessible by 4WD. Continuing in the same direction, you'll eventually arrive at the larger towns of **San Miguel** and **La Virgen**, with the nearest **banks, ATMs, hospitals,** and **post offices.** To arrive at these towns from Vara Blanca, take the bus heading from San José toward Puerto Viejo de Sarapiquí and ask to be let off at either town (San Miguel, 1hr; La Virgen, 1½hr.). Vara Blanca has a **public telephone** across from the gas station.

ACCOMMODATIONS

Cabinas El Arbollito (☎2482 2872), just 50m west of the gas station next to Soda Ardillas. Has 2 colorful, spacious *cabinas* for those wanting a more rustic or economical option. Both cabins have private hot-water baths; the larger cabin holds 4 people on the ground floor and loft area, and the smaller one has space for 2 people in its large bedroom. Cabins ¢10,000. You can also camp for free among the rubber trees surrounding enormous Laguna de Hule. Cabins ❷/Camping ❶

Vara Blanca Lodge (☎2482 2193; restaurantevarablanca@hotmail.com), a few hundred meters west of the gas station. Recently built by the popular owner of Restaurante Vara Blanca, Vara Blanca Lodge is a series of rustic wood cabins overlooking pastures and the forest beyond. The cabins are surprisingly modern inside, with hot-water baths, tiled floors, and a plethora of 3-pronged electrical outlets. Cabins US$25. ❷

Poas Volcano Lodge (☎2482 2194, fax 2482 2513; www.poasvolcanolodge.com), 100m west of Vara Blanca Lodge there is a sign. This ecotourism hotel is situated on a working dairy farm at the foothills of Volcán Poás. The lodge offers 11 well-decorated rooms, 2 with shared bathrooms. A living room with comfy couches and a romantic, sunk-in fireplace makes this place stand out, as do the filling breakfasts. While the amenities here are unsurpassed in Vara Blanca, the Lodge is remote, situated at the end of a winding road about 15km from town. Singles US$50, with bath US$60; doubles with bath US$85. Prices include breakfast, Internet, and access to the lodge's trails. ❸

Mi Casita (☎2482 2629), the first lodge you encounter as you enter Vara Blanca from San José. Features a row of bright red, dollhouse-like cabins overlooking strawberry fields. With queen beds, wrought-iron furniture, dark wood paneling, and private bathrooms, it affords both luxury and privacy without going too far out of town. Cabins with older bathrooms ¢15,500, with remodeled bathrooms and water-heaters ¢35,000. ❸

FOOD

The supermarket in town, **Super Vara Blanca,** is about 2km north of Vara Blanca. (☎2482 2650. Open daily 6am-8pm.) Though there are many *sodas* and food outlets between Vara Blanca and Sarapiquí that sell local strawberries, apples, and *cajetas*, the town of Vara Blanca has several restaurants of its own.

Restaurante Vara Blanca (☎2482 2193 or 2260 2366). The cavernous 100-year-old restaurant, built with volcanic rock, is a favorite with both locals and visitors. Food is baked in a *leña* (firewood oven), an old jukebox belts out favorite tunes, and comments of past visitors adorn the walls. Ask for a table by the windows and dine with the hummingbirds. Entrees ¢2500-3900. Open daily 7am-8pm. AmEx/D/MC/V. ❷

Restaurante Las Delicias de Tiquicia (☎2448 3267; lasdeliciasdetiquicia@gmail.com), just across from the gas station. Though not as well-known as Restaurante Vara Blanca, this family-owned and operated restaurant offers large portions of *comida típica* in a rustic wood dining area with walls decorated with old Costa Rican newspapers documenting events like the Arenal eruption, the US invasion of Panama, Kennedy's assassination, and the crash of the Challenger space shuttle. Breakfast ¢1300-2500. Entrees ¢3000-6500. Open daily 7am-5pm. ❷

Restaurant Colbert (☎2482 2776), 400m east of the gas station. While on the pricier side, Colbert is a tasty option for those tired of the standard *comida típica* fare. Entrees ₡3000-8000. Open M-W and F-Su 8am-9pm. Reservations recommended. ❷

👁 SIGHTS

LA PAZ WATERFALL GARDENS. Apart from the pristine, largely untouristed beauty of the area, the biggest attraction for most visitors to Vara Blanca is the extensive La Paz Waterfall Gardens just 6km north of town. The park's immaculate grounds and themed exhibits—including Latin America's largest butterfly farm, a serpentarium, a ranarium, an orchid garden, and a humming-bird garden—are reminiscent of an American amusement park. It's the best of both worlds: rainforest hiking without needing to actually rough it. Tours are available in English and Spanish. Wildlife sightings include toucans and parrots, honey creepers, tanagers, quetzals, sooty robins, mountain Elaenias, and black and yellow silky flycatchers. The complex includes 3.5km of paved hiking trails, including the main attraction: the **Trail of the Falls** (350m), which offers awe-inspiring views of the four waterfalls of **Templo, Magia Blanca, Encantada,** and **Escondida.** From here, you can either press on to the end of the trail, where there's an impressive view of La Paz Waterfall (the free shuttle at the end of the trail will drop you off at the restaurant), or follow the less-scenic **Bernardo's Trail** (550m) uphill back to reception. A map is available at reception. Trails are well-marked, and most people opt to venture around the 70 acres of wildlife and forest without a guide, although guides are available. *(To get to the gardens, either continue on the bus from San José toward Sarapiquí to the garden entrance or get off the bus early on your way to Vara Blanca from Sarapiquí. ☎2482 2720, for reservations call 2225 0643 or fax 2225 1082; www.waterfallgardens.com. Prices for private tours depend on the size of group; call in advance to reserve. Park open daily 8am-5pm; last admission at 4pm, though you should show up by 3pm to experience the whole park. Admission US$35.)*

VOLCÁN POÁS. The other main attraction near Vara Blanca is the active Volcán Poás, which looms in the distance. Visitors can walk around the heavily forested rim of the mountaintop lagoon and enjoy exhilarating views of the fuming volcano on the other side. Be aware that clouds can obscure the view, so try to go on a clear day. *(To get a closer look, a bus leaves from Vara Blanca toward Poás from the gas station at 7am. Get off in the town of Poasito and take another bus at 9:30am that heads to the summit of the volcano. The bus returns from the summit at 12:30pm. Transportation can be a little unreliable, so be sure to ask around before making the trip yourself.)*

LA FORTUNA

La Fortuna is known principally as the gateway to world-famous Volcán Arenal, which awoke from its 450-year dormancy on July 29, 1968, with eruptions that buried two villages and 87 people. It has been spewing orange-red lava and boulders ever since, looming above the small town of La Fortuna and filling the horizon with smoke and flames. The area offers a diverse set of wilderness exploration options: tourists flock to the hot springs at the base, while more rugged travelers hike through rainforest to catch glimpses of lava or check out the **Catarata La Fortuna** and **Las Cavernas de Venado. Laguna Arenal,** about 30min. from the town center, offers a number of adventure excursions as well.

According to local legend, La Fortuna got its name from the flotsam and jetsam that would drift down the Río Fortuna during floods—*indígena* tools and relics were scooped up by villagers as signs of good fortune. The small town's luck hasn't run out yet. The lava of Arenal, 6km to the west, flows away from town, though La Fortuna is close enough to offer spectacular views and easy visits to the volcano. La Fortuna's good luck has also meant a booming tourism industry, and the quiet streets are now almost overrun with hotels, tourist agencies, and over-priced restaurants. Luckily, the influx of tourists into the town has not spread over much into the natural sights of the area, and you can still enjoy the region's hiking and outdoor activities without too much company.

⌐ TRANSPORTATION

NatureAir operates out of Sunset Tours, offering **flights** from the small airport at El Tanque just outside of La Fortuna (☎479 9585; www.natureair.com).

La Fortuna's **bus terminal** is located 100m south of the southwest corner of the *parque*, next to the megastore. **Buses** pick up passengers and head to: Ciudad Quesada/San Carlos (1hr.; 12 per day 4:30am-5:30pm; ¢420); San José (4hr.; 12:45, 2:45pm; ¢2000); Tilarán (3hr.; 8am, 5:30pm; ¢1500) via Arenal (2hr., ¢1000); San Ramón (2hr.; 9 per day 5:30am-4pm; ¢750), where you can transfer to a direct bus to San José (45min., ¢500).

DON'T MISS THE BUS! Though La Fortuna does have its own bus station, many buses coming into town from Upala, Guatuso, and Ciudad Quesada do not enter the city, but stop a few kilometers outside at El Tanque. While you can take public buses or taxis back from El Tanque, the easiest (and cheapest) way back to La Fortuna is to wait at the bus stop and catch a ride with one of the many tour operators driving back into La Fortuna. It's usually free and the guides will often stop to pick up tourists they see waiting at the bus stop.

Taxis line up on the east side of the *parque.* There are two car rental companies offering similar services, vehicles and rates, which vary by season. **Alamo,** across the street from the west side of the church, has the largest selection of cars. (☎/fax 2479 9090; www.alamocostarica.com. Open daily 6:30am-6pm.) **Adobe Rent-a-Car** (☎2479 7902, cell 8380 8541, fortuna@adobecar.com) located 50m south of southeast corner of *parque central*, has a small selection and rents only to those 23 and up (open 8am-6pm M-Sa; MC/V).

Bicycle rental available at Cabinas Hervi, 50m south of the southeast corner of the church. (US$2 per hr.)

✳ 🛈 ORIENTATION AND PRACTICAL INFORMATION

The main street into La Fortuna runs east-west; many businesses lie here. Along its north side is the *parque central.* The church sits on the west side.

Banks:

> **Banco Popular** (☎2479 9422), on the main drag 2 blocks east of the *parque.* Currency exchange and a 24hr. ATM. Also across from the church. Open M-F 9am-3:30pm, Sa 8:30am-11:30am.

> **Banco Nacional** (☎2479 9355), 1 block east of the northeast corner of the *parque.* Open M-F 8:30am-3:45pm.

> **Western Union** (☎2479 9121), is at Grupo Coocique, 100m east and 75m south of the southeast corner of the *parque.* Open M-Sa 7am-5pm, Su 8am-noon.

Police: (☎2479 9689, emergency 911), 1 block east of the *parque.* Open 24hr.

Medical Services: Farmacia Catedral (☎2479 9518), 25m east of the southeast corner of the field. Open M-F 8am-8:30pm, Su 8am-7pm. The **medical clinic** (☎2479 9142) is 100m east and 50m north of the northeast corner of the *parque.* Open M-F 7am-4pm by appointment, 4-10pm for emergencies; Sa-Su and holidays 8am-8pm.

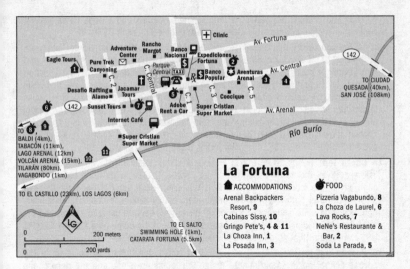

La Fortuna

🏠 ACCOMMODATIONS

Arenal Backpackers
  Resort, **9**
Cabinas Sissy, **10**
Gringo Pete's, **4 & 11**
La Choza Inn, **1**
La Posada Inn, **3**

🍎 FOOD

Pizzeria Vagabundo, **8**
La Choza de Laurel, **6**
Lava Rocks, **7**
NeNe's Restaurante &
  Bar, **2**
Soda La Parada, **5**

Telephones: You can make international phone calls at **Sunset Tours** and **Expediciones Fortuna** (☎2479 9101), opposite the southeast corner of the *parque*. Open daily 7am-10pm. Public phones are at the southeast corner of the *parque*.

Internet Access: There are several Internet cafes lining the main street on the south side of the *parque*. **Internet Cafe,** diagonally across from the southwest corner of the *parque*, has fast connections, webcams, and headsets. (☎2383 7839. ¢600 per hr., ¢400 per 30min. Open daily 8am-11pm.)

SURF AWAY. While there are several good Internet cafes in La Fortuna, the easiest (and cheapest) way to surf the web is by going to the park. The government has provided free Wi-Fi to the entire *parque*, making this sunny social destination an unlikely hotspot for businessmen and backpackers catching up on the news from home. All you have to do is access the free, keyless ICE network, and you can lie in the grass, typing away for hours.

Post Office: (☎2479 8070), opposite the north side of the church. Fax available. Open M-F 8am-5:30pm, Sa 7:30am-12pm. There is a **FedEx** office located inside PuraVida tours, 150m west of the southwest corner of the *parque*. **Postal Code:** 4417.

🏠 ACCOMMODATIONS

The most expensive resorts lie a few kilometers west of La Fortuna along the highway. In the town center, competition among hotels and B&Bs is fierce enough to ensure a wide selection of reasonably priced lodgings, and new hotels and hostels open each year. Though most locals and tourists feel that the town is safe, women traveling alone should bear in mind that certain sections along the river are poorly lit at night.

▧ **Gringo Pete's** (☎2479 8521; gringopetes2003@yahoo.com), 2 locations, one 200m west of the bus station, another 300m east and 50m south of southeast corner of *parque central*. These almost identical bright purple buildings spread about 500m apart on the river have dorm rooms and doubles with private baths, all with bunk beds. The porches and gardens are perfect for an evening barbeque, and a book exchange and communal kitchen are available. Dorms US$4; double with bath US$6.

Arenal Backpackers Resort (☎2479 7000 or 2479 7171; www.arenalbackpackers.com), 350m west of the *parque central*. Arenal Backpackers claims to be a 5-Star hostel, and it has both the prices and amenities to match. Guests can lounge in the hostel's gated complex, which features a huge lawn with hammocks, a pool and patio area, free Wi-Fi and computer access, a book exchange, and even an on-site travel desk that books local tours for discounted prices (Arenal and Baldi combination US$38). The rooms are air-conditioned (10pm-10am) and have hot water (6am-11am, 3pm-11pm). No kitchen is available, but there is a restaurant on-site (breakfast ¢1000-2500, entrees ¢1500-3500). Dorms US$14; private rooms US$54. AmEx/D/MC/V. ❷

La Choza Inn (☎/fax 2479 9091; www.lachozainnhostel.com). Down a gravel road 300m north of the northwest corner of the *parque*. This secluded hotel has summer-camp-style pine rooms with bunk beds in the older section and a modern hotel with private hot-water baths, A/C, Wi-Fi, and in-room coffee makers in comfortable singles, doubles, and quads. Laundry US$2 per kg. The owners operate Eagle Tours from the 1st fl. of the old building. Free Internet access and use of the communal kitchen. Singles US$7, with bath US$20; double US$30; quads US$40. MC/V. ❶

La Posada Inn (☎2479 9793; www.geocities.com/laposadainn), 250m east of the *parque central* on the main street. Though the rooms are small and the decorations slightly outdated, the hot-water baths, in-room fans, peaceful outdoor kitchen and patio, and accommodating owners more than make up for it. The porch is for lounging, and the owner hass an on-site tour desk. Rooms US$5 per person, with bath US$10. ❶

Cabinas Sissy (☎2479 9256 or 2479 9931), 100m south and 200m west of the southwest corner of the *parque*, facing the Río Burío. This hotel has small rooms for 1-4 people with private hot water baths, a communal kitchen, TVs, and fans. The owner works with major operators to arrange tours. Laundry service US$3 per kg. Rooms US$20 per person. Camping US$4 per person. AmEx/MC/V. ❷

🔲 FOOD

The most conspicuous restaurants in La Fortuna cater to tourists with international cuisine at high prices. Reasonably priced *típico* fare can be found at *sodas* a block or two off the main road toward the Río Burio. For The **Super Cristian** supermarket is across from the southeast corner of the *parque*. Another location is one block south of the southwest corner of the church. (☎2479 7272; both open M-F 7am-10pm, Sa 7am-10pm, Su 8am-8pm; MC/V).

Pizzeria Vagabondo (☎2479 9565), 1.5km west of the church. This patio-style eatery just outside of town serves pasta (¢3795-5300) and wood-fired pizza (¢4300-6800) and has a disco bar with pool (¢500 per hr.) and darts. Both are worth the short taxi ride on weekends (¢1500), when the DJ plays a fun mix of salsa, merengue, reggae, pop, and rock. Restaurant open daily noon-11pm. Bar open daily 7pm-2am. MC/V. ❸

NeNe's Restaurante & Bar (☎2479 9192), 200m east and 50m south from northeast corner of the *parque*. Though tucked away in an alley off of the main road, this quiet restaurant has good prices for *típico* cuisine that complements its unpretentious wooden tables and mural of tropical birds. Mixed drinks ¢1400-2000, entrees ¢2300-5800, *tres leches* ¢1000. Open daily 10am-11pm. AmEx/MC/V. ❸

Lava Rocks (☎2479 8039), on the southwest corner of the *parque*. Especially good for breakfast (fruit pancakes ¢2990). Tourists flock at dinner time for delicious fish plates (grilled Chilean sea bass ¢3950) and the view of the picturesque *iglesia* from the restaurant's open patio. Open daily 7:30am-10pm. D/MC/V. ❷

La Choza de Laurel (☎2479 7063; www.lachozadelaurel.com). While the waitresses in *ranchera* costumes, tourist info centered on 1 wall, and bananas hanging from the ceiling give this restaurant a slightly cheesy ambience, the presence of locals and a menu of fresh, light cuisine entice even the skeptical to try its steak (¢6500-8300) and sea bass (¢5700-5900). Entrees ¢3000-8500. Open daily 6:30am-10pm. MC/V. ❸

Soda La Parada (☎2479 9547), directly across from the south side of the *parque central*. The only 24hr. place in town, La Parada serves diner-style food for the late-night crowd. Breakfast ¢800-2200. *Casados* ¢1850-2400. Personal pizza ¢2500, medium ¢4000, large ¢6000. AmEx/D/MC/V. ❶

GUIDED TOURS

Numerous tour operators in La Fortuna offer a bewildering variety of activities. You can hike, kayak, bird-watch, canyon, rappel, zipline, raft, canoe, spelunk, windsurf, bike, fish, take a canopy tour, bathe in a waterfall basin, swing on a hanging bridge, ride horses or an ATV, take an aerial tram through the trees, explore the Venado caves, or raft along Río Peñas Blancas or Río Celeste.

> **TIP**
>
> **TOUR SMART.** Any of these licensed providers offers essentially the same services at similar prices. Quality across providers is comparable so long as you don't purchase the services of a non-licensed guide who approaches you on the street. In fact, each of the tour operators also sells their competitors' services, for which they receive a commission. This does not mean that the prices are higher than purchasing directly from the tour office; in fact, the prices may be cheaper. Feel free to shop around and negotiate with the tour offices before making your purchase. You should be able to lower the listed price by US$5-10 per person, especially if you are traveling in a group or purchasing multiple tours from the same provider.

Eagle Tours (☎2479 9091 or 2479 9361; www.eagletours.net), located in La Choza Inn. Offers the most popular tour in Arenal: the afternoon volcano/hot springs trip. The tour leaves La Fortuna at 3:30pm and begins with a hike around the site of old lava flows. After dusk, the tour heads to the other side of the volcano to watch the lava show, then finish with a couple hours of relaxation at the Baldi Hot Springs (US$42 per person, US$29 with a student ID). Other tour operators offer a similar package, but Eagle Tours is your best bet because they offer a lava-sighting guarantee: if it's too cloudy to see the lava on your first trip, they'll take you again the next day for free. Eagle Tours also offers day-long trips to Caño Negro (US$45, including lunch; US$30 for students) and horse-back rides to La Fortuna Waterfall (US$45/30).

Desafio Rafting (☎2479 9464; www.desafiocostarica.com), across the street to the west of the church. Specializes in rappelling and rafting tours. Enjoy the adventure of a full-day trip along the Class III and IV rapids of the Río Toro (US$85), or opt for a more tame day of rafting or inflatable kayaking down the river's class II and III rapids (US$65). You can also enjoy a horseback ride to the La Fortuna waterfall (US$40), or a rappelling and hiking trip down 8 waterfalls (4 per day, US$85). Open daily 7am-7pm. MC/V.

Sunset Tours (☎2479 9800 or 2479 9869; www.sunsettourcr.com), across the street from the south side of the church. Aside from the standard Arenal and hot springs tours, Sunset Tours also offers fishing tours (½-day US$220, full-day US$440), a dinner cruise on Lake Arenal (US$125), kayaking on Peñas Blancas (US$55), and a trip to Don Juan Eco Farm (US$55). Its Lake Arenal tour options are the most extensive of La Fortuna tour operators. Open daily 7am-8pm. AmEx/D/MC/V.

Pure Trek Canyoning (☎2479 7350 or 2461 2110; www.puretrekcostarica.com), located across the street from west side of church. Offers rappelling tours for thrill-seekers. The 4hr. trip includes 5 rappels (4 waterfalls and 1 canyon wall), hiking on the rainforest trails between each rappel location, transportation, and lunch (US$90 per person). There are 2 trips per day (7am, noon). Open daily 7am-8pm. MC/V.

Arenal Hanging Bridges (☎2231 1404; www.hangingbridges.com). A small private reserve 2km down a gravel road that branches off the main highway to Tilarán about 1km after the turnoff for El Castillo. A series of suspension bridges crisscross the primary growth forest at various levels, allowing visitors to experience the varied habitats within the forest at their own pace. The series of trails that connects the bridges is well-maintained and easily accessible, offering views of Arenal and Lake Arenal. Open daily 7:30am-4:30pm. Entrance US$22, US$17 for students; Natural History Tour US$34/29; Birdwatching Tour US$45/40. Both tours include entrance fees.

◨ DAYTRIPS FROM LA FORTUNA

EL CASTILLO

To get to El Castillo, turn left at the Ranger Station for Parque Nacional Volcán Arenal (about 17km west of town), continue on the gravel road for 10km until you reach the pueblo. The road to El Castillo is currently only accessible by 4WD, but the government is in the process of improving the road, so check with the Rancho Margot office in town about conditions before making the trek out. Rancho Margot runs a shuttle bus to El Castillo from its office on the north side of the parque central 3 times daily (7am, noon, and 4:30pm). A taxi from La Fortuna costs about US$20. If you book a trip in El Castillo through a tour operator in La Fortuna or through Rancho Margot, transportation is usually included.

Though most often visited as a daytrip from La Fortuna, El Castillo is actually a *pueblito* in its own right, and one that is quickly developing a tourism infrastructure that takes advantage of both Arenal Volcano and Lake Arenal. Numerous hotels, lodges, and attractions have been established in the area, and the only factor preventing a tourist boom in the small town is the poor condition of the road leading up to it, which requires a 4WD vehicle. However, with road construction in progress, a water-sports center under development, and new hotels opening their doors each year, El Castillo is poised to become a newer, wilder version of La Fortuna within the next couple of years.

There are an increasing variety of tourist activities available in El Castillo, most of which can be done as daytrips from La Fortuna or as part of a stay at **Rancho Margot** (see below) or other lodges in El Castillo. **Costa Rica Sky Adventures,** about 2km from the *cruce* toward the La Fortuna-Tilarán Hwy., offers a zip-line adventure through primary and secondary forests by two spectacular waterfalls. A **sky tram** takes visitors to the first platform for a more leisurely view of the forest. (☎2479 9944; www.skytrek.com La Fortuna office across from Banco Popular. Sky tram US$50. Sky tram and zipline US$60. Student discount 20%. Open daily 7am-9pm.) **Fourtrax Adventure** offers exhilarating ATV tours from a site to the south of Volcán Arenal, about 8km beyond El Castillo. (☎2479 8455 or 2479 8444; www.fourtraxadventure.com. 3hr. tour with 1-person ATV US$85; with 2-person ATV US$99.) For both the canopy and ATV tours, advance reservations are necessary; they can be arranged through most tour operators in La Fortuna or through the website.

The **WildSide BioPark,** 600m up the side-road from the *cruce,* is one of the most comprehensive and fascinating butterfly garden/botanical gardens in all of Costa Rica. Its atriums are specially designed to create distinct habitats supporting a unique variety of butterflies, from the spectacular blue morpho to the translucent "invisible" butterfly. The guided tour takes you through the botanical gardens, where you can look for edible fruits and therapeutic leaves to chew on, and finishes with a 1hr. hike through primary forest and a stop at the *ranario* to see the collection of venomous frogs. Although you can enter the park on your own for a voluntary donation, the tour with friendly, expert guides is well worth the cost. (☎8306 7390. Entrance fee is by voluntary donation. Guided tour 3hr., US$10 per person. Open daily 8am-5pm.) **Jardín Ecológico de Serpientes del Arenal,** 200m down the road from the BioPark, back toward the *cruce*, features up-close encounters with over 30 different species of snakes, frogs, lizards, and turtles. (☎8358 6773 or 8692 2087. Serpentarium US$7, with botanical garden and *mariposario* US$12. Open daily 8am-5pm.)

While most visitors to El Castillo stop by for the day, the town is actually home to one of the best accommodation options in the area for those who want to experience both the *tico* lifestyle and the natural beauty of the region. ▓**Rancho Margot ❷,** the brainchild of Chilean entrepreneur Juan Sostheim, is a sprawling complex that is part resort, part hostel, part organic farm, and part fledgling wild-life refuge. The ranch, which is completely off-grid, has its own hydro-power source and produces the meat, dairy products, and vegetables consumed by employees and guests, making it almost entirely self sufficient. While most guests come for the beautiful, hard-wood bungalows and relaxing yoga sessions, the ranch has numerous opportunities for volunteers. Those with at least a month available can help teach English, work on the organic farm, clean, or do virtually any other activity for which they are qualified; one volunteer did horse surgery. Volunteers receive free room and board in the ranch's bunkhouse; email the ranch to find out what jobs are available. Rancho Margot also offers a variety of tours, specializing in hikes around the region and horseback rides on the beautiful (and well-cared for) horses. (La Fortuna office ☎2479 7259, El Castillo office ☎8302 7318; info@ranchomargot.org. Free Wi-Fi and computer use. Doubles in bunkhouse US$45 per night including meals. More luxurious bungalows for 2 people US$160 including meals, US$30 per additional person. Fee waived for guests who volunteer on the ranch.)

OTHER DAYTRIPS

HOT SPRINGS. In the past few years, the demand for the original hot springs has increased so much that the prices have skyrocketed at the original resorts and numerous new springs have opened their doors. Of the two original hot springs, ▓**Baldi Hot Springs** is closer to town *(4km west of La Fortuna)* and much more reasonably priced than similarly popular **Tabacón.** It features an expansive set of 25 pools, sauna, spa, two swim-up bars, botanical gardens, and a Mayan pyramid replica. *(☎2479 9651. US$28 entry plus US$5 for a locker key. Open daily 10am-10pm.)* Operators in La Fortuna offer trips to the *termales* as part of the Volcán Arenal tour, which also includes a hike around the base of the volcano and a view of the lava at night. This is the best way to see the Baldi springs, as the combined price is not much higher than the individual entrance fees (approx. US$30 for the combined package with Baldi). For only US$20, you can visit the cold-water and hot-water swimming pools, waterslide, six thermal pools, butterfly garden, crocodile exhibit, and Arenal *mirador* of **Los Lagos Resort** *(☎2461 1818; fax 2461 1122; www.hotelloslagos.com. Open daily 10am-10pm. AmEx/D/MC/V. The bridge just after Tabacon has paths on each side that lead down to a hot-water stream that runs underneath and feeds a natural hot spring on each side of the bridge. Though there is no lifeguard, the springs are preferred by locals and backpackers looking for a free dip. 2 buses per day to Tilarán from La Fortuna pass the springs (8am, 5:30pm; return 3pm. Taxi for ₡5000 each way.)*

CATARATA FORTUNA. At Catarata La Fortuna, 5.5km outside of the town center, the Río Fortuna tumbles down through 70m of rainforest canopy. After a

20min. walk down the rocky trail, you come across the waterfall basin and a separate runoff area that's safe for bathing. Though the sign advising against swimming may seem nonchalant, **bathing in the waterfall basin is extremely dangerous.** The outward-flowing surface waters conceal a powerful undertow that is impossible to swim against, and there are currently no lifeguards stationed at the Catarata La Fortuna. Guided horseback tours are also available through tour operators in La Fortuna (US$45). From the parking lot, there is a trail to **Cerro Chato,** the dormant sidekick of Volcán Arenal. It's a steep, muddy slog that requires at least 2hr. each way, but an impressive crater lake at the top awaits. Local guides advise against swimming here because of the chemical composition of the water, so the hike is worth it only if you enjoy uphill treks or are in search of a cheap outdoor activity. Those looking for a safer spot to swim can check out local swimming hole ▧**El Salto,** on the left side of the bridge just past the entrance to the Catarata as you head out of town. Though there is no lifeguard here, the swimming hole is popular with locals and features a rope swing and numerous unmarked hiking trails that go around the area. *(Head south on the road that runs along the west side of the church. 1km later, a dirt road branches off to the right. After a 4km uphill walk that lasts about 1-2hr., you hit the waterfall parking lot. Taxis can take you as far as the parking lot for ₡2000—cabbing it there and then walking back to town downhill is a practical option. The road to the parking lot requires 4WD if it has recently rained. Taking a bike is another good option—you may have to walk it most of the way to the top, but you'll fly by exhausted hikers on the way back down. From the waterfall parking lot, a steep trail leads 20min. to the base of the falls. Bring plenty of water. Entrance ₡3600. Open daily 8am-4pm.)*

PARQUE NACIONAL VOLCÁN ARENAL. While the boundaries of the park stretch to Tilarán, Ciudad Quesada, and San Ramon, the paying entrance to the park is 17km west of La Fortuna (head west for 15km toward Tilaran and turn left at the sign). Though closer to the volcano, the view from the *Mirador* is not spectacular, and the park is really only worth a visit to see the volcano spew lava and rock out of its consistently active crater. One of the two paths in the park, **Sendero Las Coladas** (2.8km), crosses the 1992 lava trail and ends at a lookout point over the current lava trail. At nighttime, you can see what looks like a fireworks show as red-hot lava rocks fly down the mountain. Most hotels in the area have *miradores* from which you can see the lava flow down the mountain; sometimes it flows to the southwest, and other times more to the north. Check with guides in La Fortuna to confirm where the best lookout points are at the time of your visit. *(You can reach the station by bike, private car, or taxi. A one-way taxi ride costs US$10, but it's easier to take one of the guided tours (approximately US$20 including park entrance fee, with trip to the hot springs US$40). Eagle Tours (p. 165) offers a free 2nd chance if you don't see lava the first time around. Station open daily 8am-4pm. Park admission US$10.)*

LAGUNA ARENAL. Fifteen kilometers to the west of La Fortuna is a manmade lake that was created several decades ago after the construction of a dam as a part of a hydroelectric project. The newly formed lake covered the *pueblo* of Arenal, whose residents were compensated by the government and moved to the town of Nuevo Arenal, on the shores of the Laguna near Tilarán. The old town remains intact but decaying under water. When the water level is low, locals claim that they see the cross of the old church rising above the Laguna's gray waters. The renewable energy source now produces up to half of the country's electricity, and the lake has become a major destination for adventure seekers. Tour operators in La Fortuna and Tilaran offer kayaking (US$45; see Eagle Tours, p. 165) sportfishing (US$180 for 2 people; see Sunset Tours), and transfers to Monteverde that include a 1hr. boat ride across the lake (US$45; see Eagle Tours). The lake is popular with windsurfers, but those looking to catch the winds that rush across the lake do so from Tilarán (p. 189).

SAN RAFAEL DE GUATUSO

Rural San Rafael, commonly known as Guatuso (pop. 7000), is the capital of the *cantón* of Guatuso, called "Llanuras de Guatuso" ("Plains of Guatuso") for its expansive tropical plains. Two percent of the *cantón* is made up of indigenous **Maleku** communities, descendants of the *Guahisos*—a Corobicí tribe that emigrated from the Central Valley to establish itself in the hillsides of the rivers Tonjibe, Venado, La Muerte, and Margarita. Three of the *Maleku* towns (Margarita, El Sol, and Tonjibe) are open to tourists. Although San Rafael is not frequented by many tourists, its residents are charming hosts, and the small *pueblo* makes for an excellent base from which to explore the region's numerous natural wonders—over a fifth of the cantón is part of Refugio Nacional Caño Negro (p. 175), the **Venado Caves** and their underground waterfall are less than 10km away, and the area contains part of Volcán Tenorio National Park including the hike to the spectacularly blue Río Celeste.

▐ TRANSPORTATION

Most tourists never set foot in San Rafael, but the town's location between Upala and transportation hubs of Ciudad Quesada/San Carlos and San José means that there is a fair amount of public transportation passing through the city. **Buses** leave from Guatuso to San José (5hr.; 8, 11:30am, 3pm; ¢2000), Upala (2hr.; 8:05am, 12:30, 4:10, 7:30pm; ¢950), and Ciudad Quesada (2hr.; 5:15, 7, 9:10am, 1:30, 4:30, 6pm; ¢1250) via Fortuna (1hr., ¢950). Contact Autotransporte San José-San Carlos at ☎2255 4318.

There are about 12 licensed **taxis** in Guatuso (☎2464 0363); those looking for passengers queue up in front of Super Pague Menos. Luís Alberto (cell ☎8355 1022), who has a pickup truck that holds 12, is a popular driver who can give you plenty of information about the region on your way to your destination. Ask for him at El Turístico (see below).

✳ ▐ ORIENTATION AND PRACTICAL INFORMATION

San Rafael stretches along one main road from the bridge to Upala on the north side of town to **Bar Restaurante El Rancho Guanacaste** on the south end of town. Buses stop on the main road in front of **Super Pague Menos,** which is located 350m south of the bridge at the center of town.

Tourist Office: Enrique and William of **Restaurante El Turístico** (p. 170) (☎2464 1000) offer the best tourist information.

Banks: Banco Nacional (☎2464 0024), 300m south of El Turístico, has a 24hr. ATM. Open M-F 8:30am-3:45pm. **Coocique R.L.** (☎2464 0044), 100m east of Albergue Tío Henry. Has a Western Union. Open M-F 7am-4pm, Sa 8am-noon.

Police: (☎2464 0257), 400m south of El Turístico next to the gas station. Open 24hr.

Medical Services: Clínica Guatuso (☎2464 0161 or 2464 1004), 1.5km south of the police station. Open M-F 7am-10pm, Sa-Su 10am-8pm.

Pharmacy: Farmacia Guatuso (☎2464 0017), next to Tío Henry's. Open M-Sa 6:15am-8:30pm, Su 6:15am-noon.

Telephones: Public telephones are available in front of Restaurante El Turístico.

Internet Access: Available across from Super Pague Menos, on the 2nd fl. of the Musmanni bakery. ¢450 per hr. Open M-F 9am-8pm, Sa 9am-5pm.

Post Office: Post office (☎2464 0132), on the main road next to the police station. Open M-F 8am-noon and 1-5:30pm. **Postal Code:** 4500

ACCOMMODATIONS

Cabinas El Gordo (☎8845 0254), across the street from Cabinas Doña Chenta. Though the gated exterior over the parking lot is slightly forbidding, the amenities are the best in town: A/C, private hot-water baths, and cable TV in all rooms. Singles ¢4000; doubles and triples ¢7000. AmEx/D/MC/V. ❶

Cabinas Doña Chenta (☎2464 0023; fax 2464 0045), the 1st accommodation coming in from Upala, in the garden lot just north of Cabinas El Gordo. Has 15 family-style rooms with cable TV, fans, and private cold-water baths, along with a lounge area with a communal kitchen, dining area, and TV. Owners Gladys and Martín will cook you a *casado* and meet your tour and transportation needs. Singles ¢4000; doubles ¢8000. ❶

Cabinas Tío Henry (☎2464 0344), 100m south of El Turístico. 20 rooms with A/C, TVs, and private hot-water baths. If the gate is locked, look for owner Ignacio next door in the veterinarian's office. In addition to curing sick animals, Ignacio offers tour advice. Singles ¢7000; doubles and triples ¢10,000. ❷

FOOD

You can buy your own food at **Super Pague Menos**, next door to El Turístico. (☎2464 0672 or 2464 0373. Open daily 7am-8pm. AmEx/D/MC/V.) There are also many *sodas* that line the main road.

Restaurante El Turístico (☎2464 1000), at the bus stop on the main road. Great service and a lively social scene make it the de facto town center. Locals go through the cafeteria-style line to pick up fried chicken (¢800 per piece) and *comida típica* (¢800-2000), or just stop by to chat with friends. Open daily 6am-9pm. MC/V. ❶

Bar/Restaurante Marisquería Jimmy (☎2464 0048), next to Cabinas el Gordo. Serves Chinese, Asian, and Costa Rican dishes in a casual atmosphere. Fried rice and chop suey dishes ¢1300-2700. Seafood ¢3500-4500. Open daily 11am-2am. MC/V. ❷

Noemi's Panificadora del Norte (☎2464 0351), in front of Cabinas El Gordo and another 50m east of Bar Restaurante Marisquería Jimmy. Start your day with a pastry or homemade bread. Pastries ¢350-800. Open M-Sa 5:30am-8:30pm. ❶

Bar/Restaurante El Rancho Guanacaste, 400m south of the Banco Nacional. Of the many bars that serve food, definitely try friendly María Pineda Dávila's bar/restaurant. Though a bit of a hike from the town center, it has a laid-back vibe that is conducive to a relaxing meal. *Bocas* ¢500-2000. Beer ¢800. Open daily 11am-midnight. ❶

SIGHTS

Guatuso is a good place to visit if you want to explore rural Costa Rica while enjoying all the creature comforts of a small town. San Rafael's *fiesta patronal* (patron saint festival) is on October 24. If you have never seen a cattle auction, **Subasta Ganadero Maleco**, only 2km south of the center, is an incontestably memorable experience. Every Wednesday, auctioneers shout the weights and prices of each specimen in an infinite parade of cattle. Ask Luís Alberto (see **Transportation**, p. 169) to take you. Also ask about the *cabalgatas* that take place nearly every month, when thousands of horse riders gallop off to a nearby *pueblo* for a day-long festival to entertain the community.

NIGHTLIFE

Though Guatuso does have several bars, they are rather small, dark, and almost entirely frequented by men.

Bar/Restaurante El Rancho Guanacaste has the most female-friendly atmosphere. Its huge cement "hut" with a dance floor hosts locals grooving to a wide range of music, from 1940s tunes to current hits. Beer ¢800. Open daily 11am-midnight.

Bar Los Ganaderos (☎2464 0313), 150m east of Banco Naciona. A more laid-back locale that sees a lot of youthful traffic despite its plain white walls and random nude photo spreads. Beer ¢800. Open daily 11am-midnight.

DAYTRIPS FROM SAN RAFAEL DE GUATUSO

CAVERNAS DE VENADO

It is not possible to see the Cavernas without a guide, so visitors have 2 options: arrange their own transport and get a guide at the cave entrance, or go to the caves on a guided tour from Fortuna. Public transport to the caves is tricky; from San Rafael de Guatuso, take any bus heading to Ciudad Quesada/San Carlos or San José (25min., ¢650), and ask the driver to drop you off in Jicarito. From Jicarito, it is a 7km drive up an unpaved road to the pueblito of El Venado, at the end of which you will see the gate to the caves' entrance. Buses leave the next day from El Venado at 6:20am and 1:30pm, and head back to Ciudad Quesada/San Carlos. If planning public transportation seems too complicated, you can take a taxi from San Rafael de Guatuso (round trip ¢15,000) or set up a tour with one of the operators in La Fortuna, including Desafío (US$35-45). It is also possible to take a bus from El Tanque in La Fortuna to El Venado (1hr., 8:30am, ¢700; return 1:30pm). For information on individual visits, group rates, restaurant hours, or longer expert tours, contact the owners (Wilbur Jiménez and Yoleni Cuero) of the finca on which the cave is located. (☎2478 8008. Open daily 7am-4pm, tours usually 9am-2pm. During the rainy season, most of the tour will pass through water; expect to be almost completely submerged at points. If you don't want to trek in water-filled boots, bring hiking sandals; the caves are pretty warm throughout the year.) Standard 1½hr. guided tour of the cave costs US$15. The fee includes necessary equipment (helmet, flashlight, boots, and breathing mask) as well as access to onsite showers and towels.

Since their discovery in 1942 by two hunters chasing a *tepescuintle* (pig-like rainforest mammal), the Venado caves have lured thousands of spelunkers to their hidden wonders. On a private ranch up a gravel road from the small *pueblo* of El Venado, the caves are open to the public through guided tours. Guides can take you in to discover 10 galleries full of stalactites and stalagmites, six-million-year-old columns (called "papayas" because of their resemblance to the fruit), underground rivers, multitudes of bats, primitive insects, and fossils of the sea life that inhabited these caves millions of years ago. If you visit during the summer, gallery Boca de la Serpiente receives a magical stream of light from 11am to 1pm. During the rainy season, an 18m waterfall from **Río de La Muerte** awaits halfway through the 1½hr. tour. Though open to the public, the caves have not been developed at all. There is no electricity, and rivers run through most of the passageways. Expect to be squeezing through tunnels and scrambling up chimneys; wear clothes that you will be comfortable in while soaking wet, and bring a change of clothes for afterwards. Avoid wearing glasses, which fog up underground and could be damaged. A waterproof camera is best for pictures and necessary during the rainy season, though a professional photographer accompanies larger groups (photo CD US$20).

The town of El Venado, at the foot of the gravel driveway leading up to the *finca* where the caverns are, is charming but tiny, with more cows than buildings. The **police station** is 100m up the road from Hospedaje las Brisas, and the **clinic** is 200m down the road from the caves (open M and Th 8am-4pm).

If you bring your own tent, you may camp near the caves for free (there are bathrooms and showers at the caverns). The only *cabinas* in town are at **Hospedaje La Brisas ❶**, near the end of town that leads to the caves, which has two small, clean doubles (☎2478 8107; ¢5000 per room). If groups arrive, friendly owner María might let you stay in rooms in her house, but you should call ahead. **Bar el Venado ❶,** across from Hospedaje Las Brisas, is the only s nightlife in the town, serving up *bocas* (¢500-700) and *cervezas* for ¢650 (☎2478 4185. Open daily 11am-midnight). **Soda el Venado ❶** is the only restaurant around, preparing *gallo pinto* (¢1000) and *casados* for ¢2000 (open daily 7:30am-8pm).

🏔 RÍO CELESTE

The best way to get to Río Celeste is by driving; the closest you can get by public transport is a 3km uphill walk away from the beginning of the hike. You need a 4WD to drive to Río Celeste; from Guatuso, follow the road to Upala until km 13; take a left at the sign for Río Celeste Lodge and follow the gravel road and signs until you reach the lodge's parking lot, about 12km from the turnoff. If driving isn't an option, you can take the bus from Guatuso to Río Celeste (1hr.; 11am, 4pm; return 6am, 1pm; ¢700). The bus will leave you at a bridge that crosses the river, and from there it is a 3km walk along a gravel road to the Rio Celeste Lodge (☎2876 4382 or 8361 3510), which is the official entrance to the park. A taxi can take you all the way to the entrance from Guatuso for ¢10,000 round-trip.

An hour away from San Rafael lies one of Costa Rica's unique natural marvels: the Río Celeste. The river's name is derived from its mesmerizing, brilliant blue hue, a product of the mixing of two streams of different temperatures (one highly acidic) with volcanic minerals and gas bubbles. Though the trail along Río Celeste is officially part of **Parque Nacional Volcan Tenorio,** the entrance is on the private property of Río Celeste Lodge. The US$10 entrance fee is dispersed among MINAE, the community, and the lodge. The trail starts on a short uphill hike through the rainforest and then branches into two separate paths, one leading to the base of the magnificent waterfall, the other leading to the hot springs and the *teñidoros,* where you can see the two streams coming together and producing the celestial blue color that the water carries downstream. The unguided trip through both trails can be done in 2hr., though most guided tours take about 4hr. If you miss the bus back, you can stay at the lodge's beautiful, rustic rooms with forest views and private hot-water baths (rooms US$25, 1-4 people per room; with meals and tour US$30 per person).

PALENQUE EL TONJIBE

Palenque el Tonjibe is 6km from San Rafael de Guatuso. Buses leave from in front of El Turístico (p. 170; 30min.; 8:30am, noon, 4:30pm; return 9:15am, 1pm; ¢800). A taxi from Guatuso costs ¢4000. Few tour operators officially offer trips to El Palenque, but you can request to be taken there on trips to Río Celeste or the Cavernas Venado.

Minutes from the capital of Guatuso, a population of about 500 members of the Maleku tribe live in three small *pueblos* on a reserve for indigenous peoples. One hundred and fifty years ago, the Maleku fought a war to protect their precious rubber trees from invaders who came to steal sell them to foreigners. The Maleku were decimated by battles like that of Río de la Muerte. The few that are left today seek to continue their traditional way of life. Although many have designer clothes and cell phones, they continue to eat traditional food, use medicinal plants to treat illnesses, and participate in ancient ceremonies.

Tourists can visit the **pueblo of Tonjibe,** which offers a program combining eco-tourism with demonstrations of Maleku rituals and dancing ceremonies. The well-organized, under-touristed program includes a 2hr. hike through a plot of land that the Maleku have recently reforested, with fascinating explanations of the traditional uses of many of the plants. The guide will help you partake in edible roots, chew on plants that relieve hypertension and stomach aches, and lick leaves that work as natural anaesthetics. Eat them at your own risk. After a traditional lunch prepared by members of the tribe, the Maleku perform traditional dances and story-telling, after which you can mingle with the tribespeople, admire their native artwork, and even purchase something to take home. The entire program lasts 4hr. (US$25 per person).You can show up at any time, but most tours start between 9am and 10am, and the guides recommend calling a day in advance to make a reservation (☎2307 8972 or 2890 6509). Most of the guides speak only Maleku and Spanish—call to confirm that you can take the tour with an English-speaking guide, or organize to go with an English-speaking tour guide from a tour company in La Fortuna.

Stay in the onsite traditional huts with modern amenities (like private baths) for US$60 a night, which includes the 4hr. tour and all meals. Local guides will also take you on a unique tour of the Río Celeste (prices negotiable). The Maleku also accept volunteers, who can help with reforestation projects and building construction while staying in the on-site huts (call the reservation for details). The money raised through the tourism project is used by the Maleku to buy back land that was purchased generations ago by *tico* farmers. They hope to reforest the land and return it to its original state.

LOS CHILES

Tourism is still a novelty in Los Chiles, a town 101km north of Ciudad Quesada and 3km south of the Nicaraguan border. Its proximity to the border has shaped the town's character in conspicuous ways; today, Nicaraguan immigrants makes up almost 40% of the town's population. The town's namesake dates back to its industrial heyday, when rubber extractors passed the time by telling each other *chiles* (jokes). Today, visitors pass through on their way to Nicaragua or to the **Refugio Nacional de Vida Silvestre Caño Negro** (p. 175).

▐ TRANSPORTATION

Buses leave from the station 300m east of the northeast corner of the *parque*, behind Soda Pamela, for: San José (6hr.; 5:30am, 3:30pm; ¢4000); Ciudad Quesada (3hr.; 1 per hr. 5am-6pm; ¢3000); Upala (3hr.; 5am, 2pm, 4:30pm; ¢1500) via Caño Negro (1hr., ¢950). **Boats** go to and from San Carlos, Nicaragua. **Taxis** abound, but you should agree to a price ahead of time to avoid getting overcharged.

▗ ▐ ORIENTATION AND PRACTICAL INFORMATION

A soccer field and *parque central* mark the center of Los Chiles, with a church on the eastern side of the *parque*. The immigration office is 125m west of the southwest corner of the *parque*, and the Río Frío is another 100m to the west.

> **Tours:** Though there are no official tour companies in Los Chiles, several of the hotels in town offer information and arrange trips to Refugio Caño Negro and Nicaragua. **Hotel Rancho Tulipán** offers boat trips in Caño Negro (2 people US$70) and 2-day, 1-night tours of Nicaragua (9 people US$1900; includes boat ride, meals, hotel, and guide). **Cabinas Jabirú** can provide information and, though they do not organize trips, can help you find a tour (Caño Negro tours approx. US$80 per person) that suits your needs.
>
> **Banks: Banco Nacional** (☎2471 2020), 50m east of the northeast corner of the *parque*, changes US$, euros, and traveler's checks. Open M-F 8:30am-3:45pm. MC/V ATM. The storehouse next to the Hotel Tulipán, across from the immigration office, changes Costa Rican *colónes* into Nicaraguan *córdobas* and vice-versa. Open daily 7am-6pm.
>
> **Police: Police** (☎2471 1183, emergencies 911), 400m east and 100m south of the southeast corner of the *parque*.

Pharmacy: Farmacia Todo (☎2471 1031), 200m east of the southeast corner of the *parque*. Open M-Th 8am-8pm, Sa 8am-7pm. MC/V.

Hospital: A 24hr. **hospital** (☎2471 2000), 500m south of the police station.

Telephones: Telephones at the bus station and the northeastern corner of the *parque*.

Internet Access: Available at **Multi Servicios J&Q**, on the north side of the *parque*. ¢600 per hr. Open daily 8:30am-noon and 2-8pm. You can also acess Internet in the lobby of **Hotel Rancho Tulipán** (☎2471 1414). ¢500 per hr. Open daily 6am-11pm. If the front door is locked, check the side door in the restaurant.

Post Office: The **post office** (☎2471 1061), is in front of the courthouse, 300m east of the northeast corner of the *parque*. Open M 8am-noon and 1:30-5:30pm, Tu-F 8am-noon and 1-5:30pm. **Postal code:** 4450.

ACCOMMODATIONS

Hotel Rancho Tulipán (☎/fax 2471 1414), across from the immigration office. The cleanest, most comfortable rooms in town have A/C, satellite TV, Wi-Fi, hot-water baths, and comfy beds. Hospitable owner can answer any of your questions about Los Chiles. Singles US$30; doubles US$50; triples US$70. Breakfast included. MC/V. ❸

Cabinas Jabirú (☎2471 1496 or 8898 6357), 2 blocks east and a block north of the northeast side of the *parque*. 12 suites with private hot-water baths, a TV room with a bed, and a bedroom with a queen bed. Rooms with A/C have a fridge and microwave. Breakfast US$4. Rooms for 1-3 ¢8000 per person, with A/C ¢10,000 per person. ❷

Hotel Central (☎2471 1096), east of the south side of the *parque*. Dark, basic rooms with private cold-water baths. TV room where guests hang out. ¢2000 per person. ❶

Hospedaje Los Chiles (☎2471 1262 or 8319 6954), south of the soccer field. Small rooms with fans and shared cold-water baths. ¢2000 per person. ❶

FOOD AND NIGHTLIFE

For those looking for supplies to cook their own meal, **Supermercado Carranza** is located on the west side of the soccer field. Open daily 6am-8pm. **Palí**, next to Banco Nacional, is a larger option. Open M-Th 8:30am-7pm, F-Sa 8:30am-7:30pm, Su 8:30am-3pm. ATM inside accepts MC/V.

Bar/Restaurante Sonia (☎2471 1140), 250m south of the police station on the top of the hill. Offers breakfast and lunch *casados* in a breezy dining area with Chinese-style wall decorations. Breakfast ¢1300-1700. *Casados* ¢1500-2000. Open M-F 6:30am-10pm, Sa 6am-3pm, Su 6am-1pm. AmEx/D/MC/V. ❶

Restaurante El Parque (☎2471 1373). Though the in-house souvenir shop gives it a touristy feel, the location, large windows, and filling portions make it worth a visit. Breakfast *pinto* dishes ¢1000-1300. Entrees ¢1500-2500. Open daily 6am-10pm. ❶

Restaurante Tulipán, in Hotel Tulipán. Serves surprisingly elegant European food despite the *cabana*-style decor. Its bar offers classy nightlife and attracts an amiable crowd. *Casados* ¢2500-3000. Entrees ¢2000-3000. Open daily 6am-10pm. AmEx/MC/V. ❷

Soda Pamela (☎2471 1454), in front of the bus station. Serves as the de-facto fast food stop in town, serving tasty *empanadas* (¢350) and *casados* (¢1900-2300) to customers on bar stools. Breakfast ¢1500. Open M-Sa 6am-8pm, Su 6am-6pm. ❶

Salon-Bar-Restaurante el Roble, next door to Hotel Los Chiles. The only bar-disco in town. DJ on Saturday nights. Beer ¢500. Open daily 11am-2:30am.

REFUGIO NACIONAL CAÑO NEGRO

Where there's water, there's life, and Refugio Caño Negro has plenty of both. The refuge gets 3.5m of rain every year, and 85% of its land (100 sq. km) is flooded during the rainy season from May to December. In the heart of this aquatic wonderland is the enormous **Laguna Caño Negro,** a 9 sq. km lake that refills every summer when the banks of the Río Frío and Río Caño Negro overflow. The labyrinth of mangroves, rivers, and harbors here has been declared the world's fourth most important biological zone, with 160 species of mammals and over 315 species of birds. Reptiles like crocodiles, iguanas, turtles, and snakes abound, and rare fish, including the prehistoric gaspar, swim the waters. On the banks of the *laguna,* 23km southwest of Los Chiles, lies the village of Caño Negro. Despite its small size and remote location down a gravel road, this town is the gateway to the Refugio Caño Negro. Caño Negro is part of the protected area of the **Conservación Arenal Huetar Norte,** an organization that focuses on the improvement of the socioeconomic conditions of the community by creating sustainable development programs. Tourism in the area is largely dictated by the water; during the dry season (February to April), you can explore the *laguna* on foot. When the lake is filled, there are two options for exploring. When rains are sufficient, the park can be explored by boat. Otherwise, the easiest way to explore the park is on the consistently accessible **Río Frío.** To find out what is available, ask at the entrance or check with tour operators. (Park open daily 8am-4pm. US$10.)

TRANSPORTATION

By **car,** the best way to get to Caño Negro from San José is to head north on the road toward Los Chiles. The entrance is 1km after the Tanques Gas Zeta (19km before Los Chiles); then take the 19km unpaved road. The entire trip should take around 4hr. Despite the road conditions, **buses** leave from Los Chiles to **Upala** through **Caño Negro** (1½hr.; M-F 5am, noon, 4pm; Sa 5am, 2pm; Su 5am; ¢1100). Buses leave for **Los Chiles** (1½hr.; 3 per day M-F 6am, 12:30pm, and 5pm; Sa 6am, 5pm; Su 12:30pm; ¢1100). Buses leave for **Upala** daily at 11:30am, or approximately 1½hr. after they leave from Los Chiles. The best place to wait for the bus is in front of the mini-super, where you can see traffic coming in and out of town. Buses also stop in front of the hotels along the road to the town's entrance.

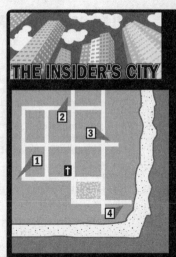

THE INSIDER'S CITY

MUCHAS MARIPOSAS

Over a decade ago, the women's association of Caño Negro started the *mariposario* project, meant to grow colonies of the winged beauties for sale. Today, you can visit 4 different *mariposarios* around Caño Negro village. Only the women's association has official hours

1. La Asociación de Mujeres de Cano Negro offers one of the biggest, most accessible gardens in town and sells fresh bread and pastries in its bakery next door.

2. Dona Claris has a smaller atrium that features the coveted and beautiful blue morpho butterfly. ☎2471 1450. ¢1000.

3. Belsis Gracia has the newest, best constructed *mariposario* in town. ☎2471 1315. ¢1000.

4. La Reinata's convenient garden has brightly colored *mariposas* that flutter around lush vegetation. ☎2471 1301. ¢1000.

ORIENTATION AND PRACTICAL INFORMATION

The bus enters the village on the **main road,** making a loop around the **parque central** before heading back out at the northwest corner of the *parque,* next to the **school.** Just north of the school is the church and, 25m to the north, a **mini-super** (☎2461 1500; open M-Sa 7am-7pm, Su 7am-5pm.) The refuge entrance is on the southeast corner of the *parque.*

The **MINAE** office (☎2471 1309, open daily 8am-4pm), 200m west of the mini-super, provides tourist information. There is **no bank,** and the nearest medical facility is **Hospital Ebais** (☎2471 1531), a small clinic 50m east from the mini-super. The **police station** (☎2471 1802) is on the southeast side of the *parque.* The town has two **public telephones,** at the mini-super and in front of the police station.

ACCOMMODATIONS AND CAMPING

It is possible to **camp** on the grounds of the Caño Negro MINAE office, which have access to cold-water showers and bathrooms. (¢1000 per person.)

Albergue Caño Negro (☎2471 2029), 200m north of the northwest corner of the *parque,* on a grassy *finca* on the banks of the Laguna Caño Negra. Simple cabins on stilts come with two twin beds, wall fans, linens, and padlocked doors. Communal cold-water baths located downstairs. Each cabin has a porch overlooking the *finca* and the *laguna.* ¢7000 per person. ❶

Cabinas Martín Pescador (☎2471 1369 or 1116), 100m past the MINAE office, in the field at the end of the road. The reception is across the street from the north side of the *parque* in the small goods store next to the *Cabinas Martín* sign. Cabins with covered porches and hot-water baths; some also have A/C and cable TV. Singles ¢11,600 (US$20); doubles ¢17,400 (US$30); each additional person ¢5800 (US$10). ❷

Natural Lodge Caño Negro (☎2471 1426; www.canonegrolodge.com), 300m north and 50m west of the mini-super. Elegant rooms decorated with abstract paintings have queen beds, A/C, safe deposit boxes, and spacious bathrooms. Amenities include a pool and hot tub. Breakfast included. Helpful and informed staff can schedule various tours. High-season doubles ¢58,000 (US$100), low-season ¢46,400 (US$80); triples ¢63,8000/¢52,220 (US$110/90); quads ¢69,600/¢58,000 (US$120/100); each additional person ¢5,800 (US$10). AmEx/D/MC/V. ❺

Hotel de Campo (☎2471 1012; www.hoteldecampo.com), on the *laguna* side of the road to the village, 400m before Albergue Caño Negro. Tidy, well-equipped rooms in stucco cottages. A manicured garden leads to the lagoon. Hot water and A/C. Breakfast included. Pool for guest use. Rooms ¢49,300 (US$85). Ask about the ecological and fishing tours. AmEx/D/MC/V. ❺

FOOD

Soda la Palmera (☎2471 1045), on the southeast corner of the *parque.* Though the menu offers few options, La Palmera cooks up tasty *comida típica* for a local clientele in its cottage-style dining area. *Gallo pinto* with eggs, an avocado slice, and coffee ¢1200. Entrees ¢2000 with drink. Bathroom use ¢100. Open daily 7am-8pm. ❶

Restaurante Danubio Azul (☎2471 1295), on the southeast side of the *parque.* A quiet spot during low season. In high season, its eating area overlooking the *laguna* becomes a popular disco. *Guapote* fish ¢3600. *Casados* of gaspar (the special lake fish) come with rice, beans, and salad ¢3500. Entrees from ¢2000. Open daily 10am-2am. ❷

Restaurante Jabirú (☎2471 1426), located in the Natural Lodge Caño Negro. The fanciest and priciest food in town. Pasta entrees (fettucine with broccoli sauce, ¢2800). Meat and seafood dishes ¢3500-5800. Imported beer ¢1300-2600.

Mango juice ¢600. Continental breakfast with bread, marmalade, coffee/tea, and orange juice ¢2800. Open daily 6am-10pm. ❷

Restaurante El Pueblo (☎2471 1419), located right before the rooms of Cabinas Martín Pescador. This restaurant serves large breakfasts for ¢3500. *Casados* (chicken, fish, or steak, includes salad and bread) ¢4000. Open daily 7am-6pm. ❷

VISITING THE REFUGE

The park is easily reached from Caño Negro village and is best seen by boat. A 1½km trail starts near the office; others emerge as the lake dries up. **Pantanal Tours,** a small unlabeled office across from Soda La Palmera (above), offers several tours in Spanish and English. (Kayaks ¢17,4000/US$30 per 4 hr.; Fish and ecological tours for 2-3 people ¢29,000/US$50 per 2hr.; horseback riding ¢11,600/US$20 per 2hr.) Open daily 6am-5pm. Antonio at **Cabinas Martín Pescador** (p. 176) takes people fishing on his canopied *lancha*. (1-4 people, ¢29,000/US$50 per 2hr.; each additional person ¢5800/US$10.) **Natural Lodge Caño Negro** runs tours of turtle and butterfly farms (¢14,5000/US$25) and 3 hr. tours of the lake (¢25,520/US$44, includes park entrance fee). There is also the **Tour and Fishing Info Office** (☎8823 4026) shortly past the Natural Lodge Caño Negro which offers fishing, butterfly and turtle tours, camping, trails, and horseback riding. Larger tour operations run out of **La Fortuna** and **Los Chiles.** Prices typically do not include park entrance (¢5800, US$10 per day) or fishing licenses (2 months ¢17,400, US$30). You can pay the ranger for park entry in the kiosk at the entrance on the southeast corner of the *parque*. **Fishing** is prohibited April through July. A license requires a photocopy of your passport and two passport-size photos. To get one, pay ¢17,400 (US$30) in any Banco Nacional and pick up your package at any MINAE office; there is one 100m north and 200m west of the northwest corner of the *parque* in Caño Negro (p. 176). You can also pay at the office. Licenses purchased within the last two months are accepted at Caño Negro. Call the **Area de Conservación Huetar Norte** with questions (☎2471 1309).

Bring waterproof boots—biting ants and 10 of Costa Rica's 17 types of venomous snakes await. For more on **Wilderness Safety,** see p. 77.

NORTHWESTERN COSTA RICA

The two mountain chains that stretch across northwestern Costa Rica guard some of the country's most famous attractions. The world-renowned Monteverde Reserve protects what remains of the cloud forests that once covered all of the Cordillera de Tilarán, while the Cordillera de Guanacaste holds three spectacular national parks further north. Volcán Arenal, Central America's most active volcano, oozes magma at a cratered peak nestled between these two majestic ranges. Though the arid lowlands of Guanacaste cannot offer such natural beauty, they have a *sabanero* (cowboy) charm all their own. They serve as good base camps for nearby attractions like Volcán Tenorio, Volcán Miravalles, and the national parks that make up the Area de Conservación de Guanacaste, which holds 65% of Costa Rica's species. The region has witnessed everything from annexation to invasions, and its dynamic history allows its rich folkloric tradition to constantly unfold and expand. While larger numbers of Nicaraguan immigrants have made diversity a source of regional pride and tension in more southern cities like San José, Guanacastan towns have managed to thrive on the harmony and vitality of their mixed populations.

MONTEVERDE AND SANTA ELENA

The Monteverde region, located 184km northwest of San José and due north of Puntarenas, is the reason that many travelers come to Costa Rica in the first place. Dry season guarantees more animal sightings and fewer lightning cancellations, but it also attracts many more tourists, making reservations a must for almost everything. Conversely, the rainy season offers a leisurely schedule and more exhilarating adventures as the ziplines are significantly faster in the rain. Private reserves in the area, including the famous **Monteverde Cloud Forest Reserve,** protect some of the country's last remaining primary cloud forest, which provides refuge for iridescent *quetzals*, foraging *coatis*, and a host of other creatures. Tourists flock to Monteverde to observe its array of flora and fauna. Others travel to these forests longing to fly through canopies on ziplines and watch sunsets on horses. Still others seek retreat, finding peace in the hikes, waterfalls, and art galleries that the region has to offer.

The town of **Monteverde** was founded in 1951 when a group of American Quakers, many of whom had served jail time for refusing to enlist in the armed forces, exiled themselves to the region. They used existing oxcart trails to bring in cows and to start up a successful cheese business. Though the largely English-speaking town has retained a sense of its roots, its population these days is as diverse as the nearby wildlife. There is a mix of *ticos*, tourists, eco-friendly expats, artists, biologists, and students gathered together in a sundry array of jungle lodges, local dives, and ordinary residential communities. The small town of **Santa Elena** hosts many of the area's tourist facilities and practical amenities while retaining an intimate ambience. Its central location provides a launching point to nearby reserves, including **Monteverde Reserve, Santa Elena Reserve,** and **El Bosque Eterno de los Niños.** Most are connected by dirt roads,

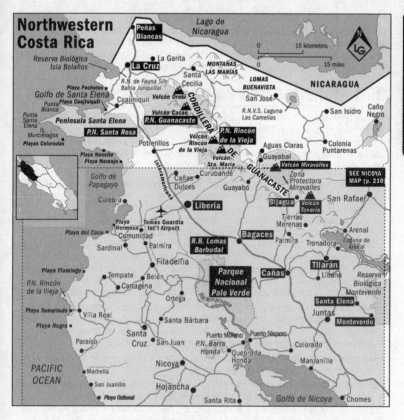

preserving a dependent community throughout the region without infringing on the area's natural splendor. Beware its spell: many visitors have been known to extend their stays indefinitely.

▛ TRANSPORTATION

Direct **buses to Santa Elena** and **Monteverde** run from **San José** (4hr.; 6:30am, 2:30pm; ¢2350), **Puntarenas** (3.5hr.; 7:50am, 1:50, 2:15pm; ¢1235), and **Tilarán** (3hr., 12:30pm, ¢1400). From **Liberia**, you can take a San José-bound bus as far as **Lagarto**, and then take a bus to **Monteverde** (8:30am, 3:00pm; ¢1200). Alternatively, go to **Puntarenas** and catch a bus from there to Monteverde. To get to Monteverde Reserve, you must change buses in **Santa Elena** (approximately 20min., times listed under Monteverde Reserve; purchase tickets for ¢600 on the bus to the Reserve).

Leaving Monteverde, buses head to: **San José** (4hr.; 6:30am, 2:30pm; ¢2350), **Puntarenas** (3hr.; 4:30am, 6, 3pm; ¢1235), and **Tilarán** (3hr., 7am, ¢1400). Buy return tickets from Monteverde to Puntarenas the morning of your bus; if going to San José, purchase the day before at the **Transmonteverde B.S.A. ticket office**, located across the street from Camino Verde in Santa Elena (☎2645 5159. Open M-F 5:45-11am and 1:30-5pm, Sa-Su 5:45-11am and 1:30-3pm.)

Many companies offer more adventurous ways to reach popular destinations. **Jeep-Boat-Jeep** (US$25) and **Horse-Boat-Car** are offered through Aventuras El Lago. **Taxis** wait outside the church in Santa Elena. Be wary of taxi-drivers looking to charge tourists unreasonable fares. Ask the tourist office what it should cost to take a taxi to your destination; it shouldn't be more than ¢5000.

✈ 🔃 ORIENTATION AND PRACTICAL INFORMATION

Buses arrive in the town of Santa Elena, which has affordable local services, hotels, and restaurants. From here, an unpaved road heads 6km southeast to the Monteverde Reserve. The actual settlement of Monteverde is strung along this road, and has more expensive restaurants and hotels. Unless otherwise noted, the following services are in Santa Elena.

Tourist Information and Tours: Camino Verde Information & Reservation Center (☎2645 6304; www.exploringmonteverde.com), across from the bus stop, offers friendly assistance when arranging a tour. Open daily 6am-9pm. Those searching for tour companies will find no shortage along the main street; it's worth shopping around as commissions vary widely. **Camara de Turismo** (☎2645 6565; fax 2645 6464), at the end of the street across from Supermercado La Esperanza, is the official tourist center. Both book reservations to the Santa Elena and Monteverde Reserve, nearby canopy tours, ATV rides, and more. Open daily 8am-8pm. Most accommodations have their own information and tour deals; often they do not receive commission and some offer refunds for tour cancellations.

Bank: Banco Nacional (☎2645 5027; www.bncr.fi.cr), around the corner from the bus station. Changes traveler's checks and US$ and gives cash advances on MC and V with passport. Open M-Sa 8:30am-3:45pm. ATM available. **Banco de Costa Rica,** up the main road toward Monteverde Reserve, next to Sapo Dorado. Open M-F 9am-4pm.

Supermarket: SuperCompro (☎2645 5068), south of the bus station, across the street from Camara de Turismo. Open M-Sa 7am-8pm, Su 7am-8pm. AmEx/D/MC/V.

Bookstore: Librería Chunches (☎2645 5147), across from Banco Nacional and Pensión Santa Elena. Overpriced and photocopied US newspapers (NY Times ¢5000) and plain overpriced magazines (US Weekly ¢5500), new and used books and music, local information, and coffee (¢600). Also sells souvenirs, batteries, blank CDs, and envelopes. Free Wi-Fi. Open M-F 8am-6:30pm, Sa 8am-6pm. MC/V.

Laundry: Most hotels and some hostels offer laundry services; more options line the main road. Available at **Librería Chunches** for ¢3000 per load.

Emergency: Red Cross (☎128 or 2645 6128).

Police: (☎2645 6248; emergency 911), across from SuperCompro, next to the Vitosi pharmacy.

Pharmacy: Vitosi (☎2645 5004), next to the police station. Open M-Sa 8am-8pm, Su 9am-8pm. AmEx/D/MC/V.

Medical Services: Clínica Monteverde (☎2645 5076), 50m west and 150m south of the sports field. Open M-F 7am-4pm, Sa-Su 7am-7pm.

Telephones: Public telephones are everywhere, including outside SuperCompro and in the Visitors Center at the Reserve.

Internet Access: Pura Vida Internet, 50m northwest of Banco Nacional. Internet ¢1600 per hr. Open daily 11am-9pm. **Atmosphera Internet Cafe** (☎2645 6555), halfway down the road to Monteverde Reserve from Santa Elena. ¢1740 per hr. Also has free coffee, gourmet meso-American food, an art gallery, and a licensed spa. Free internet for customers of the restaurant or art gallery. 12% discount for customers carrying *Let's Go* with them.

Post Office: Up the first hill on the way to Monteverde, beyond the Serpentarium. Open M-F 8am-4:30pm, Sa 8am-12pm. V. **Postal Code:** 5655.

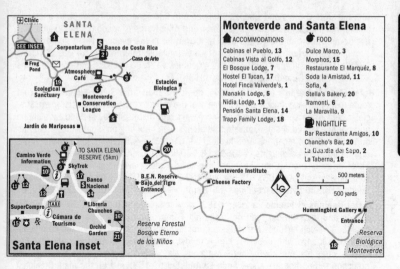

Monteverde and Santa Elena

🏠 ACCOMMODATIONS

Cabinas el Pueblo, **13**
Cabinas Vista al Golfo, **12**
El Bosque Lodge, **7**
Hostel El Tucan, **17**
Hotel Finca Valverde's, **1**
Manakín Lodge, **5**
Nidia Lodge, **19**
Pensión Santa Elena, **14**
Trapp Family Lodge, **18**

🍴 FOOD

Dulce Marzo, **3**
Morphos, **15**
Restaurante El Marquéz, **8**
Soda la Amistad, **11**
Sofia, **4**
Stella's Bakery, **20**
Tramonti, **6**
La Maravilla, **9**

🎵 NIGHTLIFE

Bar Restaurante Amigos, **10**
Chancho's Bar, **20**
La Guardia del Sapo, **2**
La Taberna, **16**

SANTA ELENA

Clinic
SANTA ELENA
Serpentarium
Banco de Costa Rica
Casa de Arte
Frog Pond
Atmosphere Café
Estación Biológica
Ecological Sanctuary
Monteverde Conservation League
Jardín de Mariposas

Santa Elena Inset

Camino Verde information
TO SANTA ELENA RESERVE (5km)
SkyTrek
Banco Nacional
SuperCompro
Librería Chunches
Cámara de Tourismo
Orchid Garden

B.E.N. Reserve
Bajo del Tigre Entrance
Reserva Forestal Bosque Eterno de los Niños

Monteverde Institute
Cheese Factory

500 meters
500 yards

Hummingbird Gallery
Entrance

Reserva Biológica Monteverde

🏠 ACCOMMODATIONS

With dozens of lodgings to choose from, travelers of all kinds can find a temporary home that fits their personality and budget in the cloud forests. Pricier hotels line the road to Monteverde, while most budget accommodations are in or near Santa Elena. Making reservations ahead of time is a good idea during the high season, but low-season visitors will find enterprising crowds waiting to solicit them at the bus stop. No need to be wary—most representatives are just trying to keep their businesses afloat. Prices are usually fixed. Most establishments list prices in US$ because the value of the *colón* is depreciating so rapidly, but most are happy to accept *colones* as well.

SANTA ELENA

▨ **Cabinas Vista al Golfo** (☎2645 6321; www.cabinasvistaalgolfo.com), 5min. walk down the dirt road heading away from time, past the police station. The extremely amicable owners Jorge and Anali and their extended family treat their fun-loving guests as close friends from the start. Sink into the snug beds and see the beautiful view of the Monteverde mountains from the enormous bedroom windows. If that's not enough, the communal kitchen, dining tables, and hammocks upstairs all boast some of the best panoramic views of the Nicoya Gulf. Many guests have hailed their stay at Vista al Golfo as their best experience in Costa Rica. Laundry and hot water available. Free Wi-Fi and internet, coffee, tea, and towels. Quiet after 10pm. Singles with shared bath ₡8700 (US$15), with private baths ₡11,600 (US$20); doubles ₡11,600/14,500 (US$20/25); quads ₡5800/6960 (US$10/12) per person. Apartments (with private bath, kitchen, fridge, and dining table): 2 people ₡29,000 (US$50), 3 or more ₡11,600 (US$20) each. AmEx/D/MC/V. ❷

▨ **Pensión Santa Elena** (☎2645 5051; www.pensionsantaelena.com; shannon@pensionsantaelena.com). Young, adventure-bound backpackers flock to this ultra-social hostel just down the street from Banco Nacional. Though some locals believe it to be somewhat unsavory, it has one of the best communal kitchens around, dining tables in the reception area, and a hammock on the porch. Travelers live and mingle like family—even with the staff. Owners and siblings Shannon and Ran spend quality time with guests to answer questions, give frank suggestions, and offer words of wisdom. Early nights may not be an option as the guests tend to loosen up in the evening. Night guard makes sure only guests enter. Laundry and hot water available. Internet free for guests. Dorms ¢3480 (US$6); singles ¢6960 (US$12); doubles ¢12,760 (US$22), with private baths ¢15,080 (US$26); *cabinas* ¢20,300 (US$35). ❶

Hotel Finca Valverde's (☎2645 5157), down the road from Santa Elena's center en route to Monteverde. Take a small bridge over the creek to this upscale oasis, where spacious cabins are connected by stone walkways and metal bridges shaded by plantain and banana leaves. A small, private trail alongside a babbling brook provides an immediate escape. The reception area hosts a bar and restaurant serving tasty mixed drinks and affordable *tico* delights (¢4060-18,560/US$7-32). Cable TV, coffee maker, and fridge in every room. Complimentary breakfast. Parking available. Prices are per person. Singles ¢40,600 (US$70); doubles ¢23,200 (US$40); triples ¢19,720 (US$34); quads ¢16,820 (US$29); *cabinas* with bathtub ¢40,600 (US$70). AmEx/D/MC/V. ❸

Hostel Cabinas el Pueblo (☎2645 6192; www.cabinaselpueblo.com), pass the police station and take the dirt road down the hill. Family atmosphere plus a bang-for-your-buck deal, which includes hot water, a floral hammock area, a fully stocked communal kitchen, a lounge with cable TV, and a tourist center. Try to catch the sloth that frequents a tree just outside the hotel. Marlenny, who waits for guests at the bus stop, will point you to her mother's *soda*, **Soda La Amistad** (p. 183), just up the road. Breakfast included. Free Wi-Fi and internet. Parking available. Rooms ¢4350 (US$7.50), with private baths ¢5800 (US$10). AmEx/D/MC/V. ❶

Hostel El Tucan (☎2645 7590; www.hoteleltucan.net), located 50m from the Banco Nacional. The brightly painted sign welcomes backpackers to small simple rooms. Leave your upstairs room to hang out in the TV room where, instead of on couches, you can relax on one of several hammocks. Fully equipped kitchen. Breakfast included. Free internet. Offers tour information. Dorms ¢4060 (US$7); singles ¢8700 (US$15), with private baths ¢11,600 (US$20); doubles ¢11,600/14,500 (US$20/25). ❶

MONTEVERDE

🟦 **Manakín Lodge** (☎2645 5080; www.manakinlodge.com), about 1km from Santa Elena toward the Monteverde Reserve. 3rd-generation owner Mario and his children make guests feel like part of the family, offering town gossip, healthy veggies, and organic meals (homemade granola, omelettes, and special requests). The porches of these beautiful rooms face the edge of the forest, where white-faced monkeys wait for bananas from guests. Horse tours (¢17,400; US$30) and trips to local *fincas* available. Breakfast included. Private bath, hot water, cable TV, and fridge. Free internet. Singles ¢11,600 (US$20); doubles ¢17,400-23,200 (US$30-40); triples ¢26,100-34,800 (US$45-60); quads ¢34,800-46,400 (US$60-80). D/MC/V. ❷

Trapp Family Lodge (☎2645 5858; www.trappfam.com). The closest hotel to the Monteverde Cloud Forest Reserve, though its distance from town necessitates transport by car, taxi (¢5000), or bus (¢600). With tall, A-frame ceilings, huge floor-to-ceiling windows, a warm orange lodge, spacious rooms, and a gorgeous location, it's easy to feel like you're already in the cloud forest. Watch the clouds roll in from the plush chairs in your room. Great restaurant on premises (entrees ¢4640-11,600, US$8-20). Parking available. Rooms with 2 double beds ¢49,300 (US$85); mountain suites (slightly higher elevation, TV, fridge, larger windows, and bathtub) ¢58,000 (US$100). AmEx/D/MC/V. ❺

El Bosque Lodge (☎2645 5221; fax 2645 5129; www.bosquelodge.com), behind Tramonti's, halfway between Santa Elena and the Monteverde Reserve. Private rooms are connected by a series of paths and bridges that weave through lovely landscaped gardens speckled with butterflies, hummingbirds, white-face monkeys, and *aguatis*. This lodge's apparent seclusion is an illusion—it is actually located right off the main road. All rooms have coffee maker, refrigerator, and hair dryer. Singles ¢26,100 (US$45); doubles ¢31,900 (US$55); triples ¢37,770 (US$65); quads ¢43,500 (US$75). D/MC/V. ●

Nidia Lodge (☎2645 5236; www.nidialodge.com), on the way to the Ecological Sanctuary. This tranquil lodge is complete with restaurant and spa (offers massages, pedicures and jacuzzi time). Ask Eduardo, the hotel owner, to give you a rundown on the intricacies of the forest. All rooms have a private bath with hot water, iron, desk, and telephone. Deluxe rooms include bathtub, private balcony, and coffee maker (¢11,600, US$20 more). Meeting room holds 30 people. Parking available. Singles in the low season ¢23,300 (US$40), in the high season ¢29,000 (US$50); doubles ¢31,900/37,700 (US$55/65); triples ¢37,700/43,500 (US$65/75); junior suites ¢66,700/69,600 (US$115/120). ●

◨ FOOD

SANTA ELENA

▨ **La Maravilla** (☎2645 6623), right across from the bus station. Serves *comida típica* to locals and tourists alike. Its convenient location and lightning-fast service make it easy to grab a ham and cheese omelet (¢1600) or a *casado* (¢2300-2850). Salads, sandwiches, soups, and seafood (fish fillet in garlic sauce ¢3450). Mango milkshake (¢800). Open daily 6:10am-9pm. AmEx/D/MC/V. ●

▨ **Soda La Amistad** (☎2645 6108), down the dirt road past the police station and next to Cabinas Vista al Golfo. Miss your *mama?* Your dynamic surrogate is waiting to serve you the most mouthwatering *tico* delights right from her personal kitchen. Cándida will plop herself down at one of the 3 tables in her home to offer warm advice and ask when she should expect you tomorrow. She can provide all of your meals: *gallo pinto* (¢1600) for breakfast, a *casado* for lunch (¢2500-3500), and vegetable spaghetti for dinner (¢1800). Open daily 6am-9pm. Cash only. ●

▨ **Coffee Bar** (☎2645 5757), in the alleyway across from the church on the main road, next to Bar Restaurante Amigos. It's all in the name: several hot coffee drinks are available (¢550-950); on warm days, the iced coffee is delightful (¢1350). Great deals include pizzas with various toppings (¢2150), burritos (¢1650), and fried garlic potatoes with bacon dressing (¢1450). Open daily 11am-10pm. ●

Restaurante El Marquez (☎2645 5918), just past Pura Vida Internet. This eatery is designed to resemble the inside of a boat, so it's not surprising that seafood is always the special of the day. Gringos and *ticos* alike enjoy the signature *mariscada au Marquez* (¢5000), combining shrimp, fish, squid, clams, mussels, and crabs in one dish. Lunch buffet of *comida típica* ¢3500. Octopus in garlic butter ¢5000. Open M-Sa 11am-10pm. AmEx/D/MC/V. ❷

Morphos (☎2645 5607), across the street from the supermarket in Santa Elena. The restaurant has taken on the phosphorescent blue Morpho (a species of butterfly) as its namesake as well as the inspiration for its decor: huge hanging butterflies fill the jungle-themed interior. A godsend for those seeking a respite from rice and beans. Double hamburgers topped with bacon, avocado, and cucumbers ¢4000. Sea bass in avocado sauce ¢6500. Top off your meal with their signature Café Morphos, a frozen concoction with coffee, coffee ice cream, and coffee liqueur (¢3200). Blackberry milkshake ¢1000. Open daily 11am-9pm. MC/V. ❷

Trio Restaurant (☎2645 7254), past the Camara de Turismo, next to the SuperCompro. This classy and elegant restaurant serves gourmet food on glass tabletops. Start with a palm heart, tomato, avocado tower ¢2030 (US$3.50), move to a delectable chicken and mango sandwich ¢3770 (US$6.50), and end with fresh fruit glazed over with frozen margarita cream

¢2030 (US$3.50). Or come in for a quiet evening to sit at one of their tables that overlooks the town with mixed drink ¢2900 (US$5) in hand. Open daily 11:30am-9:30pm. ❷

MONTEVERDE

Sofia (☎2645 7017). Take a right at Atmosphera Internet C@fé and walk up 50m on the left. Indulge in creative *nueva latina* food while guitar instrumentals strum in the background. Mango-ginger mojitos ¢2900 (US$5) are a heavenly prelude to innovative fusion dishes like the Seafood Chimichanga with shrimp and tender sea bass, guacamole, sweet potato puree, and *chayote picadillo* ¢8120 (US$14). Appetizers are a cheap, delicious treat (skewered shrimp with fresh fruits and ginger, US$5). Entrees US$12-16. Open daily 11:30am-9:30pm. AmEx/D/MC/V. ❸

Pizza Tramonti (☎2645 6120), in front of El Bosque Lodge on the main road to Monteverde Reserve. Unlike many other pizzerias in town, this one maintains authenticity through its native Italian owner, Gianni. Savor Italian specialties made with imported ingredients like Pizza Tramonti with asparagus, mushrooms, ricotta, and gorgonzola cheese ¢8700 (US$15). *Spaguetti con Pesto* ¢5800 (US$10). Open daily for breakfast 6:30-8:30am, lunch 11:30am-10pm. MC/V. ❸

Dulce Marzo (☎2645 6568), next to Moon Shiva on the road to Monteverde Reserve. The kindly American owner visited the quirky cafe and was so enamored that she bought it and moved to Monteverde. Indulge in the tantalizing chocolate creations, including cheesecakes, staggeringly large cookies, or the specialty hot chocolate (a secret homemade blend of cocoa and spices; ¢1225) and you might want to buy the place too. To temper an anticipated sugar high, the small, inventive lunch menu offers daily specials of soups, pastas, and the popular curry (¢1500). Th salsa lessons with free chips, guacamole, and of course, salsa (2hr., ¢2000). Open daily 11am-7pm. ❶

Stella's Bakery (☎2645 5560), across from El Bosque Lodge. Though Stella now spends much of her time painting and selling her work, her bakery, which displays many of her paintings, is still popular with locals and tourists. Sandwiches are customized from a selection of breads, spreads, meats, cheeses, and fillings. A chicken ham sandwich on whole wheat bread with avocado and cheese comes out to ¢1700. Fresh pastries and cakes are also available (carrot cake ¢900). Open daily 11am-7pm. ❶

LOCAL FLAVOR. US$4 *casados* beyond your budget? Shop like a *tico* at the weekly farmer's market, *La Feria*, Sa 7am-noon at the Santa Elena School, 1 block past Restaurante El Marquez, on the road to Santa Elena Reserve. Grab 3 avocados for ¢580, 3kg of mangos for ¢1160, and homemade bread, all while supporting local farmers.

🖻 NIGHTLIFE

If you're too exhausted from your daytime excursions to hit the dance floors, don't feel guilty: you're not missing much. The nightlife in Monteverde is minimal. A few small-scale clubs host modest crowds where *ticos* and American tourists engage in awkward courtship rituals and heat up on hesitant dance floors. Even so, the few modest options can be entertaining.

La Taberna (☎2645 5883), 300m from Banco Nacional on the road to the Reserve. This hip *discoteca* strewn with Bob Marley and Beatles murals attracts a large crowd of *ticos* and travelers who hit the small dance floor in the main room, dancing to everything from rap to *merengue*. On quiet nights, a young crowd lounges in a room with large couches. Beer ¢800. Open daily 4pm-2am. MC/V.

Bar Restaurante Amigos (☎2645 5071), across from the church on the main road, about 20m down a small dirt road. Drawing the largest crowds in town on the weekends, Bar Amigos resembles a sports bar with some TVs, a full menu until 10pm (chicken nachos ¢1500), and a plethora of drink options. F night live salsa, merengue, and *marcao* (a tango-esque melody unique to Costa Rica). Open daily 12pm-2am. D/MC/V.

Chancho's Bar (☎2645 5926), connected from behind with La Taberna. This small, psychedelic hangout plays *trova* (Cuban protest music), alternative rock, reggae, and house, but not too loudly. A small space in the middle of the bar allows for some *tico-turista* grinding or salsa dancing (music requests accepted). During the dry season, BBQs are held in the firepit in back. If you're lucky, Chancho may invite your group to do a welcome shot. Daiquiris ¢2500; beers ¢800-1000. Open daily 7pm-3am. Wheelchair-accessible. AmEx/D/MC/V.

La Guarida del Sapo (☎2645 7010; www.sapodorado.com), next to Banco de Costa Rica, on the road to the Reserve. This enormous dark wood house with gorgeous stained-glass windows is home to beautiful restaurant and bar known as "The Lair of the Toad." Mosaic fauna, large booths, and a long bar. Festive drinks include the delicious Monteverde Sunset (fresh blackberry syrup, OJ, and vodka; ¢1500) and the Orgasm "El Sapo" (condensed milk, amaretto, Bailey's, and coffee; ¢3000). Live music M, W and F. DJs Tu, Th, Sa-Su. Open daily 6pm-3am. Food available until 2am. AmEx/D/MC/V.

⛰ THE RESERVES

RESERVA BIOLÓGICA MONTEVERDE

The reserve is 6km uphill from Santa Elena. Walk, take a taxi (¢3500), or take a public bus from Santa Elena outside Camino Verde (every 2hr.; 6:15, 7:40am, 1:20, 3pm; return buses 6:45, 11:30am, 2, 4pm; ¢600). The Visitor Center (☎2645 5122; www.cct.or.cr) provides general info, maps, and binoculars. ¢9860 (US$17), students or ages 6-12 ¢5220 (US$9), under 6 free. 2½hr. guided tours daily 7:30am, noon, 1:30pm; ¢9860 (US$17) per person; proceeds benefit an environmental education program geared toward rural communities, as well as a recycling program. Reservations a day in advance recommended during dry season. Many local hotels and hostels arrange private tours. The Reserve only lets in 180 people at a time; get there early if you don't want to wait for entry. Open daily 7am-4pm. Night hikes 7:30pm, ¢11,600 (US$20) with transportation; if you've already been to the reserve that day, you don't have to pay the fee again. The Visitor Center lodge has dorms with 40 beds and 6 communal showers (3 female and 3 male). Prices include entrance fee and 3 meals. Private room and bath ¢37,120 (US$64), shared room ¢30,740 (US$53); includes entrance fee and 3 meals.

Positioned directly on the continental divide, this enthralling private reserve encompasses 4025 hectares of land and provides protection for over 2500 plant species and over 400 animal species. The population of this wildlife sanctuary includes jaguars, mountain lions, peccaries, and the elusive quetzal. This last animal is a shimmering red-and-green-colored bird that falls backward off perches when startled. Though visitors frequently see animals like coatis and white-faced monkeys, spotting the other inhabitants of this dense forest can prove difficult; many visitors find that guides can prove invaluable as nature-translators or human binoculars, able to pick out creatures hidden in the trees and hear monkey calls from the ground. Other visitors find that these mystical forests cloaked in clouds and bathed in mist are best appreciated uninterpreted and are content to wander unaccompanied through the dwarf elfin woodlands and the towering canopies of the higher cove forests. Reserve highlights include

La Ventana lookout (along the continental divide; take Sendero Bosque Nuboso directly to it) and a **long suspension bridge** (on the Sendero Wilford Guindon). At some points, it is possible to stand on either side of the continental divide, with one foot on the Caribbean slope and the other on the Pacific.

RESERVA SANTA ELENA

Reserva Santa Elena is 5km northeast of Santa Elena village. Walk on the road north from Banco Nacional, take a taxi (one-way ¢5000), or catch a minibus to the reserve in front of the bus stop (6:30, 8:30, 10:30am, 12:30pm; return buses 9, 11am, 1, 3, 4pm; ¢580). Make reservations for buses through Camino Verde after 6am (☎ 2645 6296). The reserve information center in town is 200m north of Banco Nacional (☎ 2645 5390); there is also a Visitor Center at the entrance. Open daily 7am-4pm. 3hr. guided tours 7:30, 11:30am; ¢8700 (US$15) not including entrance fee; must be arranged 1 day in advance. Entrance fee ¢8120 (US$14), students and ages 6-12 ¢4060 (US$7), under 5 free.

The often-overlooked **Santa Elena Reserve** was established in 1992 to diffuse Monteverde's tourism burden. During the dry season, Santa Elena makes for a less-crowded, equally beautiful alternative to Monteverde. Encompassing primary and secondary forests, it offers similar flora and fauna on more sparsely populated trails, where howler monkeys make a ruckus in the liana vines that dangle from the trees. There are **four main trails** in this old growth cloud forest, all short enough (1-5km) to be done as day hikes (45min.-5hr.). From some lookouts you can see **Volcán Arenal** 14km away. Morning hikes make for better weather (especially during the wet season), views, and animal watching. Informed professional guides help identify hidden animals and plants. Unlike the Monteverde Reserve, this Reserve is government-owned. Proceeds from the entrance fee go toward the local high school.

👁 ⛰ SIGHTS AND OUTDOOR ACTIVITIES

🎋CANOPY TOURS. Canopy tours are one of Monteverde's ecotourism highlights. These tours lead potential Tarzans through forests with less intrusion than other activities. **Original Canopy Tour,** the pioneer of this arboreal activity, provides tours, but the newer tour companies offer larger coverage and cheaper prices. In addition to ziplines, suspension bridges crossing extensive distances of canopy immerse visitors in the forest while they scout for glimpses of spectacular birds, animals, insects, and plants. Five companies offer zipline tours. Three of these companies also offer walking canopy tours. The canopy tours lead visitors along a network of bouncing suspension bridges nestled in or near the canopy of the Santa Elena Reserve. **Aventura, Selvatura, Sky Trek,** and **Extremo** all offer similar packages with harrowing ziplines, though each company has its own style. Adrenaline junkies rave about the Aventura "Tarzan swings," the "Superman," mid-forest location, and rappelling apparatus, while others prefer mixing up various lengths and speeds on Selvatura or Sky Trek cables. Sky Trek boasts the highest and longest cable among its 11 (named for popular characters like "Speedy Gonzalez"). Though Sky Trek's iron platforms offer stunning vistas and combo packages with Sky Tram gondolas, some prefer tours with less-obtrusive infrastructure. In both zipline and walking tours, be prepared for sustained exposure to the elements, especially in the afternoon during the rainy season. *(Aventura ☎ 2645 6959. Zipline tour ¢23,300 (US$40), students ¢17,400 (US$30). Original Canopy Tour ☎ 2645 5243; www.canopytour.com. ¢26,100 (US$45), students ¢20,300 (US$35). Sky Trek & Sky Tram ☎ 2645 5238; www.skytrek.com. ¢34,800 (US$60), students ¢27,840 (US$48), children ¢23,200 (US$40). Selvatura ☎ 2645 5929; www.selvatura.com. US$40, students US$30,* children US$25. Extremo ☎ 2645 6058; www.monteverdeextremo.com. ¢23,300 (US$40), students ¢17,400 (US$30), children ¢14,500 (US$25). Natural Wonders Tram ☎ 2645 5960; www.telefericomonteverde.com. Aventura, Selvatura, and Sky Trek have discounted packages for ziplines and walks on the same day. Aventura Bridges or Selvatura Walkway ¢14,500 (US$25), students ¢11,600 (US$20); Sky Walk & Sky Tram ¢29,000/23,200 (US$50/40).)

SAN LUIS WATERFALL. Tired of tour guides and over-used trails? Be free at the Leiton family *finca* that maintains this natural marvel. Follow an enchanting trail (1.7km) through the rainforest that dances across the San Luis river and finish at the enormous waterfall that snakes down two ledges before it comes crashing down. Most likely, you will be able to enjoy the waterfall all by yourself. Climb around the right side of the rocks to get close, but don't jump in—it's off limits. *(Taxi to Catarata de San Luis ¢8120/US$14. Entrance fee ¢4640/US$8. Trail maps available.)*

ECOLOGICAL SANCTUARY. The banana and coffee plantations that once operated here have been transformed into private reserves. Four different loop trails pass stunning lookouts and several cascading waterfalls, taking anywhere from 30min. to 3hr. to hike. Because the climate is hotter here than in the reserves, there are more animals to see. The forest is home to coatimundis, three-wattled bell birds, sloths, monkeys. The sanctuary is also home to the quick-footed *agoutis*, a small barking mammal that seems to walk on tiptoe as it crosses the trails. Night visits offer a very different experience than daytime walks, frequently featuring porcupines, sloths, tarantulas, kinkajous, and lots of insects. *(The well-marked turnoff from the Monteverde road is right by Atmosphera C@fe, almost 1km from Santa Elena. ☎ 2645 5869; www.ecologicalsanctuary.com. Open daily 6:30am-5pm. Guides recommended. Call a day ahead. Guides ¢14,500/US$25 for 3hr. tour, entrance fee included. Night tour 5:30-7:30pm, arrive around 5pm; ¢8700/US$15 includes entrance fee. Free printed guides available at the Visitor Center. Entrance ¢5800/US$10, students ¢4640/US$8, Costa Rican nationals and children under 10 ¢2900/US$5.)*

COFFEE TOURS. Coffee lovers everywhere will gain a new appreciation for their morning cup-o-joe on a coffee tour. Start off this educational adventure at one of Monteverde's *fincas* to see how the beans are harvested, from the drying to the roasting process, in the olden days and now. At the end of the tour, visitors can taste the different types of coffee. *(Monteverde Coffee Tour; ☎ 2645 7090; www.cafemonteverde.com. Tours 8am and 1:30pm. Don Juan Coffee Tour; ☎ 2645 7100; www.donjuancoffeetour.com. Irapiche Tour; ☎ 2645 5271. Tours 9:45am and 2:45pm.)*

CAÑAS

Sweltering Cañas sits on the Interamericana Hwy. amid dusty Guanacaste farmland and cattle *fincas*. Though the town is dull, it can serve as a useful transportation hub for those traveling between the Pacific coast and Volcán Arenal. Some also use it as a base for Parque Nacional Palo Verde, 30km to the west, or for trips on the Río Corobicí.

◪ TRANSPORTATION

Most **buses** leave from the *mercado central*, five blocks north of the *parque*, to San José (¢1330) and Puntarenas (M-Sa 4, 4:50, 5:40, 6:30, 8:30, 11:20am, 1:30, 2:30, 5:30pm; Su 6:20, 8:30, 11:20am, 1:30, 5pm; ¢800); Liberia via Bagaces (every 30min. 4:30am-5:45pm; ¢600); Tilarán (6, 8:00, 9, 10:30am, noon, 1:45, 3:30, 5:45pm; ¢300); Upala via Volcán Tenorio (M-F; 4:30, 6, 8:30, 11:15am, 1, 3:30, 5:30pm; ¢800); Bebedero (11am, 1, 3pm; 7, 9am, 5pm from the stop in front of the cemetery across from SuperCompro; ¢400).

⚡ PRACTICAL INFORMATION

The church is on the east side of the *parque*.

Banks: Banco Nacional, on the northeast corner of the *parque,* has an ATM. Open M-F 8:30am-3:45pm. There is a **Banco de Costa Rica** west of the southwest corner of the *parque* on Av. 0. Open M-F 8am-4pm.

Police: The **police station** (☎2669 0057, emergency 116) is north of the *parque* on the west side of the Interamericana.

Pharmacy: Pharmacies are everywhere, including **Farma Todo** (☎2669 0748), 1½ blocks east of Banco Nacional. Open M-Sa 7am-9pm, Su 8am-1pm and 3-7pm.

Medical Services: You can receive medical care at **Dr. Juan Acón Chen's clinic** (☎2669 0139, emergency 2669 0471), 1 block north and 1 block west of the *parque*'s northwest corner. Open M-F 8am-noon and 2-6pm, Sa 8am-noon. There is also the public **Clínica de Cañas** (☎2669 0092), 2 blocks west of the *parque*.

Internet Access: Cibercañas (☎2669 5232), 1 block north and a ½ block east of the church's northeast corner, offers Internet access and complimentary coffee. ¢400 per hr. Open M-Sa 8:15am-9pm, Su 2-9pm. AmEx/D/MC/V.

Post Office: (☎2669 1701; fax 2669 0309). Open M-F 8am-noon and 1-5:30pm) is 1 block north and 2 blocks west of the *parque*. Fax available. **Postal Code:** 50601.

🏠 ACCOMMODATIONS

Hotel Caña Brava (☎2669 5511; drcable01@ice.co.cr), 2 blocks north and 2 blocks west of the *parque*'s northwest corner and next to SuperCompro. It may be worth the higher prices if you are not traveling alone. Pool, hot tub, surveillance cameras, hotel restaurant (with the same menu as Hotel Cañas), popular bar as well as amenities like A/C, cable, flatscreen TV, Wi-Fi, and private bath in every room. Doubles US$60; triples US$80; quads US$90. AmEx/D/MC/V. ❹

Hotel Cañas (☎2669 5118), 1 block north of the *parque*'s northwest corner. Has plain white rooms with frame beds, private baths, Wi-Fi, teeny cable TV, and the option of A/C or a fan. ¢9000-12,000. AmEx/D/DC/MC/V. ❷

🍴 FOOD

Supercompro, one block north and two blocks west of the *parque*'s north-west corner, is a comprehensive supermarket that looks like a ware-house. (Open M-Sa 8am-8pm, Su 8am-noon.)

Hotel Caña Brava, 1 block north and 2 blocks west of the *parque*'s northwest corner, offers the same menu as Hotel Cañas with slightly higher prices, making up for it with the classier environment, full bar, and outdoor seating. Tasty fish fajitas (¢4400) and *casados* (¢3800). Strawberry daiquiri ¢1800. Open daily 6am-midnight. ❷

Soda Los Antojitos, ½ block west from Cibercañas, offers ordinary fast food and cheap *comida típica. Casados* ¢1900. Open daily 7am-8pm. ❶

🏞 OUTDOOR ACTIVITIES

Escape from the Cañas's dusty roads with a float trip down Río Corobicí and Río Tenorio (never exceeding Class I and II rapids, perfect for beginners and appreciating the flora/fauna). **Safaris Corobicí,** 4.5km north of Cañas on the Inter-americana, runs these tours, where you'll see everything from crocodiles to harmless parrots and cuckoos. (☎2669 6191; www.safaricorobici.com. 2hr. trips US$37 per person or 3hr. US$45, snack included; half-day US$60, lunch included. 2 person min. Trips 7am-3:30pm. Rafts are wheelchair-accessible.) Safaris Corobicí also runs **Centro de Rescate Las Pumas.** Nowhere else will give you the chance to come within an arm's length of pumas, ocelots, and various other felines, in addition to parrots, toucans, and white-tailed deer (but obey the signs: "Please don't pet the cats!"). Lilly Bodmer de Hagnauer founded the center during the 1960s to care for Guancastecan wildlife in danger, particularly species that had been poached for the pet trade or displaced by deforestation. All animals brought to the center are released back into the wild if unharmed. Those unable to survive on their own find a safe home at this reserve. The center depends on visitor donations to keep them healthy, as well as profits from the souvenir shop at the entrance. Buses running from Cañas to Bugaces and Liberia will drop you at the entrance if you ask the driver. Call ahead to arrange for a guided tour. (Open daily 8am-5pm. Visit www.lrsarts.com/PUMAS/voluntariado.html for volunteer opportunities.)

TILARÁN

The only travelers who don't breeze in and out of this gusty little transportation hub are windsurfers setting sail on **Laguna de Arenal,** 5km away. The man-made lake (initially small and natural) is the largest, most efficient hydroelectric project in Costa Rica, providing 40% of the country's energy. The lake also provides spectacular views of Volcán Arenal. High winds (up to 70kph) provide "clean energy," spinning a group of windmills at the best energy-producing wind turbine in the world. Many foreigners have made their homes here, but *ticos* still abound. The park in town is full of red benches where older *tico* couples talk quietly as the younger generations prowl the wide streets in search of wilder nights.

⎚ TRANSPORTATION

The church is east of the *parque*. **Buses** leave half a block west from the *parque's* northwest corner to: **Laguna Arenal** (45min., 4 per day 7am-4:30pm, ¢400); **Cañas** (45min.; 7 per day M-Sa 5, 6, 10:30, 11:30am, 2, 5, 7pm; ¢350); **Monteverde/Santa Elena** (3hr.; 12:30, 4:30pm; ¢1400); **Puntarenas** (2hr.; 6am, 1, 6pm; ¢1300); **San Carlos/Ciudad Quesada** (4hr.; 7am, 1:45pm; ¢1700) via **Fortuna** and **Laguna de Arenal; Guatuso** (3hr., noon, ¢1200); **San José** (3hr.; 5 per day 5, 7, 9:30am, 2, 5pm; ¢3000). Bus tickets can be bought the same day. Bus stop open M-Sa 6:30-11am and 1-5pm. **Taxis** (☎2696 5324) line the west side of the *parque* by the phones.

▚ PRACTICAL INFORMATION

Tourist Office: No official information center. Ask hotel receptionists.

Bank: Banco Nacional (☎2695 5028), across the southwest corner of the *parque*. Open M-F 8:30am-3:45pm. **ATM** on-site.

Police: (☎2695 5001, emergency 911), a block west of the bus station. Open 24hr.

Red Cross: (☎2695 5256), 100m east of the *parque's* northeast corner.

Pharmacy: Farmacia Irva (☎2695 8210), across from the northwest corner of the *parque*, to the left. Open M-Sa 7am-8:30pm. AmEx/MC/V.

Hospital: (☎2695 5093), 200m west of the *parque's* southwest corner.

Internet Access: Cyber Cafe (☎695 3319), 50m north of the northeast corner of the *parque*. ¢500 per hr. Open M-Sa 9am-11pm.

Post Office: (☎2695 6230; fax 5387), 1 block north, 2 blocks east from the northeast corner of the *parque*. Open M-F 9am-4pm. **Postal code:** 5710.

ON THE ROAD-EO

With an hour to kill before another overcrowded, sweaty bus ride to my next destination, I decided to visit a tour guide friend I had met the day before in **Bijagua** (p. 92) to try to squeeze out some more information about the *sabanero* town. When I arrived, I was surprised to see him and a friend decked out in their cowboy-best—faded, tight jeans, loose-fitting button-down shirts, mango-sized belt buckles, and leather cowboy hats and boots. They informed me that they were getting ready for the bull-riding competition, as part of the festive weekend aimed to raise money for the local elementary school. His frighteningly calm friend was part of the valiant crew from **Cañas** (p. 187) that would sacrifice their bodies for those 10 seconds of bull-riding glory.

We headed off to the stadium to see the show, which allegedly started at 4:30pm, but actually began 3hr. later (typical *tico* time delay). In the meantime, Imperial-filled cowboys enjoyed the cheap, homemade food that five women had been preparing all day in the communal kitchen. After the sun went down, everyone streamed into the rickety stadium to cheer on the friendly boxing matches between the men from the town. Not knowing that I would see anything other than bucking bulls, I was delightfully surprised to witness baby cattle auctions, raffles, and numerous skillful horseback riders guide their high-kneed horses through an array obstacle.

ACCOMMODATIONS

Hotel Tilawa (☎2695 5050; www.tilawa.com), 8km north of Tilarán. Designed in homage to Cretan palaces, its architecture is majestically imitative with "ancient" columns and hand-painted frescoes. Panoramic windows offer stunning views of Laguna Arenal and surrounding volcanoes. Hot tub, outdoor pool, Central America's largest skateboard park, tennis courts, and organic gardens. Check out the nearby **Tilawa Water Activity Center** for kayaks (¢5800, US$10 per hr.) and windsurfing. A jungle excursion on one of its 4 well maintained trails (0.60-1.70km) will reveal white-faced monkeys, toucans, butterflies, and iguanas, if you have not seen them from your window already. Free Wi-Fi. High season singles ¢40,600/US$70; doubles ¢46,400/US$80. Low season singles ¢20,300/US$35; doubles ¢23,200/US$40. Apartments with kitchen, couch, and hammock for 3-4 people low season ¢52,220/US$90, high season ¢63,800/US$110; each additional person ¢5800/US$10. AmEx/D/MC/V. ❹

Hotel Guadalupe Bed & Breakfast (☎2695 5943), 1 block south and 1 block east of the southeast corner of the park. Rustic wooden doors open up to spacious rooms with private bathrooms and cable TV. Breakfast included. Laundry US$1 per item. Free Wi-Fi. Singles ¢17,400 (US$30); doubles ¢26,100 (US$45); triples ¢34,800 (US$60); quads ¢40,600 (US$70). AmEx/D/MC/V. ❸

Hotel Mary (☎ 2695 5479), on the south side of the *parque*. Homey rooms with cable TV, hot water, and clean wall-to-wall carpeting. The restaurant and bar downstairs is popular with the locals and can get a bit loud on weekend nights. Laundry ¢300 per piece. Singles ¢5220 (US$9); doubles ¢12,180 (US$21); triples ¢15,080 (US$26); quads ¢20,300 (US$35). D/MC/V. ❶

FOOD

The town supermarket, **Almacén Samora** (☎2695 6227; open daily 7:30am-7:30pm), is located one block south of southeast corner of the *parque*. **SuperCompro** (☎2695 6050; open daily 8am-9pm) is on the south side of the *parque*. For those looking for fresher options, the **market** next to the bus station sells *comida típica* (*casados* ¢2000) along with produce. *Chorreadas* (creations that lie somewhere between tortillas and crepes, topped with cream or cheese) ¢700. Open daily, hours vary.

Taquería Las Leñitas (☎2695 8949), 50m north of the *parque*'s northeast corner. One of the few places in town that provides a break from *comida típica*. Sit inside or out and enjoy *quesadilla de honges* (tortillas filled with garlic mushrooms and cheese; ₡2200) or specialty nachos with beans, ground beef, cheese, and homemade corn chips (₡1800). Burrito Texano (flour tortilla with beef, refried beans, cheese, and guacamole) ₡2100. Open M-F 11am-9pm, Sa 1-9pm, Su 5-9pm. AmEx/MC/V. ❶

Restaurant Mary (☎2695 3281), underneath Hotel Mary on the south side of the *parque*. Serves a diverse menu from the diner-style bartop, including salads, fish, spaghetti, *comidas típicas,* and *comidas rápidas*. Get started with shrimp *ceviche* (₡2900), followed by the grilled chicken fillet (₡3000). Service may be slow when the place gets busy at night. Open daily 11am-2:30am. AmEx/D/MC/V. ❶

Restaurant Catalá (☎2695 3281), across from Hotel Mary, a bit past the south side of the *parque*. Don't let the dim lighting of this restaurant scare you off. The menu is full of pictures displaying options like their tenderloin with a special house sauce (₡5800) and the chicken breast stuffed with ham and cheese (₡4300). Fried ice cream (₡1800). Complimentary viewing of pop music videos on their big screen included. Open daily 11am-11pm. MC/V. ❷

🎬🎵 NIGHTLIFE AND ENTERTAINMENT

Equss, 12km from Tilarán, accessible by car or bus heading toward Arenal. Walk through a small patch of jungle, down a hill to an open dance floor made with rugs. Filled with a mix of *ticos* and windsurfers. Sa night salsa, merengue, and cumbia. Open 8pm-3am or when the party dies down.

Ciudad Mágica, to the right of the church. Has several rides for young children and those who are still children at heart. Every ride, including the mini roller coaster and bumper cars, requires a ₡500 ticket (bought at the booth). Open daily 4-10pm.

🏔 OUTDOOR ACTIVITIES

On the skirts of the volcano, **Laguna de Arenal** is one of the world's premier windsurfing spots, with a high season that runs from December to May and peaks in April. At the **Tilawa Water Activity Center** on the lakeshore, downhill 100m from Hotel Tilawa, instructors Tom and Evelio offer great windsurfing lessons. (Kayaks ₡5800/US$10 per hr. Sailing 1hr. ₡11,600/US$20, half-day ₡20,300/US$35, full day ₡26,100/US$45. Windsurfing 1hr. ₡14,500/US$25, half-day ₡20,300/US$35, full day ₡26,100/US$45; 3-4hr. beginner lessons ₡26,100/US$45. Open daily 7am-5pm.) Taxis run to the Center from the *parque* (₡4000).

The most striking part of the whole experience was a one-armed rider dressed in all-black. There was an event during the races when each rider had to trade horses with another rider while the horses were still moving. This man managed to grab the reins with his teeth while he used his single arm to boost himself off of his horse, and consequently onto the second horse on the side.

Although slightly disconcerting, the audience was brought to the floor in roaring laughter during the baby bull-catching event. About 10 bulls were released and, after the whistle blew, the *sabeneros* dispersed in a mayhem of lassos and leaps. The actual bull-riding only took about 10 seconds, but I learned the ever-valuable lesson of how to make the proper Costa Rican rodeo call, "Oiiii, oiiiii" which sounds strikingly (and strangely) like a drunk Miss Piggy.

If you do have an opportunity to make it to a rodeo, don't worry too much if you happen to miss your bus, as you can always ask one of the hundred *sabaneros* to give you a ride, and it will surely be more exciting. Be careful though; not all *sabaneros* are necessarily trustworthy.

—*Nadia Mohamedi*

VOLCÁN TENORIO

Although this area was decreed a *parque nacional* in 1995, the infrastructure necessary to make this grand volcano accessible to tourists and biologists was not developed until 1997. Tenorio, rising up 1916m and extending for 12 sq. km, is now accessible thanks to the growth of nearby Bijagua, where cowboys ride their horses to the few stores dotted along the main road. MINAE has been working hard at its new posts in Río Naranjo and at El Pilón, researching the flora and fauna of the volcano. This unpopulated area is rich with under-explored wonders, including bridges through the rainforest, hot and cold springs, the impressive sapphire blue Río Celeste, and its majestic waterfall. Bijagua is not only a refreshing break from packed hostels but also a chance to get familiar with the *tico* countryside, as extremely friendly and unoccupied Bijaguans will gladly take interested travelers up to their expansive *fincas*.

TRANSPORTATION

The best way to get to Volcán Tenorio is to rent a **car.** You can also take the **bus** from Upala to Bijagua (45min., 7 per day, ¢885). From San José, take the bus heading toward Upala through Cañas, which makes a stop in Bijagua. To get to El Pilón (also called Casona de San Miguel, the entrance and Visitors Center from which hikers can depart for various sights) or Albergue Heliconia (offering three trails as well as tours), you will need to seek out one of the five local (and pricey) **taxis;** there's usually one waiting at the bus stop (¢13,000).

PRACTICAL INFORMATION

Banks: Banco Nacional 200m south of the pizzeria on the main road in Bijagua. Open M-F 8:30am-noon and 1-3:45pm.

Police: The **police station,** 20m south of Bar Tropical, is open 24hr.

Medical Services: Though there is a small **clinic** 30m south of the pizzeria and to the right of Soda El Kiosco, the closest **hospital** is in Upala. Alternatively, you can direct yourself to the MINAE office in Río Naranjo, 5km south of Bijagua.

Telephones: Public phones are along the main street (calls to landlines ¢1 per min., cellphones ¢25 per min.), including in front of the bank.

Internet Access: An **Internet cafe** (☎2466 8155), lies to the left of Super Payka, 200m down the street across from the police station. ¢350 per hr. Open M-Sa 8am-8pm.

ACCOMMODATIONS

If you're just passing by looking for a good, cheap place to sleep, keep on going an hour in either direction to Cañas or Liberia for much better options. There are two *cabinas* in the town of Bijagua, which are an expensive taxi or car ride away from the most appealing natural sights. While the options in Bijagua are cheaper, staying in the mountains themselves may be more rewarding (and more beautiful). Two hotels hidden in the mountains provide premier bases for exploring the landscape of Volcán Tenorio. Although both are only accessible by car or taxi, their isolation comes as a welcome contrast to Bijagua's grit, and getting up the mountain will be a hassle even if you stay in town.

Carolina Lodge (☎2356 1656; www.lacarolinalodge.com), 10km up a windy dirt road 3km north of Bijagua on the right, provides the best lodging in the area. A hybrid of ranch and jungle, winding paths connect cabins and lead to the crystal-clear swimming hole just below a small waterfall. The private cabins of this beautiful eco-resort run without electricity, but the amenities, like delicious, home-cooked meals made from homegrown ingredients and a stone hot tub heated by a wood-burning stove, more than make up for this departure from modernity. The bargain package for 1 night's lodging includes a horseback or Río Celeste tour, as well as 3 meals. Package US$65. ➍

Albergue Heliconia Nature Lodge (☎/fax 2466 8483; www.lasheliconias.org), closer to Bijagua, offers six rustic rooms with bunk beds for four. The breathtaking view includes Lago de Nicaragua, its islands, and various volcanoes. Tours to Río Celeste, the hanging bridges, Laguna la Danta, birdwatching and much more available. Breakfast included. Singles US$40; doubles US$49; triples US$63; quads US$73. MC/V. ➌

Cabinas Samora (☎2466 8896), down a dirt road across from the pizzeria, offers 1 spacious, 3-person room in a pleasant home. Internet available. ¢2000 per person. ➊

Cabinas Bijagua (☎2466 8894), on the main road next to Carnicería Chiguin, has three sanitary, albeit seedy, rooms with private baths. ¢5000 per person. ➊

 FOOD

Pizzería El Barrigón (☎2466 8602), on the main road 200m north of the bank. Whether passing by Bijagua or staying a week, El Barrigón is an essential pitstop. Rich pizzas are homemade in a gigantic wood-fired oven right outside the dining area at this popular pizzeria. Supreme pizza ¢2500-6000. Open daily 7am-10pm. ➋

Soda y Marisquería las Tinajitas, on the main road right next to Pizzeria El Barrigón. With exotic plants hanging from the roof's edges, locals dine on inexpensive specialities like *arroz con camarones* (¢1900), *ceviche* (¢1200), and seafood soup (¢1800). Truck drivers commonly stop here on their way up to Upala. Open daily 6am-9pm. ➊

Albergue Heliconias Restaurante, overlooking Lake Nicaragua and the volcanoes. While the food is good, it's the view that makes this restaurant worth the trek. You can work off your meal on the 3 hikes onsite. *Sopa negra* US$3. *Heliconias* plate, vegetables, salad, mashed potatoes, and choice of meat US$8. Open daily 7am-8pm. MC/V. ➋

⚔ OUTDOOR ACTIVITIES

From El Pilón, you can explore a waterfall, hot springs, a *mirador*, and a small lake. The bright blue Río Celeste creates a 30m waterfall and swimming hole beneath it (about 1.5km from the entrance; be prepared to negotiate steep steps down to the waterfall). From the *mirador*, you can see volcanoes Tenorio, Montezuma, and Carmela. Continue along the path to **Laguna Azul,** where Río Roble and Buena Vista meet and cause the water to turn a radiant shade of blue, due to the minerals from the volcano. **Misteriosos del Tenorio** are hot and cold springs that lie a bit further along the trail, many of which are boiling and bubbling (use caution). There will be a sign that says *"aguas thermales."* There is a small section in the river next to the sign that is enclosed by rocks where the hot and cold waters mix to make a soothing bath in paradise. The hot springs are cooler near the river and boiling close to the trail (3hr. hike, a few steep inclines and narrow bridges; US$10). If visitors want to hike to the volcano crater (6hr. hike to the top), they must request special permission from the information center at El Pilón, since many decide to camp and make the trek down the next day. Volunteering opportunities (2-day min., room and board in lodge return), both in the lab and on the trail, are available (contact **Parque Nacional Volcán Tenorio;** ☎2200 0135 or 695 5908; www.acarenaltempisque.org). The **Albergue Heliconia Nature Lodge,** founded by the Bijagua Community Association, has a 140-hectare private reserve and three on-site trails of different length and difficulty. The **Laguna Danta** trail leads through moist, tropical forests and cloud forests to a crater that becomes a lagoon in the rainy season (with guide US$13-25 per person, depending on group size). Another trail boasts three aerial bridges, while the third offers a leisurely hike with exotic scenery (1-2hr.; US$3). The lodge also organizes botanical and birding tours as well as tours of Río Celeste (US$8-40).

Call ahead for guided tour (☎2466 8483). Albergue Heliconia also has volunteering opportunities that include room and board in exchange for work on the land and giving tours. No minimum time commitment; contact the hotel.

 STRAPPED FOR CASH? If there is no bank in your small town, be nice to the manager at the local supermarket. He/she will usually agree to charging a desired amount to your credit card and giving you cash in return. Some may charge a small fee, but it's better than eating *galletas* at every meal!

PARQUE NACIONAL PALO VERDE

Parque Nacional Palo Verde is one of Central America's most dynamic wetland areas (the wetlands make up 60% of the entire park) as well as an important site for conservation. Known primarily for its aviary life, the *parque* has 278 species in residence, among which are jacanas, herons, and egrets. From September to March, thousands of birds migrate here from Canada and South America, making for spectacular birdwatching. The *parque*'s 15 distinct habitats—including mangroves, riparian forest, and flood-plain marsh—are home to at least 1200 other species, including the largest crocodile population in Costa Rica.

AT A GLANCE

AREA: 20,000 hectares.

CLIMATE: Average temp. 27˚C; average rainfall 1300mm per year.

FEATURES: Mirador Guayacán, Isla de Pájaros, Puerto Chamorro.

HIGHLIGHTS: Boat tours to Isla Pájaros, birdwatching, hiking.

GATEWAYS: Bagaces, Liberia (p. 201).

CAMPING: Permit US$2 per night.

FEES: Entrance US$10.

TRANSPORTATION

The *parque* entrance is 20km down a primarily dirt road, near the town of Bagaces and off the Interamericana Hwy., where buses running between Cañas and Liberia will drop you off in front of the popular Bagaces gas station stop. The road is across from the gas station, and there is a clearly marked path that leads to Palo Verde. There is no public transportation between Bagaces and the *parque*, but you can get a taxi (¢12,000 one-way). If you're driving, be cautious of muddy roads during the rainy season.

ORIENTATION

Parque Nacional Palo Verde lies on the northwest corner of the Gulf of Nicoya, about 30km west of Cañas. The first ranger station, **Negritos**, is about 20km from the park entrance off the Interamericana Hwy. From the entrance, the main road traverses the park's length. After 6km, a road branches left from the main road, leading 5km down to La Bocana, a marsh popular with birds, and 9km down to Catalina. The park's second ranger station is in a denser forest but is great for seeing the colored monkey.

Back on the main road, 1km past the fork, a trail leads to Mirador La Roca. Four-hundred meters farther up sits the biological station, an independent research and education facility run by the renowned **Organization of Tropical Studies (OTS)**. Near OTS are marshes, which are home to hundreds of migrating birds and ducks December through February. Palo Verde, the third ranger and MINAE station, lies 1.5km beyond the biological station.

⚡ PRACTICAL INFORMATION

The regional **MINAE** office (☎2455 2671) overseeing **Parque Nacional Palo Verde** is on the west side of the gas station on the Interamericana Hwy. They have information and can contact ranger guides. Boat tours show off the birds in the gulf and take visitors around nearby islands, including Isla de Pájaros (2-3hr., US$70-80 per person depending on group size). Call Palo Verde National Park (☎2200 0125; park open daily 7am-5pm) or **Arenal Tempisque Conservation Area** (☎/fax 2695 5180; www.acarenaltempisque.org).

> **WHEN TO GO.** The best time to visit is between Sept. and Apr., particularly from Dec. to Feb., when there are plenty of birds to look at, identify, and inevitably envy. Keep in mind that the *parque* is most pleasant in the early morning and late afternoon (when the heat is less oppressive), and the best viewing time for mammals is at dusk (after 5pm). Don't forget to bring comfortable shoes for hiking, light clothes, bug repellent, and an umbrella or light rain jacket during the wet months (June-Nov.).

🏕 CAMPING

Puesto Palo Verde ❶ (☎2200 0125) is the only one of three ranger stations currently offering accommodations. Just 1.5km beyond the biological station, dorms have portable water, fans, and shared bathrooms. Close to many of the park's attractions, the station also serves as a good camping ground. (Kitchen available. Meals US$6-8. Dorms US$13. Camping US$2.) Although the biological station is officially for students and researchers affiliated with the OTS, it's possible to negotiate for a bed when space is available (prices vary). Volunteering opportunities are available at Puesto Palo Verde; they are very flexible in accommodating your interests. Mornings are usually dedicated to work such as trail maintenance and afternoons to exploration in the park through hiking, horseback riding, boat tours, birdwatching, etc. (Lodging and meals US$8 per night. Tours are free. 1-week min.).

🥾 HIKING

La Roca, a leisurely 540m trail, leads to a beautiful lookout point where the Palo Verde Marsh, Tempisque River, and Gulf of Nicoya are all within sight. Significantly more challenging, **El Guayacán** (1460m) leads to the best viewing points in the park, boasting vistas of El Guayacán, El Cactus, and the slithering Río Tempisque and its plains. Be ready to practically rock-climb the sharp stones to the *mirador* and clamber right back down the same way you came to get back on the main trail. The foliage-embraced trail, **El Mapache** (650m), leads through three different types of forests—lowland deciduous, evergreen, and one that grows on a limestone substrate. Also 650m, **El Querque** features enormous trees and xeroline vegetation. Finally, **La Venada** (2100m) follows the periphery of Palo Verde Marsh. **La Humedal** is a 100m boardwalk leading through the marsh that offers premier birdwatching and crocodile encounters. The rangers arrange boat tours, which are the best way to see many of the park's most interesting bird species; contact them in advance. Complimentary trail maps are available at any of the ranger stations.

RESERVA BIOLÓGICA LOMAS BARBUDAL

Lomas Barbudal (Bearded Hills) is a 23 sq. km tropical dry forest (70% decidious) that holds over 250 species of animals including the howler monkey, white-nosed agouti, jagaroundi, and 130 species of birds. However, this reserve is best known for its bees, many of which are endemic to Costa Rica. They camouflage remarkably well against the *cortezas amarilla* trees that burst into yellow bloom at the end of the dry season and can be observed from the three 2km trails within the reserve. The walk to the reserve can be long and hot without a car, but a swimming hole awaits those who make the trek. The park rangers offer complimentary guided tours.

AT A GLANCE	
AREA: 2645 hectares; 23 sq. km.	**GATEWAYS:** Bagaces.
CLIMATE: Tropical dry forest.	**CAMPING:** None.
FEATURES: La Poza el Eden de Cabuyo.	**FEES AND RESERVATIONS:** Entrance US$10.
HIGHLIGHTS: Bees, hiking, birdwatching, waterfalls, swimming.	

TRANSPORTATION

The reserve is difficult to reach without a **car.** You can take a **taxi** (¢7000 one-way) to the entrance, 6km off the Interamericana Hwy.; the turnoff is at the small community of Pijije. Visitors have been known to hitch a ride with drivers headed for San Ramón, though **Let's Go does not recommend hitchhiking.** While the dirt road is in fairly good condition, it may require 4WD in the rainy season.

ORIENTATION AND PRACTICAL INFORMATION

The reserve is located 18km southwest of Bagaces. A Visitors Center run by the neighborhood association of San Ramón is 6km from Pijije on the Interamericana Hwy., north of Bagaces. This same road reaches Palo Verde 20km later, south of Lomas. It's easier to go through Bagaces to get to Palo Verde.

The Visitors Center is open year-round and finances the reserve with donations from visitors. The center has many small exhibits on the region's wildlife and a foodcourt. Although Lomas Barbudal is no longer managed by the government, the regional MINAE office has information and may put you in touch with *guardaparques* (park rangers) who offer free tours. (☎2695 5908 or 8818 0671; lomasbarbudal@acarenaltempisque.org. Open daily 8am-4pm.)

WHEN TO GO. Although Lomas Barbudal is a tropical dry forest, it can be very wet. Hiking can be impossible during the rainy season. In addition, the many dirt roads in this area can become muddy. This makes the *parque* most easily accessible during the dry season (Dec.-Apr.).

HIKING

Most visitors never enter the actual reserve, whose northern edge is across the Río Cabuyo from the Visitors Center, since most locals take advantage of the swimming hole behind the Visitors Center, La Poza el Eden de Cabuyo. The naturally clean water allows for a dream bath that feels like it's in the middle of the jungle. Modest bathers beware; the water is surrounded by tree stumps often used for picnics. The southern side of Lomas is accessible by roads leading to Palo Verde from Bagaces. **La Catarata** and **Carablanca** (in honor of the white-faced monkeys), two 2km trails, lead to a swimming hole and waterfalls and boast a wide variety of animals, from the entertaining white-faced monkey to the less desirable bee. **Gigantes de Bosque,** a leisurely 1hr. walk, runs along the river through dense forest, affording excellent birdwatching opportunities.

LIBERIA

As the commercial center of Guanacaste and the cultural heart of this dusty cowboy region, Liberia (pop. 40,000) is more visibly entrenched in history than many other Costa Rican towns. Paradoxically, it still strives to appease a trendier crowd; surfer stores and local *sodas* line the street in Spanish-style, white-washed colonial houses while a flag waves above the *parque central.* Guanacaste maintains a strong sense of regional autonomy and identity. In suit, Liberia celebrates Guanacaste Day, which commemorates the annexation of the "Partido de Nicoya," now known as Guanacaste, from Nicaragua in 1824. The eight-day festival, culminating on July 25th, features the traditional *tope* (horse parade). Constant fiestas, dancing, concerts, bullfights, and cattle auctions in front of the University of Costa Rica make this a highly anticipated week, drawing crowds from around the country. Apart from seasonal festivities, there's not much to see in Liberia; it's more of a transportation hub than anything else. The city also serves as an excellent base for visits to national parks like Rincón de la Vieja, Santa Rosa, and Palo Verde.

⬛ TRANSPORTATION

Flights: The **Daniel Oduber Quiros International Aiport (LIR),** 13km west of Liberia, can be reached by taxi or public transportation from the 200m north of Hotel Guanacaste. **Sansa** (☎+1-877-767-2672; www.flysansa.com). Flights to **San José** (1hr.; Nov. 20-Apr. 19 7, 10:22am, 1:13, 5:18pm; Apr. 20-Nov. 19 7, 10:22am, 1:10, 3:34, 4:54pm; round-trip ₡110,200/US$190).

Buses: Schedules often change but buses are reliable; check at either the **Pulmitán** or **Central station ticket booths.** Buy tickets in advance for **Playa Hermosa, Playa Panama, Playa Tamarindo, Playa Flamingo, Nicoya,** and all international buses. Otherwise, pay on the bus. Buses fill up quickly; arrive about 30min. early. Unless otherwise noted, buses leave from **Estación Central,** across from the market, to: **Cañas** (1hr., every hr. 5am-5:30pm, ₡550); the Nicaraguan border at **Peñas Blancas** via **La Cruz** (1hr., every 2hr. 5:30am-7pm, ₡1200); **Playa Tamarindo** (1hr., 15 per day 3:50am-6pm, ₡1180); and **Playa Flamingo** (1hr., 15 per day 3:50am-6pm, ₡1165); **Playa del Coco** (1hr.; every hr. 5am-11am, 12:30, 2:30, 6:30pm; ₡350); **Puntarenas** via **Cañas** (3hr.; 5am, every hr. 8:30am-3:30pm; ₡1125); **Nicoya** via **Santa Cruz** and **Filadelfia** (2hr., every 30min. 4:30am-7:30pm, ₡785); **Playa Hermosa** and **Playa Panama** (1hr., 9 per day 4:45am-5:30pm, ₡580). Three companies depart for Nicaragua from Hotel Guanacaste (☎2666 0085), 2 blocks south of Estación Central. **Rivas, Las Virgen San Juan del Sur, Nandaime, Granada, Masaya,** and **Managua** can be reached on **Central Line** (8:30am, ₡12,000) or **Transnica** (9:30am, ₡11,400). Transnica continues to **San Salvador, El Salvador** (₡45,700). Buses to **San José** via **Bagaces** leave from the **Pulmitán terminal** (☎2666 0458), 1 block south of the main terminal (4hr.; M-F every hr. 3am-8pm, Sa every hr. 4am-8pm, Su every hr. 5am-8pm; 9am and 3pm buses stop at Playa Coco; ₡2005).

Taxis: Line up at the north side of the *parque,* as well as by the Estación Central. **Taxi Liberia** (☎2666 7070 or 3330). **Taxi Porteadores** (☎2665 5050 or 5051).

Car Rental: Sol Rent-a-Car (☎2666 2222 or +1-800-SOL-RENT/2765 7368; www.solrentacar.com), 250m south of the Toyota dealership, on the Interamericana Hwy. in

Hotel Bolero. From ¢23,200 (US$40) per day. Open daily 7:30am-5pm. Multiple rental options are also available on the road to the airport.

ORIENTATION AND PRACTICAL INFORMATION

The city is built on a typical grid with **Avenida Central** (or Av. 25 de Julio) acting as the southern border of the *parque central*, officially known as **Parque Ruiz**. Streets, however, are not well marked. **Calle Central**, or **Calle Ruben Iglesias**, is split by the *parque*. The oldest *barrios* of **Cerros, Los Angeles, Condega**, and **La Victoria** do justice to Liberia's other name, Pueblo Blanco, with their white-washed colonial buildings. In front of the church in the main plaza sits the **Frondoso Arbol de Guanacaste**, the tree after which the province was named. The **Universidad de Costa Rica** is on the west side of town.

Tourist Information and Guided Tours: Most of the hotels in town offer info on the city and on tours of nearby national parks. **Hotel La Posada del Tope, Hotel Liberia, La Casona**, and **Hotel Guanacaste** offer transportation and, during the dry season, various activities in the national parks. La Posada del Tope offers rafting trips (¢26,100/US$45), trips to Palo Verde in the dry season (¢29,000/US$50), canopy tours (¢26,100/US$45), and full adventure tours (tubing, canopy tour, and horseback riding; ¢49,300/US$85). These hotels also provide bus service to **Rincón de la Vieja** (depart 7am, return 4pm; ¢12,600) and **Santa Rosa** (depart 6am, return 3pm; ¢12,600); arrange at least a day in advance.

Banks: Banco Nacional (☎2666 1036), 3 blocks west of the *parque*. Exchanges travelers' checks. Cash advances on V. **24hr. ATM.** Open M-F 8:30am-3:45pm. **Banco de San José** (☎2666 2020), across the Interamericana Hwy., 100m along on the left, under Bar LIB. Cirrus **ATM.** Cash advances on MC/V. Open M-F 8am-6pm, Sa 9am-1pm. **Banco de Costa Rica** (☎2665 6530), north of the church. Exchanges currency and traveler's checks. Cash advances on AmEx/MC/V. Open M-F 9am-4pm.

Police: (☎2666 0213, emergency 911), 800m south of the *parque*, on the Interamericana.

Red Cross: (☎2666 0016), 200m south of the hospital, east of the *parque*.

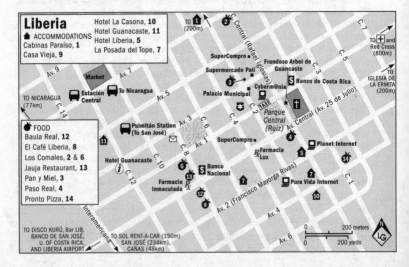

Liberia

♠ ACCOMMODATIONS
Cabinas Paraíso, 1
Casa Vieja, 9
Hotel La Casona, 10
Hotel Guanacaste, 11
Hotel Liberia, 5
La Posada del Tope, 7

🍴 FOOD
Baula Real, 12
El Café Liberia, 8
Los Comales, 2 & 6
Jauja Restaurant, 13
Pan y Miel, 3
Paso Real, 4
Pronto Pizza, 14

TO NICARAGUA (77km)
Av. 9
Av. 7
Market
Estación Central
To Nicaragua
Av. 5
Pulmitán Station (To San José)
Hotel Guanacaste
Av. 3
Av. 1

TO DISCO KURÚ, Bar LIB, BANCO DE SAN JOSÉ, U. OF COSTA RICA, AND LIBERIA AIRPORT
TO SOL RENT-A-CAR (150m) SAN JOSÉ (234km), CAÑAS (48km)

TO (200m)
C. Central (Rafael Iglesias)
SuperCompro
Supermercado Palí
Frondoso Arbol de Guancaste
Cyberm@nia
Palacio Municipal
TAXI
Parque Central (Ruiz)
C. Central (Av. 25 de Julio)
SuperCompro
Farmacia Lux
Planet Internet
Pura Vida Internet
Banco Nacional
Farmacia Inmaculada
Av. 2 (Francisco Mayorga Rivas)
Av. 4
Av. 6

Banco de Costa Rica
TO and Red Cross (800m)
TO IGLESIA DE LA ERMITA (200m)

0   200 meters
0   200 yards

Pharmacy: Farmacia Lux (☎2666 0061), 100m west of the *parque*'s southwest corner. Open M-Sa 8am-10pm, Su 8am-4pm. AmEx/D/MC/V. **Farmacia La Inmaculada,** Av. 25 de Julio (☎2666 7657), 50m west of Banco Nacional. Open M-Sa 8am-9:30pm, Su 10am-12pm and 4-8:30pm. AmEx/D/MC/V.

Hospital: (☎2666 0011, emergency ext. 325, or 911), 1km northeast of the *parque*.

Internet Access: Ciberm@nia (☎2666 7237), on the north side of the *parque*. Printing (black and white ¢100; color ¢300), international calls (¢100 per min. to US), and internet (¢300 per 30min., ¢550 per hr.). Open daily 8am-10pm. **Planet Internet** (☎2665 3737), on C. Central south of the *parque*. Internet ¢400 per 30min., ¢600 per hr. Open M-Sa 8am-10pm, Su 9am-9pm. AmEx/D/MC/V.

Post Office: (☎2666 1649), 3 blocks west and 1 block north of the *parque*. Open M-F 8am-5:30pm, Sa 8am-noon. **Postal Code:** 5000.

☎ ACCOMMODATIONS

There are many options in the city center. Some more luxurious hotels line the Interamericana Hwy. Rates may increase during the high season (Dec.-Apr.).

▨ **Casa Vieja** (☎2665 5826), 2 blocks south and 50m east of the southwest corner of the *parque*. Offers the best lodging in town without hurting your wallet. Plush couches, a full kitchen, and a covered patio with snug chairs. Dark wooden doors open up into fresh rooms with elegant curtains, private bathrooms, and cable TV. Wi-Fi and internet. Reception 24hr. Singles ¢10,000; doubles ¢17,000; triples ¢21,000. Cash only. ❷

La Posada del Tope (☎2666 3876), 1 block south of the *parque*. Entering the rustic courtyard of this 150-year-old building is like stepping into a time warp. Beds come with mosquito nets (for decorative purposes only). All rooms have cable TV. No hot water. Wi-Fi. Offers tours during the dry season and transportation to Rincon and Santa Rosa (¢12,760/US$22). Singles ¢8000, with private bath ¢12000. Cash only. ❷

Hotel Liberia (☎2666 0161), 1 block south of the *parque*'s southeast corner. Simple rooms separated from the street by the hotel's tiled patio. Make time for a conversation with the owner, Beto: he'll entertain you and give you a voucher for a free drink at Pizza Pronto, his brother's place. Backpackers gather around the TV in the common area, chatting, drinking beer, and lounging on hammocks. Tours during dry season and transportation to parks. Laundry ¢1200 per kg. Wi-Fi. Parking available. Reception 24hr. Check-out noon. Singles ¢6300, with private bath ¢7400-8600. MC/V. 16% charge for credit cards. ❶

Cabinas Paraíso (☎2666 3434), 500m north of the *parque* and 100m west of the fire station on a quiet dead-end street. Simple white rooms with large windows and balconies. The gate is not easily visible from inside, so if it's locked, yell loudly. Cable TV in some rooms (¢1000 extra). Singles ¢6000, with private bath ¢7500; doubles ¢7500/12,000; triples ¢15,000; quads ¢18,000. ❶

Hotel La Casona (☎2666 2971), 300m south of the *parque*'s southeast corner. No-frills rooms with private bathrooms and cable TV. Fully furnished apartments with private bath, hot water, A/C, television, fridge, and kitchen. Laundry ¢1200 per kg. Transportation offered to nearby parks (¢11,600/US$20 per person, 7am-3pm). Singles ¢10,000, with A/C ¢12,000; doubles and triples ¢14,000/18,000; apartment for 1 person ¢15,000, for 2 people ¢20,000. ❷

Hotel Guanacaste (☎2666 0085; www.higuanacaste.com), 500m west and 100 m north of the *parque*. Private rooms, as well as small shared rooms where you can fight with fellow backpackers over rights to the top bunk. No hot water. Tours to nearby volcanoes (¢11,600/US$20 per person) and national parks (¢11,600/US$20 per person to Santa Rosa, min. 4 people). Sells tickets for buses heading to Nicaragua. On-site restaurant; entrees ¢1800-4500. Wi-Fi. Shared room ¢4500; singles ¢6600; doubles ¢14,000; triples ¢19500. AmEx/D/MC/V. ❷

▐ FOOD

For an adventurous food experience, try the sweet traditional drink called *chan*, made from coyol or flower seeds, which can look like frog eggs in water. Also ask restaurants about the popular snack *chorreadas*—a corn pancake eaten with cream or cheese. Those shopping for supplies can browse the outdoor **street market**, five blocks west and three blocks north of the *parque*. (Open M-Sa 7am-5pm.) **SuperCompro** is one block west of the *parque*'s southwest corner. (☎2666 5242. Open daily 8am-9pm.) **Supermercado Palí** is in front of the Palacio Municipal. (☎2666 4730. Open M-F 8am-7:30pm, Sa 8am-8pm, Su 8am-6pm. AmEx/D/MC/V.)

▨ **Los Comales** (☎2665 0105), 3 blocks north of the northeast corner of the *parque*. Coopeingua RL, a cooperative of 25 women striving to bring back regional traditions and improve the lives of females, runs this authentic place. Serves hearty Guanacaste *típico* to locals. It's easy to miss this hole-in-the-wall, as there's no sign outside. The *arroz de maíz* (¢1600) is not actually rice, but broken corn chips cooked with chicken. *Pollo de salchichon* (long sausage) ¢1300. Open daily 6am-10pm. Open M-Sa 7am-5pm. MC/V. ❶

▨ **El Café Liberia** (☎2665 1660), a few blocks southwest of the *parque*. The only European-style cafe you'll find in Liberia. Serves freshly roasted Guanacastan coffee (roasted in an antique machine in the dining area) alongside homemade delicacies. Share hummus and olives (¢3000) with a friend or go solo with a toasted pesto, goat cheese, and tomato sandwich (¢3000). Finish up with some homemade cheesecake (¢1500). Breakfast combos of 100% natural juice, wheat toast with jam, coffee, and an omelette or yogurt with granola and fruit (¢3500) will fuel a day of hiking. Free Wi-Fi, multilingual book exchange, world music, and sporadic live performances. Themed movie showings (Th 7pm). Open M-F 8:30am-7pm, Sa 10am-6pm. Cash only. ❷

Pan y Miel (☎2666 0718), on the corner next to Palí and a Musamanni. The loaves of fresh bread stacked behind the counter are replenished often, as swarms of locals deplete the shelves of favorites like *pan danes* (¢1200). Pastries and cakes are also on sale. The 4 small tables don't allow much room for sit-down dining, so you may want to get your goodies to go. A less sweet but still popular option is the pan pizza topped with ham and cheese (¢1050). Open M-Sa 6am-8:30pm, Su 7am-5pm. AmEx/MC/V. ❶

Paso Real (☎2666 3455), on the 2nd fl. of a building overlooking the *parque*. A breezy outdoor balcony wraps around the high-ceilinged interior of this popular *marisquería*. Seafood and shellfish are their specialty and are prepared in every way possible. Shrimp cordon bleu fish fillet ¢6000. Shellfish casserole ¢5000. Wi-Fi. Open daily 11am-10pm. AmEx/D/MC/ V. ❸

Baula Real Bar & Restaurant (☎2666 0898), 300m south of the *parque*'s southwest corner. Decorations at this Mexican restaurant include Mexican flags, a disco ball, and sombreros. Karaoke Th-F 7-midnight. Go big with the Taco Baula (stuffed with chicken, ham, guacamole, and beans). *Fajitas* ¢3000. Open daily 4pm-2am. AmEx/D/MC/ V. ❷

Jauja Restaurant (☎2666 2061), 50m west of Banco Nacional. Cleanly presented and quickly delivered dishes served on bamboo tables. Offerings range from shrimp cocktail (¢5950) and bruschetta (¢2950) to Teriyaki tenderloin (¢7350) and pork ribs in BBQ sauce (¢5850). Finish the night with a crepe covered in chocolate, fruit sauce, and ice cream (¢2250). Live rock W 7:30pm. Wi-Fi. Open daily 7am-9pm. MC/ V. ❸

Pronto Pizza (☎2666 2098), corner of Av. 4 and C. 1. Watch the dough rise on your pizza in the clay oven. Over 26 different kinds of pizza include time-tested favorites and creative concoctions like peach pizza (tomato, cheese, peach, pineapple, honey; ¢4500). Small ¢4500-4700; medium ¢5700-6500; large ¢7800-8000. Pasta ¢4500. Sandwiches ¢3000. Open daily noon-3pm, 6-11pm. AmEx/D/MC/ V. ❷

👁 SIGHTS

Iglesia de la Ermita, six blocks east of the *parque* along Av. Central, is the oldest church in town (open daily 3-6pm, but hours vary). Enthusiastic locals converge each weekend on **Rancho Santa Alicia,** 20min. from Liberia, on the Interamericana Hwy. toward San José, where horse races, rodeos, and unrelenting heat come together to form a unique and sweaty attraction. The large horse statue at the entrance and the roaring of the crowd within make it difficult to miss (☎2671 2513; open Tu-Su).

🎵 NIGHTLIFE AND ENTERTAINMENT

Ticos hailing from surrounding villages compose the bulk of the minimal party scene here. Even with the University of Costa Rica nearby, the young crowd flocks to the beach towns for more exhilirating nights.

Disco Kurú (☎2666 0769), 300m past Burger King, across the Interamericana Hwy. One of the busiest late-night spots in Liberia. Draws include 2 bars and a dance floor with mirrors. Blasting tunes feature a mix of *merengue*, salsa, *cumbia*, and hip hop. Beers ¢1100. 18+. Open daily 9:30pm-6am. AmEx/MC/V.

Bar LIB (☎2665 0741), across the Interamericana Hwy., 100m on the left above the bank. Quieter music makes for a more talkative crowd. Tropical beats on the dance floor provide lively ambience for diners. Entrees (rice, meat, *ceviche*) ¢5000. Occasional live music events. Cover ¢1000-2000. Open W-Sa 5pm-2:13am. AmEx/MC/V.

Bar de Luna (☎2665 5640), across the Interamerican Hwy. from Disco Kurú. Blasts strictly electronica for busy weekend crowds. Mixed drinks from ¢2000. Imperial ¢1000. Sa cover ¢1000. Open Tu-Su 9pm-6am.

Mall-Plaza Centro Liberia, off the Interamericana Hwy. Taxi from the bus station ¢1000. This mall's new movie theater features recent American flicks with Spanish subtitles. Adults ¢1600, children ¢1200. Showings 2-9pm.

PARQUE NACIONAL RINCÓN DE LA VIEJA

While the rest of Costa Rica parties the night away, restless travelers head north from Liberia to seek seclusion and peace in a park full of waterfalls, turbulent rivers, and thick forests. The colorful blooms and drifting sulfur vapors make it an enthralling experience in (and for) every sense. Though its gigantic active volcano is the park's highlight, few make the grueling, 4hr. climb to the crater. Most hikers seek out the sulfuric lagoons, boiling mud pits, abundant wildlife (300 species of birds!), and thermal waters that dot its slopes.

AT A GLANCE

AREA: 14,100 hectares; 141 sq. km.

CLIMATE: Ave. Temp. 22˚C.

FEATURES: Colorado, Blanco, and Ahogados rivers; largest quantity of *guaria moradas* (the national flower).

HIGHLIGHTS: Hiking Sendero Las Pailas, La Cangreja and La Escondida waterfalls, hot springs, boiling mud pits, *fumaroles*, the crater, and swimming holes.

GATEWAYS: Although it's close to Liberia (p. 201), there is no public transportation that covers the distance to the park.

CAMPING: At Santa María ranger station; campgrounds with showers and pit toilets, US$2.

FEES: Entrance US$10, use of private road to the Las Pailas station ¢700.

⚓ 🏠 ORIENTATION AND TRANSPORTATION

The park has two entrances, Las Pailas and Santa María, each with a ranger station. Las Pailas, with trails leading past waterfalls and up the volcano, is visited more frequently, as there are many more trails here. The nearby river is perfect for swimming. The park is open M-Tu and Su 7am-3pm. Entry costs US$10. Camping at the Santa María ranger station is available for US$2 per person. The park is only 25km northeast of Liberia, but public transportation covers only 15km of this distance. A dirt road that is accessible to cars leads from Liberia's Barrio La Victoria to the Santa María entrance. Another dirt road starts 5km north of Liberia on the Interamericana Hwy. and heads 10km east to the town of Curabanda; from there it is another difficult 10km east to the Las Pailas entrance (¢700 per person to drive on the private road). Public buses go only as far as Curabanda. From there, some catch a ride with occasional traffic. **Let's Go does not recommend hitchhiking.** More reliable tourist shuttles are offered by various hotels in Liberia, including Hotel Liberia, La Posada del Tope, Hotel Guanacaste, and La Casona. (Departs 7am, returns by 5pm. US$20.) Call any of the hotels at least a day ahead. It's possible to hire a 4WD taxi in Liberia (at least ¢10,000 each way). To reach the ranger stations, call ☎2200 0399.

WHEN TO GO. While the park is accessible year-round, Rincón de la Vieja's dry climate makes this park most beautiful during the rainy season (May-Nov.), when waterfalls spill through its bright green forests, the *fumarolas* blossom, the skies are clear, and hot springs fill to capacity and bubble over. To get to the hot springs, however, you must cross 2 rivers, which is not feasible if it has recently rained heavily (usually only in Sept. or Oct.).

🏠 🏕 ACCOMMODATIONS AND CAMPING

Only the Santa María ranger station has a campground with showers and pit toilets (US$2 per person). Near Las Pailas, there are a number of lodges that offer meals and activities for those seeking refuge from Liberia's urban congestion. **Rincón de la Vieja Lodge ❹** is 2.5km before the Las Pailas entrance and offers quiet, woodsy cabins, some with bunk beds, and hammocks on the porches. Private baths, hot water, scientific library, and small pool are available. The property is a 400-hectare working *finca* with horses and a canopy tour. The restaurant serves a buffet, and the bar occasionally has live music. (☎/fax 2661 8198; info@rincondelavieja.com. Canopy tour US$60. 3hr. horseback tour to hot springs US$35. Breakfast 6-7:30am, included; lunch 12:30-1:30pm, US$10; dinner 6:30-7:30pm, US$10. Doubles US$69; triples US$90. Bungalow doubles US$80; triples US$105. MC/V.) The **Hacienda Lodge Guachipelín ❹**, 5km before the park entrance, is a 19th-century cattle-ranch-turned-hotel. Activities (at a significant extra cost) include a seven-platform canopy tour and horseback tours (US$50, students US$40, children US$30). Walking tours in the park are about US$35. For a hefty price, the hotel offers several "adventure tours," which can include hiking to the crater, horseback riding to waterfalls and hot springs, tubing on Río Negro, rappelling, and canopy tours. (☎2442 2818 or 2666 8075; www.guachipelin.com. Tours US$80, students US$75, children US$70; lunch included. Breakfast included with room price, 7-9am. Singles US$50-66; doubles US$73-83; triples US$93-107; quads US$107.)

HURT SO GOOD. Mosquitos are everywhere. If the pounds of bug repellant and full-body unitard just didn't cut it, you can still prevent those bites from being scratched into kiwi-sized welts. Pour hot wax onto the bite, let it cool, peel it off, and then relax with your itch-free self.

HIKES

The eastern trail beginning at Las Pailas ranger station is the 3km loop **Sendero Las Pailas,** which passes turnoffs to a sulfuric lagoon, a *volcancito,* boiling mud pits, *fumaroles,* and a picturesque waterfall that flows during the rainy season. At the halfway point, a well-marked branch leads another 6km east to the Santa María station. A trail west of the Las Pailas leads to the park's biggest waterfalls: **Cataratas Escondidas** (5km) is a difficult, more exciting hike with steep inclines. Most choose to hike the challenging-but-doable trail to the breathtaking **Catarata La Cangreja** (5km). If you only have time for one hike, visit Catarata La Cangreja and the beautiful, turquoise swimming hole underneath it. For a swim without the 2hr. hike, there's a crystal-clear swimming hole just 600m down the trail toward the waterfalls. It's a difficult 8km to the crater of Rincón de la Vieja; even the fittest should allow a day for the round-trip journey (about 7-8hr.) and must register at the park office in order to get a guide (US$30 per person). It is strongly recommended that solo hikers be accompanied by a guide. The crater trail can close due to poor weather conditions. (Check with rangers or lodge employees.) Most hike to a waterfall in the morning (about 4hr.), as the area is prone to floods that come with afternoon rain, and fill their afternoons with a hike along Sendero Las Pailas (about 2hr.). From the Santa María station, a 3km trail leads west through thick forests full of monkeys to the *aguas termales* (hot springs), which can get crowded during high season. Trails are subject to closing due to excessive rain (usually Sept.-Nov.).

PARQUE NACIONAL SANTA ROSA

Established in 1971, Santa Rosa preserves one of the largest remaining tropical dry forest in Central America. Encompassing most of the Península Santa Rosa, this park has managed to keep its beaches, famous for great surfing and turtle-watching, relatively tourist-free. In addition to its status as a **UNESCO World Heritage Site,** the park is part of the **Area de Conservación Guanacaste (ACG),** one of 11 conservation areas in Costa Rica. The unique flora here includes the Guanacaste, Pochote, Naked Indian, and Caoba trees, as well as 115 species of mammals, 9600 species of butterflies and moths, 460 species of birds, and more than 30,000 species of insects. There are a number of enchanting *miradores* (lookout points) on the natural and man-made trails.

The park also houses a famous historical site, **Hacienda Santa Rosa** (La Casona). On March 20, 1856, a ragtag Costa Rican army defeated invading troops sent from Nicaragua by American imperialist William Walker. Though the event consisted of only 14 minutes of fighting, this battle is one of the most famous in Costa Rican history. Invasions were again prevented in 1919 and 1955. Sadly, La Casona did not withstand its most recent invasion, on May 20, 2001, when two vindictive deer hunters snuck into the park and set fire to the site, reducing over half of the fort to ashes. The arsonists, apparently angered by recent hunting restrictions, were caught and convicted. Costa Ricans raised ₡200,350,000 to rebuild the fort. La Casona now stands restored, with roof tiles dating from 1886 and a state-of-the-art fire alarm system. Out front, you can watch cattle going through immersion baths in preparation for their truck journey from the *embarcadero* to the *corrales de piedra* (stone corrals).

⬛ TRANSPORTATION. About 12 **buses** per day pass along the Interamericana Hwy. and stop at the entrance station at La Casetilla. No buses run the 7km stretch to the administration center or along the dirt road to the beach, so those without wheels will need to find alternative means of transportation (walking takes about an hour). **Hotel Guanacaste** (p. 199) and **Hotel Liberia** (p. 199) arrange transportation but often require a minimum number of people (¢12,760/US$22 per person). Hotel Liberia is the only hotel that arranges transportation for solo travelers (¢20,300/US$35). It may be cheaper for groups to find their own **taxi** (¢34,800/US$60 round-trip).

⬛🚹 ORIENTATION AND PRACTICAL INFORMATION. The national park's **entrance station** is 35km north of Liberia and 24km south of La Cruz, on the west side of the Interamericana Hwy. From here, a dirt road leads 7km to the park's **administration center** which houses **MINAE offices** and an **information center.** A bit farther to the left is the campground; to the right, past the cabins, is the *comedor* (cafeteria). Beyond the administration center is a four-wheel-drive road (often closed to traffic during the rainy season) leading to the coast, 12km away. The road forks after 7km; the left branch leads 4km to **Playa Naranjo,** a popular campsite and famed surfing beach; the right heads 8km to **Playa Nancite.** Access to Playa Nancite requires special permission given to formal researchers. Contact the park for volunteer opportunities, mostly available before and during the turtle-hatching (June-Dec.; reservaciones@acguanacaste.ac.cr).

The park's **Sector Murciélago,** spread over the isolated northern coast of Península Santa Rosa, isn't accessible from the rest of the park (open 8am-5pm). To visit, start at **Cuajuniquil,** 8km off the Interamericana Hwy., which can be reached by taking a bus from La Cruz or Liberia. You will either need to walk 7km down the dirt road to the sector's ranger station or traverse the bumpy stretch with a four-wheel-drive vehicle. Information is available at the **administration center** (☎2666 5051, ext. 219; www.acguanacaste.ac.cr). Open daily 8am-4pm. For reservations, contact reservaciones@acguanacaste.ac.cr. The park is open daily 8am-4pm. Entrance fee US$10; beaches US$15; camping US$2 extra. Discounts offered to those working on conservation efforts.

⬛⬛ ACCOMMODATIONS AND FOOD. The park offers lodging in small houses near the main offices and decent meals in the *comedor.* An on-site snack bar selling sandwiches, drinks, and bagged cookies is open to all. Reserve lodging at least one month in advance. (☎2666 5051. Lodging US$12 per person. Meals US$6 per day. Breakfast 6:30-7:30am; lunch 11:30am-1pm; dinner 5:30-6pm. Ask in the morning to have your lunch or dinner prepared.) A campground near the administration center has drinking water, toilets, and cold-water showers. The campground at Playa Naranjo has toilets and non-potable water. Ask about camping at the administration center.

⬛⬛ SIGHTS AND HIKING. La Casona, near the administration center (follow signs past the administration center to the left), is a museum featuring historic rooms with accompanying information and an exhibition about the Area de Conservación Guanacaste. (Open daily 8am-11:30am and 1-4pm. Free.) The **Monument to the Heroes of 1856 and 1955** lies beside La Casona and offers a windy view of nearby volcanoes in Orosi, Cacao, and Rincón de la Vieja. The lookouts **Mirador Tierras Emergidas,** halfway to the administration center from the entrance on the way to the coast, and **Mirador Valle Naranjo,** starting 6km after the administration center on the way to the coast, feature stellar views of the mountains and the beach. All trails and points of interest are marked on a useful **map** available at the entrance (¢100). The short 1km **Sendero Indio Desnudo** (a.k.a. Gringo Pelado, or "Peeled Gringo") begins on the north side of La Casona next to the museum; it winds around an impressive array of regional flora. Many of the trees in this region lose their leaves during the dry season, so it's not unusual to see them bare. Look out for indigenous carvings and monkeys high in the trees. **Sendero Los Patos** (3km), 5km beyond the administration center on the road to the coast, is one of the best trails for spotting birds and the blue morpho butterfly, and features **Mirador al Cañon del Tigre.** The 2km **Sendero Palo Seco** lies 300m before Playa Naranjo. The 6km **Sendero Carbonal** also lies 300m before Playa Naranjo and leads to **Laguna El Limbo,** a crocodile hangout. On the coast, you can swim at **Bahía El Hachal, Bahía Danta** (temporarily closed), **Coquito** (temporarily closed), **Santa Elena,** and **Playa Blanca** (17km long), or hike the 600m **Poza del General** to view birds and monkeys. **Camping** is permitted in the area, but check with the park office to see if there is space, especially during *Semana Santa* (☎2666 5051). No potable water is available.

☑ **BEACHES.** The famous fast waves of **Piedra Bruja** (Witch Rock) break onto a stone off **Playa Naranjo.** Though there are great waves on the shoreline, serious surfers may want to seek out sandbars where the estuary meets the ocean at Piedra Bruja; these are best from December to April. Bring a mosquito net if you plan to use the **campground** at Playa Naranjo; beware of biting *chitras* on the beach at dawn and dusk. **Playa Nancite** hosts the country's second-largest population of Olive Ridley turtles. The nesting season, lasting from July to December, is at its height from October to November and reaches its zenith during the eight days of the crescent moon. During this time, thousands of turtles arrive at 800m of beach each night around 9pm. Access to Playa Nancite is granted by permission only, and swimming is not allowed. Bring water to these beaches, as there is none to drink. Lodging is open only to researchers and students ($10 per person, up to 20 people). Call the **administration center** (☎2666 5051, ext. 233) 20 days ahead to reserve **camping** near the beach (US$2 per day; max. 25 people per day). If you arrive at the park by car, keep in mind that driving to Nancite is not allowed. Drop the vehicle off at Playa Naranjo, where a guard will watch it for you.

THIS BEACH WAS MADE FOR WALKIN'. During the rainy season, the road may be impossible to drive, even with a four-wheel-drive vehicle. The most determined can hike the muddy trail on foot, leaving cars at the information center. Bring proper clothing for heavy mid-morning rains.

PARQUE NACIONAL GUANACASTE

Parque Nacional Guanacaste lies on the opposite side of Parque Nacional Santa Rosa, across the Interamericana Hwy.. While the western reaches of Guanacaste share Santa Rosa's lowland habitats, the environment changes as the park rises toward the summits of **Volcán Orosi** (1487m) and **Volcán Cacao** (1659m). The park, created in 1991 in part from old ranch land, is open mainly to students and scientists in the dry season and is difficult to visit without private transportation. However, there are three research stations scattered about the park at Marzita, Cacao, and Pitilla. Although the park is generally frequented by groups, tourists are rarely allowed to stay at the stations, which offer dorm beds and cold-water baths (US$14 per person, students US$6). For information, contact the Santa Rosa headquarters (☎2666 5051; fax 2666 5020). Reservation instructions are available from reservaciones@acguanacaste.ac.cr.

The most modern of the three stations, **Marzita Biological Station,** is 18km away from the Interamericana Hwy. Marzita is not open to visitors without reservations. The turnoff is to the east, at the Cuanjiniquil intersection, 8km north of the entrance to Santa Rosa. Marzita has lodging for up to 32 people, electricity, and food service (request at least 3 months in advace). At this station, research is focused on aquatic insects. The 2hr. trail hike, **Pedtroglifos El Pedregal,** is named for its approximately 800 observable petroglyphs.

A 12km trail ascends from Marzita to the **Cacao Biological Station,** which is only open to groups, students taking the biology course or occasional visitors with reservations. It begins in Potrerillos, about 9km south of the Santa Rosa park entrance. From Potrerillos, head 7km east to Quebrada Grande (take the daily 3pm bus from Liberia), then 16km north along a 4WD road to the station. At the station, there is a 900m trail called Pedregal, which is open to visitors and leads to an observatory for forest fires. You can also climb to the top of Volcán Cacao, a hard 3hr. hike into the cloud forest that starts on the east side of the lab. You will need a permission slip from the park office. Anyone can get one, but they are required to speak to you about the rules and precautions.

Pitilla Biological Station is 28km off the highway near the Nicaraguan border, around 10km south from the town of Santa Cecilia. At Pitilla, you can delight in incredible birdwatching and catch a glimpse of Lago de Nicaragua from the top of mini-Volcán Orosilito. There is lodging available at the station for up to 28 people enrolled in courses or with at least three-month advanced notice at the Santa Rosa headquarters, along with a study room, two-way radio, drinking water, parking, and a 6hr. trail.

✖ PEÑAS BLANCAS: BORDER WITH NICARAGUA

Liberia is only 1hr. away from the border at Peñas Blancas, a small frontier featuring a few houses and whole lot of police along the tree-lined road to Nicaragua. **Buses** run frequently from Liberia's **Estación Central** to the border (every hr. 5:30am-7pm, ¢1200). Buses from Liberia that continue into Nicaragua stop in front of **Hotel Guanacaste** (5hr., 3 per day 7:30-9:30am, ¢12,180). To reach Peñas Blancas from **San José,** take a bus from C. 14, Av. 3/5 (every hr. 3am-7pm, ¢4600). If you are traveling into Costa Rica, buses run from Peñas Blancas to **La Cruz** (every hr. 5am-6:30pm, ¢550), **San José** (every 1½hr. 5:30am-5:30pm, ¢4600), or **San Carlos** (5hr.; 6:30am, 2pm; ¢2800).

Crossing the border into Nicaragua usually takes about 30min.; if arriving on a bus, the process is slightly more prolonged. After getting your passport stamped at the **Costa Rica Immigration Office** (☎2677 0230 or 0064; open 6am-10pm), drive or walk to the actual crossing about 100m down the road. **Banco de Costa Rica** (open M-F 9am-4pm, Sa 9am-1pm), next to the immigration office, can exchange money and traveler's checks. Agents that catch you right as you get off the bus can also exchange money; they often offer a better deal than the bank, but **watch out for counterfeit bills.** Rates for changing US dollars to *cordobas* are better on the Nicaraguan side of the border, while rates for changing *colones* to *cordobas* are worse. **Hotel Guanacaste** in Liberia will also change money. Snack vendors line the road to the border. **Restaurante de Frontera,** connected to the immigration office, serves more substantial food (hamburgers ¢1000; *casados* ¢2000-2500; AmEx/D/MC/V).

Buses from the Nicaraguan border run to **Rivas** (1hr., every 30min. 4am-5:30pm; ¢20) and continue to **Managua.** To get to **San Juan del Sur,** catch the **Rivas bus** and change in Rivas for San Juan (30min., every 30min. 5am-5pm, ¢20).

LA CRUZ

Only 20km south of the Nicaraguan border at Peñas Blancas, the town of La Cruz is home to an equal mix of *nica* and *tico* residents. Despite the tensions that immigration has brought to Costa Rica, the breezy streets and charming plazas of La Cruz maintain a peaceful air that hearkens back to earlier days. Though the old-world buildings around town convey its age, no one is quite sure where or how its history began. Some say it was named for a mule driver who died working on the cliffs, while other say it honors the infamous Cruz de Pierda in nearby Parque Nacional de Santa Rosa. La Cruz escapes Costa Rican tourism even though it makes a great base for daytrips to beaches at Copal, Jobo, and La Rajada. The only time you'll find crowds here is on La Cruz Day in early May, when the town hosts a rodeo.

▐ TRANSPORTATION

The **bus** station is on the north side of the town, about three blocks north of the *parque*. Transporte Deldu buses from San José to Peñas Blancas via La Cruz (6hr.; 10 per day 3:30am-7pm, last bus stops in La Cruz; ¢3000). You can catch a Deldu bus from Liberia to Peñas Blancas via La Cruz at Estación Central in Liberia (1hr., every 2hr. 5am-7pm, ¢900). **Taxis** to Peñas Blancas are US$10.

From La Cruz, buses go to San José (6hr., every hr. 4am-6pm, ¢3000) via Liberia (1hr., every hr. 5:20-6:50pm, ¢700). Transportes Deldu office is in the bus terminal. (Open daily 7am-2:30pm and 2:30-5pm.) Buses to Peñas Blancas leave every hr. 6:10am-7:40 (20min., ¢500). Buses to the local beaches of Soley, Copal, Morro, and Jobo leave from 100m west of the northwest corner of the *parque* at 5, 8, 11am, 2:30, and 4:15pm; they return at 7, 10:15am, 12:30, 3, and 6pm (15min., ¢400-600). **Taxis** line up on the north and south side of the *parque* (¢5000-15,000 to the beaches, ¢1500 around town).

▐▐ ORIENTATION AND PRACTICAL INFORMATION

The town of La Cruz sits on a sharp cliff overlooking the bays, beaches, *fincas*, and mountains of the region. Playa Soley is 10km southwest of the *parque;* farther along are Playa Moro (1km), Playa Jobo (15km), and Playa Rajada (19km). **Banco Popular** is located 50m east of the *parque*. (☎2679 9352. Open M-F 8:45am-3pm, Sa 8:15-noon.) **Banco Nacional** is across the street from the police station on the Interamericana Hwy, which is 400m east of the *parque*. (Open M-F 8:30am-3:45pm.) The **police station** is next to the Clinica de la Cruz. (☎2679 9092. Open 24hr.) The **Red Cross** is 200m east of the *parque*. (☎2679 9146. 24hr. emergency service.) The main **pharmacy** in town, **Farmacía La Cruz,** is on the main road in the direction of the bus station. (☎2679 8048. Open daily 8am-8pm.) The **Clínica de la Cruz** is next to the police on the Interamericana Hwy. (☎2679 9116. 24hr. emergency service.) **Internet Moroni**, 20m east of the *parque* and next to Banco Popular, offers Internet access on new IBM computers at ¢500 per hr. (☎2679 9801. Fax, copies, and international calls. ¢50 per min. to the US.) The **post office** is 50m west of the southwest corner of the *parque*. (☎/fax 2679 9329. Open M-F 8am-noon and 1-5:30pm.)

▐ ACCOMMODATIONS

Cabinas Maryfel ❶, across the bus terminal, offers the cheapest lodging in town. The friendly owner and welcoming family provide a clean, bug-free home for people and animals alike, with rooms full of social travelers and a backyard full of whistling parrots, rabbits, and dogs. Singles with fans and private baths fill up the cute yellow and maroon building next to the church. (☎2679 9747.

Singles ¢4000; doubles ¢5000; triples ¢8000; quads ¢10,000. US$/¢.) **Amalia's Inn**
❷ is next to the Ministerio de Salud, 100m south of the *parque*. From their posi-
tion on a hilltop, the pool and porch provide a breathtaking panoramic view of
the surrounding mountains and beaches. The leather couches, antique collect-
ibles, and the numerous contemporary wall paintings in each large room make
you feel as though you have rented a fully furnished apartment for the night.
Gates close at 10pm. (☎2679 9681. Triples US$20, with bath US$35. US$/¢.)

▐ FOOD

There are four supermarkets in town: **SuperCompro,** on the east side of the
parque (open M-Sa 7:30am-8pm, Su 8am-6pm; AmEx/D/MC/V); **Supermercado
El Único,** next to SuperCompro (open M-Sa 7am-7pm, Su 8am-1pm and 3-6pm);
and **Super Palí,** across from the bus terminal and Mini Super and Licorera Jauga,
20m east of the *parque* (open daily 8am-10pm; MC/V). The best restaurant in
La Cruz is **La Negra** ❸, on the road 10km north of town. The unassuming exterior and steep prices should not deter visitors from sampling its spectacular
seafood menu. Here, *la negra* herself prepares jumbo shrimp in garlic (¢5000)
and lobster tails in butter (¢6700), served in an intimate dining room with only
seven tables. (☎2677 0150. Open M-Sa 10am-10pm. US$/¢.) A jazzed-up *comida
típica* restaurant next to the gas station, **La Orquidea** ❷ makes for a fine pit stop,
serving a huge menu ranging from meat dishes (¢4000) to fried fish (¢3500) and
soups. (☎2679 9316. Open daily 6am-10pm. US$/¢.) **Soda la Santa Marta** ❶, 50m
north of the *parque* toward the bus terminal, is one of the only authentic *sodas*
in town. The cafe is owned by a Nicaraguan couple, who have lived in La Cruz
for 26 years and still open early to serve specialties like *arroz con pollo* for
¢1600. (☎2679 9347. Open M-Sa 6am-5pm, Su 6-11am. US$/¢.)

NICOYA PENINSULA

The trip can be long, and the roads difficult, but the gorgeous beaches, nature reserves, and world-class waves of the Nicoya Peninsula will convince most travelers that it's worth the trek. Surfers come from across the world to surf at Tamarindo and Playa Negra, while the reef at El Coco draws novices and experienced divers alike. Though the inland region is often overlooked by travelers, its villages offer a rugged charm, with streets full of ambling cowpokes and *pueblos* where the residents guard a proud history. Larger cities like Santa Cruz and Nicoya are frequently used as transportation jump-offs but can offer rich cultural performances and a chance to experience authentic *tico* lifestyle, too. Since activities in these towns are scarce, it's likely you'll find yourself itching for the crashing waves and vast expanses of sand farther west.

PLAYA HERMOSA

Known as a prime swimming and diving beach for its calm waters and diverse marine life, Playa Hermosa offers beach-goers the chance to see eels, octopi, and seahorses, as well as breathtaking sunsets. With its location just outside of the Papagayo Gulf and its designation as the next "it" spot for tourism, Hermosa is experiencing tremendous growth. More villas, beachside condos, and gated communities sprout up every day. Fights to prevent environmental damage have dominated the Supreme Court for years. Despite the chaos of continual construction, Hermosa offers a peaceful and relaxing experience described by travelers and locals alike as *muy tranquilo* (very calm)—particularly in comparison to its rowdy neighbor, Playa del Coco.

⊏ TRANSPORTATION

Buses: Buses to Hermosa depart from **San José** on Av. 5/7, C. 12, one block north of the **Atlántica Norte Terminal** (6hr., 3:30pm, ¢2000) and from **Liberia** (1hr., 8 per day 4:30am-5:30pm, ¢1200). To get to San José from Hermosa, catch any bus to Liberia and transfer at the central bus station, or catch the **directo** (5am, ¢4000). Buses from **Playa Panamá** to Liberia stop in **Sardinal** (6, 7:30, 8:30, 10am, 2, 4, 5, 7:10pm; ¢1200).

Taxis: Taxis shuttle visitors from **Playa del Coco** to Playa Hermosa (15min., ¢5000).

⊞ ⛏ ORIENTATION AND PRACTICAL INFORMATION

Playa Hermosa has two entrances, both within walking distance of each other. From Playa Hermosa, **Playa Panamá** is a 3km walk along the main road to the north. **MiniSuper Dayi,** 150m south of the second Hermosa entrance, sells food products, basic amenities, beer, wine, and other liquor. (☎2672 0032; open M-Sa 7am-8pm, Su 7am-5pm.) **Lupero,** the closest *supermercado*, sits on the main road between the two entrances (☎2672 0303; open M-F 7:30am-8pm, Sa 7:30am-8:30pm, Su 8am-7:30pm). Most other services beyond those listed are available in **Sardinal.**

24hr. ATM: in the small complex of shops on the main road near the 1st entrance.

Telephones: 150m east of the beach, at the second entrance, next to **Pescado Loco.**

NICOYA PENINSULA

Península de Nicoya

Internet Access: at **Villa Huétares.** Two computers. Internet ₡1000 per hr. Open daily 7am-10pm. Many of the hotels and restaurants have free Wi-Fi.

ACCOMMODATIONS

Cabinas la Casona (☎2672 0025), 500m west of the 2nd entrance and 20m north on the road before the beach. Friendly owners and spacious rooms with private baths, cable TV, and fully-equipped kitchens offer the best deal on the beach. Apartments for 2 with large beds, futons, and A/C provide temporary havens from the heat. Low-season singles ₡14,500 (US$25), high-season ₡17,400 (US$30); doubles ₡17,400/23,200 (US$30/40); 6-person rooms ₡43,500/49,300 (US$75/85); apartments for 2 ₡43,500/52,200 (US$75/90). Cash only. ❸

Villa Huétares (☎2672 0052), 300m west of the 2nd entrance to the beach. Comfortable rooms. You will be pleased with the familial owners. A/C, cable TV, pool and jacuzzi, Wi-Fi, and internet. On-site restaurant. Low-season doubles ₡26,100 (US$45), high-season ₡37,700 (US$65); triples ₡52,200/72,500 (US$90/125); quads ₡81,200 (US$140). ❹

Ecotel (☎2672 0175), walk 500m down the road from the 2nd beach entrance and turn left at the last road before the beach. The cheapest place to stay in town, suitable for nature-lovers or those willing to rough it. Options include bunk rooms, indoor lofts, and beds in the communal space. Snorkel and canoe use included. Bunk rooms and singles from ¢8700 (US$15); doubles from ¢14,500 (US$25). Camping ¢5800 (US$10) per tent, when available. ❷

Hotel El Velero (☎2672 0036; www.costaricahotel.net), on the beach. This beautifully decorated hotel has wide, whitewashed hallways, decorative fountains, bold draperies of Costa Rican fauna, and a small aquatic-themed pool. Common area on the 2nd floor has wicker rocking chairs and a book exchange. A/C and several rooms with beach views. Sailboat tours (5hr. sunset tour ¢34,800/US$60; day tour ¢46,400/US$80 per person; both include snorkeling and open bar). Massages ¢23,200 (US$40) per hr. Yoga classes ¢4060 (US$7). Doubles ¢43,500 (US$75), each additional person ¢5800 (US$10). Ask about student discounts. Prices jump in high season. Children 9 and under stay free. AmEx/D/MC/V. ❹

Playa Hermosa Inn (☎2672 0063), on the beach next to Aqua Sports, near the 2nd entrance. Rooms and apartments with full kitchens, A/C, and hot water. Borrow a book from the mini-library's random selection of fiction. Breakfast included. Rooms ¢14,500 (US$25) per person; apartment ¢34,800 (US$60) for 2 people, each additional person ¢5800 (US$10). Ask about student discounts. AmEx/D/MC/V. ❸

FOOD AND ENTERTAINMENT

For once, *comida típica* is not the norm: restaurants are geared almost exclusively toward tourists and, accordingly, are pricier. Penny-pinchers will appreciate **Soda Dayi** right next to **MiniSuper Dayi,** where breakfast combos (¢2000-2500), burgers (¢1500), and other *comida rápida* leave both stomachs and wallets pleasantly full (open M-Sa 6am-7pm, Su 7am-3pm; cash only).

Finisterra (☎2672 0227; www.finisterra.net). At the 1st beach entrance, follow the signs to the restaurant by walking 700m toward the beach, taking a left, and walking 250m up the steep hill. Perched on a cliff, this popular Caribbean restaurant has some of the best views and food in town. Trained in Peru, the local-born chef cooks up creative dishes, including long-time favorites like purée of yucca with seared tuna, leeks, onion, and soy (¢5800) and Thai curry. Soak up your surroundings over the unforgettable passionfruit pie (¢2900). Free Wi-Fi. Open M and W-Su 5-10pm. AmEx/D/MC/V. ❸

Ginger (☎2672 0041), on stilts, off the main road. A delightful, unique tapas experience which purports to combine "all the flavors of the world on a small plate." In reality, the food is a hodgepodge of Asian and Mediterranean influences. The chef uses ample amounts of ginger, lemon-grass, cilantro, mint, and soy. Ahi Tuna (a pepper-crusted fillet served over ginger slaw and drizzled with citrus mayonnaise) ¢4000. Mojitico (guaro, passion fruit, basil, and soda) ¢2800. Large selection of wines. Open Tu-Su 5-10pm. MC/V. ❷

Pescado Loco Bar y Restaurant (☎2627 0017), 500m toward the beach (from the 2nd entrance), 50m to the right. Local food at reasonable prices served under a large wooden fish. Interesting options include squid in its own ink (¢4000), octopus *ceviche* (¢3800), and orange shrimp (¢6500). Frequented by beer-drinking locals. *Casados* ¢2800. Open daily 9am-10pm. ❷

El Velero (☎2672 1015), 600m west and 25m north of the 2nd beach entrance. Just back from the sand, watch the sunset at this restaurant while seafood experts prepare *ceviche* (¢3400) and whole red snapper (¢8000). W and Sa seafood BBQ, where fresh meat and seafood, cooked over glowing embers, are served a la carte. Chicken breast ¢4300. Filet mignon ¢7500. Daily happy hour offers 2-for-1 deals on selected drinks 4-6pm. Open daily 6am-9pm. AmEx/D/MC/V. ❷

Restaurant Aqua Sports (☎2672 0050), follow the signs from the 2nd beach entrance. Served next to Aqua Sport's extensive collection of kayaks, selections include *lomito* (ten-

NICOYA PENINSULA

derloin; ¢5690) and shrimp rice (¢4880). For a lobster with garlic butter, you'll have to shell out ¢13,820. Tequila sunrise ¢1870. Open daily 11am-9pm. AmEx/D/MC/V. ❸

Vallejos Bar Restaurant (☎2672 0187), 800m west of the 1st beach entrance. Brave souls can munch on jumbo shrimp in hot sauce (¢9000), while less adventurous eaters can enjoy chicken in mushroom sauce (¢4000) or filet mignon (¢8000). Entrees ¢3800-9000. Wine ¢2500 per glass. Open daily 10am-9pm. Cash only. ❷

Pizzeria Isabella (☎8302 3375), in front of the 1st beach entrance. Forget the *casado:* order a large pizza for the beach (¢8000-9000). Pastas ¢3800-7000. Calzones ¢5500. Salads ¢2000-4000. Open daily 5pm-10pm. Cash only. ❷

⚓ WATERSPORTS

If it rains heavily the day before, don't plan on seeing many fish when snorkeling; Pacific tides wash phytoplankton toward the shores of the Nicoya Peninsula, which reduces visibility. By and large, however, Hermosa's calm, clear water is ideal for diving, kayaking, and waterskiing.

Diving Safaris (☎2672 1259; www.costaricadiving.net), 500m west of the second entrance to the beach. Specializes in diving and snorkeling tours. Morning dives and snorkeling 8:30am-1:30pm. 2-tank dives ¢55,100/US$95, includes equipment. Beginner day-long classes and dives ¢72,500/US$125. Snorkeling ¢23,200/US$40, includes boat. For equipment only, rentals are ¢2900/US$5 per 2hr. Arranges day sails and sunset sails with open bar and the option of snorkeling, jet-skiing, or sportfishing (from ¢58,000/US$100). Also books surfing trips to Witch's Rock and Ollie's Point (7:30am-3pm; ¢174,000/US$300, 5 person max.; experienced participants only). PADI certification course available. Open daily 7am-5pm.

Aqua Sport (☎2672 0500), follow the signs from the beach's 2nd entrance. Rents kayaks (¢5800/US$10 per 3-4hr.), pedal and paddleboats (¢5800/US$10 per person), boogie boards (¢2900/US$5 per 3hr.), and sailboats (¢17,400/US$30 for 2 people per 2hr.). Snorkeling gear and tours (¢17,400/US$30 per 3hr.; includes water, fruit, kayak, and guide). Trips to Witch's Rock (¢116,000/US$200 for 4 people per 8hr.). Fishing tour (¢116,000/US$200 per 5hr.; includes water, fruit and beer). Open M-Sa 6am-9pm.

Sea Life (☎8306 1807). Snorkeling (¢26,100/US$45 per 2½hr.); sunset cruise (¢26,100/US$45 per 3hr., 10 people max.); dolphin tour (¢26,100/US$45); jet skis (¢55,100/US$95 for 1-2 people per 1hr.); ATV tour of the mountains (¢55,100/US$95 per 2hr.); tour of waterfalls, canopy, and hotsprings (7:30am-4pm, ¢55,100/US$95); horse rental (¢29,000/US$50 per 2½hr.). Call or ask for reservations through **Villa Huétares** (p. 210). Open daily 6am-11pm.

Funsealand (☎2248 0615; www.funsealand.infca.com), in front Hotel Condovac on the main road. Specializes in ATV tours (¢29,000 (US$50) per 1½hr., ¢46,400 (US$80) per 2½hr.). The megacombo package includes waverunner (1hr.), ATV (2hr.), and canopy (2hr.) tours for ¢130,500 (US$225). Student discount 25% with ID.

⯈ DAYTRIP FROM PLAYA HERMOSA

PLAYA PANAMÁ

Buses from Liberia pass Hermosa and end their route in Panamá. Buses from Hermosa to Panamá (15min.; 5:30, 8:30am, 12:30, 2, 4:30, 6:30pm; ¢300). Buses from Panamá to Hermosa (15min.; 6, 7:30, 8:30, 10am, 2, 4, 5, 7:10pm; ¢300). The two beaches are separated by 2km of well-paved road, so walking is also an option. The village of Playa Panamá lies a few kilometers beyond the beach itself.

At Playa Panamá, just 2km north of Hermosa, the arc of the coast makes for an impressively long beach. The tranquil, glassy waters are perfect for swimming, though the sand is a bit darker than on Playa Hermosa, and the vegetation is less cared-for. Budget accommodations on Panamá are non-existent; the **Four Seasons Hotel** and other luxury resorts such as **Alegro, Fiesta Premier,** and **Giardini di Papagayo** have claimed this stretch of beach. The sand, fortunately, remains free, which enables many *tico* families to sip coconut juice and sink into beach chairs on this pleasant strip. Outdoor showers, a camping zone, and a smattering of non-resort restaurants are available. Bring your own water.

PLAYA DEL COCO

The dingy Coco shores and the main street lined with tacky shops give no indication of the treasures that lie beyond them, but divers know that the nearby waters hold almost all the marine life seen in Costa Rica. It is no wonder why many say that Coco has the best diving in Costa Rica. The only plaque in the town's park commemorates the woman who brought tourism to Playa del Coco in the 1970s. Plans for better roads, a boardwalk, and modern malls and clubs are trying to greet the influx of visitors. The culture of the town revolves around snorkel and scuba, as well as the small fleets of private boats that deliver visitors to nearby islands and shores at Playas Huevo, Blanca, and Nacazcolo.

▉ TRANSPORTATION

The **bus** station is down by the beach, in front of the post office and police station. Buses from San José depart from Av. 1/3, C. 14 (☎6222 1650; 5hr.; 4am, 2, 4pm; ¢2800) and from Liberia (1hr., 8 per day 5am-9pm) and to Liberia (1hr., 8 per day 4am-6pm, ¢500) via Sardinal (5min., ¢150). To get to beaches near Flamingo and Tamarindo, catch the bus for Liberia and get off at the main highway at "La Comunidad"; from there you'll need to get another bus to Belen and then connect to your beach of choice or wait at La Comunidad for the bus from Liberia to Tamarindo. The whole process can take up to 3hr. Hermosa to the north and Ocotal to the south can only be reached by **taxi** (☎2670 0408; Hermosa US$10, Ocotal US$5). Taxis to Tamarindo cost US$40.

▉ ▉ ORIENTATION AND PRACTICAL INFORMATION

The main road runs from the highway to the beach, where you will find an unassuming *parque central* with public phones. Buses stop on the *parque*'s west side. When facing the beach, the soccer field is about a block to the left.

Bank: Banco Nacional, 750m inland from the beach on the main road. Cash advances and exchanges US$ and traveler's checks. Open M-F 8:30am-3:45pm. You can also exchange currency at **Supermercado Luperón** (☎2670 0950), directly to the right of Banco Nacional. Open M-Th 7:30am-8:30pm, F-Sa 7:30am-9pm, Su 8am-2pm.

Laundry: Lavandería (☎2670 0586), across from the Coco Verde, a few meters back from the main road. Soap, softener, drying, folding; ready in 3hr. ¢1200 per kg, US$1 per lb. Open daily 8am-7pm. US$/¢.

Emergency: ☎911.

Police: (☎2670 0258), across from the bus stop. Open 24hr.

Red Cross: (☎2679 1141). The nearest is about 20km away in Sardinal.

Medical Services: Medical Clinic Ebais (☎2670 0987). Walk 150m east on the road north of Lizard Lounge, turn right, and then left after Hotel la Puerta del Sol. Open M-Th

NICOYA PENINSULA

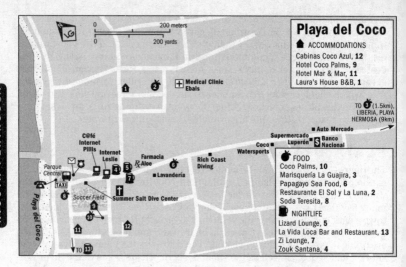

Playa del Coco

🏠 ACCOMMODATIONS
Cabinas Coco Azul, **12**
Hotel Coco Palms, **9**
Hotel Mar & Mar, **11**
Laura's House B&B, **1**

🍴 FOOD
Coco Palms, **10**
Marisquería La Guajira, **3**
Papagayo Sea Food, **6**
Restaurante El Sol y La Luna, **2**
Soda Teresita, **8**

🍸 NIGHTLIFE
Lizard Lounge, **5**
La Vida Loca Bar and Restaurant, **13**
Zi Lounge, **7**
Zouk Santana, **4**

7am-4pm, F 7am-3pm. **Farmacia Aloe** (☎2670 2050), on the main road 50m east of the Lizard Lounge. Open M-Sa 8am-8:30pm, Su 8am-1pm and 2-4pm.

Internet Access: C@fe Internet Pillis (☎2670 1772), next to Internet Leslie. ¢800 per hr. Calls to the US and Canada ¢100 per min. Open daily 8am-8pm. **Internet Leslie** (☎2670 0168). ¢800 per hr. Copies ¢25 per page. Open daily 7:30am-8pm.

Post Office: In the same building as the police. Open M-F 8am-noon and 1:15-5:30pm. **Postal Code:** 5019.

🛏 ACCOMMODATIONS

🏩 **Hostel Mar & Mar** (☎2670 0279), less than 50m from the beach, this is one of the few (and best) inexpensive options in Coco. Neat, spacious rooms have both regular beds and bunks. Cable TV and ceiling fans. Guard on-duty 24hr. Singles US$20; doubles US$28; triples US$40; quads US$48. AmEx/D/MC/V/US$/¢. ❷

🏩 **Hotel Coco Palms** (☎2670 0367; hotelcocopalms.com), at the end of the soccer field. Offers inexpensive rooms for 3, though standard rooms are significantly better. Tables with thatched umbrellas are scattered around the pool and fountains. Sushi restaurant by the pool (p. 215). A/C, hot water, safe, Wi-Fi, and cable TV. Apartments with kitchens and sitting areas also available (US$80). High-/low season singles and doubles US$59/49; triples US$69/59, quads US$85/75, ages 7-12 US$3. AmEx/D/MC/V. ❸

Cabinas Coco Azul (☎2670 0431), 100m south of the soccer field. A good option for groups of 3. Arched doorways, airy tiled bathrooms, and bright blue iron over yellow glass doors give this place more flair than many other cheap deals. If it is spring or summer, you can pick your own mangoes from the trees in the yard or have the resident monkeys help you. Well-lit at night. Parking available. Fridge and Wi-Fi in every room. US$30, 3-person max. US$/¢ only. ❸

Laura's House B&B (☎2670 0751; www.laurashouse.cr.net), 200m northeast on the road next to Lizard Lounge. Houses peaceful rooms that are well kept by their owner and namesake. The pool is surrounded by a large deck, and swinging chairs and hammocks hang from the tree overhead. Also included is the delicious breakfast of fruit, bread, eggs, coffee, and OJ is served every morning 7-10am in the outdoor dining area. Cable TV. A/C available. Rooms US$60, each additional person US$10. US$/¢. ❹

FOOD

If you're looking to cook, across from Supermercado Luperón is the new, shiny **AutoMercado**. Open M-Th and Su 8am-9pm, F-Sa 8am-10pm. You'll find no shortage of restaurants in Coco, and the handmade pastas, fresh sushi, and innovative sauces offered by a select few make them worth the *colónes*.

▨ **Restaurante El Sol y La Luna** (☎2670 0195), attached to Hotel La Puerta del Sol. Where Coco Italians bring their native flavors to the candlelit table. Handmade pastas, like *Ravioli alla Romana* (ravioli with ricotta, spinach, scremolata sauce, and parmesan cheese; ¢5000), and olive bread are to die for, and the tiramisu (¢2500) is worth the splurge. Finish off dinner with a shot of amaretto. Open M and W-Su 6-10pm. ❷

▨ **Papagayo Sea Food** (☎2670 0298), on the main road across from Hotel Coco Verde. Runs its own fleet of deep-sea fishing boats to supply the restaurant with the freshest seafood. The catch of the day can be prepared in any manner you choose, including blackened Cajun style, grilled with ginger and garlic, sautéed with an orange chili sauce, or fried with fresh pesto (¢5000-6500). It's no wonder it's considered the best seafood place in town. Open daily noon-10pm. AmEx/D/MC/V/US$/¢. ❸

Coco Palms (☎2670 0367), behind Hotel Coco Palms. A must-visit for sushi aficionados, as the selection of fish is brought in daily from the nearby shore. Fountains and statues are scattered throughout the dining area, which overlooks the hotel's pool and palm trees. Rolls about ¢4000. Sashimi ¢5000. Happy hour daily 4-6pm, national beers, house liquor, and wine US$2. Open daily 6am-11pm. AmEx/D/MC/V/US$/¢. ❷

Mariquería La Guajira, 1.5km down the main road out of Coco. Although the trek is long, the fresh fish, excellent prices, and bubbly local family is well worth it. Due to recent property laws, La Guajira had to relocate its restaurant from the beach, but it took the ocean and boat paraphernalia along with it to liven up the roadside place. Try the daily catch with garlic sauce (¢4000) and *flan del coco* (¢1500). ❷

Soda Teresita (☎2670 0665), on the main road 50m from the beach, next to the *parque*. There's no shortage of filling *comida típica* selections in this affordable local favorite. *Casado especial* ¢2000. Ham sandwich ¢1200. Papaya shake ¢1200. Open M-Sa 6:30am-9pm, Su 6:30am-6pm. US$/¢ only. ❶

NIGHTLIFE

Those looking for nighttime activity but staying in nearby Hermosa and Ocotal will want to make the short trip to Coco to find anything worthwhile.

Lizard Lounge (☎2670 0301), 150m south of the *parque*. Mellow until the weekend, when the floor packs with a crowd of *ticos* and tourists. *Ticos* take the floor when merengue, hip hop, and salsa play, while tourists are all over the Top 40 hits. The thatched roof dance floor starts to reel after a "lizard fire shot" of tequila and mint. W Ladies Night, Th Reggae Night, F and Sa Latin Night. Beer ¢800. Open daily 11am-2:30am.

La Vida Loca Bar and Restaurant (☎2670 0181). Otherwise known as "Jimbo's," this bar, reminiscent of a quirky basement, is separated from the center of town by a tiny bridge. Creek crossings become particularly adventurous for those stumbling home on weekend nights. Cluttered duck decor testifies to the owner's allegiance to the University of Oregon, while bar stools fill up with other American tourists, tapping their feet to rock hits. Check out the suggestive statues. Pool, ping pong, darts, air hockey, gambling video games, and foosball. Shots of the Quema Culo made with guaro, chili, and lime (¢1400) prove interesting for those who dare to try them. Open daily 11am-2am.

Zouk Santana (☎2670 0191; zouksantana.com), next to the Lizard Bar on the main road. Low seating and lighting lend to a bohemian interior, more conducive to chatting than Lizard next door. The owners play Italian melodies, except on Sa and Su when the dance floor gets going with salsa and merengue. Beer ¢800. Open daily 11am-2am.

Zi Lounge (2670 1978; zilounge.com), across from Lizard Lounge. For those tired of wasting away in Margaritaville, Zi offers a Miami-inspired place to sink into wicker sofas and beds. Chat with guests from the Papagayo Concessions on the 2nd fl. or with Rasta men on the outdoor gravel patio with swinging chairs. Their mixed drinks are heavenly. Caipirosca Strawberry (strawberry, lime, lemon, triple sec, sembucca, suger, vodka, and soda; ¢3000) or the Chúpame el Coco (guaro, amaretto, coconut, and coffee and chocolate liquour; ¢3500). Live international guest DJs. Bartending contest each month. Tu Martes de Maduro, free shots for women. Open daily 4pm-3am.

 WATERSPORTS

Prime dive season is from April to September. The best scuba and snorkeling sites are reachable by boat. Coco is a base for trips to Bat Island, a great place to see dolphins and manta rays (Apr.-Nov.) that roam the waters at the nearby Catalinas and one of the only places in the world to see bull sharks. Warm water and an abundance of fish make up for so-so visibility. On a dive or snorkel, dolphins, whale and whitetip sharks make frequent appearances. Bikes (available from both Internet cafes, US$10) are a great way to see the inland coast. Many of the companies listed offer the same activities and prices.

Rich Coast Diving (☎/fax 2670 0176, in the US and Canada +1-800-4-DIVING/434 8464; www.richcoastdiving.com), 300m back from the beach on the main road. The young, highly qualified staff offers diving trips (2-tank dive US$70 includes equipment), including a daytrip to the Bat Islands (US$140 per person) and to the Catalinas (US$99 per person). Training for a variety of levels, snorkeling, PADI certification, and equipment rentals available. Open daily low season 8am-6pm, high season 8am-8pm. MC/V.

Summer Salt Dive Center (☎2670 0308 or 8357 5531; www.summer-salt.com), next to Roca Bruja Surf. Also offers dives (2-tank US$75), night dives, trips to the Catalinas and Bat Islands, snorkel trips, Roca Bruja surfing trips (US$240-320, US$15 for board) and equipment rental (US$20). Open daily 8am-6pm.

Coco Extremo (☎2670 1743), 100m toward the beach from Banco Nacional. Rents kayaks (US$25 per day) and jet skis (US$85 per hr.), gives jet-ski tours (US$130 for 1hr.), and offers many water sports and ATV tours. Open daily 7am-6pm. AmEx/D/MC/V.

TIP | **DO THE SHUFFLE.** With the best diving in the country come the meanest stingrays. To avoid a painful zing, shuffle your feet along the bottom of the ocean to let them know you're coming, and they'll swim away.

OCOTAL

Breathtaking views of sparkling water and verdant islands await those who make the trek to the coved, soft, black-sand beachfronts of Ocotal. Due to its remote location, Ocotal seems to have temporarily avoided becoming a major tourist destination and retains an untouched tranquility that similar beaches have lost—it certainly feels less used and abused than Playa del Coco. A short walk around the bend leads to Bahía Pez Vela, another lovely cove. Boats are moored in the bay for diving and sportfishing, and the calm waters near the beach are ideal for swimmers and sunbathers, though high tides don't leave much of a beach. Rent snorkeling gear or go diving with **Ocotal Dive Shop** (☎2670 0321 ext, 152). Because it's attached to the fancy Ocotal Resort, prices are higher than in Coco. Except for the Ocotal Resort's employee shuttle, no buses run to Ocotal from Playa del Coco 3km away. A taxi costs ¢2500. Some people are known to hitch a ride with a local. **Let's Go does not recommend hitchhiking.**

⛰ ACCOMMODATIONS. The few places to stay in Ocotal are a bit pricey, and getting to them can be difficult without a car. With only three rooms available for guests, it hardly feels crowded at **◪Villa Vista Mar ❶**. Perched on a hill, enjoy the spectacular ocean view from either the pool or balcony. While rooms all have small kitchens, the *rancho* by the pool is the real deal; a gas oven, barbecue equipment, fridge, hammock, washer, and dryer are available. It's a steal for groups of three or four. All rooms have hot water and cable TV. (☎2670 0375; www.villavistamar.com. A/C. High-/low season small apartments US$60/50; medium apartments US$80/70; large apartments (for max. 10 people) US$90/80.) **Hotel Villa Casa Blanca ❺** has 12 richly decorated, Spanish-colonial rooms as well as two honeymoon suites. Everything in this "white house," from the manicured gardens and pool to the canopy beds and hot tub, has been arranged with style. Buffet breakfast is included for guests and is open to the public. (☎2670 0518; www.hotelvillacasablanca.com. High-/low season doubles US$105/85; family suites US$125/90; condos US$155/125. Each additional person US$10. AmEx/MC/V.)

◻ FOOD. If you're in Ocotal, the trek to **◪Restaurant Picante ❷** is more than worth it. Homemade sauces are made to order and include selections like tropical fruit curry cream and mango picante salsa. The hearty Costa Rican salad has chicken, mango, cashews, and a curry dressing (¢4000). If you're there for the Sunday brunch with live music, try the Piña Colada french toast for ¢4000. Free salsa lessons happen every W at 6pm. (☎2670 0901. Open daily 9am-10pm, Su brunch 10am-2pm.) The red barn at **Father Rooster ❹** is on the beach, with bright tables in the sand. Offers a specialty drink called the Tica Linda (US$8). The fish of the day, cooked *al gusto*, comes with rice, beans, and sweet plantains for US$19. (☎2670 1246. Open daily 11am-10pm. D/MC/V/US$/¢.)

POTRERO

Playas Potrero, Penca, Prieta, and Pan de Azúcar spread out from the village of Potrero with broad vistas of white sand, and the ancient islands off the coast seem lifted from a Japanese woodcut. While the village itself is small enough to shout across, it has begun to see more foreign traffic in recent years due to the opening of CPI, a nearby language school. The road to Flamingo through Surfside is full of new restaurants, villas, and budget accommodations. Unfortunately, public transportation hasn't adjusted accordingly, and options are still meager. Though this seclusion can prove logistically inconvenient, it does afford a beautifully empty and tranquil *tico* atmosphere.

◪ ◪ TRANSPORTATION AND ORIENTATION

The **bus** from Brasilito departs Potrero for Flamingo and Santa Cruz (8 per day 8am-5pm). Catch it on the southeast corner of the field by Supermercado Ceimy. The church is on the west side of the field. **Official Welcome Center** just north of the northeast corner of the field offers information and access to tours in a cool, organized room (☎2654 5460 and for 24hr. service 8358 4327. Open M-Sa 9am-5pm.) Self-service **laundry** available 800m away from the beach to the east near Heladeria Italiana. (☎2654 5368. Open daily 8am-6pm.) **Internet**

access is available at Heladeria Italiana (¢1000 per hr., ¢600 min.; open daily 7am-11pm) and Restaurante and Cabinas La Penca (¢1400 per hr.).

ACCOMMODATIONS

Cabinas Isolina Beach (☎2654 4333; www.isolinabeach.com), a longer walk toward Brasilito from Potrero's center, but only 100m from the beach. A popular choice among students attending the nearby language school. A/C and refrigerators in every room, and some 2-room setups have a kitchen and microwave. The bright rooms the *cabinas* encompass 2 pools and a hot tub decorated with mosaic-covered stone tables and manicured tropical flora. The poolside restaurant/thatched hut serves complimentary breakfast to guests, US$4 for non-guests. Cable TV and Wi-Fi available. High season doubles US$70; triples US$81; quads US$93. Low season US$52/81/93; US$15 extra per person. 2-bedroom villas US$35 more than standard rooms. ❹

Bahía Esmeralda (☎2654 4480; www.hotelbahiaesmeralda.com), south of the southeast corner of the *parque* as you enter Potrero center and 150m from the beach. A very comfortable hotel with a pool surrounded on all sides by mustard-yellow *cabinas* and a restaurant. In addition to 4 simple rooms with bunks and individual beds, there are 8 2-bedroom apartments with kitchens and living rooms and 4 villas with 2 double beds, a trundle in the dining area, and microwave. All rooms have A/C, TV, hot water, and views of the pool and garden. Tourist information available at reception desk. Breakfast included for the rooms without kitchens. High season singles US$60, low season US$50; doubles US$70/55; triples US$83/63; quads US$93/70; 2-person apartments US$93/70; 4-person apartments US$105/80; 6-person villas US$135/110; 9-person suite US$185/155. AmEx/D/MC/V. ❸

Restaurante and Cabinas La Penca (☎2654 4535), the closest *cabina* to Penca beach. Walk just north of the northwest corner of the field and turn left to reach this cheaper option. Behind the restaurant, rooms with A/C, TV, and private baths have good double beds and refrigerators. Low season rooms US$40, high season US$60. V/US$/¢. ❸

FOOD

The only place in town to buy food and supplies is **Supermercado Ceimy,** located on the southeast corner of the field. (☎2654 4658. Open daily 6am-7pm.)

Heladeria Italiana, where you can find of the best-tasting gelato you'll ever try. The modern decor and glowing sherbet-orange walls combine to create a hybrid Italian bar and gelato shop. Flavors like hazelnut, amaretto, and whatever local fruits are in season. 1 scoop US$1. Among the many specialties, the popular *Affogato al caffe* is made with coffee, vanilla and chocolate gelato, and espresso, topped with espresso beans and homemade whipped cream (US$5). Cappuccino US$1.60. Open 7-11pm. ❶

Marco Polo (☎2654 4664), attached to the Hotel Flor de Pacífico. The Italian chef prepares the best pizza and pasta in town, combining delicious ingredients like gorgonzola and pineapple under the heat of the woodfire oven. Phenomenal tiramisu and crepes (US$4.50) are worth saving room for, though the "individual" pizzas (US$7-14), like the trademark Marco Polo (salmon, olive, zucchini, tomato, and mozzarella, US$13), are a challenge for 1 person to finish. Open daily 7am-10pm. AmEx/D/MC/V. ❸

Maxwell's Café and Bar (☎2654 4319), on the way out of Potrero toward Flamingo. Hearty American cuisine is served beneath a simple overhang at this new cafe. The killer rack of BBQ ribs (¢6000), locally famous 1/3 lb. burger (¢3000), and meaty nachos (¢5000) are worth the prices. Happy Hour 6-7pm (free pool, ¢500 national beer, ¢1000 house liquors). Open M-Sa 5pm-11pm. Cash only. ❷

NIGHTLIFE

Multiple activities await your highness at **El Castillo,** 1km down the road to Flamingo in Surfside. Bakery and restaurant by day, this medieval-style stone castle fills up with *ticos*, *gringos*, and expats to enjoy free live music on Thursday and Friday nights and karaoke on Saturday nights (8pm-midnight). Sundays are movie nights with Spanish subtitles. (☎2654 4271. 2-for-1 Imperial and Pilsen happy hour daily 5-7pm. Beer ¢800. Open daily 6pm-midnight; open until 2am for nights with activities). A primarily *tico* crowd heats up the dance floor at **La Conchita** (just past Hotel Isolina toward Flamingo) on Saturday nights to rap, salsa, reggae, and merengue beats. (Pilsen 3 for ¢2000. Open daily 9pm-2am.)

PLAYA FLAMINGO

Lacking the birds that are its namesake, the only pink things on this beautiful beach are massive resort hotels, private villas, and the sunburned guests who pay for them. Although everything is expensive on the hill at the end of the bay, the calm, blue waters off the beach are ideal for morning swimming, snorkeling, and diving. Slightly turbulent afternoon waters offer fun, safe bodysurfing waves. Nicknamed "Flagringo" by the locals, you'll hear more English than Spanish spoken here, where wealthy vacationers come for sportfishing, pampering, and sometimes a combination of the two. Those seeking a younger scene know that backpackers, deterred by steep prices, generally stay elsewhere, but the light-colored stretches of sand are more than worth a daytrip.

TRANSPORTATION

Buses run to Flamingo from San José and Santa Cruz. Buses coming from Santa Cruz stop in Flamingo and continue on to Potrero (15min., 7am-4:15pm). To get to Flamingo from Tamarindo, take a San José or Santa Cruz bus as far as Huacas, where buses to Flamingo via Brasilito pass frequently. TRALAPA buses go from the Flamingo marina to San José (5hr.; M-Sa 2:45, 9am, 2, 4pm; ¢2700). Reserve in advance by calling the marina (☎2654 4536) or buying tickets in Supermercado Flamingo. Buses depart for Santa Cruz (1hr., 13 per day 4am-6:50pm, ¢910) and PAMPA buses go to Liberia (2hr., 6 per day 5am-7:30pm, ¢800). All of these buses go through Huacas and Brasilito. Pay on the bus.

PRACTICAL INFORMATION

The **Banco de Costa Rica,** on the hill across from Flamingo Marina Resort, has a V/Plus ATM, changes traveler's checks, and gives V advances with a passport. (☎2645 4874. Open M-F 8am-4pm.) The **pharmacy** is down the hill from the bank, near Marie's. (☎2654 8525. Open M-Sa 8am-6:45pm, Su 8am-4:40pm.) The closest **police station** (☎2654 5647) and **clinic** (☎8380 4125 for emergencies) is in Huacas. There is **Internet access** at the Mariner Inn (¢500 per 30min.).

ACCOMMODATIONS

Playa Flamingo is full of expensive resorts. The only option that won't completely empty your wallet is the **Mariner Inn ❸,** a decent hotel, but one that lacks beach views. (☎2674 4801. A/C. Cable TV. Singles/doubles US$34; quads US$45; quints US$68. AmEx/D/MC/V.)

NICOYA PENINSULA

> **THE INSIDE SCOOP.** Ditch the unenlightened resort hoppers in "Flagringo" and find a temporary home in Brasilito or Potrero. You will be closer to bluer waters, empty beaches, and more diverse food and entertainment options. The road from Portero to Brasilito, through Flamingo, is only 8km long and flat, which is perfect for a quick bike ride, leisurely walk, or a short bus trip. —*Nadia Mohamedi*

FOOD

The main supermarket in town, **Supermercado Flamingo,** is down the hill from the bank. (☎2654 4082. Open daily 8am-8:30pm.)

Marie's (☎2654 4136). One of the only restaurants in town not attached to a hotel, so it feels a bit homier than nearby options. Friendly waiters serve tasty shrimp-stuffed avocado (¢6200) and daily specials, like banana chocolate bread pudding and pineapple coconut cheesecake (¢2000). Open daily 6:30am-9:30pm. AmEx/D/MC/V/US$/¢. ❸

The Monkey Bar. A restaurant popular among older tourists, features American theme nights, Th Costa Rican Buffet (US$17), and Sa all-you-can-eat BBQ. Tables are under the thatched roof and overlook the marina. Tropical birds hang out here and won't leave until they get some of your leftovers. 2-for-1 national beers and liquors. Happy hour 5-7pm; Su 4-8pm (free snacks). Wi-Fi. BBQ chicken wings US$5. *Casados* US$8. Restaurant open daily 6am-9pm. AmEx/D/MC/V/US$/¢. ❷

OUTDOOR ACTIVITIES AND GUIDED TOURS

AQUACENTER, below Flamingo Marina Resort, offers dives at Catalinas to see sting rays, eagle rays, and tons of dazzling reef fish among other marine life (US$90, US$15 without equipment). The extremely friendly staff will also take you on boat snorkeling tours (US$49, US$45 without equipment) or on a half-day surfing trip/lesson in Tamarindo and Playa Grande for US$45. (☎8877 7420; www.aquacenterdiving.com. Snorkeling gear US$9. Open 8:30am-4:40pm.) Claudia at **Tourist Information Flamingo,** just down the hill from the Supermercado Flamingo, can answer almost any question that you have concerning accommodations, local events, banking, safety, transportation, and emergencies. They can also book your adventures for you from a wide selection of diving, sailing, sportfishing, surfing lessons, whitewater rafting, and daytrips to several places such as Volcano Arenal. Rent bicycles (US$5 per day) right from the office. (☎2654 4021 and 8377 5701; www.infoflamingo.com; info@infoflamingo.com.) **Costa Rica Outriggers** offers an excellent opportunity to paddle in a kayak or outrigger canoe to secluded beaches to snorkel and enjoy a fruit buffet. (☎8838 6783; info@guanacasteoutriggers.com. Half-day tour US$57.)

BRASILITO

Brasilito might not have much to offer besides its wonderful beach, but its rustic underdevelopment is a big part of its charm. In contrast to built-up areas like nearby Playa Flamingo, Brasilito's understated appeal defies a tourism industry that threatens to overwhelm the entire Nicoya coast. While the town currently remains relatively undeveloped, the short walk from Brasilito to the clear blue waters and shell-covered beaches of Playa Conchal are reason enough to make the trip. Brasilito brings in a share of high season crowds, but its low season calm still beckons to those looking for an empty beach on which to watch the sunrise with some coffee. This tranquility has recently attracted many expats, with the opening of two private schools as testament to the new community.

⬅ TRANSPORTATION

The TRALAPA office is just east of the soccer field on the road to Flamingo. All **buses** leave from the bus stop on the east side of the field. Buses coming from Flamingo stop in here on their way to San José (5hr.; M-Sa 2:45, 9am, 2pm; Su 9, 10:30am, 2pm; ¢3330). Reserve in advance at the TRALAPA office, especially in the high season when buses fill up fast. (☎2654 5058. Open 8am-noon and 1-5pm.) Buses also run to: Santa Cruz (11 per day 5am-7:30pm; ¢910), Flamingo (9 per day 5am-7:30pm, ¢200), and Tamarindo (8am, noon). Pay on the bus.

⬛ ❷ ORIENTATION AND PRACTICAL INFORMATION

Know that the ocean is to the west, Flamingo is north, and Huacas is south on the main road. The bank is **Banco de Costa Rica** in Flamingo. The closest **medical center** is in Huacas (☎8380 4125 for emergencies). The **pharmacy** is in Flamingo. The **police station** is 100m east of the northeast corner of the field. (☎2654 5647 for emergencies.) **Hotel Nany**, 200m south on the main road, has **Internet access.** (¢1200 per hr. fax ¢500. b/w printing and copies ¢150 per page; color ¢500 per page. ☎2654 4320; www.apartotelnany.com. Open daily 8am-9pm.) **Hotel Brasilito (Restaurant Outback Jack's)** and **Restaurant Happy Snapper** have free Wi-Fi.

⬛ ACCOMMODATIONS

Free camping is available at Playa Conchal, but the closest toilets and potable water are in Brasilito. These hotels offer beds and a break from the heat.

Hotel Brasilito (☎2654 4237; www.brasilito.com), located at the southwest corner of the soccer field. At the closest hotel to the beach, you can soak in a sunset from the chairs and hammock out in front of the festive downstairs restaurant. The location makes up for the plain, white rooms. Wi-Fi available. Cable TV. Laundry US$8 per load. Singles and doubles US$29; triples US$39; quads US$43; quints US$49; add US$7 for A/C. Beachfront rooms and high season prices add US$10. Reservations recommended. ❸

Cabinas Ojos Azules (☎/fax 2654 4346), on the main road south of the soccer field. Spacious rooms with high ceilings, sky windows, and mirrored headboards in a bright orange building surrounding coconut trees and magenta flowers. Simple rooms on the lower level house up to 8 (US$60). All rooms have a safe, fridge, cable TV, and access to a communal kitchen. Doubles and triples US$35, with A/C US$50; quads US$56. Triples with A/C and quads have access to pool and hot tub. Laundry US$2 per kg. Prices jump on weekends and high season, about 25% higher. US$/¢ only. ❸

Cabinas Diversion Tropical (☎2654 5519; www.diversiontropical.com), 200m south on the main road. For those willing to spend a bit more, they will get a lot more here. Each room comes with A/C, cable TV, hot water, refrigerator, and coffeemaker. At night, guests sit at candlelit tables in front of each room in the adobe-style building dotted with pink flowers. Singles/doubles US$37; triples US$42; quads with kitchenette US$52. Bike rental US$6 per day. Snorkeling equipment US$6 per day. AmEx/D/MC/V. ❸

⬛ FOOD

The **Mini-Super Brasilito** is on the south side of the soccer field. (☎2654 4492. Open daily 6am-7pm. AmEx/D/MC/V.) Many past local favorites have been shut down due to new ecological restrictions of proximity to the beach, but a few beachside places that just made the cut are still going strong.

Soda La Casita del Pescado (☎2654 6171), next to Hotel Brasilito. A hole-in-the-sand *soda* serving *mariscos*, including *ceviche* (¢1300), and octopus in sauce (¢4000), which locals recommend. Open M-Sa 6am-10pm and Su 8am-9pm. US$/¢ only. ❷

Outback Jack's (☎2654 4237), connected to Hotel Brasilito. Overpriced entrees might make you yell "Crikey!," but the wacky Australian-themed restaurant does offer some affordable *tucker* (Aussie slang for food). Monstrous, delicious chicken quesadilla (¢2900) or the build-your-own burger (¢2500, each topping ¢500) served in a fun, relaxed environment just steps away from the beach. The hanging parrot reminding you that "It's 5 o'clock somewhere," will invite you to indulge in a tasty treat like the Passionfruit Margarita (¢3000) or get to know other travelers over a *coldie* (Aussie for beer, ¢1200). Free Wi-Fi. Open 7am-midnight. AmEx/D/MC/V. ❷

⚑ OUTDOOR ACTIVITIES

Santana Tours, 200m south along the main road, offers ATV tours (US$65), horseback rides on Playa Conchal (US$45), sportfishing, scooters, jet skis, canopy tours, and national park tours. (☎2654 4397. Open daily 8am-4pm.) Snorkeling gear can be rented from vendors at Playa Conchal (around US$4 per hr.).

▶ DAYTRIP FROM BRASILITO

PLAYA CONCHAL. Playa Conchal is an easy 10min. walk south along the beach from Brasilito. The shore is blanketed in the characteristic pink-white sand of crushed *conchitas* (shells). With some of the clearest water on the Pacific coast, it is the ideal place to snorkel. (Various vendors on-site rent gear for US$4 per hr.) Because it's arguably one of the most beautiful beaches in the country, Conchal does get crowded with people and four-wheelers during the high season. Around Christmas and Easter, local vacationers line their tents along the shore. In the middle of the beach, there is a little open market that offers hair-braiding, massages, jewelry, souvenirs, tours, and *casados* (US$3).

SANTA CRUZ

Santa Cruz is officially "La Ciudad Folclórica de Costa Rica," steeped in history and traditions that are revived each January during **Las Fiestas Patronales de Santo Cristo de Esquipulas.** A dance troupe called Flor de Caña performs to marimbas, as the plaza fills up with traveling rodeos, parades, and overwhelming amounts of traditional Guanacastan food in honor of patron Santo Cristo. The rest of the year, the statues that stand on the four corners of Parque Bernabela Ramos serve as reminders of Santa Cruz's legacy. On the northwest corner, a stoic Bernabela wearing a *campesina* apron holds a scroll in her hand, representing the land donation that gave birth to the city. She was a wealthy Catholic Spaniard who hung the "sacred cross" on her porch and held mass for both Spanish and indigenous worshippers. A statue of Chorotega *cacique* Diriá guards the southwest corner of the *parque;* an action statue of a *montador* (bull rider) with his *vaquetero* (assistant) and a tortilla-making scene complete the display. Most tourists see the town by bus on their way to more popular destinations on the peninsula, as the bustling town serves as a convenient halfway point between beaches. A visit to the pottery village of nearby Guatil is a must if you have a few hours in or around Santa Cruz.

▤ TRANSPORTATION

From the TRALAPA bus station, on the north side of Plaza de los Mangos, **buses** depart to: San José (4hr., 5 per day 3am-5pm, ¢2935); Nicoya (45min.;

M-Sa 33 per day 5:30am-9:25pm, Su 27 per day 5:30am-9:25pm; ¢295); Liberia (1hr., every 30min. 4:20am-10:30pm, ¢500); Filadelfia (M-Sa every hr. 7am-6pm, ¢290). Buy tickets at the TRALAPA station. The Tamarindo (4 and 8:30pm) and Flamingo-Conchal-Brasilito (3:30pm, ¢600) buses also leave from this terminal, but most beach buses leave from a second station behind the *mercado munici-pal*, 200m south and 300m east of TRALAPA, to: San José through La Puente (10 per day 3am-4:30pm, 7am and 3pm bus goes through Liberia instead of La Puente; ¢2500; reserve ahead through Empresa Alfaro office at station or call ☎2680 0401); Tamarindo (1-2hr.; 7 per day 4:20am-5pm, last two buses go to Matapalo, ¢500); Flamingo (7 per day 3:40am-6:15pm, ¢960); Potrero (7 per day 6am-3:10pm); Junquillal (5 per day 4am-5pm); Marbella Ostional (12:30pm). The Santa Barbara buses stop through Guatil (8 per day 6:20am-6:15pm; Guatil at 7am, 1:30, 3:30pm); Pinilla (11:30am, 6pm); and Bolsón-Ortega (11am, 5pm). **Taxis** are everywhere, including on the west side of Mangos (☎2680 0706).

⚡ 🔢 ORIENTATION AND PRACTICAL INFORMATION

Standing in **Parque Bernabela Ramos,** Restaurante Jardín de Luna is to the north, and the church, with a visible, weathered pink tower, is to the east. **La Plaza de los Mangos** and the bus station where you will probably arrive are 400m north of this *parque;* some directions are given from Mangos.

Banks: Banco de Costa Rica, 200m north of Mangos's northwest corner, exchanges US$ and traveler's checks. Open M-F 8am-4pm. **Banco Nacional,** 600m north of Mangos, is near the entrance to Santa Cruz. Open M-F 8:30am-3:45pm. **Banco Popular,** 200km south of Mango's southeast corner. All have **24 hr. ATMs.**

Police: The **police** (☎2680 0136 or 911), 100m south and 300m east of Mangos's southeast corner, across from the *mercado municipal* and the bus station. Open 24hr.

Red Cross: Red Cross (☎2680 0330), on the west side of Parque Bernabela.

Medical Services: There is a **medical clinic,** 100m south of Parque Bernabela's southeast corner. (☎2680 0436; open M-Th 7am-4pm, F 7am-3pm; emergencies 24hr.)

Telephones: Public telephones can be found in the *parque* and the plaza.

Internet Access: Available at **Ciberm@nía** (www.cibermania.net), 100m north and 50m west of Parque Bernabela. ¢600 for 1st hr.; open M-Sa 8:30am-9:30pm, Su 2pm-8pm).

Post Office: The **post office** is 200m north and 50m east of Parque Bernabela's northeast corner. Fax available; open M-F 8am-5:30pm, Sa 8pm-noon. **Postal Code:** 5150.

🔥 ACCOMMODATIONS

Whether staying here for Las Fiestas or just stopping through on the way to surf, these hotels offer a great place to crash.

Hotel La Pampa (☎2680 0586), just west of Mango's southwest corner. The closest hotel to the bus station and the nicest place to stay in town. Rooms with private baths, cable TV, and unusually attentive service are ample compensation for slightly higher prices. Singles with fan ¢15,000, with A/C ¢19,320; doubles ¢21,000/29,100; triples ¢29,500/35,150; quads ¢35,100/¢43,400; quints ¢39,700/49,800. Huge discounts for business travelers. MC/V/US$/¢. ❸

Hotel la Calle de Alcalá (☎2680 0000; hotelalcala@hotmail.com), east of Mangos's northeast corner. Offers comfortable rooms with TVs, A/C, Internet access, and a shaded pool. Each room has a wood-carved door displaying one of Costa Rica's creatures. On-site restaurant. Parking. Singles US$52; doubles US$65; triples US$82; quints US$116; 2-person suite with hot tub US$128. AmEx/D/MC/V/US$/¢. ❹

FOOD

Santa Cruz offers three fairly predictable culinary options: Chinese, fried chicken, and *comida típica*. The town's welcome sign is written in Chinese as well as Spanish, testifying to the local Chinese population's impact on this community. The most comprehensive supermarket in town is **Kion,** on the southwest corner of Mangos. (Open M-Sa 6:30am-6:30pm, Su 6:30am-noon.)

Coope Tortillas, 200m south of the southeast corner of the *parque,* has huge iron pots simmering over wood-burning cooking pits in a large barn. Margarita Marchena started the cooperative establishment in 1975 to give mothers the chance to provide food and education for their family. Margarita, at age 85, along with 14 women and 2 men, still jokes around as they cook corn tortillas and serve them with daily specials like *arroz con maíz* (rice and chicken soup; W and Su), *empanadas,* and *sopa de albóndigas* (meatball soup). *Casado* ¢1600. Runs on *campesino* time. Open daily 4am-5pm. ❶

Soda El Mango (☎2680 0857), under a huge mango tree 400m north of Mango's northeast corner. Serves the largest, most delicious *batidos* (¢600) you'll ever have, as well as a corn-based drink called *pinolillo.* The combinations include mango, *guanabana, cas,* pineapple, *mora, maracuyá,* and passionfruit. Ham sandwich ¢850. *Casados* ¢2400. *Filet de pescado a la plancha* ¢2500. Open daily 11am-10pm. MC/V/US$/¢. ❶

El Portoncito, on the east side of Plaza de los Mangos. A welcoming, homey *soda.* The building itself feels like a little cottage; its yellow walls with wreaths and paintings and the gravel patio with a random collection of chairs looks like someone hurriedly prepared for a spontaneous party. Breakfast combo with *gallo pinto,* eggs, cheese, and coffee ¢1500. *Casados* ¢2500. Open M-Sa 6am-8pm, Su 6am-noon. US$/¢ only. ❶

FESTIVALS

Santa Cruz's history and traditions are revived every January during **Las Fiestas Patronales de Santo Cristo de Esquipulas,** honoring the faith of patron Santo Cristo. The festival lasts for five days, but it climaxes on the 15th, when a huge crowd performs indigenous and folk dances, riders mount rowdy bulls to the tune of a folkloric band, parades fill the streets, and traditional Guanacastan food is served throughout town. The week leading up to this festival is a cultural week, during which Latin American cultures are honored through celebrations highlighting native dances, art, and food. The events of the week draw large crowds from every corner of the country. Late in July, the *sabaneros* (cowboys) also show off their horses in **Las Fiestas de Santiago.**

DAYTRIP FROM SANTA CRUZ

GUAITIL. The pottery village of Guaitil surrounds the soccer field with clustered family pottery stands, selling the earthen pots on which the livelihood of the entire village depends. You can spy on 1200°C, hive-like kilns in people's yards. Some artisans will decorate jugs, vases, masks, and bowls as tourists watch. Each artist has a specialty. The art form, called *piedra,* is based on Chorotega indigenous crafts that have been passed down through generations. Currently, about 140 families, or 95% of the village, still practice these ancient ceramic techniques, and all take great pride in passing on these skills to their children. Pottery wheels are not used, and the paint is made from an all-natural clay from nearby mountains and a sand mixture called *curiol,* which yields rich grays, browns, oranges, and reds. Intricate animal motifs are often scraped out using corn cobs and stones. Some shops also make *metates,* tools historically used to grind *maíz.* Many families are willing to teach their craft to visitors for a small charge. Susan (☎2681 1696) is a local woman with a workshop on the corner of the soccer field. She holds private or group lessons with one- to three-day advance notice. Pottery prices depend on how long it takes to make. The smallest pot takes 15-20hr. and costs ¢1200. The largest pot can take up to two days to make and can be as much as US$200. *(Guaitil is a 30min. bus ride or a ¢4000 taxi ride from Santa Cruz. Buses leave the mercado station in Santa Cruz at 7am, 1:30, and 3pm. Buses pass more frequently going to Santa Barbara, from which you can walk, or where some are known to hitch a ride. As always, Let's Go does not recommend hitchhiking. Return buses to Santa Cruz leave Guaitil at 3, 4, and 5:30pm.)*

PARQUE NACIONAL MARINO LAS BAULAS

Founded in 1995, Parque Nacional Marino Las Baulas covers over 4 sq. km of land, including tropical dry forests, swampland, and several beaches. The park is known as the nesting site of endangered leatherback turtles that emerge from the ocean and deposit their eggs in the sands of Playa Grande before returning to the water. These reptiles can reach lengths of 1.5m. They are easily disoriented by light and noise; photography and shell collecting are forbidden, and dark clothing is required to observe the turtles. Playa Grande is part of the national park but is often used casually for its surfing and sunbathing.

AT A GLANCE	
AREA: 4.2 sq. km; 3.4 sq. km of beach. **CLIMATE:** Semi-arid. **FEATURES:** Playa Grande; Tamarindo estuary. **HIGHLIGHTS:** Nesting leatherback turtles; Tamarindo estuary; surfing; birdwatching. **GATEWAYS:** Tamarindo (p. 226); Playa Grande (p. 232).	**FEES AND RESERVATIONS:** Park entrance fee US$10. Guides are mandatory (US$15-20). Turtle-watching tours Oct. 20-Feb. 15. Reservations ☎2653 0470. Office open daily 8am-4pm. Reservations, with a passport, are required. Accepted 1-8 days in advance.

■▲ ORIENTATION

The Tamarindo estuary marks the park's southern border, on the northeast corner of Tamarindo village. The leatherback turtles come between mid-October and mid-February to lay their eggs on Playa Grande.

COCODRILLO CROSSING. Though many surfers swim across Tamarindo Estuary to get to Playa Grande or Parque Nacional Las Baulas, there are 2 crocodiles living in the back of the estuary that are known to come to the mouth of the river to feed. There have been no accidents yet, but if you don't want to be the first, it's worth the US$2 to go on a crocodile-free boat.

▐ TRANSPORTATION

Buses going from Tamarindo to San José stop at Huacas. From there, it's 12km to the entrance station on Playa Grande. A **taxi** from Huacas costs about ¢8000; all the way from Tamarindo to the park is US$40-50. You can also hop on a **boat** across the Tamarindo estuary at the north end of Playa Tamarindo. (Boats ¢1000 per crossing; some usually wait near the banks 7am-4pm; boat office is just beyond the police station on the main road.) During low tide, when water has emptied from the estuary, it's a 45min. walk along the beach to the entrance station, up the road from Hotel Las Tortugas. Start walking early during nesting season (when the beach is closed from 6pm-5am) and take a taxi back.

🛈 PRACTICAL INFORMATION

Entrance station: From the far shore of the Tamarindo estuary, it's a 3km, 45min. walk along the broad beach to the entrance station, up the road from Hotel Las Tortugas.

Fees and Reservations: Park entrance fee US$10. Guide US$15-20. Reserve a guide with MINAE at ☎2653 0470. Office open daily 8am-4pm. Park phone lines are often busy, so you can also use **C.R. Paradise.** Transportation from Tamarindo, entrance fee, guide, and refreshments are included. (☎2653 0981. US$45 per person.)

WHEN TO GO. If you're going to the park to see turtles, you must go during nesting season (from mid-Oct. to mid-Feb.). During this time, Playa Grande is closed to surfers and casual visitors 6pm-5am every night; only official tours are allowed on the beach. If you are visiting between Mar. and Sept., you can enjoy the park by taking a kayak or boat tour into the estuary. There are 174 species of birds, not to mention 5 species of swamp trees.

Tours: Adventure specialists in Tamarindo offer many tours and include the US$10 entrance fee in their prices (generally around US$45). Ask about kayak and boat tours into the estuary. MINAE guides bring groups of 15 people to watch the turtles, using radios and numbered signposts to track the turtles down. No more than 120 people are allowed on the beach in 1 night. Tours run every night during nesting season. Times vary based on tides. Guides (US$15-20) are mandatory. Reservations are accepted 1-8 days in advance with passport. No cameras. Wear dark clothes. Bring bug repellent.

🏠 ACCOMMODATIONS

A 45min. walk down the beach from Tamarindo, by the park entrance, **Hotel Las Tortugas** ❹ is the closest hotel to the beach, and is equipped with stone floors, tile showers, A/C, Wi-Fi, and hot-water baths. A shaded restaurant/ bar is tucked away on the premises, along with a hto tub hidden among the trees. Most rooms have small patio with colorful hammock and/or picnic table. (☎2653 0423; www.lastortugashotel.com. Standard rooms with bunk beds US$30-55; high season doubles US$90-100, low season US$85; 5-person suite with ocean view, couch, and large bath US$120. AmEx/D/MC/V/US$/¢.) **Playa Grande Surf Camp** ❷, inland from beach marker 29, offers bargains for surfers and non-surfers alike. There are two types of rooms: cabins with tent-like walls and thatched roofs, and rooms on stilts with hammocks on the porches. All have reading lamps and access to a shared kitchen, bath, and pool. (☎2653 1074; www.playagrandesurfcamp.com. Laundry US$5 per load. Board and bike rentals US$15 per day. US$15 per bed, with A/C US$25. Cash only. US$/¢.)

PLAYA TAMARINDO

Though its long shores have some rocky patches, Tamarindo is Costa Rica's most cosmopolitan, commercialized beach. Few places have so much entertainment by day—scenery, snorkeling, surfing, and shopping—and such a lively nightlife. Although the town is not as crowded as other beaches like Jacó, tourists and expats make their presence clear. Here you'll find more resort-hoppers than backpackers, more signs in English than in Spanish, and more international restaurants than *sodas*. The crowd on the beach is composed of people from

Playa Tamarindo

🔺 ACCOMMODATIONS
Cabinas Coral Reef, **5**
Cabinas Marielos, **15**
Cabinas Rodamar, **12**
Hostel Botella de Leche, **1**

🍎 FOOD
El Pescador, **7**
Frutas Tropicales, **13**
Mama's Deli and Pizza House, **9**
Olga's Coffee Shop, **3**
Pachanga, **2**
Tango & Grill, **4**

🔷 NIGHTLIFE
Aqua Discoteque, **14**
Babylon, **6**
La Barra, **10**
Monkeybar, **11**
El Pacífico, **8**

TO PLAYA LANGOSTA

Supermercado 2001
Iguana Surf Tours
Calle San Francisco
Arenas Tamarindo Adventures and Surf School
Lavendería Backwash
SuperCompro
Cyberbakanos
PLAZA CONCHAL
Maresias Surf Shop
Banco Nacional
Farmacia Pacífico
CR Paradise
Playa Tamarindo
Iguana Surf Tours
Blue Trailz Bike Shop
Best Western
Tamarindo Blvd.
Witch's Rock Surf Camp
PACIFIC OCEAN
TO ISLA CAPITÁN
Emergencias Tamarindo
TO PN MARINO LAS BAULAS (3km)

0   200 meters
0   200 yards

NICOYA PENINSULA

all walks of life: *tico* families, retired *gringos*, surfers from the north and south, teens awaiting happy hour, and backpackers seeking respite from rice and beans. Socialites can find plenty of people to schmooze with, and surfers are happy to amuse themselves around town when they get struck by low-tide blues. Despite recent construction of resorts and restaurants, surfing is the center of the culture, which keeps the young and fit traveling through budget hostels, surf shops, and beach-wear stands. If your time in Tamarindo starts to feel like a Cancun spring break, it's always easy to escape at beaches in Parque Nacional Las Baulas.

TRANSPORTATION

Flights: Flights from San José are run by **Sansa** (50min.; 7 daily 5:15am-3:50pm, return flights 7 daily 6:20am-4:55pm; US$90) and **NatureAir** (50min.; high season 3 daily 6:30am-3:20pm, low season 4 daily 9am-1:40pm, return high season 7:45am-4:20pm, low season 7:25am-4:35pm; US$80). Planes arrive at the airstrip 3km north of town (☎USA and Canada +1-800-235-9272; www.natureair.com).

Buses: Buses to Tamarindo come from Liberia (2-2½hr., 10 per day 3:50am-6pm, ¢1000). From Nicoya, first take the bus headed to Liberia and get off in Santa Cruz (45min.; 32 per day 3:50am-10pm; ¢400), then walk to the *mercado* bus station, 300m south and 300m west of where the bus drops you off. Buses from there leave to **Tamarindo** (1-2hr., 7 per day 4:20am-5pm, ¢500). Buses from Tamarindo to **San José** leave from the Alfaro office in the Tamarindo Resort driveway, located 200m east down the road 200m north of the semicircle (6-7hr.; M-Sa 3:30, 5:45am; Su 5:45am, 12:30pm; ¢3000). Reserve tickets at least 1 day in advance. From the semicircle, buses go to **Santa Cruz** (1-2hr., 5 per day 6am-4:15pm, ¢500) and **Liberia** (2-2½hr., 8 per day 5:45am-6:30pm, ¢1000). They can also be flagged from anywhere along the main road. Private shuttle buses are also available, running to major tourist destinations like **San José, Quepos, Mal País, Santa Theresa, Sámara, Nosara, Jacó, Monteverde,** and **Volcán Arenal.** (US$47 per person. Book at Costa Rica Paradise or various hotels.)

Car Rental: Renting a car with 4WD for a day averages just under US$50, including insurance and tax. **Thrifty** (☎2653 0829) is in the Best Western. **Alamo** (☎2653 0737; www.alamocostarica.com). **Adobe** (☎2653 1414; www.adobecar.com). **Budget** (☎2436 2000; www.budget.co.cr), inside Hotel Zullymar, rents to those under 21.

Bike Rental: Blue Trailz (☎2643 1205; www.bluetrailz.com), next to Iguana Surf on the main road, rents bikes (US$20 per day) and beach cruisers (US$10 per day).

✦ 🔃 ORIENTATION AND PRACTICAL INFORMATION

The main road in Tamarindo extends 2.5km, from Parque Nacional Las Baulas at the far northeastern end of town to the main bus stop in a semicircle of shops and restaurants on the southwest edge. The **Best Western,** on the northeast end, is a key landmark. There are two main beach entrances with parking, one off the semicircle and another in the middle of the strip. Everything along the main street is geared to travelers' needs and luxuries. **Centro Comercial Aster** is a small strip of shops 200m north of the circle. A road south of the strip leads east to more restaurants, and tour agencies. **Hotel Zullymar** is another key landmark, on the corner of the intersection between the main road and a road running east, leading to many restaurants, supermarkets, and accommodations.

Tourist Office: C.R. Paradise (☎2653 0981), 15m south of Banco Nacional. Full bus and flight schedules posted on the wall. Guides offer information on local activities, book tours and shuttles, and answer any specific questions. International phone calls US$0.90 per min. Internet access on 2nd fl. Open daily 7:30am-6pm. English spoken.

Tours and Surfing Equipment: Surf shops and tour companies are everywhere.

Witch's Rock (☎2653 1238), 50m south of the Best Western on the main road. Proud to be the most qualified around with a 2007 Official Document of Regulation from the ISA. Small classes for comparable prices to larger groups and runs tours to nearby surf breaks. Surf lessons US$35 per 1hr. class, 3 people per instructor. Reservations recommended. Board rentals US$8 first hr., US$12 for 4hr., US$20 per day, US$100 per week. Open daily 6am-10pm. AmEx/D/MC/V.

Maresia's Surf Shop (☎2653 0224; www.maresiassurfcostarica.com), next to the bank. Offers 1hr. lessons for US$25. Board rental US$2-4 per hr., US$18 per day. Open M-Sa 9am-7pm.

Iguana Surf Tours (☎2653 0148 or 2653 0613; www.iguanasurf.net) has 2 main locations: 800m north of the circle and up the street, immediately south of the Supermercado 2001. Wide variety of tours including 2hr. group surf lessons (US$30 per person, includes Iguana Surf T-shirt), kayak and estuary tours, sunset cruises (US$65, with snorkeling US$75), diving (US$90), sportfishing, snorkeling tours (US$50), canopy tours (US$40), and ATV tours (US$65, US$15 for extra person). They also offer daily shuttles to San José, Arenal, Jacó, and Manuel Antonio (all US$33). Shuttle to Monteverde US$43. Surfboard rentals US$1.50-4 per hr., US$18 per day. Open daily 8am-6pm.

Tamarindo Adventures and Surf School (☎2653 0108), up the street running east of the main intersection, below Hightide Surfshop. Offers ATV tours. Rents ATVs and motorcycles. Surf lessons US$30. Stand up in the 1st lesson, or get a 2nd free. Open M-Sa 8am-8pm, Su 9am-6pm.

Bank: All have **24hr. ATMs. Banco Nacional,** 75m north of the circle. Changes traveler's checks and gives V cash advances. Lines are long, especially on F, so get there early. Open M-F 8:30am-3:45pm. **HSBC** is next to Interlink on the main road. Open M-F 9am-

6:30pm, Sa 9am-12:30pm. **Banco de Costa Rica** (open M-Sa 8am-6pm, Su 8am-5pm) and **BAC San José** (open M-F 9am-6pm, Sa 9am-1pm) are in Plaza Conchal.

Laundry: Backwash (☎2653 0870), on the road near Plaza Conchal, does laundry for ₡700 per kg. Open M-Sa 8am-8pm.

Emergency: ☎911. Medical emergencies ☎2653 0611 or 2653 1226.

Police: (☎2653 0283), 100m north of Best Western on the main road.

Hospital: Tamarindo lacks a proper hospital or clinic, but **Emergencias Tamarindo** (☎2653 1226) is north of the Best Western.

Pharmacy: Farmacia Pacifico (☎2653 0711), across from the bank. Open M-Sa 9am-7:30pm. MC/V.

Internet Access:

> **InterLink,** 200m north of Banco Nacional. ₡1050 for 30min., ₡2100 per hr. Printing ₡150 B/w, ₡250 color. CD burning ₡2000. International calls ₡50 per min. Open daily 9am-9pm.

> **Internet Cafe del Mar** (☎2653 1011; www.cafedelmarinternet.com), 50m up the road east of Hotel Zullymar. ₡1600 per hr. International calls ₡300 per min. Open M-Sa 9am-9pm, Su 10am-8pm.

> **Cyberbakanos,** just north of the circle. ₡1000 per hr. International calls ₡100 per min. to USA. Open daily 9am-10pm.

ACCOMMODATIONS

While Tamarindo is notoriously expensive, there are a few great budget accommodations (primarily hostels) with fun atmospheres and creative decor.

Hostel Botella de Leche (☎2653 0189; www.labotelladeleche.com), up the hill past Pachanga (you can't miss the big bottle of milk and cow-spotted walls on your right). Not only the best place to meet other travelers but also the cheapest, most creative, comfortable, and colorful hostel in Tamarindo. The Argentinian owner and her sons make you feel at home with an impeccably clean communal kitchen. Guests lounge on the colored hammocks, picnic tables, bean bags, and couches watching TV and chatting. Some rooms have A/C and private baths. US$10 per person. Cash only. US$/₡. ❶

Cabinas Marielos (☎/fax 2653 0141), next to Iguana Surf. Brilliant *cabinas* are set back from the road, with sparkling baths, fans or A/C, and access to a stocked kitchen and garden with painted tables. Some rooms have balconies. Surf and boogie boards for rent; ½-day US$5, full-day US$10. Low season singles US$25-35, high season US$35-45; doubles US$35-45/45-60; quads US$60-70/70-80. AmEx/MC/V. ❸

Cabinas Coral Reef (☎2653 0291), 50m up the road from Hotel Zullymar. This social hostel has turquoise walls and an outdoor communal kitchen strung with hammocks. While the shared bathrooms aren't in great shape, the dirt-cheap price and fun-filled atmosphere more than compensate. Inexpensive restaurant on-site. Surf lessons US$20. Free coffee and Internet access. If you stay for more than 2 days, surfboard use is free. US$1 breakfast. Low season/high season dorms US$8/10; singles US$18/20; doubles US$24/30; triples US$36/40. AmEx/D/MC/V/US$/₡. ❶

Cabinas Rodamar (☎2653 0109), behind Frutas Tropicales on the main road. Lacks the community of backpacker hostels, but makes up for it in proximity to the beach and low prices. Simple, bright teal rooms line 2 long buildings with tiled patios and benches. Rooms US$10, with bath US$13; doubles with A/C and bath US$38. US$/₡ only. ❶

FOOD

There are no amazing deals in Tamarindo, though it's a good place to splurge at inventive fusion restaurants. The supermarkets are the best budget option in town. **SuperCompro** (☎2653 1410) is 100m northeast on the road that heads northeast after Plaza Conchal and Tango's Bar and Grill (open M-Sa 7am-9pm,

TOP TEN WORDS YOU NEED TO KNOW TO BE A SURFER

If you find yourself on the Pacific coast, it'd be hard for you to miss the surfing culture. Surf shops are everywhere, and you may look out of place without your board. Try to blend in by at least knowing some of the terminology. Costa Rica is one of the world's surfing hot spots, and you don't want to stick out because you have no idea what a point break or a grom is.

1. **A-Frame:** large wave with double shoulders that can be surfed by two people.
2. **Dropping in:** standing up and taking off down the wave
3. **Filthy:** awesome.
4. **Grom or Grommet:** a young surfer, probably not making you look very good.
5. **Gnarly:** intimidating, scary. Often shortened to gnar.
6. **Hollow:** a curling wave with a pocket to ride inside.
7. **Overhead:** wave heights higher than the surfer is tall.
8. **Point break:** peeling waves breaking perfectly around a point.
9. **Shredding/Ripping/Shralping :** tearing it up.
10. **Smashed:** wiped-out; what happens a lot to beginners.

Su 8am-9pm). **Supermercado 2001** (☎2653 0935) is across from the police station (open M-Sa 7am-9:30pm, Su 8am-8:30pm).

Tango & Grill (☎8867 5184), just before SuperCompro on the road that branches off after Plaza Conchal. Mariana (owner of Hostel Botella de Leche) and family recently opened another Buenos-Aires-inspired establishment; this one brings Argentinian cuisine to Tamarindo. The decor embraces the combination of old colonial and cosmopolitan with an antique street lamp and photos of Argentinian houses, famous people, tango, and soccer. If you have been avoiding the not-so-impressive meat in Costa Rica, the wide variety of tender cuts (which the owner's sons/waiters will explain), such as *vacío* (¢5500), will satisfy that carnivorous desire. Try the perfectly cooked grilled seabass fillet (¢5500). Sa Tango show. Open daily 5:30-10:30pm. ❸

El Pescador (☎2653 0786 or 2653 1001), on the beach 200m south of the circle; turn right (west) on the road beyond Iguana Surf. Seafood brought in fresh 3 times per week is served on glass tables full of shells and coins from around the world. Grilled or steamed fish fillet ¢4000. Scallop *ceviche* ¢4000. Breaded squid ¢3500. If your mind is twisted from all the options, throw them all together in the iconic seafood soup (¢5000). Open 24hr. AmEx/D/MC/V. ❷

Pachanga (☎8368 6983), about 400m east of the intersection in front of Hotel Zullymar. The French-trained Israeli chef, Shlomy, combines Mediterranean and European flavors using the freshest ingredients from the nearby coast. Daily specials accompany well-known staples to create dishes like seared yellowfin tuna in a honey chili marinade (¢6800), shrimp-stuffed rigatoni in a light cream sauce (¢3800), and Moroccan couscous (¢6300). Open M-Sa 6-10pm. Cash only. ❸

Mama's Deli and Pizza House (☎2653 0178), across from the Copacabana on the main road. Serves up hearty sandwiches, entrees, and genuine Italian pizza on homemade sourdough loafs and freshly baked focaccia. With a *heliconia* and white candle on every table, the atmosphere lends to sipping wine with that beach fling or chowing down on a large, delicious chicken *milanese* with hungry surfers (¢3800). The plastic banner surrounding the sides of the patio, featuring old Italian images, contrasts with the American music. Pizza with mozzarella, edam cheese, and parma ham ¢5000. Delivery available with ¢500-1000 delivery charge. Open M-Sa 11:30am-10pm. US$/¢. ❷

Frutas Tropicales (☎2653 0041), 200m south of the Best Western. Serves the most-popular *comida típica* in a small, gated patio painted in warm, festive colors. The breezy interior with minimal decor resembles a high-end *soda*. *Gallo pinto* and eggs ¢2000. *Casados* ¢2600. Open daily 7am-9pm. AmEx/MC/V. ❷

Olga's Coffee Shop (olgascoffeeshop.com), next to Supermercado 2001. Serves fantastic organic teas, coffee, and smoothies, as well as a variety of treats like granola and yogurt (¢1200) and create-your-own salad (¢2500). Although Olga started her "baby" making only US$10 per day, the 5-year-old just celebrated its birthday with 200 guests in the new elegant space. Sip ginger-mint lemonade (¢1000) or green tea with a shot of ginseng (¢1000) on the natural wood tables on the patio or the barstools on the 2nd fl. Free Wi-Fi. Open M-Sa 7am-9pm, Su 8am-2pm. US$/¢. ❶

NIGHTLIFE

Although high season nightlife is thumpin', the low season scene generally consists of folks relaxing at beachside bars with a beer to some music, unless one of the clubs is having a special night. The **Monkeybar** at the Best Western throws huge sunset poolside parties on Friday nights reminiscent of a high-school rager. Once in a while, the nearby town of Villa Real has events where you'll hear merengue or salsa rather than the customary American music that spills out onto the streets of Tamarindo.

La Barra (☎2653 0342), across from the Copacabana. Colored lights and loud music create a fun, tropical mood. The place is packed with twirling ladies and suave men on W Latin Night, which gets lively with live salsa (¢1000 cover). Sa features DJs playing disco, dance hall, reggae, or 80s favorites. Beer ¢1000. Open daily 6pm-2am.

Aqua Discoteque (☎2653 AQUA/1781; lindsayaqua@gmail.com), right on the main road 300m north of the circle. Looming above the strip with its huge glass windows, 2-story Aqua might as well be an exclusive club in Manhattan with its pearl padded walls, dark leather seating, swirling lights, and pulsating dance floor. Mostly young travelers don their finest finds from the Tamarindo boutique stores, and sip on creative drinks like the Adios Gringo (vodka, rum, gin, guaro, triple sec and sweet and sour syrup; ¢4000). Thirsty Th (cover for women ¢2500, for men ¢3500) gets crazy with national beers (US$0.25) and house margaritas. F nights 2-for-1 shots. International DJs spin hottest club music. Open M and Th-Su 10pm-3am.

Babylon (☎2653 1434), 100m behind the Mambo Bar. Looks makeshift with scattered chairs and tables. A mismatching fence surrounds an open dance floor that gets crowded with *ticos* and *gringos* alike. Th Reggae music and Sa Ladies' night, when ladies are entertained by shirtless male dancers (¢2000 cover). Open daily 9pm-3am.

El Pacífico, on the circle. The circular dance floor attracts crowds on feature nights, usually playing a mixture of salsa, reggaeton, and American rap. Same owners as Babylon, so the look and atmosphere are very similar. W ladies' night (ladies drink free 10:30pm-12:30am). Su reggae night. M Latino night. Tamarindo iced tea ¢2500. Beer ¢500-1000. Open M-W and F-Su 8:30pm-2:30am.

OUTDOOR ACTIVITIES AND GUIDED TOURS

Though there's plenty of incredible surf around Tamarindo for beginners and experts alike, visitors should also come ready for crowds. Those looking for more personal surf school options have a number of alternatives nearby: 10km south is **Playa Avellana,** home of the right reef-break "Little Hawaii"; 15km south is **Playa Negra,** which is more hollow than the rest; or **Playa Langosta,** which has a left and right break at the mouth of the river. **Playa Grande,** farther north, is another good beach break and home to "La Casita." Playa Grande is one of the most consistent beach breaks in Costa Rica, and the waves are almost always bigger than in Tamarindo. Nature-seekers can also head to Playa Grande, now part of the 420 hectare **Parque Nacional Las Baulas,** on the northeast end of the village. From mid-November to mid-February, the park is a nesting site for the *baula*, the leatherback turtle (beach closed 6pm-5am during nesting season).

Sportfishing is another great option; many tourist offices and surf stores offer trips. **Agua Rica Diving Center,** by Banco Nacional, is the most professionally equipped diving coordinator. PADI certification available (two dives US$95). The snorkeling tour (US$50) goes to Catalina Islands. (☎2653 0094; www. aguarica.net. Snorkel equipment rental US$8. Open daily 9am-7pm.) Estuary tours, on both boats and kayaks, are an active way to explore Tamarindo's wildlife, as are canopy and ATV tours. **C.R. Paradise** can explain all your options and help book tours. (☎2653 0981. Open daily 7:30am-6pm.) You can explore inland areas on bikes. (☎2643 1705; www.bluetrailz.com. US$20 per day)

PLAYA NEGRA

Once you've seen Playa Negra, it's immediately clear why the small town's reputation as a surf destination is well-deserved. The whole place runs on an early surf schedule, all the hotels seem to be equipped with surf racks, and after sunset there's not much to do in the area but watch a surf movie, go to sleep, and get ready for the next morning's session. A picturesque reef produces a consistently fast and hollow right made famous by the movie "Endless Summer II," but this isn't the best place for beginners unless they enjoy a good beating and getting "pitched with the lip." Negra's waves are good enough to induce many experienced surfers to brave the rough, sometimes-washed-out road to get here. Novice (or non-) surfers will enjoy the black-sand beaches and forests in the area; a walk to nearby Playa Lagartillo is particularly worthwhile.

⊟🔋 TRANSPORTATION AND PRACTICAL INFORMATION

Playa Negra is located next to the town of Pargos, about 4km north of the village of Paraíso, where there is a stop for **buses** running from Santa Cruz to Junquillal. The dirt road may require 4WD in the rainy months. Travelers are known to hitchhike along the road. However, **Let's Go does not recommend hitchhiking.** Walking from the bus stop takes about 1hr., and it's also possible to walk along the beach from Junquillal (4km south of Paraíso) at low tide. Playa Avellana (4km) and Tamarindo are farther north. A bus runs twice a day from Pargos to Santa Cruz (7:45am, 1:30pm), but there are more buses from Paraíso (5, 6, 9am, 12:30, 4:30pm). Major services can be found in Paraíso, 27 de Abril, and Santa Cruz (p. 222). **Internet access** is free for guests/clients at **Kon-Tiki** and **Cafe Playa Negra**. Both have Wi-Fi, and Cafe Playa Negra has a computer.

♦ ACCOMMODATIONS

▨ **Kon-Tiki** (☎2652 9117; kontikiplayanegra@yahoo.com), on the main road 1km from the entrance to Oasis toward Playa Negra. Designed by its owner to feel like a treehouse, Kon-Tiki offers the most distinctive lodging in town. In the pink and green paradise, you'll feel like a long-lost relative—the family and guests eat home-cooked meals together every night, including a BBQ every Sa. Tired surfers relax in hammocks, lining the common area. Board rentals US$15-20, with lessons from the owner's son. BBQ and brick oven available. Work-out room. Breakfast ¢2000; lunch or dinner plate ¢3000; free coffee. Laundry ¢3000 per load. Free Wi-Fi. Rooms sleep up to 6. Shared baths are dark but spacious. US$10 per person; US$8 per person for groups larger than 4. ❶

Mono Congo Lodge (☎2652 9261; www.monocongolodge.com), on the main road toward Avellana. Elevated rooms on stilts sit in the lush greens of the canopy. Dark wood rooms feature white captain beds and pottery from around the country. 3 rooms share 2 hot-water tiled baths, while the 4th and 5th have their own. An outstanding American breakfast is served every morning (US$5-10) on the 2nd fl. balcony. Guests enjoy free coffee. Don't be surprised when monkeys swing by the hammocks that line the wrap-around terrace. If you're feeling up to it, check out the crocodile family that lives nearby. A/C, TV with DVD player and movies, and hot water. Doubles US$65-95. MC/V. ❹

Aloha Amigos (☎2658 9023), a 15min. walk down the main road, beyond the soccer field. Owned by a former resident of Hawaii, Aloha Amigos brings Hawaiian style to a new Pacific coast. Spaced out, white *cabinas* with hammocks share nice baths and cluster around an open, manicured garden (the owner's pride and joy). A kitchen, BBQ, an eating area with hammocks, circuit machine, and an extensive book collection are all housed under a circular, thatched *rancho*. Laundry included. Haircuts available. Some cabins have a fridge. *Cabinas* US$10 per person, with bath US$12.50. US$/¢ only. ❶

Cabinas La Playa (☎2652 9162; www.cabinaslaplaya.com), a tan-colored house and art gallery 20m before the entrance to Oasis and 100m from the beach. A killer deal for larger groups. The owner just built these 2 *cabinas*, which are basically air-conditioned mini-apartments big enough for groups of 4 or 5. Features high ceilings, shared hot-water baths, daily cleaning service, secure gates, and an open common room, complete with kitchen, fridge, and glass table with chairs. Laundry US$3 per load. *Cabinas* US$50 for up to 2 people, US$60 for 4. Extra mattress for 5th person US$5. US$/¢ only. ❷

Piko Negro (☎2653 2441; www.pikonegro.com), next to the soccer field in Pargos. Another new budget accommodation, which is one of the few locally run places around, attracting young surfers who swing in the common room's hammocks and play cards on the 2nd fl. Cabin-like rooms with lime green walls have beds constructed of logs and private baths with green and blue tiles. Monkeys hop from tree to tree and a crocodile lurks in a creek in the back. On-site restaurant with satellite TV. Breakfast included. Cable TV. Rooms US$25 per room, with A/C US$40. 4-person max. US$/¢ only. ❷

Cabinas Cafe Playa Negra (☎2652 9351; www.playanegracafe.com), right before the fork leading to Playa Negra. Just-opened, these Peruvian-inspired *cabinas* are unmatched in their proximity to Negra. The soft mattresses covered with traditional Peruvian cloths lie on a thick, dark-gray cement bed. Rooms have private bath with mosaic decorations. Guests can relax on the 2nd fl. balcony with green couches, bed, large hammock, bean bags, and a hidden pool. Wi-Fi and continental breakfast included. Singles US$20, with A/C US$32; doubles US$26/48; quads US$64/78. AmEx/D/MC/V. ❷

🔳 FOOD

Options are limited for those looking to cook. **Minisuper los Pargos,** in the nearby town of Pargos, is the only supermarket around. (Open daily 6am-7:30pm.) **El Mapache,** in Lagartillo, also has a small selection of neccesities.

Cafe Playa Negra (☎2652 9351; www.playanegracafe.com), just before the fork leading to Playa Negra. The most popular place in town due to its huge menu, vegetarian specialties, and surfing movies. The Peruvian owners whip up native specialties like *tiradito* (marlin carpaccio with capers; ¢2900) and Peruvian-style, diced-and-breaded fish with fried yucca (¢3900). Desserts like passion fruit pie, homemade sorbet, and cheesecake

keep people coming back for more. Offers book exchange and free Wi-Fi and Internet access to guests and clients. Open daily 7-10am and 6-9pm. US$/¢ only. ❷

La Vida Buena (☎2658 8082), before the fork to Playa Negra. Serves pizza and diners pre-game their meal with foosball. Shrimp and spinach pizza ¢4200. *Ceviche* ¢2500. Ginger fish ¢4000. Open daily from 11am to when people leave. US$/¢ only. ❷

El Mapache (☎2652 9114), just before the entrance to Oasis. Israeli owner brings new flavor to Playa Negra and Avellana with options like a falafel sandwich (¢1500) and waffles with Nutella and ice cream (¢1400). Their roadside stand is covered with a large, tattoo-style mural of a girl in the jungle with a *mapache* (raccoon). Hammocks and streched white cloths form triangles overhead. Also has a minisuper. US$/¢ only. ❶

Flor de Lis (☎2652 9218), across from La Vida Buena. Dishes out *comida típica* with a few twists. 2 tables outside and 2 in the restaurant, which is also the owner's house. *Casados* ¢2500. Yucca fries with red sauce ¢1000. Open daily 1-9pm. Cash only. ❶

PLAYA AVELLANA

Playa Avellana is a surfing beach that has everything: lefts, rights, reef, and beach. Even better, it requires less experience and skill than Playa Negra does, 4km to the south. The outside reef with the rights with the largest swells is called Little Hawaii and can get crowded, but the beach is so big that you'll usually have a peak to yourself. Surfers at **El Estero**, a local favorite, can enjoy swells with long rights and left barrels. Low, gnarly trees line the empty stretches of sand to offer a shaded spot to sit and take in the beauty of the dark-brown rocks, clear waters, and frothy waves. The beach is a great place for rock collecting, shell searching, and picnicking to the sound of crashing waves.

🚌 🛈 TRANSPORTATION AND PRACTICAL INFORMATION

There's no real town, and no buses stop at Avellana; the nearest stop is Paraíso, about 10km south, or Pargos, 3km south, which has only one bus per day stop there. Some people are known to hitchhike, but **Let's Go does not recommend hitchhiking.** You can take a **taxi** from Paraíso to Avellana (about ¢8000) or from Tamarindo to Avellana (US$25). Bluetrailz (see below), goes back and forth frequently, and may offer a ride from Tamarindo (☎2643 1705).

🏠 ACCOMMODATIONS AND CAMPING

Blue Trailz Surf Camp (☎2652 9153). Coming from the north, bear left 400m past Cabinas Las Olas to reach the best budget option for non-campers. A new, brightly painted hostel, the dorm-style rooms are clean, sleep 4, and have fans. The large common room features a TV and stereo. Hammocks, a pool table, and BBQ pit under the thatched roof *rancho* make for great socializing. Miguel, trained at the Culinary Institute of America, can provide you with delicious meals from the on-site Karma Kafe. A very small *supermercado* is located next door. Surfboards and bikes US$15 per day, mountain bikes US$20 per day. Group surf lessons US$35 per person. Laundry US$4 per load. Dorms US$10 per person. US$/¢ only. ❶

Cabinas El León Bed and Breakfast (☎2652 9318; www.cabinaselleon.com), 500m on the main road before the beach. Committed Italian owners keep immaculately clean rooms and serve breakfasts with rich black coffee (US$5). 3 spacious rooms have hot-water baths and effective fans. The dining area, decorated with an interesting collage of Rastafarian posters and Italian flags, also has satellite TV. Laundry services available on request. High season/low season US$17.50/15 per person. US$/¢ only. ❷

Mauna Loa (☎2652 9012), about 500m before El León (away from the beach). The nicest lodging in town, also Italian-owned. Recently built cabins are colorful, sleek, and playful, with chalkboards by each door making it reminiscent of a college dorm. Huge sage-green and mustard-yellow baths. The gorgeous pool is surrounded by palm trees and has an island with chairs in its center. The small communal kitchen is surrounded by dining tables with tree-stump seats. On-site restaurant has an eating area of huts, swinging chairs, tables, and hammocks. Ping pong, foosball, and small workout area. Doubles US$70; triples US$90; quads US$120. AmEx/D/MC/V/US$/¢. ❹

Dos Lunas (☎8866 4423), 400m south of the main entrance. It may look dingy from the road with a rusty roof, but the blue-and-white house with bamboo walls and a straw roof over the communal space offers the best deal for camping on the beach. The kitchen is used by a chef who will gladly cook for you. BBQ, toilets, and showers are available. Visit on a full moon, when people from Playa Negra and Tamarindo dance to a DJ by the fire. Board rental US$12 per day. Camping US$5; dorms US$10 per person. ❶

Casa Camping Avellana (☎2652 9230), 200m south of the main entrance. A camping option with toilets, showers, and kitchen. ¢2500 per person. Tents available. ❶

🍴 FOOD

Lola's On The Beach ❹, located at the main beach entrance, earns its high prices with huge portions, good ingredients, and beach location. Tables with large, dark-blue umbrellas are set up right on the sand. Veggie pizzas on homemade tortillas (8-slice margarita; ¢4600) are served on wood boards. Vegetarians will love Lola's Burger, a veggie, soy burger with onion, cheddar, avocado, and fries (¢5400). Watch Lola, the resident pig, on one of her many adventures. (☎2652 9097; lola@playaavellana.com. Yoga W and F at 8:30am. Open Tu-Su 11am-5pm, full menu available 11am-3pm, *bocas* and drinks available 3-5pm. Cash only.)

NICOYA

Nicoya, 78km south of Liberia, is the main settlement on the peninsula. The town was named after Chorotegan Indian Chief Nicoya, who ruled the region and welcomed the Spanish in 1523. In many museums throughout Europe, Nicoya is one of the main places marked on early colonial navigation maps. Though it sees less traffic these days, Nicoya still has its charms. The *parque central* is home to ancient stone benches, cobblestone barriers, and one of

Costa Rica's oldest churches. The city serves as a good base for spelunking in Parque Nacional Barra Honda. Nicoya also features more tourist services and transportation options than nearby towns, though many find that the city lacks the personality to be a destination in and of itself.

TRANSPORTATION

Buses: The **main station** is 200m east and 200m south of the *parque*. Buses leave for: **Nosara** (3hr.; 5, 10am, noon, 3, 5:30pm; ¢1000); **Playa Sámara** (1hr., every hr. 8am-9:30pm, ¢800); **San José** (4hr. via ferry, 8 per day 3am-5pm, ¢2430; 5-5½hr. via Liberia, 7:30am and 3pm, ¢4190). Buy tickets for San José at the window at least a day in advance to guarantee a seat. (☎2685 5032. Open daily 7am-5pm.) From another stop 100m north and 150m east of the *parque*, buses run to **Filadelfia** (1hr.; 10pm, additional bus Su and holidays; ¢680) and **Liberia** (2hr.; M-Sa 55 per day 3:30am-9pm, Su and holidays 9 per day 5am-7pm; ¢1000) via **Santa Cruz** (45min., ¢310).

Taxis: (¢17130/US$30 to Sámara) line up just about anywhere, including in front of the bus station, *parque*, and hospital.

ORIENTATION AND PRACTICAL INFORMATION

The two landmarks in the city center are the **parque central** and the main road, **Calle 3**, which runs north-south a block east of the *parque*. The bus might drop you off at various locations, so your best bet is to ask for the *parque central*. Once in the *parque*, Hotel Venecia is north, the *municipalidad* is south, Banco de Costa Rica is west, and Soda el Parque is east.

Tourist Information: MINAE (☎2686 6760), on the north side of the *parque*. Info on the national parks in Guanacaste. Open M-F 8am-4pm.

Banks: Banco de Costa Rica (☎2685 5010), on the west side of the *parque* with Visa/Plus **ATM,** cashes traveler's checks and gives Visa cash advances. Open M-F 9am-4pm. **Banco Nacional** (☎2685 3366), next to the Super Compro. Open M-F 8:30am-3:45pm. **24hr. ATM.**

Police: (☎2685 5559, emergency 911), 150m south of the bus station, near the airport.

Red Cross: (☎2685 5458, emergency 911), 500m north and 50m west of the *parque*.

Medical Services: Hospital de la Anexión (☎2685 8400), 100m east and 600m north of the *parque*. **Farmacia and Clínica Médica Nicoyana** (☎2685 5138), 100m east and 10m south of the northeast corner of the *parque*. Pharmacy open daily 8am-7pm, Sa 8am-6pm. Clinic open M-Sa 8am-5pm.

Internet Access: Planet Internet (☎2685 4281), 100m south of the southeast corner of the *parque*. Internet ¢500 per hr. Open M-Sa 8am-10pm, Su 10am-9pm. **Good Times Internet** (☎8893 8891), on the south side of the *parque*, has new flatscreen computers. Internet ¢400 per hr. Black and white copies ¢100, color ¢250-1000. Open daily 9am-10pm. **Cyber Center** (☎8886 0730), below Hotel Jenny. ¢500 per hr. Black and white copies ¢100, color ¢250 and up. **Cyber Plus Internet** (☎2686 7607), 100m south of the southeast corner of the *parque*, has webcams and headphones. Internet ¢400 per hr. Open daily 8am-10:30pm.

Post Office: (☎2686 6402), across from the southwest corner of the *parque*. Open M-F 8am-5:30pm, Sa 7:30am-noon. **Postal Code:** 5200.

ACCOMMODATIONS

Unless you're willing to completely empty your wallet for a room in the truly impressive **Hotel Tempisque**, lodging options here are not the height of luxury.

NICOYA PENINSULA

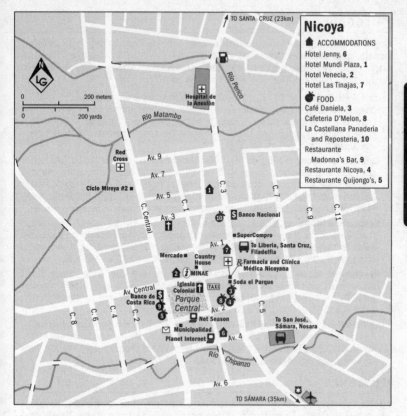

Nicoya

🏠 ACCOMMODATIONS
Hotel Jenny, **6**
Hotel Mundi Plaza, **1**
Hotel Venecia, **2**
Hotel Las Tinajas, **7**

🍴 FOOD
Café Daniela, **3**
Cafeteria D'Melon, **8**
La Castellana Panaderia
    and Reposteria, **10**
Restaurante
    Madonna's Bar, **9**
Restaurante Nicoya, **4**
Restaurante Quijongo's, **5**

Hotel Mundi Plaza (☎2685 3535 or 6702), 50m north of Banco Nacional. Pastel pink hallway and mirrors lead to bright, comfortable rooms with blue tiled floors and matching toilet-sink sets; some have balconies with mountain views. A/C and cable TV. Breakfast included. Towels provided. Secure parking. Singles ₡14,276 (US$25); doubles ₡23,984 (US$42); triples ₡34,263 (US$60). AmEx/MC/V. ❸

Hotel Jenny (☎2685 5050 or 867 5309), 100m south of the southeast corner of the *parque*. Rattier than Hotel Mundi, but becomes a real bargain if you're traveling in a group. Simple rooms with small beds, decent baths, A/C, and cable TVs. Parking available. Singles ₡10,000; doubles ₡14,000; triples ₡18,000; quads ₡20,000. AmEx/MC/V. ❷

Hotel Las Tinajas (☎2685 5081), across from the bus station to Liberia. Simple but clean rooms with small desks, shelves, and cable TVs. Public telephone available. Singles ₡6950, with A/C ₡9965; doubles ₡9800/13,600; triples ₡13,400/17,300; quads with A/C ₡22,000; quints ₡25,000; 6-person rooms without A/C ₡22,400. MC/V. ❶

Hotel Venecia (☎2686 5325), on the north side of the *parque*. High ceilings. Basic rooms with shared baths and a fan. TV and A/C also available. If you don't need a TV or A/C, this is the most economical option, though not the most comfy or sanitary. If you're going to spring for these amenities, look elsewhere. Free Wi-Fi. Lockout midnight. Singles ₡7000, with TV ₡9000, with TV and A/C ₡12,200; doubles ₡9000/10,200/13,500; triples ₡11,000/12,700/15,500. Cash only. ❷

FOOD

Casados and Chinese food joints dominate Nicoya. Pick up groceries at **Super Compro,** next to Banco Nacional. (☎2686 6314. Open M-Sa 8am-8pm, Su 8am-noon.) **Country House,** north of the northeast corner of the *parque*, sells produce. (☎2686 4800. Open M-F 8am-7pm, Sa 7am-7pm.)

Café Daniela (☎2686 6149), 100m east and 50m south of the northeast corner of the *parque*. The most popular spot for *comida típica*, with vegetarian *casados* (¢1800) that come with large green salads—a rarity in *sodas*. Large meat *casados* (¢1800-2700) come with beans, salad, rice, tortilla, and pasta. The fresh lemonade (¢800) is incredible. Open M-Sa 7am-9pm. MC/V. ❶

Cafeteria D'Melon (☎2658 4674), 100m east of the *parque*, on Av. 2. Cute coffee shop with lime green and orange walls has 67 options for hot or cold coffee, tea, and hot chocolate. Creative drinks include the Shiver *café* (coffee, chocolate cookie, vanilla ice cream, and milk; ¢1600) and the mint choco-orange (¢1000). Breakfast combo (¢2900) served with pancakes, juice, and fruit. Free Wi-Fi. Open M-Sa 9am-7pm. ❶

Restaurante Nicoya (☎2658 5113), next to Café Daniela. With the best Chinese food in town, Restaurante Nicoya is a local favorite. Large portions of fresh seafood with various Asian and Indian flavors, like sweet-and-sour shrimp (¢3480) and chicken and shrimp with cashews (¢4000). Open daily 10:30am-3pm and 5-10:30pm. MC/V. ❷

Restaurante Madonna's Bar (☎2685 4142), on the west side of the *parque*. Don't cry for her, Costa Rica—Madonna has made it to small towns here, if only in poster form. Try the *casado* (¢1900) or the fried chicken with fruit and veggies (¢1600). Entrees ¢1500-2000. Open daily 11am-2am. ❶

La Castellana Panaderia and Reposteria (☎8861 4205), across from the Banco Nacional. Locals come for the pan pizza (¢800) and bread with pineapple and coconut (¢700). Americans feeling homesick will feel better after a slice of chocolate cake (¢600). There isn't much seating, so take it to go. Open M-Sa 5am-7pm, Su 6am-1pm. ❶

SIGHTS

Iglesia Colonial, on the northeast corner of the *parque*, is one of the oldest churches in Costa Rica. It was constructed in 1644 from stone, brick, and *cal*, a unique local sand. The church was damaged by earthquakes in 1822 and rebuilt in 1831. Several religious artifacts, including a baptismal font and a 16th-century confessional booth, are worth a look. (Open to visitors M-F 8am-4pm, Sa 8am-11pm, Su 8am-5pm.) The folks at **Ciclo Mireya #2,** 400m north of the northwest corner of the *parque*, rent bikes, the perfect way to explore the surrounding countryside. (☎2685 5391. Bikes ¢8000 per day; mountain bikes ¢15,000.) Nicoya is full of shops, selling imported Panamanian clothes at unbeatable prices.

NOSARA

The town of Nosara is normally sleepy, but on weekends it seems like everyone—teenagers, grandparents, and children alike—is out dancing or at a local bar. The town spreads across 6km of dirt roads, which often get muddy during the rainy season. Rent a bike to explore; it's hard to get lost and easy to spot wildlife. It should be noted that the town of Nosara is not a tourist destination in itself, but rather the backbone (medical clinic, post office, bus station, etc.) of Playas Guiones and Pelada, 5km away, where most of the action appealing to travelers takes place. While prices do seem to go up with each step you take in the direction of the beach, there are a few great steals.

TRANSPORTATION

Flights arrive at the airstrip 50m south of the southeast corner of the soccer field. Sansa flies from San José (1hr.; 11:31am, return 12:35; US$89), as does NatureAir (50min; low season 9:45, 10am, return 10:50, 11:05am, 2:20pm; high season 10am, 1:20pm, return 11:05am, 2:30pm; US$109). NatureAir (San José office ☎2299 6000, Guiones office 2682 0181; www.natureair.com) is 1km south of the post office and has representatives in Casa Romantica in Guilones. You can take the **bus** from Nosara toward Nicoya/San José and ask the bus driver to let you off at Playa Guiones. Buses leave from Farmacia San Antonio to Nicoya (3hr.; 8am, 12:40, 3, 5:30pm; ¢1050) and San José (8hr., 12:45pm, ¢4000). Renting a **bike** or **all-terrain vehicle (ATV)** is a necessity if you plan to explore Nosara, Playa Guiones, and Playa Pelada. Some travelers are known to hitchhike, though **Let's Go never recommends hitchhiking.**

ORIENTATION AND PRACTICAL INFORMATION

The main road into Nosara from Nicoya and Sámara runs north to south. All directions are in relation to the **soccer field**. Don't confuse the soccer field with the grassy area that seems to serve as a grazing field for horses, a few hundred meters to the west field. Beaches are far from the town center (6km to Playa Guiones, 4km to Playa Pelada), and there are no buses to them.

The town has no bank or ATM, but **Supermercado Nosara,** 300m west and 400m south of the soccer field, changes US$ and traveler's checks. They can also call a cab for you. (☎2682 0141. Open M-Sa 8am-7pm, Su 8am-3pm.) The **24hr. police station** (☎2682 1104) is on the southeast corner of the field. The **Red Cross** (☎2682 0175) is next door to the police station. The **Ebais Clinic** (☎2682 0266) is 300m south of the southeast corner of the soccer field. **Paradise Medical Service** is on the east side of the field. (☎2682 0347. English spoken. Open M-F 8am-5pm, emergencies 24hr.) **Public phones** are outside the police station, just west of the soccer field, next to the post office and supermarket. **Farmacia San Antonio** is on the northwest corner of the soccer field. (☎2683 0168. Open M-F 8am-noon and 2-6pm, Sa 8am-noon and 2-5pm.) **Rey de Nosara,** on the northeast side of the field, is the most convenient place for **Internet access.** (☎2682 0215. ¢2500 per hr. Hours vary, but the owner is usually there 11am-3pm and will stay as long as you need.) The **post office** is 50m south of the southeast corner of the soccer field. (Open M-F 8am-noon and 1-5:30pm.) **Postal Code:** 5233.

ACCOMMODATIONS

Legends Bar (☎2682 0184), just north of Supermercado Nosara. Offers white rooms with just the basics: beds and a fan. Shared bath. High season singles US$12; doubles US$14. Low season singles US$7; doubles US$10; 1 apartment with A/C, private bath, and patio that sleeps up to 6 US$30. ❶

Cabinas Agnnel (☎2682 0142), 200m west of the northwest corner of the soccer field near the bus stop. Has bright-green, clean rooms with private baths and powerful ceiling fans. ¢4000 per person. US$/¢ only. ❶

FOOD

La Casona (☎2682 0442), a 7min. walk south of Rancho Tico, near the fork in the road to Ostional. Has reasonable prices and is one of the only dining options close to Nosara center. Impressed by the size of the thatched roof? Wait until you see the pizza. Pepperoni ¢4500. Open daily 12:30pm-9pm. MC/V. ❷

Soda Vanessa, 80m west of the soccer field, is a reliable place for *casados* (¢1800), cheap eggs and *gallo pinto* for breakfast (¢1200), and tasty fast food. Chicken sandwich ¢850. Fish fillet ¢2300. Open daily 6am-7pm. ❶

Legends Bar, decked out in American and Canadian sports paraphernalia, this restaurant serves a huge menu of bar food until 2am. Huge ½ lb. burger ¢2000. The best deal is a bucket of 5 beers for ¢3500 before 6pm. Open daily 11am-2am. ❶

🎵 📻 ENTERTAINMENT AND NIGHTLIFE

For those itching to bump and grind to reggaeton, **Tropicana Disco Bar,** on the northeast corner of the field, is the best place to satisfy your craving. Glow-in-the-dark drawings of popstars like Santana and Madonna hang on the walls, and a huge projector screen shows random TV channels. (Open F-Sa 9:30pm-3am.) **Bar Buena Nota,** on the southeast corner of the field, has a niche for all types: Friday and Saturday, revelers can flaunt their moves on the dance floor and at the pool table. However, most prefer the tables on the sidelines, where they can people-watch and make use of the late-night menu. (☎2682 0292. Beer ¢800. Open daily 1-11pm, later F-Sa.) If all that dancing gets in the way of your drinking, try **Bambú Bar,** on the northwest side of the field, where folks sip extra-cold Pilsens and Imperials to a solely reggae beat.

Meanwhile, a crowd of travelers heads to **Kaya Sol,** in Guiones, each night for the relaxed surfer vibe. There's live Latin funk and folk music on Wednesdays, a classic rock cover band on Thursdays, Reggae Night on Fridays, and the talented *guitarrazo* Juan Peregrino for Sunday Brunch 10am-5pm. Other locales with live music, mostly classic rock and funk, are the **Gilded Iguana** on Tuesdays and **Casa Tucan** on Thursdays from about 7 to 10pm (all in Guiones). At sunset, stop in at **Lagarta Lodge,** 4km south of central Nosara in Pelada, which offers spectacular views of Ostional, the mountains, and the forest reserve. While meals are pricey, a few drinks won't break the bank. (Sunset drinks ¢2000. Open M and W-Su 4:30-7:30pm.) **Olga's,** on the beach in Pelada, has karaoke Sunday nights, providing good fun for families and groups of friends.

PLAYA PELADA AND PLAYA GUIONES

No buses pass through here from Nosara center, so most travelers stay by the beach, hitchhiking and biking into Nosara. **Let's Go does not recommend hitchhiking.** Playa Pelada, a short crescent beach with a rocky point and some stony outcroppings breaking up the waves, has relatively calm waters that are ideal for both swimmers and beginning surfers. It is separated from Playa Guiones by a small inlet, which is filled more with crabs and tide pools than it is with people. Signs for specific establishments abound on the main road from grittier-sanded Nosara, which first branches west toward Pelada and then toward Guiones a few kilometers later. Generally, Pelada is less crowded and more private than Guiones, which is generally teeming with surfers in the high season (Dec.-Apr.). Guiones, to the south of Pelada, is referred to by its *tico* residents as "Proyecto Americano" due to the plethora of young surfers and wealthy families that are starting to call it home. Guiones also offers the longest uninterrupted coastline of all the beaches in the area and a beach break that surfing novices and pros alike will appreciate and enjoy. When the waves reflect the vast clouds during the sunset, the views are incredible.

⚑ 🛈 ORIENTATION AND PRACTICAL INFORMATION

The fastest way to travel between Pelada and Guiones on foot is to take the beach. A short trail branches inland and cuts through the woods between the beaches in order to avoid the rocks on the point (about 20min.).

Important services (buses, post office, police) are in Nosara, but the mini-mall in Guiones has most daily necessities. **Pharmacy Botiquín San Antonio** is at the mini-mall (open M-F 8am-noon and 1:30-5pm, Sa 8am-noon and 1:30-4:30pm), as is the **laundromat** (open daily 8am-noon and 1-4pm). **Banco Popular,** next to the mini-mall, gives Visa cash advances with a passport and exchanges US$ and traveler's checks. (☎2682 0011. Open M-F 8:30am-3pm, Sa 8:30am-11pm.) **Internet access** is available at the cafe (US$3 per 30min.), as are a **mailbox, phone cards,** and **public phones. Mini-Super Las Delicias** is down the road from the Gilded Iguana (open M-Sa 8am-7pm) and has phone cards.

⚲ ACCOMMODATIONS

PELADA

Hotels are spread out along the beaches, over circuitous roads, and nestled in trees. In general, accommodations tend to be pricey, but bargain options do exist for those who are willing to look. Many hotels have negotiable rates depending on the season, group size, and length of stay.

Refugio del Sol (☎2682 0287; www.refugiodelsol.com). The best bang for your buck in Pelada. Masks and local art hang on the adobe walls creating a classic Costa Rican ambience. Rooms have private baths, and 2 have kitchens. New owners have brought their *tropi europeo* cuisine and share it in the on-site restaurant, Sarah's Smile by day, Sarafina by night. My Big Fat Greek Omelette US$8, coconut salmon US$18. Hammocks line the patio. Doubles US$45; junior suite for 3 with A/C and kitchen US$65; suite for 4 with kitchen, A/C, and private terrace US$75. Cash only. ❸

Rancho Congo (☎/fax 2682 0078; rcongo@infoweb.co.cr), midway between Pelada and Guiones. Offers 2 very spacious rooms with large private baths and an above-ground pool. Though it is closer to the road than to the beach, you're more likely to hear monkeys than cars, and the flora surrounding the hotel gives it seclusion. The owner takes immaculate care of the place and serves one of the best breakfasts in town, including homemade marmalade. Laundry US$5 per load. Doubles US$50; triples US$55. ❸

Camping, on the beach in front of Olga's Restaurant, which offers showers (¢500) and the cheapest food in town. Those who camp on the beach should be careful to keep their valuables in sight. There is no guard, and theft is common. Free. ❶

GUIONES

Kaya Sol (☎2682 0080; www.kayasol.com), 100m from the beach. Oozes youth and reggae. The colorful wall murals feature mermaids watching over a pool and restaurant/bar with hammocks and TVs. More crowded than most other nearby options, it also offers 1 hexagonal bungalow with 5 beds, with shared baths and hot water, for US$10 per person. When the sun sets, you're already at the party at this social place. Yoga M-Th at 3:30pm; donation-based. *Cabinas* US$35; apartment with kitchen for 6 people US$80; beach house US$100. Get 1 night free if you stay longer than a week. Cash only. ❸

Hostel Solo Bueno (www.solobuenohostel.com), down the road from the mini-super. The only hostel in the area and a good place to meet other travelers. When bunks get full in the high season, travelers claim hammocks, couches, and even the floor for a night's rest. Shared hot-water baths. Communal kitchen. Surfboards US$15 per day. Surf lessons US$25 per hr. Bunks US$12; camping US$7 per person. Tents US$5. ❶

El Punto (☎2682 4041; www.juansurfohouserental.com; juansurfo@yahoo.com), across from Kaya Sol. 5 cute *cabinas* surrounding a *ranchito* hung with hammocks. *Cabinas* have books and fully equipped kitchens. Doubles US$45; quads US$100; apartments for 4 with kitchen, hot water, and fans US$95. Houses for rent available. Cash only. ❸

Hotel Café de Paris (☎2682 0087; www.cafeparis.net), on the main road above the mini-mall. Has a poolside restaurant and wood-paneled rooms. All rooms have A/C and fan. Doubles US$90; triples US$100, with kitchen US$120; bungalow for 4 US$180. Weekly rental US$360/480/720. AmEx/D/MC/V. ❺

Giardino Tropicale, on the main road before the mini-mall. Solar powered rooms have sinks, A/C (for an extra US$10), an outdoor lounging area, coffeemaker, fridge, hot water, and private bath. Access to a lap pool, fitness room, and Internet access. Wheelchair accessible. Breakfast US$9. High season standard single US$60; double US$80; triple US$80. Low season US$50; double US$60; triple US$70. Huge bungalows for up to 5 people with TV and kitchen also available US$120/135. AmEx/D/MC/V. ❹

🍴 FOOD

PELADA

You can find groceries and cooking supplise at **Panchos Market,** across from Refugio del Sol. (Open daily 8am-9pm.)

Olga's (☎2682 0511), only 20m from the beach. Inexpensive seafood and *comida típica*. This *tico* favorite serves *mariscos* that are brought in fresh daily. *Huevos rancheros* ₡1500. *Casados* ₡1600. Open daily 8am-10pm. Cash only. ❶

La Luna, on Playa Pelada. An international menu with a Mediterranean twist due to the Greek owner. The elegant house has a beach view. All entrees have an interesting sauce, like Thai lime coconut curry or green peppercorn. The Mediterranean platter is popular (₡4500). Great pizzas in high season (₡2400). Open daily noon-10pm. ❷

GUIONES

Rosi Soda Tica, up the hill across from Café de Paris. The smell alone will carry you here for great *comida típica*, but it's the low prices and welcome break from Nosara's typically tourist-based culture that will keep you there. *Gallo pinto* with eggs ₡1300. *Casados* ₡1600-2200. Fish soup ₡20,000. Open M-Sa 8am-3pm. Cash only. ❶

Robin's (☎2682 0617), in the mini-mall. If you find yourself craving something sweet and fresh, come here for ice cream and sorbet made on the premises. With 20 years of culinary experience under her belt, Robin offers delicious design-your-own crepes. If you're trying to keep that bikini bod, try one of the whole wheat focaccia sandwiches. Crepes ₡7500. ₡500 per topping. Avocado and hummus sandwich ₡2500. Ice cream or sorbet ₡1500 single scoop. Open 7:30am-7pm, or upon request. ❷

Giardino Tropicale (☎2682 0258). Its large pizza menu (all wood-fired) draws diners to a huge 14-seat medieval table. The carpaccio (fish in lime juice, black pepper, olive oil, celery, and garlic; ₡2700) and focaccia (₡1900) are delicious. Serves fish, chicken, and pasta entrees, and desserts à la flambé. 2-person pepperoni and ham pizza ₡5300. Open daily 7:30-9:30am and 6-10pm. Open for lunch in high season. Cash only. ❷

🎫 GUIDED TOURS

Casa Río Nosara runs horseback tours guided by true cowboys. Tour the beach, see the wildlife, and visit Maia Noche waterfall, all on horseback. Advanced riders can explore "secret" locations. Also rents canoes, bikes, and kayaks. (☎2682 0117; 3hr. horseback tour US$45.) **Boca Nosara Tours** hosts a variety of

3½hr. horseback tours. (☎2682 0280; www.bocanosaratours.com. Single US$90, 4-6 people US$60 per person.) **Nosara Boat Tours,** down the road from Lagarta Lodge in Pelada, offers birdwatching boat tours in the reserve. (☎2682 0610. Single US$60, 2 or more people US$30 per person. Reserve a day in advance.)

🖈 LOCAL ACTIVITIES

Many hotels offer various tours and rentals. Several surf shops and schools in Guiones offer board rentals and surf lessons. The **Nosara Surf Shop,** down the road from the mini-mall, rents boards (US$15-20 per day) and gives lessons (US$40 per hr.). ATV rentals available by the day (US$35-45) and by the week, with a US$150 deposit and a passport. (☎2682 0186. Open daily 7am-6pm.) **Coconut Harry's,** across from Café de Paris, rents boards for US$20 per day and gives lessons for US$45 per hr. (☎2682 0574; www.coconutharrys.com. Snorkeling gear US$5 per day. Open daily 7am-5pm.) **El Punto Surf Shop,** across from Kaya Sol, rents boards for US$15 per day. (☎2682 1081; juansurfo@yahoo.com. Lessons US$45. Open daily 8am-5pm.) Snorkeling tends to be best and calmest at nearby San Juanillo beach—ask about rentals and tours at hotels. There are some natural waterfalls with swimming holes (the falling water makes for an intense all-natural massage) during the rainy season in the hills behind Nosara; call the **The Gilded Iguana,** near Guiones (☎2682 4089, ask for Joe Davis). If you're just trying to find a secluded piece of beach to call your own, take the 1-2hr. hike past Playa Guiones to the pink beach of **Playa Rosada.** Ask for directions at the hotels on your way south. Take a walk or guided tour (US$6 self-guided, US$12 with guide) in the biological reserve run by Lagarto Lodge in Pelada, where encounters with the local wildlife are common and the birdwatching is fantastic. Multiple, well-marked trails take about 2hr. to hike (entrance US$6). One of the town's most unique meditation spots is the **Nosara Yoga Institute,** which draws large numbers of aspiring yoga teachers to Nosara with its month-long training sessions. Single classes are open to the public (US$30) in a stunning studio in the treetops of Nosara. The institute's main office is in Guiones's mini-mall (as are the monthly schedules), but the studio is a 5min. walk south down the main road past Café de Paris. Follow the signs on your right. (☎2682 0071; www.nosarayoga.com. 1hr. public classes US$10. Office open M-F 8:30am-4:30pm, Sa 9am-3pm.)

OSTIONAL

This gritty strip of black-sand beach is Costa Rica's most important breeding ground for olive ridley turtles. During the moon's fourth quarter, female turtles flock here by the thousands to lay their eggs. During this time, the tiny town comes to life: the few modest hotels in the area fill up and the fires at the two restaurants remain lit. Luckily, daytrips to Ostional from Nosara, Sámara, and even Tamarindo are available.

📧 **TRANSPORTATION.** The trip between Nosara and Ostional (8km) makes for a pleasant 1hr. **bike** ride over dirt roads lined with cow pastures; bring a buddy. Alternatively, hop on one of the many **buses** from the bigger hotels in the surrounding towns. One bus makes the bouncy 3hr. ride between **Santa Cruz** and Ostional, leaving from Cabinas Guacamaya in Ostional and stopping at all the small towns along the way. (5, 7am, 4pm; from the *mercado* in Santa Cruz 12:30 and 4pm. It passes through Restaurante Las Tucas in **Paraíso** at 1pm. ¢2100.) The bus can't make the trip during heavy rains. Some travelers report finding rides, though *Let's Go* never recommends hitchhiking. Inquire for a **taxi** at local businesses, like Soda Conchito.

⚡ ACCOMMODATIONS AND FOOD. Cabinas Guacamaya ❶, 150m south of Soda La Plaza, is the best deal in Ostional, with spacious orange rooms that have private baths, fans, and large patios. (☎2682 0430. ¢4000 per person.) **Arribadas ❷,** across and slightly to the left of Soda La Plaza (p. 244), offers more amenities for a higher price. Each of the five rooms has a private bath with hot water and large windows. (☎8816 9815; www.hostcasaatmos.com. Breakfast included. Kitchen available. Two computers with internet available. Free Wi-Fi. Rooms ¢14,313/US$25 per person.) **Cabinas Ostional ❷,** across from Soda La Plaza, has simple triples and quads with private baths, a few hammocks, and small, private porches. The reception area is hidden, so just walk straight across from Soda La Plaza. (☎2682 0428. ¢5000 per person.) **Camping ❶** is allowed during the summer for ¢2,290/US$4 per day. You'll need to speak with the guard and pay at the ADIO booth, 150m to the left of Soda La Plaza when facing the beach. (Portable outdoor toilet.)

The central **Soda La Plaza ❶** is one of the few restaurants in town and has a menu of all the *típico* staples at bargain prices. (*Casados* ¢2500. *Batidos*—fresh fruit juice shakes—¢500. Open daily 7am-8:30pm.) An attached **pulpería** stocks snacks and very basic cooking supplies. (Open daily 6:30am-noon and 2-7pm.) **Tony ❷,** next door to Cabinas Guacamaya, is your only other option and a break from the ubiquitous *casado*. Favorites include the Thai chicken (¢3900) or one of the many pizzas (¢4200). Free Wi-Fi for customers. (Open daily noon-10pm.)

⚡ OUTDOOR ACTIVITIES. Turtles come almost every night in small numbers, beginning around 9pm. During the moon's fourth quarter is the **arribada** or **flota,** the synchronized arrival of thousands of turtles to a specific section of the beach. In those special periods (generally 3-8 days) when the *arribada* occurs, most turtles arrive at the beach between 3pm and 7am. They travel from as far away as Peru and Baja California to give their offspring a chance to begin life in the same place they themselves were born. This makes Ostional the second largest olive ridley sea turtle breeding ground in the world. During the *arribada*, the sand is barely visible beneath the massive number of turtles digging cozy holes for their eggs. With guides holding red lights, you can watch a mother turtle dig a hole, drop all her eggs, scramble to cover the hole, and then camouflage it. This fascinating process takes about 30min. Including the ascent to the laying spot and return to the water, expect a viewing to last about an hour and fifteen minutes. Sometimes the beach gets so full with turtles that they overflow onto the town's roads. To make sure you don't miss this event, contact biologist Rodrigo Morera (☎ 682 0470; www.ostionalcr.tripod. com/index.html) at **La Asociación de Desarollo Integral de Ostional,** 100m north of Soda La Plaza. The **National Wildlife Directorate** (☎8233 8112 or 8222 9533) can also provide information about the *arribada*. You can also check in with the tourist agencies in Nosara or Sámara. If you do miss the *arribada*, wait a few weeks to see the baby turtles make their way to the water. During the *arribada* and at night, **guides are required.** Contact Rodrigo Morera, who can refer you to a guide, or any tourist agency in the area. (¢5,725/US$10. 10-person maximum per group. Flash cameras, flashlights, and surfing are prohibited during the *arribada*.) You will not be able to see the many crabs that roam the beach in the dark, so wear closed-toed shoes. To learn more about the volunteer opportunities available here, contact Rodrigo Morera. Fore more information on volunteering in Costa Rica, see **Beyond Tourism,** p. 60.

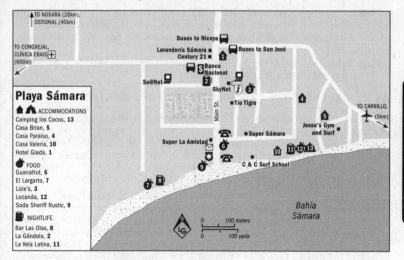

Playa Sámara

▲ ⌂ ACCOMMODATIONS
Camping los Cocos, **13**
Casa Brian, **5**
Casa Paraíso, **4**
Casa Valeria, **10**
Hotel Giada, **1**

🍴 FOOD
Guanafrut, **6**
El Largarto, **7**
Lizie's, **3**
Locanda, **12**
Soda Sheriff Rustic, **9**

🍸 NIGHTLIFE
Bar Las Olas, **8**
La Góndola, **2**
La Vela Latina, **11**

PLAYA SÁMARA

Sámara has always been, and remains to this day, a *tico* beach. Come holiday time, *tico* families flock to its sandy shore and pristine blue waters. Protected by a reef, the beach is swimmable, and its gentle, shallow waves are perfect for beginning surfers. The arrival of a language school has attracted loads of foreigners, evident by the restaurant menus, which are often translated into many languages. Even with the impending development by a large international population, Sámara still has managed to remain quieter and more authentic than many of Costa Rica's better-known hot spots.

▐ TRANSPORTATION

Since the roads in the southwestern Nicoya Peninsula are in poor shape, getting to Sámara on public transportation from Montezuma or Mal País in the southern Nicoya Peninsula involves going back to Paquera, catching the ferry to Puntarenas, taking a bus to Nicoya, and then taking a final bus to Sámara. Even if you're on the first bus to Paquera in the morning, you'll likely have to spend the night in the town of Nicoya and catch a bus to Sámara the next morning. You'll be better off arranging for private transportation to Sámara in a 4WD vehicle or coming via bus from San José (5hr., 12 per day 6am-6pm, ¢3050), Liberia, Tamarindo, or other points in northwestern Costa Rica.

Flights: Sansa flies from San José to **Sámara** (45min., 8:23am, US$89) and back to **San José** (9:43am). Book at SkyNet Tours, Hotel Giada, or call ☎2656 0131.

Buses: Complete schedule posted in SkyNet Tours on the main drag near Century 21. Buses drop passengers in front of Hotel Giada on the main drag or just past the soccer field. Buses leave from San José to **Sámara** (6hr., 12 per day 6am-6pm, ¢3050) and back (11 per day 3am-5:30pm, Su extra 3pm bus and no 4:30am bus). Buy San José tickets at least 1 day in advance at the Alfaro office just northeast of Hotel Giada. (Open M-Sa 4:30am-8:30am, Su 8:30am-3pm.) Buses leave for **Nicoya** via **Congregal,** a tiny village 1km west, (1hr.; M-Sa 11 per day 4am-5:30pm, Su 9 per day 6:30am-5:30pm; ¢650). Buses from Nicoya to **Sámara** (M-Sa 13 per day 5am-9:45pm, Su 11 per day 6am-8pm) continue on to **Carrillo,** 8km east (25min., ¢350). Pay on bus. Buses to

Nósara leave from a gas station 5km from the town center. (Ask the driver to stop at La Bomba; 1hr.; 5, 7am, noon, 3pm; ¢600.) Interbus (☎2283 5573) offers shuttles to tourist destinations like **Mal País, Monteverde, Quepos** and **San José,** among others (most US$35). Book at most hotels as well as at SkyNet Tours.

Taxis: No local number, but the town lists numbers of specific taxis (☎8356 4288, 8390 3271, and 8656 0802). To **La Bomba** US$6.

◄▓ ▧ ORIENTATION AND PRACTICAL INFORMATION

Playa Sámara is on the west coast of the southern Nicoya Peninsula, 8km east of Playa Carrillo and 35km southwest of Nicoya. **Main Street** runs south into town, is crossed by two main side streets, and ends just before the beach; orient yourself by remembering that the beach is south. *Cabinas*, hotels, restaurants, and houses line the beach going east of Main St. Another road branches off the main drag to the west and leads to the tiny village of **Congrejal.**

Tourist Office: Most hotels have an abundance of information, but **SkyNet Tours** (☎2656 0920; www.samaratours.com), 20m south and across the street from Century 21, is the best place in town to help direct you to the tour that's right for you with their numerous excursion options. Books tours, flights, hotels and buses. Rent scooters (US$35 per day) and bikes (US$12 per day). Book exchange and Internet available as well (¢800 per 30min.). Open daily 8:30am-9:30pm. Sámara also has a collective website, **www.samarabeach.com,** with information and links for tourists.

Bank: Banco Nacional (☎2656 0089), across from Century 21, on the road that branches west from Main St. **24hr. ATM.** Open M-F 8:30am-3:45pm.

English-Language Bookstore: Koss Art Gallery, a 500m walk east along the beach. Keeps a few English-language paperbacks for exchange. Usually open M-Sa 9am-5pm.

Laundry: Lavanderia Sámara, across from Hotel Giada. US$2 per kg. Open M-Sa 8:30am-5:30am.

Police: (☎2656 0436), at the far south end of Main St., near the beach.

Pharmacy: Farmacia Sámara (☎2656 0727), across from Century 21. Open daily 9am-5pm.

Telephones: Common around town, especially near the beach on the main drag. **Hotel Giada** has a credit card phone for calls to Canada and the US.

Internet Access: At **SkyNet Tours** (¢800 per 30min.; open daily 8:30am-9:30pm). **Se@ net,** on the north side of the soccer field (¢800 per 30min.; open daily 8am-8pm).

Post Office: Next to the police station at the far south end of the main drag. Open M-F 8am-noon and 1:15-5:30pm. **Postal Code:** 5235.

▐▀ ▞ ACCOMMODATIONS AND CAMPING

Because of its popularity with all kinds of travelers, from backpackers to pampered tourists to vacationing *tico* families, Sámara has accommodations to fit every budget. Many offer similar quality and amenities at similar prices. If the first place you check is full, just walk a little farther down the road.

▓ **Casa Brian** (☎2656 0315; afro_dad@hotmail.com), 1km east on the beach in the beginning of Matapalo. The only hostel in town. The owner, Brian, makes you feel like family with stories, a communal kitchen, long dining room table, and complimentary breakfast. A room with 3 bunk beds shares a bath. Private bedrooms are available with a double bed, bath, mosquito net, and fan. At 20m to the beach and a common space with hammocks, chairs and books, it is clear why many people intend on coming for a day but stay for months. Brian uses part of his profits to give back to the community, such as buying computers for local schools. Bunks US$15; private rooms US$35. ❷

Casa Valeria (☎2656 0511), 50m east of Super Sámara on the side street closest to the beach. The best rooms are the *casitas* (little houses) set apart from the rest of the hotel. However, even the simpler rooms are cozy—pink walls, ceiling fans, patios, and hot-water baths. Fully stocked communal kitchen, large dining area, and a beachside dining area with hammocks and chairs. Doubles US$25, with TV, A/C, and fridge US$35, 3 person max.; *casitas* US$50/60, 4 person max. US$5 more for each person. ❷

Casa Paraíso (☎2656 0741; hotelcasaparaiso@hotmail.com), down the street from Super Sámara. Sports the cheapest private rooms in town. Good deal for solo travelers. Private hot-water baths, comfortable beds, and patios in every room. Parking, free coffee, and communal kitchen available. US$20 per person. ❷

Hotel Giada (☎2656 0132; www.hotelgiada.net), 300m north of the beach on the main drag. One of Sámara's nicer options, full of international students from nearby language schools. The spacious rooms have comfortable beds, bamboo furniture, private balconies, and hot-water baths. Breakfast is included near one of the 2 pools. High season singles US$60; doubles US$85; triples US$95; quads US$105. Low season singles US$50; doubles US$75; triples US$90; quads US$100. AmEx/D/MC/V. ❹

Camping Los Cocos (☎2656 0496), 300m east of the main drag. The best campsite in town, with shady palms and sandy floors. Small covered patio for campers who want to stay dry. Showers, sinks, and bathrooms. Electricity until 10pm. ¢2500 per person. ❶

🍴 FOOD

Sámara's increasing population of foreigners has resulted in the increasing popularity of ethnic cuisine and multilingual menus among area restaurants. Not surprisingly, everything is a bit pricier, but the food is generally worth it, and the beachfront cafes have picture-perfect views. **Super La Amistad,** on Main St. next to the police station, is the cheapest market and has a great selection. (Open daily 7am-8pm.) **Super Sámara,** 100m east on a road off of Main St., is a little more comprehensive. (Open daily 7:30am-9pm.)

🍴 **Guanafrut,** across from Super Sámara, sells a beautiful selection of raw fruit and vegetables, and makes fantastic *batidos* (¢500-800). Try the fruit plate, a selection of seasonal fruit that includes especially delicious mangoes (¢1000)—it's the perfect refresher after a day in the sun. Open daily 7am-7pm. ❶

🍴 **Lizie's,** take a left on the road just after Guanafrut and then the next right. Offers a large, spunky menu that will satiate any craving—from sushi to *gallo pinto* with the Tropical Typical Tico Breakfast (*pinto*, eggs, bacon, fried Turrialba cheese, and *picadillo; ¢2500*). Each dish is crafted beautifully, even the veggie quesadilla (¢2800). Sip one of the crazy mixed drinks like the Cool Lizie (Midori, peach schnapps, vanilla, ice cream, and blue curacao ¢2200) in the spacious, covered gazebo beside a charming bridge that hops over the small stream and garden. Free Wi-Fi. Open daily 7am-10pm. ❷

Locanda (☎2656 0036; www.locandsamara.com), next to La Vela Latina on the beach. Has the biggest cups of coffee and the best *gallo pinto* (with eggs; ¢1800) in Sámara. The reclined chairs sink into the sand and are shaded by coconut trees. The perfect setting to watch surfers ride the waves with a Locanda Sunset (Cacique, pineapple juice, and grenadine; ¢2000) during happy hour (3-6pm, buy 2 get 3rd free). Offers *casados* (¢3000), lasagna (¢4500), and lamb red curry (¢4200). Open daily 7am-10pm. ❷

Soda Sheriff Rustic, at the south end of the main drag. Beach-lovers in bathing suits sit on chairs chiseled from tree stumps for tasty *casados* (¢2900) and fish specials (¢3000). Papaya-pineapple-mango *batidos* ¢700. Open daily 7:30am-3:30pm. ❷

El Lagarto (☎2656 0750; signa5@hotmail.com), on the beach, 250m west of main drag. Offers vegetables, seafood, chicken, and meat fresh from the wood-fire grill. The wood table under trees right on the beach is the perfect place to celebrate a special occasion. Start off your meal with mussels in white wine and garlic sauce (US$7.50) and then enjoy the steak tenderloin (US$15.50-17.50), chicken (US$7.50), or mixed mushrooms (US$10). If you still have room, try the homemade lemon pie (US$4.50) or cheesecake (US$5). Large mixed drink selection. Vanilla Sky (rum, Bailey's, vanilla ice cream, and whipped cream) US$6.50. Open daily 5-11pm. AmEx/D/V/MC. ❸

NIGHTLIFE

Sámara's nightlife is lively and crowded during the high season and school holidays, when teenagers from nearby Nicoya pack the beachside bars and lounges. In the low season, count on smaller crowds, composed primarily of foreign students from the language school.

Bar Las Olas (☎2656 1100), on the beach before El Lagarto. Whether it's the midday crowd playing pool or the more energetic dance throng on Th, F and Sa, this place is a local hot spot attracting students and tourists. Beer ₡1000. Open daily 11am-2:30am.

La Góndola, 175m north of the beach on the main road. A prime spot for games and revelry of all sorts. Pool, darts, foosball, and ping-pong entertain crowds. The genre of music varies nightly, depending on what the crowd wants to hear. Live bands and special shows weekly during high season. Beer ₡1000. Open M-Sa 5:30pm-2am.

La Vela Latina, on the beach 200m east of Main St. The best place to meet other young travelers. Open in the late afternoon for drinks, it draws a slightly more mellow crowd to its leather-covered rocking chairs. After sunset, international travelers and students from the language school mingle while hip hop, reggae, and rock selections play in the background. Occasional bonfire parties. Appetizers served until 10pm. Open daily 8am-late.

OUTDOOR ACTIVITIES AND GUIDED TOURS

If you tire of the beach, several hotels and tour operators can offer tours and trips to suit every interest. Most are geared toward the water, as there is excellent fishing, snorkeling, and surfing nearby. Dolphin-watching is also popular; when they migrate along the coast they often get quite close to the shore.

Jesse's Gym and Surf (☎8373 3006), 500m east of the main drag, next to Koss Art Gallery and 20m back from the beach. Although the original Sámara surf school retained its name, Jimmy, one of the best surfers in Costa Rica, runs the place. Has weights and machines if you need to work out (US$5 per day, weekly and monthly rates and personal instruction available). Rents surfboards (US$6 per hr., US$20 per day) and boogie boards (US$3) and offers surf lessons (1hr. lesson plus 1hr. with a board US$40, additional 1hr. US$5). Beach yoga 7:30am (US$10, lessons US$20. 3 lessons, board, and access to yoga and gym for a week US$140. Open daily sunrise-sunset. Cash only.

Tío Tigre (☎2656 0098, 2656 1060, or 8372 6521), 100m north of Hotel Casa del Mar. A friendly staff leads dolphin tours (US$45, 4-person min.), kayaking, and snorkeling tours (US$30-45), inshore fishing (US$200 per boat, 2-person max.), and combinations of the 4. Open daily 8am-6pm. MC/V.

C&C Surf School (☎2656 0628; www.samarasurfcamp.com), the rival school to Jesse's. Rents boards for slightly higher prices, but donates 10% to the Turtle Project in Buena Vista and to schools in Sámara. Boards US$4 per hr., US$20 per day. Lessons US$30.

PLAYA CARRILLO

Anyone seeking beautiful, palm-lined beaches with white sand and calm waves will probably find Carrillo euphoric. It is also significantly less developed than its budding neighbor Sámara. It is popular with *Samareños* escaping the tourists. Grab this tranquility while you can, as plans are developing for 10-story condos and a boardwalk crammed with shops. Occasionally, sun-worshippers share the beach with fishermen who like to anchor their boats in the bay's shallow waters, but you'll almost always be able to find a little patch of shore to call your own. If you can't spend much time here, at least swing by in the evening to witness some of the country's best sunsets from the hills of the village.

TRANSPORTATION. The easiest way to get to Carrillo from San José is by **plane** (same flight info as Sámara, p. 245). Flights arrive at the small airstrip right in front of the beach. Transportation between Carrillo and Sámara has improved since the construction of a well-paved road that winds between the two towns. **Buses** from Sámara to Carrillo (15min.; M-Sa 13 per day 6am-10:45pm, Su 10 per day 7am-9:30pm; ¢350) leave from outside Hotel Giada and drive east into Carrillo, stopping near the beach before ascending a steep hill and dropping off passengers on the main street. To get back to Sámara, flag a bus down near the intersection of the beach road and the main drag (M-Sa 13 per day 4am-5:45pm, Su 9 per day 6:45am-5pm; ¢350). You can also **walk** (45min.) to Playa Carrillo east along Playa Sámara through a small trail that cuts through the cliff between the two. **Carrillo Tours** has private shuttles to major tourist destinations. (☎2656 0543; www.carrillotours.com. Prices are listed by the bus, 8-person max. Liberia US$110, San José US$200, among others. Open daily 7am-6pm.) Schedules change often, so check for the most up-to-date times. If you find you need a **taxi**, have a hotel call one for you.

ORIENTATION AND PRACTICAL INFORMATION. Playa Carrillo is tucked in a small, protected bay about 8km southeast of Sámara. Unlike most beachside towns, the main drag does not end on the sand. A palm tree-lined road runs parallel to the beach but turns up a hill into the village of Carrillo, which leads for about 500m along a road that starts about 200m from the beach. Walking on the main street away from the beach, you'll be facing north.

Most services are in Sámara, so take care of essentials before coming. **Carrillo Tours** (p. 249) has **Internet access. Onda Latina** (☎2656 0434; ondalatinainternet@ gmail.com), 100m past Hotel Esperanza, has services for Internet access (¢800 for 30min., ¢1200 per hr.), international calls (US$0.33 per minute), copies (¢30, ¢200 for color), fax (¢150 national or same price as international call), and office supplies. Also has mini-golf course in back (¢1200 per person).

ACCOMMODATIONS. Staying in Carrillo is quieter and more relaxed than Sámara, but it can be expensive. **Cabinas Congo Real ❸**, just west on the street past Hotel Esperanza, has the best deal in town. Cute rooms with mixed-pattern decorations have fully equipped private kitchens. (☎2656 0608. Doubles US$26, with kitchen US$40, each additional person US$3.) **Popo's ❹**, just past Cabinas Congo Real, has two treehouse *cabinas* elevated on stilts that make you feel one with your tropical surroundings. Each room has reading lamps and access to a private bar, fridge, and kitchenette in a large thatched *rancho*. (☎2656 0086. CantrellTad@yahoo.com. High season US$65; low season US$55, each additional person US$10.) **Cabinas El Colibrí ❷** is around the corner from the side street past Hotel Esperanza. A good option for large groups, Colibrí's spacious rooms (3 with kitchens) have hot water, A/C, and private porches with hammocks, tables, and benches separated by wooden screens. The rooms themselves are all decorated in slightly different ways and have huge shelving units. (☎2656 0656; www.hotelcabinaselcolibri.com. Restaurant on-site. High-/ low season doubles US$25/20; triples US$30/25; quads US$35/30. US$/¢.)

FOOD. The **MiniSuper** is conveniently the closest store to the beach, 50m up the hill next to Carrillo Tours. (Open daily 7am-6pm.) Palm trees provide shade, making the beach a perfect and popular place to picnic. Most local dives glean their charm from the sea—ocean views and fresh seafood delight sunworn travelers at restaurants all along the shore. **Pizzería El Tucán ❷**, 50m east on the road across from Hotel Esperanza, offers a secluded atmosphere and good Italian food. Soul and bluegrass music will keep you entertained while your four-cheese pizza (¢4800-5700) is baking. (☎2656 0305. Pasta gorgonzola ¢3600. Open daily 5-10:30pm. US$/¢ only.) The Argentine owners of the restaurant attached to **Cabinas Colibrí ❷** make "classics" like meat with bread crumbs (¢3500) and *choripan* (sausage sandwich and chimichurri, ¢850) from an oven located right in the main dining area. (☎2656 0656. Open daily 6-10pm. MC/V.) Further down the road, on the south side of the soccer field, is **Soda La Plaza ❶**, which serves basic *comida típica* at budget prices. (*Gallo pinto* breakfast ¢1500. Fish fillet ¢3000. *Casados* ¢2500. Open daily 7am-9:30pm.)

⚠📷 OUTDOOR ACTIVITIES AND GUIDED TOURS. Carrillo Tours, 100m up the main drag, runs tours around Carrillo and beyond, including trips to Monteverde Cloud Forest and Arenal (about US$150), kayaking/snorkeling in Playa Camaronal and Río Ora (US$45-50), Playa Ostional and Camaronal turtle nesting excursions (US$35-40), canopy tours (US$85), Palo Verde National Park and crocodile tours (US$85), Barra Honda National Park tours (US$85), dolphin tours (US$160 per boat, 5-person max.), and horseback rides (US$35). (☎2656 0543; www.carrillotours.com. Open daily 7am-6pm.) **Kingfisher Sportfishing,** east on the road past Pizzeria El Tucan, takes fishermen out on their 10m boat. (☎2656 0091; www.costaricabillfishing.com. ½-day US$700, full-day US$900.) **Kitty Cat,** 200m north up the main drag, is manned by "Captain Rob," who runs trips on his custom-built, 28 ft. aluminum sportfisher. Hotel Esperanza and Hotel Guanamar can also book tours and help with information.

PLAYA CARRILLO TO MAL PAÍS

The 30km stretch of coastline extending south of Playa Carrillo to the southern tip of the Nicoya Peninsula is one of Costa Rica's least-traversed areas. After the well-paved section from Carillo to Estrada (before Punta Islita), which curves up an enchanting hill, the road here becomes rough, signs start to dwindle, and public transportation disappears. Those attempting the drive should prepare with a sturdy 4WD vehicle. At the road's best, you'll be bouncing along a caked lane with steep potholes that will intermittently turn to gravel; during the worst days of the rainy season, expect to be window-deep in rivers. Make sure to speak with locals for current river and road conditions before starting the trek. Fuel up on gas before and bring along all the supplies you'll need. That said, the drive is spectacular and full of adventure. The coast hides some of Costa Rica's picture-perfect beaches, and the area's inaccessibility means you'll have little trouble escaping crowds.

📷 BEACHES

PLAYA CAMARONAL. About 8km south of Playa Carrillo is Playa Camaronal, a gorgeous, 3km rock-engulfed beach stretching from the mouth of the Río Ora in the west to the cliffs of Point Camaronal in the southeast. Local surfers from Sámara and Carrillo rave about its strong and consistent left and right beach breaks, but it remains almost completely unknown by travelers who opt for more-touristed and accessible surf spots. In fact, it is not unusual to be the only person there. Even non-surfers can revel in the seclusion and scenery that define Playa Camaronal; the dark-brown-sand beach is surrounded by volcanic hills covered with exotic vegetation like spiny cedar, stinking toe (a Caribbean fruit), and balsa wood. In addition, leatherback and Pacific ridley sea turtles use the beach to lay their eggs in the rainy season. Camaronal has no facilities, but camping is possible near **Playa Vuelta del Sur,** on the other side of the river, and the **Refugio Nacional de Vida Silvestre Camaronal,** 200m after the Camaronal Quebrada estuary, has showers, bathrooms, and potable water (US$4). Those without their own wheels can take a boat ride here from a tour operator in Playa Carrillo (p. 248) or Playa Sámara (p. 245). Volunteer opportunities are available at the **Refugio Nacional de Vida Silvestre Camaronal.** Contact either Julian Garcia or Dominica Alarcon (☎8332 3339).

PUNTA ISLITA AND PLAYA COROZALITO. These two little beaches are just 5km farther down the coast from Camaronal and 15km southeast of Carrillo. Cattle ranching is the area's primary activity, and a sparse local population lives in tiny hamlets scattered at the foot of the hills. Islita and Corozalito are separated by volcanic rocks more than 80 million years old. Islita, with a shore that is barely 1km long in a protected bay, is fed by two clean streams ideal for swimming and boogie boarding. After driving down a bumpy, windy road with small turnoffs to admire the stunning views, you will come to neighboring Corozalito, which is a swampier 1.5km area with an estuary, mangroves, and fresh water. Both sections of coastline have rough cliffs and tide pools that harbor an exotic collection of brilliantly colored fish and sea urchins. Driving between Islita and Corozalito, you'll pass Barranquilla Ranch. Just north of here is a 5km mule track that ascends over 500m to **Potal Peak,** from where you can enjoy a fantastic view of over 20km of Nicoya coastline. The only real services in the area are at a posh luxury hotel frequented by honeymooners and resort hoppers in search of ultimate peace and quiet. Islita also has an **airstrip;** book flights through NatureAir or Sansa from San José (p. 83).

PLAYA SAN MIGUEL. The gray sands of little-known San Miguel are 4km from Bejuco and 21km southeast of Carrillo. In addition to a secluded bay nestled in the shadows of an imposing mountain range, San Miguel has a small lagoon with calm waters and a sandy bottom that's perfect for wading. Parrots and armadillos are among the most-commonly sighted animals in the area.

PLAYA COYOTE. Of the beaches along this stretch of coastline, Playa Coyote is among the most-frequently visited, although you'll still find very few people who have made the trek out. The large horseshoe bay and small village, San Francisco de Coyote, are about 5km down the coast from San Miguel and 26km from Carrillo, almost exactly halfway between Sámara and Mal País. The beach is picture-perfect, with soft sands, a wide bay fringed by coconut trees, and water so shallow you can sometimes walk 200m into the sea and still stand on your feet. Just past the beach near Punta Coyote, a 20min. walk along the rocky beach formations, is an excellent surf spot often overlooked because it is not visible from the beach. The right point and the long break are the most popular. Coyote has a few small bars, restaurants, supermarkets, and an **Internet cafe** in the village 5km north of the beach. There are also some basic *cabinas,* like **El Muco** (☎2656 1015; US$20, 3-person max.; private bath and fan),

PLAYA MANZANILLO. About 42km southeast of Carrillo, Manzanillo is the last spot along the coast before Mal País, about 5km south. Mal País locals can't stop praising Manzanillo for its idyllic beach, whose sands are draped by stout palms and twisted almond trees. Though low tide exposes some risky ocean rocks, you can wade, swim, and snorkel in the tide pools between them. Most people come from Mal País either by driving through river estuaries or by biking 1hr. past Santa Teresa. Coming from the north is impossible during the rainy season, as the river between Coyote and Manzanillo overflows. Instead, drivers must take a 2hr. route around the river. The roads are often impassable in the rainy season, however, so ask locals about conditions before heading off.

MAL PAÍS AND SANTA TERESA

Don't be fooled by the name of this remote surfing village near the southern tip of the Nicoya Peninsula; with long, empty beaches, stunning rock formations, and scenic coves, Mal País is hardly a "bad country." Settled by a small community of locals and currently home to a growing contingent of foreigners, this area is slowly developing into a haven for excellent ethnic restaurants and unique accommodations. You'll find more hotels, restaurants, and shops clumped together in Santa Teresa. Bad roads can make travel to Mal País difficult and time-consuming, but the constant surf and peaceful vibe make the trip worth the effort.

TRANSPORTATION

Buses: Most travelers take the **ferry** from Puntarenas to **Paquera** and drive directly to Mal País, or take buses directly to **Cóbano** (2hr., 7 per day 6am-7pm, ₡1200). If you're lucky, there may be extra space on the **San José** bus coming off the ferry that will go directly to Mal País. You can also head first to **Montezuma** and then take buses to Mal País. From Montezuma, take the bus to **Cóbano** (15min., 6 per day 5:30am-4pm, ₡300) and catch a connecting bus from the same stop to **Santa Teresa** via **Mal País** (1hr.; 10:30am, 2:30pm; ₡700). Return buses leave from Santa Teresa and pick passengers up at hotels and the main crossroads by Frank's Place before heading back to **Cóbano** (7:30, 11:30am, 3:30pm). Buses leave from Frank's Place to **San José** (M-F 5:45am, Sa-Su 5:45, 8:15am, 3:45pm; ₡6500). Ask your accommodation for more information about bus stops in town.

Taxis: Taxis drive around town but are not common. If you can't find one, call a local taxi (☎8819 9021). Taxis to **Cóbano** ₡8588 (US$15) leave from the intersection.

Private Transportation: Bad roads and infrequent public transportation make moving on from Mal País time-consuming and complicated, so transfer services, though expensive, may prove well worth it for the convenience. **Montezuma Expeditions** (☎2642 0919), which can be booked at **Tropical Tours** (☎2640 0384) by the crossroads, has shuttles to major destinations (Arenal, Jacó, Manuel Antonio, Monteverde, San José, Tamarindo; ₡22,900-25,763/US$40-45) and can arrange other shuttles. Most leave around 8am.

Car Rental: Alamo (☎2640 0526), on the right, on the road into town from Cobano. Rentals from ₡22,900 (US$40). 21+. Open daily 8am-5pm. **Budget** (☎2640 0500), 100m from Frank's Place on the road to Santa Teresa. Rentals from ₡25,763 (US$45). 21+. Open M-Sa 8am-6pm, Su 8am-4pm.

Bike and ATV Rentals: Getting around Mal País is easiest with a **bike** or **4WD vehicle. Alex's Surf Shop** (☎2640 0364), 600m toward Santa Teresa from the main intersection, rents bikes for ₡5725/US$10 per day and quads for ₡34,350/US$60 per day. Open daily 8am-6:30pm. MC/V. In Mal País, **Isla Red Snapper** (☎2640 0490), 400m south of Mal País Surf School and Resort. Look for a sign that says "bikes, sportfishing, snorkeling." Low-season bikes ₡4580 (US$8); high-season ₡5725 (US$10). **Tropical Tours** (☎2640 0384). ATVs for ₡25,763 (US$45) per 6hr., ₡31,488 (US$55) per 10hr., ₡42,938 (US$75) per 24hr.

ORIENTATION AND PRACTICAL INFORMATION

The area that most surfers and locals refer to as Mal País is actually three separate beaches stretching along 6km of shoreline on the southwest corner of the Nicoya Peninsula, 11km southwest of Cóbano. Buses from Cóbano stop first at the **crossroads,** which marks the center of the bumpy **dirt road** that runs parallel to the beaches. All accommodations and services are off this main drag. The

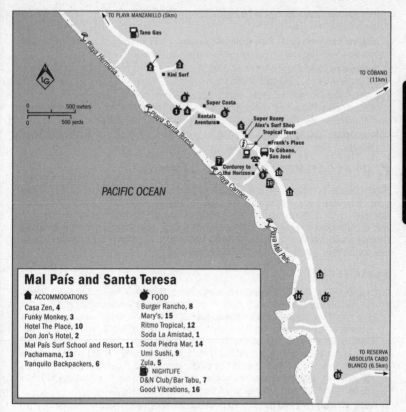

NICOYA PENINSULA

Mal País and Santa Teresa

🏠 ACCOMMODATIONS
Casa Zen, **4**
Funky Monkey, **3**
Hotel The Place, **10**
Don Jon's Hotel, **2**
Mal País Surf School and Resort, **11**
Pachamama, **13**
Tranquilo Backpackers, **6**

🍎 FOOD
Burger Rancho, **8**
Mary's, **15**
Ritmo Tropical, **12**
Soda La Amistad, **1**
Soda Piedra Mar, **14**
Umi Sushi, **9**
Zula, **5**

🌙 NIGHTLIFE
D&N Club/Bar Tabu, **7**
Good Vibrations, **16**

closest thing you'll find to a town center is at this main crossroads and just to the right into **Santa Teresa,** which stretches 3km north. On the opposite end from the crossroads, **Mal País** stretches 3km south, ending at the tiny marina where fishermen unload their daily catch. Establishments are pretty spread out in Mal País. **Playa Carmen** is 100m west, down a gravel road in front of the bus stop.

Tourist Office: Tropical Tours (☎2640 0384 or 1900). 2 locations, 1 by Frank's Place and the other by Super Ronny. The most comprehensive tourist information center, offering private transportation, internet, and organized tours. Open daily 8am-8pm. Hotels and various surf shops are also glad to help with information and book tours.

Currency Exchange: Banco Nacional (☎2640 0640), in the Playa Carmen Mall, 50m north of the main intersection. **24hr. ATM.** Open M-Sa 1pm-7pm. **Banco Costa Rica** (☎2640 1019), to the left of Frank's Place. **Currency exchange** and **ATM.** Open M-F 9am-4pm.

Laundry: Many hotels and hostels do laundry for their guests, but locals often offer cheaper rates. Heading north toward Santa Teresa from the main intersection, look for the many signs on the right advertising laundry. Most places charge around ₡1000 per kg.

Gas Station: Tano (☎2641 0009), 3km toward Santa Teresa. Open M-Sa 7am-5pm.

Police: ☎911 or 117.

Pharmacies: Amiga Farmacia (☎2640 0539), next to the Banco Nacional. Open M-Sa 8am-8pm. AmEx/MC/V.

Medical Services: Costa Rica Medical Response (☎2640 0976 or 2417), in the Playa Carmen Mall. The only clinic in the area. English spoken. Open 24hr.

Telephones: Several along the main drag, at the crossroads, and at Super Santa Teresa. Super Ronny's (p. 255) sells phone cards.

Internet Access: Tropical Tours, next to Super Ronny's. ¢1500 per hr. Open daily 8am-9pm. **Frank's Place** has similar rates. Open daily 8am-6pm. Other options throughout Santa Teresa. Many restaurants offer free Wi-Fi with purchase of a meal.

Post Office: Closest full-service office is in Cóbano, but there's a **mailbox** at **Pizza Tomate,** 1.5km toward Santa Teresa.

ACCOMMODATIONS AND CAMPING

Santa Teresa is where you'll find most of the budget places, while Mal País has several newer and more upscale options. Many rooms come equipped with full kitchens to accommodate surfers, many of whom stay for weeks at a time. A few camping areas provide sandy grounds for the bare-bones traveler. **Zeneida's Cabinas y Camping ❶** is a good option on the beach. Sites have bathrooms, showers, and water. (☎2640 0118. ¢2000 per person.)

SANTA TERESA

▧ **Casa Zen** (☎2640 0523; www.zencostarica.com), 1km down the road to Santa Teresa. The highlight of this peaceful palace is its centerpiece: a 2-story, octagonal common area and Thai restaurant with elephants painted on the walls. In high season, Zen offers massages and nightly shows, including live music, trapeze artists, and fire entertainment. Small climbing wall on-site. Th and Su free movie nights. Yoga classes ¢4015 (US$7) per class or ¢14,338 (US$25) for 5 classes. Laundry ¢800 per kg. Internet ¢1200 per hr. Dorms ¢6882 (US$12); private rooms for 2-5 people ¢13,764-27,528 (US$24-48); huge apartment with kitchen, satellite TV, and bath for 2 people ¢31,543 (US$55), can accommodate up to 14 for ¢83,158 (US$145). ❶

▧ **Funky Monkey** (☎2640 0272; www.funky-monkey-lodge.com). One of the town's most popular surfer hangouts. Two-story, unpainted wooden dorms are spacious and include gardens, showers, and sinks. Bungalows are similar, with floor-length shutters that open up onto porches with hammocks. The lounge area has a pool table and mattresses for lying out on while you watch TV. Close to a good surf break. The on-site restaurant is open daily for breakfast and dinner and serves sushi Tu and Sa. Wi-Fi, a pool, and a communal kitchen also available. High-season dorms ¢9750 (US$17); bungalows ¢45,880 (US$80). Low-season dorms ¢6882 (US$12); bungalows ¢34,410 (US$60). Each additional person ¢5735 (US$10). Apartments for 4 with ocean view ¢57,350 (US$100), with A/C ¢68,820 (US$120). V. ❶

▧ **Tranquilo Backpackers** (☎2640 0614; www.tranquilobackpackers.com), 400m down the road from Frank's Place in Santa Teresa. The rooms aren't fancy, but live music during high season, a communal kitchen, cable TV, free internet, a pool table, and plenty of hammocks draw a social bunch of backpackers. The young and helpful staff offers complimentary coffee and tea and flips free pancakes every morning. ¢2000 room key and linens deposit. Security guard 6:30am-6:30pm. Dorms ¢6309 (US$11), with bath ¢7456 (US$13); doubles ¢17,205/20,073 (US$30/35). ❶

Don Jon's Hotel (☎2640 0700), past Pizzeria Tomate on the road to Santa Teresa. Tight-fisted but simply can't live without A/C? You're in luck. This hotel boasts brand new, spacious dorms with log bunk beds, high ceilings, and, yes, A/C. Common room shows surf movies all day, and a restaurant serving breakfast and lunch is located on-site. Communal kitchen. High-season dorms ₡8603 (US$15), low-season dorms ₡6882 (US$12); triples and quads ₡25,808/22,940 (US$45/40). Two-bedroom apartment with kitchen, bathroom, and DVD payer ₡34,410/43,013 (US$60/US$75). Cash only. ❶

MAL PAÍS

▨ **Hotel the Place** (☎2640 0001; www.theplacemalpais.com). Elegance and style don't have to come at prohibitive prices. The modern, outdoor lounge next to the swimming pool has low tables, chairs, and pillowed seats, all accented with African and Costa Rican masks and patterns. The private bungalows all have their own themes: from "Mediterranean Breeze" and "Out of Africa" to "El Nido de Amor" (The Love Nest). The chic bar serves just about any drink you could want. Rooms come with A/C, private baths, and Wi-Fi. Satellite TV in common area. Doubles ₡40,145 (US$70); quads ₡45,880 (US$80); bungalows for 4 ₡57,350 (US$100); 2-bedroom house ₡114,700 (US$200). Discounts in low season and for stays of 6 nights or more. MC/V. ❹

▨ **Mal País Surf School and Resort** (☎2640 0061; www.malpaissurfcamp.com), 500m down the road to Mal País. Prides itself on a relaxed surfer atmosphere. Has rooms for all budgets. Its 10 acres of land feature a bar, restaurant, 17m pool, gym, and pool and ping-pong tables. With a flat-screen TV showing surfing videos and a projection screen for movies at night, there's always something to watch. Surf lessons (₡22,940/US$40), board rental, tours, and laundry also available. Check-out noon. Surfer package with 3 meals, board rental, and basic accommodations ₡34,410 (US$60). High-season open-air dorms ₡8603 (US$15); cabins for 2 ₡20,073 (US$35); villas for 4 ₡48,748 (US$85); suite with kitchen and living room ₡86,025 (US$150). Low-season dorms ₡5735 (US$10); cabins for 2 ₡14,338 ($25); villas for 4 ₡37,278 ($65); suite with kitchen and living room ₡57,350 ($100). AmEx/D/MC/V. ❶

Pachamama (☎2640 0195; www.pacha-malpais.com), 1km from Frank's Place, toward Mal País. Lemon, mango, and papaya trees surround the buildings, while monkeys move in the treetops. A 30m trek up to the hotel's lookout point offers the most breathtaking sunset view in the area. The friendly Austrian owner, Franz, offers fishing trips, kitesurfing, and board rentals. Three bungalows sleep 2-5 and have private hot water baths, kitchens, and porches with hammocks. Bigger groups will love the 2-story house, which sleeps 5 and includes a kitchen, bath, BBQ pit, outdoor dining area, loft, and porch. Free Wi-Fi. Adjoining bungalows ₡34,410 (US$60); stand-alone bungalows ₡45,880 (US$80); house ₡80,290 (US$140). 3-floor tipi ₡5735 (US$10) per person. Cash only. ❹

▐ FOOD

The long road running through Mal País and Santa Teresa is sprinkled with cafes, restaurants, and *sodas*. Many keep unpredictable hours despite their "official" schedules. Additionally, some restaurants close entirely in the low season. Those looking to cook at home can go to **Super Ronny's,** about 750m down the road to Santa Teresa. (☎2640 0297. Open daily 7am-9pm.) Farther into Santa Teresa is **Treble Maya Super.** (☎2640 0645. Open daily 7am-9pm.) **Super Costa** is across the street from Casa Zen. (☎2640 0530. Open daily 7am-9pm.) An **organic produce market** is held every Saturday afternoon near the main beach entrance of Playa Carmen.

SANTA TERESA

Zula, 700m down from Frank's Place toward Santa Teresa. This Israeli restaurant comes highly recommended. Hummus served with falafel (₡3500) or chicken on homemade pita bread (₡3500) are fantastic. Vegetarians will drool over the delicious avocado pita (₡3000). Larger dishes come with salad and fries. If you're feeling adventurous, try the *shakshuka,* a traditional meal with eggs poached in tomato sauce (¢3600). Free Wi-Fi. Glass of house wine ¢2000. Shisha ¢2500 per tablet. Open M-F and Su 10am-4pm and 6:30-10pm. ❷

Umi Sushi (☎2640 0968), in the Playa Carmen Mall, at the intersection of the road to Cóbano. The cool Japanese decor and extensive sushi menu will make you forget you're in Costa Rica. Eat indoors or under an umbrella in the pebble-filled courtyard. Sushi (¢1750-2780) and sashimi (¢2650-5150) are made with both local and imported fish. Start with edamame (¢1900) or miso soup (¢1155), and sip on an imported Sapporo (¢2250). Open daily 11:30am-10:30pm. MC/V. ❷

Soda La Amistad (☎2640 0452), slightly past Casa Zen. This small soda comes highly recommended by surfers. Owner Stanley serves yummy *comida típica*. *Casados* ¢2000-2200. Rice with seafood ¢3000. Open daily 8am-10pm. ❶

Burger Rancho (☎2640 0583), 200m south from Funky Monkey, in front of the *futból* pitch. "Free Love" is listed on the menu, but chicken sandwich (¢2900) and hummus and pita (¢2600) are better bets. Daily specials listed on the black board. Belgian meatballs ¢4500. Free Wi-Fi for customers. Open daily 9am-11pm. ❶

MAL PAÍS

▨ **Mary's** (☎2640 0153), 3km down the road to Mal País. Hand-made lanterns made of pressed flowers hang over private booths. The wood oven bakes delicious red snapper; the seared yellowfin tuna is scrumptious as well. All of the fish are caught by fishermen in Mal País. Pizzas (¢5000-6500) are all made with their special tomato sauce. Entrees ¢4500-6500. Open M-Tu and Th-Su 5:30-10pm. ❷

▨ **Soda Piedra Mar** (☎2640 0069), 2km down the road to Mal País and then 200m down a dirt path toward the beach. Set back from the main road and nestled between the rocks and waves that crowd the beach, this quiet *soda* remains hidden from most travelers. The standard *típico* entrees are as scrumptious as they are affordable. Sit out on the patio and enjoy spectacular ocean views and picture-perfect sunsets. Ask about fishing trips and kite-fishing lessons. *Casados* ¢1800-2000. Chicken fajitas ¢3000. Breakfast pancakes with honey ¢1800. Fruit drinks ¢900-1000. Open M-Sa 8am-8pm. ❶

Ritmo Tropical (☎2640 0174), 700m down to the road to Mal País. Come here for good Italian food. Sit under the palm-leaf umbrellas and listen to the ocean in the distance. Pizza ¢3600-5200. Four-cheese pasta ¢4000. Open daily 8am-11:45am and 5-10:30pm. ❷

🔊 NIGHTLIFE

In general, the surfer lifestyle makes for subdued nights in Mal País. That said, three main bars still get crowded on some nights.

La Lora (☎2640 0132), 3km up the road to Santa Teresa. The place to be on Th nights for reggae. Latin dance music separates the foreigners from the *ticos* on Sa. Cover ¢2000-3000 for live music events. Open daily in high season noon-2:30am, in low season 6pm-2:30am.

D&N Club (☎2640 0353), right off the beach, just south of the town center. Formerly Bar Tabu, D&N hosts full-moon parties with fire dancers, trapeze artists, and trippy techno music during the high season. M night reggae. W Latin night. Sa electronica. The club also holds BBQs on the beach and is planning to set up night lighting for surfers. Open daily 4:30pm-2am.

Good Vibrations (☎2640 0007), just south of the Playa Carmen Mall at the main intersection. Formerly Howling Monkey Sports Bar and Grill. Not much of a party scene unless the reggae (or Beach Boys) is blasting, but has a flatscreen TV permanently tuned to surfing or big sports games. Tasty bar food ¢3000-4800. F 10pm jam sessions. Beer ¢1000. Happy hour 5-7pm, beer ¢800. Open daily 11am-2am.

◪ BEACHES AND SURFING

The Mal País area is known as a **world-class surf spot** with consistent waves and a faithful crowd. Its location between the Central Pacific coast and Guanacaste creates big southern swells in the rainy season and gnarly offshore breaks in the dry season. The currents are strong here, so swimming can be dangerous. There are several surf spots along the coast with slightly different conditions. South of the crossroads, **Playa Mal País** is inconsistent and better for tide pool exploration. Three kilometers south of the crossroads, **Punta Barrigona** at Bar Mar Azul develops great waves around the point when the swell is big. One kilometer farther south is **Playa de Los Suecos** (or Sunset Reef). The break here is shallow, inconsistent, and for high caliber surfers only. **Playa El Carmen,** directly ahead of the crossroad, has a long right wall. The best spot on **Playa Santa Teresa** is 3km north of the crossroad behind Cabinas Santa Teresa. The A-frame break here is more powerful and consistent than El Carmen; it also holds a better wave at low tide. **Playa Hermosa,** the next beach north of Santa Teresa, has almost no crowds and fast peaks rise along the beach. This beach is becoming increasingly popular for kite-surfing. The beach farthest north in the area is **Playa Manzanillo,** an idyllic spot 8km from the crossroads. It has an offshore reef and less hairy waves than its neighboring beaches. It's only accessible by 4WD or a 1hr. bike ride on rough roads and through shallow rivers. Still, it's worth the daytrip just to see the unspoiled scenery.

Several surf shops in Mal País and Santa Teresa rent boards and provide instruction. **Kina Surf,** 2.2km down the road to Santa Teresa, next to Pizzeria Tomate, is one the best-run surf shops, with plenty of boards and gear to pick from and a knowledgeable, friendly staff. It also sells pop art made from items found on the beach. (☎2640 0627; www.kinasurfcostarica.com. Surfboard rental ¢5735/US$10 per day; 2-3hr. surf lessons plus day board rental ¢20,073/US$35. Open M-Sa 9am-5pm, Su 10am-4pm.) **Alex's Surf Shop,** 200m toward Santa Teresa from Frank's Place, rents boards (¢5735/US$10 per day) and offers lessons (private ¢28,675/US$50, group ¢20,073/US$35), which include board rental. (☎2640 0364. Open daily 8am-6:30pm. MC/V.)

◪ ◪ OUTDOOR ACTIVITIES AND GUIDED TOURS

Although the hollow beach break is what most people come to town for, the Mal País area offers an array of outdoor activities for non-surfers; even die-hard wave-riders might find themselves diverted by the plethora of beach activities. **Fishing** is the second-most popular activity around here. The small marina at the end of the road to Mal País is always bustling with fishermen and tourists counting their catches. The adventurous and bus-weary can walk 2.5km along the road to Mal País until they reach the fork in the road, then turn left and continue 9km more to the **Reserva Natural Absoluta Cabo Blanco.** Otherwise, rent a snorkel and explore the **tide pools** just behind Sunset Reef Hotel. To get there, walk 2.5km down the road to Mal País, turn right at the fork, and continue another 500m until you see the hotel at the end of the road. Those with a bit more cash can take one of the package tours or organized trips offered around town. Check out a wide range of options at **Tropical Tours.** They offer **canopy tours** (¢20,073/US$35), **snorkeling** at Isla Tortuga from Montezuma with BBQ and drinks (¢25,808/US$45), and daytrips to Monteverde and Arenal (☎2640 1900; www.tropicaltoursmalpais.com). Located on the beach next to D&N Club, **Adrenaline Surf and Kite School** offers kite-surfing lessons to beginners and advances surfers alike. (☎8324 8671. 2hr. beginner lesson ¢57,350 (US$100); 4hr. ¢103,230 (US$180). You can also talk to Franz, the owner of **Pachamama,** about kite-surfing tours up to Nicaragua; he also knows about some inexpensive **sportfishing** (☎2640 0195; www.pacha-malpais.com).

MONTEZUMA

Rooted in 1960s surfer and Rasta culture and now dealing with an influx of tourists, Montezuma offers plenty of modern amenities and maintains some of its hippie charm. Craft stands abound, and vegetarian cafes and yoga classes are readily available. Its dirt roads and endless beaches lead to some of the peninsula's best waves, and nearby hills are full of an array of waterfalls.

⌐ TRANSPORTATION

If you're coming from towns in the northern half of the peninsula, note that backtracking to Puntarenas and taking the **ferry** to Paquera is the fastest way to reach Montezuma, even though other routes look shorter on a map (the roads are tediously slow and have infrequent public transportation). **Buses** go to Paquera (1hr.; 6 per day 5:30am-4pm, return 6 per day 6:15am-6:15pm; ₡2000) and Cabo Blanco (50min.; 8, 10am, 2, 4, 6pm, return 7:10, 9:10am, 1:10, 3:20, 6:30pm; ₡600) via Cabuya (25min., ₡500). To go to Santa Teresa via Mal País, take the 10am or 2pm bus to Cóbano, where the Mal País bus to Santa Teresa will be waiting (1hr.; 10:30am, 2:30pm, return 7, 11:30am, 3:30pm; ₡700).

◾✦ 🛈 ORIENTATION AND PRACTICAL INFORMATION

Near the southern tip of the Nicoya Peninsula, Montezuma is 41km southwest of Paquera and 8km south of Cóbano. Most services are in Cóbano. Montezuma consists almost entirely of accommodations, restaurants, and souvenir shops. The bus into Montezuma from Cóbano stops in an unpaved parking lot with Hotel el Parque on its south side. The **beach** is immediately to the east. The main road continues to Cabuya and **Reserva Natural Absoluta Cabo Blanco**, 11km away. To reach the town center, walk north 100m up the small hill and take the first right. At the far end of this street, Chico's Bar is the center of Montezuma.

Banks: The closest bank is a **Banco Nacional** (☎2462 0210) in Cóbano. Open M-F 8:30am-3:45pm. This is the only bank along the coast between Playa Naranjo and Montezuma, so be prepared for long lines. Since many foreign cards do not work at the ATM, you may need to obtain cash from the teller inside. Passport required. If you're in dire need of *colónes*, try the tour agencies or the supermarkets. The tourist services center at **Zuma Tours,** near Soda Monte del Sol, will exchange traveler's checks and major international currencies at the current exchange rates. Office open M-Sa 8am-1pm and 4-7pm. The closest Western Union is in Cóbano.

Car Rentals: Cocozuma Traveler (☎2642 0911 or 8835 0270). Rents cars (prices vary) and ATVs (½-day US$50, full-day US$70). **Montezuma Eco-Tours** (☎2642 0467) also rents ATVs (US$50/70), as does **Zuma Tours** (☎2642 0224. US$60/70).

HIDDEN COSTS. While ATVs are a fun, affordable way to explore the beaches and unpaved roads of the Nicoya Peninsula, make sure to ask about the deposit required to use the vehicle. Rental agencies will typically place a hold on your credit card for an amount ranging US$500-1000, sometimes without letting you know. While the agency lifts the hold when you return the vehicle, many an unsuspecting tourist has rented an ATV only to see their credit card bounce at dinner.

Private Transportation: Montezuma Expeditions (☎2462 0919; www.montezumaexpeditions.com), **Montezuma Eco-Tours** (☎2642 0467), and **Zuma Tours** (☎2642 0024) provide shuttles (2-person min.) to popular destinations, including Arenal, San José, Monteverde, Sámara, Tamarindo, Manuel Antonio, and Nicoya. Most places US$35-45 per person. Make reservations 1 day in advance, as they leave in the morning.

Bookstore: Librería Topsy (☎2642 0576), 100m north of Chico's. A huge selection of fiction, magazines, and travel books in several languages. Annual blow-out sale in Jan. You can buy used books, but check out the books for rent in the back room and save money by exchanging your old books for store credit. Book rental ¢900 for 2 weeks with a ¢5000 deposit. Open M-F 8am-4pm, Sa-Su 8am-noon.

Laundry: Hotels have the cheapest prices. **Pension Areneas,** n3ext to Hotel el Parque (p. 260), and **Hotel La Cascada** (p. 259) charge ¢1000 per kg.; turnaround times vary.

Police: ☎911, Cóbano police ☎2642 0770.

Pharmacy: The nearest is in Cóbano (☎2642 0685), 100m south of Banco Nacional on the road to Montezuma. Open M-F 8am-7pm, Sa 8am-6pm. AmEx/MC/V.

Medical Services: Clínica de Cóbano (☎2642 0056 or 8380 4125), next to the pharmacy toward Montezuma. Open M-Sa 8am-5pm, 24hr. for emergencies. AmEx/MC/V.

Telephones: Public phones 25m south of the Bakery Cafe and 25m north of Hotel Lucy. Phone cards are sold at the supermarket and at the surf shop next to Hotel Lucy. Sun Trails, across the street from Chico's, charges ¢400 per min. for international calls. The tourist services office at Zuma Tours also allows international calls for US$1 per min. to the US and US$1.50 per min. to anywhere else in the world.

Internet Access: Most places charge ¢20 per min. (¢1200 per hr., min. 10min.) **El Sano Banano** (p. 261) has the newest computers. Open daily 10am-10pm. **Zuma Tours,** next to Soda Monte del Sol. Discounts with a 3 or 5hr. Internet access card. Open M-Sa 8am-1pm and 4-7pm. **Sun Trails** (☎2642 0808) has a slower connection but cheaper rates. Internet ¢20 per min., ¢1000 per hr. Open M-F 8am-9pm, Sa-Su 9am-5pm.

Post Office: The closest **post office** is in Cóbano, 300m west of Banco Nacional toward Paquera (open M-F 8am-5:30pm). **Librería Topsy** has stamps and mails letters.

📷 📷 ACCOMMODATIONS AND CAMPING

Montezuma is packed with hotels, catering to both the budget-conscious and those looking for more luxurious digs. The hotels listed below are the best of the budget set, but many others exist as well. The most quiet and scenic spots are just a short walk along the road to Cabo Blanco; if you stay near Chico's, you'll definitely need earplugs to drown out the music. Camping on the beach is free, relatively safe, and popular, especially in the high season.

📷 **Amor de Mar** (☎/fax 2642 0262; www.amordemar.com), a 10min. walk down the road to Cabo Blanco. A river runs alongside, the ocean crashes at the edges of the tiny private peninsula, and there's never a shortage of hammocks. Rooms are gorgeous, with dark wood and adobe. All but 2 rooms have beautiful baths; most have hot water. Breakfast, including crepes at the 1st fl. restaurant. Borrow equipment to play lawn games on the grass overlooking the sea. Laundry service priced by item. Reception 7am-noon and 2-5pm. High season US$50-95, low season US$45-85; cabins US$180/160. ❸

Hotel La Cascada (☎2642 0057), just before the river on the road to Cabo Blanco. An excellent value for groups. Wood paneling makes every room feel like a cozy cabin. You'll fall asleep to the sounds of the ocean and a nearby waterfall. The spacious balcony has plenty of hammocks and is a great spot to meet fellow travelers. Private hot-water baths. Laundry ¢1000 per kg. The attached restaurant has a huge menu and reason-

Montezuma

ACCOMMODATIONS
Amor de Mar, **14**
Camping, **2**
Hotel La Cascada, **13**
Hotel Lucy, **12**
Hotel El Parque, **8**
Luna Llena Hostel, **3**

FOOD
Bakery Cafe, **4**
Bar Moctezuma, **9**
Orgánico, **6**
La Playa de los Artistas, **11**
El Sano Banano, **5**
Ylang-Ylang Restaurant, **1**

NIGHTLIFE
Bar Moctezuma, **10**
Chico's Bar, **7**

able prices. High season singles and doubles US$45, with A/C US$60; low season US$35/50; triples, quads, and quints US$15/12 per person. US$/¢ only. ❸

Luna Llena Hostel (☎2642 0390), 100m up the hill to the right on the road out of town (away from Cabo Blanco). A true backpackers' hostel in Montezuma, Luna offers bare-bones bungalows and simple dorms with metal bunks, sky-blue walls, and shared hot-water baths. A great place to meet fellow travelers: the porch area has ocean views, satellite TV, bean bags, a hammock, and a swing. The entire property is illuminated at night by funky lanterns and candles. Kitchen available. Safe deposit box for valuables in each room; the staff recommends keeping all belongings locked up. Singles US$20-30; doubles US$30-40; triples US$36-50. US$/¢. ❷

Hotel Lucy (☎2642 0273), about 400m down the road to Cabo Blanco. Its prime beach-front location, family management, and rooms with shared cold-water showers make this the best of the truly budget options. Rooms with shared baths are the cheapest option. Laundry ¢1000 per kg. ¢5000 per person; double with bath ¢12,000. US$/¢. ❶

Hotel el Parque (☎2642 0164), conveniently located next to the bus stop, has the cheapest rooms in town and hammocks out back, overlooking the town harbor. The friendly owner, Kevin, takes care of all your needs. Rooms available with shared bath for 1-4. US$10 per person. MC/V/US$/¢. ❶

Camping (☎2642 1000) is available in the small blue building, a 10min. walk down Playa Grande. Rustic bathrooms and cooking utensils provided. ₡1000 per person. ❶

▐ FOOD

Montezuma eateries offer a diverse array of cuisines, with international food, organic vegetarian meals, and *comida típica* readily available. Many places in Montezuma do not include gratuity or taxes in their listed prices. Some add both to the bill at the end of the meal, and some only add the taxes in the hopes that international tourists will tip more than the 10% customary in Costa Rica. Check for a note at the bottom of the menu or ask a server to be sure. To purchase your own food, head to **Super Mamatea**, next to Chico's (☎2642 0578; open daily 7am-11pm; all credit cards accepted) or **Super Montezuma**, next to El Sano Banano (☎2642 0370; open daily 7am-10pm; MC/V/US$/₡).

▨ **Bakery Cafe** (☎2642 0458), 100m down the road to the right of Chico's, opposite Librería Topsy. No place in town does breakfast better. The portions are generous, and everything is vegetarian and incredibly fresh—just be sure that the monkeys in the shady trees nearby don't snatch away your food. The lunch menu includes a variety of international options ranging from ▨**falafel** (₡3200) to nachos (₡3500) to Thai chicken satay (₡3800). Don't miss the Avemi (₡10,700), a delicious shake with regular or soy milk, oats, honey, and cinnamon. Open daily 6am-4pm. MC/V/US$/₡. ❷

▨ **Ylang-Ylang Restaurant and Bar,** at the Ylang-Ylang resort, a 15min. walk down Playa Grande. Meals are beautifully presented—sometimes as extravagant food sculptures. Experiment with the extensive vegan, and raw food menu, or have the delicious eggplant lasagna (US$15). Don't miss the tiramisu-stuffed crepe, with ice cream and praline sauce (US$9) for dessert. Most entrees US$10-25. Try one of the bar's creations, such as Monkey Business (vodka, coffee liqeur, banana, coconut, and milk). Happy hour daily 3-6pm (2 drinks for US$7). Open 7am-9:30pm. AmEx/MC/V/US$/₡. ❸

La Playa de los Artistas (☎2642 0920), on the beach, 400m down the road to Cabo Blanco. This is a fantastic choice for a romantic setting with style. Moonlit waves reflect the lantern light from the palm-leaf roof. The Mediterranean menu changes daily, but always includes seafood and a few veggie dishes. Entrees ₡3000-12,000. Open high season M-Sa noon-11pm; low season M-W noon-4:30pm, Th-Sa noon-11pm. Hours vary, so call ahead; you'll want a reservation for dinner anyway. US$/₡. ❹

Bar Moctezuma (☎2642 0657), next to Montezuma's main beach. A popular nighttime hangout, Bar Moctezuma keeps busy during the daylight hours as well, serving tasty breakfast crepes (₡1200-2400) and seafood dishes (₡2400-3700) at great prices. Conveniently located on the beach and at the center of town, the view of the ocean is 2nd to none. Shrimp omelette ₡2400. Salad ₡1900-2800. Pastas ₡1900-3600. Restaurant open daily 7:30am-10pm, bar open late. MC/V/US$/₡. ❶

El Sano Banano (☎2642 0638), 50m up the road leading west from Chico's. The menu is pricey, but nightly English movies (free with min. ₡3000 order) draw tourists every night. Have sushi with locally caught fish (₡3500-5000), or test out the aphrodisiac penne made with seafood, avocado, onion, and mushrooms (₡7000). Don't leave without trying the homemade frozen yogurt, ideally as part of a banana split (₡1500). Most entrees ₡4500-10,000. Open daily 7am-10pm. AmEx/MC/V/US$/₡. ❸

Organico (☎8359 4197), just north of Super Mamatea. Serves an exclusively organic, vegetarian menu, and is pricier than other lunch places. Go for a veggie burger (₡3500) or have the hummus wrap (₡3850). If the tropical heat is getting to you, take a few minutes to cool down in the cafe's no-shoes, air-conditioned "chill room." Finish your meal with a scoop of homemade ice cream (¢1500). Open M-Sa 8am-6pm. US$/¢. ❷

🎵 🎭 ENTERTAINMENT AND NIGHTLIFE

Masses of tourists head to the **Tucán Movie House** in El Sano Banano to see English-language movies. (Movies daily 7 or 7:30pm. Free with minimum ¢3000 food or drink order.) After the movie, everyone moves on to either **Chico's Bar** (beer ¢1000; open daily 7am-2am) or **Bar Moctezuma** (beer ¢900, mixed drinks ¢1500; open daily 7:30am-late), underneath Hotel Moctezuma, to meet up with the locals and sip Imperials in a quieter bar scene or enjoy two Sex on the Beaches for ¢800 from 4 to 6pm. Chico's has more of a club scene, with music ranging from reggae to salsa to old US rap. Nights at Chico's are quiet earlier on, as the crowd gathers around the bar and pool table, but dancing starts around 10:30 or 11pm. If you tire of local beer, Chico's has hot *cucarachas* (¢2500), a spicy tequila and coffee mix that is lit on fire and slurped through chilled straws. **Luz de Mono** hosts dance parties Thursday through Saturday at 10pm. (Th reggae, F tropical, Sa house music. Beer ¢1000-1500.)

🏖 BEACHES

Montezuma's shoreline is scenic but rugged, and thus, swimming is difficult. Parents should be especially cautious with children, since water depth changes rapidly and is uneven along the shore. For safer swimming, head to one of the hotel pools or **Isla Tortuga,** where the water is pristine and calm.

The beach south of the town center is tightly bordered by rock formations and is used as a harbor, so take precautions when swimming. During low tide, it's possible to continue farther south along the beach by walking on the rocky headlands. Here you'll find safe, shallow tide pools teeming with fish and aquatic plants; rent a snorkel from a tour agency for the best view. Most people choose to go to the beach north of town, south of the Ylang-Ylang restaurant, but stretches of open beach continue up the coast for miles. These beaches, the largest appropriately called **Playa Grande,** are usually less crowded than beaches closer to Montezuma and are fantastic for swimming, horseback rides, or long walks along the soft sand. **Playa Las Manchas** and **Playa Cedros,** 1km and 2km south, respectively, along the road to Cabo Blanco, are also popular, especially for sunbathing. Beaches tend to be more crowded in the high season.

🏔 📷 OUTDOOR ACTIVITIES AND GUIDED TOURS

Montezuma's most rewarding and inexpensive activity is a hike to the several waterfalls near town. The best one is also the closest, about a 7min. walk along the road to Cabo Blanco; a sign just past Hotel La Cascada marks the entrance. You can see an impressive set of rapids just steps up the trail from the road. From there, the trail continues uphill to where an 80 ft. waterfall and second, smaller waterfall fall into a common pool. The ground is very wet, and it is easy to slip or fall. Be sure to wear sturdy shoes for the hike and don't expect to keep your feet dry. From the road, it takes about 30min. to reach this waterfall. **Let's Go does not recommend jumping into the pool at the base of the waterfall or attempting to explore further upstream.** A small waterfall with good swimming is a 2hr. walk north up the coast. The waterfall flows directly into the sea—a rare sight. You can't go wrong just following the water's edge, but it is easier to follow the horse trails around them.

Several tour agencies in Montezuma will organize trips to nearby sights and activities. **Cocozuma Travelers** (☎2642 0911), **Eco-Tours** (☎2642 0467), and **Zuma Tours** (☎2642 0024) offer the most comprehensive ranges of packages through their arrangements with other local businesses. The tour companies charge slightly different rates and vary prices by season, so it may be possible to save a few dollars by shopping around—all three are on the same block. Full-day snorkeling trips to Isla Tortuga include equipment, lunch, and refreshments (US$40). Those with PADI certifications scuba dive the reefs instead (1 dive US$100, 2 dives US$140). Scuba certification lessons are avaialable as well (US$140). Fishing charters are available starting at around US$160 for a few hours, but prices are much higher for full-day and offshore trips. If you would rather spend time in the treetops than in or on the water, go on a zipline canopy tour that will take you to several waterfalls (US$35). If you're looking for dance lessons, any of these tour companies will likely be able to arrange something or will at least point you in the right direction. Zuma Tours also functions as a travel agency and can make flight reservations with Sansa and NatureAir, while Cocozuma works with only NatureAir.

 KICK IT. It's well known that it's important to choose comfortable and supportive shoes when on the road, but think twice about your footwear: the shoes you wear can set you apart as a tourist almost immediately, which can put you at risk for high prices, pickpocketing, and even harassment. Stay away from fancy brands and showy kicks. With the right footwear, you'll be one step closer to a happy travel experience.

⚡ DAYTRIPS FROM MONTEZUMA

RESERVA NATURAL ABSOLUTA CABO BLANCO. A bumpy road runs the 8km from Montezuma to the Reserva Natural Absoluta Cabo Blanco, Costa Rica's first protected tract of land and the cornerstone of the country's reserve system. The reserve extends 1km from the shore to protect marine life and is home to the Peninsula's population of pelicans and Central America's largest concentration of brown booby birds. Foliage here is less dense, and animals are easy to spot. The beach is one of the best on the peninsula.

MONTEZUMA MOVIES

Cannes. Sundance. Montezuma?

In November 2007, the small town brought new levels of art and culture to the Nicoya Peninsula by hosting the first **Montezuma International Film Festival** to kick off the high season for tourism. Book your tickets now, because Montezuma is making the 5-day festival an annual event.

Movies are shown at El Sano Banano, Luz de Mono, and Los Mangos, with a variety of categories ranging from comedy to animation to drama. The festival celebrates features and shorts by both local and international talent.

But the fun doesn't stop when the credits roll and the curtain falls; Luz de Mono and Chico's Bar host nightly after-parties, while many hotels and tour companies offer discounts on lodgings and local adventures for the duration of the festival. Around movie showings, backpackers mingle with directors during yoga lessons and snorkeling trips to Isla Tortuga. Crowds gather in the street to watch fire-dancers perform. As always, the beaches beckon to those looking to catch the perfect wave or just to get a tan.

It's just one more reason to go to Montezuma.

Annually in mid-November. Visit www.montezumafestival.com for details.

The ranger station is about a 10min. walk from the entrance. The **Sendero Sueco (Swedish Trail)** begins at the station. About 800m up the trail, the 1300m **Sendero Danés** branches off to the right and meanders through the hills, while the Swedish Trail takes a more direct route. Both trails come back together. From there, it is about 3200m to the beach. Trails are steep but well-maintained. The trip to the beach and back should take about 4hr., leaving you just enough time to catch the 1:10pm bus back to Montezuma if you arrive on the 8am bus. Bring insect repellent and closed-toed shoes. Camping is not permitted. *(From Montezuma, take the Cabuya/Cabo Blanco minibus from the stop next to Hotel el Parque (30min.; 8, 10am, 2, 4, 6pm; return 7:10, 9:10am, 1:10, 3:20, 6:30pm; ¢600). Park ranger station ☎2642 0093. Open W-Sa and Su 8am-4pm. US$10, children US$3.)*

TAMBOR

Looking at Tambor's quiet gravel roads and volcanic, silver-gray beach, you'd never guess it had such an extravagant past. Temporarily abandoning its humble beginnings as a quaint fishing village, Tambor became a mecca for resort-hoppers with the construction of several luxury hotels in the early 90s. A few years later, it gained international fame as the site of the American reality program Temptation Island 2. These days, Tambor's shorelines pale in comparison to many other, more picturesque beaches of Guanacaste. The small town draws modest crowds of vacationing *ticos*, mellow budget travelers, retired foreigners, and a few whales that swim by during their annual migrations.

◪ TRANSPORTATION

The quickest way to arrive in Tambor is by **plane.** Flights run from San José through Sansa (30min.; 6, 6:20, 8:10, 10:30am, 12:30, 1:50pm; return high season 8:30, 9, 11:20am, 1:15, 2:35, 5:05pm; US$71) and NatureAir (30min.; 8:20am, return 9am, 2pm; low season 9am; US$72). Flights arrive at the airstrip by Playa Barcelo and Hotel Tambor, about 5km north of Tambor. The Paquera-Montezuma **bus** passes Tambor about 1hr. after departing from Montezuma and 30min. after departing from Paquera (6 per day 6:15am-6:15pm, ¢800). When arriving, be sure to tell the driver to let you off at Tambor *pueblo*, not the airstrip, next to which several large international resorts are located.

◪ ◪ ORIENTATION AND PRACTICAL INFORMATION

Tambor is located on the southern end of Bahía Ballena (Whale Bay), 27km north of Montezuma and 14km south of Paquera. Buses stop on the main road, which runs south to Cóbano and north toward Paquera. Everything in town is located either on the main drag, the beach, or a short street that connects the two. The town has little in the way of services, so you'll have to head to Cóbano, 19km south, for a **bank**, a **post office**, and **medical services. Super Lapa**, 50m down the side street heading east just past the bus stop, has food, toiletries, and a small mailbox. (☎2683 0082. Open M-Sa 8am-noon and 1-8pm. MC/V/US$/¢.) **Amiga Farmacia** is 250m north of the bus stop on the main road. (☎2683 0581. Open M-F 9am-12:30pm and 1-7pm, Sa-Su 9am-12:30pm and 1-5pm.) You can do laundry (¢4000-5000 depending on size of load) at **Cabinas El Bosque** (p. 265). The **police station** (emergency ☎911) is next door to the market on the street heading east past the bus stop. **Internet access** is available upstairs at **Tucan Boutique,** next to the pharmacy. The store sells clothing, crafts, and coffee products. (☎2293 2654. ¢20 per min. Open M-F 9am-8pm, Sa-Su 9am-6pm.)

ACCOMMODATIONS

All of Tambor's budget places are along the main drag in town, with a few luxury lodgings sprinkled on the outskirts.

Cabinas el Bosque (☎2683 0039), on the main drag 150m north of the bus stop. Spacious common areas make it great for groups. Rooms have private baths and patios. Laundry ₡4000-5000 per load. Breakfast (₡1800) and dinner (₡2500) available. Singles and doubles ₡12,000, with A/C ₡15,000; triples and quads ₡16,000/20,000; cabin for 6 with fridge and coffee maker ₡35,000. Tax not included. US$/₡. ❷

Cabinas Cristina (☎2683 0028), 25m down the side street. An excellent value for its proximity to the beach. Rooms are small and sparsely decorated, but clean. Singles ₡12,000; doubles ₡15,000, with A/C ₡22,000. Room configurations available for up to 6. ₡5000 per additional person. MC/V/US$/₡. ❷

FOOD

Surprisingly, tiny Tambor has several delicious dining options, well worth the visit even if you're staying elsewhere.

FRESH CATCH. Head to the dock next to Bahía Ballena midday to buy fresh-caught fish from local fisherman or just to see the day's catch. Mahi mahi, tuna, squid, and shark are all available for just a few dollars per kilogram—far lower than in any store. On Saturdays, you can do the rest of your shopping here as well. The mother of the owner of Bahía Bellena runs a market featuring local produce, including veggies, herbs, yogurts, and cheeses.

Trattoria Mediterranea (☎2683 0400), just south of the bus stop. Run by a couple originally from a town near Venice, this trattoria serves incredible meals made with freshly caught Costa Rican fish and ingredients imported from Italy. You can't go wrong with either a pasta dish (₡4800-4900) or one of the seasonal seafood dishes (₡5700). Don't leave without trying one of the homemade desserts (₡1500). Salad ₡4800. Glass of house wine ₡1500. Open W-Su 5:30-10:30pm. Pizza only on Su. MC/V/US$/₡. ❸

Bahía Ballena (☎2683 0213), overlooking the marina outside of town. Turn left at the sign 800m south of the bus stop, then continue for 500m on the dirt road. This friendly bar and restaurant offers the freshest seafood and a congenial atmosphere at night. On weekends in the high season, the owner's father and brother will sometimes perform live music. *Ceviche* ₡2500-3000. Fish fillets ₡3500-7000. Open daily 10am-midnight during high season; M-Tu and Th-Su noon-midnight during low season. US$/₡. ❷

ENTERTAINMENT

From live music to swinging karaoke festivals, Tambor's casual bars offer low-key entertainment for locals and tourists alike. Head to **Los Gitanos** for a large, casual bar on the beach due east of the bus stop. (☎8376 0746. Karaoke Th and Sa nights. Beer ₡900. Mixed drinks ₡1500. Open Tu-Su 11am-10pm.)

CENTRAL PACIFIC COAST

The Central Pacific shore is Costa Rica's poster child: snapshots of its sunsets grace the covers of travel brochures and postcards, man-sized marlin lure sportfishermen from all over the world, and rugged rainforests sprawl just steps from the region's soft, sandy beaches. From vacationing *ticos* and foreign backpackers to resort-hopping honeymooners, a diverse group of travelers flocks to costal towns where they can take advantage of a well-developed tourist infrastructure. Popularity brings inevitable drawbacks, and major beach towns like Jacó, Quepos, and Manuel Antonio are invariably more crowded and more expensive than Costa Rica's more-remote Caribbean side. Diehard peace-seekers, however, need only move on to Playa Esterillos Oeste or Uvita for unspoiled, magnificent scenery and long stretches of deserted beach.

OROTINA

Known as "the city of fruit," the small town of Orotina abounds with vendors hawking locally grown mangos and melons. Despite its bustling streets and abundant produce, Orotina has never been a major stop on tourist itineraries; instead, its central location along the route from San José to the Pacific makes it a convenient stop for locals buying cheap and tasty treats on the way to the beach. The town itself is quite pleasant, and the *parque central* is relaxing, filled with towering palm trees and and small benches perfect for watching the activity on all sides. Orotina also makes for a convenient base from which to try the Original Canopy Tour or visit Turu Ba Ri eco-park; it is well worth a short stop on the way to more heavily-touristed destinations such as Puntarenas or Jacó. Interestingly, none of the roads have names, and nothing has an address. The only way to give directions or send mail is to describe a building's relationship to a major landmark and approximate distance. This makes finding things a little harder than normal.

▐▄ TRANSPORTATION

The main **bus** terminal run by Transportation H.R.C. is located 200m south of the southwest corner of the *parque* in a large yellow building (☎2427 9146). **Buses** to San José via San Mateo leave from the main station (3hr.; 6, 7:15, 10am, 2:50, 4, 6pm with an additional bus at 1pm every day but Su; ₡710). Buses to Jacó leave from the same station (2hr.; every hr. 5am-5pm; priced around ₡1000, but ask the driver). Buses to Puntarenas via Esparza leave from a stop 150m west of the northwest corner of the *parque* (1hr.; 5, 6, 7, 8, 10am, 12:30, 3, 5, 7pm; ₡600). Direct buses to Esparza leave from the northeast corner of the *parque* between the church and the Red Cross building. (Daily 9am and 12pm; ₡400.) Schedules change often, so check with locals for up-to-date times. Taxis wait on the north side of the *mercado municipal*. **Alexis Jimenez** is recommended by many people in town (☎2888 0706).

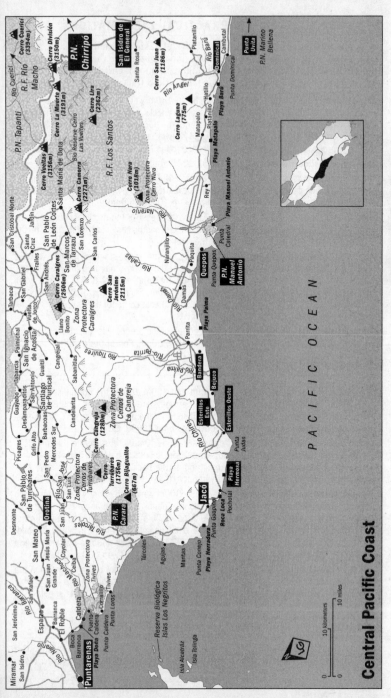

Central Pacific Coast

PACIFIC OCEAN

◼ 🔁 ORIENTATION AND PRACTICAL INFORMATION

Orotina is located 66km west of San José and 42km northeast of Jacó. Major centers of activity are the *parque central* and the *mercado municipal*, located one block north (open M-Sa 6am-6pm, Su 6am-noon). Orient yourself by putting the church on the east side of the *parque* and the railroad on the north.

Banks: Banco de Costa Rica (☎2284 6600), 100m west of the northwest corner of the *parque*. Changes $US and cashes traveler's checks, open M-F 8am to 4pm. **Banco Nacional** is located on the southwest corner of the *parque*, open M-F 8:30am-3:45pm. Both have 24hr. ATMs. **Coope Orotina** (☎2428 8045 or 2428 8052), on the north side of the *parque* and has a Western Union office (open M-F 8am-4pm, Sa 8-11:30am).

Police: The **police station** (☎2428 8010), 200m south of *parque*'s southeast corner.

Pharmacy: Farmacia Vega (☎2428 7733 or 2428 8526) is located just west of the *mercado*. (Open daily 6am-8pm.) **Farmacia Nueva Orotina** (☎2428 7997 or 2428 7969) is located next to the Red Cross. (Open M-Sa 9am-10pm, Su 9am-9pm.)

Red Cross: (☎2428 8304, emergency 911), 100m east of the northeast corner of the *parque*. Public telephones can be found on the south, east, and west sides of the *parque central* and on the east side of the market.

Internet Access: Jatcafe.net (☎2427 9027), up the spiral staircase behind Nachos King one block north of the northwest corner of the *parque*, has free Internet access. Open M-Th 9am-8pm, F 8am-5:30pm. The **Website Cafe** (☎2427 8869), a block north of Nachos King, ¢400 per hr. Open M-Sa 9am-9pm, Su noon-9pm). **CFC Computer Solutions** (☎2428 0103), 300m north of the northeast corner of the *parque*. ¢300 per hr.; open M-Sa 9am-10pm, Su 10am-10pm.

Post Office: 200m south of the southeast corner of the *parque*, just past the police station. ☎2428 8481; open M-F 8am-noon and 1-5:30pm. **Postal Code:** 4021.

⌂ ACCOMMODATIONS

Cabinas Kalin (☎2428 8082), 100m north and 100m east of the northeast corner of the *parque,* is closest to the town center. The rooms are simple, quiet, and clean, with double or single beds and fans. Don't be offended if the pet green parrots in the courtyard call you bad names. Doubles ¢5000, with bath ¢6000. ❶

Hotel Yadi (☎2428 8329), opposite the MegaSuper Orotina, just before the turnoff to Orotina. Has simple, clean rooms with either 2 single beds or a double bed each, private cold-water baths, TVs, fans, and a small pool in the back. A few rooms also have A/C. Check-out 1pm. Singles and doubles without A/C ¢11,639; with A/C ¢13,966. ❶

Iguana Verde (☎2428 4498 or 2428 4295), 300m west of the northwest corner of the *parque*. Has new rooms surrounding a patio with palms and cacti and a swimming pool with a small waterfall. All rooms have A/C, cable TV, a hot-water shower, and Internet access. Some of the larger rooms feature a kitchenette. Breakfast included. Smaller rooms with a double bed ¢20,000 for 1, ¢25,000 for 2; bigger doubles with kitchenette ¢30,000/35,000 large room with 3 beds; ¢35,000/40,000 /45,000. MC/V. ❹

Hotel Los Faroles (☎2428 9320 or 2428 8035), off the highway 100m behind the Pura Vida Restaurant before the turnoff to Orotina. Offers clean, spacious rooms with double beds, TV, and private hot-water baths. The dark wood furniture and white sheets offer details to the otherwise typical rooms. All rooms ¢15,000. ❸

◖ FOOD

The cheapest place to get a bite to eat is at one of the *soda* stands behind the main bus station in the *mercado municipal*, where you can snag a good *plato del día* or *casado* for just ¢1200. Several more *sodas* scatter the highway. To stock up on your own, **Perimercado,** north of the *mercado municipal.* (☎2428 8683. Open M-Sa 8am-9pm, Su 8am-6pm. AmEx/MC/V.) The **Megasuper Orotina** is located on the highway at the corner of the turnoff to Orotina. (Open M-Th 7am-9pm, F-Sa 7am-10pm, Su 7am-8pm.)

> **Chicharonera Capulin** (☎2428 8024), across the highway from the MegaSuper The large, clean *rancho* dining room feels more like a restaurant than a *soda. Gallo pinto* breakfasts ¢1300-1800 and *casados* ¢2000-3800. Specials are advertised on a banner out front. Open M-F and Su 10am-10pm, Sa 9am-11pm. ❶

> **Bar/Restaurante Tropical** (☎2428 7755), 300m north of the northeast corner of the *parque,* is a great place to escape the midday sun with a cool drink or enjoy a quiet dinner at 1 of the blue tables with red-checkered table cloths. *Casados* ¢2100. Fettuccine alfredo or spaghetti ¢2600. Fajitas ¢2600. Open daily 11am-10pm. AmEx/MC/V. ❷

> **Nachos King** (☎2427 8935), a block north of the northwest corner of the *parque.* Serves cheap cheeseburgers (¢700), tacos (¢800), burritos (¢1000), and pizza sandwiches (¢2000) for a late night bite. Open daily 6am-midnight. ❶

▶ DAYTRIPS FROM OROTINA

ORIGINAL CANOPY TOUR AT MAHOGANY PARK. It was the very first, and it still claims to be the best in all of Costa Rica. When Darren Hreniuk fulfilled his childhood dream of creating a rainforest zipline in 1994, people said he was crazy. Hreniuk remained confident in his forest-spanning creation, and today, copycat tours are offered in nearly ever village and hamlet of *ticolandia.* The Original Canopy Tour at Mahogany Park, named for its location in one of the only mahogany reserves in Costa Rica, is right off the highway and is accessible by bus or taxi from Orotina. Just meters from the highway, the adventure begins at the main office, where thrill-seekers are outfitted with harnesses, helmets, and gloves and given a tutorial on zipline hand-braking techniques before heading out into the park. The 11-platform, nine-line journey allows viewing of howlers, capuchins, scarlet macaws, and tremendous iguanas, with bursts of speed punctuated by platform pauses where groups catch their breath and relish the beauty and splendor of the canopy ecosystem. *(From Orotina, take any bus headed toward Esparza and ask to be let off at the Canopy Tour near Jesús María village (30min., ¢400. You can also take a bus headed to Puntarenas, but make sure that the bus goes through Esparza (30min., ¢600). Tours last 2 hr. and leave at 8, 10am, noon, and 2:30pm. US$45 for adults, students US$35, under 12 US$25. All-inclusive tours can also be arranged. Puntarenas/ San José: 2 people US$100 per person, 3 people US$95, 4 people US$85, 5 or 6 people US$80. Jacó: US$110/100/90/80. ☎ 2291 4465; www.canopytour.com. Reservations recommended.)*

TURU BA RI ECO-ADVENTURE THEME PARK. For 15 years, this majestic land between the Río Grande Tarcoles and Parque Nacional Carara was used solely for cattle production. In 1997, the decision was made to create a new breed of attraction in Costa Rica, and in April 2003 the new Turu Ba Ri Eco-Adventure Theme Park was opened. Besides the extensive tropical garden that dominates the park's 583 acres, there is also a 12,400 sq. ft. butterfly garden with over 25 species, 12km of well-kept trails, and a botanical garden with over 500 types of bromeliads and orchids. The adventure begins at the park entrance, with a 10min., 80.7m-high aerial tram ride with views of the surrounding landscape including the Río Grande Tarcoles.

In addition to these attractions, Turu Ba Ri includes lunch and one complimentary adventure tour with the price of admission. Most notable of these tours is the **Sensational Cable,** an experience unique to Turu Ba Ri that is only for the truly adventurous. Participants opt out of the traditional aerial tram ride into the park, and instead enter the park by cable, flying through the canopy on a unique, Superman-style zipline that reaches speeds up to 80kph. The 1min. flight begins every hour 9am-3pm. Other activities include a 17-platfom canopy tour (1½ hr.), 75m climbing wall, horseback riding, and a Tarzan swing. *(There are no buses to the park, so the easiest means of transportation from Orotina is a taxi. With any driver, the fare should be about US$10. Turu's 1-day package tour includes lunch, tropical park or adventure tour, and round-trip transport to and from San José/Jacó/Puntarenas. US$80, ages 3-11 US$60, student discounts can be negotiated by phone in advance; with lunch and 1 activity only adults US$60.* ☎ 2250 0705; www.turubari.com. Open daily 8:30am-5:30pm with the last entrance into the park at 3pm. AmEx/MC/V.)

PUNTARENAS

After the Spaniards granted Costa Rica a monopoly on tobacco production in the 18th century, Puntarenas appeared on the map as an important port town. When the railway connected it to the Central Valley in 1910, its fate seemed sealed as a lucrative vacation magnet for beach-seeking *ticos*. However, modern developments have not been kind to this city; its beach has become alarmingly polluted while infrastructure developments have drawn commerce away from its port. Puntarenas is now a shadow of its former self, with vacant lots, eroding buildings, and rising crime rates. On the positive side, the stone church in the central *parque* and the newly renovated Capitania de Puntarenas are reminders of the city's former glory. Many *ticos* still loyally vacation here, especially during fiesta season, but most tourists only pass through to catch a ferry to the beautiful beaches of the Nicoya Peninsula.

◗ TRANSPORTATION

Buses: From Av. 1, C. Central/1, in front of the Farmacia Andrea, buses run to **Orotina** (1hr.; 6, 8, 9, 10am, noon, 2, 5, 6:30, 8:15pm; ¢600). From the stop on Av. 1/3, C. 2, just south of the *mercado central*, buses leave for **Caldera** (40min., every 2hr. 7:30am-5:30pm, ¢325). Buses to **Esparza** stop on Av. Central, C. 9/11 and C. 7/9 (40min., every 45min. 6am-8pm, ¢275). From the stop on Av. 1, C. Central/2 in front of the Restaurant Hong Tu buses leave to **El Roble** (25min., every 10 min. 5:30am-8pm, ¢200) and to the **Barrio Carmen Ferry Terminal** (10min., every 20min. 6am-9:30pm, ¢100.) Buses to **Barrio Carmen** also stop at the southwest corner of the *parque* at the intersection of Av. Central, C. 7. Schedules change frequently, so its good to ask a hotel manager or other locals. The main intercity terminal is in a blue building on the southeast side of town at the corner of C. 2 and the beachfront road, Paseo de los Turistas. From inside the terminal, buses leave for **San José**, dropping passengers at the Alajuela **airport** en route (2hr., every hr. 4am-7pm, ¢1610) and for **San Ramón** (1hr., every hr. 4am-9pm, ¢785). From the covered stop just across the street from the terminal, buses run to: **Filadelfia/Nicoya/Santa Cruz** (3hr.; 6am, 4pm; ¢1300); **Monteverde** (☎2645 5159; 3hr.; 7:30am, 1:15, 2:15pm; ¢1510); **Miramar** (45min., every 30min. 6am-9:40pm, ¢1000); **Quepos** (5hr.; 5, 8, 11am, 12:30, 2:30, 4:30pm; ¢1350); **Jacó** (3hr.; 5, 8, 11am, 12:30, 2:30, 4:30pm; ¢1350); and **Liberia** (☎2663 1752; 5hr.; 5, 8:30, 9:30, 10:30, 11:30am, 12:30, 2:30, 3:30pm; ¢1300). Buses to **Filadelfia/Nicoya/Santa Cruz, Monteverde, Miramar, and Liberia** accept payment upon entry, but tickets for buses to **Quepos** and **Jacó** must be purchased in advance from the **Transporte Quepos-Puntarenas S.A. ticket office** located on the west side of C. 4 between Av. 2/Central (☎2661 1345 or 2777 0743).

Ferries: Boats leave from the main dock near Av. 3, C. 35 on the far northwest side of the peninsula. Ferries to **Paquera** are run by the Naviera Tambor company (☎2661 2084 or

Puntarenas

▲ ACCOMMODATIONS
Hotel Cabezas, **6**
Hotel Chorotega, **3**
Hotel Don Robert, **4**

🍴 FOOD
El Fela Restaurant and
  Marisquería, **2**
Restaurante Hong Tu, **5**
Soda La Maravilla, **1**

Río Naranjo Estuary

Golfo de Nicoya

Playa Puntarenas

Muelle

TO ⊞ HOSPITAL
  MONSEÑOR
  SANABRISAS (8km),
  PLAYA DE DOÑA
  ANA & BOCA
  BARRANCA (14km),
  ESPARZA (20km),
  OROTINA (35km),
  JACÓ (75km),
  SAN JOSÉ (115 km)

C. 6
C. 4
To San José
To other
  destinations
Ticket office
  for buses to
  Jacó and Quepos
C. 2

El Roble,
Barrio Carmen
To ⊞
Banco
  Popular $
Banco de
  Costa Rica $

Mercado
  Central ⓘ
To Caldera
To Orotina
Av. 3
Banco de
  Costa Rica
Banco
  Nacional $ $
BAC $
Palí $
Supermarket
Farmacia
  Puntarenas
Cibernet
C. Central
C. 1
C. 3
C. 5
C. 7
C. 9
C. 11
C. 13
C. 15
C. 17
C. 19
C. 21
C. 23
C. 25
C. 27
C. 29
C. 31
C. 33
C. 35
C. 37

Av. 3
Parque
  Central
To ⊞
Barrio Carmen
To Esparza
Museo
  Histórico
  Marino
Red Cross ⊞
Av. 1
Av. Central
Av. 2
Av. 4 Bis
Av. Central
Av. 2
Paseo de los Turistas/ Av. 4
Paseo de los Turistas/Av. 4
Laundry
Connecte2

Ferries to
Paquera and Puerto Naranjo
Coonatramer
Naviera Tambor
Av. 3
Av. 1

0   200 meters
0   200 yards

2661 2160. 1hr.; 5, 7:30, 10am, 12:30, 3, 5:30, 8, 10pm; ¢530, children ¢300, cars ¢6230). From Paquera, buses connect with ferries to **Montezuma** via **Tambor, Pochote,** and **Cóbano.** Ferries also leave for **Puerto Naranjo** from the **Coonatramar Terminal** (☎2661 1069; www.coonatramar.com; 1hr.; 6:30, 10am, 2:30, 7:30pm; return 8am, 12:30, 5:30, 9pm;¢750, children ¢455, cars ¢5200.). From **Puerto Naranjo,** buses connect to **Nicoya,** where you can take a bus to **Playa Sámara, Playa Nosara,** or **Santa Cruz,** for connections heading to beaches farther south.

Taxis: Local company Coopepuerto (☎2663 5050 or 2663 3030); national company Coopetico (☎2663 2020).Taxis line the street on the south side of the *mercado central* on the northeast side of the peninsula. Crossing town from the San José bus terminal to the ferry dock costs around ¢1000.

✦✱ 🔢 ORIENTATION AND PRACTICAL INFORMATION

Puntarenas is a long, skinny peninsula 115km west of San José. Over 35 *calles* run north to south across the city's 1km width, while only 5 east-west *avenidas* span its length. The center of town is marked by the *parque central,* which houses the Puntarenas cathedral, and is bordered by Av. Central to the south, Av. 1 to the north, and C. 7 and 3 to the west and east respectively. Along the peninsula's southern border runs Av. 4, more commonly referred to as Paseo de los Turistas because it holds the upscale restaurants and hotels once popular with wealthier tourists. Travelers should note that no part of Puntarenas is safe after dark, especially around the *mercado central* and the western point of the peninsula. If you must go somewhere at night, it's best to take a cab.

Tourist Office: The main **tourist office** (☎2661 2980) is located above the Banco de Costa Rica opposite the main pier (Muelle) on the *paseo* and distributes tourist maps, changes currency, and provides information. Open M-F 8am-5pm, Sa 8am-noon.

Banks: The peninsula's banks cluster along Av. 3 between C. 3 and Central, with branches on the eastern end of the *paseo* near the main tourist office. All have **24hr. ATMs. BAC** open M-F 9am-6pm, Sa 9am-1pm. **Banco Popular** open M-F 8:15am-3:45pm, Sa 8:15am-11:30pm. **Banco Nacional** open M-F 8:30am-3:45pm, Sa 9am-1pm. **Banco de Costa Rica** open M-F 9am-4pm.

Laundry: Lavandería Millenium (☎2344 7199) is located behind a thick white fence on Paseo de los Turistas. The fence is locked, but call out to Luisa the proprietor and she'll let you in. Machine wash (up to 10 lbs.) ¢1300, dry ¢1300. Detergent and softener ¢300. Drop-off service charge ¢700. Open daily 8am-6pm.

Public Toilets and Showers: Toilets and showers available in a large, blue complex halfway down the Paseo de los Turistas (¢300).Toilets available in the main bus terminal on the southeast side of town (free).

Police: (☎2661 4869 or 2661 4839, emergency 911), on the northeast edge of town behind Banco Nacional, north of the post office.

Red Cross (☎2661 1945 or 2661 0184) is located 250m west of the northwest corner of the *parque.* Open 24hr.

Medical Services: Farmacía Puntarenas (☎2661 5558 or 2661 5559), next door to Palí supermarket, is well stocked. Open M-Sa 8am-8pm, Su 8am-5pm. **Hospital Monseñor Sanabria** (☎2663 0033), 8km east of town. Take any bus for Esparza, Miramar, Barranca, El Roble, or Caldera.

Internet Access: The convenient **Internet Café Puntarenas** (☎2661 4024) lies east of the church in the *parque.* ¢500 per hr. Open daily 10am-8pm. The fastest most reliable access is at **CIBER NET** (☎2661 3181); where tech-savvy kids come to play RPGs and instant message in the modern, air-conditioned cafe. ¢500 per hr.

Library: The **public library,** inside the Museum in the *parque.* Open M-F 10am-6pm.

Post Office: (☎2661 2156), Av. 3, C. Central/1, look for the sign across from the BCR. Open M-F 8am-5:30pm, Sa 7:30am-noon. **Postal Code:** 5400.

ACCOMMODATIONS

Camping on the beach in Puntarenas is unsafe and unsanitary, but plenty of good budget accommodations are available; rooms range from clean and spacious *cabinas* with full amenities to dirty dives that charge by the hour. Be careful about where you choose to stay. Tourists who wander into the wrong hotel are easy targets for cockroaches and unscrupulous owners alike. Paseo de los Turistas is generally safe with a few good places near the *parque central*, but try to avoid the *mercado central* and areas that aren't heavily populated.

Hotel Cabezas, Av. 1, C. 2/4 (☎2661 1045), a cozy place with pink walls and tropical decorations. Over 30 small rooms with fans and communal cold-water baths. You might find yourself watching hours of Spanish programs from the rocking chairs in the lobby. ¢4000 per person. Triple with private bath ¢15,000. ❶

Hotel Chorotega, C. 1, Av. 1/3. (☎2661 0998), diagonally across from Banco Nacional. Offers spacious rooms with cable TV. Singles ¢9000, with bath ¢11,000, with bath and A/C ¢13,000; doubles ¢12,000/16,000/17,000; triples ¢16,000/20,000. ❷

Hotel Don Robert, Av. 1, C. 3/5 (☎2661-4610), across the street on the north side of the *parque central*. This hotel's scenic location near the *parque* and dark wood paneling add a more homey feel to the spacious rooms and bathrooms. All rooms feature cable TV, Wi-Fi, private cold-water baths and fans. Singles ¢10,000, with A/C 14,000; doubles ¢18,000/20,000; triples ¢24,000/27,000. ❸

FOOD

Several mid-priced restaurants serving seafood and *típico* fare line Paseo de los Turistas. A small strip of *sodas* draws those waiting for a ferry on the other side of town while others are scattered throughout town. **Palí** (☎2661 1962) is the largest and best-stocked supermarket in town. (Open M-Th 8am-7pm, F-Sa 8am-8pm, Su 8:30am-6pm.) While many of the restaurants and *sodas* aren't worth mentioning, there are several noteworthy exceptions.

Soda La Maravilla (☎2661 1586), on the south side of the *mercado central* serves satisfied *tico* customers all day long. A dozen different *pinto* breakfasts (¢1300) and a dozen more *casados*

PUNTARENAS PIRATE PUNKS

Over 100 years ago, the port city of Puntarenas and the small inland trading post of Esparza were subject to frequent raids by pirates and other plunderers. However, as Costa Rica moved into the 20th century and Puntarenas' role as a major port city diminished, it seemed that the threat of pirate attack had disappeared for good. That is, until 2008, when a wave of pirate attacks began to plague the waters of Puntarenas again.

In June of 2008, over 15 fishing boats were caught by surprise and boarded by a small group of armed sea bandits. Instead of stealing fish and trade items like the pirates of the past, these men took modern-day valuables such as motors, gasoline and cellphones. Some of the instances involved violence; many of Puntarenas's fishermen fear repeated attacks in the future and some have put a hold on their daily excursions to sea.

Local authorities, alarmed by the spate of sea crimes, are looking for these criminals while also trying to come up with protective measures for fishermen— no easy task, given the vast, unbounded nature of ocean territory. While no attacks have been made so far on boats carrying tourists, Costa Rican fishermen will surely be more cautious.

(¢1500-1800) grace the billboard menu. Mild, homemade salsa tops nearly every meal. Open M-Sa 6am-5pm, Su 6am-3pm. ❶

Restaurante Hong Tu, Av. 2, C. Central/1 (☎2661 2753). While Chinese food may seem out of place in Central America, Hong Tu is one of the best eats in town. A/C, framed silk paintings, and a large TV keep patrons comfortable and entertained. Chinese *casados* (¢2900), Cantonese rice (¢1600), and fried egg rolls (3 for ¢1800) are favorites. Take-out available. Open daily 10:30am-11pm. MC/V. ❷

El Fela Restaurant and Marisquería, Av. 3, C. 1/3 (☎2661 3132), serves seafood and more typcial Costa Rican fare. The small bar in front gives way to a deck overlooking the Río Naranjo Estuary with great sunset views. *Arroz con pollo* (¢2200), spaghetti (¢2200), and numerous fish filet dinners (¢2750-3500). Open M-Sa 10am-10pm. ❷

◢ SIGHTS

MUSEO HISTÓRICO MARINO DE LA CIUDAD DE PUNTARENAS (CASA DE LA CULTURA). The museum is located in the *parque central* and recently underwent a renovation during summer 2008. The museum highlights the history of Puntarenas and its inhabitants with exhibits on archaeology, customs, local artistry, and trade relations, as well as a brief display on the region's natural resources. Bilingual information panels stress the city's importance as a cultural melting pot, while pre-Columbian artifacts are used to scrutinize and examine ancient funeral rituals. Additionally, exhibits of skeletons re-create a macabre array of burial postures. An exhibit on Isla San Lucas, Costa Rica's island prison, includes pictures and replicas of its graffiti. (☎2661 0387. Open M-F 10am-6pm. Free.)

◢ BEACHES

PLAYA PUNTARENAS. Running along the south side of the peninsula is Playa Puntarenas, a long, dirty-brown beach that gets cleaner as you move west along the coast, but has powerful currents. Locals frequent the beach on weekends, but few swim because of the dirty water. A 15min. bus ride takes you to a cleaner and less crowded beach located behind Cabinas de San Isidro, 7km from Puntarenas. (Take any bus toward Barranca, or El Roble from the stop on Av. 1, C. Central/1, and ask the driver to let you off at the beach. 15min., every 10min. 4:15am-10:25pm, ¢120.)

PLAYA DE DOÑA ANA AND PLAYA BOCA BARRANCA. Playa de Doña Ana, 14km from Puntarenas and 2km from the port of Caldera, is the only beach in the area that is even slightly developed for tourists. You'll find picnic tables, toilets, showers, and a bag guard (¢300). Two pink pillars mark the way to a ticket booth and the entrance to a short trail to the beach. Just 500m north along the highway (take a left after the bridge onto the sandy road) is rocky Boca Barranca, enticing surfers with a left break from the cliff between Barranca and Ana to the Fiesta Marriott Hotel. However, without a swell, there isn't much appeal—dirty water, strong currents, and the occasional dead cow keep most visitors away. Beware of nets from the local fishermen. The long, skinny strip of beach at Puerto Caldera, 3km south, is frequented mostly by *tico* families or local surfers. Watch out for strong riptides. (When someone's on duty, Doña Ana is open daily 7:30am-5:30pm. Both Doña Ana and Barranca are accessible via the Caldera/Mata Limón bus, leaving from Puntarenas at Av. 1/3, C. 2. 20min.; every 2hr. 7:30am-5:30pm, return from Caldera every 2hr. 6:20am-4:20pm; ¢325. Beach admission ¢1000, vehicles add ¢600.)

PARQUE NACIONAL CARARA

Encompassing over 5200 hectares, Parque Nacional Carara features the only remaining transitional rainforest in Costa Rica, where the drier rainforest of the North Pacific meets the humid rainforest of the South Pacific. The highly varied flora of these two distinct ecosystems provides homes for numerous rare and endangered species, including the giant anteater, the white-faced monkey, the scarlet macaw, and over 50 American crocodiles that lounge on the banks of the Río Tarcoles and the Meándrica Lagoon. Archaeological sites in the surrounding area have dug up artifacts of ceramic, rock, and jade. The park's well-maintained trail system also features **Acceso Universal,** the first and only wheelchair-accessible trail in any national park in Central America.

AT A GLANCE

AREA: 5242 hectares. Approx. 10% trail-accessible.

CLIMATE: Mean annual temperature 27˚C. Annual rainfall 2.8m. Highlights: Fully paved, wheelchair-accessible trail; several rare and endangered species; the only remaining transition forest in Costa Rica; crocodiles.

FEATURES: Río Tárcoles, Meándrica Lagoon.

GATEWAYS: Jacó (p. 277), Orotina

CAMPING: Not allowed in the park.

FEES: Admission ₡5735 (US$10), children 6-12 ₡574 (US$1), children under 3 free; Costa Rican nationals ₡1147 (US$2).

⌐ TRANSPORTATION

Buses traveling along the **Costanera Highway** pass by the reserve regularly. From **Jacó** or **Playa Hermosa,** take any Puntarenas-, Orotina-, or San José-bound bus (see **Transportation** sections), and ask the driver to let you off at the park entrance. In case your driver is forgetful, watch for the sign and large white ranger station. From **Puntarenas** or **Orotina,** take any Jacó- or Quepos-bound bus. **To return,** you'll have to rely on the buses that pass along the highway from San José or Puntarenas to Jacó or Quepos. A schedule of buses is posted on the information desk at the entrance to the park. Buses to Jacó and San José typically pass by every hour starting at 7am. Buses to San Jose pass by every 2hr., and to Jacó or Quepos every hour. Because buses pass by on different schedules, you may find yourself waiting anywhere from 10min. to 2hr. for the correct bus. (The park is open daily from Dec. to Apr. 7am-4pm; from May to Nov. 8am-4pm. Last tickets sold at 3pm.)

◤ ORIENTATION

Located 17km northeast of Jacó and 90km west of San José, Parque Nacional Carara was originally created to facilitate scientific studies and investigations. Three of its trails leave from the main entrance and are good for casual hikers, as they are easily traversed, evenly sloped, and well-shaded. The fourth, **Sendero Laguna Meándrica,** is a bit more challenging, especially during the wet season.

WHEN TO GO. Because most of the trails take about 1-2hr. to walk, Carara is best visited as a short daytrip. Get an early start and bring insect repellent, food, and water. Birdwatching is best in the morning (as soon as the park opens). Crocodiles are most likely seen at midday; scarlet macaws and monkeys are usually visible between noon to 2pm on the Laguna Meándrica trail. The **ranger station** has bathrooms, a picnic area, and potable water but no food.

HIKING

Only 10% of Carara is accessible by trail, but these trails are all well-marked and maintained. One trail leaves from the main ranger station and connects with two others, while the fourth, Sendero Laguna Meándrica, leaves from a trailhead off the highway 2km north of the main entrance. Wheelchair-accessible **Acceso Universal,** or **Sendero Cemento,** is a flat, paved 1.2km loop that takes about an hour to hike. It begins at the ranger station, moves through primary rainforest, and connects to **Sendero Quebrada Bonita.** Bonita is 1.5km long and takes about 1hr. to complete. It begins after a small metal bridge and is linked to a third trail, the 1.2km loop of **Sendero Las Aráceas,** by another small bridge. While all trails pass through similar primary forest, you're more likely to see wildlife on the Bonita trail. The less-trodden fourth trail, **Sendero Laguna Meándrica,** begins at the yellow gates 2km along the Costanera from the ranger station, where even more animals are to be found. Meandering alongside the **Río Grande de Tárcoles** for 4km, Laguna Meándrica leads to a lagoon **viewpoint,** which is the best place in the park to spot monkeys, scarlet macaws and crocodiles. This trail, however, offers little shade and is muddy year-round due to the high waters of the lagoon, so the rangers recommend rubber boots (₡1000 for rental at the ranger station). When the lagoon floods in September the trail becomes impassable. All visitors to the park must **register** and buy their **tickets** at the **MINAE office** (☎8383 9953) before hiking. Freelance guides can be hired to spot creatures and help keep your feet dry; they are recommended for visitors taking the Laguna Meándrica path. (₡11,470/US$20 per person. Guides available in English, French, German and Spanish. Antonio Vindas, ☎2645 1064, is recommended by the park, and during the dry season he can guide overnight backpacking trips into the park for ₡57,350/US$100, up to 15 people.) Scouts will guard cars for tips (recommended contribution ₡2868/US$5). There is also a secure parking lot (guarded M-Sa 8am-2pm) lot near the station if you don't mind walking to the farther trails. Don't leave valuables in the car. Carrying them is no safer, as **muggings** have been known to occur.

SIGHTS

The **Río Tárcoles Bridge** is about 3km north of Parque Nacional Carara's ranger station on the highway to Puntarenas and San José. It is known more commonly as the **Puente de los Cocodrilos** (Crocodile Bridge) because of the scores of crocodiles that reside in the muddy waters of the river and doze along its banks. The rangers say that the crocodiles prey on farm animals that roam the surrounding pastures. While there have been a few (probably apocryphal) reports of people being eaten alive or having their limbs chewed off, the animals can be safely viewed from the edge of the bridge. If you're lucky, you might see a crocodile lumbering around or floating log-like down the river, but it's more likely you'll see 20-40 crocodiles lounging immobile by the water. Locals sometimes stir up activity by throwing plants or even live chickens into the water (not recommended). The bridge is hardly worth its own visit, but if you're passing by on the highway you might stop for a quick peek. Just look for several people peering off the edge. If you want a closer look, call **Jungle Crocodile Safari** (☎2236 6473 or 2385 6591; www.junglecrocodilesafari.com) in Tarcoles for a 2hr. tour down the Río Tárcoles, complete with a bilingual guide who will perform some daring crocodile tricks. (¢14,338/US$25. Tours at 8:30, 10:30am, 1:30, and 3:30pm.)

JACÓ

Swimmers might be intimidated by the waves that beat against Jacó's cinnamon-colored sands, but surfers from around the world flock here to enjoy the consistent conditions and energetic atmosphere. Beginners will find that this is a great spot to pick up surfing skills, as the waves are not as enormous as other Pacific beaches, and surfing lessons are almost as common as the *casado*. Even during the low season, the town bustles with activity as surfers hit the water and tourists enjoy the numerous shops on Jacó's main drag. On the weekends, *ticos* flock to Jacó for the parties and waves. Of course, all this popularity comes with a price: restaurants charge a little more, budget accommodations aren't quite as cheap, the streets are littered with tour agencies, the beaches are not as pristine as they once were, and drugs and prostitution grow more common with each passing year. The party scene is fast-paced and runs from dusk until dawn every night. To avoid trouble, always walk with friends or take

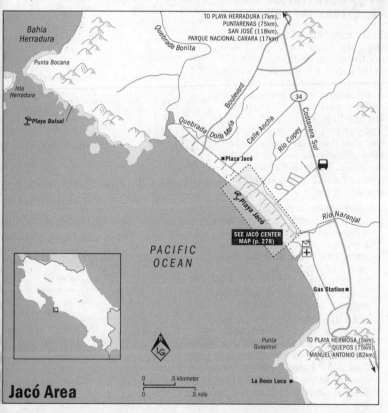

Jacó Area

a taxi at night. Travelers looking to relax can find more peace on the black sands of Playa Hermosa, a getaway just a few kilometers south.

▐ TRANSPORTATION

Buses: Buses to **San José** (Transportes Jacó S.A., ☎2290 2922; 3hr.; 5, 7, 9, 11am, 1, 3, 5pm; ¢1510) arrive and depart from Plaza Jacó, opposite the Best Western, 1km north of the town center on Ave. Pastor Diaz. Buy tickets early from the office at the southeast corner of the plaza. Other buses stop at various locations along the main road so ask around for the nearest stop; a good place to catch them is from the benches near the Más X Menos. Buses to **Orotina** (1½hr.; 4:30, 5:30, 7, 9am, noon, 2, 4pm; ¢1000) and **Puntarenas** (3hr.; 6, 9am, noon, 2, 4:30, 5, 7pm; ¢1350) stop on the east side of the street, and buses to **Quepos** (1hr.; 6:30, 9:30am, 12:30, 2, 4, 6pm; ¢800) stop on the west side.

Taxis: (☎2643 1919, 2643 2121, or 2643 2020) line up in front of Más X Menos (Playa Herradura ¢3500; Playa Hermosa ¢3000). Except for those coming from San José and Puntarenas, buses drop off passengers along the main road. Otherwise, buses passing near Jacó along the Costanera Sur Hwy. stop at the south end of town. It is a 1km walk or a ¢600 taxi ride to Jacó center.

◆▐ ORIENTATION AND PRACTICAL INFORMATION

Jacó center stretches about 1km along the main road, which runs northwest to southwest, parallel to the beach. For simplicity's sake, we describe the road here as north-south, with the northernmost end of town marked by the Best Western and bus station and the far south end by the post office. Several side roads and paths branch west off the main road and lead to the beach. Playa Herradura is 7km north of Jacó; Playa Hermosa is about 5km south.

Tourist Information: Jacó has no official tourist office, but many tour operators and shop owners are attentive and speak English. Maaike, the attendant at **Pacific Travel and Tours** (☎2643 2520; open M-F 9am-6pm, Sa 10am-1pm), arranges tours and transportation, and provides maps and other general information.

Banks: Banco Nacional, in the center of town. Open M-F 8:30am-3:45pm. **BAC,** ion the top floor of the Il Galeone shopping center. Open M-F 11am-6pm. **Banco Popular,** 100m north of Banco Nacional next to Il Galeone. Open M-F 8am-4pm, Sa

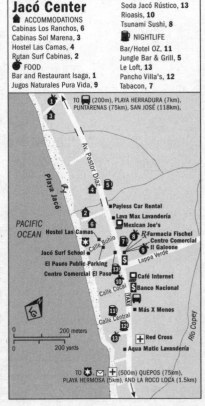

Jacó Center

♠ ACCOMMODATIONS
Cabinas Los Ranchos, **6**
Cabinas Sol Marena, **3**
Hostel Las Camas, **4**
Rutan Surf Cabinas, **2**

♦ FOOD
Bar and Restaurant Isaga, **1**
Jugos Naturales Pura Vida, **9**
Soda Jacó Rústico, **13**
Rioasis, **10**
Tsunami Sushi, **8**

▮ NIGHTLIFE
Bar/Hotel OZ, **11**
Jungle Bar & Grill, **5**
Le Loft, **13**
Pancho Villa's, **12**
Tabacon, **7**

TO 🚌 (200m), PLAYA HERRADURA (7km), PUNTARENAS (75km), SAN JOSÉ (118km),

Av. Pastor Diaz

Playa Jacó

PACIFIC OCEAN

■ Payless Car Rental
■ Lava Max Lavandería
■ Mexican Joe's
Hostel Las Camas
Jacó Surf School ■
El Paseo Public Parking
Centro Comercial El Paso
Calle Bohio
℞ Farmacia Fischel
Centro Comercial
Il Galeone
Lappa Verde
Café Internet
Banco Nacional
Calle Cocal
Más X Menos
Calle Central
Rio Copey
Red Cross
Aqua Matic Lavandería

TO 🏥, ✉, ✚ (500m) QUEPOS (75km), PLAYA HERMOSA (5km), AND LA ROCO LOCA (1.5km)

0   200 meters
0   200 yards

8:30-11:30am. All have **24hr. ATMs.** A **Western Union** office is located next door to Mexican Joe's. Open M-Sa 9am-1pm and 2-6pm.

Car Rental:

Budget Car Rental (☎2643 2665; www.budget.co.cr), in the Pacific Shopping Center, 50m north of the Jungle Bar. 21+. Drivers 18-20 pay ¢11,600 (US$20) extra per day. ¢435,000 (US$750) deposit. Cars in high season from ¢578,600 (US$57) per day, ¢208,800 (US$360) per week; in low season from ¢19,100/134,560 (US$33/232). Open daily 8am-5:30pm. AmEx/D/MC/V.

Economy Rent a Car (☎2643 1719), on the north side of town across from W.O.W. Surf. 18+ for Costa Rican residents, 21+ for non-residents. ¢1,160,000 (US$2000) deposit. Open daily 8am-6pm.

Laundry: Lava Max (☎2643 1617), just north of Mexican Joe's. Self-service wash and dry ¢4000 per 5kg; full-service ¢5000 per 5kg. Pick-up and delivery service also available. Open daily 8am-5pm. AmEx/MC/V. **Aqua Matic Lavandería** (☎2643 2083), 50m south of Banco Nacional. Self-service wash and dry ¢3000 per 5kg; full-service ¢3400 per 5kg. Open M-Sa 7:30am-5pm. AmEx/MC/V.

Parking: in El Paso Parqueo on C. Bohio across from Hotel Poseidon. ¢600 per hr., ¢400 per hr. for 24hr.

Emergency: ☎911.

Police:(☎2643 3011 or 2643 1881), in front of the Plaza de Futbol. Take C. Bohio down to the beach and walk 50m north. Open 24hr. An office for the transit police is located next to Clínica de Jacó.

Red Cross: (☎2643 3090), 50m south of Más X Menos. Open 24hr.

Pharmacy: Farmacia Fischel (☎2643 2089; www.fischel.co.cr), on the ground floor of Il Galeone. Has a knowledgeable staff. Remedies for jellyfish stings and board burn. Open daily 9am-9pm. AmEx/MC/V.

Medical Services: Clínica de Jacó (☎2264 3176 or 2643 3667), a 5min. walk south of town along the main road, just past the post office. English spoken. Open daily for consultations 7am-4pm. Open 24hr. for emergencies.

Telephones: Most internet cafes offer international calls and Skype access. **Public telephones** are located near the beach at the end of C. Bohio and all over town.

Internet: Mexican Joe's Internet Café, next to Tabacon in the center of town. 2nd location on the north end of town near W.O.W. Surf. Internet ¢250 per 15min., ¢700 per hr. Wi-Fi ¢550. International calls ¢100 per min. Private rooms available for Skype. Open daily 7am-11pm. **Cafe Internet @** (☎2643 2089 or 2643 1518), just north of Banco Nacional. Internet ¢500 per 15min., ¢1000 per hr. International calls ¢80 per min.

Post Office: On the south side of town, near the clinic. Follow the main road south as it curves left and make a right in front of the *municipalídad;* turn right on the 2nd side-street. Open M-F 8am-4:30pm, Sa 8am-noon. **Postal Code:** 4023.

ACCOMMODATIONS

Jacó's main drag and its surrounding side streets are lined with small *cabinas* and hotels, the majority of which have budget or mid-range rooms located less than 200m from the beach. A few more luxurious places cluster around the northern and southern ends of town. Rooms fill quickly on weekends and during the high season; it's not a bad idea to reserve a few days in advance. In the low season, bargain down the prices for groups and extended stays.

Rutan Surf Cabinas (☎2643 3328), 400m north of the bridge. Turn toward the beach at Mexican Joe's; the cabinas are on the left just past Isaga. Formerly known as Chuck's Cabinas (and still known by that name to locals). Myriad surf-slang bumper stickers testify to the hundreds of surfers who have crashed here. There's always a handful relaxing in the courtyard and giving free advice to beginners. Rents beginner epoxy boards from

W.O.W. Surf across the street for ¢1740 (US$3) per hr., ¢8700 (US$15) per day. Free Wi-Fi. Dorms ¢5800 (US$10) per person; doubles ¢130,500 (US$15). ❶

Hostel Las Camas (☎8377 3459), 50m north of the bridge across from Plaza Coral. This 4-story complex with brightly painted walls and funky accents is a haven for backpackers. Well-equipped common area and rooftop patio with spectacular views of the mountains to the east and the ocean to the west. Each room has A/C, cable TV, and lockers. Wi-Fi. Check-out 11am. Dorms ¢8120 (US$14); doubles ¢17,400 (US$30). ❷

Cabinas Los Ranchos (☎2643 3070; fax 2643 1810), 100m down the first sidestreet south of the bridge. A beautiful complex just 50m from the beach with private patios, lazy-day hammocks, and a pool surrounded by towering palms. Simple, spacious rooms with comfy beds, overhead fans, and private hot-water baths. All rooms are quads. Wi-Fi available. Check-in 8am-10pm. Check-out noon. Rooms ¢26,100 (US$45); with kitchen ¢31,900 (US$55). Discounts for long stays and in the low season. AmEx/D/MC/V. ❸

Cabinas Sol Marena (☎2643 1124), next door to Rutan. High-ceilinged rooms with cable TVs, fridges, and private baths are kept cool by overhead fans or A/C. Internet available. Singles ¢10,000 with fan, with A/C and hot-water ¢20,000; doubles ¢15,000/18,000; triples ¢18,000/30,000. ❷

🍴 FOOD

A wide range of food options, from traditional *tico* fare to sushi and Argentinean steaks, are available in Jacó. This variety comes with a price: even the *sodas* in Jacó are more expensive than normal. Watch out for nightly tourist-trap promotions. For those looking to cook for themselves, the **Más X Menos** (☎2643 2528) supermarket, just south of Banco Nacional, is well stocked. (Open daily 8am-10pm. AmEx/MC/V.). A **Megasuper** (☎2643 2764) is also located in Plaza Coral just north of Budget Car Rental. Open daily 8am-10pm.

Soda Jacó Rústico (☎2643 1721), 50m down the south side of Pancho Villa's. Inexpensive, but tasty, *típico*. Filling buffet-style lunch and dinner with rice, beans, your choice of meat, salad, and drink ¢2000. Open daily 7am-7pm. ❶

Bar and Restaurant Isaga (☎2643 1467 or 2643 1412), on the north end of town, across from Rutan's Hostel. *Gallo pinto* ¢1500. *Ceviche* ¢2700. *Casados* ¢1600-2300. Beer ¢700. Free Wi-Fi. Open daily 10am-2am. ❶

Tsunami Sushi (☎2643 3678), upstairs in the Il Galeone complex, 100m north of Banco Nacional. Classic Japanese dishes like California rolls (¢3045), dragon rolls (¢6400), and shrimp and vegetable tempura (¢4900). Tu 2-for-1 tuna roll special. Watch your rolls being made in the open sushi-making area. Open daily 5-11pm. MC/V. ❷

Rioasis (☎2643 3354 or 2643 0119), 25m down C. Cocal, on the side street just north of Banco Nacional. Creatively topped wood-oven pizzas. Munchies pizza with ham, onions, sweet pepper, salami, and oregano ¢5209. Mexican burrito ¢3000. Tortellini alfredo ¢5890. Free delivery in Jacó for any order over ¢5000. Open daily 11:30am-10pm. ❷

Caliche's Wishbone Restaurant and Bar (☎2643 3406). Signed surf boards and a palm tree motif constitute the decor at this popular eatery. Stuffed potatoes with cheese and choice of chicken or broccoli ¢3300. Wishbone pizza (BBQ chicken, onion, cilantro, mozzarella; ¢6100). Guacamole and chips ¢3800. Open M-Tu and Th-Su noon-10pm. ❷

Jugos Naturales Pura Vida (☎2643 6221), in the Pacific Shopping Mall. This small juice shop concocts thirst-quenching drinks with fresh produce. Drinks ¢1000. Fruit salad topped with condensed milk, cornflakes, and granola ¢1600. Open daily 7am-8pm. ❶

🕹 GUIDED TOURS

King Tours (☎2643 2441, toll-free from the US 800 213 7091; www.kingtours.com), 150m north of Banco Nacional. Friendly, knowledgeable staff arranges tours to satisfy all manner of adventure cravings. Tours to Isla Tortuga (¢69,600, US$120), Manuel Antonio (¢51,600, US$89), Poas (¢72,500, US$125), and Volcán Arenal (¢72,500, US$125) include lunch and transportation. Canopy tours ¢49,300 (US$85). Rafting ¢69,600 (US$120). Dolphin-watching ¢40,020 (US$69). Horseback riding ¢43,500 (US$75). Open daily 8am-8pm. AmEx/D/MC/V.

Green Tours (☎2643 1984 or 2643 1021), directly across from Il Galeone. Extensive selection of tours and services. Canopy tours at Vista Los Sueños and crocodile tours ¢31,900 (US$55). Rafting near Quepos ¢58,000 (US$100). Rainforest ATV tours ¢40,600 (US$70). Meals, water, and A/C transportation included. Transportation services to Manuel Antonio ¢16,800 (US$29) per person. Full-day sportfishing tours with meals, drinks, bait, and transportation provided ¢377,000 (US$650). Open daily 8:30am-8pm.

Ricaventura ATV Tours and Motorcycle Rentals (☎2643 5720; www.ricaventura.com), just north of the bridge next to Subway. Arranges comprehensive ATV tours. Tours include waterfall views and swimming time in naturally formed pools. (2hr. tour ¢37,700/US$65; 3hr. ¢49,300/US$85; 4hr. ¢63,800/US$110). Scooters ¢17,400/US$30 per day. Motorcycles ¢34,800/US$60 per day. Open daily 8am-6:30pm.

An Xtreme Rider (☎2643 3130 or 8867 5089; www.axroad.com), just north of the Red Cross across from Pancho Villa's. Runs ATV tours and rents motorbikes, scooters, bicycles, and surfboards. Bicycles ¢5800 (US$10) per day, ¢17,400 (US$30) per week. Scooters ¢23,200 (US$40) per day. Motorbikes ¢40,600 (US$70) per day. Credit card required to rent. Open daily 8am-7pm.

🔊 NIGHTLIFE

Jacó has no shortage of clubs and bars: nightlife here is serious business. Be aware that Jacó's drug problems are on the rise and prostitutes linger in many bars at night.

Le Loft (☎2643 5846), across from Lappa Verde St. Up-and-coming bar with Asian-inspired decor. Plays all types of music, but if you want to salsa, head elsewhere. Open bar W midnight-2:30am. Cover for men only ¢3000. Open 9:30pm-2:30am.

Jungle Bar and Grill (☎8643 3911), 50m north of Payless Car Rental, above Subway. Live DJ plays mostly Latin and Reggaeton to accompany revelers on the enormous dance floor. Pool and beer pong tables. Tu and Sa Ladies nights 10pm-midnight (free tequila, vodka, and rum). W Latin night. Open 6pm-2:30am.

Tabacon (☎2643 3097), in the center of town opposite C. Bohio. Classy, relaxed atmosphere is a welcome break from the high-party feel of its peers. But that doesn't mean that you won't find a party here: live rock and reggae bands on weekends draw a dance crowd. Tasty drinks include the Jamaica banana (¢2500) and the mango and peach margarita (¢2200). Appetizers ¢2700-5800. M Ladies night 10pm-midnight. Open daily noon-midnight.

Pancho Villa's (☎2643 3571), toward the southern end of town across from the Red Cross. After the other bars close, a largely male crowd stumbles to this all-night joint for pricey grub and gambling on the in-house slot machines. Mariachis regularly stop by. Free Wi-Fi. Appetizers ¢2000-6500. *Casados* ¢2000. Lobster ¢16,500. Open 24hr. Loosely affiliated with **Divas Night Club** (☎2643 1978), an adult entertainment lounge located upstairs. Cover ¢4000; includes 2 beers. Open daily 8pm-3am.

Bar Oz (☎2643 2162), down a side-street across from Más X Menos. Large, airy bar. Pool tables, darts, and TVs playing American sports. Open daily 10am-2:30am.

CENTRAL PACIFIC COAST

BEACHES AND SURFING

Long renowned as some of Costa Rica's most famous surf spots, the waters around Jacó have some of the country's most consistently diverse waves. Jacó's main beach has gentler swells that mellow southward—ideal conditions for beginners and intermediates. Experts craving more challenging surf head to the mouth of the river, north past Plaza Jacó, or to La Roca Loca, a sizable right break about 1.5km south of Jacó that crashes over a large submerged rock on Punta Guapinol (read: no beginners). **La Roca Loca** is a 30-45min. walk from the center of Jacó Beach—just head south and climb out over the rocks. Or, make the 5-10min. drive and tiptoe down a gnarly cliff. Just 5km away, Playa Hermosa (opposite page) has a challenging beach break also popular with advanced surfers. Farther south of Jacó are **Esterillos Oeste, Esterillos Centro, Esterillos Este, Playas Bandera**, and **Bejuco**. North of Jacó is **Boca Barranca.** Most of these beaches have isolated surf spots.

Jacó is a popular daytrip for surfers from all over the country, and most surf tourists pay it a visit. The main road is loaded with surf shops that buy, rent, sell, trade, and repair boards. Most offer similar services and prices, but some unusual deals exist.

W.O.W. Surf (☎2643 3844 or 2643 1108; www.wowsurf.net), on the northernmost part of the main road, 50m past Beatle Bar. The largest selection of surfboards, boogie boards, and surf gear in town. Beginner epoxy boards ₡8700 (US$15) per 24hr., fiberglass boards ₡11,600 (US$20) per 24hr. ₡464,000 (US$800) credit card deposit. Surf lessons (₡37,700/US$65 for a 3hr. group lesson, ₡69,600/US$120 for a private lesson). Open M-Sa 8am-8pm, Su 8am-6pm. AmEx/MC/V.

El Pana (☎2643 2125), directly across from Tabacon. Great deals on board rentals (₡5800, US$10 per day). One of the most affordable places to buy a used board in good condition (from ₡58,000/US$100). Pana himself is almost always around to help you make the best selection. Open daily 7am-9pm.

El Roka Loka (☎2643 1806), 50m south from Pana. Good selection of used boards (from ₡87,000/US$150). Board rentals ₡8700/US$15 per 24hr.

Jacó Surf School (☎8829 4697 or 2643 1905 after 7:30pm; www.jacosurflessons.com). Operates out of a small tent on the beach at the end of Bohio Rd. Run by Gustavo Castillo, a pro who spent a decade with the Costa Rican national team, this school offers the best, most comprehensive surf lessons in town. If you don't stand up, you don't pay. All instructors are certified lifeguards and speak English and Spanish. 3hr. group lessons (₡29,000, US$50 per person) include water, fruit, and full-day board use. Private lessons ₡43,500 (US$75).

PLAYA HERRADURA

Not long ago, Playa Herradura was little more than a quiet fishing village. Now, the northern shore is dominated by the luxurious Los Sueños resort, and the rest of the beach is beginning to show the effects with classier restaurants and higher prices. The southern end of the beach still offers privacy and beautiful views. Beside the resort, most of the tourists are *tico* families who string hammocks between the almond trees that line the narrow black beach in town. During the day, keep busy exploring the crescent-shaped bay, or, during low tide, wade out to nearby Isla Herradura, a deserted patch of land a few hundred meters off shore, and relax under the shady trees. Again, make sure you go during low tide. Public bathrooms available next to La Puesta del Sol (₡200).

Anyone seeking a drastic contrast from *gringo*-filled Jacó will enjoy a quiet daytrip here or a night of camping on the calm, palm-lined, black-sand shore. You can set up your tent for free along the beach with quieter spots farther south on the beach. For those without tents, the lime-green **Cabinas El Almendro ❷**, on the paved road 250m before the beach, offers pink and green motel-style rooms with fans, cable TV, and private hot-water baths (☎2637 8156. Singles ₡10,000, doubles and triples ₡15,000, 4-person rooms ₡20,000.)

A few beachfront restaurants make pleasant lunch stops. **La Puesta del Sol ❷** (☎2637 8003), the first place off the road to the beach, is a favorite among fishermen who bring in lobster or fish to be prepared on the spot. Barflies agree that Puesta has the best *ceviche* in Costa Rica for ₡1500. (Open daily 9:30am-2am, serves food after 12:30pm.) **Marisquería Juanita ❸** (☎2637 8073), is the best place to sample locally caught seafood, offering culinary consolation to those who can't catch their own. **Plato Juanita** with fish filet, lobster and vegetables ₡16,000; lobster ₡16,000, tuna filet ₡4300; *casado típico* ₡2400. Open daily 11am-10pm. AmEx/MC/V.) A few meters down the shore is **El Pelícano ❷** (☎2637 8910), a fancier restaurant that specializes in exotic seafoods (mahimahi sauteed in garlic ₡5975; shrimp *ceviche* ₡3795). They also make a killer homemade guacamole (₡3400) with tortilla chips. (Open daily 10am-10pm)

The easiest way to get to Playa Herradura is to take a taxi (₡3500) 7km north from Jaco. Buses running to San José, Puntarenas, or Orotina can drop you off at the left-hand beach turnoff; it's a 4km walk along a paved road to reach the beach. When you're ready to come back, call a taxi or take one of the hourly buses that run from the beach, past Jacó on the highway and then up through Jacó from the south (6am-10pm, ₡150). Be sure to flag it down, as the buses make a fairly fast turnaround.

PLAYA HERMOSA

Veteran surfers at Hermosa will tell you to skip Jacó entirely and head directly to this idyllic surf community. A stark contrast to the ritzy beach with the same name on the Nicoya Peninsula, Hermosa is a virtual paradise for those seeking to spend long days swinging in hammocks or catching the consistent, hollow, and nearly perfect waves. These swells can easily spring up to double overhead at high-tide before rushing up the steep grade of a 7km long black-sand beach. As in Dominical, the large number of *gringos* make this a fun choice for backpackers looking to make friends, but a poor place to practice their Spanish.

☐ TRANSPORTATION

Any Quepos-bound **bus** from San José, Puntarenas, Orotina, or Jacó will drop you off in town. A slightly more expensive option is to take a **taxi** from Jacó. (☎2643 1919, 2643 2020 or 2643 2121; ₡3000.) Arrange a time to return or ask a hotel to call a taxi when you're ready to return. From Hermosa, buses stop at a small palm-covered awning 25m south of the MiniSuper for Puntarenas (3½hrs.; 6, 9am, noon, 2, 4pm; ₡1000), Quepos (2hr.; 7, 9, 10am, 12:30, 2, 4pm; ₡800); and San José (3hr.; 6:15, 8, 9am, 3:30pm; ₡1250). Since Hermosa is only a pick-up point and not a major destination, allow 20min. in both directions on all bus departures, and check with locals for the most up-to-date times.

▨ ▧ ORIENTATION AND PRACTICAL INFORMATION

The small community of Playa Hermosa clusters around a 1km stretch of the **Costanera Sur Highway**, 5km south of Jacó and 70km north of Quepos. The highway actually runs northeast to southwest, but all directions here are simplified to north and south. From Jacó, you will ride south into town, passing **Hotel La Terraza del Pacífico** and then **Cabinas Rancho Grande** (at the north end of town). The **Backyard Bar** marks the southern end of town. All businesses are located between the highway and the beach with entrances on the road. On the northern end of town, **Pizzeria Bocha** (☎2643 3696), a wildly painted blue and orange building next to the Jungle Surf Café, offers **Internet.** (¢1000 per hr. Open daily noon-9pm.) Located just south of Bocha in the back of the Jungle Surf Cafe, **Black Sand Tours** (☎2643 5615, 2643 1495 or 8812 2860) offers tourist information and can arrage a variety of adventure tours as well. (Open M-W, Th-Su 7am-3pm.) The nearest **banks, pharmacies, clinics** and other services are in **Jacó.**

ACCOMMODATIONS

All accommodations face the beach to take full advantage of spectacular views. Generally catering to surfers who play in the surf for several weeks at a time, most of Hermosa's hotels and *cabinas* are pricier than their counterparts in other small towns, but you can still find some good deals. Accommodations in Hermosa are generally full year-round, so call ahead for reservations.

Cabinas Las Olas (☎2643 7021; www.lasolashotel.com), near the center of town. The wooden lodge and *cabinas* seem more appropriate for the Swiss countryside than the beach, but the sound of the waves crashing into the shore just meters away is more than enough to bring you back to Costa Rica. The small pool is perfect for breaks between the tides. All rooms have tile floors, private hot-water baths, and fridges. Discounts available for large groups and during low season. A-frame ranchos with 5 beds and fans US$20 per person; standard doubles in the lodge US$20 per person; doubles with A/C US$25 per person. The skybox suite, a 4-person, 3rd-story bungalow with balcony and breathtaking ocean views US$25 per person. ❷

Costanera Bed and Breakfast (☎2643 7044; www.costaneraplayahermosa.com), between Cabinas Las Olas and Las Arenas. Travelers can spend a day relaxing and taking in the incredible beach views from Costanera's amber-tiled terrace just feet away from some of the best food in town. All rooms are freshly furnished with private baths and tile floors. Doubles with fan and cold water US$35; triples US$40. With A/C and hot water add US$10. Breakfast included for singles and doubles. ❸

Cabinas Rancho Grande (☎2643 7023), located at the north end of town, offers the best price in Hermosa for the eclectic group of surfers and backpackers who fill its rooms. Several 4-person rooms with A/C, TVs and private baths make up the lower floors of the bamboo and wood structure, while the top floor offers a more primitive 5-person room accessible only by a difficult ladder climb, with no A/C. Doubles as a sauna by day. Communal outdoor kitchen and pool table. A/C rooms with private bath US$12.50 per person, top-floor rooms with fans and communal outdoor shower US$10. ❶

Cabinas Las Arenas (☎2643 7053 or 2643 7013) near the center of town behind Restaurante Coco Bongo. Has comfortable wood-paneled rooms with great beach views. All rooms have private hot-water baths and TV. With fans, singles US$33; doubles US$35; triples US$50. With A/C, US$50/54/60. Discounts available for long stays. Arenas also allows camping on a grassy patch of land right in front of the beach with showers available. US$12; bring your own tent. ❸

FOOD AND NIGHTLIFE

Like Jacó, most food at Playa Hermosa is geared toward American visitors. Although the *gringo* food and prices feel a bit touristy, the demand leads to a variety of options and make the higher prices almost worthwhile in Hermosa. **Supermarket MiniSuper Pochotal** is near the town center but offers only a very limited selection. (Open M-Sa 7am-9pm, Su 8am-noon.)

▨ **Pizzeria Bocha** (☎2643 3696), just north of the Jungle Surf Cafe, offers a huge selection of dishes, all big and savory enough to fill even the hungriest of stomachs. Start out slow with a tall fruit smoothie (¢1500-2000) or a homemade empanada (¢900). Then move on to a loaded deep-dish pizza with melt-in-your-mouth crust (¢5000-6800), but make sure to bring a friend along to help. The Maradona with 10 veggie and meat toppings is a popular choice. Open daily 11:30am-9:30pm. ❶

▨ **Costanera Cafe** (☎2643 7044), 2 doors north of Cabinas Las Olas in the Costanera B&B. Chef and owner Nadia prepares delicious homemade breakfasts year-round, which include banana pancakes, bacon and eggs, and fruit and granola with endless coffee and tea. All breakfasts US$3-5. During the high season, there's a rotating menu of pasta dishes made from imported Italian ingredients (US$5-6). Open daily 8-11am. High season open daily 8-11am and 6-9pm. Call ahead if you want dinner. ❶

Jungle Surf Cafe (☎2643 1495), on the north end of town, just past the soccer field. Offers inexpensive and tasty *típico* breakfasts (¢1500) as well as a variety of lunch entrees including the popular Baja Fish Tacos (¢2800). The short, rotating dinner menu offers creative selections and fantastically fresh fish, such as sesame-seared teriyaki tuna. All dinners include rice or mashed potatoes and sauteed veggies (¢5500). Open M-Tu and Th-Su 7am-3pm and 5-9pm. ❷

The Backyard Bar (☎2643 7011), at the southern end of town. A restaurant by day and a bar and dance club by night. As the only late-night option in Hermosa, large numbers of visiting surfers and fun-loving *ticos* fill its split-level bar, pool tables, and large dance floor almost every night of the week. W ladies' night features live music and even draws some of the crowd from Jacó. Burgers and buffalo wings US$8. Daily happy hour (4:30-7:30pm) offers ¢600 beers, ¢700 shooters and free *bocas*. W ladies drink free 9pm-midnight. Open daily 7am-2am. AmEx/D/MC/V. ❷

◉ ▨ SIGHTS AND GUIDED TOURS

Hermosa's waves might be where most of the action is, but the surrounding forests and tamer waters offer enough activities to keep non-surfers busy for a day or two. Although the various canopy tours and rafting adventures may be a bit pricey, the steep **Monkey Trail,** which begins on the dirt road across from the old Bar Palmarenos and sees steady wildlife traffic, is free. If you're around between July and December, you'll have a good chance of seeing the 3000-4000 olive ridley turtles that emerge from the water to lay their eggs, with sightings most common in August. Ask the manager of your hotel where the best sightings have been recently. Gilberto Rodriguez of **Black Sand Tours,** located in the back of the Jungle Surf Cafe, can set you up with a variety of activities in the area. (4hr. canopy tour US$70, Parque Manuel Antonio tour US$120 per person with 2 people, US$85 with 4, or horseback riding along Hermosa Beach US$90.) (☎2643-5615, 2643-1495 or 8812-2860. Open M-Tu and Th-Su 7am-3pm.) **Hotel La Terraza del Pacífico,** 300m north of town, arranges a number of adventure tours as well. Canopy tours US$70, ATV tours US$70, rafting tours US$90, and two-tank scuba diving US$65. (☎2643 3222. AmEx/D/MC/V.)

◿ SURFING

Intermediate and expert surfers swear by Hermosa's perfectly cascading waves, which regularly reach heights of 8-13 ft. before slamming onto its seemingly endless black-sand beaches. One caveat to note is that the waves have a tendency to hold a fallen surfer under, and the impact zone is famous for splitting boards and crushing faces against the sandy bottom. Still, near-perfect conditions at high-tide regularly call dozens of skilled surfers in and out of the white foam. Even with this traffic, except for a few busy weeks in the high season, there are enough peaks along the 7km beach that you won't have to dodge boards to catch a wave. For a memorable moon-lit ride, Hotel La Terraza illuminates the beach break in front of the hotel with flood lights on Saturday nights from 8 to 9pm (8pm-midnight when there's a local competition going on). True experts flock to Hermosa for the annual Quiksilver qualifying event held by the Hotel La Terraza, which is usually held for several weeks in the month of July. For those still learning, Hotel La Terraza can also set up surf lessons with a local pro (US$70 for a private 2hr. lesson).

SOUTH OF JACÓ TO QUEPOS

The well-paved Costanera Sur Hwy. curves along the Central Pacific coast, connecting Jacó to Quepos and passing many quiet, largely deserted beaches on the way. These tiny beach communities can barely be called towns; they are mostly remote residential pastures with a few *cabinas* and hotels scattered along the beaches. These shores draw vacationing *tico* families and some local surfers during the Christmas holiday and *Semana Santa* (Easter), but otherwise the pristine beaches and their powerful waves are only crowded by the surfers and tourists trading in the nightlife and crowded streets of Jacó for better waves and more relaxation. Surfing is especially good at Esterillos Oeste and Playa Bejuco, where big waves break on the sand, and waves become larger heading south to Playa Bandera. These beaches are best for large groups of skilled surfers or anybody who would rather enjoy the beach or the breaks without the crowd. Beaches are listed north to south from Jacó to Quepos.

PLAYA ESTERILLOS OESTE

The first major beach south of Jacó and Playa Hermosa is Esterillos Oeste, 22km south along the Costanera Sur Hwy. and 47km north of Quepos. Here, the beach is long and shady, with bowl-shaped waves beginning at the *esterillo* (estuary). An outcropping of coral and volcanic rock formations at the north end of the beach break the waves and provide a great area for safe swimming. Esterillos Oeste is also the most developed of the beaches between Jacó and Quepos with a variety of accommodations and restaurants to choose from, which is good as camping is not allowed on the beach. From the highway follow the uphill fork 2km to the supermarket and the beach 100m further.

F ACCOMMODATIONS. Accommodations and restaurants in Esterillos cluster around the two roads that lead to the right and left of the supermarket. The north road is the right-hand turn just after the supermarket, and the south road is the left just before it. The main road continues past the Supersol to the beach. One of the best values in town for people traveling alone or in smaller groups, **Cabinas/Soda Mary ❶,** is located 50m up the north road. Accommodating four or six, these large cement-floored rooms have cold-water private baths, fans, and access to a communal kitchen. They are inside the owner's house, and overlook a yard cluttered with plants and old surfboards (US$10 per person. One double also available.) The owner, Brett, also teaches surfing lessons. (US$50 for a 2hr. lesson. Board rental US$20 per day.☎2778 7058) Find a more luxurious version of the basics at **La Sirena ❹,** about 500m along the north road; look for the large copper mermaid statue on the reef just in front of the hotel and brightly colored mermaid paintings on the gate. The rooms are large and cheery with TVs, private cold-water baths, A/C, and plenty of fans. Guests also have access to the large pool and a hammock-filled patio. (☎2778 8020. Quads ₡25,000; 8-person rooms with full kitchen ₡40,000.)

◘ **FOOD.** Travelers who want to pack their own picnics can pick up supplies at the **Supersol,** just before the main beach entrance. (☎2778 8097. Open daily 6am-10pm. AmEx/MC/V.) Several good restaurants cluster near the beach.

The **Lowtide Lounge,** a.k.a. **Bubba's on the Beach Bar ❶,** is the main surfer hangout in town, and it embraces that fact with surf stickers, rock music and board rentals (US$25 per day; boogie boards US$8 per hr). To get there,, continue down the main road past the Supersol to the beach. Surf families enjoy the simple menu of chicken, beef, fish, or breakfast tacos (¢2250). Add the combo plate of rice, beans, and grilled sweet corn for ¢800 more. (☎2778 7013. Daily happy hour (4-7pm) serves national beers (¢750) and imports (¢1000). Open daily 9am-9pm. Cash only. **Restaurante Azul ❷,** between the north and south roads, has a pleasant atmosphere with bamboo-thatched roof, wooden fish decorations, and a colorful bar. A diverse menu, including vegetarian options like *ensalada azul* with hearts of palm (¢2500) as well as fish burritos (¢2700) and lobster (¢11500), fits the eclectic decor. (Open daily 7am-11pm). At the end of the south road where it meets the beach, **Bar y Restaurante Barrilito ❶** is a popular nighttime hangout. When the crowds pick up on the weekends, locals and visitors belt out karaoke favorites. (*Chalupas* ¢1500. Fried plaintains with meat and beans ¢1500. Open daily 10am-2am.) Once Barrilito dies down, people usually head to **Discoteque Azul,** next door to the restaurant of the same name. The bar, popular with young locals, has an expansive dance floor and hosts live music once a month. (☎2778 7318. Open Th-Su 7pm-2am.) A slightly older crowd (20s and 30s) looking for a more laid-back atmosphere winds down at **Shake ❶,** in a coral pink building where the north road ends on the reef. The second-floor bar overlooks the beach and serves tasty dishes like seafood soup (¢2000) and spaghetti (¢1900) on a pleasant patio. Pool, foosball and a good selection of arcade games are available inside. (☎2778 8285. Beer ¢900. Mixed drinks ¢2000. Open M and W-Su 10am-10pm, but on the weekends the crowd sticks around until 1 or 2am.)

PLAYAS BANDERA (PALMA) AND BEJUCO

Farther south of Jacó and inching toward Quepos is a long stretch of beaches that see little visitor traffic. The sand darkens as coconut palms and *almendro* trees thicken around the coast. Fishing and swimming are favorite activities for the *tico* families who come to stay in beach houses here, though foreigners are becoming a more significant presence in local life. All enjoy decent surfing conditions when the swells are firing. At **Playa Bejuco,** 3km south of Esterillos Este, stay at **Hotel El Delfín ❺,** an elegant place on the beach, complete with a large pool and hot tub with a dolphin mosaic on the bottom. A sweeping staircase leads to 14 heavily amenitied rooms with private gas-heated baths, A/C, full orthopedic beds, satellite TV, Internet access, and private balconies. Over two miles of teak were used to make the impressive high-domed bar where patrons enjoy the free continental breakfast. (☎2778 8054; www.delfinbeachfront.com. High season doubles US$128, low season US$105. AmEx/D/MC/V.)

Playa Bandera, also known as Playa Palma because of the mountain of African palms that preceed it, is a 9km long shady beach that is a bit more popular with surfers than swimmers and has more of a small-town atmosphere than Playa Bejuco, while seeing few tourists. From Parrita 16km south of Esterillos, head northward and turn left at the first sign for Playa Bandera, or, from the north, turn right at any of the three entrances and continue on the main road until the small yellow sign for **Restaurante Que Comemos ❷,** where all the entrances to Playa Bandera intersect. The dining room is surrounded by a gorgeous botanical garden from which he gathers herbs such as basil and oregano to use in his dishes. Pito taught himself to cook and takes pride in the fact that many diners declare his steaks to be the best in Costa Rica. Many who discover this treasure refuse to dine anywhere else during their stays in Bandera. (Steaks ¢4500. Open daily 10am-10pm)

To get to the beach from Comemos, take the first left, then follow the main road 4km as it winds down toward a large yellow sign that warns of the dangerous undertow. Continue past the sign and take a right on the beach road to get to **Cabinas Maldonado ❸**. Good for families or large groups planning to stay a while, its six huge rooms sleep four, six, or 10 people and have full kitchens, fans, and cold-water private baths, along with access to a pool, hot tub, and grill outside. (☎2779 6350 or 2227 5400. Quads ¢35,000 high season, ¢24,000 low season; 6-person ¢35,000/50,000; 10-person with 2 baths ¢70,000/75,000.) Just a few doors before Maldonado, **Las Brisas del Mar ❶**, just behind the *abastecedor* with the same name, is the cheapest option in town. The dark rooms offer ceiling fans, TVs, and private baths. (☎2779 6555. Quad ¢10,000.)

QUEPOS

Located 3hr. south of San José, the city of Quepos is one of the Central Pacific's most well-trodden destinations. The town's appeal lies more in its proximity to tourist-magnet Parque Nacional Manual Antonio than in its urban hustle or unremarkable beach. Quepos also serves as a base for dozens of competing tour operators who run trips through the turbulent rivers and wild mountain terrain just outside town. Tourism has definitely jump-started the economy here; sportfishing easily rakes in more money than the banana crops on which the town once depended, and the soldier-straight rows of African palms along the shore are quickly forgotten en route to raftable rivers and canopy tours. If the adventures offered don't fit your budget, Quepos is a convenient (and wallet-friendly) base from which to explore Parque Nacional Manuel Antonio.

▉ TRANSPORTATION

Flights: Flights arrive at the airstrip 5km northwest of town. Sansa (☎2777 0676 or 2777 0683; www.flysansa.com) flies to **San José** (25min.; high season 15 per day 6:45am-2:15pm, US$78; low season 6 flights per day 6:45am-2:15pm, US$72) and to **Palmar Norte** (45min., 1 flight per day 9:30am, US$98). AmEx/D/MC/V. NatureAir (☎2220 3054; www.natureair.com) also flies to **San José** (high season 8 per day 7:45am-2:30pm, US$80; low season 4 per day 7:45am-2:30pm, US$75). Because these planes hold very few passangers, reservations should be made several weeks in advance during high season. Check online for the most up-to-date prices and schedules. You can reserve tickets at Lynch Travel (☎2777 1170 or 2777 0161; www.lynchtravel. com), located 1 block north and west of the bus station across the street from Banco Nacional. Open daily 7am-6pm. Closed Su during low season. AmEx/MC/V.

Buses: To Quepos from San José, buses depart from Av. 1/3, C. 16. (Direct 3hr.; daily 6, 9am, noon, 6, 7:30pm; indirect 5hr.; M-F 7, 10am, 2, 5pm; ¢1800.) From the main bus station in Quepos, buses go to: **Manuel Antonio** (25min., approx. every 30min. 5:30am-9:30pm; ¢115); **Parrita** (45min.; M-Sa, 15 per day, Su, 9 per day; ¢300); **Puntarenas** (4hr.; 4:30, 7:30, 10:30am, 12:30, 3, 5:30pm; ¢1350) via **Jacó** (1hr.; 4:30, 10:30am, 3pm; ¢1000); **San Isidro** (2hr.; 5:30, 11:30am, 3:30pm; ¢1500); **Uvita** via **Dominical** (2½hr.; 6:30, 9:30am, 5:30pm; ¢1500); **San José** (direct 3hr.; 4, 6, 9:30am, noon, 5pm; ¢2615; stops in **Jacó** en route; 4½hr.; 5, 8am, 2, 4pm; ¢2105).

Taxis: (☎2777 3080, 2777 1207, or 2777 0425) line up across the street from the bus station. A taxi to Manuel Antonio should cost about ₡2500-3000.

Car Rental:

Payless Rent-a-Car (☎2523 9007 or 2523 9000; www.paylesscr.com), past the *lavandería*. Drivers Economy car high season US$59 per day, US$371 per week; low season US$52 per day, US$330 per week. US$1000-2000 credit card deposit required, depending on size of vehicle and duration of trip. Open daily 7:30am-5:30pm. AmEx/D/MC/V. 21+.

Budget Car Rental (☎2774 0140; www.budget.co.cr), 100m north of the field on C.7. High season US$50 per day, US$330 per week; low season US$38/US$195. Open daily 9am-6pm. 21+.

CENTRAL PACIFIC COAST

Quepos

🏠 ACCOMMODATIONS
Cabinas Mary, **13**
Hotel Malinche, **7**
Mar y Luna, **4**
Wide Mouth Frog, **11**

🍎 FOOD
Bar/Restaurant Quepoa, **9**
Café Milagro, **2**
Escalofrío, **12**
L'Angolo Gastronomía Ristorante, **8**
Soda Sanchez, **10**
Tropical Sushi, **5**

🍸 NIGHTLIFE
Discotheque Arco Iris, **1**
Licorería Ramu's, **6**
Republik Lounge, **3**

Fast Eddie's Scooter Rentals (☎2777 4127 or 8888 8111), located across the street from Budget, has scooters. US$55 per day. Weekly rates are available upon request. Open daily 8am-5pm during the high season. Closed Su during the low season.

■✦ ORIENTATION AND PRACTICAL INFORMATION

Quepos is 172km southeast of San José, 65km south of Jacó, and 7km north of Parque Nacional Manuel Antonio. The bus station marks the center of town; the beach is on your right (west) when you face the supermarket with your back to the terminal, and the soccer field and road to Manuel Antonio are two and three blocks to your left (east), respectively.

Banks: All have **ATMs.**

Banco Popular (☎2777 1055), 1 block east and 1 block south of the bus terminal, changes traveler's checks. Open M-F 8:15am-3:30pm, Sa 8:15-11:30am.

Banco de Costa Rica (☎2777 0285), directly east of the bus terminal. Exchanges US$ and changes traveler's checks. Open M-F 10am-6pm.

Banco Nacional (☎2777 1157), across the street from Lynch Travel, cashes traveler's checks. Open M-F 8:30am-3:45pm.

Laundry: Aquamatic Lavandería (☎2777 0972), 50m down the curving road southwest of the soccer field. Wash and dry self-service ¢2800, full service ¢3200, detergent and dryer sheets ¢300. Open M-Sa 9am-noon and 1-5pm. AmEx/MC/V/¢.

Emergency: ☎911.

Police: (☎2777 0196), 100m south of Av. 2 on C. 2, facing the ocean. Open 24hr.

Red Cross: (☎2777 0116, 2777 3380, or 2777 3381), 25m east of the bus station. Open 24hr. Call the first number first.

Pharmacy: Farmacia Fischel (☎2777 0816 or 2777 0527), across the street and just west of the bus station, is well-stocked and has a knowledgable pharmacist on staff. Open M-Sa 7am-10pm, Su 8am-7pm. AmEx/D/MC/V.

Medical Services: The **hospital** (☎2777 0922), 5km northeast of town on the Costanera Sur Hwy., is accessible by buses to Londres, Naranjito, Inmaculada, and Uvita (every hr. 4:30am-6pm, ¢115). Taxi ¢3000.

Telephones: Located just east of the bus terminal and scattered throughout town. The supermarket and pharmacy both sell phone cards.

Internet Access: Tropical Café Internet (☎2777 2368), across the street from Cafe Milagro, has the cheapest, most reliable Internet in town (¢800 per hr.) as well as photocopy and fax service (¢150 per page). Open M-Sa 9am-9pm. **K.I.T. (Keep In Touch) Internet Café** (☎2777 7575), on the 2nd fl. of Centro Comercial La Garza just east of Hotel Ramu's, has Skype-capable computers and will also let you hook up your own computer (¢1000 per hr.). Open M-Sa 9am-10pm, Su noon-6pm. **Compunet Internet** (☎2777 4698 or 8832 7852), next door to Lynch Travel, offers the same prices as Tropical Café Internet (¢800 per hr.) but their computers are a little older.

Post Office: (☎2777 1471), facing the soccer field. Fax available (☎2777 0279). Open M-F 8am-noon and 1-5pm, Sa 8am-noon. **Postal Code:** 6350 or 60601.

⛁ ACCOMMODATIONS

Budget accommodations are more plentiful and less touristy here in Quepos than in Manuel Antonio, making it a cheaper (albeit a bit less scenic) base for visits to the park and nearby beaches. Most places in town have similar offerings—simple rooms with fans and cold water—but some provide an atmosphere with a little bit more character. Due to the area's popularity, reservations are recommended during the high season.

■ **Wide Mouth Frog Hostel** (☎2777 2798; www.widemouthfrog.org), 2 blocks east of the bus terminal. Offers the newest facilities with the most character and community in town. Basic lodging is complemented by a large communal kitchen, free Wi-Fi, swimming pool, and a shared space with cable TV and DVD rental. Guests come from a variety of backgrounds, but most are friendly backpackers from around the world. Parking available. GBLT-friendly. Laundry service available for guests, US$6-8. Dorm beds US$9. Doubles and triples with fans and shared bath US$28. Doubles and triples with private hot-water bath US$38. With A/C add US$10. ❶

Mar y Luna (☎2777 0394). With your back to the bus station, walk toward the beach, turn right at the corner, and then make a left at the corner with Lynch Travel. Mar y Luna is a few meters down on the right. While the rooms are simple, the walls throughout the building are covered with colorful aquatic murals and the common area features comfy chairs and a TV. Singles with fan and shared cold-water bath US$13; doubles with fan and bath US$26; triples US$39. Add US$5 per person for hot-water bath. ❶

Hotel Malinche (☎2777 0093), across from Mar y Luna. This yellow building with white-railed balconies holds large, well-furnished rooms with plenty of sunlight suitable for a variety of budgets. Doubles with fans and private cold-water bath US$26 in the low season, US$30 high season. Doubles with A/C, cable TVs, and private hot-water baths US$50 low season; US$60 high season. ❷

Cabinas Mary (☎2777 0128), next to the *pelequería* on the road across from the soccer field. Mary's offers simple and clean rooms at reasonable prices. Each room holds 2 -4 people and is equipped with powerful fans and private cold-water bath. Parking available. ₡5000 per person. ❶

▣ FOOD

With the influx of American and European tourists to the Quepos area, a wide variety of restaurants have emerged to satiate their palates, offering everything from Italian gelato to Japanese sushi. Though these options may be more expensive than the food in less-touristed areas, the numerous *sodas* that surround the bus station offer more affordable *típico* fare. Visitors can also pick up their own groceries at the **Super Mas** across from the bus station. (☎2777 1162. Open M-Sa 8am-8pm, Su 8am-1pm).

■ **Soda Sanchez** (☎2777 2635). Over the past few years this humble establishment, located just east of the Red Cross office has earned a reputation as the best *soda* in the Quepos/Manuel Antonio area. The original cooks are still around and have perfected the menu's *típico* fare, so the small but comfortable dining room is never empty. Don't miss the seafood soup (₡3000): its ingredients change based on what's fresh, but it often includes calamari, shrimp, half crabs, and other shellfish. *Gallo pinto* breakfasts ₡1000-1400. *Casados* ₡1500-2000. Open M-Sa 6am-9pm, Su 9am-4pm. ❶

Café Milagro and El Patio Restaurant (☎2777 1707 or 2777 4982; www.cafemilagro. com or www.elpatiodecafemilagro.com), located near the bridge leading northwest out of town. Buy a bag of fresh roasted beans or enjoy a cup of coffee (₡625) in the cafe, or head to El Patio just next door for banana and macadamia nut pancakes (₡2100) or *nueva latina* dinner entrees such as tuna with avocado salsa and Brazilian spice rub (₡5850). Dinner reservations recommended. Open M-Sa 6am-10pm, Su 6am-6pm. ❷

L'Angolo Gastronomía Ristorante (☎2777 4129). This small Italian deli located a block south of the bus station uses some imported ingredients to create authentic dishes. Though the menu of panini (₡1400-2900) and pastas (₡3000-5000) may be basic, it sure is tasty. Try the tomato, mozzarella, and pesto panini (₡1400) or fettuccine alfredo with seafood (₡4200). Italian groceries also available. Open M-Sa 8am-1pm. ❷

CENTRAL PACIFIC COAST

Tropical Sushi (☎2777 1710 or 8387 2308), just west of Hotel Ramu's's. Glass tables and warm, scented hand towels lend the place some class, and the creations of Japanese chef Fuji seem especially exotic to those used to a monotonous diet of *ceviche*. The selection includes tempura appetizers (¢3550): rolls with crabmeat, cucumber, and fried banana (¢3550) and vanilla ice cream fried in tempura for dessert (¢1250). All-you-can-eat 5-7pm (¢8000). One of the few places in the country to enjoy Sapporo (¢1800) and sake (¢1900). Open daily 4:30-11pm. AmEx/D/MC/V. ❸

Escalofrío (☎2777 0833 or 2777 1902), a block south of the bus station. Though the large rainforest murals on the walls may be a bit misleading, the food at Escalofrío is exclusively Italian. 4 types of bruschetta (¢1600-2200) will whet your appetite for a selection of brick-oven pizzas so large they'll leave you loosening your belt (¢2700-5600). Save room for the creamy gelato dessert, served in a cone (¢600) or in a fancy sundae (¢2000). Open Tu-Su 2:30-10:30pm. ❶

Bar/Restaurante Quepoa (☎2777 4050), across the street from the bus station. One of the few places in town that serves authentic *típico* fare in a large, pleasant setting. Locals gather here for filling *casados* (¢2500-3600) and chicken platters (¢2200-3800) before belting out karaoke tunes (W and F 9pm-1am). Open daily 7am-2am. ❶

🔊 NIGHTLIFE

For a fairly small city, Quepos has quite a few bars and clubs. These places can fill up during the high season but calm down in the rainy months when most *gringos* take the bus straight through town and continue to Manuel Antonio.

Discotheque Arco Iris (☎2777 2061 or 8834 6726), 1 block after the bridge out of Quepos heading northwest, is the only real late-night option in Quepos. Salsa, merengue, and reggae beats get bodies moving on both dance floors in this huge, fortress-like building that comes complete with its own moat. Nightly cover includes 2 beers. Cover ¢2000 before 12:30pm, ¢5000 after. Open daily 9pm-4am.

Licorería Ramu's's, next door to Hotel Ramu's. A neighborhood bar that is particularly popular with older male *ticos* and a welcome option for those seeking a quieter local atmosphere. The drink selection is extensive, but dining options are limited to prepackaged snacks and *ceviche*. Open M-Sa noon-9pm.

Republik Lounge (☎8394 7350), 1 block north and 2 blocks west of the bus station across from El Gran Escape features a modern silver interior with artistic, egg-shaped bar stools. But the visual is only part of the appeal. Latin and electronic beats keep the dance floor crowded year-round. W ladies nights are especially popular; ladies drink free all night, ¢1000 cover for men. Open daily 6pm-2:30am.

🏔 📷 OUTDOOR ACTIVITIES AND GUIDED TOURS

Most tourists find themselves in Quepos to make plans for an outing—the environs offer a variety of tempting options, including rafting, canopy tours, mangrove exploration, and some of Costa Rica's best sportfishing. Plan ahead and bring your credit card because most trips will make a pretty sizeable dent in any budget traveler's wallet.

Tours2Go (☎2777 1754 or 2777 7222), next to Cabinas Hellen, west of the school on Ave. 2. Susan can set you up with nearly any tour in town, probably for less than if you did it yourself. Multilingual book exchange, tourist information, and Internet access (¢400 for 30min.) Open M-F 9am-1pm and 3-6pm, Sa 10am-1pm and 3-5pm.

Iguana Tours (☎2777 2052; www.iguanatours.com), at the southeast corner of the soccer field. Arranges hiking and horseback tours of Parque Nacional Manuel Antonio (US$42) or Parque Nacional Carara (US$65), mangrove boat trips to Damas Island (US$60), and kayaking tours (US$65). Experienced guides specialize in day white-water rafting trips (Río Naranjo US$65; Río Savegre US$95; includes lunch). Rescue kayakers accompany all rafting trips. Open daily 7am-7pm. AmEx/D/MC/V.

H2O Adventures (☎2777 4092 or 2777 4094; www.aventurah2o.com), in the red building across from the *lavandería*. Offers the best prices for white-water rafting on the Río Savegre (half-day US$70 includes snack and transport; full day US$98 includes breakfast, lunch, and transport) and the only Class V rafting in the area on the El Chorro river (US$98; only during the high season). 3hr. ocean and mangrove kayaking trips are also available (US$70). Also organizes an annual 2-day foot, bike, kayak, and canopy line race called the Central Pacific Challenge (Oct. 9-10; www.cpchallenge.com).

Estrella Tour (☎/fax 2777 1286; stefano@estrellatour.com), located across the street from Tours2Go. Run by a group of ex-professional bikers, Estrella Tour offers mountain biking excursions as well as indoor cycling classes. Trips range from casual 6 mi. rides (US$45) to 17 mi. expert rides (US$75). Custom rides and multi-day adventures can also be arranged. Open M-Sa 9am-12:30pm and 2:30-7pm.

Fourtrax Adventure (☎2777 1829 or 2777 1825; www.fourtraxadventure.com), near the southeast corner of the soccer field. Offers exhilarating 4hr. ATV tours to the town of Naranjito in the mountains. Singles US$95, doubles US$125. Includes pickup, transport, bilingual guides and 2 meals. Open daily 7am-9pm.

MAD Manuel Antonio Diving (☎2777 3483; www.manuelantoniodiving.com), across from Ramu's's. A PADI-certified Instructor Development Center with multiple classrooms and their own pool, MAD offers everything from Discover Scuba Diving courses (US$155) to a 3-day open-water certification course (US$365). 10% student discount.

PARQUE NACIONAL MANUEL ANTONIO

Parque Nacional Manuel Antonio offers a popular combination of Costa Rica's most scenic terrains: warm, jade-green waves cascade onto white sand beaches that lead into lush tropical forest. *Ticos* treasure the park, and most tourists choose to visit here at some point during their stay. Despite government efforts to regulate local development, this once-pristine park is beginning to show the effects of heavy tourist traffic. Trinket vendors solidly block the beach view, huge crowds fill guided tours, and cars travel all the way up to the park entrance. With souvenir shops lining the streets and families toting beach chairs and picnic coolers along the trails, the park sometimes feels like it's playing host to a massive family vacation, but that doesn't make its beauty any less incredible: birds fill the trees with color while armadillos amble through the underbrush. An encounter with the park's most outgoing inhabitants, white-faced monkeys, is almost guaranteed. They have neither fear nor shame; they'll snag your snacks, ham it up for your camera, and toss mangoes at your head. If you're willing to do a little walking, you can reach the park's more isolated beaches, which still enjoy the charm of a newly discovered paradise.

AT A GLANCE

AREA: 683 hectares of land and 42,016 marine hectares.

CLIMATE: Tropical humid.

FEATURES: Punta Catedral Peninsula, Playa Espadilla, Playa Espadilla Sur, Playa Manuel Antonio, Playa Escondida, pre-Columbian tortoise traps.

HIGHLIGHTS: Hiking, canopy tours, parasailing, kayaking, diving, snorkeling, and rambunctious wildlife.

GATEWAYS: Quepos (p. 288).

FEES AND RESERVATIONS: US$10; closed Mondays.

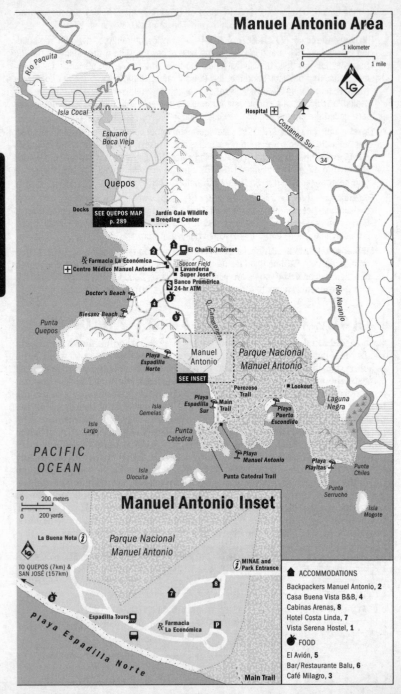

⚑ ORIENTATION AND TRANSPORTATION

Parque Nacional Manuel Antonio is located 7km south of Quepos, 157km south of San José, and is preceeded by a small, very touristy neighborhood that bears its name. From Quepos, the **bus** will drop you off at the T intersection in front of Restaurante Marlin (25min., every 30min. 5:30am-9:30pm, ¢115). From here, you'll see a small street winding uphill and inland, marked by the Restaurante Marlin on the left. This road eventually leads to the park entrance after passing several budget and mid-range accommodations along the way. The direct buses from San José to Quepos also continue to Manuel Antonio (3hr.; 9am, noon, 6, 7:30pm). A **taxi** from Quepos shouldn't cost more than ¢3000.

WHEN TO GO. Manuel Antonio is one of Costa Rica's most-visited national parks, so if you prefer less-crowded trails and don't mind overcast skies, come during the rainy (low) season (May-Nov.), when fewer people are on vacation. Sundays tend to be particularly crowded in any season. Bring light clothes, comfortable shoes, sunscreen, and water. A word on responsible tourism: because it disrupts the animals' natural patterns, visitors are advised to refrain from feeding them.

ⓘ PRACTICAL INFORMATION

The park entrance, MINAE office, and main ranger station are located at the end of the side road heading northeast from the Farmacia La Económica. (Park open Tu-Su 7am-4pm. Entrance fee US$10 for tourists, ¢1600 for nationals.) English-speaking guides are available just outside the ranger station and can help you spot the more elusive treetop wildlife, although they are not necessary for spotting common animals or taking short hikes. (US$20 per person for a 2-3hr. tour; negotiable based on group size.)

Banks: Banco Promérica (☎2777 5101). **ATM** is located 100m north of the La Mariposa turnoff along the main road.

Laundromat: Laundry service is available at the **Lavandería** (☎2777 5050), 50m southwest of the soccer field. Full service wash and dry ¢4000. Open daily 8am-8pm.

Police: Quepos police also serve Manuel Antonio (☎911 or 2777 0196).

Pharmacy: Farmacía La Económica (☎2777 5370 or 2777 2130) has 2 locations, across the street from the *lavandería* and the other near the beach across from Restaurante Marlin. Open daily 8am-8pm. AmEx/D/MC/V.

Medical services: English-speaking **Centro Medicó Manuel Antonio** (☎2777 2422 or 8367 7256 for emergencies) is across the street from the *lavendería* next door to the pharmacy. Open M-Sa 9am-9pm.

Bookstore: La Buena Nota (☎2777 1002 or 2777 1946; buenanota@sol.racsa. co.cr.)is an English-language bookstore, 800m northeast of Restaurante Marlin near Cabinas Piscis. Owner Anita opened the first tourist shop in the area 28 years ago and has since built up a store full of tourist information and trinkets. A large selection of American magazines and newspapers and thousands of used English-language books are available upstairs. Changes traveler's checks. Open daily 9am-6pm. MC/V.

Internet Access: The cheapest Internet service is at **El Chante Internet** (☎2777 3307) just in front of Vista Serena. ¢400 for 15min.; ¢1000 per hr. International calling. US$0.15 per min. Open M-Sa 9am-10pm, Su 9am-noon. Internet is also available inside **Espadilla Tours** (☎2777 5334) next door to Restaurante Marlin.¢1000 for 30min.; ¢1500 per hr. Open daily 9am-8pm. The **Regalame** gift shop (☎2777 0777),

IN RECENT NEWS

A NEW PROJECT COMES INTO HARBOR

For the last few decades, the town of Quepos has served primarily as an entryway into Manuel Antonio National Park. Most tourists make use of the less expensive lodging and dining options in Quepos but spend the bulk of their days on the more beautiful and pristine beaches of Manuel Antonio just 7 km southwest. But soon, Quepos itself may have something more to offer.

In 2007, construction began on the 35-acre Marina Pez Vela. The marina, scheduled to open sometime in 2009 or 2010 will be the first, and for the time being, only full-service marina in Central America. The marina will house 250-plus boats and provide dock space for multiple cruise ships.

The marina promises to substantially increase tourism in the area, drawing sportfishermen, cruise-goers and boat-lovers alike. Residents hope that they will bring good tidings for the town of 20,000. The marina will provide hundreds of jobs and could mean thousands of dollars in foreign investment. This money could be used to clean up the town's cluttered streets, address the rising crime rates, and make Quepos a better place to live in and to visit.

Though Quepos may not be the place to be right now, in two years time, people may begin to think differently. Particularly those who can appreciate a nice marina.

300m down the main road from La Mariposa, offers a faster connection at slightly higher prices. (US$2 per 30min.) Open daily 7am-10pm. Other services and conveniences can be found in Quepos.

ACCOMMODATIONS

While staying in the touristy town of Manuel Antonio may be more expensive than staying in Quepos, it is definitely a far more scenic experience. Camping is only allowed on public beaches but is discouraged due to the high incidence of burglary. Water shortages in the area cause most hotels and *cabinas* to only change the sheets every other day and ask that you do your part to conserve.

Casa Buena Vista B&B (☎2777 1002 or 2777 1946; www.casabuenavista.net). Ask the bus driver to stop at La Mariposa and take a right 500m downhill. This charming B&B is in a small, cream-colored building with a triple covered driveway on the left. Flanked by several astronomically priced resorts, it offers 8 spotless doubles with fans, tank-heated water, home-cooked breakfast, and priceless views of Punta Catedral. Owner Anita of La Buena Nota can also provide information about Manuel Antonio.Call ahead for reservations. High season singles US$35; doubles US$50. Low season US$25/35. Add US$10 for A/C. ❸

Vista Serena Hostel (☎2777 5162; www.vistaserena.com). You'll pass it on your right as you take the bus into town. Get off at the soccer field stop and backtrack 150m to the best backpacker view in town. All rooms have A/C. Attractively decorated dorms share heated showers, kitchen, living room with cable TV, and hammock views of spectacular sunsets over the ocean (US$15). Private doubles share heated bath and kitchen with 1 other room. Low season US$45; high season US$50. ❷

Backpackers Manuel Antonio (☎8820 4621), across from the soccer field and below the pharmacy on the road into town. Though it's short hike to the park entrance, this hostel is conveniently located near most of Manuel Antonio's more practical services. Clean dorm rooms share hot-water baths, communal kitchen, and a TV room with comfortable couches and DVDs for rent. Free Wi-Fi is also available. Dorm rooms US$9; doubles with shared bath US$30. Add US$10 for each additional person up to 5. ❶

Cabinas Arenas (suwama@hotmail.com). This small but colorful establishment located just meters from the park entrance offers 2 brand-new *cabinas*. Both *cabinas* feature huge ceilings and colorful blue tile floors as well as more practical amenities such as A/C, cable TV, and private hot-water baths. Both are triples, US$30. ❸

Hotel Costa Linda (☎2777 0304; costalindamicha@yahoo.de), 300m up the inland road from Restaurante Marlin. The closest backpacker digs to the park entrance. Basic cement-floor rooms have fans and sturdy beds. Courtyard cold-water baths lack privacy, but the brightly painted common room is great for meeting other travelers. Breakfasts of fruits, pancakes, and *gallo pinto* are served daily (¢1500). Laundry ¢3500 per load. Dorm beds US$9; doubles with baths and fans US$19; triples US$28. ●

FOOD

There's no shortage of upscale and pricey restaurants in Manuel Antonio, and finding a reasonably priced restaurant or *soda* is more difficult than in most Costa Rican towns. Budget travelers can still eat well without breaking the bank at more basic restaurants closer to the beach. Travelers who want to cook for themselves can stop up at the **Super Josef** market (☎2777 1095), located 150m past the soccer field toward the park. Open daily 7:30am-9pm.

Bar/Restaurante Balu (☎2777 0339), 100m down the beach from the 1st drive-through loop near the beach, has a very relaxed beachfront atmosphere. In fact, the "floor" is nothing but sand. The place is so close to the breaking waves that sea foam sometimes moistens customers' toes as they munch on *tico* fare like *gallo pinto* (¢1700) and rice with shrimp (¢3500). Daily happy hour 4:30-6:30pm with 2 for 1 drinks. Open daily 8am-9pm. V. ●

Café Milagro (☎2777 0794; www.cafemilagro.com) at the intersection of the main road and the side road to La Mariposa. Serves a wide variety of breakfast dishes and sandwiches to go with signature coffee drinks and homemade pastries. Try the french toast for breakfast (¢2350) or the chicken pesto sandwich with avocado (¢3350) and top it off with an espresso milkshake (¢1450). Open daily 6:30am-6pm. ●

El Avión (☎2777 3378; www.elavion.net), located 300m up the hill from La Buena Nota. It's hard to miss the giant C-123 airplane thats sits in the middle of this mountainside restaurant. A relic from the Reagan era, the plane houses a classy bar and inspires great conversation to go along with incredible ocean views and delicious seafood dishes such as the blackened tuna sandwich (¢3700) and salmon with fried plantain and sour cream (¢5900). Open M-Th 2-10pm, F-Su noon-10pm; bar open until 2am daily. ●

BEACHES AND HIKING

Although it is the smallest of Costa Rica's national parks, with only 683 terrestrial hectares, Manuel Antonio is second only to Volcán Poas in the number of visitors it receives each year. The park is easily explored in a leisurely 3-5hr. jaunt through its interconnecting trails, including stops to observe the wildlife. Once lured into the warm waters of the fine, white-sand shores of its four beaches, however, you can easily watch the entire afternoon slide by. To exit the park, follow the signs back to the Perezoso Trail and go back through the gate in front of the ranger station and MINAE office.

PLAYA ESPADILLA. Just outside the park, this is the large public beach that runs parallel to the town's main drag. Flanked by mangroves and estuaries, this scenic shore is often crowded because it is free. Vendors also line the road and beach selling everything from fried chicken to jewelry. The waters are nice for wading, although swimmers and novice surfers should be aware of the possibility of strong riptides. Find beach-comber Evan near the small turnoff road near Restaurante Balu to rent plastic recliners (US$10 per day), but beware of the crocodiles that chill on the north end of the beach. The nine-footer that the guides refer to as "Juancho" has not yet harmed a person, but once snapped up an unsuspecting and unfortunate dog.

PLAYA ESPADILLA SUR. Playa Espadilla Sur, popular with both visitors and monkeys, stretches from the north limit of the park to the Punta Catedral Peninsula and is accessible by following the main Perezoso Trail 1½km into the park and then following the trail northwest from Playa Manuel Antonio. Shaded by almond trees, this slender white beach is so enticing that some tourists make it no further into the park.

PLAYA MANUEL ANTONIO. The Perezoso Trail that leads from the main entrance into the park take visitors right to Playa Manuel Antonio, also known as Playa Tres (Third Beach). Picnic areas, bathrooms, showers, and a refreshment stand are all available here. As the park's most popular and idyllic beach, Playa Manuel Antonio lives up to visions of a tropical paradise. Set in a rocky cove, it has calm surf, narrow shores, and turquoise water that's perfect for bathing, swimming, and snorkeling. If you happen upon the beach at low tide, don't miss the most visible of Manuel Antonio's pre-Columbian tortoise traps on the northernmost edge near Play Escondida. The Quepo Indians built these curved rock walls in the intertidal zone to catch mating turtles as the tide went out.

PLAYA PUERTO ESCONDIDA. From the junction of the Perezoso Trail with the various beach trails, take the eastern trail to Puerto Escondido (1.6km). The beach is only accessible during low tides, so check with the rangers before attempting it. Though this beach is the farthest from the main entrance, the short hike is well worth it as this "hidden beach" is significantly less crowded than the others and is equally spectacular.

SOUTH TRAIL (PEREZOSO TRAIL). This 1.3km trail originates at the park entrance and connects to the Puerto Escondido Trail before reaching Playa Manuel Antonio. The trail itself mainly serves to provide access into the park, connecting to other more scenic trails, but the trail has earned its name—*perezoso*—for the numerous sloth sightings frequent along its route.

PUERTO ESCONDIDO TRAIL (PUNTA CATEDRAL TRAIL). This 1.4km loop begins at the southwest end of Playa Manuel Antonio and circles Punta Catedral, a former island that has become linked to the land by sediment build-up, forming a sandy bridge between the fertile terrains. The trail winds through the rainforest on the peninsula before leading to several spectacular views of the ocean.

 FRESH KILLER. Mosquitoes got you down? Try a homemade bug spray. Listerine® works great as bug spray. Spray it on (just watch for open wounds or old mosquito bites) and it may work better than Deet.

DOMINICAL

With rocky chocolate-brown beaches and reliable waves, the tiny surfer town of Dominical (pop. 300) lies 50km south of San Isidro on a straight shot down the highway toward the Pacific coast. Though it attracts a constant stream of surfers year-round, the influx really picks up during the wet season, when great waves bring surfers in droves. This three-road town is more than just a surfer stop; it also has a small, close-knit community of *ticos* who've lived here all their lives and expats who came here on vacation and never left. The constant stream of visitors, however, have replaced the more traditional *sodas* and bars with American-style food and entertainment, making Dominical a less-than-ideal destination for those more interested in encountering *tico* culture. Travelers will enjoy the tree-canopied shoreline, mountainous backdrop, expansive beach, and consistently enjoyable nightlife.

TRANSPORTATION

Buses: The 2 main bus stops are the covered benches across from Arena del Sol in the middle of town and Bar and Restaurante El Co Co and the southern end of town, but you can catch a bus anywhere along the main road. Schedules are posted in nearly every business establishment, but it's best to come a bit early, just in case the bus isn't running on schedule. Buses head to: **San Isidro** (1hr.; 6:30, 7:30am, 1:30, 2:30, 5:30pm; ¢1300); **Uvita** (30min.; 8:30, 10, 10:20, 11:30, 11:45am, 5:15, 7:30, 9pm; ¢500); **Quepos** (2hr.; 5, 5:30, 8:15, 11:30am, 1, 1:40, 5, 5:30pm; ¢1300); **Ciudad Neily** via **Cortés** (3hr.; 4:30, 10am, 3pm; ¢1200).

Taxis: The town of Dominical doesn't have a taxi company, but taxis can be called from surrounding areas. If you need one, ask a business to call one for you.

ORIENTATION AND PRACTICAL INFORMATION

The north end of Dominical's 1km main road hits the **Costanera Sur Highway.** A side street forks off the main drag across from the large, gated ICE complex, forming a well-trodden shortcut to the beach road, which runs parallel to the main road. They intersect at the southern end of town just past Bar/ Restaurante El Co Co. Orient yourself by remembering that the ocean is always west.

Banks: The only bank in town is the **Banco de Costa Rica** located in the Centro Comercial Plaza Pacífica across the highway from the main entrance road into Dominical. Offers money exchange and a **24hr. ATM.** Open M-F 8am-4pm.

Laundry: The cheapest is **Lavandería Las Olas** (☎8881 3594), in the town center across from San Clemente. ¢900 per kg. **Arena y Sol** toward the southern end of town also does laundry. ¢1000 per kg. Open daily 7am-10pm.

Public Bathrooms: In the Centro Comercial, where the main road meets the highway.

Emergency: ☎911.

Police: (☎2787 0011), on the main road, south of the side street.

Telephones: There are 2 public phones in front of San Clemente, 1 in front of the police station, and a few scattered along the beach.

Internet Access: Arena y Sol, on the main road across from the ICE complex has several Skype-capable computers and Wi-Fi. ¢500 for 20min., ¢1000 per hr. Open

LOCAL LEGEND

BLING BLING, I CAN'T FIND A THING

Most visitors to Manuel Antonio come in search of beaches and wildlife, but perhaps they should be in search of something a little more valuable. Over five centuries ago, the land that Parque Nacional Manuel Antonio now occupies was inhabited by the Quepos Indians, a subgroup of the Boruca people. The Quepos had a reputation of being brave warriors who possessed great quantities of gold and other valuables won from conquered tribes and from the panning of the river. It remains unknown, however, what happened to these treasures when the Indians began to move out of the Quepos territory.

Some claim that the treasure was even supplemented by 16th century pirates looking to unload their ships heavy with gold. English privateer John Clipperton traveled to the area in the early 16th century in hope of finding this lost treasure. Though he uncovered many an anecdote to support his theories, Clipperton never found any treasure and died without finding any evidence of the treasure.

Today, the history of the Quepos Indians is even less present in Manuel Antonio. Luxury resorts and condos now stand on the old Indian hunting and crop areas. Though this beachfront property may be worth a bundle in its own right, it may be sitting on even more valuable grounds.

daily 7am-10pm. **Dominical Internet Café and Calling Center** (☎2787 0191), on the 2nd fl. of the business complex next to San Clemente, also has Internet access. ¢1000 per 30min. Open M-Sa 8am-10pm, Su 9am-6pm.

Post Office: There is no official post office building in town, but **San Clemente Bar & Grille** on the northern end of town, can send and receive mail and has a post office drop box. It also sells envelopes and stamps (¢155 for a postcard to the US).

ACCOMMODATIONS

The logistics of staying in Dominical vary quite a bit by season, though accommodations are available for every budget range no matter when you go. Prices rise and availability drops during the high season (Dec.-Apr.), when reservations are necessary. Generally, you won't get as much luxury for your buck in Dominical as you can in less-touristed towns. Camping on the beach is possible, although belongings and equipment should never be left unattended. Check with the police for up-to-date security information. Campers can typically negotiate a cheap shower from one of the nearby *cabinas*.

Tortilla Flats (☎2787 0033), the 1st place right where the access road meets the beach is the center of most of the social life on the beach side of Dominical. While the eponymous bar and restaurant draws a crowd on most nights, the brightly painted hotel with lazy hammocks and floral murals draws a fun group of backpackers and surfers as well. All rooms are quads and offer private lukewarm baths and fans. The rooms on the road are newer, but a bit louder at night. High season US$30, low season US$25. ❸

Hostel/Cabinas Piramys (☎2787 0196), stands alone 100m south of the intersection of the main and beach roads at the end of town. Piramys features a pitched roof over the tent loft and walls decorated with splatter paintings and hieroglyphics. There's an outdoor kitchenette on the premises, and easy-going owner Angel will let you rent a surfboard for US$10 per day. Mosquito-netted beds with shared hot-water showers high season ¢5000, low season ¢4000; doubles with private bath ¢15,000/10,000; camping in the loft ¢3000, includes tent. ❶

Posada del Sol (☎2787 0085), on the south end of the main road just before Arena y Sol. The owners have created a quiet atmosphere, an oasis in the middle of Dominical. Their private garden features an array of flowers and porch-side hammocks, and the well-lit private rooms feature hot-water baths, 2 fans, and a small safe. Singles US$25; doubles high season US$35, low season US$30; quads US$45/40. ❸

Hostel and Camping Antorchas (☎2787 0307). Follow the side road past Diu Wak Resort to the beach and take the 1st right after Tortilla Flats. Cheerful rooms have high ceilings, mosquito-netted beds, and shared outdoor bath. Guests also have access to a communal kitchen, half-basketball court, and a *rancho* with tables and cable TV. Free coffee all day. Singles US$15; high season doubles US$25, low season US$24; quads US$60/40. Camping under a low-roofed loft with electrical outlets, firepole, tent, and mattress provided US$9/8. Open-air camping in the small yard US$7. ❶

Cabinas El Co-Co (☎2787 0225), at the south end of the beach road, where it intersects with the main road. Offers the cheapest (but small) *cabinas* around. Singles with shared cold-water bath ¢6000, with bath and TV ¢12,000; doubles ¢8000/16,000; triples ¢10,000/20,000; with A/C add ¢5000. AmEx/D/V/MC. ❶

FOOD

The influx of surfers and other foreigners to Dominical has led to a wide variety of dining options for such a small town. Within km you can find everything from Tex-Mex to Sushi with some typical *sodas* in between. The biggest supermarket in town, **Supermercado Dominical** , is located in the Centro Comercial on the opposite side of the highway. ((☎2787 0143. Open M-Sa 8am-8pm, Su 8am-6pm.) On the corner of the side and main roads, **Bajcra Supermercado** has all the basics in a more convenient location, but at slightly higher prices. Locals buy their greens from **Fernando's Frutería El Mercadito** (☎2787 0621), near the highway where the main road turns down toward the beach. (Open daily 8am-8:30pm.)

▨ **Maracatú** (☎2787 0091), along the main road before San Clemente. Serves up vegetarian and Caribbean fusion cuisine, like veggie *casados* (¢2200), fish tacos (¢3500), and salad with pineapple and mango (¢3400). Tu open-jam night, W ladies night; and Th "Rasta Pasta"—all-you-can-eat pasta and reggae. Happy hour daily 4-5:30pm. Drink specials daily 10pm-midnight. Open daily 11am-10pm. Bar open until 2am. ❷

Chapy's (☎2787 0283), next door to Blowfish Surf on the north end of town. This small, 1-man cafe serves up delicious fruit smoothies with your choice of milk, soy milk, or yogurt (¢1500) to go with creative, huge sandwiches made from all-organic ingredients. Try the hummus and avocado (¢2300) or the eggplant and gouda (¢2800). ❶

Tortilla Flats (☎2787 0147 or 2787 0033; www.tortillaflatsdominical.com) has a beachfront restaurant attached to its *cabinas* and is the favorite hangout for surfers and is usually the center of the town's nightlife until other places get going. Flats has everything from a simple grilled cheese with avocado (¢1700) to mahimahi with cheese (¢3500). Happy hour daily 4-6pm. Ladies night Th. Open daily 7am-10pm. ❷

San Clemente Bar & Grille (☎2787 0045). A local hangout that serves Tex-Mex and beer in a fun atmosphere in the center of town. Guests enjoy the heaping *casados* nicknamed "The Starving Surfer" (¢3000) while they spend the night relaxing in the restaurant's reconstructed school bus, watching surf videos, and playing pool (¢500). Taco Tu features ¢800 tacos and ¢1000 margaritas. Open daily 7am-10pm. ❷

Restaurante Su Raza (☎2787 0105), across the street from San Clemente, is one of the few places in town that serves traditional Costa Rican cuisine. This is one of the cheapest local options for good food all day. *Gallo pinto* with eggs ¢1300. *Casados* with steak, veggies, or fried chicken ¢2500. Open daily 7am-10pm. ❶

◗ NIGHTLIFE

Ticos, surfers, and other tourists usually tend to pack into the same spots, which vary in popularity depending on the day and the drink specials.

Roca Verde, 1km south (20min. walk; ¢2000 taxi) of Dominical along the highway. Every Sa night *ticos*, surfers and everyone else looking to party in the Dominical area fill this large open-air bar and dance hall. A live DJ blasts Latin dance beats while disco balls illuminate the brightly painted walls. After 11pm even the *gringos* are dancing. Cover ¢2000. Domestic beers ¢800. Sa 9pm-3am.

San Clemente Bar & Grille (☎2787 0045). Half-price margaritas and tequila shots are a big draw on Th, though even bigger crowds come on F nights, when a DJ comes in to mix salsa, merengue, pop, and funk. Bar open daily 11:30am-10pm.

Qué Nivel (☎2787 0127). The only place in town that stays open late on weeknights. Crowds don't show up until the other bars shut down, but when they do they find pool tables, foosball, and a long-lasting party. The bar also hosts weekly beer pong tournaments and a power-hour pregame every Sa night before the party at Roca Verde. Happy hour 6-8pm with 2 beers for ¢12,000. Open daily 10am-2am.

◪ OUTDOOR ACTIVITIES

Going swimming in untouristed **Dominicalito** is a relaxing change of pace from *gringo*-fied Dominical. Swimmers have two options: the mild waves of the all-but-deserted beach, or **La Poza Azul** (the Blue Pond) farther inland, which features a small waterfall, natural swimming hole, and rope swing. The waves in Dominicalito, gentle in comparison to those that crash into the beach in Dominical, are great for beginning surfers. To get to either destination, travel south on the highway 4km by **car** (5min.), on a bus headed to Uvita (5min.; 8:30, 10, 10:20, 11:30, 11:45am; ¢100); by **bike** (10min.), or by **foot** (20min.). Across the highway from the beach, a soccer field marks the center of town. Numerous paths lead to the shore. To get to the pond, follow the main road inland, past the soccer field and church, and take a right at the top of the hill.

Dominical Surf & Adventures (☎8897 9540 or 2787 0431; www.dominicalsurfadventures.com), just north of Arena y Sol, is a one-stop shop for adventurous alternatives to surfing. Day-long rafting trips on the Guaro and Savegre rivers (Class III-IV) include transportation and meals (US$75-100 depending on river). Guided mountain bike tours (3-4 hr. US$45). They can also arrange other adventure tours throughout the area, rent bikes (US$20 per day), and offer surf lessons (US$35-45 depending on group size). Prices decrease with multiple lessons. **Blowfish Surf** (☎2787 0420), near the center of town next to Chapy's, has a good selection of new and used boards for sale as well as a surf board testing area for those looking to try before they buy. They also offer board rentals (US$20-30 per day) and lessons. (US$40 for 2hr.; includes board. Open M-Sa 9am-5pm.) Angel of **Cabinas Piramys** has the best deal on surfboard rentals (US$10, hourly rates vary).

◪ DAYTRIP FROM DOMINICAL

HACIENDA BARÚ NATIONAL WILDLIFE REFUGE

From Dominical, take a left on the Costañera Sur and cross the bridge; walk 3km down the gravel road toward Quepos, and take the 1st left after the gas station. From Dominical or San Isidro, any Quepos-bound bus will drop you off at the same place. The staff can arrange taxis (¢4000 one-way), though buses (¢250) returning to Dominical or Uvita pass by at 7, 8, 11, 11:30am, 1, 5, 7, 8:30pm. (☎2787 0003; www.haciendabaru.com.) US$6 entrance fee covers a full day of adventures including 7km of rainforest trails, butterfly and orchid gardens, and birdwatching tower.

Indigenous development began in this area as early as 100 BC, but the region remained mostly virgin rainforest until the 20th century, when increased settlement brought hunting, deforestation, and the threat of extinction for many animals in the area, such as the spider monkey and jaguar. The refuge opened to the public in 1987 when founders Jack and Diane Ewing decided to give up farming in favor of supporting the various endangered species living within their property. Now protecting 330 hectares and 3km of beach, Hacienda Barú offers 7km of pleasantly uncrowded jungle trails through over five different ecosystems inhabited by over 359 species of birds. The **Strangler Trail** (2km) leads through primary rainforest full of strangler figs, beautiful parasitic vines that twine themselves around their hosts, and eventually to the beach. The trail also connects to the 1.5km **Pizote Trail,** crossing through wetlands full of caimans sunning themselves. This is the best trail for birdwatching. Hiking both of the trails together takes about 2hr. unless you decide to spend the afternoon on the seemingly deserted beach. The 2.5km **Lookout Trail** is the steepest hike in the area, but well worth it for the chance to spot white-faced capuchin monkeys. All trails have informative signs about the local flora and fauna. Access to all trails is included in the US$6 entrance fee as well as to the **orchid garden, birdwatching tower,** and **butterfly garden,** which features the most colorful of the 38 species found within the refuge. In addition to their basic daytrip, the reserve also offers lodging and more extensive guided tours. Six **cabins ❸** are available for overnight stays. Cabins come equipped with hot-water baths, kitchenette, a cozy living area and two or three bedrooms that can accommodate five people. (High season US$58 for 1 person; low season US$35; each additional person approx. US$10.) A small **restaurant** ❷ near the entrance serves *típico* food and standard fare for all meals. (*Casados* ¢3400. Fish fillet with salad, potatoes, and veggies ¢3700-4400. Open daily 7am-9pm. Reservations recommended.)

Hacienda also has a variety of tours available that require reservations, such as their popular "Flight of the Toucan" **zipline canopy tour** or the 36m vertical tree climb by rope (each US$35 per person), which focus on ecology rather than adrenaline and are appropriate for visitors of all ages. Hiking tours through the mountains or crocodile- and caiman-populated mangroves (US$20-25 per person), an early morning birdwatch (US$35), and a climb to the top of a 34m canopy observation platform (US$35) all offer unique opportunities to scope out the resident wildlife. The bold may also consider an overnight trip into the jungle or a night hike to a beach where tree frogs, caimans, and fishing bats await (US$60 per person includes breakfast and dinner).

UVITA

Over the last few years, the newly paved highway from Domincal to Uvita has facilitated development of this previously isolated village. Though the beach remains uncrowded, the town itself now offers many of the same conveniences of larger cities. The only good surfing can be found during low tide, when waves break on the whale-tail-shaped reef out on Punta Uvita. A wooden sign on the beach indicates the northern boundary of Parque National Marino Ballena, whose unspoiled waters are populated by tortoises, whales, and the largest live coral reefs on the Pacific coast. If you visit the park at night, be sure to carry a flashlight, wear close-toed shoes, and watch out for venomous snakes.

⊏ TRANSPORTATION

Buses in Uvita go to San José via Quepos (7hr.; 4:30am and 1pm; ¢3000); San Isidro (2hr.; 6am and 2pm; ¢1000); Dominical (30min.; 5, 6, 10, 11am, 1, 2, 5, 5:30pm; ¢500); Quepos (2½hrs.; 11am and 5pm; ¢800); and Ciudad Cortés (1hr.; 5, 11am, 3 and 5pm; ¢700). In Ciudad Cortés you can connect with buses to Neily and Palmar Sur. All buses leave from the fork of the main road in Bahía and stop again for pick up along the Costanera near the Banco Costa Rica at the northern end of Uvita. There is no official **taxi** service in Uvita, but two private cab drivers are recommended. Call Marcos (☎8879 2756) or Hermes (☎8855 3850). A ride from Uvita to the beach should cost around ¢1500.

⚔ 🛈 ORIENTATION AND PRACTICAL INFORMATION

The town of Uvita is split into two distinct sections: the town that lies along the highway near the mountains called **Uvita** and **Playa Bahía Uvita,** or Bahía, which lies along the beach 2½km southeast of Uvita. Bahía can be reached by taking one of two gravel roads down from the highway, the first just after the bridge north of Banco Nacional and the second 500m farther south. The two roads meet at a fork just past the soccer field and continue to make a T intersection in front of Bar/Restaurante Los Delfines. Take a left at this intersection to reach **Parque Nacional Marino Ballena.** Most buses to Uvita continue into Bahía or drop passengers off at the start of the main gravel road, a 20min. walk to the beach. Accommodations and restaurants can be found in both Uvita and Bahía, with most services located in Uvita.

Tourist Office: The Uvita Information Center (☎8843 7142 or 2743 8889; www.unita. info), along the highway at the north end of town across from the Banco de Costa Rica.

Provides tourist information, maps, and arranges a variety of adventure tours throughout the Osa Peninsula. Open M-Sa 9am-12:30pm and 1:30-6:30pm.

Banks: Banco de Costa Rica is located across the highway from the Info Center and offers money exhange M-F 9am-4pm. Open M-F 8am-4pm, Sa 8am-noon. **Banco Nacional** (☎2743 8437) is located across the highway from Restaurante Marino Balleno. Open M-F 8:30am-3:45pm. Both have **24hr. ATMs.**

Police Station: Local businesses and hotels have radio contact with the police station, 3km from Bahía (emergencies ☎911).

Pharmacy: (☎2743 8310), located 25m north of the BCR toward the mountains. Open M-F 7am-10pm and Sa 8am-8pm.

Telephones: Located in front of the Information Center.

Internet access: Hotel Tucan, 50m north of the BCR away from the highway. ¢800 per hr. Open daily 6:30am-10pm. **Rainforest Café** (☎2743 8933), upstairs in the white building next to the Supermercado Don Israel, 500m east along the highway from the Info Center. ¢220 per 15min. Open M-Sa 8am-6pm, Su 11am-6pm. The cafe also serves coffee, bagels, cakes, and smoothies.

ACCOMMODATIONS

▨ **Hotel Tucan** (☎2743 8140; www.tucanhotel.com), just 50m north of the 1st bus stop, offers the best digs in town with the most character. Tucán is decorated Eastern style with Chinese cloth hangings, paper lamps and creative murals. Guests have access to a common area with hammocks, a pool table, free Internet, and a communal kitchen. A small restaurant also serves meals (¢1500-2900). Daily beach shuttle (US$4), bike rental (US$10 per day), surfboards (US$15), snorkels and boogie boards (US$5). Dorm with shared hot-water bath and fans US$10; triples with private hot-water bath and A/C US$30; camping in the yard or treehouse US$6. ❸

Cabinas Hegalva (☎2743 8016), occupies an acre of grassy land 25m right of Delfines from the T intersection. Newly remodeled rooms have large beds, TV, A/C, and handicap-accessible private hot-water baths. Separate huts have Spanish tile roofs, outdoor toilets, and showers. The hotel's *soda* offers an extensive menu that includes salads (¢900), French toast (¢300), and other favorites. Restaurant open daily 8am-8pm. Double with fan and private bath ¢10,000; rooms for 2-4 people with A/C ¢15,000 for 2; ¢20,000 for 3 or 4. Huts ¢5000 per person; camping in the yard ¢2000. ❸

Cascada Verde Eco Lodge (☎2743 8191; www.cascadaverde.org), a 20min. walk into the mountains from the highway. Follow the gravel road past the Toucan 700m and take the 1st left after the cemetery. Follow this road uphill 400m and turn left at the abandoned blue building. Cascada Verde lends ocean views from the wooden lodge containing a camping loft and yoga deck. Dorms US$8-10 depending on the view; doubles with private cold-water bath US$14-24 per person with higher prices for ocean views. ❷

Cabinas Punta Uvita (☎2743 8015), 50m toward the beach from the front of Delfines. Has older rooms with bamboo facades, fans, and hammocks in a private garden and dining area. Elba, the owner, has earned fame as a jewelry maker, selling earrings (¢1000) and necklaces (¢1500) made from fish bones, seeds, and bamboo. 2-5 person rooms with baths and fans ¢5000 per person. Camping ¢2000 per person. ❷

FOOD

Basic *típico* food is plentiful in Uvita, and even travelers well-acquainted with typical *sodas* will probably be astounded by their concentration here. Most places have two menus: one in Spanish and the other in English. The number of supermarkets in the small town is also impressive. The biggest supermarket in the Uvita area is **Supermercado Don Israel,** located along the highway at a rest stop 200m past the first bridge east of the first bus stop in front of BCR. (☎2743 8031. Open daily 6am-10pm. AmEx/MC/V.) **Supermercado La Corona** (☎2743 8423) is on the north side of the highway. (Open M-Sa 8am-8pm and Su 8am-7pm. All of the basics, besides fresh fruit, are available closer to the beach at the extremely -well air-conditioned **Supermercado Tatiana.** Take the left fork at the soccer field 600m toward the highway from the T intersection in Bahía. (☎2743 8078. Open M-Sa 7am-8pm, Su 7-9am and 1-8pm. MC/V.)

Restaurante Marino Ballena (☎2743 8104), next to the Rainforest Café on the highway, is conveniently located for those staying in town, but is a bit of a trek from the beach. The open-air eatery boasts the largest menu around in the most upscale, albeit touristy, dining room in Uvita. Friendly waitstaff serve entrees like fish fillet in mango sauce (¢5000) and rice with octopus and shrimp (¢2800). If you want them to change the TV channel, just ask. Open daily 7am-10pm. AmEx/MC/V. ❷

Restaurante Doña María (☎2743 8787), located next door to the Info Center, is a favorite among locals and visitors alike. The spacious open-air dining area is a comfortable place to sit and enjoy a *típico* breakfast of *gallo pinto*, juice and coffee (¢2900) or a buffet-style lunch or dinner plate with rice, meat, beans, salad, fried plaintains, and various other options (¢3000). The daily dessert special is also worth a try. ❷

Soda El Ranchito (☎2743 8019), across from Cabinas Punta Uvita, serves the cheapest food in town and is the closest *soda* to the park entrance. *Gallo pinto* breakfasts ¢1800, rice with shrimp ¢3000, fish *ceviche* ¢2000. Open daily 6:30am-9:30pm. ❶

📷 🎵 ENTERTAINMENT AND NIGHTLIFE

In the mountains past Uvita is **Restaurante Mistura at La Cascada de Uvita** (☎8855 8148 or 2743 8308; NOAH_ART@yahoo.com) where bright, blue-eyed German owner Noah Poppe has established an exciting hangout destination for the local *tico* and expat clientele. To get to Mistura, follow the gravel road past Hotel Tucan and take the first left after the cemetery. Continue up the hill 50m past the blue building marking the entrance to Cascada Verde. It's about an hour's walk to Mistura from Bahía, but calling a taxi is only ¢2000. Though the schedule of events is not set in stone, visitors can count on fun and creative entertainment almost every night of the week. Monday nights typically feature live music, Fridays are sushi nights, and Saturday night parties often feature meals home-cooked by Noah and a bonfire.

The real party happens on the full moon of each month, when a potluck celebration mixes all of the local flavors with live music, dancing, and whatever else the spirit desires until daybreak. Mistura is also home to a number of gentle waterfalls that start from and empty into convenient swimming holes. Noah only asks for ¢300 from visitors, which he uses to maintain the trail. Noah recently constructed a new art studio as well where he holds art lessons, with a special focus on stained-glass creations. Mistura opens for breakfast at 7am and closes "whenever, sometimes never."

📷 GUIDED TOURS

Though there are several professional tour companies in Uvita, hotels and individuals often arrange horseback riding and snorkeling excursions for lower prices. Most of the hotels will direct you to a man in Uvita named Beltrán, who is affectionately known as "Cuca" (☎8847 6791 or 2743 8116). His 4hr. **horseback tours** are US$25 per person. At the T intersection in Bahía, next door to Restaurante Delfines, **Dolphin Tours** (☎2743 8013 or 8825 4031; www.dolphintourcostarica.com) offers day-long tours of Caño Island or Corcovado and San Josécito that include lunch and snorkeling (US$100). They also offer 4hr. snorkeling tours of Marino Ballena and Punta Uvita that include ocean caves and whale and dolphin watching (US$65-70 depending on season; AmEx/MC/V.) **Fernando Guerrero** (☎8827 8705) is recommended by Dolphin Tours and the park rangers for kayak tours through the ocean and mangrove forests to the north. He is also a great source of information about the park and surrounding area.

◢ DAYTRIP FROM UVITA: PARQUE NACIONAL MARINO BALLENA

The Parque Nacional Marino Ballena was founded in 1989 as the first (and only) national aquatic park in Costa Rica. If you enter past one of the four ranger offices, they will require an entrance fee (US$6 for tourists; ¢1000 for nationals). All proceeds are used to help preserve Marino Ballena. In general, the park is very loosely run, with flexible hours and stray chickens wandering the grounds. The park consists of 115 terrestrial hectares and 5375 marine hectares, with an extensive reef in the marine portion that contains five types of coral.

The park is made up of four main beaches located south of the whale tail-shaped Punta Uvita. From north to south they are: Playa Uvita, Playa Colonia, Playa Ballena, and Playa Piñuela. The majority of visitors enter at Playa Uvita through the ranger station at Bahía Uvita. Vacationers with tents usually chosen to camp at Playa Colonia where they can find bathrooms and showers near the ranger station. Snorkeling is possible off Punta Uvita when the tide is right (check the tide chart at the ranger office or ask at Villa Hegalva).

From December to early March, you may spot *ballenas* (whales) migrating from Southern California with their newborns. July through September, whales return from the south through the park. Also June through September, baby tortoises hatch in a sand pit next to the ranger station. You can camp in the park with your own tent and permission from the rangers, but they may encourage foreigners to stay in Bahía hotels to promote economic development. Picnic tables are located throughout the park. Toilets and showers are available at Playa Colonia, Playa Ballena, and Playa Piñuela. (☎/fax 2743 8236 or 2743 8236. Ranger offices are located at all 4 of the major entrance points to the park. North to south these are: **Punta Uvita** (located in Bahía), **Playa Colonia, Playa Ballena,** and **Playa Pinuela.** To get to any of the other entrances, take a bus heading to Ciudad Cortés and ask the driver to stop where you want to get off. US$6 entry fee collected at all ranger stations.)

SOUTHERN COSTA RICA

With the notable exception of Parque Nacional Chirripó, this relatively isolated area doesn't really cater to tourists. In its small towns, which are either business hubs of fruit producers or gateways into the secluded wilderness of the region, foreigners often receive inquisitive stares, or an emphatic "hellooooo" and laughter from children practicing their English. Travelers who choose to explore the even more remote areas are richly rewarded; Parque Nacional Chirripó offers lush cloud forests, stunning waterfalls, and ridgeway views of both coasts, while the less visited Parque Internacional La Amistad features hikes into Panama and expeditions to seek out the quetzal and its iridescent tail. It is the area's diversity—from its concentration of indigenous reserves to the unexpected Italian flavors of San Vito—that keeps its small-town life uniquely vibrant.

SEE PENINSULA DE OSA AND GOLFO DULCE MAP (p. 332)

Southern Costa Rica

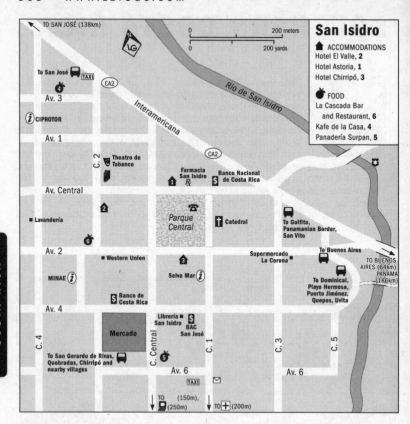

SAN ISIDRO

One hundred and thirty-eight kilometers southeast of San José, the city of San Isidro de El General, also known as Pérez Zeledón, is an urban centered circumscribed by rural villages. Though the urban streets are unusually clean and friendly, the attractions of the asphalt terrain pale in comparison to the living greenness of nearby parks. The city makes an ideal springboard for trips into the surrounding national parks and other areas of southern Costa Rica, where you can get away from the bustle of city life and relax amidst natural splendors. Shoe fanatics may find it difficult to leave San Isidro, however; *zapaterías* line every corner, making it likely that you will finally find those blue sneakers with neon green laces you've always known, deep down, that you needed.

TRANSPORTATION

While finding the right **bus** out of San Isidro is complicated by the fact that the five different companies that share the town don't share destinations, all five have well-staffed and well-marked stations, which makes travel a bit easier. From the local bus terminal on the south side of the *mercado*, buses leave to nearby villages including **Quedabras** (15min., 11 per day 6:45am-7:25pm, ¢250) and **San Gerardo** (1hr., 2pm, ₡900). Another bus to San Gerardo leaves from the west side of the *parque* at 5am.

Musoc (☎2771 0414). Buses go to **San José** from the terminal on the Interamericana Hwy. between C. 2 and 4 (3hr., M-F 4:30am and daily every hr. 5am-6:30pm, ₡2190). Bathroom ₡150. Ticket office open daily 4:30am-6pm.

Transportes Blancos (☎2771 2550), on the curve between Av. 2 and Av. 4 on the east side of town. Marked by a Soda Quepos sign. Buses to: **Dominical** (1½hr.; 7, 9am, 4pm; ₡800); **Puerto Jiménez** (6hr.; 6:30am, 3pm; ₡2300); **Quepos** (3½hr.; 7, 11:30am, 3:30pm; ₡1300); **Uvita** (2hr.; 9am, 4pm; ₡950). Ticket office open daily 6:15-11am and 1:30-4pm.

Tracopa (☎2771 0468), on the corner of the Interamericana Hwy. and C. 3. Service to **Golfito** (3½hr.; 10am, ₡3760; 6pm, ₡5800); **San Vito** (3½hr.; 5:30am, 2pm; ₡3995); the Panamanian border at **Paso Canoas** (4hr.; direct at 10am, ₡7000; indirect at 2, 4, 7:30, 9pm, ₡3760). Ticket office open M-Sa 4:30am-7pm, Su 4:30am-3pm.

Gafeso (☎2771 0097), next to Transportes Blancos. Buses to **Buenos Aires** (1½hr.; direct at 5:15, 7:20, 10am, 12:15, 3, 5pm; indirect at 6, 8:30, 11:30am, 1:30, 4, 7:45, 10pm; ₡685).

Taxis: On the north and west sides of the *parque central,* south of Av. 6 between C. Central and C. 1. Next to the MUSOC bus terminal. To San Gerardo ₡10,000.

▰✦ ▰ ORIENTATION AND PRACTICAL INFORMATION

Unlike most other towns in Costa Rica, San Isidro has well-marked streets with signs on almost every corner. **Avenida Central** and **Calle 0** meet at the northwest corner of the *parque central.* Overlooking the eastern side of the *parque central,* the spires of the large modern cathedral, visible from most places downtown, serve as useful landmarks. The Interamericana Highway forms the northern boundary of the *parque* and is a good reference for finding other streets.

Tourist Information:

CIPROTUR, Av. 1/3, C. 4 (☎2771 6096 or 2771 2003; www.camaradecomerciopz.com), in the back of the blue Coopealianza building. Provides free maps. Answers questions about San Isidro and offers information about tours and activities in the surrounding area. Internet ₡300 per hr. Open M-F 7:30am-noon and 1-5pm.

Selva Mar, Av. 2/4, C. 1 (☎2771 4582; www.exploringcostarica.com; www.selvamar.com). Information on kayaking, canopy, and snorkeling tours to Bahía Drake, Delfines, Golfo Dulce, Isla del Caño, Parque Nacional Chirripó, Parque Nacional Corcovado, and Tortuguero. Open M-F 7:30am-5:30pm, Sa 8am-noon. AmEx/MC/V.

Oficina Regional de Cultura-Zona Sur (☎2771 5273; dirculturazonasur@gmail.com), inside the *mercado* near the entrance to the bathrooms and buses. Works to support cultural activities within southern Costa Rica. Provides information on artisan groups and other cultural events in the area. Open M-F 8am-4pm.

Banks: All offer currency exchange and have **24hr. ATMs.**

Banco Nacional de Costa Rica (☎2785 1000), on the northeast corner of the *parque* at Av. Central, C. 1. Changes traveler's checks and gives V cash advances. Open M-F 8:30am-3:45pm.

Banco de Costa Rica, Av. 4, C. 0/2 (☎2770 9996). Open M-F 9am-6pm.

BAC San José, Av. 4, C. 0/1(☎2771 3080 or 2295 9797). Open M-F 9am-6pm, Sa 9am-1pm.

Western Union, Av. 2, C. 0/2 (☎2771 8535 or 2771 3534), on the 2nd fl. of the large yellow building. Open M-F 7:30am-4:30pm, Sa 7:30am-noon.

Bookstore: Librería San Isidro (☎2771 7802; www.libreriasanisidro.com), next to the BAC San José on Av. 4. Office supplies and copying services available on the 1st fl. (black and white ₡12, color ₡290). 2nd fl. has books, magazines, and posters, mostly in Spanish. Open M-F 8am-7pm, Sa 8am-6pm. AmEx/MC/V.

Library: Biblioteca Municipal (☎2771 3816), on the corner of Av. Central and C. 2. Travelers can read in the pleasant, well lit library but cannot check out books. Open M-F 8am-7pm, Sa 8am-noon.

Laundry: Av. Central, C. 4 (☎2771 4042). ¢800 per kg. Open M-Sa 8am-6pm.

Public Toilets: On the north and south sides of the *mercado*. ¢150. Open M-Sa 6am-6pm, Su 6am-4pm. Additional location on the north side of the cathedral. Open M-F 7am-5:30pm.

Police: (☎2771 3608 or 2771 3447), less than 1km from the *parque;* walk 200m to a small bridge over Río San Isidro, then 300m farther on the left, or speak with one of the many officers on duty around town.

Red Cross: Emergency ☎911. Toll-free ☎128. Ambulance ☎2771 0481.

Pharmacy: Farmacia San Isidro (☎2771 1567), on Av. Central, north of the *parque*. Open M-Sa 7am-8:30pm. AmEx/MC/V.

Hospital: Hospital Clínica Labrador (☎2771 7115 or 2772 6464), 5 blocks south of the cathedral on C. 1. Open daily 7am-8pm for appointments and 24hr. for emergencies. Some English-speaking doctors.

Internet Access:

Connect@ Internet Café, Av. 10, C. 0/2 (☎2771 6023), across from the soccer stadium, 400m from the *mercado*. Computers are Skype-capable. Internet ¢350 per hr. Open daily 8:30am-10pm.

Fofo's Internet, Av. 1 & C. 4 (☎2770 1186), 1 block south of Hotel Diamante Real. Internet ¢350 per hr. Wi-Fi ¢200. International calls to the U.S. ¢50 per min. Printing services black and white ¢50, color ¢300. Open M-F 7am-10pm, Sa 7am-7pm, Su noon-8pm.

Post Office: Av. 6/8, C. 1 (☎2771 0346). Offers fax service. Open M-F 8am-5:30pm, Sa 9am-1pm. MC/V. **Postal Code:** 11901.

▛ ACCOMMODATIONS

Most of San Isidro's budget and mid-range accommodations are clustered around the *parque central*. Other, more expensive accommodations line to the perimeter of town.

Hotel Chirripó, Av. 2, C. 0/1 (☎2771 0529), on the south side of the *parque*. Behind a small restaurant of the same name. Large windows light up pleasant, peach-walled and tiled hallways. Bright rooms have fans, cable TVs, and hot-water baths. Wi-Fi available. Singles with shared baths ¢6500, with private baths ¢9500; doubles ¢10,000/16,000; triples ¢20,000; quads ¢27,000. ❶

Hotel El Valle, Av. Central/2, C. 2 (☎2771 0246), 1 block west and 1 block south of the *parque's* northwest corner. Well kept establishment lined with signs commanding *"silencio,"* especially after midnight. A "no visitors, no exceptions" policy. Parking available. Singles with shared baths ¢6000, with private baths and cable TV ¢8000; doubles ¢9000/12,000; triples ¢18,500. ❶

Hotel Astoria (☎2771 0914), on Av. Central facing the north side of the *parque*. 2nd entrance on the Interamericana Hwy. across from the courthouse. Somewhat institutional feel. Small rooms with just as small armoires may lack windows, limiting ventilation to a small space near the ceiling. Singles ¢4000, with private baths ¢6000; doubles ¢13000; triples ¢12,000, with private bath and cable TV ¢18,000. ❶

▟ FOOD

In addition to *sodas* and restaurants, you can stock up on essentials at **Supermercado La Corona** on Av. 2 between C. 3 and the Interamericana Hwy. (☎2771 5252; open M-Sa 7:30am-9pm, Su 8am-7pm; AmEx/MC/V) or at the even larger **Supermercado Central Coopeagri,** just south of the local bus terminal. (☎2785 0227. Open M-Sa 7pm-9pm, Su 8am-4pm.) Dominated by *sodas,* raw meat shops, and produce vendors, the **Mercado Municipal** smells of fish and fried food all day. (Located between Av. 4/6, C. 0/2. Open M-Sa 5am-6pm, Su 5-11am.)

Kafe de la Casa, Av. 3 between C. 3 & 4 (☎2771 7000). Homey coffee shop. Extensive menu features everything from cinnamon pancakes (¢1800) and banana chocolate coffee (¢2000) to eggplant stuffed with meat (¢3500) and baked potatoes filled with spinach (¢3500). Leave your mark by writing your thanks on one of the walls. Open M-F 6am-9pm, Sa 6am-7pm, Su 8am-5pm. MC/V. ❷

La Cascada Bar & Restaurant, Av. 2 and C. 2 (☎2771 6479). This open-air restaurant always hosts hungry customers munching on chicken kebabs (¢4000), Caesar salad (¢4200), or stroganoff tenderloin (¢5500). Mixed drinks and virgin daiquiris ¢2500-3000. Open daily 11am-2am. ❷

Soda Chirripó, Av. 2, C. 1 (☎2771 8287), on the southeast corner of the park. Catering mostly to locals watching sports on its small TV, this restaurant feels more like a diner than a traditional *soda*. Cheese and ham omelettes ¢1800. *Casados* ¢1950-3200. Also has a less expensive fast-food menu (¢1200-1850). Open daily 6:30am-6pm. MC/V. ❶

⬡ SIGHTS

COMPLEJO CULTURAL. This cultural center hosts local shows and performances. Dates and times posted on an announcement board just outside the building. *(On Av. 1, C. 2, next to the municipal library. ☎2771 2336 . ¢1500).*

FUNDACIÓN PARA EL DESARROLLO DEL CENTRO BIOLÓGICO LAS QUEBRADASN (FUDEBIOL). This reserve is managed by a group of devoted volunteers. Learn about conservation at Las Quebradas, hike through bird-filled trails to impressive waterfalls, visit the reserve's butterfly garden, or simply enjoy its streams and lagoon. Its isolated location makes this reserve as relaxing as it is educational. Up to 30 people can stay at the center's **mountain lodge** (¢7000 per night). Join the staff every Sunday for a traditional *tico* breakfast (Su 8-11am; ¢3000). Ask about volunteer opportunities. *(In the mountains above the Quebradas River Basin, 7km from downtown San Isidro. Take the bus to Quebradas from the main bus station (every hr., 15min. past the hr., starting at 8:15am) and get off at the last stop. Walk 2.5km up to the dirt road, turning right at the FUDEBIOL sign, and continue until the end of the road. ☎2771 4131 for information and reservations. Open M and W-Th 7am-3pm. US$2 entrance fee.)*

ON THE MENU

CHILLY AND SMOOTH(IE)

While most visitors will have had enough rice and beans to last them a lifetime by the end of a trip to Costa Rica, there is one *tico* specialty that never gets old: the refreshing, tasty fruit shake, or *batido*. A Costa Rican favorite for breakfast, lunch, dinner, and snacktime, *batidos* come in nearly every fruity flavor possible and can even be spiced up with a bit of local *guaro* for a night-cap.

Luckily for travelers, *batidos* are easy to make and don't need any special, tropical ingredients to whip up. To conjure up your own "Batido de Fresa y Plátano con Leche," gather together:

8 strawberries
1 banana
1 small container of natural yogurt
1L of 2% milk
4 ice cubes (as desired)
Sugar to taste

Simply cut the banana and strawberries into small pieces. Add the milk, yogurt, sugar and ice, and mix in a blender until the *batido* reaches a liquid consistency. Finally, enjoy a taste of *pura vida*—wherever you may be. For a truly chilled drink, put the fruit and milk in the freezer for an hour or so before mixing.

CHIRRIPÓ AND SAN GERARDO DE RIVAS

A popular destination for nature enthusiasts, Parque Nacional Chirripó is home to the tallest peak in Costa Rica and the second tallest peak in Central America, Cerro Chirripó (3820m). A well-marked route to the summit ascends through steep pastures before winding through cloud forest and into alpine-tundra-like *páramo*. The name Chirripó means "land of eternal waters" and is well-suited to the many rivers that originate from sparkling lagoons on its summit and rush down its glacial valleys to both the Pacific and Caribbean. If the weather cooperates (during high season Jan.-Apr., or very early in the morning), you can see both the Atlantic and Pacific Oceans from Cerro Chirripó. The 20km trip up the mountain is an manageable climb for the average traveler in three days, though the especially experienced and motivated can make it in two. Sports extremists and foolhardy masochists from around the world come to challenge the mountain every year for the Chirripó Marathon in February; the record to beat for the 29km to and from Base Crestones stands at just over 3hr. San Gerardo, the gateway to Parque Nacional Chirripó, although unavoidably situated on steep hills, is otherwise geared toward accommodating the sore legs and hungry bellies of visiting hikers. Since the park's opening in 1975, the families of San Gerardo have learned to embrace tourism while still maintaining their rural authenticity. To the weary hiker, the town offers natural hot springs, local trout and coffee, home-grown vegetarian food, and an abundance of hospitality.

▐ TRANSPORTATION

The **bus** from San Isidro (5:30am or 2pm) will drop you off at the edge of town in front of the ranger station (2km from the trailhead), or at the town center in front of the soccer field. Catch the return bus at the ranger station (1½hr.; 7am, 4pm; ¢900) or from the church (5min. before the ranger station bus).

▟ ▞ ORIENTATION AND PRACTICAL INFORMATION

San Gerardo stretches for 2km along an uphill section of road from the ranger station at the bottom to the park entrance at the top. The town center consists of a large yellow church and a school with a soccer field across from the *pulpería* (small grocery store) **Las Nubes** (☎2742 5045; open daily 6:30am-8pm). Another smaller *pulpería* is at Hotel El Urán. The owner, Hans Arias, and his family can provide a wealth of information about San Gerardo and the national park.

> **Tourist Information:** Extensive tourist and volunteer information can also be found online at www.sangerardocostarica.com.
>
> **Public phones:** outside the ranger station and in front of Las Nubes. Both establishments also have free restrooms.
>
> **Internet Access: Reserva Talamanca** (☎2742 5080), 1km uphill from the soccer field. ¢3000 per hr. Open M and W-Su 11am-10pm.
>
> **Taxis:** ☎2770 1066.

▐ ▐ ACCOMMODATIONS AND FOOD

After arriving in town, some travelers get dropped off at the ranger station, check in, and then find a nearby hotel. Most others prefer to find a hotel near the trail, stash their gear, and then walk down to check in at the ranger station. Reservations are recommended for those planning to stay at hotels near the trail during the high season (Jan.-Apr.).

Casa Mariposa (☎2742 5037; www.hotelcasamariposa.com), 50m from the trailhead. This unique stone and bamboo structure offers the closest beds to the trailhead. Cozy dorms have great window views of the rainforest and the surrounding mountains. All rooms have access to shared hot-water showers, a communal kitchen, and a relaxing gazebo with hammocks. The owners, John and Jill, are a wonderful source of information on the area. Free tea and coffee complement the priceless hospitality. Provides transportation to and from the ranger station upon request. Laundry ¢2500 per load. Internet ¢350 per hr. Dorms ¢6000 (US$12); singles ¢8000 (US$16); doubles ¢12,500 (US$28). ●

Hotel El Urán (☎2742 5003 or 2742 5004; www.hoteluran.com), 25m below Casa Mariposa. Picks up visitors from the ranger station for free. The on-site **restaurant** ● offers hearty *comida típica* (*casados* ¢2000-2400, sandwiches ¢850-1200, pancake breakfast with fruit ¢1200, coffee ¢350; open 4:30am-8pm), while the attached grocery store sells bread, eggs, milk, spaghetti, beans, and snacks for the trek up. Free pick-up from the ranger station. Free internet for guests; for others, ¢600 per hr. Free parking. Sleeping bag rentals ¢1500 per night. Stoves ¢1500. Dorms ¢6000; singles ¢11,300; doubles ¢16,950; triples ¢23,000. ●

Cabinas El Descanso (☎2742 5061). Small, pastel rooms with cramped, shared hot-water baths. The owner, Francisco, has run the race up the mountain 21 times (check out his impressive trophy cabinet). On-site **restaurant** ● (open daily 5am-9pm) serves coffee (¢500), vegetarian dishes made with homegrown produce (spaghetti with vegetables ¢2000), and fresh *batidos* (milkshakes ¢800). Free parking and complimentary rides to the trail entrance after 5am. Trail maps provided upon request. Laundry ¢400 per item. Internet ¢1000 per hr. Sleeping bags ¢2000 per night. Stoves ¢3000 for 2 nights. Camping on the lawn or on Francisco's nearby coffee farm ¢2320. Rooms ¢5800 per person, with private baths ¢8700 per person. ●

Cabinas El Bosque (☎2742 5021), across from the ranger station. Basic cement-floored rooms with access to hammocks on the 2nd fl. balcony. The attached **restaurant** ● serves *comida típica* (open daily 10am-9:30pm; earlier upon request). Breakfasts ¢1600-1800. *Arroz con pollo* ¢2300. Salads ¢2400-2700. Chicken fingers ¢2600. Rents sleeping bags for ¢2000 per night. Doubles ¢5000; each additional person ¢5000. ●

Hotel El Marin (☎2742 5091), next to the ranger station. Transportation to the park at 5am. Restaurant open 5am-10pm. *Casados* ¢2500-2700. Omelettes ¢1200. Doubles ¢14,000. ❷

⚠ OUTDOOR ACTIVITIES

PARQUE NACIONAL CHIRRIPÓ. Hikers almost always stay at **Base Crestones,** a rugged, well-equipped lodge at the base of the peak, as a layover point on their way to the summit. Reservations are required as only 40 spaces are available, but cancellations are frequent. You may be able to nab a spot from the San Gerardo rangers. It's usually easier to reserve in the rainy season (May-Nov.). Reservations can be made one month in advance by calling the San Gerardo ranger station (☎2742 5083; M-F 6:30am-4:30pm) and then making a direct deposit into a P.N. Chirripó Banco de Costa Rica account. Reservations can also be made in person one day in advance. (Ranger station open daily 6:30am-4:30pm. Park admission ¢8700 per night plus ¢5800 for lodging at Base Crestones and ¢3000 for camping.)

CLOSED GATES. During two weeks in May and the entire month of Oct., the park closes to allow for trail and facility maintenance. Visitors can still check with the rangers in San Gerardo to find out if any trails are open.

Most hikers take two or three days to summit the mountain and return using Base Crestones as a stopping point. The 14.5km to Base Crestones is almost entirely uphill and takes a good hiker anywhere from 6-10hr. To ensure that hikers get an early enough start to reach the shelter before night falls, the park entrance is open only between 5am and 10am, and rangers suggest starting as early as possible. Make sure you keep an extra keen lookout for the park entrance on the right; you will have gone too far if you hit the Cloudbridge research station. Rangers also discourage hiking in the dark because of jaguars and other dangerous wildlife that emerge at night. When hiking in the wet season, it is especially important to start early, as rain can begin as early as noon and often continue throughout the afternoon.

Base Crestones, officially named Centro Ambientalista el Páramo, is a top-of-the-line facility, located 500m vertically below the summit. It offers dorm beds with mattresses, bathrooms with running water and extremely cold showers, a communal kitchen with cooking utensils (but no stoves), a phone, and high-speed internet. The facility is powered by solar energy and has electrical light beginning at 6pm. One thing it doesn't have is heat—the temperature at the base can drop to 3°C (45°F) at night from May to December and as low as 0°C (32°F) from January to April—so plan accordingly. The lodge can provide blankets and stoves in an emergency, but in general, sleeping bags and stoves should be rented from hotels in San Gerardo. Most offer rentals for around ¢2000 per night.

DAYHIKES FROM BASE CRESTONES. The trail up Chirripó is not the only hike from Base Crestones. **Cerro Crestones** is another popular summit located 1.7km from Base Crestones. Topped by towering exposed rock, it is the most recognizable rock formation in the park. A popular day-long route is to climb Cerro Chirripó early to watch the sunrise, and then take the other turn at Valle de Los Conejos that leads over **Cerro Terbi** (3760m) and to Los Crestones for the sunset. Hikers may then stay in a shelter nearby and hike down to Base Crestones in the morning. Other hikers may opt to take the extremely steep hike up from Base Crestones (2hr., 2.5km) and try to scale La Aguja ("The Needle"), a 60m vertical face for advanced rock climbers. Sendero Ventisqueros (6km) leads to the *cerro* of the same name. Other trails include the flatter hike to the Valle de Las Morenas (Valley of the Moraines; 7km), where lagoons reflect the mountains, Sabana del Los Leones (The Lion's Savannah; 3.9km) flanked by paramo flowers in the wet season (May-Nov.), and Laguna Ditkebi (3.3km).

AN ALTERNATIVE ROUTE. Serious hikers—only about 80 per year compared with the 8000 others who hike Chirripó—have recently begun exploring a three-day, 40km hike along the **Cordillera Talamanca,** the highest mountain range in the country (Chirripó is one of its peaks). This range divides the Atlantic and Pacific sides of the country, and 80% of the trail (about two days) consists of a ridge path that offers stunning views of both coasts. Some say that Cerro Urán, a distinctive two-peaked mountain, provides an even more beautiful view of the country than Chirripó does. The trail, **Urán Chirripó,** originates in the village of Herradura, 3km uphill from the San Gerardo Ranger Station. The rangers require that hikers take a guide from Herradura with them. Contact Rudalfo Elizondo of Herradura (☎2742 5006), a knowledgeable, kind man who can set you up with guides and lodging in Herradura. (Up to 10 people US$50; 11-16 people US$65.)

BEYOND CHIRRIPÓ. Although the more athletic or motivated can make a round trip in two full days, most overnight trekkers spend three days in the park: the first to hike to **Sirena,** the second to explore using Sirena as a base (the route to

Los Patos is most popular), and the third to hike out. Rangers arrange lodging options and meals. (Breakfast US$10. Lunch and dinner US$15. Dorm beds US$8; bring sheets and mosquito net. Camping US$4 per person; only allowed in designated areas at the stations.) Where the *colectivo* truck stops in Carate, there are last-minute meals (coffee ¢300; *gallo pinto* ¢1500; steak and eggs ¢2000). A public restroom is available for ¢300.

If your legs have enough energy left for a bridge crossing on Río Blanco and another steep hike, you'll be rewarded by soothing *aguas termales* atop a nearby hill, where hot water (32.5°C/97°F) from a natural spring bubbles up into two stone pools. These **thermal waters** are popular in the dry season (Jan.-Apr.) but often under-touristed during the wet season. Take the road that forks left at the large cement bridge for 100m. Proceed uphill about 500m to a bridge well-marked as the entrance to Aguas Termales. Don't forget your towel! The ¢1500/US$3 entrance fee is collected at the small *soda* at the top of the hill run by Gerardo Alvarado and his family (☎2742 5210. Open daily 7am-5pm.). Gerardo also has three small *cabinas* for rent (¢15,000 per night).

Francisco Elizondo of Cabinas El Descanso (p. 313) and his family offer guided treks in English through their Finca El Mirador **coffee farm,** complete with views of the entire valley and a lesson on coffee harvesting and production (3hr., ¢11,600 per person). Francisco will also guide Chirripó hikes for small groups (¢23,200), although you may have to ask him to take it slowly: he has run the Chirripó Marathon over a dozen times. He can also arrange **horseback rides** and other tours throughout the area (price varies depending on duration and group). **Truchero los Cocolisos,** a short walk up the left fork 200m past the church, offers **trout fishing** at its farm. Visitors can take fish to cook later, or, on weekends, the owner will fry them up for you. Arrive before 4pm to be guaranteed trout action. (☎2742 5054 or 2742 5023; ¢3,000 per person; open Sa-Su 9am-6pm.)

For less-adventurous nature enthusiasts and those exhausted from Chirripó's relentless inclines, the **Cloudbridge Reserve** (www.cloudbridge.org) offers mellower hikes. The Reserve's goal is to preserve and reforest former pasture lands. Researchers study the ecology of the surrounding cloud forest at the reserve year-round. Ask for volunteer opportunities through the website. For hiking, follow the main road 1km past the Chirripó trailhead until it ends at the Cloudbridge Station. Hikes make 1hr., 3hr., and day-long loops. Eric, a Seattle native at the first house past the Chirripó trailhead, is available to guide tours. It is best to contact him in advance through the Cloudbridge website. For those who only have one day but want to experience both Chirripó and Cloudbridge, a solid 5-6hr. day hike starts at the park entrance and ends 7km at the Refugio Llano Bonito, a resting point with a bench table and some toilets. On the return from this point, about 150m past the 4km mark, you can take the more scenic trail on your right into Cloudbridge Reserve, which leads back to the main road and affords several waterfall sightings.

BUENOS AIRES

Hemmed in on all sides by lucrative pineapple plantations, Buenos Aires is a typical farming town: busy with business by day and deserted by night. In contrast to the bustling city of San Isidro, 64km northwest, the town has few attractions, though tourists often find it a necessary layover on southbound bus routes. Buenos Aires may also serve as a base for exploring nearby Reserva Indígena Boruca, an environmentally sustainable Durika community as well as the under-appreciated Parque Internacional La Amistad.

⊏ TRANSPORTATION. Two **bus** companies operate in town. GAFESO (☎2771 1523, 2730 0215, or 2771 0419) is across the street from the southwest corner of the *mercado*. Buses go to San Isidro (1½hr.; 12 per day 5:30am-6pm; ¢685). The TRACOPA (☎2730 0205) ticket office is in a small passageway in the center of the *mercado* (Open daily 7am-4pm) and buses leave from a terminal on the north side of the *mercado*. Buses leave for: San José via San Isidro (4.5hr.; 5:45, 9:15am, 4:15pm; ¢3370), San Isidro (1½ hr.; 9 daily 5:45am-5:45pm; ¢1720), Cortés (2hr.; 1:15 and 7pm; ¢1920), Ciudad Neily (3.5hr.; 6, 8am, 1:45, 5:45pm; ¢2585) San Vito via Las Tablas (2½hr.; 6:45am and 3:15pm; ¢2240). **Taxis** wait between the market and the park (☎2730 0800).

▣ ▨ ORIENTATION AND PRACTICAL INFORMATION. Facing uphill, the city center from west to east includes a central marketplace with the *parque*. Facing the *parque central*, the modern pink church is on your east, and the *mercado central* is on your west. The GAFESO station is south of the *mercado*, and the Banco Nacional is north of the *parque*. **Banco Nacional** (☎2730 0210) can exchange money with a passport and a **24hr. ATM** that accepts MC. (Open M-F 8:30am-3:45pm.) A **Banco de Costa Rica** 24hr. ATM is located on the corner just north of Cabinas Violeta. Accepts MC/V. **Public bathrooms** (¢150) are available in the market. The police station is 50m north of the front of the church. (☎2730 1324 or 2730 0103. Open 24hr.) The **Red Cross** (☎2730 0078 or 911) faces the TRACOPA terminal in the market. **La Clínica Buenos Aires** (☎2730 0116) is about 2km north of the police station. **Farmacia CVS** (☎2730 0154) is located near the southeast corner of the market. They also have a small English-speaking clinic behind the main pharmacy. (Both are open M-Sa 7:30am-7pm, Su 8am-2pm. MC/V.) The **fire department** (☎2730 0251) is west of the north end of the market. **Public phones** are located on the southeast corner of the *parque central* next to the taxi stop. **Internet** access is available in the **Internet cafe** (☎2730 4526) on the second floor of the MegaSuper building. (Open M-Sa 8am-10pm, Su 8am-8pm. ¢300 per hr.) **Terranet,** just 50m east of the MegaSuper, has Internet access and copying services. (☎2730 5050; ¢350 per hr.; b/w copies or faxes each ¢10; open daily 9am-9pm.) The post office is next to the police station. (Open M-F 8am-noon and 1-5:30pm.) **Postal Code:** 60301.

▨ ◖ ACCOMMODATIONS AND FOOD. Most tourists don't stay longer than is necessary to make their bus connections, so options are limited. **Cabinas Violeta ❷,** is next to the fire station just 50m southwest of the *mercado*. This orange and blue motel-style building is located at the end of a quiet street and houses clean, well-lit rooms with private cold-water bath, cable TV and fans. It also offers plenty of parking spaces. (☎2730 5252. Singles and doubles ¢6000; triples ¢7000; quads ¢8000.) **Cabinas Fabi ❷** is conveniently located next to the GAFESO bus terminal (just look left). Though the noise of traffic can continue until late at night, the spacious rooms boast fans, cable TVs, and private cold-water baths. Ample parking exists here as well.(☎2730 1110, 8812 8863 or 8828 1763. Singles ¢6000; doubles ¢8000; triples ¢10,000; quads ¢12,000.)

Groceries and essential toiletries are available at the **MegaSuper,** one block south (downhill) of the southeast corner of the market. (☎2730 0938. Open M-Sa 8am-8pm, Su 8am-6pm. AmEx/MC/V.) **Soda El Dorado ❶** faces the GAFESO terminal on the downhill side of the market and offers some of the best *comida típica* in town. Locals gather here for their morning coffee and filling *gallo pinto* (¢1300). There's also empanadas for ¢300 and *plata del día* for ¢1000. (Open daily 5am-5pm.) **Soda Pope's ❶** is across the street from the GAFESO bus terminal. Offers the same filling *tico* fare at slightly better hours, and the lacy, peach-colored drapes and floral decor will make you feel like you're sitting in

Grandma's kitchen. (☎2730 1142. *Gallo pinto, arroz con pollo,* and *plato del día* ¢1000. Coffee ¢300.) The town's best seafood is at **Marisquería Felipe ❶,** a block south of the GAFESO bus terminal, where local families gather to enjoy fish and *patacones* (¢2200) while watching Spanish music videos on a small TV. (☎2730 1050. Open daily 8:30am-9:30pm.) Nightlife in the city consists of small local bars scattered around the market. The largest and busiest option is **La Orquieda,** next to Terranet, a bamboo-furnished bar that fills up at night with locals listening to folksy Latin music, drinking Imperials (¢700), and munching on appetizers (¢1300-2500). Open daily 2pm-2:30am.

⚡ DAYTRIPS FROM BUENOS AIRES. The **Reserva Indígena Boruca** is a vibrant, welcoming community of indigenous people 20km south of Buenos Aires, the same area where they have lived since pre-Columbian times. Although the Boruca have adopted modern dress and the Spanish language, many traditional customs persist. The primary occupation of the village is *artesanía,* vocational crafts that include weaving, painting, and carving. Approximately 80% of the members of the community do this work, cooperating in family groups to produce masks and woven goods. They also carve balsa drums of all sizes and richly decorated canteens traditionally used to dispense *chicha,* an alcoholic beverage made from corn. The vibrantly painted masks are used during the **Fiesta de los Diablitos (Festival of the Little Devils),** which takes place from the night of December 30 through January 2. The celebration depicts the indigenous peoples' struggle against the Spanish. When the Spanish moved to the area, they referred to the indigenous people as *"diablitos"* (little devils). During the four days of the festival, men wearing traditional dress and hand-carved devil masks play a game of chasing and dancing to drive away the "Spaniard," a villager dressed in a burlap bag and bull's mask. On the final day the Spaniard, *"El Toro,"* takes off his mask and throws it to the group, signaling his defeat.

For those who can't visit during the end of the year festival, the **Museo de Boruca** (☎2730 2462; www.borucacr.org), a one-room museum located 100m uphill from the bus stop, is open daily 9am-4pm. The museum features an exhibit on the *artesanía* process and the year-end festival. Just outside, a display of crafts is set up for perusal and purchase, including hand-woven bags, belts, money purses, elaborate masks, drums, and bows and arrows. The Borucan people are also eager to share their artwork with tourists. Doña Marina Lázaro Morales (☎2730 1676), a town matriarch and head of the **La Flor Co-Operativa,** can arrange demostrations of the craft-making process and tours of the community. A series of three waterfalls good for both swimming and views is also located just a 20min. walk from the museum.

For those visitors wishing to spend more than the day in the village, which may be required for those arriving by bus, Doña Marina can also arrange **homestays ❸** in her own home and in the homes of various members of the community. The community doesn't explicitly ask for payment, but for a night's stay with prepared meals, artisan demonstrations, and incredible hospitality, a contribution of US$30 per person is appropriate. If something more private is desired, non-indigenous Memo Gómez of the Bar/Restaurante Boruca 100m uphill from the museum, has several small *cabinas* for rent. The basic, cement-floor *cabinas* can accommodate up to three people and offer fans, hot water and parking. (☎2730 2454; ¢5500 per person). The attached restaurant is open daily 11am-midnight. Visitors can also pick up snacks and basic supplies at the **Coope Brunca** located next to the bus stop at the bottom of the hill. (☎2730 1673. Open daily 8am-1pm and 3-10pm.) **Buses** leave Buenos Aires for the Reserve from the TRACOPA station (1½hr.; 11:30am, 3:30pm; ¢550) and arrive next to Coope Brunca 100m downhill from the museum. Buses leave from the covered bus stop near Coope Brunca for Buenos Aires at 6:30am and 1pm. A round-trip taxi ride to the village from Buenos Aires should cost around US$60.

PALMAR NORTE

As a major transportation hub for southern Costa Rica, most travelers will pass through this medium-sized town (pop. 10,800) on the way to more popular destinations on the Osa Peninsula. Palmar also happens to be at the center of a major banana growing region and offers phenomenal fresh fruit at roadside stands and supermarkets. Its variety of speedy Internet options make it a great place to get back in touch with home.

TRANSPORTATION. Most likely, the bus stations in the center of town will be the focus of your stay here. TRACOPA **buses** (☎2786 6511) will take you to: Golfito (2hr.; 12:30, 9pm; ¢1505); Neily (1½hr.; 8, 9, 11am, 3, 5:30pm; ¢1200); Paso Canoas (2hr.; 11am, 7pm; ¢1585); San Isidro (3hr.; 8:30am, noon, 2:45, 5pm; ¢2315); San José (6hr.; M-Sa 7 per day, ¢4255). Office open M-Sa 6am-5pm. Buses to Cortés leave from a stop just north of the FarmaSur (20min., every 30 min. 6:30am-8pm, ¢425.) From this same stop buses leave for Dominical (1½hr.; 8:30am, 5pm; ¢1125). Buses to Sierpe leave from a stop across the street from the Importadora Monge (25min., 6 per day, ¢350). **Taxis** (☎2786 6457) line up across from the TRACOPA station, but the trip to Sierpe is pricey, even post-bargaining (around ¢6000).

PRACTICAL INFORMATION. In the small shopping center across the Interamericana Hwy., the friendly staff at Osa Costa Rica Travel can make hotel reservations and provide a great deal of **tourist information** (☎2786 7825, fax 2786 9003. Open M-Sa 8am-5pm. D/MC/V.) Next door, Banco Popular has a **24hr. ATM** (V) and cashes traveler's checks. (☎2786 7073. Open M-F 8:45am-3pm, Sa 8:15am-2pm. Banco Nacional also has a MC/V **24hr. ATM**. (☎2786 6263. Open M-F 8:30am-3:45pm.) **Western Union** is located in the blue and white Coopealianza building 100m east of the shopping center along the Interamerica. (☎2786 7128. Open M-F 8am-5pm, Sa 8am-noon.) Other services include: 24hr.

SOUTHERN COSTA RICA

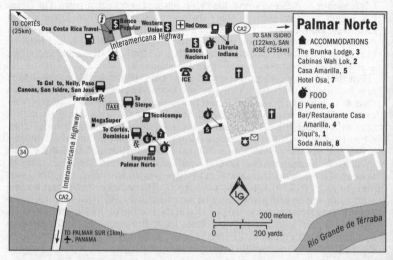

Palmar Norte

TO CORTÉS (25km)
Osa Costa Rica Travel
Banco Popular
Western Union
Red Cross
CA2
Interamericana Highway
Banco Nacional
Librería Indiana
TO SAN ISIDRO (122km), SAN JOSÉ (255km)
ICE
To Goluto, Neily, Paso Canoas, San Isidro, San José
FarmaSur
TAXI
To Sierpe
Tecnicompu
MegaSuper
To Cortés, Dominical
imprenta Palmar Norte
Interamericana Highway
34
CA2
TO PALMAR SUR (1km), PANAMA
Río Grande de Térraba

| 0 | 200 meters |
| 0 | 200 yards |

ACCOMMODATIONS
The Brunka Lodge, **3**
Cabinas Wah Lok, **2**
Casa Amarilla, **5**
Hotel Osa, **7**

FOOD
El Puente, **6**
Bar/Restaurante Casa Amarilla, **4**
Diqui's, **1**
Soda Anais, **8**

police (☎911 or 2786 6320); **Red Cross** (☎2786 6204); **pharmacy,** Ibarra #2 (☎2786 6757; open M-Sa 7:30am-8pm, Su 8am-noon) and closer to the bus stop Farma-Sur (☎2786 6686; open M-Sa 8am-8pm, Su 8am-noon; V) **public phones,** within a block anywhere in the business district and at the ICE office (see map) **public restrooms** in Restaurante Wah Lok (¢100); **Internet access** in a variety of locations—fastest connection and Wi-Fi at **Tecnicompu** (☎2786 6584; ¢600 per hr.; open M-Sa 8am-8pm, Su 1-7pm) across the street from Hotel Osa at **Imprenta Palmar Norte** (☎2786 7556; ¢600 per hr.; open M-Sa 7am-7pm) or at the stationary store **Librería Indiana** (☎2786 6224; open M-F 8am-noon and 1-6:30pm, Sa 9am-noon and 1-5pm; ¢650 per hr., b/w copies ¢15, color ¢250; MC/V). The **post office** is currently closed. **Postal Code:** 8150.

⌂ ACCOMMODATIONS. Palmar Norte has two basic accommodation options: typical hotel rooms or *cabinas*. **Cabinas Wah Lok ❶** offers inexpensive motel-style rooms just off the highway and near the bus stop. The spacious rooms include parking, private bath, and fan. (☎2786 6262. Singles ¢3000; doubles ¢6000. With TV ¢6000/8000.) **Casa Amarilla ❶** has many rooming options, with hotel rooms opening onto a plant-filled deck upstairs and modern *cabinas* out back. (☎2786 6251. Singles with shared bath and fan ¢3000; doubles ¢5000; triples ¢7000. With bath ¢5000/7000. In the *cabinas* with A/C, TV and bath ¢11,000/13,000.) **Hotel Osa ❷** offers spotless *cabinas* with cable TV, A/C, free parking, hot water, and lots of shelf space, and is conveniently located near numerous Internet cafes. Bus schedules and inspirational posters surround large beds. (☎2786 7272, 8848 9491, or 8819 4731; www.hotelosa.com. Singles US$20; doubles US$30; triples and quads US$40. With A/C add US$5. Hotel rooms with shared bath ¢4000). **Brunka Lodge ❷,** located south of the Banco Nacional, is the newest, most luxurious place in town. Each free-standing wooden *cabina* has its own porch and spacious rooms with tile foor, A/C, mini-fridge, TV, and hot-water baths. Guests also have access to a small pool and hot tub. (☎2786 7489 or 8382 9936. Singles US$40; doubles US$46.)

▯ FOOD. The largest supermarket in town, **MegaSuper,** has everything a hungry traveler could desire. (☎2786 6434. Open M-Th 8am-8pm, F-Su 7am-8pm.)**Soda Anais ❶** is the best place in town to get an inexpensive *típica* meal. Filling *gallo pinto* breakfasts (¢800) and *casados* (¢1200) are served in a colorful dining room covered with landscape murals. (Open daily 7am-6pm.)A family-style franchise, **Diqui's ❶** has an inviting and colorful open front and one of the most expansive menus in town. It has everything from *comida típica*, to spaghetti, to a selection of five specialty hamburgers (¢2000-3000). For dessert try one of the many ice cream flavors or a milkshake (cones ¢300; milkshakes ¢1600). (☎2786 7944. Open daily 6:30am-10pm.) **El Puente ❷** caters to tourists who missed their bus connection with a bilingual menu, cable TV, Latin beats, and *típica* and fast food. Whole fish fillet (¢3500), shrimp dishes (¢5000), hamburgers (¢2000) are served. (☎2786 7265. Open daily 4pm-midnight.) **Bar/Restaurante Casa Amarilla ❶,** on the first floor of the yellow building, has a wide variety of *bocas* (¢1000-1500), tasty *casados* (¢2500), good deals on Imperial (¢600 per bottle), and late hours, making it a local favorite. (☎2786 6251. Open daily 10am-1am.) It is near the bus stop and above the pharmacy.

SAN VITO

Hilly San Vito stands 980m above sea level, offering a respite from the humid southern heat with its mild days and cool nights. When Italian settlers arrived here late in the Industrial Revolution, they carved this town out of the woods and established the coffee plantations that still comprise most of its economy. After clearing one of the area's defining landmarks—a massive, 55m ceibo tree that they feared would cause damage if it fell on its own—they planned their new town around its remains. Today, there is a cultural center on the tree's roots and the town's most upscale hotel is named in its memory. A convenient base for exploring the Wilson Botanical Gardens or Parque Internacional La Amistad, San Vito is still home to 20 of the original founding Italian families, and the Italian flavor of its cuisine is one of its most distinctive highlights.

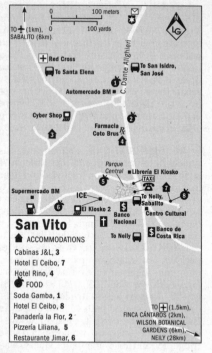

San Vito

ACCOMMODATIONS
Cabinas J&L, **3**
Hotel El Ceibo, **7**
Hotel Rino, **4**
FOOD
Soda Gamba, **1**
Hotel El Ceibo, **8**
Panadería la Flor, **2**
Pizzería Liliana, **5**
Restaurante Jimar, **6**

TRANSPORTATION

Buses to San José run through San Isidro with stops (6hr.; 7:30, 10am, 3pm; ¢4965) and direct (5am, ¢5150), departing from the TRACOPA terminal (☎2773 3410), located 300m north of the park on the main street. Additional buses to San Isidro run at 6:45am and 1:30pm (3hr., ¢2895). Buses to Ciudad Neily stop on the south side of the park and at the covered stop across from the Banco de Costa Rica (2hr.; 5:30, 7:30, 9, 11am, 2, 5pm). Cepul (☎2773 3848) buses to Santa Elena and other nearby towns leave from the terminal next to the Red Cross. Most buses also stop on the corner across from the museum to pick up their passengers before leaving town—just look for the signs. **Taxis** line up on the uphill (northern) edge of the park (☎2773 2929).

ORIENTATION AND PRACTICAL INFORMATION

Marked by the *parque central*, the town center proudly displays the *fuente de fraternidad* (fountain of fraternity), which symbolizes the enduring friendship between Costa Rica and Italy. The Centro Cultural faces the park and is located on the main street, **Calle Dante Alighieri**, which leads uphill to the Wilson Botanical Gardens and downhill to the TRACOPA bus station and post office.

Banks: Banco Nacional (☎2773 3601), on the south side of the park, has 2 **ATMs** and exchanges traveler's checks. Open M-F 8:30am-3:45pm. There's also **Banco de Costa Rica** (☎2773 3901), 100m south of the Centro Cultural. Open M-F 9am-4pm.

Police: The **police station** (☎2773 3225, for emergencies ☎911) is on the main street north of the TRACOPA station.

Red Cross: (☎2773 3191), just past the Cepul bus station.

Pharmacy: Coto Brus (☎2773 3076), the pharmacy next door to Hotel Rino, has a decent selection. Open M-Sa 8am-12:30pm and 1:30-6:30pm. MC/V.

Hospital: (☎2773 4125 or 2773 4103), 1½km north of town, past Banco de C.R.

Internet Access: Internet, copy and fax services are conveniently located at **El Kiosko** (☎2773 5040), is next to the ICE building west of the park. Open M-Sa 7am-6pm. Internet access ¢500 per hr.; b/w copy ¢20; fax ¢150 and up. **Cyber Shop** (☎2773 3521), also offers Internet. Open M-F 8am-7pm and Sa 8am-6pm. ¢500 per hr.

Bookstore: The original **Librería El Kiosko** (☎2773 0303), just north of the park, sells magazines and other writing materials. Open M-Sa 7am-6pm

Telephones: Public phones are in the *parque central* and on most street corners.

Post Office: The **post office** is on the main street next to the police station. (☎2773 3130. Open M-F 8am-5:30pm, Sa 7:30am-noon.) **Postal Code:** 8257.

ACCOMMODATIONS

Cabinas J & L (☎2773 3319), farther from the center of town, offers the best budget accomodations in San Vito. A small wood-paneled hallway opens onto spacious, well-kept rooms with fans, cable TV, and private hot-water baths. ¢5000 per person. ❶

Hotel Rino (☎2773 3071, 8815 6967, or 2777 4030), located 50m north of the park. Reminiscent of an Italian villa, with spacious rooms near a 2nd-fl. balcony with beautiful wood ceilings. Well worth the extra *colónes*, with cable TV, tiled hot-water bathrooms (some with bathtubs), and fans or A/C. Singles ¢8400, with A/C ¢9600; doubles ¢13,300/19,000; triples ¢17,200. Laundry US$2 per kg. AmEx/MC/V. ❷

Hotel El Ceibo (☎2773 3025), tucked away on a quiet street east of the park, has 40 luxurious rooms with orthopedic mattresses, cable TVs, large, private, ceramic hot-water baths, fans, and Internet access. Rooms on the 2nd fl. have private balconies. Singles US$35; doubles US$45; triples US$55; quads US$60. V. ❸

FOOD

Automercado BM, tucked into the corner of a small roundabout near La Panadería Flor, is the most convenient grocery store in town. (☎2773 3525. Open M-Sa 7am-8pm, Su 7am-7pm.) Their additional location near the gas station has a slightly larger selection (☎2773 3855).

Panadería y Repostería Flor (☎2773 3251) has delicious Euro-style pastries (¢430 and up) and fresh bread; owners are Italian. For an evening dessert, try their cake with pineapple or almonds (¢430 per slice) or their signature raisin bread (¢430 half, ¢860 whole). Open daily 5am-8pm. ❶

Pizzería Liliana (☎2773 3080), up the road from the taxi lines and with lanterns around its sign. The town's first Italian restaurant still remains the local favorite. Diners enjoy specialty pizzas (house specialty bacon and mushroom ¢2700-5600) on a breezy terrace near a palm tree garden. Open daily 10:30am-10pm. V. ❷

Hotel El Ceibo (☎2773 3025) dining room down a small driveway east of the park has a greater variety of Italian fare, including Italian-cooked filet mignon (¢3500) and *cannelloni* (¢2700). After a meal in the elegantly-decorated, high-ceilinged dining room, relax in plush chairs clustered around a large TV. Open daily 7am-10pm. ❷

Restaurante Jimar (☎2773 4050), downhill from the park and the ICE office, serves fast food. Hamburgers ¢1200; fries ¢1000; green salad ¢1200, with chicken ¢1900) in colorful diner-style seating. The hillside patio seating is spacious and has a good view of the treeline. Open daily 10am-10pm. Express service available. ❶

Soda Gamba (☎2773 3072), across from the TRACOPA bus terminal, is one of the best places to find traditional Costa Rican food around town. *Gallo pinto* (¢800-1300), special *casados* (¢2000), and fried chicken (¢2000) are served in the very clean and brightly lit dining room. Open daily 7am-6pm. ❶

👁 SIGHTS

CENTRO CULTURAL DANTE ALIGHIERI. The center has a small classroom and museum dedicated to the town's Italian heritage. Housed in a beautiful wooden building, black-and-white photographs document the arrival of early settlers, the towering ceibo tree they felled, and even their first marriage ceremonies. A side room contains Italian periodicals and reference books, along with a sizeable collection of Italian videos. The center also offers Italian classes for all ability levels. Classes cost ¢6000 per month or ¢12,000 per quarter including books and materials. (*☎2773 4935; fax 2773 3570. Open M-F 1-7pm. Free.*)

FINCA CÁNTAROS. 2km outside town, features 10 hectares of trails and a lagoon full of birds. Picnic tables under a *ranchito* are convenient for family outings, and the lookout presents a panoramic view of red-roofed San Vito. The lodge has a children's library and a craftwork store selling indigenous *artesanía* from the Boruca and Guaymi, as well as pieces by Panamanian artists. You can also camp for US$5 per person. (*The finca is reachable by taxi for ¢11,100, by foot uphill about 1hr., or by any bus headed to the Wilson Botanical Gardens (daily 6, 6:30, 9, 9:30am, 2, 3, 4, 6pm) from the stop in front of Banco Costa Rica; ¢200. ☎2773 3760. Park ¢500, ages 6-12 ¢250, ages under 6 free. Open daily 9am-5pm. If the lodge door is shut, just knock.*)

🗻 DAYTRIP FROM SAN VITO

🏛 WILSON BOTANICAL GARDENS
The gardens are located 6km south of San Vito. Buses headed to Neily from the stop opposite the Banco de Costa Rica can drop people off at the gardens (10min.; 6, 6:30, 9, 9:30am, 2, 3, 4, 6pm; ¢300). Buses headed back to San Vito pass by the covered bus stop outside the park entrance (5:30, 7:30, 8:45, 10:30am, 12:15, 2:30, 4:15, 4:30, 7pm). Some people walk (2-3hr.) or take a taxi (¢2700). ☎2773 4004, reservations 2524 0628; www.ots.ac.cr. or www.esintro.co.cr. US$8. Open daily 8am-5pm.

Founded in 1963 by tropical plant-lovers Robert and Catherine Wilson, the botanical gardens' 30 acres overflow with a mind-boggling variety of plants from around the world and countless native animals. There are over 700 species of palms alone, the second-largest collection in the world. International biologists and botanists spend months here, though the park's self-guided trails make it accessible to the casual visitor as well. In addition, the gardens recently purchased over 250 hectares of former *finca* (farm) for the purpose of reforestation, which is viewable on either of two **Jungle Trails** (20 or 40min.) Most trails and tours in the area should take 2hr., but one could easily spend all day meandering throughout the beautifully-landscaped garden and adjacent rainforest. The **Natural History Trail** is the best way to see the most of what the garden has to offer in the shortest amount of time. The trail makes a large loop around the gardens and features violet bananas, colossal bamboo shoots, and the entertaining "marimba palm." Rub a stick along its spines to watch it dance. You can also follow trails like the **Palm Tour,** which shows off an astounding array of different kinds of palms: palms "ridged," "stemmed," "fringed," or "laced." Check out the **Orchid Tour,** the **Hummingbird Tour,** and the **Anthurium Trail,** designed by famous Brazilian landscaper Roberto Burle Marx, a Picasso disciple. His creation is a maze-like path that loops back onto itself at unexpected moments, winding between vistas and nooks. The longer **Río Java** and **Primary Forest** (2-3hr.) trails lead across several creeks and through stunning secondary forest, but access to these trails is limited to overnight guests only. The garden provides overnighters with walking sticks and rubber boots.

Maps of the hikes are included with entrance fee, but more detailed tour books are available at the entrance shop; the most broad-based is the **Natural History Tour Guidebook** (¢2500). For a more in-depth look, 2hr. guided tours are offered daily at 8am and 1:30pm. Call ahead for reservations. (☎2773 4004. US$18 per person.) Reserve a spot before 10am if you want to eat in the garden's dining room with resident scientists and students (US$12 per person). Comfortable *cabinas* are also available on-site for those who want to explore the gardens at greater length. (Singles US$86; doubles US$82 per person; US$72 for each additional person. All meals included.)

CIUDAD NEILY

Although this town is a major center for the African palm-oil industry and an important transportation hub, it doesn't offer many tourist attractions. If you find yourself staying here for more than one night, ask the English-speaking pharmacy owner for directions to the mysterious caves 2km from town.

▐ TRANSPORTATION

All **buses** leave from one main terminal uphill from the center of town. Transgolfo (☎2783 4880) runs to Golfito (1hr.; 12 per day; ¢750.) TRACOPA (☎2783 3227) runs to San José (7-8hr.; 4:30, 5, 8:30, 11:30am, 5pm; ¢5430) and San Isidro (3-4hr.; 7, 10:30am, 1:15, 3:30pm; ¢3205). Transportes Térraba (☎2783 4293; www.terrabasur.com) goes to Palmar via Ciudad Cortés (1hr.; 4:45, 8, 9:15am, 12:30, 4:30, 5:45pm; ¢525); Dominical (5hr.; 6, 11am, 2:30pm; ¢1680) and Puerto Jiménez (4hr.; 7am, 2pm; ¢1685). CEPUL runs buses to San Vito (2hr.; 6, 9, 11am, 3, 5:30pm; ¢745). Local buses run to Zancudo (3hr.; 9:30am, 2:15pm; ¢1000.) **Taxis** line up on the diagonal street at the southeast corner of the park. Call one to meet you anywhere in town (☎2783 3374).

▐ ▐ ORIENTATION AND PRACTICAL INFORMATION

The town's commercial center lies between the park and the Interamericana Hwy. Facing north, the main drag starts one block to the right of the big gas station. The **Banco de Costa Rica,** across from the gas station, changes money and traveler's checks and has two **24hr. ATMs.** (☎2783 3535. Open M-F 9am-4pm.) Farther north, the **Banco Popular** has another ATM and offers the same services as well as free **public bathrooms.** (☎2783 3300 ext. 9001 or 9002. Open M-F 9am-4:30pm, Sa 8:15am-11:30am. AmEx/MC/V.) The **police station** is located at the north end of town (☎2783 3150). The **Red Cross** is across the street from the police station. (☎2783 5205. For emergencies ☎911). The **pharmacy** Farmacia Santa Lucia, located at the center of town, is well-stocked and has a knowledgeable pharmacist on staff. (☎2783 3666. Open M-Sa 8am-8pm.) The **hospital** (☎2783 4111) is 2km east of town along the Interamericana Hwy. **Public phones** are available in the *parque central* and scattered throughout town. **Internet access** is available at **PC-Doctor** near Banco Nacional (☎2783 9020 or 8844 9799. ¢500 per hr. Fax ¢150, photocopies ¢15. Open M-Sa 8am-10pm; MC/V.), or at **Computer Systems Fixe,** north of the Banco Popular. (☎2783 9022. Open M-Th

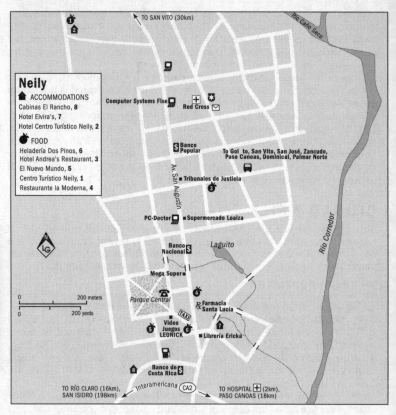

Neily

ACCOMMODATIONS
Cabinas El Rancho, **8**
Hotel Elvira's, **7**
Hotel Centro Turístico Neily, **2**

FOOD
Heladería Dos Pinos, **6**
Hotel Andrea's Restaurant, **3**
El Nuevo Mundo, **5**
Centro Turístico Neily, **1**
Restaurante la Moderna, **4**

8am-5pm, F 8am-8pm. ¢500 per hr.) Local kids play Xbox at **Video Juegos LEON-ICK** on *parque central.* (☎8822 2304. ¢500 per hr. Open M-Sa 4pm-10pm.) The **post office** is next door to the police. (☎2783 3500. Open M-F 8am-noon and 1-4:30pm, Sa 7:30am-noon.) **Postal Code:** 8250.

ACCOMMODATIONS

The city is full of affordable places to sleep, most of which are clustered around the gas station and at the northern end of town.

Cabinas El Rancho (☎2783 3060), has rooms at every price level. Turquoise *cabinas* with tiled floors and baths, as well as optional cable TV and A/C, are spread across a gravel parking lot. Simple singles with fan ¢4500; doubles ¢7000. With TV add ¢2000; with TV and A/C add ¢3500. ❷

Hotel Centro Turístico Neily (☎2783 3031), located in a quiet area at the north end of town, offers simple *cabinas* as well as more luxurious lodging in the grand yellow hotel with Roman columns across the street. Free Wi-Fi in restaurant. Swimming pool is open on weekends and is free for guests. Prices range from a enormous single in the *cabinas* with cold bath and ceiling fan for ¢5000 to a triple suite in the more nicely decorated hotel with A/C, TV, ceramic bath, and veranda (¢28,000). ❷

Hotel Elvira (☎2783 3057). Has rooms grouped around a plant-filled courtyard. Guests share a common room with cable TV and either share cement and chicken wire bathroom stalls or enjoy private tiled bathrooms. Small singles with fan and shared cold-water bath ¢4000. Singles and doubles with bath ¢5000/7000. ❶

🚩 FOOD

For groceries, **MegaSuper** has all the basics at cheap prices. (☎2783-3015. Open daily 7:45am-9pm. AmEx/MC/V.) For a larger selection in a newer building try **Supermercado Loaiza**. (☎2783 3152. Open M-Sa 6am-9pm.)

🌄 **Centro Turístico Neily** (☎2783 1116). Roman columns and white tile adorn a cozy dining room surround by 4 large TVs. They specialize in Mexican food (burritos ¢2500), but the *tico* food is filling and cheap as well. *Casados* ¢1500. Open M 3-10pm, Tu-F 6am-10pm, Sa 8am-4pm, Su 7am-10pm. ❶

Restaurante La Moderna (☎2783 3097). *Tico* families gather to feast on pizzas (¢1750-3500) and soups (¢1200-3500) in a large wooden dining room with an indoor play-set complete with artificial grass. Open daily 7am-11pm. AmEx/MC/V. ❶

Hotel Andrea's Restaurant (☎2783 3745). Splurging on breakfast here is a great way to enjoy the ambience without paying for a room. Fruit plates and honey pancakes (¢1400) taste even better on a swanky veranda. Lunch and dinner prices hover around ¢3500. Open daily 6:30am-10:30pm. ❶

El Nuevo Mundo (☎2783 3111). For a break from *comida típica*, enjoy a sampling of chop suey (¢2850) and other Chinese dishes here. Open daily 11am-11pm. ❷

PARQUE INTERNACIONAL LA AMISTAD

Because of its remote location and lack of publicity, Parque Internacional La Amistad remains one of the best-kept secrets of Costa Rican ecotourism. Offering gorgeous vistas and stunning scenic variety, the park borders the southern edge of the Cordillera de Talamanca, which stretches well into Panama. This frontier-crossing accounts for the park's name, which refers to the friendship between Costa Rica and Panama. La Amistad's colossal size (199,147 hectares) and mountainous terrain make the majority of the area fairly inaccessible. In 1983, Amistad was designated a World Heritage Site by UNESCO. The government is wary of the dangers of its increasing popularity. Its priority is protecting the park, not promoting it.

AT A GLANCE

AREA: 199,147 hectares

CLIMATE: Average temp. 20°C near sea level; 10°C at high altitudes, reaching -8°C on the highest peaks

FEATURES: the town of Biolley; Cerro Kámuk (3549m); Cerro Dúrika (3280m), Cataratas Melissa y La Dama.

HIGHLIGHTS: Hiking Valle del Silencio.

GATEWAYS: San Vito (p. 319), Buenos Aires (p. 315).

CAMPING: US$6 per person for beds at Estación Biológica de Altamira; US$5 at designated campsites.

FEES AND RESERVATIONS: Call the Altamira station (☎2200 5355 or 2200 5675) to alert them to your arrival. An additional park office is located at Potrero Grande (☎2742 8090), or call MINAE in Buenos Aires (☎2730 0846). Park admission US$5 for foreigners, ¢500 for residents. For more information about the park, visit www.invio.ac.cr/pila.

✴ ORIENTATION

The easiest place to begin exploring La Amistad is the **Puesto Altamira** entrance point. Altamira is most readily accessible from Buenos Aires via Las Tablas, or from San Vito via Las Tablas. The park is not really a feasible daytrip with public transportation, so plan on staying overnight at Altamira.

> **WHO YOU GONNA CALL?** Because there are fewer tourists during the rainy season, you may have **Estación Biológica Altamira,** the park station, entirely to yourself; however, it is best to call the **MINAE** office in Altamira to alert them to your arrival. (☎2200 5355 or 2200 5675. Open M-F 8am-4pm.) If you need more information and can't get a hold of the Altamira station, try the Buenos Aires MINAE office (☎2730 0846), or try the one in San Vito. (☎2773 3955 or 2773 4090. Open M-F 8am-4pm.) The ranger station at **Potrero Grande** also has a phone (☎2742 8090).

▐ TRANSPORTATION

To get to Puesto Altamira, you must first travel through Las Tablas and the small town of Altamira. Departing from San Vito, head to the TRACOPA station and take any **bus** headed for San José or San Isidro and get off at Las Tablas (45min.; 5, 6:45, 7:30, 10am, 1:30, 3pm; ¢1200). Another option is to take the GAFESO bus from San Isidro to Buenos Aires and then switch to a bus for Las Tablas (1½hr.; noon and 4pm, ¢850). From Las Tablas, buses run directly to Altamira (45min.; 2 and 5pm, ¢900).

▐ ACCOMMODATIONS

Estación Biológica Altamira ❶ is well-equipped with bathrooms, potable water, 24hr. electrical outlets, and a picnic area. There are tents with beds set up. Bring your own food or restock in the town of Altamira, 2km down the hill. Even in the dry season, reservations are usually unnecessary, though visitors should call ahead to the station. (☎2200 5355 or 2200 5675. Open M-F 8am-4pm. US$6 per person.) Campground facilities also available at the base of Cerro Kámuk with potable water and toilets (US$5).

◈ HIKING

If you think the views from the station are gorgeous, just wait until you get on the trails. It's important to note that some trails are more difficult to follow than others, and some become impassable in the rainy season. **Sendero Gigantes del Bosque** is the only trail for solo hikers, as guides must accompany visitors on all other trails. Park rangers can arrange a guide from a group of 30 locals who have undergone extensive training from the park for ¢5000 per person.

SENDERO GIGANTES DEL BOSQUE. The Sendero Gigantes del Bosque, named for its towering 40m trees, is a well-marked 3km stroll through primary and secondary forest and the only hike possible without a guide. The trail generally hovers around 1300m and never reaches more than 1500m. At the end of the trail, the birdwatching observatory on the border of the primary forest is a great place to spot feathers early in the morning. The hike out to the observatory and back takes about 2hr., and along the way you'll see strangler figs, numerous species of butterflies, and maybe even a toucan or a quetzal. Wear long pants; the grass is scratchy and hip-deep on the second half of the route.

SENDERO VALLE DEL SILENCIO. This hike is an 8hr. 20km round-trip journey through the "Valley of Silence." This beauty is the best-known and most highly recommended trail in La Amistad. Hikers attest to the cloud forest's eerie tranquility, claiming even the nearby rivers are silent. As the trail climbs, unique *páramo* ecosystems dominate the land above 2700m, where trees are stunted by the high elevation and the panoramic view becomes unobstructed. Guides are required for visitors wishing to undertake this hike. Call ahead. (¢5000 per person. Discounts available for large groups.)

SENDERO ALTAMURA-SABANAS ESPERANZAS. This trail takes you past an indigenous cemetery to natural savannahs that are 1808m above sea level and have dizzying views of the towns below. Keep an eye out for the birds, including quetzals. To reach the trail, turn left at the fork in the road next to the church in Altamira. This road leads to the town of **Biolley** (5km), which has a ranger station where you can get directions to the trailhead. A guide is required.

✖ PASO CANOAS: BORDER WITH PANAMA

Sprawling out from the immigration offices at the Costa Rica-Panama border, Paso Canoas is hardly scenic. Though shoppers mosey from one side to the other without hassle, the fairly painless passport and tourist card process is necessary for those advancing further into either country. Most travelers with proper papers have no problem passing through easily.

⌁ TRANSPORTATION. To get to the border from the Costa Rican side, take a **bus** to Ciudad Neily and transfer onto one of the buses that run regularly to Paso Canoas (30min., every 30min., 6am-6pm, ¢300). They will drop you at the main intersection. **Taxis** travel between Ciudad Neily and Paso Canoas for ¢3000 (US$6). Paso Canoas is 50km from the Panamanian town of David, with Padafront (☎2727 7230) buses running between them nearly every other hour. (US$1.75). Padafront buses also run to Panama City at the same times (7½ hr.; US$15). Bus terminals are located 100m from the border on the Panamanian side. On either side, TRACOPA (☎2732 2119 or 2786 3227), 100m west and east of the intersection, sells tickets to San José (8hr.; 4, 7:30, 9am, 3pm; US$11) and one-way tickets from San José to David (9hr.,US$15, valid for 3 months). You'll have to pay even if you have no intention of visiting either city, unless you have a plane ticket out of Panama, which is the only other proof of exit accepted.

◪☷ ORIENTATION AND PRACTICAL INFORMATION. Costa Rica is west; Panama is east. Three main streets run north to south along the border. All establishments take US$, and almost all the Panamanian stores accept *colónes*. The **Interamericana Highway** from Neily and San José cuts straight through town toward David and Panama City.

Though the border process doesn't usually take more than 45min., timing depends completely on lines. To cross the border, go to the **Costa Rican General de Migración,** located in the large blue complex 175m west of the main intersection, and get your passport stamped. (☎2732 2150. Open daily 6am-10pm.) **Customs** is next door. (☎2732 2801. Open daily 6am-10pm.) Then head to the large white complex at the border that houses the Panamanian migration offices. Entering Panama, travelers need a passport, a tourist card (available at the border checkpoint; lasts 30 days; US$5), proof of economic solvency, and a return ticket with a bus line. Entering Costa Rica has the same requirements. For more information visit **www.ipat.gob.pa. Tourist cards** are sold at **Instituto Panameño de Turismo** in the Panamanian complex. (☎2727 6524. Open daily 6am-11pm.) Both sides have additional checkpoints 1km down the Interamericana, so keep your passport handy. **Money changers** abound, especially near the crossing, and are easily identified by the stiff leather packs slung across their chests. **Bolsijeros** on the Panamanian side give the best exchange rate, but check the rate before you approach them to avoid getting hustled. In Panama, the **Banco Nacional de Panamá** is 300m south down the main shopping stretch and has a **24hr. ATM** (☎2727 6522. Open M-F 8am-3pm, Sa 9am-noon.V.) **Police** are 50m from both borders. (Costa Rica ☎2732 2402, for emergencies 911 in Costa Rica and 104 in Panama.) Buses arriving from Neily drop off in front of the **post office** in Costa Rica. (☎2732 2029. Open M-F 8am-noon and 1-5:30pm.) A Panamanian post office is located on the second floor of the white migration complex. (☎2727 6592. Open M-F 7am-6pm, Sa 7am-5pm.) **Internet** is available at **Libreria Viviana** about 300m south down the Costa Rican strip closest to the border (☎2732 2515. Open M-Tu and Th-Su 7:30am-8pm, W 10am-7pm. ¢500 per hr.) or at **Intercall**, across the border on the Panamanian side (☎2727 7727. Open daily 9am-10pm. US$0.80 per hr. International calls US$0.15 per min.)

⚐⚑ ACCOMMODATIONS AND FOOD. Though it might lack major points of interest, Paso Canoas certainly won't leave you hungry. **Cabinas/Bar/Restaurante Interamericana** (*cabina* ❶ /restaurant ❷), 200m south of the Highway Interamericana, has an excellent restaurant that can also deliver a variety of entrees (seafood dishes ¢4000-7000, appetizers ¢500-1000) to its relatively cheap and well-kept rooms. (☎2732 2041 or 2732 2196. Restaurant open daily 6am-11:30pm. Singles with bath US$12, US$6 for each additional person. V/US$/¢.) **Cabinas Hilda** ❷, just 50m past Interamericana offers slightly newer rooms at a variety of prices. Simple rooms with cement floors and fans are located on the first floor, and more pleasant, tiled rooms with A/C and TV are located on the second level. Single with fan ¢6000, double ¢7000/¢10,000. Midway between Migración and TRACOPA and across the street, **Cabinas/Restaurante/Bar Antares** ❶, offers some of the cheapest rooms in town. Small rooms with bath are fairly worn, but fulfill all basic needs. (☎2732 2123. Singles US$8; doubles US$12; triples US$18.)

Expect the same fast food from either side of the border: everything will be fast, filling, and fried. **Soda Los Comales** ❶ is next to the TRACOPA office, and though they don't have a formal menu, all the standard *tico* favorites are available. (*Casados* ¢1300. Open M-Sa 6am-6pm.) Located next to the Costa Rican post office, **Chicken Bros** ❶ has clean tables and fast food. (☎2732 1075. Combo meals ¢2250-2950. Open daily 10am-11pm. MC/V.) **Super El Ahorro** sells any basic groceries you might need. (☎2732 2083. Open daily 6:30am-9pm.)

PENÍNSULA DE OSA AND GOLFO DULCE

 For those seeking natural wonders, the Península de Osa offers unparalleled seclusion and splendor. The amazing concentration of diverse plant and animal life includes species that cannot be found anywhere else in the world. From the wetlands around Sierpe to the sprawling forests of Parque Nacional Corcovado, no other Costa Rican region has kept itself away from tourist hordes with such great success. Bounded only by wide expanses of empty beaches, the untouched wilderness seems endless. Puerto Jiménez is the most convenient base for exploring Corcovado, but the intrepid explorer will find that entrances to the park can be found in nearly every port town on the peninsula. If the jungle isn't enough of a challenge, escape to the beaches, and try surfing on one of the world's longest lefts in Pavones, or snorkel among rainbow fish and dolphins off the coast of Reserva Biológica Isla de Caño.

SIERPE

Founded about 60 years ago, tiny Sierpe was originally a community of banana plantation farmers. The 15km road from Palmar leading to this serene, rural town is now lined with palm tree farms and cattle ranches. Ecotourism is the crux of Sierpes's economic livelihood, so residents are friendly to travelers and eager to pitch boat tours of the area's abundant flora and fauna. In addition to ferrying visitors back and forth to Bahía Drake, local boat owners offer numerous tours of the surrounding mangroves, Isla de Caño, and Parque Nacional Corcovado. These voyages all begin on the charming Río Sierpe, which meanders around the edge of town.

TRANSPORTATION. To get to Sierpe from anywhere in Costa Rica, you must first travel to Palmar Norte (p. 318). From there, **buses** run to Sierpe (30min.; 5:30, 6:30, 9:30, 11:30am, 2:30, 5pm; ¢350.) Buses leaving Sierpe depart from the bus stop across the street from El Fenix (30min.; 7:30, 8:30, 10:30am, 1:30, 4, 6pm; ¢350). **Taxis** leave from the other side of the park (¢6000).

ORIENTATION AND PRACTICAL INFORMATION. The *parque central* and Bar/Restaurante Las Vegas on the *parque*'s southwest corner comprise the heart of the tiny village. Facing the *parque central*, a large building called El Fenix holds a convenience store of the same name, offers tourist information, and sells tickets for the TRACOPA buses to San José from Palmar (¢4255). The 24hr. **police** station (☎2788 1439) is located across the street from Las Vegas. **Internet access** is available at Las Vegas. (☎2788 1082. US$6 per hr. US$1 per 10min. Open daily 6am-10pm.) **Public phones** are scattered throughout town with a large cluster located on the north side of the park.

ACCOMMODATIONS. If you do spend the night in Sierpe, **Hotel Margarita ❶**, 200m inland from the northwest corner of the *parque central*, past the soccer field, offers the best rates in the area. The friendly owner will put you up in brightly furnished rooms with powerful fans and access to a lukewarm communal bath.

Península de Osa and Golfo Dulce

(☎2788 1474. Laundry available. Singles ¢4000; doubles ¢8000; triples ¢12,000. Singles, doubles, triples with private hot-water bath ¢15,000. US$/¢.) Two hundred meters east of the soccer field on the main road out of town, **Cabinas Sofia** ❸ has the some of the nicest rooms in town. Brand new rooms feature A/C, hot water, bath, and Internet access as well as shared use of an enclosed patio with comfy chairs and a river view. (☎2788 1229. Singles, doubles, and triples US$40.) The more posh **Hotel Oleaje Sereno** ❺ is just down the street from Las Vegas as you walk west from the park. Wood-furnished rooms have enormous private bathrooms with hot water, parking, and A/C. Guests eat breakfast at the open-air *soda* on the riverfront (pancakes, cereal, coffee, and *gallo pinto* ¢3500 for non-guests). Upscale dinner options include shrimp fettuccini (¢5500) and filet mignon (¢5600). (☎2788 1111; www.oleajesereno.com. Laundry service ¢300 per item for guests only. Soda open daily 6am-9pm. Singles US$40; doubles US$60. Breakfast included. MC/V/US$/¢.)

🍴 **FOOD. El Fenix,** the largest grocery store in town, offers a wide variety of fresh produce as well as tourist information including bus schedules and advice about traveling to Bahía Drake. (☎2788 1233. Open daily 6am-6pm.) **Riverfront Bar/Restaurante Las Vegas** ❷ is the place to be during the crowded months of the dry season. Information on Bahía Drake and Borucan *artesanía* is plastered all over the wooden walls. The kitchen serves American fast food to quell homesick *gringo* appetites (chicken wings and fries ¢2000), though the pricier *tico* food (*casados* ¢2900-3000) is actually much better. (☎2788 1082; www.lasvegassierpe.com. Kitchen open daily 6am-10pm; bar 10am-midnight.) **Pizza y Pollos Los Vagos de Sierpe** ❸, located just north of the northwest corner of the *parque*, serves fast food and pizzas. They serve up specials such as fried chicken and fries (¢2700) and pizzas (¢4500-7500). Try "The Other Side of the Moon," with gorgonzola, onion, and parmesan. (☎2788 1005. Open daily 11:30am-8:30pm.)

🎣 **OUTDOOR ACTIVITIES.** Countless tour companies with similar prices line the riverfront. Rates per person decrease for larger groups, so try to make friends to split the cost if you're traveling alone. It's also a good idea to reserve your tour a few days in advance at all times of the year, but especially during the dry season (Dec.-Apr.). **Tour Gaviotas de Osa** (☎2788 1212 or 8815 8557; www.tourgaviotasdeosa.com), next door to Las Vegas, offers day-long tours of Corcovado and Caño Island that include meals, transport, guide services, and park entrance fees. (Corcovado US$110; Caño Island US$110 includes snorkeling equipment.) Gaviotas also has shorter (2hr.) mangrove kayaking tours on the Río Sierpe (US$50 per person). **Costa Rica Adventures** (☎2788 1016; cradventures@gmail.com), on the northwest corner of *parque central,* offers some of the most interesting tours in town. The 2hr. poison dart frog and bird exploration tour at Sierpe waterfall is best in the early morning or late afternoon (US$25 per person). They also offer half-day horseback tours to Isla Violin (US$75), kayaking tours of the Sierpe River to the mysterious Diquis stones (US$35), and diving tours at Caño Island (US$120). All tours include lunch or a snack. Costa Rica Adventures also rents kayaks (US$20 per day) and snorkeling equipment (US$5 per day). Though expensive, sportfishing is also popular in Sierpe. **Aldea del Río** (☎2788 1313; www.aldeadelrio.com), on the south side of the park, specializes in sportfishing and can arrange unique trips for each individual. They also offer standard day-long river and ocean trips that include bait, food, and beverages (US$400 river; US$700 ocean; max. 4 people). Costa Rica Adventures also offers ocean fishing for the same price.

BAHÍA DRAKE

As the legend goes, Sir Frances Drake moored at Drake in the 1570s to bury treasure along its lush green coast. Although locals say that small pieces of Spanish currency wash ashore on a regular basis, all serious treasure hunts have ended unsuccessfully, and no pirate stash has ever been found. Divers might not come from all over the world to look for plunder, but they do come for the chance to swim with marlins, rainbow fish, dolphins, and pilot whales in some of the country's clearest waters. Those who prefer to keep their feet on (relatively) dry land can explore Corcovado's diverse wildlife (including four species of monkeys and over 400 species of birds); which is just a short hike away. Though Bahía Drake (pronounced DRAH-keh by locals) is not conducive to budget traveling, few who travel here end up regretting the expense.

▐ TRANSPORTATION

Flights: Sansa (☎2290 4100; www.flysansa.com) and **NatureAir** (☎800 235 9272; www.natureair.com) both run daily flights between **San José** and **Drake Bay.** From San José Sansa flights depart to Drake Bay (50min.; 6am and 10:53am; and return 7:02am and 11:55am; US$91). NatureAir flights depart San José (40min.; 8:30am and 11am; and return 9:20am and 11:50am; US$125). The airstrip is located 5km north of town and most hotels can arrange taxi transport to and from for guests.

Bus: Bahía Drake can also be reached by bus from Puerto Jiménez via La Palma. Buses to **La Palma** depart across the street from the Super 96 (1hr.; every 30min. 6am-5:30pm; ¢450). From La Palma a *colectivo* truck runs twice daily to Bahía Drake (1½hr.; 11:30am, 4:30pm; ¢2500). Though buses are less expensive than boats, mud often make the roads impassable and the bus a less reliable means of transport.

Boat: Motorboats run back and forth between Bahía Drake and the Restaurante/Bar Las Vegas in Sierpe. (1hr.; most boats depart around 11:30am; US$15 if arranged through a hotel, much pricier if arranged through the lounging captains.) If you don't have a reservation, make sure to speak to several captains to negotiate the best price. You can often wiggle your way onto another hotel's boat for around US$15, though it's most convenient to get one that docks somewhere near your own lodgings. Jorge, the owner of the Las Vegas, is usually working the cash register and can help you find the best option. Once you've found transportation, enjoy the ride and ask about the wildlife as the boat snakes through dense mangrove jungles and past the legendary Isla Violines, where Sir Frances Drake's treasure is said to be buried. During the rainy season, the mouth of the river can become quite turbulent. Better captains will require passengers to put on life vests, while less-experienced boatmen will probably inspire the rest to wear them.

▐ ORIENTATION AND PRACTICAL INFORMATION

All hotels are along the bay's coast, while farms and uninhabited jungles lie farther inland. **Agujitas,** the main *pueblecito* on Bahía Drake, lies approximately in the center of the bay. The main thoroughfares in town are the beach and a dirt road hugging the coast. Most boats make land near the **pulpería** (☎2770 8210 or 2770 8051, open M-Sa 6:30am-6pm, Su 7am-2pm) where main roads intersect. A **public phone** can be found inside. **Internet access** is available 150m west of the school at Corcovado Expeditions. (☎8818 9962 or 8850 5387. Open daily 9am-8pm. ¢1000 per hr.) **Public restrooms** are available inside as well (¢300). The **medical clinic,** Hospital Clínica Bíblica, is located 200m down the road.

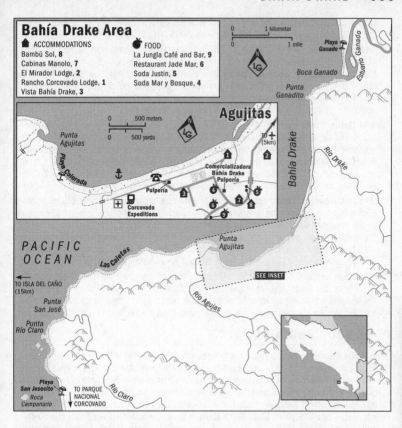

Bahía Drake Area

⌂ ACCOMMODATIONS
Bambú Sol, **8**
Cabinas Manolo, **7**
El Mirador Lodge, **2**
Rancho Corcovado Lodge, **1**
Vista Bahía Drake, **3**

🍎 FOOD
La Jungla Café and Bar, **9**
Restaurant Jade Mar, **6**
Soda Justin, **5**
Soda Mar y Bosque, **4**

SEE INSET

OSA PENINSULA

ACCOMMODATIONS

The following hotels are the least expensive in town, though the average resort cost is three times as much—Bahía Drake's seclusion has its price. All supplies must be brought in by boat from Sierpe or via the unreliable dirt road from La Palma, until recently, all electricity has been either solar or generator-driven. Nearly all activities are organized through hotels, with more extensive offerings at larger resorts. All of the following hotels can arrange boat rides from Sierpe (1hr., US$15), and it's a good idea to make reservations in advance, particularly from November to April. Most hotels also include meal packages in their price, though several inexpensive *sodas* can be found throughout town.

🏨 **El Mirador Lodge** (☎8334 4438 or 8836 9415; www.miradordrakebay.com). A 15min. walk east from the *pulpería*. Facing inland, walk to the left along the beach until you reach a stream. Climb up onto the road and walk right to a sign that will direct you left and 35m uphill. Nestled amid fruit trees, wooden cabins overlook the gently rolling ocean. Home-cooked meals include local fish, produce from the hotel's organic garden. The owner, Michael, speaks English and can arrange individual and group tours. Rooms have private cold showers and porches. While the main building where meals are served has electricity, rooms are lit only by candlelight. Laundry US$4. Internet access US$2 per hr. US$45 per person, including 3 meals. AmEx/MC/V/US$/¢. ❸

Cabinas Manolo (☎8885 9114 or 8825 4825; www.cabinasmanolo.com), located 100m south of Soda Justin on the main road. Though it may lack ocean views and easy beach access, Cabinas Manolo offers one of the best deals in town. Spacious rooms share cold-water baths and hammocks on a small porch while newly remodeled rooms have baths and balconies. All rooms have fans. Rooms US$10 per person, with bath US$15. Breakfast included. Laundry available. ❶

Vista Bahía Drake (☎8837 2955, 8837 6925, or 8816 9172; www.drakebayvista. com). For those who didn't bring a tent, the owner, Emilio, has some pitched just up the hill from the *pulpería* on covered platforms with electricity, fans, and beds insideand hammocks outside. Campers share cold-water baths, picnic tables, and stunning views of the bay. Tent with double bed US$15; with 2 single beds US$20. Breakfast included.It costs US$5 to pitch your own tent. ❶

Rancho Corcovado Lodge (☎8315 2361; www.ranchocorcovado.com), 600m north-east along the beach from the *pulpería*. The González family offers one set of cabins in the shade of the rainforest and another right on the beach. On their nearby *finca*, the family grows papayas and pineapples for the delicious meals they serve in a thatch hut. All rooms have ceiling fans and private hot-water baths with showers. US$38, with meals US$70. Camping with cold-water baths US$10. ❸

Bambü Sol (☎8334 4438 or 8836 9415), 500m back from the beach, up the road from El Mirador and under the same management. Although these small, dark rooms sit in the low ground between 2 streams and have no view, they are clean and are the cheap-est digs in town. Shared cold-water bath. Rooms have electricity and fan. US$9. ❶

FOOD AND NIGHTLIFE

Soda Justin ❶, next door to Bambu Sol, has a small menu with *casados* (¢2300-2500), rice dishes (¢1500), and hamburgers (¢800) written on the chalkboard on the wall. The fish *casado* made with fresh sea bass is particularly tasty. Though the dining room may be small, the dishes are not, and locals can be found eating and chatting with the owner at any time of day. (☎8877 6508. Open daily 7am-8:30pm.) **Soda Mar y Bosque ❶**, across the street from the Com-ercializadora Bahía Drake, has a bigger selection of the same *típica* fare and a slightly better view. *Casados* (¢2000-2500) and fresh fruit *batidos* (¢600) are served on an open-air patio that offers glimpses of the bay. (☎8313 1366. Open daily 6am-8pm.) **Restaurant Jade Mar ❶** is 100m up the road from Hotel Jade Mar and serves *gringo* food. The English-language menu offers fast food (¢2000), pastas and lasagna (¢2500-3300), and a variety of steaks including filet mignon (¢5500). Join the locals watching TV on the large flat-screen television while you wait for your order. (Open daily 6am-1am. Mixed drinks ¢2000. US$/¢.) Just up the road from Jade Mar, the recently opened 🐾**La Jungla Café and Bar** has the best nightlife in town. Packed with locals and a few tourists, the wood-paneled bar has plenty of comfortable seating and a relaxed atmosphere. If you get there before sunset you might even get lucky enough to see sloths and other wildlife out the bar window. (☎8818 9962 or 8850 5387. Happy hour daily 4-6pm with 2 for 1 Imperials. Open daily 4pm-2am.)

OUTDOOR ACTIVITIES

All of the excursions that Drake Bay has to offer can be arranged through hotels. Prices are negotiable for large groups. Most hotels offer two options for exploring Corcovado National Park from either the San Pedrillo or Sirena ranger station. Some tours include horseback riding. The cost of guides varies widely, but the average is around US$75 per day including boat transport and lunch. From Bahía Drake, visitors are strongly discouraged from entering Corcovado without a guide. For solo treks, the park is more easily accessible from the southern part of the peninsula around Puerto Jiménez (p. 346). Visitors interested in an adventure excursion will find opportunities are available to kayak through the mangroves, zip-line through the rainforest canopy, whale watch in the bay, and snorkel and scuba dives in the coral and rock formations of San Josécito or Isla del Caño. Most snorkel trips to Isla de Caño are priced around US$70 per person. There are also daytrips available for early morning birdwatching, as well as night hikes to view insects and nocturnal mammals through night-vision goggles. The only independent tour company, **Corcovado Expeditions** offers all of the above tours for visitors whose hotels do not. (☎8818 9962 or 8850 5387; www.corcovadoexpeditions.net. Corcovado day tours US$70-95; Caño Island snorkeling US$70; mangrove kayaking US$45; dolphin and whale watching US$80; birdwatching US$35; mountain biking US$45. All tours include guide, transport, and lunch or a snack. Open daily 9am-8pm.)

DAYTRIP FROM BAHÍA DRAKE

ISLA DEL CAÑO

Located 17km west of Osa Peninsula. Because Isla del Caño is a protected area, only 10 divers are allowed at each of the 5 dive sites at a time. Most hotels in Bahía Drake offer tours to the island that include transportation, snorkeling or scuba diving, and lunch for about US$70. Boats depart between 7 and 8am; approx. 1hr.

Trips to the stunning Isla del Caño National Preserve are in many ways the best way for a traveler on a short stay to experience the best of Drake Bay. Snorkeling and diving boats typically depart from hotels around 7am and return around 2 or 3pm. Captains are happy to interrupt the 1hr. voyage to observe passing pods of humpback and pilot (or "false killer") whales, or to play with the dolphins.

Boats may choose to wait at one site or move to another while other divers are exploring. Once at these crystalline depths, divers may encounter manta rays, Pacific sea turtles, and bull sharks and white-tip reef sharks among rock caves, canyons, and coral. While divers explore the ocean floor, snorkelers float and dive from the surface through large schools of rainbow runners, big-eyed jack, butterflyfish, and abnormally friendly barracuda that congregate near large rocks and coral. These teeming waters are also home to

THE HIDDEN DEAL

ROLLING STONES OF ISLA DEL CAÑO

Most visitors to Isla del Caño Island come to see the coral reef and tropical fish. And though these fish are often strange creatures, the most perplexing features of Isla de Caño are the mysterious Diquis stones located at the center of the landmass.

The stone spheres on Isla de Caño are believed to have originated in the Diquis Valley on the Costa Rican mainland around the same time as similar stones in Palmar Sur. It is not known who made them or when, but they are believed to be over 300 years old. Made in a time without advanced tools or modes of transportation, the stones (ranging in diameter of a few centimeters to over two meters and weighing up to 16 tons) are almost perfectly round. The Diquis stones are even more impressive when one thinks about how far they must have traveled to reach their destination.

Though the specific purpose of the stones is not known, it is believed that they may have had religious significance or were used to mark the passage of time with the stars. Those with wilder imaginations have suggested that they were created by aliens or supernatural powers. Aliens or not, it's worth the hike to the center of the island to see them and come up with one's own theory.

exotic tropical loners such as bluetail tigerfish, spotted porcupinefish, parrotfish, giant damselfish, and the rather elusive reef shark.

After the divers' first tanks are depleted, dive boats moor off the beach of Isla del Caño's northern shore, which only opened to tourists 20 years ago. Trees and palms give shade to the beach and picnic areas where boat crews and tourists prepare lunch. The ranger station, located where a cool stream meets the warm surf, is the only building on the island. Though the majority of the station is only open to rangers, it does have flushing toilets and a porch with a small display of indigenous artifacts open to the public.

Just behind the ranger station, concrete steps mark the beginning of Isla del Caño's hiking trail. The hike is initially quite steep, rising to an altitude of 110m in less than a mile before leveling out to a large plateau. Partway through the hike, the trail splits. The eastern trail (turn left at the fork) leads to a Pre-Columbian burial ground where the mysterious *diquis* stones (granite spheres) can be observed. The western trail (turn right at the fork) ends at a vista on the southwest edge of Isla del Caño. Either hike will take about 45min., and both can be seen in about 2hr. Most day tours to the island include diving or snorkeling in the morning and a guided hike in the afternoon after lunch.

GOLFITO

Golfito (pop. 18,000), former home of the United Fruit Company headquarters, sits on the northeast coast of the Golfo Dulce. Drastic banana production cutbacks in 1984 led officials to revive a weakening local economy by establishing a duty-free zone in the northern end of the city. This well-known shopping area fills the hotels year-round (especially on the weekends) with *ticos* who come to buy appliances, clothing, and alcohol without tariffs or taxes, while industrial ships bring in fertilizer and export palm oil from surrounding farms. Unlike surrounding surfing towns, the numerous bars create a noisy local nightlife until they are shut down at midnight. Water taxis and private boats in the harbor ferry tourists to more hospitable locales like Pavones, Zancudo, Cacao, or Puerto Jiménez. Its convenience, however, makes Golfito worth stopping at for a few days—it's a great base for touring the bays and beaches of Golfo Dulce or for exploring nearby nature reserves and Parque Nacional Piedras Blancas.

▌ TRANSPORTATION

Flights: Sansa (☎2775 0303) has flights daily between **San José** and **Golfito** (1hr.; US$108 for tourists, US$83 for residents). Flights depart San José at 5:30, 11:40am, and 1:50pm. Flights depart Golfito at 6:40am, 12:54, and 3:03pm. The Sansa office, is 100m north of *muellecito,* on the other side of the street. **Golfito Vive Information Center** near the hospital also arranges tickets.

Buses: Depart from the **TRACOPA** bus terminal (☎2775 0365) to **San José** (7hr.; 5am, 1:30pm, ¢5430) via **San Isidro** (4hr., ¢3520). Ticket office open daily 4:30am-4:30pm. Down the main street, 200m north of TRACOPA, buses go to **Neily** (1hr., 6-7pm, ¢520) via **Río Claros** (30min.; ¢420) before continuing on to the Panamanian border at **Paso Canoas,** 17km beyond Neily. These buses also stop at the covered bus stops throughout the main road in **Golfito.**

Boats and Ferries: For connections in the high season, plan to arrive early to secure a seat. From the *muellecito* (between Hotel Golfito and the gas station), ferries run to **Puerto Jiménez** (30min.; 5, 9:30am, 1:30, 3:30, 4, 5pm; ¢2000; a longer trip at 1½hr.; 11:30am; ¢1000). Private taxi boats can also be arranged at the *muellecito* with the numerous captains hanging around during the day. Taxis run to **Playa Zancudo**

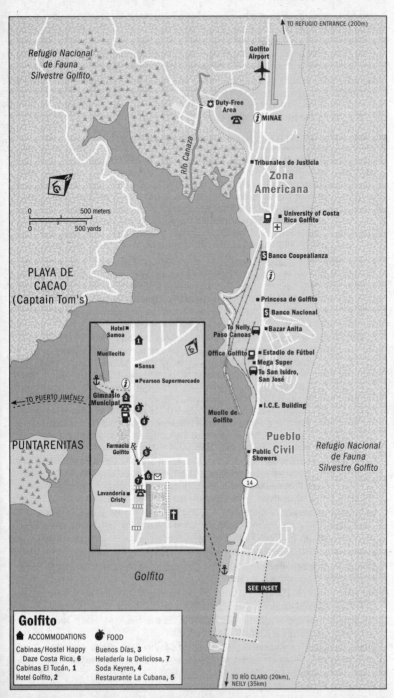

TO REFUGIO ENTRANCE (200m)

Golfito
Airport

Refugio Nacional
de Fauna
Silvestre Golfito

Duty-Free
Area

MINAE

Río Canaza

Tribunales de Justicia

Zona
Americana

0   500 meters

0   500 yards

University of Costa
Rica Golfito

PLAYA DE
CACAO
(Captain Tom's)

Banco Coopealianza

Princesa de Golfito

Banco Nacional

Hotel
Samoa

To Nelly,
Paso Canoas

Bazar Anita

Muellecito

Office Golfito

Estadio de Fútbol

Sansa

Mega Super

TO PUERTO JIMÉNEZ

Pearson Supermercado

To San Isidro,
San José

Gimnasio
Municipal

I.C.E. Building

PUNTARENITAS

Farmacia
Golfito

Muelle de
Golfito

Pueblo
Civil

Refugio Nacional
de Fauna
Silvestre Golfito

Lavandería
Cristy

Public
Showers

14

Golfito

SEE INSET

OSA PENINSULA

SEE INSET

TO RÍO CLARO (20km),
NEILY (35km)

Golfito

ACCOMMODATIONS

Cabinas/Hostel Happy
   Daze Costa Rica, **6**
Cabinas El Tucán, **1**
Hotel Golfito, **2**

FOOD

Buenos Días, **3**
Heladería la Deliciosa, **7**
Soda Keyren, **4**
Restaurante La Cubana, **5**

(US$30), **Playa Cacao** (US$12), **Casa Orquídeas** (US$80), **Pavones** (US$120), **Playa Azul** (US$30), and other locations. Boats hold around 7 people and you pay per boat, so gathering up a group reduces individual fares. A daily taxi boat runs to **Zancudo** (1hr., noon, ¢2000) leaving from the dock at the Hotel Samoa. Other private boats can be found about 1km north near and upon the gigantic *muelle bananero*.

Taxis: (☎2775 1170 or 2775 2020), line up next to the gas station and can be flagged down anywhere on the main road (¢500 anywhere on the map, ¢350 if split with another party). **Local Bus:** Run along the main drag from 5:30am-10pm and stop on either side of the road at the bench. Bus stops every 20min. (¢155 anywhere on the main road).

✴ 🛈 ORIENTATION AND PRACTICAL INFORMATION

Golfito runs along a 4km north-south stretch of beach road, with the gulf to the west. The city is physically and economically divided into two sections. The swankier **Zona Americana** lies near the duty-free zone and airport and includes everything north of the hospital. It's home to a mix of US retirees and better-off *ticos*. The bus terminal, the Puerto Jiménez ferry dock, called *muellecito* or "little dock," and many smaller businesses and *sodas* occupy the shabbier **Pueblo Civil** to the south. Red, white, and blue buses marked "Golfito Centro" (¢155) and taxis (¢500) run up and down Golfito between these two areas.

Tourist Office: The **Cámara Ecoturística de Golfito** (☎2775 1820), just north of the *muellecito*. The friendly staff offers information on transportation, lodging, and tours in Golfito and the surrounding area. They also have maps and free Internet access. Open M-F 8am-noon and 1-4pm. The **Golfito Vive Information Center** (☎2755 3338), south of the Banco Coopelianza. Provides general information and can arrange flights from Golfito and guided tours. Open M-F 8am-5pm, Sa 8am-noon.

Guided Tours: It is more convenient to hire tour guides in Puerto Jiménez, but if you want to stay in Golfito, adventure trips are available. The best option is **Dolfin Quest** (☎2775 0373; www.dolphinquestcostarica.com), run by an expat named Ray who owns 700 acres of virgin rainforest in San Josécito. He offers horseback tours of his land and butterfly farm (US$10 per hr.), guides snorkel trips and jungle hikes (US$5 per hr.), as well as 4hr. dolphin tours (US$200 for a group of up to 15). All equipment included. Water taxis can take you directly to his farm (US$20-40). The main **MINAE** office is located in the large white and blue building just south of the airport, but better information can be obtained from the office at the Golfito Refuge park entrance 800m down the gravel road south of the airport (☎2775 2620 or 2775 0075. Open M-F 8am-4pm).

Bank: Banco Nacional (☎2775 1101), 100m north of the TRACOPA bus terminal, has a **24hr. ATM,** changes traveler's checks, and gives cash advances. Open M-F 8:30am-3:45pm. **Banco Coopealianza** (☎2775 0025 or 2775 0800) also has an ATM and a **Western Union** office inside. Open M-F 8am-5pm, Sa 8am-noon.

Laundromat: Lavandería Cristy (☎2775 0043), inside the Hotel Delfina on the flat road south of the gas station. Go up the stairs and ring the bell. A load takes a few hours. ¢1000 per kg. Open 24hr.

Police: (☎2775 1022), located on the west side of the duty-free zone.

Pharmacy: Farmacía Golfito (☎2775 2442), across the street from Lavandería Cristy. Open M-Sa 8am-noon and 1-7pm. MC/V.

Hospital: (☎2775 1001), 2km north of the *muellecito*. It's the complex of green buildings with red roofs.

Telephones: Available outside the gas station, in the duty-free zone, next to Heladería La Deliciosa, and at regular intervals along the main road.

Internet Access: Free Internet is available at the **Cámara Ecoturística de Golfito.** Open M-F 8am-noon, 1-4pm. For access at night and on weekends, try **Office Golfito** (☎2775

0718), just north of the MegaSuper. ¢600 per hr. ¢250 min. Open daily 8:30am-8:30pm. An unnamed office across from the University of Costa Rica also has Internet for ¢500 per hr. B/w photocopies ¢20. (☎2775 2187). Open M-Sa 8am-8pm.

Post Office: (☎2775 1911; fax 2775 0373), uphill from the *muellecito* and the 2nd left before the soccer field. Offers fax services. Open M-F 8am-noon and 1-4:30pm, Sa 8am-noon. **Postal Code:** 60701

⚑ ACCOMMODATIONS

There are numerous cheap, simple accommodations in and around Pueblo Civil. Quieter accommodations away from the bustle of the city can be found both north and south of town, but these tend to be a bit pricey.

Hotel Golfito (☎2775 0047), just south of the *muellecito*. Offers some of the nicest, cleanest and most reasonably-priced rooms in town. Bright rooms have soft beds, showers with hot water, and A/C. Some rooms have waterfront views. Doubles with industrial fans ¢7000, with A/C ¢12,000; triples ¢18,000. ❶

Cabinas/Hostel Happy Daze Costa Rica (☎2775 0058; www.happydazecostarica. com), 50m north of the soccer field and set back from the noise on the high road. Though the barred windows and floor-to-ceiling cement may be less than inviting, the basic rooms are spacious. Rooms come in a variety of sizes, all with private bath. A balcony overlooks the gulf. Communal kitchen, Internet access, and laundry service also available. Rooms US$6 per person. Pay in advance. ❶

Cabinas El Tucán (☎2735 0553), 50m north of the *muellecito* on the right. Doña Daisy offers simple rooms with private cold-water baths and fans. Parking available. Singles with fan and TV ¢4000; doubles ¢7000. With A/C, ¢12,000/¢20,000. ❶

Cabinas y Marisquería Princesa de Golfito (☎2775 0442), across the street from the Banco Nacional. This cozy 2-story white house with red roof and trim has a well-kept garden and offers comfortable rooms complete with private bath, fans, TV, and lacy sheets. Laundry service available. Singles ¢6500; doubles ¢9500. With hot water, add ¢500. A more spacious 4-person suite is also available (¢16,000). ❷

◐ ♫ FOOD AND ENTERTAINMENT

You can grab a meal anywhere along the road between the pharmacy and the Banco Nacional. There are more *sodas* than anything else, and prices hover consistently between ¢1500 and ¢2500 for a full meal. Alternatively, go to **MegaSuper** across from the soccer stadium. It has all the necessities, from fresh fruit to hygiene products. (☎2775 2274. Open M-Th 8am-8pm, F-Sa 6am-9pm, Su 6am-7pm. AmEx/MC/V.) **Supermercado Pearson** is nearer to the Pueblo Civil. (☎2775 0054. Open M-Sa 7am-7pm, Su 7am-6pm. AmEx/MC/V.)

Buenos Días (☎2775 1124). A local family favorite is just south of the *muellecito* in the center of Pueblo Civil. This unusually clean, air-conditioned diner is reminiscent of those that serve all-day breakfast in the US. The difference is that this Spanish-English menu includes a full beer selection as well as enormous *casados* (¢2500-3250) and *gallo pinto* breakfasts (¢1500-2550). Open daily 6am-10pm. MC/V. ❷

Restaurante La Cubana (☎8313 1411) offers the tastiest *tico* food in Golfito in a breezy dining room with more style and less grease than other *sodas*. Enjoy a fish fillet with salad and fries (¢2600) or a fruity *batido* (¢600) while watching the bustle of the main street from the balcony seating. Open M and W-Su 7am-10pm. ❶

Soda Keyren. Great for ill-timed hunger pangs, this *soda* is one of the most convenient and friendly restaurant around. Substantial *casados* with chicken, beefsteak, or ribs (¢1500) are served over a high counter from a cozy kitchen. The handwritten menu is posted on the wall above the pinball machine. Open 24hr. ❶

Heladería La Deliciosa (☎2775 1674), across from Cabinas Happy Daze, is known around Golfito for unbeatable desserts. Ice cream flavors like vanilla caramel and rum with fruit come in cones (¢600) or more elaborate banana splits (¢1600) that can be enjoyed in the cheerful pink dining room with glass-top tables. Flan and rice pudding (each ¢500) are unfrozen favorites. Open daily 2pm-10pm. ❶

▌▌ DAYTRIPS FROM GOLFITO

The "outdoors" lie deceptively close to the edges of town: just minutes outside Golfito, the sounds of urban bustle give way to the gurgling of nearby streams and the twitters of bickering birds. And though the beaches and forests feel remote, their proximity to the city makes them susceptible to many of the same threats as the surrounding urban environment. Travelers should be wary of exploring these areas alone at night.

PLAYA DE CACAO. Though this beach is easily accessible from Golfito, it's rarely crowded. The vegetation reaches all the way down to the water in many places, but there are plenty of smooth sandbars as well. Here, the warm water of the Pacific calmly caresses the shore. Because the Cacao peninsula and Puntarenitas island make a natural marina of Golfito Bay, the water here is extremely calm and rarely rises more than a foot with the tide. Cacao is known locally as Captain Tom's, so beachgoers should ask the taxi to drop them there. Tom's wrecked ship remains a point of interest on the southern edge of the main beach. *(6km north around the bay from Golfito; a pleasant 1hr. walk. Taxis cost about ¢6000, but the water taxis from the muellecito or muelle bananero are a cheaper, more enjoyable option, especially during the rainy season when the road can become impassable. 10min. ¢3000.)*

REFUGIO NACIONAL DE FAUNA SILVESTRE GOLFITO. Poorly publicized Refugio Nacional de Fauna Silvestre Golfito protects the steep, lush hills of primary rainforest above Golfito, encompassing distinct terrains that are home to 125 species of trees. This forest area is visible from the town, and extends from the edges of its residential areas to Playa Cacao. The reserve has the advantage of remaining fairly dry even during the rainy season and makes a good alternative to more demanding routes in **Parque Nacional Corcovado** (p. 350).

The park includes four principal **trails** beginning at various locations throughout Golfito. The main park entrance provides access to the easiest and best-marked trail just north of the Golfito airport. Take any of Golfito's local buses and get off at the entrance to the duty-free zone near the airstrip. Walk past the airstrip to the marked trailhead. The park office is located 800m down the dirt road. A short, well-marked trail begins behind the park office and leads through impressive primary rainforest to a small waterfall about 20min. away. Follow the main trail for about 10min. until the trail encounters a stream. Follow the stream the rest of the way to the waterfall.

Another waterfall trail begins near the police station on the road toward Playa Cacao. The **waterfall** is on the property of the public water supplier, so to take this trail you must have a note from the park office or a guide. Take the gravel road on the south side of the police station and follow it straight through the neighborhood of Llano Bointo. The road winds through beautiful countryside with flower-covered pastures on one side and trees on the other for 30min. before reaching a fork. Bear left there and follow the road for another 15min. Here you'll reach a small house where the guard for the water supply lives, and you'll have to present permission to continue. Behind the house the trail narrows before crossing a stream and climbing uphill for another 10min.

The waterfall here is more impressive than the one near the park entrance and has several cascades. The hike should take about 2hr. round-trip.

Another trail through more difficult territory begins behind the Banco Nacional. Nicknamed **"Las Torres,"** this trail (2hr.) leads uphill through the forest to the radio towers at the top of the hill and offers spectacular views of Golfito and all of the Golfo Dulce from the top. To find the trailhead, take the side road just south of the Banco Nacional and follow it through the residential area. At the point where the road starts to loop back around, there is a small dirt road leading uphill on the right marking the beginning of the trail. Because the trailhead can be tricky to find, a guide is recommended for visitors. This hike is not recommended at night or for solo travelers since the urban location makes it susceptible to crime. There is a US$10 per person park entrance fee, but it is rarely collected. As of now there are very few facilities within the park and none for overnight stays. *For more information, contact Susan at the MINAE office in Golfito (☎2775 2620 or 2775 0075. Open M-F 8am-4pm. For guided tours the park recommends Pedro Caballo who offers 6-hr. horseback tours of the refuge and Playa Cacoa. (☎2775 2240, 8876 7357 or 2732 1229.) Don Martin of the Ecotour Development Foundation (☎2775 1813 or 818 2433) will also guide hiking or horseback tours of the waterfalls (Hiking: 6hr. US$60 per person. Horseback: 8hr. US$80per person. 5-person min.)*

OSA WILDLIFE SANCTUARY. Located on Cana Blanca beach, on the western edge of Piedras Blancas National Park, the sanctuary is only accessible by water taxi (1hr., US$100-125 per boat). The purpose of the sanctuary is to rescue, rehabilitate and release animals into the rainforest. The sanctuary receives little government funding, so directors Earl and Carol Crews rely on the donations of visitors and the work of volunteers. The Crews lead 2hr. tours of the sanctuary that focus on environmental awareness and animal protection. Visitors are able to interact with several of the animals currently under the sanctuary's care including toucans, spider monkeys, and sloths. *Tourists can arrange tours by calling Carol and Earl at least a day in advance (☎8861 1309) and should leave food and children under 6 in the boat. (osawildlife.org. US$20 donation requested with visit.)*

PAVONES

Named after the flocks of Great Curasaw turkeys that used to roam here, Pavones is home to the second longest left-break waves in the world— at times over a mile long—and for this reason is

GIVING BACK

BRINGING CUDDLY BACK

Many animals arrive at the Osa Wildlife Sanctuary as young orphans. Some were meant for the pet trade but were rescued at the border. Others lost their parents at the hands of poachers or to the tires of a car. However the animals arrive, they are received with outstretched arms by the staff, many of them volunteers.

Sanctuary directors Carol and Earl Crews welcome a small group of volunteers into their cabins. In addition to preparing food, cleaning cages, and maintaining trails, each volunteer is paired with one young animal to feed and care for during their entire stay. Volunteers, who stay for a minimum of a month, find themselves developing special relationships with the baby animals on-site, including tropical birds, various primates, and predatory cats.

Carol and Earl give preference to volunteers who plan on longer stays but will take people for as little as 30 days. Many volunteers who come are interested in biology or veterinary medicine or are receiving college credit; others are simply interested travelers or wandering surfers. A US$15-20 fee per day is asked of volunteers, which is used to cover expenses and to hire an additional Costa Rican staff member for the sanctuary. After that, all that is needed to participate is compassion and a nurturing heart.

known as a goofy-footed (right foot forward) surfer's paradise. Bronzed international surfers may sit for months awaiting the level of swells that can create triple overhead faces, and a vibrant community of farmers has called this place home for years. There's little in the way of nightlife since most people are on a surfer schedule and get up early to hit the first waves. A few can be found lounging on the beach or boogie-boarding, but daytime activity is mostly confined to surfing. Vast expanses of sand with fewer surfers can be found at Punta Banco, 5km southeast. Follow the dirt road along the coast until the beach becomes less rocky (1km) and continue your trek on the dark sands.

🚌 🛈 TRANSPORTATION AND PRACTICAL INFORMATION

The center of town is marked by a group of colorfully-painted, tin-roofed buildings with a parking lot near the soccer field. Two parallel roads run along the coast connected by a path that runs between the Abastecedor (Supplier) Willy Willy and Bar/Restaurant la Plaza. Two **buses** run daily from Pavones to Golfito leaving from the stop where the path meets the inland road (2hr.; depart 5:30am, 12:30pm; return 10am, 3pm; ¢1000 plus ¢50 for a **ferry** ride en route). The Golfito bus stops in Conte, where a bus from Neily to Playa Zancudo waits for people who want to make the connection from Golfito (noon and 4pm).

Public phones are located near the Supermercado Río Claro and Bar Esquina del Mar. The **police station** is located behind the soccer field next to Puesta del Sol. (Open 24hr.) **SeaKings** surf shop on the site of the original "Turkey Town," the first surf shop in Pavones, is located across the street from Esquinas and sells surf gear, Pavones trinkets, and used boards for US$125-800. (☎2776 2015. Open M-Sa 10am-5pm.) **Clear River Sports and Adventure,** located in a small red building 100m outside of the town center, can satisfy all rental needs. They also have **computers** with Skype capability for use. (☎2776 2016, 2776 2017 or 2776 2403. US$3 per hr. Surf boards US$20 per day. Bikes and boogie boards US$10 per day. Open M-Sa 8:30am-4pm.) Next door to Sea Kings, **Ylang Ylang** sells handmade earrings, bikinis, and bags as well as other tourist items, such as hand-painted postcards. (☎2776 2401. Open M-Sa 11am-4pm.)

> **ON THE ROAD.** When thinking about travel times, it's not enough to just consider the distance. Travelers should ask about road conditions and elevation changes. Also keep in mind that conditions change with the seasons, so it's best to check with tour offices for the most up-to-date road conditions.

🏠 ACCOMMODATIONS

The gravel road that begins near Restaurante La Plaza and connects the beach road and the parallel inland road is lined with *cabinas* that are perfect for a variety of budgets. These places understand the mysticism awaiting a Pavones swell and will negotiate rates for longer stays.

Cabinas Caza Olas (☎2776 2381 or 8876 4874), along the main gravel road around the bend from La Plaza. Neatly-decorated rooms in a 2-story blue house include access to the family's kitchen. Laundry US$6 per load, or do it yourself for free. Check-out 11:30am. Quiet hours after 10pm. Doubles with shared bath US$20; triples US$30. With A/C and bath US$35/45. ❶

Cabinas Willy Willy (☎2776 2024), just up the road from Maureen. Newly renovated Willy Willy is 1 of the cleanest *cabinas* in town. Each room has A/C and bath with either 2 or 3 wooden beds. Double US$30; triple US$40. ❷

OSA PENINSULA

Cabinas Jasmin (☎8836 7196), 50m left from the bus stop where the gravel road meets the bus road. Has clean *cabinas* with cold ceramic bath, fans, wooden ceilings, and cement walls that keep rooms cool. Doubles US$25; triples with A/C US$45. ❷

Cabinas Maureen (☎2776 2002). In the same building complex as Sea Kings, Cabinas Maureen offers basic rooms with high wood ceilings, fans, and cold communal baths. The windows have screens, but bringing a mosquito net wouldn't be a bad idea. Large rooms with shared bath US$10 per person. Rooms with bath US$15. ❶

Oceanside Cabinas Esquina del Mar, a cheap surfer hangout with a popular *cantina*. The bar is open irregularly, but it blares music during the day and offers a one-of-a-kind view of surfers enjoying the waves. Bring a mosquito net, as there are no screens on the windows. Ask for room #1, as it offers the best view of the sweeping lefts. ¢3000 per person with shared cold-water baths. ❶

FOOD

The biggest grocery store in town, **Supermercado Río Claro,** is up the gravel road, and left on the bus road for 200m. It offers everything from fresh fruit to pharmacy items. (☎2776 2012. Open M-Sa 7am-7pm, Su 7am-4pm.) Right in the center of town is **Abastecedor Willy Willy,** which sells basic groceries. (☎2776 2024. Open daily 7am-8pm.)

Bar/Restaurante La Plaza (☎2776 2021), where the gravel road meets the main beach road. Locals and surfers alike fill up looking for huge portions of the best *tico* food in town. Diners eat on park benches and large patio chairs under a covered veranda. *Casados* ¢2500, with fish ¢2800; burger and fries ¢1500. Open daily 6am-8:30pm. ❶

Café de la Suerte (☎2776 2388; www.cafedelasuerte.com). Run by a pair of Israeli graphic designers, this cafe caters to California surfer palates with an all-vegetarian menu. Treat yourself to one of their creative sandwiches, like the guacamole, hummus, cheese, and pesto (¢3800), which will fill you right up. Open daily 7:30am-5pm. ❶

Restaurante La Bruschetta, located 2km south of town on the inland road (follow the signs for La Ponderosa). A colorful open-air Italian place with nice open views. The tasty Italian food and romantic atmosphere are worth the walk. Pizzas ¢5300. Pastas ¢5500. Try the gnocchi with gorgonzola. Open daily 11am-9pm. ❸

Puesta del Sol, just behind the goal of the soccer field, is a tourist-pleasing hut with irregularly-shaped wooden tables. It serves breakfast from a bamboo booth on the river's mouth, right around where the lefts begin. *Gallo pinto* ¢1500; pancakes with fruit ¢1500. Open daily 8am-8pm. ❶

ZANCUDO

With five kilometers of black sand beaches, top-notch ocean swimming, consistent waves for surfing, and world-record sportfishing, Zancudo should be full of tourists and outrageously high prices to match—but it's not. Though a small expat community cruises the main road in golf-carts, this beach town has remained mostly undiscovered by foreign travelers. Its seclusion is only interrupted during major Costa Rican holidays (the weeks around Christmas and Easter) and during the first week of February, when Roy's Zancudo Lodge hosts a large fishing and blues festival that features world-famous musicians.

TRANSPORTATION

The public taxi **boat** from Zancudo returns from Golfito at 12:30pm (¢3000). From Pavones, **buses** headed toward Golfito (1 hr.; 5:30am and 12:30pm; ¢500) let passengers off in Conte where a bus from Neily heading to Zancudo waits for people to make the connection (noon and 4pm, ¢500). From Zancudo, the only public transport is a ferry to Golfito that leaves from the docks on the north end of town (7am, ¢3000) or a bus to Neily that leaves from Bella Vista (5:30am). Private **taxi boats** to Golfito and Puerto Jímenez can be arranged through Cabinas Los Cocos (☎2776 0012. US$20 per person).

ORIENTATION AND PRACTICAL INFORMATION

Situated on a peninsula jutting out into the Golfo Dulce, Zancudo is 15km south of Golfito and 10km north of Pavones (35km by car or bus). The town runs along a 5km beach road with the gulf to the west and the Río Sabalo estuary to the east. The Bella Vista *pulpería* and bus stop mark the center of town. Waves at the southern end of the beach build enough for some decent surfing, while the northern end mainly attracts swimmers and sunbathers. Mangrove forests surround the Río Sabalo, which runs inland from the middle of town. The dock is located on the estuary, 500m before the northern tip of the peninsula. Most businesses have handmade signs and may be hard to recognize.

There is no tourist office in Zancudo, but for the best **sportfishing information,** contact **Roy's Zancudo Lodge** (☎2776 0008). Adventure tours such as kayak tours of the gulf or mangrove forests can be arranged through the bigger lodges in town.The main *pulpería,* **Bella Vista,** occupies a large green building in the center of town, where all buses drop off. (☎2776 0101. Open M-Sa 7am-1pm and 2-7pm, Su 7am-4pm with extended hours during high season.) **MiniSuper Tres Amigos,** 3km south of the town center, has a slightly larger selection and rents **surfboards** on the beach, right in front of some of the best breaks. (☎2776 0158. US$15 per day, US$7 per half-day. Open M-Sa 7am-6pm, Su 7am-1pm.) **Coloso del Mar,** across the street, also rents boards and arranges surf lessons. (☎2776 0203 or 2776 0050. US$20 per hr. lesson.) The **police station** (☎911 or 2776 0212) is across the street from the school at the north end of the peninsula. **Telephones** are numerous, but they only work with Costa Rican calling cards. If you don't have your own computer, **Cabinas, Bar and Restaurant Oceano** has **computers** and free Wi-Fi (☎2776 0921; ¢3000 per hr.; open daily 11am-10pm). **Coloso del Mar** also offers free Wi-Fi at almost any hour of the day.

ACCOMMODATIONS

Accommodations are generally divided into two categories: backpacker dives and luxuriously-equipped cabins. If traveling in a large group, sharing a cabin with a kitchen might actually turn out to be a more affordable—and comfortable—option. The best backpacker deals are usually attached to *sodas* or bars and are located a few meters from the beach.

Cabinas Sol y Mar (☎2776 0014), 2km south of the town center, is for those looking for luxury at a good price. It offers clean and spacious *cabinas* with hot-water baths, large decks, and ocean views. Boogie boards and hammocks free for guests. Bike rentals US$10 per day. *Cabinas* for 1-3 US$15-42. Rental house with 2 bedrooms and kitchen US$800 per month high season, US$550 per month low. The attached restaurant and bar offers some of the best food and nightlife in Zancudo. *Cabinas* ❸/Restaurant ❶

Cabinas, Bar and Restaurant Jafeth (☎2776 0078), also known as Rafa's place, has the best deal on basic rooms: bare concrete floors, foam mattresses, and whitewashed walls go for ¢3500 in the high season and ¢3000 per person in the low season. Rooms with ceramic bath ¢4000/5000. The restaurant lacks a physical menu but serves affordable *tico* food (breakfast ¢1100; lunch ¢2500; fish and chips dinner

¢2800) in a *rancho* dining room. Restaurant open daily 6am-9pm. *Cabinas* ❶/Restaurant ❶

Cabinas Sussy (☎2776 0107), 500m south of the town center, is a bit farther from the bus stop. Sussy has lively backpacker rooms available in a 2-story blue house with gardens, a pool table, ping pong, darts, dance floor, and book exchange. The bar also houses a local artist's studio. ¢3000 per person with fan and cold bath. Negotiable for larger groups and longer stays. Camping across the street is free. ❶

Cabinas Los Cocos (☎/fax 2776 0012; www.loscocos. com). Somewhat pricier but worth the money. Artists-owners Susan and Andrew offer fully equipped cabins with palm frond roofs, hammocks, kitchenettes, coffee makers, canopy-style mosquito nets, and European-tiled bathrooms. An assortment of bamboo plants and broken tile murals adorn the property. Laundry US$3 per load. Cabin for 2-3 US$60 per night; low season US$50. Week-long packages available. ❸

🍴 FOOD

🍽 **La Puerta Negra** (☎2776 0181), offers first-class Italian dining in the colorful open-air dining room. Italian chef Alberto makes his own pasta using his Mama Rosa's best recipes. His flavorful dishes (homemade ravioli with Mama Rosa's sauce ¢4000) have made this a favorite spot for locals as well as tourists. Dinners (US$10-15) include salad and bread. Open daily 5:30pm until the last customer leaves. Lunch by reservation. Closed mid-Sept. to mid-Oct. ❸

Bar/Restaurante Tranquilo (☎2776 0121), 3km south of the town center. The restaurant offers both *tico* and Italian food (*casados* ¢2000-2500. Spaghetti ¢2000.) Restaurant open daily 6am-9pm. Offers modest and well-kept *cabinas*. Room with communal, cold bath ¢3500; double with bath ¢7500; triple with A/C and TV ¢15,000. *Cabinas* ❶/ Restaurant ❶

Macondo (☎2776 0157) up the stone walkway and through the flowered arch just a bit south of Tío Froilan Way. Another equally charismatic Italian place. The owner, a former friar-in-training, prepares pastas with your choice of one of 13 sauces (¢2200) to accompany specialty garlic bread (¢600). Open daily noon-2pm and 5:30-9pm. ❶

🎵 NIGHTLIFE

Salon and Bar El Coquito (☎2776 0010.) A local joint with a small bar in front that plays music ranging from reggaeton to country all day long. The salon opens later in the day and has the biggest dance floor in town. Slower nights play host to karaoke. Open daily 11am-10pm or until the crowd diminishes.

THE LOCAL STORY

BLACK SAND, BRUSCHETTA, AND TH BLUES

Most visitors to Zancudo woulc expect to find nothing more thar an average *soda* or two. Little d they know that Zancudo feature some of the best Italian food tha Costa Rica (and maybe even Italy has to offer at Alberto Ferrini's L Puerta Negra restaurant.

Originally from Genoa, Italy Alberto fell in love with Zancudc and decided to leave Italy to oper his own restaurant. Alberto serve homemade Italian cuisine in a airy dining room that he decoratec himself. He carved the tables anc chairs from local trees, craftec the wall hangings, and picks fresh flowers daily from the yard sur rounding his house.

Alberto also sets his owr unique mood with his choice o music. A fan of southern blues al his life, Alberto's playlist feature soulful acoustic blues standards as well as less-known pieces.

However, the atmosphere isn' everything at La Puerta Negra Alberto cooks up amazing foot to match. He makes his owr ravioli almost daily and his deli cious bruschetta and Mama Rose tomato sauce are recipes from his Mama Rosa back home in Italy.

☎2776 0181; albertolapuer tanegra@yahoo.com. *Reserva tions are necessary for lunch Open daily for dinner 5:30pm o until the last customer leaves Closed Sept.-Oct. when Albertc goes back home to Italy.*

PUERTO JIMÉNEZ

Named in honor of three-time Costa Rican President Ricardo Jiménez, Puerto Jiménez has become known as the backpacker alternative to Bahía Drake, offering far lower prices and many more options for collective transportation and tours into the nearby Parque Nacional Corcovado. The town is undeniably convenient and has adapted well to the high concentration of passing tourists without losing the traditional Costa Rican feel. The nearby beach is a serene yet unimpressive counterpart to a town center well-populated by confused foreigners and the numerous stores that cater to them. A glimpse of the gregarious scarlet macaws that feed in the almond trees along the soccer field, however, is a reminder to most visitors of the spectacular wildlife that draws so many travelers here in the first place.

RAINDROPS KEEP FALLIN' ON MY HEAD. It is best to take one of the early morning or afternoon taxi boats from Golfito to Puerto Jiménez, especially during the rainy season, as afternoon rains can leave you and your things soaking wet after the 30min. trip. Boats don't have excellent roof protection, so it's better not to take the chance.

TRANSPORTATION

Flights: Sansa and **NatureAir** both have offices in the small airport terminal across from the cemetery. Both fly to and from **San José:** Sansa (☎2735 5890; 50min.; 4 flights daily in the low season 6:55, 10am, 12:20, 2:20pm; 9 daily high season 6:55am-5pm; US$108 for tourists, US$83 for residents); NatureAir (☎2735 5428; www. natureair.com; 50min.; departs daily 7:15, 9:45am, 12:15pm with an additional 4:30pm flight during high season; US$79-119.) Reservations are necessary, and tickets sell out quickly during the dry season (Dec.-Apr.) but are more available during the wet season (May-Nov.). Both airlines also arrange rental cars and other transportation.

Buses: Operate out of a terminal 1 block west of the soccer field's southern edge. 1 daily bus to **San José** (8hr., 5am, ¢3620) via **San Isidro** (5hr., ¢2500). An additional bus runs to San Isidro (5hr., 1pm, ¢2500). 2 buses depart daily for **Nelly** (3hr.; 5:30am and 2pm; ¢1865). Getting to **Golfito** is easiest by ferry, but it's possible to take a Neily bus and transfer at **Río Claro.** Ticket office (☎2771 4744) open M-Sa 4:30-5am, 7:30-11am, 12:30-4:30pm, Su noon-1pm.

Ferries: There are 7 ferries daily to **Golfito** from the pier at the north end of town. (1hr.; 5:45, 6am, noon, 3, 4pm; ¢2000; 1½hr., 6am, ¢1000.) Private boats to Golfito cost about US$60-70.

Taxis: Line up on Calle Comercial. Taxis hold 5 people at most. With some bargaining, you can reach: **Carate** (US$80), **La Palma** (US$40), **Los Patos** (US$70), **Matapolo** (US$40), **Playa Preciosa** (US$10), and **Puntarenita** (US$15). All prices per taxi.

ORIENTATION AND PRACTICAL INFORMATION

The **Calle Comercial** (main road) runs from the soccer field in the north to a gas station in the south. Buses arrive one block to the west of the soccer field. The beach road runs just north of the soccer field and heads east to the ferry pier and airstrip. The airstrip area is mostly residential and is often referred to as *gringolandia* for the high concentration of foreigners who live there.

Tourist Office: Almost every tour company and shop in town advertises tourist information. **CafeNet El Sol** (☎2735 5719), 1 block south of the soccer field on C. Comercial.

Though it's not a formal tourist office, this Internet cafe connects visitors to general information about area adventures and higher budget lodgings. Enjoy the A/C and use the maps on the walls to figure out your hiking itinerary. Open daily 7am-11pm. The **MINAE** office is located in a large orange building on the west side of the airstrip. For more specific tour information, see **Guided Tours,** p. 349.

Bank: Banco Nacional de Costa Rica (☎2735 5155), 4 blocks south of the soccer field. Cashes traveler's checks and has an MC/V **ATM.** The nearest source of cash for any other cardholder is Golfito. Open M-F 8:30am-3:45pm.

Laundry: Lavandería Kandy (☎2735 5347), 2 blocks south of the bus terminal beneath Soda y Heladería Antojitos. Same-day service. ₡800 per kg. Open M-F 7am-6pm.

Pharmacy: Farmacia Hidalgo (☎2735 5564), across the street from Carolina. Open M-Sa 8am-8pm. MC/V.

Police: (☎2735 5114, emergency 911). South of the field on the main street.

Red Cross: (☎2735 5109), across from the clinic.

Medical Clinic: (☎2735 5029 or 2735 5063; fax 2735 5601), 10m west of the southwest corner of the soccer field. Open 24hr. For mosquito nets, sunblock, or other essentials, try **Tienda el Record,** next door to Osa Discoveries. Open daily 8am-6pm.

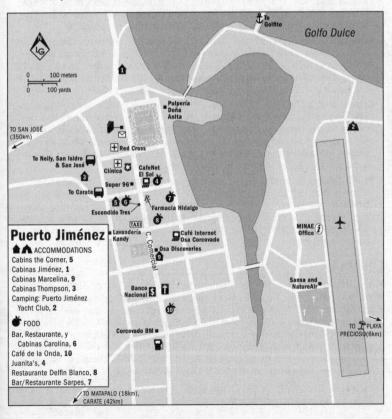

OSA PENINSULA

Internet Access: Cafe Internet Osa Corcovado (☎2735 5757), 2 blocks south of the southeast corner of the soccer field, has the cheapest and fastest Internet in town on Skype-capable computers. ¢1000 per hr. ¢250 per min. B/w printing ¢150. Open M-F 9am-8pm, Sa 10am-8pm. **CafeNet El Sol** (☎2735 5719; www.soldeosa.com), 1 block south of the soccer field on Calle Comercial, has higher prices, but better hours. ¢1500 per hr. ¢500 per min. International calls ¢500 per min. Open daily 7am-11pm.

Library: just north of the post office. Has a sizable English-language book selection and free 2-week lending for residents and tourists. Open M-F 9am-noon and 1-3pm.

Post Office: (☎2735 5045), on the west side of the soccer field. Open M-F 7:30am-noon, 1-5:30pm. **Postal Code:** 60702.

ACCOMMODATIONS AND CAMPING

Cabins the Corner (☎2735 5328), 1 block south of the bus station and to the right. Cabins has a large, well-kept dormitory and several clean and simple private rooms for up to 3 people. All rooms have ceiling fans and share hot-water showers. Laundry service and communal kitchen available. They'll watch your bags for free while you explore Corcovado. Tents, stoves, and mattresses available for rent. Dorm ¢3500; singles ¢8000; doubles ¢10,000; triples ¢12,000. ❶

Cabinas Thompson (☎2735 5148), behind Soda Thompson, 1 block south of the bus station and to the right. Spacious rooms have peach walls with rainforest paintings, fans, and cold-water baths. Popular with backpackers. US$6 per person. ❶

Cabinas Marcelina (☎2735 5286; fax 2735 5007; cabmarce@hotmail.com), 3 blocks south of the soccer field on Calle Comercial on the left. Rooms are luxurious and comfortably sized, with bedside lamps, private hot water baths, and fans. Laundry service available. Breakfast served daily in the main house (US$6). High season singles US$24; low season US$20. Doubles US$40/US$35; with A/C US$48/40. ❷

Cabinas Jiménez (☎2735 5090; www.cabinasjimenez.com), 150m north of the northwest corner of the soccer field. A waterfall graces the lobby and rooms have patios overlooking the bay. Offers everything from standard and deluxe rooms to a private bungalow with mini-fridge and private deck. All rooms have A/C, ceiling fans, hot- water baths, parking, and aquatic murals. Prices range from a standard single (US$30) to 4-person in the bungalow (US$110). Reduced rates for long stays. ❷

Puerto Jiménez Yacht Club (☎2735 5051), near the water at the eastern end of the beach road through the same entrance as the Parrot Bay Village. It has drinking water, bathrooms, cold-water showers, and access to the gulf. The grassy camping area is slightly elevated, so you stay a bit drier than on the beach. Adonis, the camp manager, will also take you to watch him feed the caiman and crocodiles in the nearby mangroves for free. US$3 per person. Bring your own tent. Camping on the beach free. ❶

FOOD

For such a small town, Puerto Jiménez has a wide variety of dining options. While restaurants can be a bit pricey, there are plenty of *sodas* offering cheap, filling food as well. **Corcovado BM,** across the street from the gas station, is the largest grocery store in town. (☎2735 5009. Open M-Sa 7am-9pm, Su 8am-8pm. **Super 96** supermarket is more centrally located, one block south of the soccer field across from CafeNet El Sol. (☎2735 5168. Open M-Sa 6am-6:30pm, Su 7am-noon.) For a quick meal, **Pandería Monar** (☎2735 5523), north of Super 96, sells calzones and sweet bread (¢300). Open M-Sa 5am-6pm, Su 5-9am.

Café de la Onda (☎2735 5312), just south of Banco Nacional. This colorful coffee shop has a variety of tasty breakfast and lunch offerings and always plays good music.

Everything from a simple bagel and cream cheese (₡1500) to crepes with banana, whipped cream, and chocolate sauce (₡2200). Try the bagelwich, your choice of bagel with garlic/basil cream cheese, egg, melted mozzerela, and tomato (₡2000). Book exchange and frequent live music performances. ❶

Bar/Restaurante Sarpes (☎2735 5373), 2 blocks south of the southeast corner of the soccer field. Recently opened, Sarpes has already become a local favorite with its masterfully prepared fish dishes like grilled tuna with garlic and ginger marmalade and grilled mahimahi with papaya chutney. All dinner plates come with salad and potatoes or rice (₡4500). Lunch ₡2500-3500. Open M-Sa 11am-11pm, Su 4-11pm. ❷

Bar, Restaurante, y Hotel Carolina (☎2735 5185), 2 blocks south of the soccer field on C. Comercial. Always packed with tourists, this is a great place to chat with other travelers, people-watch, or plan your next trip. *Tico* and American food available at slightly inflated prices. Granola, fruit, and yogurt breakfast ₡1900. Rice dishes ₡2100-2700. Garlic fish fillet ₡2500. Open daily 7am-10pm. ❶

Juanita's (☎2735 5056), east of CafeNet El Sol. With its cavernous wooden adobe interior, Juanita's looks a little out of place on the Osa Peninsula but serves decent semi-authentic Mexican food. Happy hour (4-6pm) serves beer on tap (₡600). Mixed drinks ₡1200-1500. Most entrees, including some vegetarian, ₡1500-3500. Open daily 9am-11pm; bar may stay open longer depending on crowd. ❶

Restaurante Delfin Blanco (☎2735 5998), in the white and blue building a block south and east of Carolina. The new, spacious dining room features a huge flat-screen TV and sizable bar. The food is an eclectic assortment of Chinese-American (chop suey ₡2400-2700), Italian (fettuccine alfredo or carbonara ₡2700), and Costa Rican cuisine (*ceviche* and *casados* ₡2200-2500). Open daily 7am-11pm. ❶

🐾 GUIDED TOURS

Puerto Jiménez serves as a launching point for the Osa Peninsula, and tour operators have a variety of options to satisfy this demand. Tours are not exactly "budget," but they do provide access to places that would be difficult to reach on your own. The high level of tourism also means that most guides speak fluent English. **Escondido Trex,** inside Restaurante Carolina, one block south of the soccer field on C. Comercial, is the oldest and most extensive operation in town. They offer everything from budget to deluxe tours, with student and group discounts available. Trips are led by English-speaking naturalists, and include sunset dolphin watching (US$35), mangrove kayaking (US$35), waterfall-rappelling (US$75), rainforest day treks (US$50), two to ten day kayaking expeditions (US$250-850) and multi-day hikes through Corcovado. (☎2735 5210; www.escondidotrex.com. Open daily 8am-8pm.) Three blocks south of the soccer field, **Osa Discoveries** specializes in beach tours but also offers birdwatching, snorkeling, gold prospecting, sportfishing, and horseback riding excursions. Guided ATV tours are also offered during the high season (6, 9:30am, 2pm). Drivers US$129, passengers US$20, lunch included. (☎2735 5260. www.osadiscoveries.com). The helpful and friendly staff at the **Ministerio del Ambiente y Energia (MINAE)** office, on the inland side of the airstrip, takes reservations for overnight stays in the park (US$8 hostel; US$4 camp), and supplies free tide charts, detailed maps of the park's trails, and up-to-date information on which trails are waterlogged. (☎2735 5036. Reservations can also be made online at www.pncorcovado.blogspot.com or by emailing pncorcovado@gmail.com. Open daily 8am-noon and 1-4pm.)

🏖️ 🎆 BEACHES AND NIGHTLIFE

Though the beach in Puerto Jiménez may be unimpressive, one doesn't have to journey far to find a superior substitute. **Playa Preciosa,** located 6km east of the airport, offers 5km of black-sand beaches and impressive views of the gulf and of Zancudo and Pavones on the other side. Here the beach is clean and the sand is plentiful. Though visitors should watch out for riptides, swimming and boogieboarding are possible during low tide. The beach is rarely crowded, and when it is it's usually because there's a local beach volleyball game going on. (1hr. walk or 20min. bike ride. Taxis should cost around US$10 round-trip.) Bathrooms and bag storage are available at **La Perla de la Osa Hotel and Restaurant.** The restaurant also offers a nice bar and tasty sandwiches for those who didn't bring their own supplies. Every Friday night, La Perla hosts the biggest party in town. *Ticos* and tourists show up for a hearty buffet-style dinner (US$6) followed by several hours of Latin dancing (6-9pm). (☎8829 5865 or 8848 0752; www.thepearloftheosa.com. Open daily 11am-8pm.)

PARQUE NACIONAL CORCOVADO

Sprawling along the western coast of the Osa Peninsula, Parque Nacional Corcovado feels like an Edenic garden. Cool, clear streams spill out of the rainforest and into the warm surf of the Pacific. While these deserted beaches are truly tempting, luring hikers to swim or bodysurf, the real draw of Corcovado is its variety of flora and fauna. Though the peninsula comprises only 4% of the land mass of Costa Rica, it offers 50% of its biodiversity. The park protects the last portion of tropical humid forest in the world, and the hundreds of species of trees are overhung with bromeliads, orchids, and other epiphytes. There was no land access to the park until 1978. Despite its popularity in recent years; Corcovado still awaits full exploration; hundreds of species still await identification by the students and scientists who frequent the area.

AT A GLANCE

AREA: Land 440 sq. km; sea 24 sq. km.

CLIMATE: Tropical humid forest: hot, rainy; and very humid. Dry (high) season Dec.-Apr., rainy (low) season May-Nov.

HIGHLIGHTS: Contains 50% of Costa Rica's biodiversity, including unidentified animals and vegetation.

GATEWAYS: Puerto Jiménez (p. 346), Bahía Drake (p. 332).

CAMPING: Camping permitted only in designated ranger stations areas.

FEES AND RESERVATIONS: Entrance US$10 per day for foreigners,₡1600 for Costa Rican residents. Camping US$4. Beds at Sirena US$8; meals US$12-17. Reservations strongly recommended, especially for longer trips.

📋 **TRANSPORTATION. Puerto Jiménez** is the largest town on the peninsula and offers the most affordable transportation into the thickets of the national park. Most independent hikers choose this town as their base of exploration. To get to the ranger station at **La Leona,** take the **colectivo truck** from Puerto Jiménez to Carate (2hr., daily 6am and 1:30pm, return 8am and 4pm, US$8, with Costa Rican residency US$2), which leaves from Soda Thompson, one block south and one block west of the soccer field. From Carate, turn right onto the beach. It's about an hour's walk to the park entrance at La Leona. To get from Puerto Jiménez to Los Patos, take the bus to **La Palma** that leaves from in front of the Super 96 (1hr., 6 per day 5am-3pm, ₡500.) From there, hike to **Guadalupe** (2km, 1hr.) and from there another 1km to **Río Rincón** (30min.). Finally, from Río

Rincón, hike 13km (3hr.) to the ranger station at Los Patos, on a path along the river's banks that crosses water over 20 times and ascends a steep ridge toward the end. Because of the river crossings, this path is often impassable during the rainy season; check with MINAE in Puerto Jiménez before heading out. In the dry season, you may be able to take a **taxi** from Puerto Jiménez (2hr., US$80) or a **taxi tractor** from La Palma to Los Patos (2hr., US$60-80).

From **Bahía Drake** (p. 332), the only way to get to the eastern and southern parts of the peninsula is by car or boat. Roads are very rough and often require passing through rivers and creeks. Boats, on the other hand, are very expensive. To reach the ranger station at San Pedrillo from Bahía Drake, either hike 18km (6-8hr.) along a shaded trail that hugs the beach, or hire a boat from one of the Drake hotels for US$60-80 per trip. The trail may be flooded and it may be necessary to take a boat when water levels are high; contact the Puerto Jiménez MINAE for more information. (☎2735 5036. Open daily 8am-4pm.) Most hotels in Bahía Drake also offer guided tours of Corcovado including transportation to San Pedrillo for around US$80.

◼️🔢 ORIENTATION AND PRACTICAL INFORMATION. There are four ranger stations inside the park boundaries, each of which has water, bathrooms, and campgrounds. Three of these form a triangle connected by trails—**Sirena** on the southwest tip, La Leona on the southeast tip, and Los Patos to the north between them. In addition to a camping area, Sirena also offers beds, electricity and a lodge with food service. San Pedrillo, on the northwest tip of the park, is accessible from Sirena only during the dry season (Dec. 1-Apr. 31) or by beach from Bahía Drake with a guide. Los Patos and La Leona are best reached from Puerto Jiménez; San Pedrillo is most accessible from Bahía Drake.

> **WHEN TO GO.** Corcovado is tropical year round, with a rainy season from May to Nov. and a dry season from Dec. to April. Some trails are only accessible during the dry season and the park tends to be more crowded during the dry months. Tidal changes make parts of some trails impassable at certain times of day. Corcovado is a rainforest, but protection from the sun and proper hydration are absolutely essential; hikes are long, and some stretches offer little or no shade.

◼️🔢 ACCOMMODATIONS AND CAMPING. Although the more athletic or motivated can make a round trip in two full days, most overnight trekkers spend three days in the park: the first to hike to Sirena, the second to explore using Sirena as a base (the route to Los Patos is most popular), and the third to hike out. Rangers arrange lodging options and meals. (Breakfast US$12. Lunch and dinner US$17. Dorm beds US$8; bring sheets and mosquito net. Camping US$4 per person; only allowed in designated areas at the stations.) Where the *colectivo* truck stops in Carate, there are last minute meals and snacks available at the *pulpería* (coffee ¢500; *gallo pinto* ¢1500; steak and eggs ¢2000). A public restroom is available (¢300). Camping is also possible in a field across the street with access to showers and bathrooms (US$5 per tent).

There are two other options along the beach before La Leona. At the posh **Corcovado Lodge ❹**, travelers can stay in large tents with real bed frames and mattresses and take it easy in the hammock seating of the bar. (San José office ☎2257 0766 or 2222 0333; www.corcovadotentlodge.com. High season singles US$74; doubles US$54 per person. Low season US$68/51. 3 meals included.) The more affordable **La Leona Lodge Camping ❸**, has 13 tents with air mattresses, sheets, towels, and beachside hammocks for relaxing after a day of exploration in Corcovado. Newly built, the site has a kind staff and clean facilities. (☎2735 5705 or 2735 5704; www.laleonaecolodge.com. High season singles US$45; doubles US$35 per person. Low season US$35/25. Ages under 3 free, ages 4-10 50% off. With lodging, trail use, three meals, and unlimited coffee, tea, and juice: high season US$85/75 per person. Low season US$75/65.) Both lodges are well-marked along the beach within 100m of the La Leona ranger station.

▣ **HIKING.** In addition to a tide chart, guides are recommended for attempting the three major long-distance hikes inside the park. The first trail goes from La Leona to Sirena (16km, 6-7hr.) along a sandy beach with several parallel forest trails that are fairly well-marked. Two sections (Salsipuedes and Punta La Chancha) are impassable at high tide. It is best to speak with the rangers before heading out. The second hike, from Los Patos to Sirena (18km; 6-8hr.), is especially difficult during the rainy season, particularly where it crosses the Río Pavo. This trail passes through the heart of the rainforest near a swampy lagoon, and is the best place to find wildlife. The third trail, from **Sirena** to **San Pedrillo,** is only open from December 1 to April 31. It hugs the beach and ends in the forest. (25.5km; 8-10hr.) Beware: this is a dangerous hike, as the first 18km are on beaches that offer little shelter from the sun; your guide may want to pass here by night. In any case, stay hydrated. The last 7.5km is considered by many to be the most majestic ecological terrain in Central America, with gargantuan trees reaching heights of 75m spread throughout. Two hours from the end of the trail, stop for a break on **Playa Llorona,** where a magnificent waterfall awaits. Shorter dayhikes are possible from each of the ranger stations. Behind the San Pedrillo station, the short **Sendero Catarata,** on the right facing away from the sea, loops near a waterfall (45min.). **Sendero Río Pargo** begins across the Río San Pedrillo, which runs along the station. This trail through the woods leads to the Río Pargo (Snapper River), where you can swim near the mangroves while watching the fresh water run straight into the ocean (1-2hr. loop). **Sendero Playa Llorona** is 6hr. round-trip, much of it along the coast. Retrace your steps to return. From La Leona, out and back day hikes of varying lengths are possible down the park's main trail. Many people choose to hike out on the trail past the Río Madrigal where inhabitants used to pan for gold, to Punta La Chanca and then return on the beach. Hikers must be aware that sections of the beach become rocky, requiring a return to the forest trail.

Sirena is encircled by six trails that run the gamut of wildlife exploration, making it the most popular destination in the park. **Guanacaste** (1hr.) and **Espaveles** (2hr.) explore the swampy lowlands where most mammals can be found. The steep ascent of Ollas (1hr.) leads to the ridge of Corcovado (3hr.), an excellent place to watch birds and the sunrise through the rainforest canopy. The Río Claro trail (3hr.) runs adjacent to the river of the same name and is a great place to observe freshwater wildlife. Finally, the **Naranjos** trail (1hr.) returns to Sirena along a beach lined with palm trees. Any one of these trails can be explored individually, but many hikers choose to hike two or more on end before returning to Sirena. Many visitors choose to stay two nights in Sirena to take the day to explore all of these trails in one large loop. You can also return to Salsipuedes and explore the sea caves that are exposed during low tide.

CARIBBEAN LOWLANDS

Water, palms, and reggae music abound in the coastal lowlands along Costa Rica's Caribbean shore. From the turtle-filled wetlands of Tortuguero and Parismina to the seaside wildlife and reefs of Cahuita to the reggae and surfing hotspot Puerto Viejo, the Caribbean has almost every type of sandy shore imaginable. Though tourism on the coast is on the rise, the region's most famous visitors are the nesting sea turtles that fill the beaches of Barra del Colorado, Tortuguero, Parismina, and Manzanillo. Puerto Viejo is becoming a surfing and party mecca as Cahuita and Manzanillo are defining themselves as more low-key beachside towns. Just south of the border in Panamanian archipelago Bocas del Toro, travelers can island-hop their way through scuba diving, sea kayaking, and sunbathing trips. Lacking the dramatic peninsulas and higher prices of the Pacific Coast, the Caribbean offers budget travelers a haven of volunteer opportunities, endless sandy beaches, and low-priced options of reasonable quality.

Though under-touristed until recent years, the Caribbean Coast has long been a hot spot for immigrants from around the world. The most prominent cultural groups in the area are the indigenous Cabécar and Bribrí tribes and

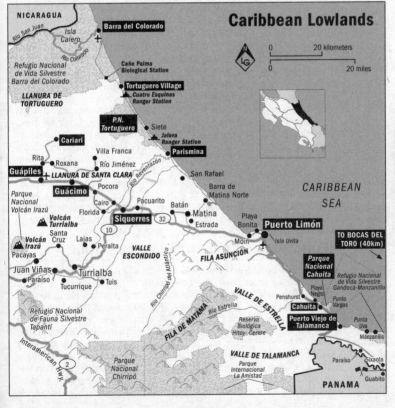

Caribbean Lowlands

NICARAGUA

Río San Juan
Isla Calero
Barra del Colorado
Río Colorado
Refugio Nacional de Vida Silvestre Barra del Colorado
Caño Palma Biological Station
Tortuguero Village
Cuatro Esquinas Ranger Station
LLANURA DE TORTUGUERO
P.N. Tortuguero
Siete
Cariari
Villa Franca
Jalova Ranger Station
Parismina
Rita
Roxana
Río Jiménez
Guápiles
LLANURA DE SANTA CLARA
San Rafael
Pocora
Barra de Matina Norte
CARIBBEAN SEA
Parque Nacional Volcán Irazú
Guácimo
Cairo
Pácuarito
Batán
Florida
Matina
Playa Bonita
Volcán Turrialba
Siquerres
32
Estrada
Puerto Limón
Santa Cruz
Lajas
Peralta
VALLE ESCONDIDO
Moín
Isla Uvita
TO BOCAS DEL TORO (40km)
Volcán Irazú
Pacayas
10
FILA ASUNCIÓN
Juan Viñas
Turrialba
Tuis
Parque Nacional Cahuita
Paraíso
Tucurrique
VALLE DE ESTRELLA
Penshurst
Playa Negra
Refugio Nacional de Vida Silvestre Gandoca-Manzanillo
Refugio Nacional de Fauna Silvestre Tapantí
FILA DE MATAMA
Río Estrella
Cahuita
Punta Vargas
Reserva Biológica Hitoy-Cerere
Puerto Viejo de Talamanca
Punta Uva
Interamerican Hwy.
2
Parque Nacional Chirripó
VALLE DE TALAMANCA
Parque Internacional La Amistad
Paraíso
Manzanillo
Sixaola
Guabito
PANAMA

0   20 kilometers
0   20 miles

the Afro-Caribs and Chinese, who immigrated in the 1800s to work on banana plantations and railroads. Though Spanish is still spoken by most residents, the local dialect, especially in the south, is a Jamaican-influenced Spanglish, almost indecipherable to everyone but locals. The most delicious result of the Afro-Caribbean influence here is the twist on *típica* food; instead of the traditional *casados*, enjoy rice and beans simmered in coconut milk, gumbo-style *rondón* soup, Jamaican, jerk-flavored meats, and an abundance of curries.

GUÁPILES

Though rarely visited by tourists, Guápiles is a convenient stopover before heading south to the Rainforest Aerial Tram or northeast to Barra del Colorado or Tortuguero. An important city on the old banana train route, Guápiles is now a pit stop for banana-hauling trucks heading toward San José or Limón, and its dusty streets are surrounded by auto shops and car garages. However, the town is also a popular local shopping area, and there are lots of bargains to be found in its open-air stalls, vintage *importadora* clothing stores, and boutique shops selling everything from furniture to clothing and umbrellas.

TIP **BARGAIN HUNTING.** While the majority of Guápiles' boutiques simply re-sell basic American fashions, some of the so-called *"importadoras"* are real bargain basements; some stores will let you walk away with a bag of 80s and 90s wear for under US$5. With that kind of price, you can't go wrong.

TRANSPORTATION

All intercity **buses** arrive and depart from **Guapileños Bus Station** at the south end of town. Buses depart from specific terminals; the destinations served by each terminal are posted on signs at the entrances to the terminals. Many buses stop in smaller towns en route to those listed below (information ☎2710 0808 or 2710 6075). Buses go to: Puerto Limón (express bus 1½hr., 1 per hr. 4am-7pm, ¢550), Puerto Limón via Guácimo, Pocora, and Siquirres (2hr., 12 per day 6am-8:15pm, ¢550); Calle Vieja via Guácimo (1hr.; 6, 8:30, 11:10am, 4pm; ¢250); Cariari (direct every 30-40min. 7:15am-7:15pm; indirect every 30-40min. 6am-10:20pm; ¢220); Río Frío via Las Finca (6, 7:30, 9:30am, 12:30, 4:15pm; ¢685); Río Frío via La Victoria (8:30am, 2, 3:30, 6pm; ¢685); Puerto Viejo de Sarapiquí (1½hr., 10 per day 5:30am-6:30pm, ¢735); San José (1½hr., every 30min. 5am-9pm, ¢1000). Local buses shuttle passengers around town; ask anyone at a bus stop where the bus is headed. **Taxis** abound, although they tend to overcharge. A taxi from the bus station to the town center runs ¢500-800.

ORIENTATION AND PRACTICAL INFORMATION

Guápiles is a relatively large town, but most visitors will not need to go beyond the town center during their stay. The bus station is at the southern tip of the town center. The road in front of the bus station runs north, down the hill, intersecting with the town's main street, which runs east from the Mas X Menos about 500m to the church to the west. Just to the east of the church is the *parque central*, which stretches several blocks north toward the **Palí** supermarket, which is 50m north of the northeast corner of the park. Heading west down this street, you will encounter a series of pharmacies and clinics, along with the Musmanni bakery and Caffe Ristorante Nona. **Clínica del Caribe** handles emergencies. (☎2710 1445 or 2710 2164. Open 24hr.) Thirty meters west of Palí is a **Banco Popular** with a **24hr. ATM.** (☎2710 0259. Open M-F 8am-5pm, Sa

8-11:30am.) There are also several full-service banks on the west and east sides of the *parque central*. The **post office** is 100m north and 50m west of the church. (Open M-F 8am-noon and 1-4:30pm, Sa 7:30am-noon.) Though Guápiles has many **Internet cafes,** the most-convenient ones are **Cafe Internet,** across the road from the south end of the bus station, and **Cafe Internet del Caribe,** 100m north of the bus station on the second floor of the strip mall on the left (☎2711 0631; ¢500 per hr; open M-Sa 9am-9:30pm, Su 9am-8pm).

ACCOMMODATIONS

Though not very touristed, Guápiles does have several basic, comfortable budget options. Make sure to see the room and verify the price before lodging, and be aware that guests in hotels near the church will be serenaded by the ringing of the bells each morning at 6am.

Cabinas Irdama (☎2710 7034). While its location 70m north of the Mas X Menos is on the outskirts of town, the low prices and amenities more than make up for it. Be sure to ask for a room with hot water—not all rooms have it, but the price is the same as for cold-water baths. All rooms have cable TV, fans, and private baths. Singles ¢5900; doubles ¢7000-9400, triples ¢14,000; quads ¢16,300. MC/V. ❶

Cabinas San Carlos, on the main road, 30m west of the intersection with the road from bus station. Though its location down a dark hallway in a concrete atrium makes it less than ideal for claustrophobes, Cabinas San Carlos offers reasonably priced rooms with private hot-water baths, cable TV, and efficient fans. Free parking. Singles ¢8000. ❷

Cabinas Orquideas (☎2710 7271), on a side road just east of Palí supermarket. Though a bit of a trek from the bus station, Cabinas Orquideas offers good prices for basic, clean rooms with TV, fans, and private cold-water baths. It's a good deal for couples. Singles and doubles ¢6000; *cabinas* and triples ¢9000. Cash only. ❶

Cabinas Car (☎2710 6124), 20m west of the church on the main road. This family-run hostel next to a hamburger and ice cream shop offers some of the nicer rooms in town, though the prices are a bit higher as well. The comfortable rooms have private hot-water baths, fans, TVs, and large closets. Singles US$22; doubles US$35; triples US$45; taxes included. Prices can be negotiated for long-term stays. ❷

FOOD

Like most Costa Rican cities, Guápiles is filled with small, family-run *sodas* and bars that serve standard burgers, *casados*, and *gallo pinto*, although there are a few sit-down restaurants. **Más X Menos** supermarket (open M-F 9am-9pm, Sa-Su 9am-7pm) is located 200m west of the main intersection, and a **Palí** supermarket is 50m north of the northeast corner of the *parque central*. (Open M-Th 8:30am-7pm, F-Sa 8am-8pm, Su 8:30am-6pm.)

Caffe Ristorante Nona (☎2710 0041), 100m west of Palí. Offering a mix of Costa Rican and Italian cuisine, this small street-side cafe caters to a crowd of families and businessmen drinking its wide selection of coffee concoctions (¢375-1250). Entrees ¢900-3500. Open M-Sa 8am-8pm. MC/V. ❶

Super Tacos Guápiles (☎2710 5353), 30m west of the church across the street from Hotel el Tunel. While its tacos are more accurately described as *taquitos*, Super Tacos's strengths are in its sides: massive portions of french fries and toppings that grow in size and mess-potential all the way up to the Taco Elefante—a yummy, indistinguishable mass of meat, french fries, cheese, sour cream, and various veggies (¢2625). Open M-F 2-10pm, Sa 11am-10pm, Su 4pm-10pm. ❷

Restaurante El Unico (☎2710 6250 or 2710 7004), 200m north of the bus station at the intersection with the main road. Patrons at this Costa-Rica-fied Chinese restaurant can enjoy an inexpensive meal while catching up on *tico* soap operas on the restaurant's big-screen TV. The menu is one of the most varied in town, with rice dishes (¢2000-2400), wontons (¢2200), chop suey (¢2000-2400), and large entrees served with french fries (¢2300-3700). Open M-F 10am-11pm, Sa-Su 10am-midnight. ❷

▐ DAYTRIP FROM GUÁPILES

RAINFOREST AERIAL TRAM

From Guápiles, go to the San José ticket window at the bus terminal and ask for a ticket to the teleférico; be sure to ask the bus driver to drop you off there, even if the destination is written on the ticket. (25min., every 30min. 5am-9pm, ¢800.) Though the tram is only 20km from Guápiles, most people visit from San José. A free shuttle takes visitors the 1.5km from the entrance of the park to the tram platform. Tours from San José can be arranged through the tram office on Av. 7, C. 7. (☎ 2257 5961; www.rfat.com. US$85, students US$57; includes round-trip transportation from your hotel, guided trips on the tram line, a 45min. nature trail hike, and breakfast or lunch.) Whether coming from Guápiles or San José, you can dispense with the meal and transportation and make a reservation for the guided tour and nature trail hike (US$55, students US$27.50); keep in mind that catching a bus back to Guápiles or San José could take an hour or so, as most buses are express and do not stop between destinations. The zipline is another exhilarating way to experience the rainforest, and one of the safest in Costa Rica with double cables (US$65 per person). Thick-walleted travelers can spend the night at one of the park's cabinas, which feature hot-water baths and balconies and include 3 meals a day and unlimited rides on the teleférico (US$109 per person per night). If you're hiking, pants, sturdy footwear, and bug repellent are recommended. Reservations recommended, especially for high season visits. Tram trips 7am-3pm.

At the edge of the Braulio Carillo National Park, the Rainforest Aerial Tram was designed by naturalist Don Perry and completed in 1994. After spending years exploring the rainforest canopy on ropes suspended high atop the trees, Perry designed a simple pulley system with 22 ski-lift-like cars suspended along an almost 2km aerial track. The construction of the Tram involved minimal damage to the surrounding rainforest, thanks to the Nicaraguan Sandinistas, who loaned their fighter helicopters to deliver large steel poles to the site.

The tram ride is 45min. in each direction, taking visitors from the heavy brush on the floor of the rainforest to the top of the canopy over 30m above. Once the journey begins, the only reminders of human interference are the dark green cable poles and the small wood and concrete walkways that occasionally criss-cross through the forest. The mating calls of thousands of cicadas, which combine to make a sort of synchronized hypnotic hum, are a constant soundtrack to the journey. For the first half of the adventure, guests lie low, brushing up against the lush vegetation of the rainforest floor while learning about the different ecosystems of the three levels of rainforest. Particularly prominent in this section are the philodendron "elephant ears" and the *labios ardientes*, or "hot lips"—named for its curled red protective sheaths as well as the supposedly aphrodisiacal fruits inside. After getting up close and personal with the plants below, visitors are whisked upward into the top of the canopy, where they can enjoy a birds-eye view of the vegetation below as well as fleeting glimpses of the many streams and rivers that pass through the forest.

The lack of human influence here means that the wildlife in the area is very diverse. However, visitors should remember that vegetation is dense and most animals are nocturnal, so many will be identifiable only by their unique calls. The best way to see wildlife is to go early in the morning, when many of the animals rummage around for food. The 475-hectare reserve area around the tram also has a few nature trails open to visitors; check with the rangers before heading out to make sure trails are open to self-guided tours.

SIQUIRRES

Though dusty, dry, and not very touristed, Siquirres keeps visitors coming as a transportation hub for Puerto Limón, Guápiles, and Parismina. Its sprawling suburbs are filled with markets and banana fields, a testament to the importance of the fruit to the local economy. Formerly, Siquirres was primarily a banana-train city; today, it is filled with more road traffic than railways, but the bananas and the tourists keep coming through.

⌐ TRANSPORTATION

Siquirres has two bus terminals. The first is much more tourist-oriented. From **Gran Terminal Siquirres** (☎2768 8732), at the southeast corner of the soccer field, **buses** leave for Caño Blanco (2hr.; M-F 4am, 1pm; Sa-Su 7:30am, 3:15pm; ¢1000); Guápiles (1hr., 36 per day 4:50am-7:50pm, ¢580) via Guácimo (35min., ¢500); Limón (3hr., 32 per day 5am-8:10pm, ¢800); San José (4hr., 18 per day 5am-7pm, ¢1245). From the bus stop north of the soccer field (☎2768 8172), local buses head out for La Florida (30min., 5 per day, ¢370) and Alegria (20min., 12 per day 5:30am-7:15pm, ¢265). **Taxis** (☎2768 4141 or 2768 9333) line up along the roads east of the northeast corner of the soccer field and circle around the bus terminal every 10min. or so.

◼◼ ☒ ORIENTATION AND PRACTICAL INFORMATION

The soccer field is in the center of town, and the circular church is on its west side. The municipal offices are on the south side of the soccer field, and the main bus station is at the southeast corner. Keep in mind that the area around the *mercado central*, 300m north and 200m east of the northeast corner of the soccer field, is poorly lit at night and should be avoided after dark.

Banks: Banco de Costa Rica (☎2768 8353), 100m north and 50m west of the northeast corner of the soccer field. Open M-F 8am-4pm. AmEx/MC/V. Next door is **Banco Nacional. 24hr. ATM.** (☎2768 5767. Open M-F 8:45am-3pm, Sa 8:30am-noon.)

Police: The **police station** is 100m south of the southeast corner of the soccer field. (☎2768 8797, emergencies 911).

Medical services: You can visit **Farmacia Génesis,** just north of the main bus terminal (☎2768 5942; open daily 7am-7pm; AmEx/D/MC/V), or **Farmacia El Ahorro,** 50m north of the northeast corner of the soccer field. (☎2768 6273; open M-Sa 8am-9pm, Su 8am-4pm; MC/V).

Telephones: You can find telephones at the **Instituto Costarricense de Electricidad (ICE)** office, on the northwest corner of the soccer field. (☎2428 8123. Open M-F 7:30am-5pm, Sa 8am-noon.)

Internet Access: Café Internet Caribe, 50m north of the northeast corner of the park, across from Farmacia El Ahorro. ¢300 per hr. Open M-Sa 8am-9pm, Su 8am-6pm.

Post Office: The **post office** is in front of the police station, 100m south of the southeast corner of the soccer field. Open M-F 8am-noon and 1-5:30pm. **Postal Code:** 7200.

⌐ ◖ ACCOMMODATIONS AND FOOD

Siquirres is a relatively small town, and because of its proximity to the more-touristed destinations of Guápiles and Limón, most visitors do not stay for the night. The closest accommodation option to the town center is **Centro Turistico Pacuare ❷,** located about 1km southeast of town. From the main bus station, walk south 500m, turn left at the stop sign, and walk another 500m; the hotel will be on your left. A taxi costs ¢500. Pacuare's modern facilities include a restaurant/bar with big-screen TV, karaoke at night, pool tables, swimming pool, conference hall, and simple but comfortable rooms with fans, cable TV, and private hot-water baths, and it is popular among *tico* businessmen and their families. (☎2768 6482. Singles ¢10,000, with A/C ¢13,000; doubles ¢13,000/16,000.)

The **Palí** supermarket is 100m north and 100m west of the northwest corner of the soccer field. (☎2768 7532. Open M-Sa 8am-7pm, Su 8am-6pm. MC/V.) For a relaxing, tasty meal close to the bus station, head to **Soda Lorena ❶,** where the friendly family owners serve up filling portions of *comida típica* in a welcoming dining area with fake flower centerpieces and simple white tablecloths. (☎2768 6334. *Casado* and drink ¢2000. Open daily 6am-5pm.) Those who don't mind a little noise to go along with their food will find every hunger satisfied at **Panaderia, Reposteria, y Cafeteria La Castellana ❶,** which, as the name suggests, houses a baker, confectioner's shop, and cafe in one large pink building at the northeast end of the park. (☎2768 8703. Hamburgers ¢750. *Casados* ¢1500. Pastries ¢300-800. Salads ¢1000-2000. Open daily 4:30am-7:30pm.)

◄ DAYTRIP FROM SIQUIRRES

ESCUELA DE AGRICULTURA DE LA REGIÓN TROPICAL HÚMEDA (EARTH). Created in 1990, Escuela de Agricultura de la Región Tropical Húmeda (EARTH) is a private, international, non-profit university that educates students from the Americas, Spain, and Southern Africa in agriculture, environmental conservation, and sustainable management of resources in tropical regions. The university's on-campus educational farm functions as a lab for hands-on projects, while the commercial farm, which includes forestry, agricultural, and cattle activities, generates profits to support the academic programs. Since its inception, the school has been at the forefront of research and development in environmentally friendly and sustainable agriculture, training scientists and farmers around the world how to best manage resources of tropical areas. The university offers tours of its classrooms, labs, and land, but arrangements should be made in advance. (☎2713 0000; www.earth.ac.cr. 5- to 10-person groups preferred. Call in advance to arrange a tour. From Guácimo, take any bus to Siquirres or Pocora (15min., 20 per day 6:30am-6:30pm, ¢180) or from Siquirres, take any bus to Guápiles (30min., 23 per day 4:50am-7:20pm, ¢580) and have the driver let you off at the front entrance to EARTH.)

PUERTO LIMÓN

A major port city and the end of the Atlantic railway line, Puerto Limón is Costa Rica's gateway to the Caribbean. Its large population of laborers from the West Indies and China, combined with a growing industrial economy and a laid-back Rasta vibe, maintains a balanced, calm atmosphere despite the constant action. Though the streets are more prone to crime after dark, the daytime is peaceful and beautiful, with vendors hawking everything from Bob Marley bags to hunks of meat in the *mercado municipal* and children frolicking feet from the Carribean at waterfront parks. Most visitors to Limón stay just long enough to catch a boat or bus on to Tortuguero, Cahuito, or Puerto Viejo, but those that take time to explore the city will come to appreciate its vibrant, diverse community. Larger, busier, and more complex than most Caribbean towns, it is still reasonably easy to navigate. The constant stream of shoppers, vendors, and loitering pedestrians means you will never have to look far for a helping hand.

📰 TRANSPORTATION

NatureAir (☎2232 7883) and Sansa (☎2666 0306) run **flights** to and from San José and other destinations. The airstrip, reachable by **taxi**, is 4km south of town. Auto Transport Caribeños and Prosersa **buses** (in San José ☎2222 0610, in Limón ☎2758 0385 or 2758 2575) leave from the spic-and-span station Gran Terminal del Caribe, Av. 2, C. 7/8, three blocks west of the *mercado municipal*, and go to: Guápiles (2hr., approx. every 45min. 6am-6pm, ¢1195); Moín (20min., every hr. 5:30am-7pm, ¢230); San José (3hr., every 30min. 5am-7pm and Su 8pm, ¢2000); Siquirres (1hr., every hr. 5am-7pm, ¢800). Buses depart from the spread out, marked stands across from the MEPE station (☎2758 1572 or 2758 3522), one block north of the northeast side of the market. Buy tickets at the cashier for buses to: Manzanillo (2hr.; 6, 10:30am, 3, 6pm; ¢1800); Puerto Viejo de Talamanca (1½hr., every hr. 5am-6pm, ¢1330) via Cahuita (45min., ¢890); the Panamanian border at Sixaola (3hr., every hr. 5am-6pm, ¢2345). All the Sixaola buses pass through Bribrí (1½hr., ¢1625). Taxis line the north side of the Gran Terminal; a taxi to Moín should cost about US$4, but many taxi drivers will try to charge as much as US$8. Be prepared to bargain hard for a good deal, especially if you don't speak Spanish.

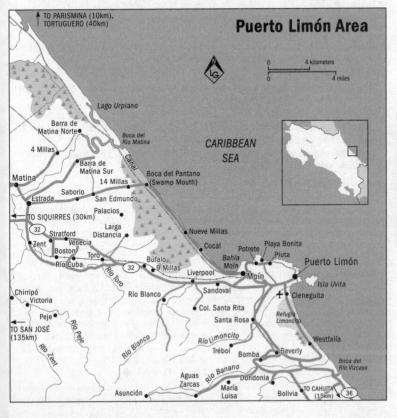

Puerto Limón Area

ORIENTATION AND PRACTICAL INFORMATION

Like most major Costa Rican cities, Puerto Limón is laid out in a grid of north-south *calles* and east-west *avenidas*, but finding street signs is nearly impossible. Orient yourself by the **mercado municipal**, Av. 2/3, C. 3/4. Most hotels and restaurants are within a few blocks of the *mercado*, which serves as the center for Limón's business and social activities. A walled-in area runs along the north side of town, while the east is bound by the shores of the Caribbean.

Tours: Caribbean Costa Ricans (☎2798 2203; www.caribbeancostaricans.com) is the only tour agency in town, but its services focus on international trips and cruises. Boat captains in nearby Moín offer tours to Parismina and Tortuguero; arrive at the docks before 5pm to bargain for transport or talk to the captains.

Banks: Banco Nacional (☎2758 0094), at the southeast corner of the market. Exchanges US$ and traveler's checks (2% commission) and offers V cash advances. Open M-F 8:30am-3:45pm, Sa 9am-1pm. **Banco San José** (☎2798 0155 or 2798 0167), 50m east of the northeast corner of the market. **ATM** available. Open M-F 8am-6pm, Sa 9am-1pm. MC/V. Both accept Cirrus. Maestro/Plus card users can use the **24hr. ATM** at the **Scotia Bank,** 100m east of the northeast corner of the market.

Emergency: ☎911.

Police: (☎2758 0365), at the southwest corner of the market.

Red Cross: (☎2758 0125 or 911), 1 block south of the southeast corner of the market. English spoken. Open 24hr.

Pharmacy: Farmacia de Limón (☎2758 5450), 50m west of the southwest corner of the market. Open M-Sa 7am-9pm, Su 8am-5pm. MC/V.

Hospital: Hospital Tony Facio (☎2758 2222), 300m north of Av. 7 on the boardwalk.

Telephones: Public phones are located all around the city, including on the north and south sides of the *mercado municipal.*

Internet Access: Instituto de Computación (☎2798 0128), on the 2nd fl. of the Gran Terminal. ₡500 per hr. Open daily 8am-9pm. There are also numerous Internet cafes in the blocks surrounding the *mercado municipal.*

Post Office: Across from the southwest corner of the market. Open M-F 8am-5:30pm, Sa 7:30am-noon. **Postal Code:** 7300.

ACCOMMODATIONS

Budget accommodation is par for the course in Puerto Limón, but beware of any ultra-cheap options; some of the city's hotels are quite run-down and others have noticeable traffic of prostitutes or drug sales. Make sure your hotel of choice has an electric lock, and ask to see rooms before agreeing to pay. All of the hotels listed below are tourist-friendly.

Hotel Miami (☎2758 0490 or 2758 4888), ½ block west of the southwest corner of the market. Though within sight of the *mercado,* Hotel Miami retains a calm, quiet atmosphere, offering a clean and surprisingly upscale option without forking over too many *colónes.* Its chair-lined balcony is one of the best people-watching spots in town, and the rooms are spacious, comfortable, and secure. All rooms include phone and TV, while more expensive rooms come with hot water and A/C. The hotel has free Internet access, Wi-Fi, and water for guests. Singles, doubles, and triples with cold-water baths and fans ₡10,000/13,500/18,000, with hot-water baths and A/C ₡13,500/18,000/20,000; quads with hot-water bath and A/C ₡21,500. AmEx/MC/V. ❷

Hotel Internacional (☎2758 0434), 2 blocks north and ½ block east of the northeast corner of the *mercado.* Like its sister hotel across the street, Hotel Internacio-

To Hospital Tony Facio (300m), Playa Bonita (4km), Moín (7km)

Av. 7

Av. 6

Av. 5

Av. 4

Av. 3

Av. 2

Av. 1

C. 7

C. 6

C. 5

C. 4

C. 3

C. 2

C. 1

Reef

Reef

Reef

Reef

Reef

Malecón

Puerto Limón Center

🛏 ACCOMMODATIONS

Hotel Continental, **1**
Hotel Miami, **8**
Hotel Internacional, **3**

🍊 FOOD

Soda Black Star Line, **2**
Restaurante Internacional, **4**
Soda La Estrella, **6**

🍸 NIGHTLIFE

Discoteca Aquarius, **7**
Ninja's Bar, **5**

To Cahuita, Puerto Viejo, Sixaola, Manzanillo

Iglesia Metodista

Más X Menos

Scotia Bank

Banco de San José

Cathedral

Caribbean Costa Ricans Tours

Mercado Municipal

TAXI

Municipalidad de Limón

Parque Vargas

Mirador

Banco Nacional

Gran Terminal del Caribe

Farmacia de Limón

Instituto de Computación

CARIBBEAN SEA

0   200 meters
0   200 yards

nal has basic, simple rooms with private cold-water baths and ceiling fans. The rooms here are a bit cheerier than those next door, with brightly patterned bedspreads and a sunny hallway leading out to a small balcony. Singles, doubles, and triples with fans ₡3700/5900/9200, with A/C ₡4900/7700/11,000; quads with fans ₡11,000. ●

Hotel Continental (☎2798 0532), directly across the street from the Hotel Internacional. Though the austere white walls and lack of decor are a bit forbidding, the rooms at this secure hotel are clean, organized, and quiet, with private cold-water baths and mounted ceiling fans. Singles and doubles with fans ₡3700/5900, with A/C ₡4900/7700. ●

🍴 FOOD

Limón's cosmopolitan atmosphere has contributed to its diverse selection of dining options. Visitors can enjoy some of Costa Rica's best Chinese food at the many Chinese-owned establishments near the center, hunker down with tasty Caribbean or traditional *tico soda* fare, and even watch their health at one of the many macrobiotic and healthfood eateries in town. Most of Limón's restaurants are within three or four blocks of the *mercado municipal* in the center of town, 300m west of the beach. (Open M-Sa dawn-dusk.) A supermarket, **Más X Menos,** is across from the northeast corner of the market. (☎2798 1792. Open M-Sa 8am-8pm, Su 9am-5pm. AmEx/D/MC/V.)

Soda Black Star Line, corner of C. 5 and Av. 5 (☎2798 1948). Popular with families, students, and businessmen alike, this cheery, quiet eatery in a seafoam-green building serves traditional Caribbean fare in its high-ceilinged dining area. Enjoy *casados* or rice and beans (¢2750-3000 including drink), *bistec de bochinche* (spicy beef with pasta and salad; ¢2300), and *sopa de mondongo* (stew with tripe, chicken, potatoes, and vegetables; ¢1000-1300). Open M-Sa 7am-10pm, Su 11am-5pm. AmEx/D/MC/V. ❷

Soda La Estrella (☎2798 4658), 100m west of the northwest corner of the *mercado*. One of the cheapest eateries in town, this *soda* provides extensive options for *tico* and Chinese food, all served up quick in a white-tiled dining area with youngsters watching cartoons. *Casados* ¢1200-1800; chop suey, chow mein, and fried rice dishes ¢1100-3000. Open daily 8am-8pm. ❶

Restaurante Internacional (☎2758 0423), next door to Hotel Internacional 2 blocks north of the northeast corner of the *mercado municipal*. One of the many Chinese options in town, this simple restaurant is popular with a takeout crowd, serving up large portions of chow mein (¢2600-3400), chop suey (¢1500-3100), and meat entrees (¢2700-3100) to a largely local clientele. Open daily 11am-11:30pm. Cash only. ❷

NIGHTLIFE

Nightlife in Limón is lively and filled with partying *limonenses*, but being out alone after dark is not advisable; the safer bet is to go out in a group. During *carnaval* in mid-October, nightlife gets really wild, as the city fills with tourists from around the world looking to enjoy parades, music, and parties at all hours of the day. **Ninja's Bar,** on the north side of the cathedral, overwhelms guests with a greenhouse entrance, three bars, seven TVs, house beats, and what feels like more lights than New York's Times Square at New Year's. Roofed-in stalls near the entrance cater to patrons seeking privacy. (☎2758 2833. Beer with complimentary *bocadillo* ¢800. Open M-Sa 2pm-late.) **Discoteca Aquarius,** a dance club on the top floor of the Hotel Acón, across the street from Más X Menos, pounds reggae and salsa rhythms into the night. (☎2758 1010. Cover ¢1000. Sa 8pm-midnight women free and 2-for-1 drinks. Open Th-Sa 10pm-4am.)

SIGHTS

Vendors at the *mercado municipal* hawk jewelry, clothing, electronics, and typical Caribbean fare: coconuts, bananas, fish, and lobster. The market is open from dawn to dusk, though its numerous *sodas* often stay open later. While the *mercado municipal* seems calmer and more organized than most central *mercados*, it's still pickpocket territory. The most spectacular sight in Limón is the new **Catholic cathedral** being built on the site of the old Vicariato Apostólico. Construction began in November 2001, but progress has been slow due to issues with funding. Even unfinished, the cathedral's towering spire and modern, angular design are still impressive. **Parque Vargas,** in the southeast corner of town, is a picturesque refuge from the town's bustling center. Waves pound against the seawall while children enjoy the nearby playground equipment. To get to the *parque*, head two blocks east from the southeast corner of the *mercado*, toward the dense, towering coconut palms; you can see the seawall from the market's edge. Be sure to check out the impressive seaside mural by artist Guadalupe Alvarea. Though the paint is chipping, the work remains a powerful depiction of Limón's rich and tangled history. On a clear day, the **Isla de Uvita,** 1km away, is visible from a *mirador* in the northeast edge of the park.

A young crowd looking for waves and rays usually heads over to **Playa Bonita,** 4km northwest of Limón. On one side, the water is calm and perfect for wading; on the other, broad, powerful waves give surfers the lift they need. Though it is close to the town center, the road to Playa Bonita has little room for pedestrians and drivers tend to speed precariously along, so it is a better idea to take the Moín bus from the Gran Terminal del Caribe (every 30min. 5:30am-6:30pm, ¢230). Buy a ticket at the window and get off at one of the first stops (ask the driver and other passengers if you're unsure). You can also take a taxi (¢1500). While you're there, enjoy a meal or a *trago* on the outdoor patio of **Reina's Restaurant ❷**, overlooking the crashing waves and dense forest beyond. (*Casados* ¢2200-2800. Seafood dishes ¢4000-6000. Open daily 8am-9:30pm.)

PARISMINA

Drier, dustier, and even more secluded than its northern neighbor, Tortuguero, the tiny island hamlet of Parismina (pop. 400) attracts hundreds of leatherback, green, and hawksbill turtles every year, along with surprisingly small numbers of tourists. Where Tortuguero has developed an ecotourism industry based on short-term stays and guided tours, Parismina has created several volunteer programs that allow visitors to become "park rangers," doing 4hr. night watchman shifts while living with local families in homestays. Visitors looking to enjoy the island's calm ambience for only a few days will also find Parismina a welcoming stop; locals drink with tourists at the Mono Carablanca Lodge, and everyone who can stand the heat joins in the impromptu soccer games that pop up continually on every flat surface available.

TRANSPORTATION

Buses: From the Gran Terminal Siquirres, where the bus drops off, walk to the old bus station on the north side of the soccer field and catch a bus to Caño Blanco, from where a boat heads to Parismina (2hr.; M-F 4am and 1pm, Sa-Su 6am and 2pm; ¢300).

Boats: Parismina has no roads and is only accessible by boat. From Caño Blanco, a public boat meets the bus and shuttles passengers to Parismina (8min., ¢1000). If you arrive at Caño Blanco from Siquirres by taxi (¢17,400, US$30) or private car, you can hire a private boat from the Caño Blanco dock to Parismina (¢14,500, US$25) or take one of the public boats leaving that day (8min., ¢1000). Be sure to arrive at Caño Blanco at least 30min. before 6pm as boats leave the dock early and there are no overnight facilities. Coming from farther south, hop on a boat from Moín to Tortuguero and tell the captain you only need to go to Parismina. Jumping on an already hired boat should run about ¢14,500 (US$25) to Moín and ¢11,600 (US$20) to Tortuguero. The tourist info center can arrange a pick-up for 5pm; notify them by 3pm that day. Public boats usually pass by each day in each direction between 10:30am and noon. Private boats organized on Parismina will cost upwards of US$100 for the trip; as usual, the best way to go is to buddy up or join another traveling group. To return to Siquirres, take the boat from Parismina to Caño Blanco (open M-F 5:30am and 2:30pm, Sa-Su 8:30am and 4:30pm; ¢1000) and catch the bus back to Siquirres (open M-F 6am and 3pm, Sa-Su 10am and 5pm).

Tour agencies: From Parismina, the easiest way to continue onto Tortuguero or south to Moín is to contact one of the Tortuguero tour agencies, most of which arrange round-trip transportation from Moín to Tortuguero. The agencies will notify the boat captains heading in each direction that they should stop for passengers at Parismina.

ORIENTATION AND PRACTICAL INFORMATION

Though the island of Parismina is quite long, the town itself is small and easy to navigate. There are two main docks in town; both are 100m west of the main path. Just south of town, the first docks service boats to Caño Blanco, while the second dock, about 250m north, services private boats including those going to Moín and Tortuguero. The main path stretches from the Caño Blanco docks in the south and ends at Sayleen del Caribe, where a right turn leads east toward the waterfront and the soccer field. There is a *pulpería*, 100m east and 50m south of Sayleen del Caribe (open daily 7am-5pm). There are **no banks or ATMs in town,** and the only place that accepts credit cards is **Mono Carablanca Lodge and Restaurant** (MC/V), so plan accordingly.

Tourist Office: The **Parismina Information Center,** located 200m north of the Caño Blanco docks, has a poster board with up-to-date info about traveling to and from the island as well as volunteer opportunities. The center also has a English and Spanish **book exchange** (open M-Sa 2-5pm).

Internet: The information center houses the only computer with internet in town (¢1500 per hr.; be prepared for lines).

Medical Services: There is no clinic in town, but a **doctor** visits every few days; details of the visits are posted in the Information Center.

Telephones: in front of both docks.

ACCOMMODATIONS

Though most visitors to Parismina are students on school trips or long-term volunteers participating in homestay programs, the town has several good value budget options for short-term, independent travelers.

Carefree Ranch Lodge (☎2710 3149), east of the Information Center. This small B&B-style lodge feels like home, with peach-colored sideboards and forest-green doors. Offers some of the most comfortable accommodations in town, with high ceilings, private hot-water baths, and wide balconies. A charming on-site restaurant serves family-style meals. Rooms ¢5800 (US$10), with 3 meals ¢15,660 (US$27). ❶

Cabinas La Iguana Verde (☎2798 0828), 100m east of Salon Naomi. The yard of this small hotel looks like a jungle: the resident parrot erratically spouts greetings to passersby, and massive beetles hang continually from tree branches near the fence. The rooms, however, are animal-free, with private hot-water baths and large beds. Rooms ¢5500, with A/C ¢10,000. ❶

Mono Carablanco Lodge (☎2798 1031), 200m east of Sayleen El Caribe, just past the soccer field. The stark blue block of rooms is easily outshined by the *cabana*-style bar and restaurant, small blue pool, and palm-tree-filled lawn. All rooms have fans and private cold-water baths. ¢5000 per person, with A/C ¢7000. ❶

FOOD AND NIGHTLIFE

Because most visitors to Parismina have meals with their home-stay families, the options for food and nightlife are pretty basic. Expect a lot of *comida típica* and not much else.

Restaurante Mono Carablanca (☎2798 1031), in the Mono Carablanca Lodge. Serves upscale versions of staples. Popular for locals and tourists looking for a beer between soccer games (¢500-1800). Breakfasts ¢3000. *Casados* and rice dishes ¢3000. Open daily 8am-8:30pm. MC/V. ❶

Rancho La Palma (☎2798 0259), in front of the docks where boats depart for Tortuguero. An older crowd enjoys Parismina's cheapest, most basic eats in this open-air dining area. *Casados* ¢2500. Sandwiches ¢1200. Open daily 5am-7pm. ❶

Carefree Ranch Restaurant (☎2710 3149), in the Carefree Ranch. Home-cooked, family-style meals. Drop by during breakfast hours for scrambled eggs, fruit, fresh bread, cheese, coffee, and orange juice (¢2500). Lunch and dinner ¢3000. ❶

Salon Naomi, in the center of town. The Salon is the only disco in Parismina, though the size of the local population means that the cavernous building only starts to fill on weekends or when a particularly large tourist group is in town. Beer ¢700. Mixed drinks ¢1000-2000. Dancing on Sa night. Open daily 11am-10pm. ❶

Soda Xine, in the center of town near Salon Naomi. *Casados* ¢2400-3600. Hamburgers ¢1500. *Gallos* ¢1000. Rice and beans ¢2800. Open daily 8am-7pm. ❶

⚠ OUTDOOR ACTIVITIES

There are no official tourist agencies with offices in Parismina, but you can get information and phone numbers for tour guides at the Information Center. Parismina's biggest tourist attraction is the *deshove* (turtle nesting), whose high season runs between March and September, though turtles nest sporadically throughout the year. Green turtles primarily nest between June and October, leatherbacks from February to June, and hawksbills at various times. Visitors can explore the wildlife-filled canals around Parismina village and go whitewater rafting, hiking, fishing, and horseback riding.

Rainforest World (☎2556 0014 or 2556 2678; www.rforestw.com). Runs 2- and 3-day all-inclusive rafting and turtle-watching trips down the Reventazon to Parismina, where guests stay in Rainforest World guide Rick Knowles's hotel Iguana Verde. 2-day, 2-night packages start at ¢150,800 (US$260). Whitewater rafting on the Pacuare or Reventazon ¢52,500-72,500 (US$90-125) per day.

La Asociación de Boteros de Parismina. A small, private group of boat captains that offers tours of the river canals from Caño Blanco. Several captains are bilingual and excellent at spotting the wide variety of wildlife lurking on the river banks. Prices range from ¢2900 (US$5) for the short ride to Parismina to ¢87,000 (US$150) for a round-trip ride to Tortuguero. Look for the boat captains at the Caño Blanco docks; be sure to get there by 5:30pm at the latest.

Mola Fish (☎2798 1034 or 8308 5518; www.molafish.com). Daniel, the owner, has offered sportfishing trips for the past four years in Parismina. 1-day trip US$580 (¢336,400) for 1 person, US$780 (¢457,000) for 2-people. All equipment is provided. English spoken.

Paradise Island (☎2298 0989; www.junglejessietours.com), near Mono Carablanca. Jorge Alberto has 30 years of experience offering sportfishing (¢145,000/US$250) and wildlife tours at sea (¢11,600/US$20; min. 6 people). English spoken.

GIVING BACK

TURTLE-WATCH

While Tortuguero has become famous for its unique brand of ecotourism that has helped save the local sea turtle population from extinction, the citizens of Parismina have developed an even more hands-on approach to teaching tourists about their precious creatures' livelihood.

Instead of going on nightly *deshove* tours, visitors to Parismina can actually become honorary park rangers, which means participating in the nightly guards that protect the endangered turtles from poachers and predators.

For about US$20 a night, volunteers are put up in homestays with local families in town and are taught to perform the 4hr. guard periods that happen each night from March to September. The rangers walk along 5.6km sections of the beach, looking for signs of turtles in shifts 8pm-midnight or midnight-4am. While volunteers can stay as short as 3 days, most stick around for weeks, long enough to learn about the turtles and finish their "apprenticeship," after which they are deemed capable of doing the patrols on their own, without supervision.

For more information on joining the nightly patrol or about Parismina's sea turtles, contact La Asociación Salvemos Las Tortugas de Parismina (☎2710 7703; www.parisminaturtles.org, parisminaturtles@gmail.com).

TORTUGUERO VILLAGE

Famed for the vast number of turtles that nest on its beaches every year, the small village of Tortuguero has managed to parlay its ecological wealth into a thriving tourism industry that has both improved the local economy and reduced the impact of poaching. Completely separated from the mainland by a maze of canals and situated on the shores of the Caribbean, Tortuguero cannot be conveniently accessed from San José or any of Costa Rica's major transport hubs, but the effort required to get here is entirely worth it. Though the village is charming and the sunbathing quite pleasant, the real reason for visiting Tortuguero is a night-long event: the *deshove* (turtle nesting). From June to September, visitors to Tortuguero can witness the impressive efforts of nesting leatherback, green, and hawksbill turtles on the shores of Tortuguero village and the adjacent Tortuguero National Park. For those who don't get their fill of animal watching at the *deshove*, Tortuguero has many opportunities for boat, canoe, and kayak trips in its surrounding canals, where visitors can get practically face-to-face with caimans, monkeys, turtles, and a fantastically diverse array of birds.

Though thousands of tourists follow the turtles to Tortuguero's beaches each year, the onslaught of *cabinas* and tourist information centers has not completely destroyed its small-town appeal. Here, ecotourism has truly taken hold, and many of Tortuguero's residents are employed in the tourism industry. The influx of tourist money that comes from the nightly *deshove* has stabilized the local community and helped to decrease the prevalence of turtle poaching in the area.

▌ TRANSPORTATION

Flying from San José (p. 83) to the airstrip, a few kilometers north of Tortuguero, is the most convenient way to get to the village, but it is also the most expensive. **Sansa** offers flights from San José and from Juan Santa María International Airport in Alajuela. (☎2221 9414; www.flysansa.com. Approx. US$100.) **NatureAir** departs from Tobías Bolaños Airport in Pavas. (☎2220 3054, reservations from US +1-888-535-8832. Approx. US$100/¢58,000.) Except for flying, all routes into Tortuguero require a boat trip, as the island is separated from the mainland by a network of canals. There are two main starting points for transport into Tortuguero: **Cariari**, in northeastern Costa Rica, and **Moín**, next to Limón on the Caribbean coast.

From Cariari: Buses leave each morning for Cariari from the **Terminal de los Caribeños** in San José (☎2221 2596; 2hr.; 9 per day). Once in Cariari, there are 2 options for transport to Tortuguero. The cheapest route from Cariari is by bus to Pavona (1hr.; 6, 11:30am, 3pm; ¢1100). Take this bus to the end of the line at the river's edge, where **lanchas** (small boats) will speed you through a swampy river to Tortuguero's main docks (1hr.; departs upon bus arrival; ¢1600, buy tickets on board). If you are traveling by **car**, park your car in Pavona and then take the boat to Tortuguero.

From Moín: The trip to Tortuguero from Moín is completed entirely in a boat and is known for providing opportunities for crocodile, bird, and monkey sightings. *Lanchas* depart early in the morning for Tortuguero from Moín's small dock behind **Restaurante Papá Manuel** (10am and 3pm, but try to arrive at least 1hr. early to bargain prices and get a captain). The *lancha* trip is 3-5hr. through canals teeming with wildlife (¢20,300/US$35). It's best to arrange in advance, either at the docks or through a hotel or tour company in Tortuguero. If you're traveling alone, a tour guide may request up to ¢87,000 (US$150) for the trip; arrive early to buddy up with other travelers (see **Tour Smart,** p. 370).

From Tortuguero: Private boats depart from Tortuguero at almost any hour desired, though boats are only allowed to travel in the area's waterways from 6am to 6pm. Most tour companies in Tortuguero organize return trips to Moín, Parismina, and Cariari via

Pavona. To schedule a trip, talk to any of the tour companies listed; prices should run about ¢14,500 (US$25) per person to **Moín,** ¢11,600 (US$20) per person to **Parismina,** and ¢5800 (US$10) to **Pavona** and on to **Cariari.** Boats depart regularly for Pavona from the main docks at 6am, 11:30am, and 3pm, where a bus waits to travel the rest of the way to Cariari. Make sure to book in advance to ensure an available boat, and be aware that prices may become much steeper if traveling alone. By booking in advance, you can join a group and pay a significantly lower price.

Tour Companies: Most tour companies in Tortuguero can arrange transportation from San José or cities along the Caribbean coast to Tortuguero. However, there are several companies throughout Costa Rica that offer pre-arranged trips to the park. **Fran and Modesto Watson's tours** (☎2226 0986; www.tortuguerocanals.com) on their riverboat, *Francesca,* are highly recommended. Their most popular trip to Tortuguero includes round-trip transportation from San José to Moín in a van and from Moín to Tortuguero in a boat, in addition to 2-day, 1-night lodging at the Laguna Lodge, 5 meals, a canal boat tour, a turtle tour, a visit to Caribbean Conservation Center, and park entrance fees (¢95,700-113,100/US$165-195) per person. **Turtle Beach Lodge** (☎2248 0707; info@turtlebeachlodge.com) also offers transportation from San Jose (7½hr.; 6am; ¢20,300/US$35).

⚑ 🛈 ORIENTATION AND PRACTICAL INFORMATION

The main village of Tortuguero is only about 500m long, with sandy gravel paths winding their way through the scattered buildings. The airstrip is a few kilometers north of town and is only accessible by boat. Most travelers arrive at the dock in the center of town. From the docks, with your back to the water, north is to your left and south is to your right. The docks lead on to the canals and rivers, and across the island, only about 200m from the docks, is the Caribbean Sea. The main path, **Calle Principal,** runs from the **Caribbean Conservation Center** at the far north end of the village all the way to the **ranger station** at the park entrance on the southern end of town. If you are walking around at night, you should consider bringing a flashlight; there are very few streetlights, and the paths through town beyond the main road near the docks are mostly dark and covered by trees.

Tourist Office: Tortuguero boasts an impressive number of buildings along the river's edge purporting to be "free information centers," each of which adjoins a for-profit tour company. Information guru Victor Parientes runs the 🛈**Tortuguero Information Center** (☎2709 8015), opposite the church, 100m north of the docks. At the **Sansa Ticket Office** (☎2709 8015 or 8838 6330), in the same building, you can arrange plane, bus, and boat reservations, as well as rafting, hiking, and turtle-watching excursions. Open daily 8am-1pm and 2-7pm.

Banks: There are no banks or ATMs in Tortuguero, so try to stock up on *colones* before you arrive. If you are in a bind, the **Super Morpho,** located in the town center across from the docks, gives cash back on credit card or debit card purchases. (Open daily 7am-9pm. AmEx/MC/V.)

Police: The **police station** (☎2767 1593), in the blue building, 75m north of the dock to the left of the C. Principal.

Medical Services: For medical emergencies, call ☎8841 8404 or 8304 2121. For serious emergencies, the Sansa ticket office can arrange charter flights to the hospital in San José.

Telephones: Available at **Miss Junie's,** the Super Morpho in front of the docks, and in front of the **ICE office,** 25m south of the police station. Local calls ¢20 per min. International calls require a calling card; some phones require a calling card regardless of destination.

Internet Access: Internet Cafe, 150m north of the main dock on the right. Offers 6 computers with sometimes-slow internet (¢2000 per hr.). Open daily until 9pm.

ACCOMMODATIONS

Despite its remote location, Tortuguero Village has an extensive selection of accommodations, most of them well within a student traveler's means. Hot-water baths and fans are standard fare on the island, and many *cabinas* have on-site breakfasts and hammocks available. Because of the large number of tourists visiting the island, it is important to make reservations in advance if you wish to stay at a particular place, especially during the Tortuguero's high season (July-Oct.). Those who aren't too fond of bugs should remember that the buildings near the canals, where the water is slow-moving, are much more mosquito-friendly than those closer to the drier air and quicker currents of the beach. **Camping** is not allowed on the beach. Backpackers can pitch tents for US$12 (¢6960) per person at the **Jalova ranger station** (includes park entry, accessible only by boat; p. 370) in Tortuguero Village (includes access to kitchen and hot-water showers).

Cabinas Aracari (☎2709 8006). From the docks, head south on the path and take the 1st left after the mini shopping center; Aracari is at the end of the path. Though its prices are relatively low, the *cabinas* scattered throughout the tropical garden are spotless, with tile floors, private hot-water showers, fans, and porches. Singles ¢5800 (US$10); doubles ¢9260 (US$16); triples ¢13,920 (US$24). ❶

Casa Marbella (☎8833 0827 or 2709 8011), between the Tortuguero Information Center and Dorling's Bakery. Beautiful views and a friendly owner make it a charming option, but swarming mosquitoes detract from the experience. Each of the 10 rooms has high ceilings, soft beds, and hot water. Breakfast included, as well as access to the fridge and microwave. Free Wi-Fi. Singles ¢17,400-29,000 (US$30-50); doubles ¢20,300-31,900 (US$35-55); triples ¢26,100-37,700 (US$45-65). ❸

Miss Miriam's (☎2709 8002), on the soccer field, next door to Miss Miriam's Caribbean restaurant. A 2-story house with sunny, yellow-walled rooms with private, but temperamental, hot-water baths and fans. Across the soccer field, at **Miss Miriam's II**, 9 slightly larger cabins with similar amenities are just as close to the ocean but farther from the traffic. Singles ¢11,600 (US$20); doubles ¢14,500 (US$25); triples ¢17,400 (US$30). ❷

Cabinas y Restaurante La Casona (☎2709 8092 or 8860 0453), on the northeast corner of the soccer field. The best deal at this popular complex is the *casita*, a 3-bedroom apartment with its own kitchen, hot-water bath, and open-air porch with stellar views of the Caribbean beach. Breakfast included. Free Wi-Fi and internet. Reserve in advance. *Casita* ¢4060 (US$7) per person for up to 8 people; singles ¢13,340 (US$23); doubles ¢17,400 (US$30); triples ¢23,200 (US$40). AmEx/D/MC/V. ❶

FOOD

Though a small town, Tortuguero has a fair number of restaurants, most of which are on the expensive side as they cater to an almost entirely tourist clientele. To pick up your own trimmings, head to **Super Morpho,** directly opposite the docks (open daily 7am-9pm; AmEx/D/MC/V), **Super Las Tortugas** (☎27098022), 200m north of the docks (open daily 7am-9pm; AmEx/D/MC/V), or **Super Bambu** (☎2709 8108), 200m south of the docks (open daily 7am-9pm; AmEx/D/MC/V).

■ **Miss Junie's,** 250m north of the docks. When it is not overrun by tourist groups, this Caribbean restaurant conjures up fresh and flavorful regional specialties. Breakfast ¢1160-4060 (US$2-7). Entrees ¢5220-8120 (US$9-14). Open daily 7am-10pm. ❸

■ **Miss Miriam's** (☎2709 8002), next door to Miss Miriam's *cabinas* on the north side of the soccer field. Serves family-style "make your own *casado*" meals with coconut-simmered rice, salad, *gallo pinto,* french fries, and a variety of Caribbean-flavored proteins including whole fish, chicken, steak, and pork chops (¢4400 per person). Stop by in the morning for a traditional *tico gallo pinto* breakfast with a kick of coconut flavoring (¢3300). Call out if no one is in sight. Open daily 7:30am-9pm. ❷

Cabinas y Restaurante La Casona, on the northwest corner of the soccer field. Nestled in a thatched-roof porch in the gardens of Cabinas La Casona, this relaxing restaurant prepares a variety of tasty dishes for customers at picnic-style wooden tables. Hanging plants and the sweet smell of burning incense add to the intoxicating vibe. Delicious *casados* ¢3200, heart of palm lasagna ¢4200, and garlic and butter grilled shrimp with rice ¢5600. Open daily 7:30-11am and 1:30-8:30pm. AmEx/D/MC/V. ❷

Buddha Bar (☎2709 8084), 50m north of docks. Though its prices are a bit higher than those of other restaurants in town, the lounge-like atmosphere, spacious riverside terrace, and pleasant ambient music bring a fair-sized crowd to the relaxed Buddha Bar. Guests can relax on couches in the night-club-style interior or enjoy their meal *al fresco* at the dock-side tables along the river. *Batidos* ¢2000-2800. Pizza ¢4000-8000. Lasagna ¢3800. Crepes ¢3700-4300. Sangria ¢2800. Desserts (¢2000-2700) are tasty, though tiny. Reservations recommended for after 6pm. Open daily 11:30am-8:30pm. AmEx/D/MC/V. ❷

♪ NIGHTLIFE

Punto Encuentro, 100m north of the docks. Look for writing on the left side of the wall. The hippest place in town, right on the water's edge. Just try not to fall in after too many cold *Imperiales* (¢1000). Large screen displays music videos showcase old-school Caribbean music and Latin pop. Rice and shrimp ¢2500. Open daily 11am-2am. AmEx/D/MC/V.

Mala Culebra, across from the SuperMorpho at the docks. Not as busy as Punto Encuentro. Groups of tourists gather to show off their moves to the reggae-heavy soundtrack. *Imperial* ¢1000. Open daily 11am-2am.

◉ SIGHTS

CARIBBEAN CONSERVATION CORPORATION NATURAL HISTORY VISITOR CENTER. Before going to see the turtles, check out the non-profit Caribbean Conservation Corporation Natural History Visitor Center (CCC). Founded by Archie Carr, who later prompted the creation of Tortuguero National Park, the CCC specializes in research and education on sea turtles. The center has videos, exhibits, and information on the decimation of the sea turtle population and the efforts taken by conservationists to save the endangered animals. In the 50 years since its inception, the CCC has tagged over 50,000 turtles, making it the world's largest green-turtle-tagging program. Visitors can "adopt" a turtle with a ¢14,500 (US$25) donation and, in turn, receive an adoption certificate, photograph, turtle fact sheet, and information about the tagged turtle when it is found. Those who want to get up close and personal with the turtles can sign up for the center's internship positions, where interns hole up in research facilities and aid the center's scientists in their work. Interns can pick which type of turtle they want to research. Prices for internships run ¢816,000-1,573,800 (US$1400-2700) for 1-3 week programs. The center's admission fee is used to further the efforts of the CCC. *(At the north end of town. Head north on the main path for* *about 200m, where you will see the center's signs; turn right and follow the path a few hundred meters farther until you reach the center. ☎ 2709 8091; www.cccturtle.org. Open M-Sa 10am-noon and 2-5:30pm, Su 2-5:30pm. US$1/¢580. MC/V.)*

TOUR SMART. While tourism has certainly reinvigorated the local economy in Tortuguero, it has also resulted in a wave of new tour agencies, some of which hire unqualified guides and require travelers to patronize certain establishments. To ensure that you are getting your money's worth, ask about a guide's qualifications before signing up for a tour and try to compare the offers of several individuals or companies before making a decision. Keep in mind that tours that uncover the sand where eggs are located disrupt the hatching process, kill the newly hatched baby turtles, and are illegal.

PARQUE NACIONAL TORTUGUERO

Sheltering the most important nesting site for marine turtles in the Western Hemisphere, Parque Nacional Tortuguero encompasses 261 sq. km of coastal territory and 501 sq. km of marine territory 84km north of Limón. It is almost exclusively accessible and navigable by boat. The park's 35km beach, where thousands of turtles return each year to lay their eggs, has brought the park international fame and thousands of visitors. Not content to surrender the show, howler monkeys echo in the treetops, toucans coast overhead, and caimans glide through the canals that flow into the park's swampy regions.

Despite decades of research, scientists still do not know why the turtles flock in such numbers to Tortuguero or how they are able to find their way back here to nest over 30 years after they first hatched. They do know that as the turtle leaves the beach, it records the details of the beach and its location relative to its next destination. Despite an extinction scare in the 1960s brought on by poaching and egg-stealing, conservation efforts have tremendously helped the turtle population, and the famous green turtles continue to nest in the park (from the end of June to Sept.), along with leatherbacks (Mar.-July), hawksbills (May-Sept.), and loggerheads (June-Oct.). All of these species are endangered, though the recent focus on ecotourism in the area has helped the turtles considerably; they are now worth more as a tourist attraction than as an ingredient in turtle soup. However, the turtles still face an immense number of natural predators. If they make it to the sea, baby turtles are prime meat for sharks, big fish, and other sea creatures. In the end, only one out of 1000 sea turtles will make it. To help save the baby turtles from human predators, proceeds from designated turtle stickers ¢2320 (US$4) sold at souvenir shops and tourist booths fund the guards who watch over the eggs.

Today, researchers tag turtles and use satellite tracking to determine patterns of birth dates, routes, and travel patterns in an attempt to uncover the mystery behind these forever-returning females. Tagging turtles has revealed amazing information about their migratory and mating habits: one turtle tagged near Tortuguero was found just one month later on the coast of Senegal, Africa, and many reports show that female turtles, after visiting hundreds of beaches around the world, return to their birth site to nest 30 years later.

▣ TRANSPORTATION. Tortuguero Village is the gateway for Parque Nacional Tortuguero. See p. 366 for transportation to and from Tortuguero. The entrance to the park, at the Cuatro Esquinas Ranger Station, is a 400m walk south of the

Caravan.com is Going Places in Costa Rica from $995.

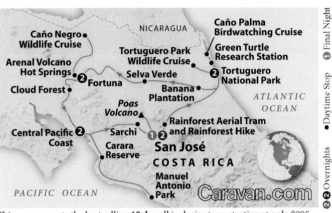

main docks in Tortuguero Village. The less-frequented Jalova Ranger Station is accessible by a 1½hr. boat ride—arrange transportation at the main docks.

WHEN TO GO. Tortuguero has an average yearly rainfall of 5-6m. The rainy season is officially June-Oct., but expect it to rain a lot year-round. The driest months are Feb.-May. Unlike most of Costa Rica, high season in Tortuguero is during the rainy season, when the four different species of turtles come for the *deshove* (turtle nesting). The famous *tortugas verdes* nest on Tortuguero's 35km beach June-Sept.; leatherbacks nest Mar.-July; hawksbills nest May-Sept.; and loggerheads nest June-Oct. Be sure to bring good, waterproof footwear (rubber boots work well), rain gear, sunblock, insect repellent, a hat, and cash. Frequent blackouts in rainy season make a flashlight highly advisable.

🛈 PRACTICAL INFORMATION. Most journeys into the park begin at the **Cuatro Esquinas Ranger Station,** where rangers sell entrance tickets, provide maps, and answer visitors' questions. The entrance is open daily 5:30am-6pm. Although the park closes at 6pm, tickets must be purchased before 4pm, and the last entry is at 4pm. If planning a boat trip, remember that many of the canals around Tortuguero are part of the national park and thus are only open daily 6am-6pm. Most of the canals also have speed and motor restrictions; check with the park rangers (☎2709 8086) for more details. Entrance ₡5800 (US$10); children ₡580 (US$1).

🥾🔭 HIKING AND GUIDED TOURS. There are two official land hikes in Tortuguero National Park. Starting from the Cuatro Esquinas Ranger Station, **Sendero El Gavilán** (1hr., 2km) used to be the only hike available, but it is currently under construction. Though it is not a difficult hike, it can be muddy and buggy. The trail winds through the forest and ends on the beach, where you can take a left and walk back to town. Rubber boots are required for the hike and can be rented for ₡580 (US$1) per person at a hotel or tourist center. If it is still under construction, you can take the **Sendero Jaguar,** a 4 km (1½hr.) circular hike that both begins and ends at the Ranger Station. Venomous snakes can be found on both trails, but will not attack unless aggravated. **Caño Harold** is one of the best waterways in the Park for caiman, turtle, monkey, and kingfisher sightings.

The best way to explore the park is by canoe or kayak on its numerous canals and rivers. Although it's possible to go alone, hiring a guide makes for a much more informative and fun experience. Keep in mind, however, that guides abound in Tortuguero, and the competition between guides can be fierce. If you want a particular guide, stick with them, even if competitors try to mislead you. Most guided boat tours cost about ₡8700 (US$15) per person, plus park entry fees. The hike to the top of Cerro Tortuguero offers one of the most spectacular views of Parque Nacional Tortuguero, but is under-frequented due to its location across the canals from the village. Guided tours of the hike last about 3hr. and include transportation (₡11,600, US$20 per person).

Tinamon Tours (☎2709 8004 or 8842 6561; www.tinamontours.de), in the purple house 100m past Cabinas Tortuguero. Owner Bárbara Hartung leads canoe, hiking, and village tours in English, French, German, and Spanish. She prefers groups of 4-5 people. Tours ₡2900 (US$5) per hr. per person. Book several days in advance as tours fill up quickly.

Mundo Natural Tours (☎8341 1359 or 8811 7919), next to the cafe. Owners Jorge and David offer canoe trips (₡8700, US$15), turtle night walks (₡11,600, US$20), a frog night tour on private trails (₡8700, US$15), and an 8hr. "extreme adventure" tour (₡34,800, US$60).

Bony Scott (☎2709 8139 or 8320 5232), 50m south of the docks. Offers canoe tours each morning (3hr.; ₡145,000, US$25, includes park entrance fee). Kayak rentals ₡9800/US$18 per day; includes park entrance fee.

TURTLE WATCHING. The park's feature presentation is the nightly *deshove*, when turtles come to lay their eggs. The female turtle emerges from the sea and makes her way up the sand, pausing frequently to check for danger. When she finds the perfect spot, she uses her flippers to dig a body pit about 1ft. deep, and then a smaller pit for her eggs. After laying her eggs and using her flippers to bury them in the sand, she leaves them, never seeing the final product. The intriguing process lasts about 2hr.

Visitors must be with a guide certified by the park (ask to see a license). The beaches are guarded by 18 rangers whose sole job is to find and protect the turtles; if you try to watch the *deshove* without a guide, they will throw you out. (Tours leave nightly around 8 and 10pm. ₡11,600/US$20 per person. Park entrance ticket required for beaches south of Cuatro Esquinas Ranger Station.)

Talk to any of the guides mentioned above to arrange a tour or ask around town to find an experienced local guide. It is best to find a guide in town before 4pm because the guides must purchase permits before the park closes. Wear good walking shoes and dark clothing (light clothes may scare the turtles).

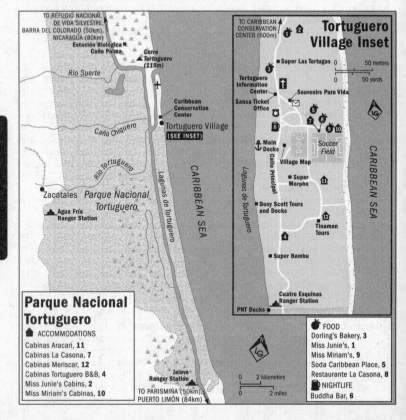

Flashlights are useful for the hike to the beach, but cameras and flashlights cannot be turned on once at the beach, as the light disturbs the turtles and causes them to stop the nesting process. Make sure to bring a bottle of water along with you, as some of the hikes are upwards of 2km long, and you may end up waiting up to an hour for the first turtle to arrive. Official park rules state that once a tour group has seen the egg-laying process, they must leave, regardless of whether or not the two hours have elapsed. The park rangers take any offenses very seriously and may deny future entry to any visitor who violates the rules.

> **ECO-FRIENDLY TOURS.** Visitors should always exercise responsibility and sensitivity when exploring the wildlife. Official park rules require boats to switch from gas to electric motors, which do not disturb the animals as much as the roar from loud gas engines. Tour boats should also glide along the canals extremely slowly to avoid causing wakes, which disrupt animal and insect life on the shores. Most tour guides observe these rules, but some ignore them for financial reasons. As an informed and eco-sensitive tourist, do your best to ask non-rule-abiding guides to slow down and be quiet.

 CERRO TORTUGUERO AND CAÑO PALMA BIOLOGICAL STATION. Located just off the canals en route to Tortuguero Village from Pavona, **Caño Palma Biological Station** offers similar naturalist attractions and fauna to Tortuguero without the large numbers of tourists. Staffed by a small group of employees and volunteers from the non-profit **Canadian Organization for Tropical Education and Rainforest Conservation (COTERC),** the station has numerous hiking trails for day visitors and opportunities for long-term volunteer work. Though technically part of Barra del Colorado Wildlife Refuge, the entrance to Caño Palma is more easily accessed from Pavona or Tortuguero. (☎2709 8052; www.coterc.org. 1st week ¢145,000/US$250, each additional week ¢104,400/US$180; includes dorm-style lodging, meals, hiking, and pickup from Cariari or Tortuguero. Station admission ¢1160/US$2.)

From Pavona, take the boat heading for Tortuguero and ask to be dropped off at the station (30min.; 9am, 1:30pm; ¢1600). From Tortuguero, catch any of the boats heading back to Pavona and ask to be dropped off at the station (30min.; 6, 11:30am, 3pm; ¢1600).

BARRA DEL COLORADO

Even more remote than Parque Nacional Tortuguero, the swampy terrain of Barra del Colorado lies 25km to the north, close to the Nicaraguan bor-der. At first glance, Barra could be Tortuguero's long-lost twin; both national parks are accessible only by boat or plane, are nearly ecologically identical, and are traversed on quiet boats through lagoons that meander through the dense vegetation. However, while Tortuguero has cultivated an eco-friendly and backpacker-based tourism industry, Barra del Colorado remains almost entirely undeveloped and lacks any public or tourism infrastructure outside of its extremely pricey sportfishing lodges. The adventurous—especially those with some extra cash—may enjoy the undisturbed wildlife and beautiful fish-filled canals of the Barra, but for most travelers, this northeastern section of Costa Rica will remain a bit too much off the beaten path.

AT A GLANCE

AREA: 920 sq. km; 50km of coastline.

CLIMATE: Hot and humid; avg. temp. 26°C (79°F).

FEATURES: Remote, jungle-like Refugio Nacional de Vida Silvestre Barra del Colorado.

GATEWAYS: Cariari.

HIGHLIGHTS: Some of Costa Rica's best sportfishing, as well as turtle nesting and wildlife-sighting opportunities similar to those at Parque Nacional Tortuguero.

CAMPING: Not allowed in the park.

FEES: Park admission US$10; fishing license US$30.

ORIENTATION

The Barra del Colorado refuge is immense, covering 920 sq. km of swampy wetlands and mangrove-lined rivers. Within the refuge, there is only one touristed area, located 99km northeast of San José and 35km north of Tortuguero. It is actually composed of two separate small slivers of land, Barra Sur and Barra del Norte, which sit directly opposite each other at the mouth of the Río Colorado. Barra del Norte is almost entirely residential, and Barra del Sur, while still relatively under-touristed, has the only accommodation and dining options available to visitors. While there are a few other lodges further to the north and south of the main *pueblo*, these are only accessible by boat.

TRANSPORTATION

The easiest way to get to Barra is by flying into the local airstrip on one of the daily **flights** offered by Sansa (30min.; 6am, return 6:45am; US$70) or NatureAir (30min.; 6:30am, return 7am; US$70).

Outside of flying, there are two ways of getting to Barra del Colorado, and both involve a solid day of traveling. The cheapest way to get to Tortuguero is from Cariari, which can be accessed by **bus** from San José (El Caribe Bus Terminal; 2hr.; 6:30, 9am; ¢1200) or Guápiles (40min., every 20min., ¢200). From Cariari, there are two buses that leave each day for the long, bumpy trek to Puerto Lindo (3hr.; 4:30am, 2pm; ¢1200), where boats wait to take passengers on a picturesque journey down the canals of the Refugio to the docks of Barra del Norte and Barra del Sur (1hr., on arrival of buses from Cariari, ¢2500). Though the bus to Puerto Lindo is often labeled "Tortuguero," it services a different destination entirely than the Tortuguero buses, which go to Pavona instead of Puerto Lindo. Make sure to ask the bus driver if the bus goes to Barra del Colorado or you may end up several hours away from your intended destination. Leaving Barra del Colorado, boats stop at the Barra del Sur docks daily at 5am and 2pm to bring visitors back to Puerto Lindo and on to Cariari.

The second way to get to Barra del Colorado is much pricier. From Moín or Tortuguero, you can ask around at the docks and tour companies for a **private boat** to Barra del Colorado. There are no regular services, so expect prices starting at ¢35,000 per boat from Tortuguero and ¢80,000 per boat from Moín. Prices may be even more expensive leaving Barra del Colorado because most captains in the area do not sail outside of the refuge. While this route is very expensive for the individual, it is a better deal for groups (most boats hold up to 10 people) and a better option for those who get queasy at the thought of the bumpy, muddy 3hr. school-bus haul from Cariari.

CARIBBEAN LOWLANDS

🔃 PRACTICAL INFORMATION

Barra del Norte (pop. 1200) is almost completely residential, while Barra del Sur (pop. 700) is home to the **main dock, airstrip,** and the few accommodations and services in the area. The remote location of the town and lack of any real infrastructure (including roads) means that only the most basic goods and services can be found in town. In case of a **medical** or **police emergency,** have the guards near the main dock contact doctors and authorities in Guápiles on their radio. **Los Almendros Bar y Pulpería,** about 150m on the right side of the airstrip away from docks, has a **public phone** (local calls ¢10 per min.; to US, Mexico, and Canada US$0.60 per min.; to Europe US$0.80 per min.), a Sansa ticket office, and basic supplies. (Open daily 7am-noon and 3-7pm.) **Pulpería Clark,** on the left side of the airstrip, sells basic food and supplies. (Open daily 6am-9pm.) Another **public phone** is available at **CYD Souvenir,** 100m down the airstrip from the docks and to the right. (☎2710 6592. Local calls ¢15 per min., to US ¢500 per min. Open daily 6am-8pm.) Across from Los Almendros, **Diana's** has the local monopoly on non-lodge **Internet access;** service is skittish, slow, and pricey, and Diana will charge for each dial attempt. She can also provide phone numbers for Barra's residents and lodges. (☎2710 6592; ¢50 per min.)

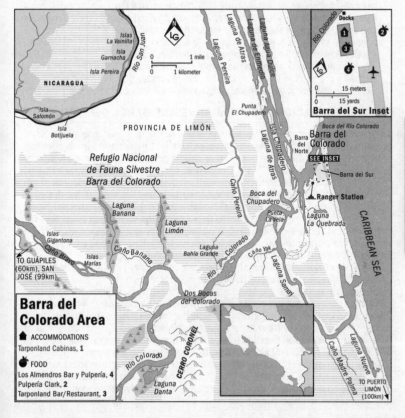

Barra del Sur Inset

Barra del Colorado Area

🔺 ACCOMMODATIONS
Tarponland Cabinas, **1**

🍎 FOOD
Los Almendros Bar y Pulpería, **4**
Pulpería Clark, **2**
Tarponland Bar/Restaurant, **3**

CARIBBEAN LOWLANDS

WHEN TO GO. Barra del Colorado is hot and humid year-round, with an average yearly rainfall of 6m. The rainy season is officially June-Oct., but expect it to rain a lot year-round. The driest months are from Feb.-May. Differing from most of Costa Rica's national parks, Barra del Colorado has no hiking trails, since the area is almost exclusively covered with swamps, wetlands, and lagoons. Leatherback and green turtles nest on Barra's beach from July to Sept., and the snook and tarpon fishing season reaches its peak Jan.-May and Sept.-Oct. Be sure to bring good, waterproof footwear (rubber boots work well), rain gear, sunblock, insect repellent, a hat, cash, and any medical supplies you might need, since not many supplies are available in Barra.

ACCOMMODATIONS AND FOOD

There is only one relatively budget accomodation and dining option here:

Tarponland (☎8818 9921), a.k.a. Memo's, about 30m down from the dock by the airstrip. Though not marked by a sign, it's hard to miss—its blue and white buildings are sprawled along the right side of the airstrip just 30m away from the docks. The complex, connected by concrete and wooden walkways, contains large, simple rooms with 2-4 beds and hot showers. Farthest away from the docks is a large, empty dining room backed by a small bar where locals gather to watch TV and enjoy a variety of *casados* and other Costa Rican standards. The menu often features catch-of-the-day snook and tarpon, as well as fresh chicken from owner Guillermo Cunningham's farm (breakfast ₡2000, entrees ₡2500-3000). Guillermo also offers a tour of his coconut farm that includes rides through nearby canals, lagoons, and a beach for US$40 per person, less for groups of 2 or more. Rooms US$30. Full fishing package US$300, includes food and lodging. Inquire about the details of other wildlife tours, including whale watching. ❸

REFUGIO NACIONAL DE VIDA SILVESTRE BARRA DEL COLORADO

The Barra del Colorado Wildlife Refuge is one of Costa Rica's largest protected areas, with almost 920 sq. km of swampy tropical forest and canals teeming with wildlife. It is drenched with 6m of rain yearly, and the average temperature hovers around 26°C (79°F). Created in the mid-1980s, the area remains relatively untouched except for quite a bit of illegal logging in the depths of the park. The park's **Ranger Station,** accessible by boat, is 1km west of the docks at Barra del Sur on the Río Colorado. Though Barra del Sur and Barra del Norte are both part of the refuge, visitors to these *pueblitos* do not pay entry fees for the park, and most guided sportfishing trips will arrange passes and fishing licenses if reservations are made in advance. (Open daily 6am-6pm. US$10 per day. Freshwater fishing license US$30, valid for 60 days.)

Very little of Barra is accessible by foot, since the area is swampy (especially in the rainy season) and no trails have been cut through the upland areas; the most popular activity is sportfishing. Locals make much of their living fishing for spiny lobsters and exporting them throughout the country, while most of the tourism centers on the enormous fighting fish known to lurk in the Barra waters. Tarpon and snook season is best from January to May and September to October (wet-season flooding makes the water cloud with mud and obscures bait lures), but locals will tell you that fishing is good year-round.

Some comparatively cheap alternatives to sportfishing are local wildlife tours, which can be arranged at any of the lodges in Barra. These tours offer the chance to see jaguars, three-toed sloths, spider and white-faced monkeys, manatees, and a huge variety of birds such as laughing falcons, keel-bird toucans, and green macaws. Green, leatherback, and hawksbill turtles also nest in Barra, but in smaller numbers than at Tortuguero. The **Río Colorado Fishing Lodge** offers an all-inclusive two-day, one-night jungle safari package with transportation from San José and tours of the Barra canals for US$196.

CAHUITA

Tourism may have turned the isolated Caribbean outpost of Cahuita into a *gringo*-filled vacation spot, but luckily, the natural charms that lured the first visitors to the small town have not gone away. Sun-kissed beaches, lush jungles, and coral reefs draw even the crowd-shy to Cahuita's shores, where howler monkeys screech above white sand beaches and manta rays lurk in the waters of hidden inlets and lagoons. Parque Nacional Cahuita boasts the largest coral reef on Costa Rica's Caribbean coast, while those who prefer to stay on land can choose from the white sand of the park's Playa Blanca or, on the northern end of town, the sun-bathing hot spot of black-sanded Playa Negra.

TRANSPORTATION

The MEPE **bus** company (in San José ☎2257 8129, in Limón ☎2758 1572) has buses departing from 200m west of the park to: Bribrí (1hr., every hr. 6am-7pm); Limón (1hr., every hr. 6:30am-8pm, ¢890); Manzanillo (1hr.; 6:45, 11:15am, 3:45, 6:45pm; ¢590); Puerto Viejo (30min., every hr. 6am-7pm, ¢335); Sixaola (2hr., every hr. 6am-7pm); San José (3hr.; 6, 10am, noon, 2, 4pm; ¢4200). There are no public **taxis** in Cahuita, but Mr. Big J, one block southeast of the bus stop, can help you contact a private operator. (☎2755 0328. Open daily 8am-6pm.)

ORIENTATION AND PRACTICAL INFORMATION

A road branching off the Limón-Puerto Viejo Hwy. runs for 1km before entering downtown Cahuita. The bus station is in a shopping center 700m down the road, just outside of the town center. Cahuita's main road, **Avenida Alfredo González Flores,** goes from northwest to southeast. It intersects the road from the highway at the town center, where there is a small park. **Playa Negra** is 1km west of the northwest end of the main road, and **Playa Blanca** lies in **Parque Nacional Cahuita** over the bridge at the southeast end of the road. Most hotels and restaurants are within several blocks of the park and town center.

Tourist Information: Your best bet for information is **Mr. Big J** (p. 380).

Banks: Banco de Costa Rica, in the shopping center next to the bus station accepts V/Cirrus/Plus. Open M-F

Cahuita

🏠 ACCOMMODATIONS
Cabinas El Safari #1 Hotel, **5**
Cabinas Sol y Mar, **9**
Spencer Sea-Side Lodge, **4**
Kelly Creek Hotel-Restaurant, **10**
New Cabinas Arrecife, **2**

🍴 FOOD
Café El Parquecito, **6**
Cha Cha Cha, **3**
Miss Edith's, **1**
Kelly Creek Hotel-Restaurant, **11**
Restaurante Tranquilo Cahuita, **7**

🌙 NIGHTLIFE
Coco's Bar, **8**

0   200 meters
0   200 yards

CARIBBEAN SEA

TO PLAYA NEGRA (1km)

Willie's Tours
Supermercado Safari
Parque Alfredo González Flores
Mr. Big J's
Roberto's Tours

Clínica Cahuita
Banco de Costa Rica
Farmacia Cahuita
MEPE

TO AVIARIOS DEL CARIBE/ BUTTERCUP FOUNDATION (12km), CAHUITA BUTTERFLY FARM (500m), PUERTO LIMÓN (40km)

TO KELLY CREEK RANGER STATION (25m)

8am-4pm. At **Mr. Big J's,** you can pay with traveler's checks for 0% comission. Most restaurants and hotels take major credit cards.

Luggage Storage: Mr. Big J stores valuables for the day in a steel case. ¢1500 per day.

Laundry: Mr. Big J offers wash, dry, and fold. AM dropoff, PM pickup; ¢3500 per load. Open daily 8am-6pm.

Emergency: ☎911.

Police: (☎2755 0217), at the northwest end of the main road, next to the post office. Open 24hr.

Pharmacy: Farmacia Limon, in the shopping center next to the bus station. AmEx/D/MC/V.

Medical Services: Clínica Cahuita (☎2755 0383). Offers basic medical services. Walk 250m south of the bus stop toward the main highway; it is the light blue building on your right. Open M-Th 7am-4pm, F 7am-noon.

Telephones: At the shopping center in front of the bus station, in the *parque municipal,* and in front of the police station.

Internet Access: The cheapest Internet access is in the shopping center by the bus station at **Internet Caribbean Adventure,** which has new computers and a sometimes-quick connection. ¢800 per hr. Open M-Sa 10am-6pm. **Spencer Sea-Side Lodge** (☎2755 0027) has slightly higher prices but good connection speed. Offers a bank of computers overlooking the Caribbean. Open daily 8am-8pm.

Post Office: (☎/fax 2755 0096), at the northwest end of the main road, next to Miss Edith's. Open M-F 8am-noon and 1:30-5:30pm. **Postal Code:** 7302.

ACCOMMODATIONS

Cahuita has a seemingly endless selection of accommodation options, but most places offer similar amenities for similar prices. The average *cabina* charges US$15-20 for a single and US$25-30 for a double; any less is a deal and any more may be a rip-off. Expect simple rooms with fans, tempermental hot water in private showers, and hammocks almost everywhere.

Spencer Sea-Side Lodge (☎2755 0027 or 2755 0210). Foamy waves splash over the rock seawall at the banks of this idyllic hotel, situated in a hammock-filled, wooded yard. The rooms are just as pleasant; hardwood, cabin-style walls add to the rustic ambience despite the private hot-water showers, mosquito nets, and fans in each room. Guests looking for the perfect morning yoga spot (or just more of a splurge) can climb the homemade mosaic stairs to the 2nd fl., where rooms are twice as expensive but larger, with private hammocks on porches with a lovely sea view. Internet access ¢1000 per hr. Daily reef tours US$25 per person. Rooms downstairs US$10 per person; upstairs US$20. Accepts traveler's checks. AmEx/D/MC/V. ❶

Cabinas Safari #1 (☎2755 0405; www.cabinassafari.com), 50m east of the park. In the middle of town and less than 3 blocks from every part of it. These quiet *cabinas* prevents noise with a tree- and plant-filled garden buffer. The comfortable *cabinas* have twin and queen beds, private hot-water baths, fans, and porches with hammocks and tables, perfect for late-night lounging. The locked gate and barbed-wire fence ensure the safety of your belongings. Singles US$15; doubles US$25. AmEx/MC/V. ❷

New Cabinas Arrecife (☎2755 0081), 25m southeast of Miss Edith's. Several blocks from the town center, this dark-wood complex offers spotless tile rooms with ceiling fans and private hot-water baths. Located just steps from the beach, it has a pool with lawn chairs and a covered hammock area for lounging. Breakfast overlooking the ocean ¢1500-2000. Singles US$20; doubles US$25; triples US$30. AmEx/D/MC/V. ❷

Cabinas Sol y Mar (☎2755 0418; cabsolymar@hotmail.com), 1 block north of the park entrance on the main road. In between the town center and the park entrance, this older hotel has clean, bright-green rooms with fans and private hot-water baths at some of the lowest prices in town. The upstairs balcony overlooks the street, park entrance, and beach. Singles US$12; doubles US$20; triples US$25. MC/V. ❶

Kelly Creek Hotel-Restaurant (☎2755 0077; www.hotelkellycreek.com), to the right of the park entrance, just before the bridge. Though pricier than most options in town, Kelly Creek has peaceful, enormous rooms with 2 beds, hand-woven (and somehow elegant) mosquito nets, pink sheets, ceiling fans, huge, private hot-water baths, and closets. Singles US$40; doubles US$45, each additional person US$10. ❸

FOOD

Most restaurants in Cahuita cater to tourists and serve tasty dishes at relatively high prices. However, the benefit of more tourists is larger variety and higher quality of food; during your stay, you can enjoy Spanish, Costa Rican, Jamaican, Italian, Chinese, and American-style dishes without leaving the town center. Stock up at the **Supermercado Safari** or get an inexpensive meal at the *sodas* two blocks from the bus station into town.

■ **Cha Cha Cha** (☎8368 1725), 200m north of the park. Chef Bertrand Fleury conjures up fresh, delicious combinations of meat, seafood, and vegetarian platters, all served in a candlelit, open-air dining room. The prices are high, but the quality is unparalleled in Cahuita. The chocolate cake (¢2200) is heavenly. Salads ¢3000-4000. Entrees ¢3000-8000. Desserts ¢2200-2600. Open daily 5:30pm-10:30pm. Cash only. ❸

■ **Miss Edith's** (☎2755 0248), northeast of the post office. Known around Cahuita as the epitome of high-class Caribbean cooking, Miss Edith's serves succulently flavored Caribbean specialties at prices that are a well-deserved splurge. Feast on incredible vegetable soup (¢1500); fish with coconut, curry, and yucca (¢2800); or lobster (price varies depending on season). The Jamaican jerk dishes (¢3000-7000) are extra spicy. Be sure to call ahead for the *rondón* (¢3000-6500). Open daily 11am-10pm. ❷

Cafe del Parquecito (☎2755 0279 or 8993 1517), on the east side of the park. This delightful cafe serves up scrumptious, healthful breakfasts and lunches in its open-air dining area, while hummingbirds and Caribbean-influenced hip hop and reggae from throughout the Americas serenade you. The restaurant serves dinner as well (¢3000-5000), but it's more popular for earlier meals of massive crepes (¢2000-2400), egg and *pinto* dishes (¢1100-3000), and specialty sandwiches (¢1800-4000). The *batidos* are some of the best in town: try one with pineapple in milk (¢850). Open M and W-Su 6am-3pm for breakfast and lunch, dinner 6pm-late. ❷

Kelly Creek Hotel-Restaurant (☎2755 0007), to the right of the park entrance. Tucked into the gardens of Kelly Creek Hotel, this small Spanish restaurant offers haute cuisine in a quiet, country dining room. The hands-down favorite is the homemade paella (¢6800 per person, min. 2 people, call at least 6hr. in advance to request), best enjoyed with a jar of the homemade sangria (¢6000). Appetizers ¢2200-3200. Seafood entrees ¢4000-6000. Open M-Sa 6:30pm-9:30pm. MC/V. ❸

Restaurante Tranquilo Cahuita, 50m west of the park. With its cheery, faux-flower decor, open-air seating, and friendly staff, this small *soda* serves up *comida típica* at lightning speed for some of the lowest prices in town. Breakfast ¢1600-1900. Lunch and dinner entrees ¢1500-4500. Open Tu-Su 6am-10pm. AmEx/D/MC/V. ❶

NIGHTLIFE

Though Cahuita attracts a number of surfers and backpackers, its nightlife scene is comparitively very small. The only late-night option is the popular **Coco's Bar** (☎2755 0003), across the street from the park. With a large dance floor and a balcony perfect for people-watching, Coco's attracts a crowd of locals and tourists looking for live music, which starts up around 7 or 8pm and usually runs until about 10pm or so. On the weekends, the crowd generally gets bigger and stays later. (Open daily noon-2:30am. Live music most nights; inquire for details. MC/V.)

GUIDED TOURS

Mr. Big J (☎2755 0328). Run by Mañuela and the amiable Mr. Big J himself (a.k.a. Joseph), one of the best sources of information in Cahuita. Aside from his laundry, storage, and book exchange services, Mr. Big J also arranges almost any type of tour in the area, including snorkeling around Cahuita (3hr., includes gear, drinks, and local guide; US$25), and horseback trips along beaches (½-day trip with refreshments US$40).

Roberto Tours (☎/fax 755 0117), 2 blocks northwest of the park entrance. Roberto personally leads his adventure-filled, highly successful fishing trips (daytrips 4hr., US$50; equipment included). Cook your own catch at Roberto's Caribbean-style seafood restaurant next door. He also offers early-morning dolphin tours (5hr. or until dolphins are found, US$55). Open daily 7am-10pm. AmEx/D/MC/V.

Willie's Tours (☎2755 0267; www.willies-costarica-tours.com), 50m north of the *parque municipal*. Run by German expat Willie, this tour office with a boom box and couch offers trips all over the Caribbean coast of Costa Rica and Panama. River rafting on the Pacuare and Reventazon (US$95), all-inclusive 3-day, 2-night Tortuguero trips (US$265), canopy tours (US$45), and his unique multi-day trips to Panama, including Bocas del Toro and Bastimentos (4-person min., US$195 per person). Free Internet access for trip participants. Open daily 8am-noon and 2-9pm.

Cahuita Butterfly Farm (☎2755 0361; fransoha@hotmail.com). Walk 1km back to the main highway, turn right, and continue for a few min. until you see the sign on your left. One of the most elaborate *mariposarios* in the region, the Cahuita Butterfly Farm has 20 varieties of butterfly, including the sought-after, deep-blue Morpho peleides. Visitors interested in the history and science of butterflies can check out the informative exhibits on the stages of a butterfly's life. US$8, students US$6. Open daily 8:30am-3:30pm.

DAYTRIPS FROM CAHUITA

AVIARIOS DEL CARIBE/BUTTERCUP FOUNDATION. In 1992, three girls from a *pueblo* near Cahuita found an abandoned sloth in the forest and took it to local wildlife refuge Aviarios del Caribe, run by Judy and her husband Luis. The family fell in love with Buttercup, the contented, smiling three-fingered *perezoso*, and decided to dedicate their refuge to saving Costa Rica's sloth population. Since Buttercup was adopted, Aviarios has become the largest sloth refuge and rehabilitation center in the world, with over 100 sloths in residence at the hospital, nursery, and protected island. The center performs medical procedures and physical rehabilitation for sloths injured from power-line electrocution, hunting, violence, and falls. The work at Aviarios has proved groundbreaking in sloth research, helping to dispel myths that the two- and three-fingered creatures are dirty or evolutionary flukes. In fact, the mosses and moths that live on these sloths are an important part of the forest ecosystem, and their slow movements are not pure laziness but rather a camouflage technique to shield them from predatory birds flying above the trees.

While the medical facilities of the refuge are closed to visitors, the center offers two-part tours starting with a canoe trip around the island, where sloths, caimans, monkeys, and over 300 types of birds can be spotted, after which visitors are shown a video on sloths and a presentation on the differences between two- and three-toed sloths. The tour concludes with visiting five sloths cared for by the sanctuary; if the sloths are in a good mood, they may let you pet them. The refuge also has a gift shop, which opens onto a beautiful veranda where Buttercup lives in her private chair-swing, and baby sloths as young as six weeks old are fed goat's milk, greens, and carrots by volunteers. Though visitors cannot touch these sloths, they are free to watch them cuddle and hide under their blankets or teddy bears for a drowsy nap. For those who can't bear to leave their new friends, the refuge has seven luxurious rooms on-site, with breakfast and a sloth tour included. All rooms have tile floors, comfortable beds, hot-water showers, and fans. More expensive rooms have A/C, bathtubs, and/or a sitting room. *(Singles US$75; doubles US$87-99; triples US$105-116; quads US$122-134. 20min. away from Cahuita, just 1km past the bridge after the turnoff to Penshurt. To get to the refuge, take any bus headed from Cahuita to Limón and ask for a ticket to the Cruce Penshurt (¢345). Ask the driver to let you off at the entrance to Aviarios. Tours of the refuge cost US$25 per person; book in advance for larger groups. The center also offers a birdwatching tour that begins at 6am. It includes a 2hr. canoe birdwatching trip, breakfast, and a sloth tour afterwards. US$35 per person. ☎ 2750 0775 or 2750 0725; www.slothrescue.org. Open daily 6am-3pm.)*

PARQUE NACIONAL CAHUITA

Parque Nacional Cahuita's claim to fame is its spectacular 600-hectare coral reef. Though the vast majority of the park is underwater, most visitors come to lounge on the white sands of Playa Blanca or hike through the seaside jungle, which is home to sloths, monkeys, vipers, and other creatures.

AT A GLANCE	
AREA: 22,400 hectares of ocean; 1067 hectares of land.	**CAMPING:** The park does have sites for camping, but park rules and availability vary seasonally; check with the staff at the ranger station for more details.
CLIMATE: Hot and humid; average temp. 29°C/84°F.	
FEATURES: Punta Vargas on the 600-hectare coral reef, Playa Blanca, hiking in the rainforest, surfing, snorkeling.	**ENTRANCE FEES:** Suggested donation from Kelly Creek station; US$10 from Puerto Vargas station.
GATEWAYS: Cahuita (p. 377).	

▐ TRANSPORTATION

Cahuita is the gateway town for Parque Nacional Cahuita. The Kelly Creek park entrance is in the town of Cahuita, and the Puerto Vargas entrance is 6km south of Cahuita on the **bus** route toward Puerto Viejo. See **Transportation** (p. 377) for transportation to and from Cahuita.

▐ ORIENTATION

Parque Nacional Cahuita lies on the south end of the Atlantic coast in the province of Limón. The park has two ranger stations accessible from Cahuita. The southeast end of the main road takes you over a bridge to the **Kelly Creek Ranger Station,** which is used by most visitors. **Puerto Vargas,** the second station, is off the main highway between Puerto Viejo and Limón. To enter the park through the Puerto Vargas ranger station, take the Puerto Viejo de Talamanca bus in Cahuita and ask to be dropped at the Puerto Vargas *entrada* (entrance).

▐ PRACTICAL INFORMATION

If you enter through the **Kelly Creek Ranger Station,** you must register in their logbook. No admission fee is required, but they ask for a voluntary donation;

most visitors leave about ¢1000. (Station open daily 6am-5pm; last entry 4pm.) A standard US$10 national park admission fee is required if you enter from the **Puerto Vargas Station**. (☎2755 0461, 2755 0302, or 2755 0060; aclac@ns.minae. go.cr. Open daily 6am-5pm, last entry 4pm.)

> **WHEN TO GO.** The Cahuita area is very hot and humid year-round, and especially wet from May to November. For this reason, most people visit during the dry season (Dec.-Apr.). Be sure to bring a bathing suit to enjoy the ocean. Swimming is permitted at many locations throughout the park, but conditions can change quickly and currents can be dangerous, especially after a storm. Riptides are also common. Check with the rangers before you get in the water. Snorkeling without a guide is prohibited.

HIKING

An easy 9km (2hr.) **Rainforest Trail** leads from the Kelly Creek Station in Cahuita to Punta Cahuita for 4km and continues 3km until it reaches Puerto Vargas. The hike finishes 2km past the station along the main highway, where you can catch a bus back to Cahuita (6km, every hr. 6am-7pm, ¢250). The trail often seems more like a narrow road than a path, with bikers riding through and local mothers pushing strollers. Because the path is close to the water, it is known to flood. About 1.5km along the path is the Río Suarez which can be 1m in depth during high tide. Plan accordingly and be prepared to get wet.

The views along the 2hr. hike make the trek worthwhile. On one side, the rolling waves of the Caribbean drum against secluded, white-sand Playa Vargas; on the other, swampy forests clash with towering coconut palms. The treetops of Cahuita are among the best in the country for spotting howler monkeys and white-faced monkeys; at sunrise and sunset, the reclusive primates sometimes come down from their perches to meander along the shoreline.

Numerous *cawa* trees (Cahuita's namesake) line the path; the tree is recognizable by its thick folds, which make it look as though they're resting on a wrinkled base. The tree is also called *sangrillo*, for the blood-like sap it "bleeds;" Bribrí shaman have been known to prescribe concoctions of the sap to pregnant tribeswomen as a natural abortive. Look for the white trees that locals call *gringo pelado* under their breath: the trees peel in the sun like pale *gringos*. Boiled in milk, the peelings are thought to promote weight loss.

Though the majority of Cahuita's animals are harmless, the park is known for **yellow vipers,** which are deadly and live in and around the park. Though they are often seen on the trail, they are timid and won't attack unless disturbed. However, avoid wandering off the trail and give the snake space if you see one.

THE CORAL REEF

Fish of all kinds populate Cahuita's 600-hectare coral reef; over 35 coral species line the ocean floor. In the past few years, the reef has shrunk due in part to the accumulation of eroded soil from banana plantations. Additionally, banana pesticides have drained into the water, contaminating the reef. Earthquakes have also deteriorated the reefs and have left dead coral in their wake, thus obscuring the sites. With the help of a guide (**Guided Tours,** p. 380), you can find some of the best snorkeling on the Caribbean coast. Snorkeling without a guide is prohibited. The most popular spot is Punta Vargas.

DAYTRIPS FROM PARQUE NACIONAL CAHUITA

RESERVA BIOLÓGICA HITOY-CERERE. *Sixty-seven kilometers from Limón, Hitoy-Cerere is usually visited from Cahuita. Getting there by public transportation is possible, but the long journey necessitates starting early in the morning. Take any bus heading north from Cahuita and ask to be let off in the tiny town of Penshurt (20min., ¢170). Wait at the gas station for the hourly bus to Valle Estrallada, Finca 6. If you are coming from Límon, take the hourly bus from the MEPE station to Valle Estrallada (Ask to be let off at Finca 12; 30min., ¢360). From there, it is a 4km uphill hike along a winding dirt road winding through local banana plantations. There are no signs until you arrive, but it is the only road in the area. The ranger station has a large common space with TV, sheetless beds, outdoor and indoor bathrooms, and a friendly staff. ☎2798 3170; fax 2758 3996; aclaca@ns.minae.go.cr. Beds US$7. Open daily 8am-4pm. Camping not permitted.*

Parque Nacional Cahuita

Punta Cahuita

Cahuita

Sector Playa Blanca
(Swimming Allowed)

Kelly Creek

Reef

Punta Vargas

CARIBBEAN SEA

Playa Vargas
(Swimming Allowed)

Puerto Vargas

(Swimming Prohibited)

TO PUERTO VIEJO DE TALAMANCA (15km)

Sector Carbón

TO PUERTO LIMÓN (44km)

Río Suárez

Río Perezoso

Quebrada Kelly Creek

Rainforest Trail

36

You can usually catch a ride back to Penshurt with one of the rangers, who descend daily in their 4WD vehicles. From there, wait for the hourly bus back to Cahuita or Limón. Guided tours of Hitoy-Cerere are available through agencies in Cahuita (p. 377) and Puerto Viejo (p. 384); they usually run about US$65. Private taxis from Cahuita can be hired for about US$55; from Penshurt they run about US$25. Admission US$10.

The Reserva Biológica Hitoy-Cerere is cradled between the Talamanca Mountain Range and the Estrella Valley, as well as by the three indigenous reservations of Tayni, Telire, and Talamanca. With an estimated yearly rainfall of 3500mm, the reserve has no dry season—merely a less-wet season. Because of the rain and the isolation, few tourists make it here, though it is a biologist's paradise. Nature-lovers will enjoy the pristine, rugged trails and the vast knowledge of the rangers and local guides; there is even a collection of (dead) poisonous snakes and insects at the station. Guides are not customary, but rangers will gladly arrange one. These guides are cheaper (¢8000-10,000 per day) than any arranged in Cahuita or Limón, and have experience in the area. Except for the two trails below, rangers request that visitors travel with a guide.

SENDERO CATARATA. This trail begins with a 10min. path starting from the station that eventually intersects the Río Cerere. Build a cairn (small pile of stones) to help you recognize the exit when returning. The rest of the trip is not a trail, but rather an effort to follow the river. Depending on recent rainfall, you could end up crossing the river seven to 15 times to reach more manageable, dry paths. Never wander far from the river, but follow it for 2km until you reach the first waterfall. The trail isn't marked, but it is easy to follow. You may get soaked, so dress accordingly. The waterfall at the end provides luxurious bathing. A second waterfall, 1km farther, is off-limits without a guide.

SENDERO TEPEZCUINTLE. This is a tiny loop (1km, 45min.) through the woods near the ranger station. This trail offers the best views of Hitoy-Cerere's flora and fauna. It is a safe, well-lit, well-marked path, but watch out for the tiny, bright red frogs—they are poisonous, even to the touch.

SLIPPERY WHEN WET. A common anecdote about the Reserve is that the name in the indigenous language Cabécar means "fuzzy rocks" (Hitoy) and "clear water" (Cerere). Most of the hikes involve crossing the rivers over moss-covered rocks. However, this beautiful feature can also be a major safety hazard, especially since wet moss makes for slippery crossings. Normally, the first segment of the river reaches knee level, but common thunderstorms can fill the river to neck level. Be sure to ask the rangers about recent rainfall. Always cross the river by crab-walking and facing against the current. Swimming against the current is impossible. Bring a machete for trail underbrush and a bamboo stick that is your height to measure the depth of waters before crossing. Long pants and boots are important when hiking in the jungle areas. The Sendero Catarata also requires significant sun protection, since the nearby forest offers little shade.

PUERTO VIEJO DE TALAMANCA

Life in Puerto Viejo combines the cosmopolitan air of cities like Puerto Limón and Heredia with the relaxed, calm pace of life that exemplifies the Caribbean Coast. A growing expat and local population dedicate their time to finding the best ways to relax; surfing, snorkeling, sunbathing, and just chilling are the main enticements here. Arguably the most Afro-Caribbean of Costa Rica's cities, Puerto Viejo has transformed itself in recent years into a tourist hub and one of the most affluent, commercially active towns on the coast. However, as the lingering sounds of reggae and ocean waves can attest, the city's affluence hasn't damaged the way of life at all; in Puerto Viejo, slower is better, relaxing is ideal, and the best place to be is the sunniest beach or the biggest breaks.

TRANSPORTATION

Buses: Buy bus tickets at the small MEPE office across from the basketball court (☎2750 0023) or on the bus. Buses head to: **Bribrí** (30min., 16 per day 6:30am-8:15pm, ¢360); **Limón** (1hr., 12 per day 6:30am-7:30pm, ¢830) via **Cahuita** (30min., ¢365); **Manzanillo** (30min.; 7, 7:30am, noon, 4:30, 7:30pm; ¢315) via **Punta Uva** (30min., ¢170); **San José** (4hr.; 7:30, 9, 11am, 4pm; ¢2545); the Panamanian border at **Sixaola** (1-1½hr., 12 per day 6:30am-8:15pm, ¢810).

Taxis: Though most of Puerto Viejo's attractions are within walking or biking distance of each other and bus service is fairly extensive, taxis are available in front of the bus stop. For private taxis, call OMP Private Transport Services (☎2750 0439 or 8827 4219 or 2750 0562) or Taxi Kale (☎8340 2338).

ORIENTATION AND PRACTICAL INFORMATION

The main road comes in from the west, crosses the bridge near an abandoned barge, and cuts through town before heading east to Manzanillo. The bus drops people off diagonally across from the ATEC office in the center of town.

Tourist Information: Many tour offices overstress the need for a guide; a more neutral source may be your hotel owner. You can also take your questions to the **Talamanca Association for Ecotourism and Conservation (ATEC;** ☎2750 0398; www.greencoast. com), in the center of town. This nonprofit organization was founded to promote local tourism while preserving the region's heritage and ecology. Offers tours of Yorkín, Shiroles, and Kékôldi Reserves with native guides (half-day tours start at US$25). Photocopy services (¢20 per page). Open M-Sa 8am-9pm, Su 10am-6pm.

Banks:

Banco de Costa Rica (☎2284 6600), 200m south of the bus stop. **24hr ATM.** Open M-F 8am-4pm, Sa 8am-noon. Cirrus/MC/V.

Los Almendros (☎2750 0235), around the block from ATEC. Exchanges US$ (1% commission) and cashes traveler's checks and money orders (2.5% commission for *colónes*, 5% for US$). Cash advances available on AmEx/MC/V with a passport (11% commission). Open daily 7am-6pm.

Comisariato Manuel León (☎2750 0422; fax 2750 0246), on the beach 1 block west and 2 blocks north of ATEC. Offers similar services at similar rates. Open M-Sa 8am-5pm, Su 8am-3pm.

Laundry: (☎2750 0360), 1 block west and 1 block south of ATEC. Wash US$3; dry US$3. Locals or long-term tourists often negotiate special rates. Open M-Sa 9am-7pm.

Police: (☎2750 0230, emergencies 911), 1 block east and 1 block north of ATEC facing the beach. Open 24hr.

Red Cross: The closest one is in Bribrí (☎2751 0008). There is also one in **Limón** (☎2758 0125 or 911; p. 358). English spoken at both. Both open 24hr.

Pharmacy: Farmacía Amigas (☎2750 0698), 200m west of ATEC, across from the post office. Open M-Sa 9am-noon and 1-6:45pm. AmEx/D/MC/V.

Medical Services: (☎2750 0079), next to Banco de Costa Rica. Open 24hr.

Telephones: ATEC offers international phone service. US$0.31 to North America; US$0.40 to Central America and Caribbean; US$0.56 to Europe, New Zealand, Australia, US$1 to other countries. **Real World Forest** (☎2750 0365), next to ATEC. Has international phone service for approx. the same rates as ATEC. Open daily 7am-9pm. There are pay phones right outside and more across from the MEPE ticket office.

Internet Access: Real World Forest and **ATEC** both have quick connections for ¢20 per min. **Puerto Viejo Tours** offers access for ¢1500 per hr.

Post Office: (☎2750 0698), 200m west of ATEC. Open M-F 8am-noon and 1-5:30pm.

ACCOMMODATIONS

Puerto Viejo offers every type of accommodation imaginable. Luxury lodges and resorts abound, but budget travelers will find plenty of options in the numerous *cabinas* in town and along the road toward Manzanillo.

Jacaranda Cabinas (☎2750 0069), 1 block west and 2 blocks south of ATEC. Bright yellow, hand-painted rooms, a cool veranda and lush gardens, and mosaic pathways greet weary travelers at this central hotel. Rooms are immaculate, with private hot-water baths, mosquito nets, and ceiling fans. Pricier rooms have patios with hammocks. Communal kitchen open 7am-9pm. Massages offered in the on-site pagoda (professional

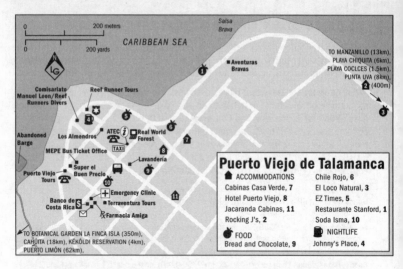

Puerto Viejo de Talamanca

🏠 ACCOMMODATIONS
Cabinas Casa Verde, **7**
Hotel Puerto Viejo, **8**
Jacaranda Cabinas, **11**
Rocking J's, **2**

Chile Rojo, **6**
El Loco Natural, **3**
EZ Times, **5**
Restaurante Stanford, **1**
Soda Isma, **10**

🍖 FOOD
Bread and Chocolate, **9**

🍸 NIGHTLIFE
Johnny's Place, **4**

reiki or *shiatsu* US$50 per hr.). Singles start at US$25; doubles US$32; triples US$35; quads US$40. Commission of 16% with credit card payment. AmEx/MC/V. ❷

Rocking J's (☎2750 0657; www.rockingjs.com), 800m east of town. Massive, occasionally overwhelming, and almost always cheap, Rocking J's attracts a crowd of surfers, spring-breakers, and tight-budget travelers in its sprawling complex of hammocks, tents, dorms, library, movie area, bar, restaurant, and grassy quad. Located right next to the beach, the hostel is perfect for travelers who can't bear to leave the surf or the party—just don't expect much quiet or privacy. Tent space US$4, with equipment rental US$6; hammocks US$5; *cabinas* US$7, with private bath US$20; treehouses US$60. ❶

Hotel Puerto Viejo (☎2750 0620; www.hotelpuertoviejocr.4t.com), 1 block east and ½ block south of ATEC. Popular with traveling *ticos*, Hotel Puerto Viejo offers cheap rooms in the center of town with bright communal baths. The hotel has free gated-in parking, and a massive communal kitchen and dining area. For more comfort and quiet, ask for a room with a fan, away from the communal spaces near the entrance. US$5-10 per person, depending on season and availability. ❶

Cabinas Casa Verde (☎2750 0015; www.cabinascasaverde.com). From ATEC, continue 1 block east on the main road and turn right, then turn left at the 1st street; the entrance gate is clearly marked. Though it's in the center of town, Cabinas Casa Verde has an air of idyllic relaxation, with a rock-rimmed pool, frog farm, and tropical garden nestled in between 4 groups of *cabinas*. Cheaper rooms have shared baths; pricier rooms have private baths and some have cable TV. All baths have hot-water. Singles US$32-60; doubles US$40-72; triples US$42-86; quads US$78-98. AmEx/D/MC/V. ❸

🍴 FOOD

Puerto Viejo is one of the Caribbean Coast's most popular destinations, and many visitors never manage to leave. The town's diversity is reflected in the abundance of dining options, from *rondón* to more exotic curries, pastas, and other fine cuisine. A supermarket, **Super el Buen Precio,** is opposite the bus stop, facing the beach. (☎2750 0060. Accepts payment in US$ and gives *colónes* in exchange for a decent rate. Open daily 6:30am-8:30pm. AmEx/MC/V.)

▨ **Chile Rojo** (☎2750 0250), currently located at the beginning of the road toward Manzanillo but moving within the year to a larger, 2-story location across from ATEC. The picnic tables fill up nightly for popular 2-for-1 happy hour specials, and stay full with guests enjoying delicious, well-presented Thai Green Curry with Coconut Milk (¢4800) and delectable "Death by Chocolate" brownies with homemade ice cream (¢1800). Happy hour 6-8pm in high season, 6pm-10pm in low season. 2 for ¢2000 fresh fruit daquiris and piña coladas. Open M-Tu and Th-Su 7:30am-10pm. Cash Only. ❷

▨ **El Loco Natural** (☎2750 0263), 400m east of town toward Rocking J's and Manzanillo. With a new, lounge-like location in a swath of trees just outside of town, El Loco Natural entices customers with delectable curries, entrancing music, and a relaxed ambience, with warm colors, Indian-style wall-hangings, mosaic floors, and multicolored mushroom-shaped paper lamps reminiscent of *Alice in Wonderland.* Curries ¢4000-6000. Calypso and reggae complete the relaxed atmosphere Th, Sa, and Su nights. Reservations recommended. Open daily 6-10pm, bar open until later. MC/V. ❸

Bread and Chocolate (☎2750 0733), just before Cabinas Jacaranda coming from the main street. The most happening breakfast spot in town, Bread and Chocolate serves up hearty dishes with homemade breads, jams, sauces, whipped cream, and, of course, chocolate. Its breakfast (¢1000-2600) and sandwich (¢2000-2800) menus are served all day; try the Cinnamon Oatmeal Pancakes (¢2300), the 3 types of ultra-rich chocolate cakes (¢1200-1500), or a fresh truffle (¢500). Pastries ¢600-900. Open W-Sa 6:30am-6:30pm, Su 6:30am-2:30pm. Cash only. ❷

EZ Times (☎2750 0663), 50m east and 50m north of ATEC. EZ Times is the local spot for live music from all over the world. Shows begin at 8 or 9pm, but guests show up earlier to the outdoor dining area, indoor bar, or open-air lounge area to enjoy tasty, unique dishes, like shrimp papaya salad with avocado (¢5500) and sandwiches on homemade focaccia with fresh fish (¢4400). The gourmet pizzas (¢2500-3500 plus ¢400-800 for toppings) are the most popular item on the menu. Open daily noon-1:30am. ❷

Soda Isma (☎2750 0738), 1 block west of ATEC on the main road, it's the open-air restaurant with the yellow balcony. Famous for its *rondón,* a dish made with fish in coconut sauce that must be ordered a day in advance (¢5000 per person). Spur-of-the-moment types feast on delicious coconut bread (¢100), tiny sandwiches (¢850), tasty *gallo pinto* (¢950), or *casados* (¢1200-3500). Open M and W-Su 7:30am-9pm. ❷

▨ NIGHTLIFE

Widely considered the reggae capital of Costa Rica, Puerto Viejo is pretty chilled out at night, especially in low season, with the majority of visitors and locals relaxing at open-air bars and restaurants or listening to live music at EZ Times. Those looking for a bit more dancing fun can head over to **Johnny's Place,** on the water 200m north of ATEC, where tourists and locals hit up the open-air dance floor, grooving to reggae (M and F), world music (Tu), hip-hop (W), and mixed favorites (Sa). The party often spills off the dance floor onto the sand. (☎8832 0971. Mixed drinks US$5. Open daily 1pm-3:30am or later.) **Restaurante Stanford's,** 200m east of ATEC on the main road, may look like a laid-back *marisquería,* serving up international fusion cuisine (US$5-20) by day, but at night it is transformed into the rocking Discoteca Stanford. The two-story complex has an upstairs patio area, strobe-lighted dance floor, and outdoor lounge area on the sand with music videos playing on a projector screen. The dance floor stays quiet in low season but fills up during busier times of year. (☎2750 0016. Open daily noon-midnight or later. AmEx/MC/V.)

SIGHTS

FINCA LA ISLA'S BOTANICAL GARDEN. A 20min. walk west of town (look for the sign that says "Pan Dulce"), Finca La Isla's Botanical Garden is an abandoned cacao plantation that has been transformed into a working tropical farm. Tours focus on education on spices (black pepper and cinnamon, among others), herbs, and medicines that are produced on the farm. Organic permaculture is stressed. Tours last 2hr. and end with juice and fruit samples. Labels help those without a guide, but the information provided in the tour, along with the complimentary samples, make a guided visit a better option. (☎2750 0046. *Open M and F-Su 10am-4pm. US$5, with 2hr. guided tour US$10.*)

RESERVA INDÍGENA COCLES/KÉKÔLDI. The majority of Costa Rica's indigenous population resides on reservations throughout this region. The most accessible is the Reserva Indígena Cocles/Kékôldi, 4km west of Puerto Viejo. Established in 1977, it is home to approximately 40 Bribrí and Cabécar families. You must have an authorized guide, available through ATEC, Puerto Viejo Tours, and Terraventuras. The ATEC guides are members of the reservation. Tours include a hike on ancient trails through old cacao plantations, secondary forests, and farms. Tours concentrate more on nature than culture to create privacy and respect between the community and tourists. At the entrance to the reservation is the Iguana Farm, a project begun by two Bribrí women to bolster the reservation's declining iguana population. A guide is not necessary to visit the farm. (*Take the bus to Bribrí and ask the driver to let you off at the "Abastecedor El Cruce," 4km from Puerto Viejo. 5-10min., ₡335. To get back, catch one of the buses that pass the Abastecedor every hr. ATEC advises that you stop by their office first to get more up-to-date and specific directions before making the trip. 1-day trips US$45-65.*)

OUTDOOR ACTIVITIES AND GUIDED TOURS

Most surfers head straight over to **La Salsa Brava** ("Angry Sauce"), an extraordinary surf-hole east of the village where waves break over a coral reef. However, if you're less experienced with a board and averse to getting drilled into coral, **Beach Break** is a 15min. walk east along the beach, where comparable waves break on soft sand. **Playa Cocles,** one of the most popular surfing spots in the Caribbean, lies 1.5km southeast of town and is immediately recognizable by the rocky, tree-covered *islita* that lies just 30m off shore. Its long, tall waves are most popular with the highly skilled local crowd. **Playa Chiquita,** 6km southeast of town, is another exciting surfing destination.

ATEC (p. 385) offers tours similar to those offered by Terraventuras and Puerto Viejo Tours, but it specializes in trips guided by members of local communities, especially to the indigenous reservations around Puerto Viejo (½-day US$25-45), hiking trips to Punta Uva (US$20), and leatherback turtle-watching tours in Gandoca (prices vary).

Terraventuras (☎2750 0750; www.terraventuras.com), 150m west of ATEC. Offers guided snorkeling in Parque Nacional Cahuita (US$35). Also offers a hiking tour of Gandoca-Manzanillo Wildlife Refuge (US$65), walking and canopy tours of the Kékôldi and Talamanca Bribrí Indian reserves (US$60), and trips to Tortuguero (US$135-190). All tours include transportation and fruit. Arranges for car rentals (US$40-70 per day, basic insurance included). Open M-Sa 8am-7pm. AmEx/D/MC/V.

Aventuras Bravas (☎2750 2000; www.costa-rica-adventure.net), in front of Stanford's. Rents surf and boogie boards and ocean kayaks (full day US$15). John Wheatley of Aventuras offers surf lessons (US$40) proclaiming that you'll stand up by the end of the lesson. John and his staff offer tours, including a sunset kayak tour when the waters are calm (US$25), and whitewater rafting (starting at US$65). Open daily 8am-7pm.

Puerto Viejo Tours (☎/fax 2750 0440), across from the bus stop. Offers informal tours similar to Terraventuras's. Surfing (US$45 per person), dolphin-watching trips (US$60 per person), and tropical birdwatching (US$55 per person). They can also arrange car rentals (starting at US$40 per day, basic insurance included) and trips through the forest on ATVs (call for prices). Internet access ¢1500 per hr. Open daily 8am-8pm.

Reef Runner Divers (☎/fax 2750 0480 or 2879 1537), 1 block west and 2 blocks north of ATEC. The biggest scuba company around. Offers PADI certification courses (US$325) and diving excursions to the Gandoca-Manzanillo Refuge. All dives include full equipment, guide, boat, fruit, and beverages. 2hr. excursions US$70. Night dives start at US$45. 8% surcharge with credit card. Open daily 8am-6pm. AmEx/MC/V.

◤ DAYTRIP FROM PUERTO VIEJO

PUNTA UVA

Most visitors come on bike (30-40min., ¢1500-2500 per day from any bike shop in town), bus, or car (taxis ¢5000) from Puerto Viejo, though it is possible to walk the approx. 8km on the road or on the beach (2-3hr.). Any bus heading from Puerto Viejo to Manzanillo will stop in Punta Uva; catch a bus anywhere along the road heading south out of town (7, 7:30am, noon, 4:30, 7:30pm; return 5:15, 7:15, 8:45, 10:45am, 1, 5:30pm; ¢265). Ask the bus driver to let you off in Punta Uva.

The road from Puerto Viejo down to Manzanillo is lined with beaches, resort-style lodges, and palm trees with the occasional group of howler monkeys. However, while **Playa Cocles** (2km from Puerto Viejo) and **Playa Chiquita** (5km) are surfer-filled beaches with waves usually too big for safe swimming, Punta Uva remains an idyllic retreat, with calmer light-blue waters, winding beaches, and more palm trees than people. Though primarily a swimmer and sunbather hot spot, Punta Uva is also perfect for sea-kayaking and long-board surfing, or, on lazy days, admiring the beautiful view from a hammock in the trees.

Punta Uva itself consists of a couple of bars, some upscale lodges and *cabinas*, and one lightly-stocked *abastecedor* (small grocery). There are three paths to the beach. The first, closest to Puerto Viejo, is next to Selvin's Restaurant. The second is at the sign for Punta Uva Bar, and the final is past the Abastecedor, just in front of the Punta Uva bus stand. Though the first two paths are connected by

ONE LOVE, MANY BANDS

While Puerto Viejo is known year-round as the central reggae-party in Costa Rica, the atmosphere changes during each March and April for the annual South Caribbean Music Festival. Held at the Playa Chiquita Lodge, the festival has concerts on Friday and Saturday night with live reggae, classical, and calypso music from around the Caribbean coast.

Though the music itself is enough of an attraction for most visitors, the festival doesn't stop there. In true Caribbean tradition, you can also enjoy home-cooked Caribbean specialties at the open-air concerts, watch dance recitals of local and foreign groups, and join in workshops where local musicians teach kids and tourists to play Caribbean-style music.

With stellar music, great food, and a picturesque backdrop against the calm, palm-tree-dotted beaches of Puerto Viejo, the South Caribbean Music Festival is the epitome of the area's chilled-out lifestyle; a few days jamming to the relaxed beats and you may find yourself joining the dread-locked locals for a longer stay.

The South Caribbean Music Festival is held each year in March and April. Check with the Playa Chiquita Lodge (☎ 2750 0062 or 2750 0408; festival@playachiquitalodge.com) for more details.

beach, the third one is separated by the area's namesake **"Grape Point,"** a natural rock tunnel in a tiny peninsula that juts into the water.

There aren't a wide array of dining opportunities in Punta Uva, though Puerto Viejo is within easy reach. Bring as much food and water as you plan on using; the few restaurants and bars in town keep somewhat erratic hours and occasionally do not even open during scheduled hours.

MANZANILLO

Blessed with the rich jungles of the Gandoca-Manzanillo National Wildlife Refuge and sandy palm-tree-lined beaches, Manzanillo is a refuge from the comparatively bustling streets of Puerto Viejo. Unlike the other beaches between the two towns, Manzanillo has enough restaurants and accommodation options to keep more laid-back travelers occupied for more than a daytrip. It is famous for Maxi's Restaurant, known throughout the coast for its Caribbean food, and it also provides the small beachy town with a fun, social atmosphere.

TRANSPORTATION. Buses run daily from Puerto Viejo to Manzanillo (7, 7:30am, noon, 4:30, 7:30pm; returns 5am, 12:45, 5:15, 8:30pm; ¢590), passing by Punta Uva, Playa Cocles, and Playa Chiquita. Buses to Manzanillo leave from the front of the MEPE ticket office in Puerto Viejo. You can also take a **taxi** (¢4500), rent a **bike** (1hr.), or **walk** (3hr.) from Puerto Viejo. The walk along the beach, though lengthy, is gorgeous and peaceful. Check the tides before leaving as some of the beaches are almost entirely submerged at high tides.

ORIENTATION AND PRACTICAL INFORMATION. The local **MANT headquarters** is the green-and-yellow house on your left as you enter Manzanillo along the main street. The guides can provide details on the park and the preservation efforts inside the refuge (including dolphin and turtle projects often looking for volunteers). A little farther down the road on the right, facing the beach, is the bright-green **MINAE office.** (☎2759 9100 or 2754 2133. Open M-F 8am-4pm.) A map and history of the refuge are available with donation. Rangers have a few beds and baths for those who want to volunteer in the refuge assisting with park maintenance or performing research. The **police station** is in the blue building across from the MANT office. (Open 24hr.) **Public phones** are near Restaurant Maxi. Laundry services are at **La Lavendería Caribeña** (☎2759 9043), on the right just before you enter town, in a house labeled "Local Guide."

ACCOMMODATIONS. The most central, popular lodging spot in town is the newly redone **Cabinas Maxi ❶,** just to the right of Restaurante Maxi as you enter town. The simple row of cabins has modern, private hot-water baths and clean rooms with double beds and fans. (☎2759 9061. Singles ¢6000; doubles ¢9000. AmEx/D/MC/V.) Visitors looking for a more personal atmosphere outside of the hustle and bustle of Maxi's can head to **Faya Babi ❸,** 100m to the right from the end of the path next to Soda El Rinconcito. Its four rooms are nestled in the upstairs floor of the owners' house, with an open-air kitchen and lounge area. Rooms are compact but elegantly furnished with mosquito nets, fans, and private hot-water baths with mosaic-lined showers. (☎2759 9167. Doubles US$30; triples US$35. Cash only.) No camping is allowed on the beaches of Manzanillo. In the refuge itself, camping is allowed in designated areas. Camping varies by season, so be sure to speak to a ranger before heading in with a tent.

One of the most popular alternatives to hostels is ◪**Steve Brook's Organic Farm** in Punta Mona. Volunteers flock to this secluded destination to help with the farm work and learn about permaculture, a form of sustainable agriculture (the farm offers a 5-week permaculture certification course). Volunteers, who range from 18-year-old students to 60-year-old doctors, can stay for one week for US$125, food and lodging included, or one month for US$300. It is possible to hike to Punta Mona from Manzanillo (see below), but the farm also runs a boat to town and back upon request. (US$15 1-way. www.puntamona.org/)

🗋 FOOD. 🏠**Maxi's Restaurant ❸**, in the center of town at the end of the main street, is the uncontested social center of Manzanillo and is famous throughout the region for its large, delicious portions of Caribbean cooking. Decorated with banners of European soccer teams, Maxi's is usually full of locals and tourists alike enjoying the sea breeze and beautiful views from its patio overlooking the water. (☎2759 9073; restmaxis@racsa.co.cr. Rice and beans ¢2400-7500. Grilled entrees ¢2800-5950. Lobster specials ¢8250-27,500. Open daily 11am-10pm. AmEx/D/MC/V.) Some of the cheapest food in town is 50m down the side street from Aquamor at **Soda El Rinconcito Alegre ❶**, where owner Patricia serves up large portions of *casados* and rice and beans (both ¢1800-3000) on a cheery red, yellow, and green-painted patio. (☎2759 9104. Breakfast ¢700-1500. Open daily 6am-8pm.) For groceries, **Mini Abastecedor Más X Menos** is on the main road 100m past the house labeled "Local Guide." (☎2759 9021 or 2759 9050. Open M-Sa 7am-noon and 2-7pm, Su 8am-noon and 5-6pm.)

⊙ SIGHTS. The main reason to come to Manzanillo is to visit the breathtaking **Refugio Nacional Gandoca-Manzanillo.** A dense jungle trail stretches from the village, through the refuge, and all the way to Panama. Founded in 1985 to protect endangered flora and fauna, the refuge includes 5013 hectares of private and public land—65% of which is tropical rainforest—and 4436 hectares of ocean. The wetlands teem with crocodiles, alligators, sloths, pumas, and monkeys, while sandy beaches and fossil-lined coral caves offer gorgeous previews of the beauty beneath the water. Five different types of coral make this reef a particularly rewarding spot for underwater exploration. A red mangrove tree swamp, unique to the Costa Rican Caribbean coast and situated beside the Gandoca Lagoon, protects the only natural population of mangrove oysters on the coast. The lagoon is also home to the nearly extinct manatee. The waters off rocky 🏠**Punta Mona** are frequented by tucuxi, bottlenose, and Atlantic spotted dolphins. One of the only drawbacks of the refuge is that trails are not well-marked, and heavy rains make them difficult to maintain. Because of this, guides are mandatory for hiking in the refuge. MANT provides some of the best guide services, with local guides who are very familiar with the area.

📷 GUIDED TOURS. **Guías MANT** (☎2759 9064, guiasmant@yahoo.com.mx) is composed of MINAE-certified guides who are native to Manzanillo and have formed a coalition uniting their profession and their devotion to conserving land in the region. A portion of their earnings goes toward supporting local farmers in order to minimize agricultural expansion and deforestation. The MANT office is on the left as you come into town, but if it is closed, the staff at Aquamor can give information about different tour options. The guides give various tours, including hikes, turtle-watching, night walks, horseback rides, snorkeling, and just about any other adventure a traveler might want to tackle in the refuge. (Most tours US$15-45 per person. Hiking tour in Manzanillo refuge US$35. Dolphin tour US$40. Sportfishing US$350-400 for 2 people.)

If you want to explore the park from the water, check with the watersports shop **Aquamor,** the last right off the main road before Maxi's. The main dive

BEACH PATROL

While most visitors to the sandy beaches of southeastern Costa Rica come for the surfing, swimming, and snorkeling, a new organization in the seaside town of Gandoca is drawing tourists in for another reason. Volunteers at the **ANAI Sea Turtle Project** participate in nightly patrols of the beach, like volunteers in Parismina (see **Turtle-Watch,** p. 365), but they are also involved in a bigger project: tagging turtles, relocating nests, and aiding baby turtles in their trip from the hatchery.

The project accepts volunteers from February to August, who work 4hr. shifts each night (8pm-midnight or midnight-4am) on the beach, patrolling for turtles. During the day, volunteers can help in the hatchery or enjoy the beaches and Gandoca/Manzanillo Refuge. The minimum stay for volunteers is 1 week, and the organization has particular need for individuals with backgrounds in first aid, biology, statistics, organic chemistry, hiking, and environmental science. Volunteers live in homestays (US$15 per day, includes room and board), at field station dorms (US$15 per day, solar panel electricity only), or in campsites around the village (US$8-10 per night, covered campsite, dish use, and well water included). There is an inscription fee of US$35.

For more information on the project and logistics of getting involved, check out www.anaicr. org or call ☎2224 3570.

school of the Gandoca marine refuge, it also rents kayaks and snorkeling gear and offers diving and dolphin observation excursions. (☎2759 9012; www.aquamor.com. Kayaks US$6 per hr., with guide US$25 per hr. Snorkel gear US$5 per hr., with guide US$16-45. Dolphin tours US$40 per person, group discounts available. Open daily 8:30am-8pm.) All guides in the area are associated with MANT and Aquamor, so prices are fairly consistent.

Aquamor also serves as a coral reef educational center and helped start the **Talamanca Dolphin Foundation,** an organization that hosts volunteers who aid in investigations and help protect the precious dolphins and their ecosystem. The organization sponsors eco-friendly dolphin tours through Aquamor. Get in touch with Aquamor for information on how to volunteer for the TDF or contact them directly. (☎2759 0715 or 2759 0612; www.dolphinlink.org.)

SIXAOLA

This small, dusty border town serves as little more than a stop to or from Panama (see "Border with Panama" p. 392). **Buses** let passengers off next to Soda el Buen Sabor, a small, blue building 25m off the main road. Buses from Sixaola head back to San José (6hr.; 7:30, 9, 10am, 3pm; ₡5000) and Limón (2hr.; every hr., 6am-7pm; ₡2300) via Puerto Viejo. Passengers leaving Sixaola may need to show their papers, so don't put your passport away just yet.

There are a limited number of services in town. **Ferratería California** changes US dollars to *colónes* at a decent rate. (☎2754 2030. Open daily 7am-10pm.) The nearest bank is in the town of Bribrí. The Costa Rican **police station** sits opposite the migration office. (☎2754 2160. Open 24hr.) **Telephones** are just before the bridge on the left-hand side of the tracks.

Few travelers spend the night in Sixaola, but if you do stay there, you can head to **Cabinas Sanchez ❶**. From Soda el Buen Sabor, walk toward the bridge, turn right for 20m, go through the tunnel, and head straight for another 100m. It is an orange building with barred windows on your right. Though a walk from immigration, this small *hospedaje* has many amenities, such as TVs, private cold-water baths, and fans. (☎2754 2126. ₡6000 for singles and doubles.) **Soda El Buen Sabor ❶** will make you a *casado* for ₡1500. (Open daily 5am-6pm.)

☒ SIXAOLA: BORDER WITH PANAMA

The Panamanian side of the border in **Guabito** (p. 393) is open daily 8am-6pm (☎2759 7019). The

Costa Rican side, in **Sixaola** (p. 392), is open daily 7am-5pm (☎2754 2044), but because of the time zone difference, both places are always open at the same time. The Panamanian side of the border closes each day for lunch; the Costa Rican side closes for lunch on weekends only (noon-12:30 or 1pm). To enter Panama from Costa Rica, visitors fill out a Central American entry card at the Costa Rican border indicating their intention to enter Panama. The border guard at the office will take this card, stamp the passport, and you can continue on across the rickety wooden bridge, being sure to avoid the holes in the wooden planks on the old railroad track. On the other side of the bridge, there are two Panamanian entry offices. All visitors must pass through the long, slow-moving line of the first office, where passports are stamped. However, travelers from most countries will have to pay a tourist tax (US$5) at the second office and then get a ticket stamped at the first office again. To avoid standing in this office's long lines twice, head to the tourist tax office first to pick up a ticket before getting in line to have your passport stamped. Travelers from the UK do not have to pay the tourist tax. Visitors from South Africa need a special visa to enter Panama; make sure to get one before entering Costa Rica as there is no South African embassy in Costa Rica. To enter Costa Rica from Panama, be prepared to show proof of finanical independence (about US$500 will suffice) and a ticket or itinerary showing how you plan to leave the country. There is a US$5 entry tax to Costa Rica. Remember to get your passport stamped on the Panamanian side (the same line used to enter) before crossing the bridge. The Panamanian currency, the *balboa*, is directly linked to the US dollar (and effectively is the dollar). US bills are quite often used, though Panama mints its own coins. Panamanian telephone numbers are preceded by the code 507, and most cell phone numbers are preceded by a 6.

BOCAS DEL TORO, PANAMA

White-sand beaches, jungle-filled coastlines, light-blue waves, and rainbow-colored coral reefs draw hordes of tourists to the Bocas del Toro archipelago in northeastern Panama. Just a couple hours from the Costa Rican border, Bocas is just now starting to become a major tourist destination. However, while the streets of Bocas Town are now paved and lined with expat-owned hotels and restaurants, Isla Bastimentos retains its authentic, small-town feel alongside its diversity of natural attractions. Boats speed between the islands throughout the day, enabling tourists to island-hop between beaches, diving spots, and nightlife options. However, despite the influx of tourists, the long, picturesque beaches remain relatively empty, creating the illusion of a secluded paradise while only minutes away from the amenities of a relatively large town.

Getting to Bocas del Toro from Costa Rica is simple. After crossing the border into Guabito, take a bus to Changuinola and, from there, a boat to Bocas.

GUABITO

For those entering Panama, the first stop will be Guabito, though it will probably be a brief one. **Buses** run from Guabito to Changuinola every hour or less (40min., US$0.80) until about 7pm, leaving from the Super Guabito, on your right as you enter the town. Collective **taxis** leave from the Soda el Amanecer, on the left side of the crossing, for the docks at Changuinola (US$5 per person) and Almirante (US$3 per person). Special taxis leave for Almirante from Restaurante La Fortuna, next to Super Guabito, but charge US$10 per person.

A single telephone sits in front of the Aduanas (customs), next to the migration offices. The migration offices are across the street from national **police** posts (☎507 759 7940, emergency 104), which are connected to one another by a decrepit bridge. Guabito has no accommodations and just a few *sodas*, and most visitors simply pass through on their way to other destinations. **Restaurante Fortuna ❶** and **Soda el Amanecer** (formerly Kiosco Dalys) ❶, just across the bridge from Costa Rica in Guabito, both serve *comida corriente* (US$2.50). Fortuna is open daily 7:30am-10pm and Amanecer is open daily 5am-8pm.

CHANGUINOLA

Changuinola has some services and accommodations, but most don't stay except to change buses or planes, as the real destinations are farther along. Changuinola has a number of hotels, but, as most Bocas-bound visitors pass quickly through without stopping, few of the local accommodations are geared toward tourists. The best option is **Hotel Golden Sahara ❸**, 350m north of the Shell, which offers clean, central rooms with TV, A/C, fridges, and private hot-water baths. (☎507 758 7908 or 507 758 7910; hotelgoldensahara@yahoo.com. Single or double US$32; triple or quad US$45.) The main street is lined with *sodas* and pizzerias. Those seeking respite from the chaos of the town should head 100m north of Hotel Golden Sahara to the cool, dark interior of **Steak Mar ❷**, a Chinese restaurant with one of the biggest menus in town. (☎507 758 9057. Chow mein US$4-5, entrees US$5-11. Open daily 11am-11pm. MC/V.)

The town is about 10min. from the Changuinola Finca docks and about 30min. from the Almirante docks. Sincotavecop Gran Terminal de Transporte, next to the Shell station in the center of town, handles short-distance travel by bus and taxi. **Buses** leave daily for Almirante (every 15-30min. 5am-9pm, US$1.20); Guabito (every 25min. 5am-9pm, US$0.80); San José via Puerto Limón (9hr., daily 10am, US$10); and a variety of local destinations in Panama. Buy your ticket on the bus. **Taxis** leave from the bus station to the docks (7min., US$2), where you can catch a **boat** to Bocas. **Bocas Marine and Tours** (☎507 757 9033) makes the scenic 45min. boat trip to Bocas (every 1hr. 8am-5:30pm, return 7, 9:30, 11am, 1, 2:30, 4, 5:30pm; US$7). It is possible to take a bus to Almirante and then from there a shorter boat ride to Bocas. **Bocas Marine and Taxi 25** (☎507 757 9028) makes this trip (every 30min. 6am-7pm or whenever the boat is full, US$4), though the trip is a bit longer and costs US$2 more than the Changuinola route. Collective taxis are parked under specific destination signs. Changuinola's main street is flooded with public taxis which will take you to Changuinola and Guabito (40min., US$2) or to Almirante (45min., US$5).

Facing the Shell station, north is to your left. There is a **Banco Nacional de Panama** with a **24hr. ATM** 200m south of the station on the main road. (☎507 758 0445. Open M-F 8am-3pm, Sa 9am-noon.) **El Centro Deportivo del Cid,** 100m north of the Shell station, has a Western Union. (☎507 758 9635. Open M-Sa 8:30am-12:30pm and 1:30-5:30pm.) **Farmacia Universal** is 100m south of the Shell station. (☎507 758 8888. Open daily 7am-11pm. MC/V.) **The Centro Medico Dental Los Angeles,** near the pharmacy, provides medical care. (☎507 758 8008. Open M-Sa 8:30am-midnight.) **Internet Oriente,** 200m north of the Shell on the left, offers Internet access. (☎507 758 5341. US$1.50 per hr. Open M-Sa 9am-9:30pm.)

ALMIRANTE

From the terminal, **buses** leave for Changuinola (30min., every 30min. 6am-9pm, US$1.40). Two **water taxi** companies, Taxis 25 (☎507 758 3498) and Taxis Marítimos (☎507 758 4085), take passengers to Bocas del Toro (30min., every hr. or less when boats are full 6am-6pm, US$4 each way). Walk 20m away from the bus terminal, make your first left down a small dirt path, and continue another 100m until you see the docks. Taxis Marítimos is the first building on the road and Taxis 25 is another 40m beyond that. A ferry also leaves from the opposite side of town (M-Sa), but the hour of departure varies greatly.

ISLA COLÓN AND BOCAS TOWN

The cosmopolitan face of Bocas del Toro, Bocas Town flits between small-town easy living and fast-paced, expat-fueled development. It has the most extensive nightlife, restaurants, and paved roads of the islands' towns, and most amenities are located within blocks of the docks. Farther away from the main street, Bocas becomes residential, with the houses eventually giving way to beaches, caves, and excellent spots for watersports. While some visitors are turned off by the obvious presence of tourists in Bocas Town, the reasonable accommodation prices and easy access to other islands continue to lure in travelers.

▐ TRANSPORTATION

Water Taxis: Bocas Marine and Tours (☎507 757 9033), next to El Pirate in the middle of C. 3. Runs boats to **Changuinola** (7, 9:30, 11am, 1, 2:30, 4, 5:30pm; US$7, US$3 extra for surfboards). **Bocas Marine and Taxis 25** (☎507 757 9028; www.bocasmarinetours.com), next to the police station on C. 1. Boats leave whenever they are full. Both run water taxis to **Almirante** (every 30min. 6am-6:30pm, US$4 1-way).

Ferry: Makes the trip from Almirante to **Bocas** and back M-Sa, once per day, departing from the southern end of the island closest to C.3. The hour of departure varies greatly.

Local Boats: Locals with boats hang out at the public docks south of the police station or at the pier next to Le Pirate on C. 3 (especially in the morning). Prices to different locations in the archipelago are negotiable (usually US$2-5), although the price to **Old Bank** on **Isla Bastimentos** is set (US$2.50).

▐ ▐ ORIENTATION AND PRACTICAL INFORMATION

Tiny Bocas town is laid out in an L-shaped grid; lettered *avenidas* run east-west and numbered *calles* run north-south. With the docks at your back, north is to the right and south is to the left. Just about everything is on C. 3, the main street, or on C. 1, which branches off to the right of C. 3 about 100m south of the *parque*. Water cuts across the grid from C. 3 at the southern end of town to C. 1 at the eastern end. The *parque* lies between Av. D and F and C. 2 and 3. Av. G, at the northern end of town, is the only road that leads out to the rest of the island. Billboard maps are posted around town, including in front of the IPAT office, though maps for sale are hard to find.

Tourist Office: IPAT (☎507 757 9642; www.ipat.gob.pa), near the police station, on the 2nd fl. of a yellow house on C. 1. labeled "tourist info." Has an exhibit on the history and ecology of Bocas del Toro. Friendly staff answers questions. Open M-F 8:30am-4:30pm. **ANAM** (☎507 757 9244; www.anam.gob.pa), on C. 1 north of the police station. Offers info and permits to Parque Nacional Isla Bastimentos. Open M-F 8am-4pm.

Immigration: (☎507 757 9263), in the government building north of the *parque*. Open M-F 9am-noon and 12:30-4pm.

Banks: Banco Nacional Panama, Av. F, C. 1/2, 1 block north and 1 block east of the *parque*. Cashes traveler's checks. **24hr. ATM.** Open M-F 8am-2pm, Sa 9am-noon. There is also an ATM next to the police station on C. 1.

Library: On C. 3, in the green-and-yellow building 100m north of the *parque*. Has slow but free Internet access. Open daily 8am-noon and 2-5pm.

Laundry: Mr. Pardo's Laundromat, across from Casa Max on Av. G, washes and dries clothes quickly for US$3 per load (he doesn't fold). Open daily 8am-9pm.

Police: (☎507 757 9217, emergency 104), on C. 1 by the water.

Hospital: (☎507 757 9201), on Av. H, a few blocks west of town. 24hr. emergency.

Internet Access: Bocas Internet Café (☎/fax 507 757 9390), on C. 3, 2 blocks south of the *parque*, has fast connections, lots of computers, A/C, and high prices. US$2 per hr. Open daily 8am-10pm. **Don Chicho Internet,** next to El Lorito, offers fewer computers but has Internet at a cheaper rate. US$1 per hr. Open daily 8am-9pm.

Post Office: In the sign-less, run-down-looking government building 30m north of the northeast corner of the *parque*. Open M-F, hours vary.

ACCOMMODATIONS

The popularity of Bocas town among budget travelers has resulted in an increase in high-quality budget options. The most popular hostels are often full, though, and if you are traveling in a group, it is best to reserve or call ahead to make sure space is available. Most hotels and *hospedajes* are on C. 3 or Av. G.

- **Mondo Taitú** (☎507 757 9425; www.mondotaitu.com), across from Casa Max on Av. G. The most social hostel in Bocas Town, Mondo Taitu fills up quickly with surfers, backpackers, and budget travelers who hit the waves by day and fill up the hostel's popular, relatively cheap bar by night. There is a lounge area, book exchange, kitchen, bar, and TV room downstairs, while the winding staircase leads upstairs to wooden rooms with large windows. Bathrooms are shared but clean, and the owners will shave their tree-logo onto your chest for free. The owners have another hostel on Av. G, next to El Lorito. While that one, **Hostel Heike,** has no private rooms or bar, it has a roof deck and balcony overlooking the main street and a quieter atmosphere. The prices are the same, and Heike also has a communal kitchen, lounge area, small book exchange, and hot-water bathrooms. Dorm-style rooms US$9; singles and doubles US$10 per person. ●

- **Hostel Hansi** (☎507 757 9085), on a side street between Starfleet Tours and IPAT off of C. 1. A well-maintained, cheery establishment named after the owner's cats. Its budget-priced rooms are a great deal for solo travelers looking for a private atmosphere. Each room comes with a ceiling fan, hot-water bath, desk, chair, and colorful striped beds. Singles US$10, with bath US$15.40; doubles US$22. ●

- **Hostel Gran Kahuna** (☎507 757 9038; www.grankahunabocas.com), on C. 3, 50m left of the docks. The newest hostel in Bocas, Gran Kahuna has a central location but a little less of a party atmosphere than the other hostels in town. However, its airy common room with hammocks and a big-screen TV is perfect for a relaxing afternoon and evening. The rooms are pleasant as well, with high ceilings and huge windows that let in the breeze. Kahuna also has free Wi-Fi, 15min. of free computer use at check-in, a communal kitchen, and discounts on drinks at local bar La Iguana. US$5 deposit for blanket, towel, and locker key. Dorms US$10. Cash only. ●

- **Hotel Las Brisas** (☎507 757 9549; www.brisasboca.com), where C. 3 dead ends in Av. G. Though the rooms are a bit drab, they are filled with extensive amenities. Rooms have A/C, cable TV, and private hot-water baths. More expensive rooms are larger, and the there are 2 suites with kitchens, living rooms, and balconies (6-person suite US$80, 10-person suite US$175). Doubles US$22-40; triples/quads US$30-60. ●

- **Casa Max** (☎507 757 9120), on Av. G, 50m west of C. 3. A budget hotel with the friendly, social atmosphere of a hostel. Enjoy the on-site restaurant, lounge area with TV, and a hammock-filled yard, all while indulging in the privacy of double rooms with fans and private hot-water baths. More expensive rooms are larger and have private balconies. Breakfast US$2.50-5. Doubles US$30-35. Discounts for longer stays. D/MC/V. ●

FOOD

The main street of Bocas is lined with cheap *sodas* and moderately pricey restaurants with international cuisine. Luckily, there are high-quality options in both categories, so delicious food is possible whatever your budget. There are several supermarkets on C. 3, and most are open daily until midnight. There are fruit and vegetable markets along the main street with dirt-cheap prices; just make sure to wash, cook, or peel all produce, as the water in Bocas is not clean and most places do not have filters for their water.

▨ **El Chitre,** on C.3, 1 block south of the *parque.* Favored by locals and tourists alike. Serves up heaping portions of delicious *bocatareño* food in a small cafe-style dining area, and amazing smells waft from the food line. The low prices make even full stomachs hungry for more. Meat, salad, and rice US$3-4. Open M-Sa 6am-9pm. ❶

▨ **Om Café** (☎507 603 3591), at the intersection of Av. G and C. 4. This family-owned Indian restaurant conjures up delicious curries (US$7-10) and breakfast specialties (US$2.50-7) in a calm, breezy upstairs patio. With veggie options and Indian versions of American breakfast specialties, Om has something for everyone at some of the most reasonable prices in town. Open M-Tu and Th-Su 8am-noon and 6-10pm. ❷

Lemongrass (☎507 757 9630), upstairs from Starfleet Scuba (p. 397). Beautiful sea views, red drapes, and an eclectic music selection greet visitors at this high-class restaurant with some of the best food in Bocas Town. The inventive, tasty Asian fusion cuisine is enhanced by constantly changing specials and a nightly happy hour 5-7pm. Appetizers US$4-6. Entrees US$8-12. Open daily noon-3pm and 6-10pm. ❸

El Lorito, on C. 3 across from the *parque.* This fast food hangout, popular with locals, offers cheap, quick *comida corriente* in a good location. *Casados* with beans, rice, and choice of meat (US$2.50-3). Big breakfasts US$2-3. Open daily 6:30am-midnight. ❶

The Reef (☎507 647 5302), on a polished wooden pier at the southern end of C. 3. One of the few places left in Bocas Town to get tasty *bocatareño* food. Excellent seafood meals accompanied by rice, potatoes, or *patacones* are US$4.50-7. After 8pm or so, the restaurant shifts into bar mode. Open daily 7am-11pm. ❷

◖ NIGHTLIFE

The bar scene, like everything in Bocas Town, swells substantially during the high season (especially around Christmas). But even rainy nights bring an amiable mix of locals, tourists, and expats out to the dock-side *cabañas* and comfortable pool halls. Things generally pick up around 9 or 10pm and run until 1 or 2am. Sunday nights are often quiet. One of the best places to party at night is ▨**Barco Hundido** (a.k.a **Wreck Bar**), on C. 1, near Taxi 25. This maze of ramps and open-air pavilions blasts hip hop and reggaeton until the crowd clears and occasionally has performances by local bands. (Beers US$1-2.50. Mixed drinks US$3-4. Open daily 8am-12:30am, until 3am on weekends.) Near the end of C. 3, across from Hospedaje EYL, is **Bar El Encanto,** a dimly lit joint frequented by locals dancing to dance hall and *cumbia.* (Beer US$1-2.50. Open daily noon-3am.) The boys at **Mondo Taitú** (p. 396) have a bar where they serve up cheap mixed drinks (US$2) and a special happy hour every night of the week. (Happy hour 7am-8pm, ½-price drinks. Open until 12:30am or later.)

◖ ▨ WATERSPORTS AND OUTDOOR ACTIVITIES

With a local economy almost entirely dependent on tourism, nearly every hotel, restaurant, and shack offers some form of tour or rental. The listings here provide an overview of what's available from a few dependable businesses.

The best dive rental/tour operator is PADI-certified ▨**Starfleet Scuba,** on C. 1 where it curves east at the southern end of town. It is run by amiable English expat and diver expert, Tony Sanders. A two-tank dive is US$60, including boat and equipment, and a three- to four-day PADI certification course is US$250. Starfleet offers snorkel tours for US$20. (☎/fax 507 757 9630; www.starfleetscuba.com.) Dives vary depending on the time of year, time of day, and weather, although operators can tailor a trip to the conditions and your preferences.

Most dive shops rent snorkeling gear (US$5-8 per day) and offer tours (US$15-25, equipment included). Local boat owners by the **Le Pirate Bar** docks on C. 3 often offer cheaper rates than tour companies—try to bargain.

Equipment rentals are available for just about any outdoor activity that you can imagine. Always check rentals, especially bikes, for quality. Rent bikes at the stand at **Bocas Bikes** on the corner of C. 3 and Av. G (US$2 per hr., US$10 per day). Rent kayaks at **Bocas Water Sports** (US$3 per hr.). A few motorcycles (US$8 per hr.), dirt bikes, and surfboards (US$2 per hr.) can be rented on a patch of grass next to the handicrafts stands across from the *parque* on C. 3. Hostels Mondo Taitu and Heike rent surfboards as well (US$10-15 per day).

DAYTRIPS AND SIGHTS

From Bocas Town, Av. H leads west across a small isthmus to the main body of the island. From here, the road forks; the left side leads 15km through the island past **La Gruta** to **Boca del Drago,** and the right fork follows the eastern coast, passing **Big Creek, Punta Puss Head, Playa Paunch,** and **Playa Bluff.** Many of these beaches are infested with *chitres* (tiny sandflies with an irritating bite), especially in the late afternoon. Walking and biking are the cheapest transportation options around the island, but roads are alternately bumpy and muddy— bring sturdy shoes or a well-maintained bike, especially after rain.

EASTERN BEACHES. The best of these beaches is the relatively *chitre*-free **Playa Bluff.** The sand stretches almost 2km, with good surfing or casual swimming on more mellow days. Between March and September (especially June to July) the beach fills with sea turtles laying their eggs. Go to the **ANAM** office (see **Tourist Information,** p. 395) to arrange to see nesting turtles on the island's east coast. *(About 8km north of Bocas Town. Biking takes about 45min. Turtle trips depart at 8pm or midnight; call or stop by earlier in the day. Turtle tour US$10 per person.)*

LA GRUTA CAVE. A small cave filled with bats and bat guano, this sight is a 45min. bike ride from Bocas Town. If you want to do some amateur spelunking, make sure to bring a flashlight and good boots. (Open to the public.) La Gruta is also considered a religious shrine and is the site of an annual pilgrimage celebrating Nuestra Señora de la Gruta, La Virgen del Carmen. A torch-lit parade down C. 3 takes place every July 16 in celebration of the Virgin; the pilgrimage to her cave occurs the following Sunday.

ISLA BASTIMENTOS

While Bocas's paved roads and international restaurants are testament to its cosmopolitan air, Isla Bastimentos's simpler buildings, slower pace of life, and muddy beach trails reflect a different attraction altogether. With long stretches of isolated white-sand beaches, an indigenous Ngobe village, and Parque Nacional Marino Isla Bastimentos all in its territory, Bastimentos is laden with natural attractions and native culture. And, only 10min. from Bocas by water taxi, Bastimentos is perfectly positioned as a daytrip for Bocas residents or as a home base for those wishing to escape the constant party of Bocas Town.

OLD BANK

◼◫ ORIENTATION AND TRANSPORTATION. The village of Old Bank (a.k.a. Bastimentos) has no roads, only a semi-paved 1km path running along the water. With your back to the water, west is to the left. A park lies toward the western end of town, as do most of the docks, where you can catch **boats** to Bocas del Toro. The **police station** is near the park. They have no telephone, and communicate with the station in Bocas by walkie-talkie. The **Clínica** is farther to the west. (Open M-F 8am-4pm.)

Boats leave Bocas Town from the Taxi Marítimo pier next to Le Pirate and head to Old Bank (more frequent in the morning, 6am-6pm; US$2.50). To get back to Bocas, head back to the dock and wait for a boat to come by (usually 1 every 10min. or so). To reach Cayos Zapatillas on the other side of the island, your best bet is a tour operator. An equally good option is to ask around at the docks for a boat—independent operators are all over. Agree on a fare beforehand (approximately US$25).

⌂ ACCOMMODATIONS. All the accommodations in town are budget, although facilities vary widely. Up a hill just right of the docks is the cheery **Hostal Bastimentos ❶,** which offers the most backpacker-style accommodations on Bastimentos, with cold-water baths, great views of the water and town, and a "Chill-Out Bar" with hammocks and a big TV. (☎507 757 9053. Free kitchen access. Singles US$12; doubles US$18, with bath US$30.) **Hotel Caribbean View ❹** offers the most luxurious accommodations in Old Bank. Victorian style architecture, dark-wood furniture, and the most amenities in Bastimentos. Rooms have A/C, TV, and private hot-water baths, and upstairs rooms have balconies. (☎507 757 9442; hotelcaribbeanview@yahoo.com. Doubles US$62; triples US$77.)

⬚ FOOD. When it comes to restaurants, what Old Bank lacks in variety, it makes up for in quality. **Alvin Kecha ❷,** a few blocks west of the main docks, is perhaps the best deal for hungry visitors to the island, with tremendous savory portions of *bocatareño* fare (US$3-7) on a small deck with colorful tables and chairs. (☎6700 6109 or 6517 7053. Open daily 4am-9:30pm.) A few blocks west of the docks is locally owned **Restaurante Roots ❸,** where guests sit on tree-trunk chairs in the open-air patio enjoying seafood dishes US $6-17. All food

ON THE MENU

LOCO FOR COCO

According to acclaimed chef Miss Edith (see **Cahuita: Food,** p. 379), Caribbean cuisine in a nutshell is "anything with coconuts." Miss Edith has been serving Caribbean delights in Cahuita for 37 years and regularly teaches a popular Caribbean culinary class.

At her classes, Miss Edith teaches beginners how to cook the basics; fish and vegetables with coconut ingredients. According to her, it takes an intermediate student to perfect rice and beans in coconut milk, and only advanced students can prepare the pinnacle of Caribbean cuisine: *rondón,* roots, vegetables, plantains, and meat in coconut milk. To prepare it, chefs simmer the basic ingredients for several hours in the milk, letting it all "run down" in a big pot. Most chefs request a half-day's notice to prepare. Be wary of restaurants that claim to serve *rondón* immediately upon request; this is usually less tasty and more watery than the authentic variety. There's one more ingredient in Miss Edith's *rondón* that she wouldn't reveal to Let's Go, but she promises to let visitors know if they come to class on time.

To participate in one of Miss Edith's classes, drop by her restaurant in Cahuita or call ☎ 2755 0248. She prefers small groups, and offers 3hr. classes for beginners for US$20-30, including the cost of ingredients.

is served to the tune of reggae music. (☎6491 5494. Open daily 11:30am-11pm.)

BEACHES. The island's beautiful beaches are connected by a series of trails along the northern and eastern coast. To get to **Wizard's Beach,** take the path (marked with a sign for "Wizard") that branches inland near the eastern end of Old Bank's main cement path and proceed for 20min.; after rain, it might be worth taking a boat (US$2) to avoid a 30min. walk through mud. If you do walk after rain, be aware that the mud here is mixed with clay and will not come out of clothing, so wear something you don't mind getting tinted red. Beware: extremely strong currents make swimming dangerous. The next beach to the east is **Playa Segunda,** also known as **Red Frog Beach** for the little red frogs that are found only here (the frogs are harder to spot on sunny days). This is a favorite tourist destination, and it has good surfing during the dry season.

A popular beach farther down is **Polo's Beach,** one of the best beaches in the entire archipelago. The sole inhabitant of Polo's is Don Polo, an amiable hermit who's lived there for over 40 years. He'll let you camp on his land for US$10 per day, with three meals included (if you don't mind eating grilled iguana and bush rat, among more traditional seafood). There are no services, but that's part of the charm. Don Polo is famous around Bocas (he was even featured on *Wild on E!*), so any boat will know how to get there (approximately US$15-20).

At the opposite end of the island from the town of Old Bank lies **Punta Vieja,** a secluded beach that offers astonishingly clear water and great snorkeling. Not only do many turtles nest here during the night, but there is an awesome reef right out front and the Ngöbe village of **Salt Creek** is nearby. Many tour operators in Bocas Town run tours to both the reef and Salt Creek (US$15-25).

PARQUE NACIONAL MARINO ISLA BASTIMENTOS

After a 3hr. hike along the beach and trails from Old Bank, you'll reach the spectacular 14km **Playa Larga,** an important turtle-nesting site. The beach has a ranger station and an entrance to Parque Nacional Marino Isla, which protects Playa Larga, the interior of Isla Bastimentos, the extensive mangrove swamps on the island's western side, and the two **Cayos Zapatillas** farther out in the ocean to the southeast, accessible only by boat. (Negotiate at the docks next to El Pirate. Approximately US$15-20 per person or US$60-80 for a whole boat.) Volunteers can work on the island tagging the leatherback turtles and taking care of the eggs until they hatch. (Contact Clara at ☎507 6584 2451; turtlevolpanama@yahoo.com. US$140 per week; includes food, accommodations, transportation, and a valuable donation to the project.)

TRAIL MIX. Though the trails on Bastimentos are not too difficult to hike, they are not very well-marked and can occasionally be confusing. To avoid getting lost on the trails, check with locals before heading out to ask for directions, and always hike in pairs or groups on the first trip through.

The inland forest on Isla Bastimentos is home to fantastic wildlife, and the southernmost of the two Cayos Zapatillas has a forest trail that leads to beaches and underwater caves. The ranger stations on the island and on the southern Cayo Zapatillas both have simple *refugios* and allow camping. There are no facilities; bring everything you need, including mosquito nets and a water purifier. Before heading to the park, you have to get permission from ANAM in

Bocas Town (see **Tourist Information,** p. 395) and pay an entrance fee. They can ensure that rangers will be there. Park rangers guide for free, although a tip is expected. (Camping US$5 per person. Park admission US$10.)

OTHER ISLANDS

ISLA CARENERO

For an island only a few hundred meters off the east docks of Bocas Town, Isla Carenero is remarkably undeveloped and untouristed. Its residents, many of them of Ngöbe origin, survive on subsistence farming and fishing. Just a handful of relatively upscale hotels and restaurants line an otherwise vacant and peaceful shoreline. There is one great budget accommodation option in Carenero; **Aqua Lounge ❶,** 50m south of the docks, has sundecks, a massive water trampoline, and some of the longest happy hours in Bocas Del Toro (daily noon-7pm). Reasonably priced dorm rooms (US$10 per night) include a free breakfast. To explore these relatively empty beaches, take a water taxi from Bocas (US$0.75). To get back, flag down a boat returning to Bocas.

CAYO NANCY

Cayo Nancy is famous for **Hospital Point,** one of the best and most readily accessible snorkeling and scuba-diving spots around. You'll find a variety of rainbow-colored corals, some barely submerged, others 100 ft. deep down along a huge wall, and a staggering variety of reef fish, spotted eels, and light-blue shrimp. You may even get to see one of the resident nurse sharks. Any boat can transport you, but the guides at Starfleet are more informed about changes in local ecology and visibility. If you decide to go with a boat, bring your own snorkeling gear. There are a few good places to snorkel in the protected waters between Bocas town, Isla Carenero, Isla Bastimentos, and Cayo Nancy. If you go by private boat, ask the driver to wait, because these are open-water sites.

APPENDIX

CLIMATE

Costa Rica has two seasons: summer and winter. The summer (also known as the dry season) is December through April and the winter (also known as the wet season) runs from May to November. Temperatures vary little by season, but significantly by altitude. San José and towns at higher elevations tend to be temperate and dry, while the coasts are hotter and more humid.

AVG. TEMP. (LOW/ HIGH), PRECIP.	JANUARY			APRIL			JULY			OCTOBER		
	°C	°F	mm	°C	°F	mm	°C	°F	mm	°C	°F	mm
Caribbean Lowlands	21/29	69/84	300	22/31	71/87	270	23/31	73/87	450	22/30	71/86	220
Northern Lowlands	19/27	66/80	120	23/30	73/86	75	24/31	75/87	400	22/30	71/86	425
San José and Central Valley	14/24	57/79	15	17/26	63/79	46	17/25	63/77	211	16/25	61/77	300
Northwestern Costa Rica	21/33	69/91	10	23/36	73/96	45	23/32	73/89	150	22/31	71/87	275
Central Pacific Coast	21/31	69/87	50	23/32	73/89	110	23/31	73/87	450	23/30	73/86	550
Southern Costa Rica	22/33	72/91	100	23/33	73/91	250	22/31	71/87	450	22/31	71/87	600

To convert from degrees Fahrenheit to degrees Celsius, subtract 32 and multiply by 5/9. To convert from Celsius to Fahrenheit, multiply by 9/5 and add 32.

°CELSIUS	-5	0	5	10	15	20	25	30	35	40
°FAHRENHEIT	23	32	41	50	59	68	77	86	95	104

MEASUREMENTS

Costa Rica uses the metric system. The basic unit of length is the **meter (m)**, which is divided into 100 **centimeters (cm)** or 1000 **millimeters (mm)**. One thousand meters make up one **kilometer (km)**. Fluids are measured in **liters (L)**, each divided into 1000 **milliliters (mL)**. A liter of pure water weighs one **kilogram (kg)**, the unit of mass that is divided into 1000 **grams (g)**. One metric **ton** is 1000kg.

MEASUREMENT CONVERSIONS	
1 inch (in.) = 25.4mm	1 millimeter (mm) = 0.039 in.
1 foot (ft.) = 0.305m	1 meter (m) = 3.28 ft.
1 yard (yd.) = 0.914m	1 meter (m) = 1.094 yd.
1 mile (mi.) = 1.609km	1 kilometer (km) = 0.621 mi.
1 ounce (oz.) = 28.35g	1 gram (g) = 0.035 oz.
1 pound (lb.) = 0.454kg	1 kilogram (kg) = 2.205 lb.
1 fluid ounce (fl. oz.) = 29.57mL	1 milliliter (mL) = 0.034 fl. oz.
1 gallon (gal.) = 3.785L	1 liter (L) = 0.264 gal.

LANGUAGE

Spanish is the official language of Costa Rica. While many *ticos* speak English, in more rural areas, Spanish will be the only language spoken. Despite Costa Rica's small size, there are still different dialects and indigenous languages spoken throughout the country.

PRONUNCIATION

Spanish pronunciation is very simple. Each vowel is pronounced only one way: **a** ("ah" in father); **e** ("e" in "convey"); **i** ("ee" in "beet"); **o** ("oh" in "tote"); **u** ("oo" in "boot"); **y**, by itself, is pronounced like the English "ee." Most consonants are pronounced the same as in English. Important exceptions are: **j** ("h" in "hello"), **ll** ("y" in "yes"); **ñ** ("ny" in "canyon"); **rr** (trilled "r"); **h** (always silent); **x** (either "h" when in the middle of a word or like in English when at the end). The letter **c** is pronounced like an English "s" before "soft vowels"—e and i—and like the English "k" before "hard vowels"—a, o, and u. **Z** sounds like the English "s."

By rule, the stress of a Spanish word falls on the second-to-last syllable if the word ends in a vowel, n, or s. If the word ends in any other consonant, the stress is on the last syllable. Any word in which the accent does not follow the rule carries an accent mark over the stressed syllable.

PHRASEBOOK

ESSENTIAL PHRASES

ENGLISH	SPANISH	PRONUNCIATION
Hello.	Hola.	OH-la
Goodbye.	Adiós.	ah-dee-OHS
Yes/No	Sí/No	SEE/NO
Please.	Por favor.	POHR fa-VOHR
Thank you.	Gracias.	GRA-see-ahs
You're welcome.	De nada.	DAY NAH-dah
Do you speak English?	¿Habla inglés?	AH-blah EEN-glace
I don't speak Spanish.	No hablo español.	NO AH-bloh ehs-pahn-YOHL
Excuse me.	Perdón.	pehr-DOHN
I don't know.	No sé.	NO SAY
Can you repeat that?	¿Puede repetirlo?	PWEH-day reh-peh-TEER-lo

YOUR ARRIVAL

ENGLISH	SPANISH	ENGLISH	SPANISH
I am from (the US/Europe).	Soy de (los Estados Unidos/Europa).	What's the problem, sir/madam?	¿Cuál es el problema, señor/señora?
Here is my passport.	Aquí está mi pasaporte.	I lost my passport.	Perdí mi pasaporte.
I will be here for less than six months.	Estaré aquí por menos de seis meses.	I have nothing to declare.	No tengo nada para declarar.
I don't know where that came from.	No sé de donde vino eso.	Please do not detain me.	Por favor no me detenga.
Where is customs?	¿Dónde está la aduana?	Where do I claim my luggage?	¿Dónde puedo reclamar mi equipaje?

DIRECTIONS

ENGLISH	SPANISH	ENGLISH	SPANISH
(to the) right	(a la) derecha	(to the) left	(a la) izquierda
next to	al lado de/junto a	across from	en frente de/frente a
straight ahead	derecho	turn (command)	doble
near (to)	cerca (de)	far (from)	lejos (de)
on top of/above	encima de/arriba	beneath/below	bajo de/abajo
traffic light	semáforo	corner	esquina
street	calle/avenida	block	cuadra

GETTING AROUND

ENGLISH	SPANISH	ENGLISH	SPANISH
How can you get to...?	¿Cómo se puede llegar a...?	Is there anything cheaper?	¿Hay algo más barato/económico?
Does this bus go to (Grecia)?	¿Va este autobús a (Grecia)?	On foot.	A pie.
Where is (Mackenna) street?	¿Dónde está la calle (Mackenna)?	What bus line goes to..?	¿Qué línea de buses tiene servicio a...?
When does the bus leave?	¿Cuándo sale el bús?	Where does the bus leave from?	¿De dónde sale el bús?
I'm getting off at...	Bajo en...	I have to go now.	Tengo que ir ahora.
Can I buy a ticket?	¿Podría comprar un boleto?	How far/near is...?	¿Qué tan lejos/cerca está...?
How long does the trip take?	¿Cuántas horas dura el viaje?	Continue forward.	Siga derecho.
I am going to the airport.	Voy al aeropuerto.	The flight is delayed/cancelled.	El vuelo está atrasado/cancelado.
Where is the bathroom?	¿Dónde está el baño?	Is it safe to hitchhike?	¿Es seguro pedir aventón?
I lost my baggage.	Perdí mi equipaje.	I'm lost.	Estoy perdido(a).
I would like to rent (a car).	Quisiera alquilar (un coche).	Please let me off at the zoo.	Por favor, déjeme en el zoológico.
How much does it cost per day/week?	¿Cuánto cuesta por día/semana?	Does it have (heating/air-conditioning)?	¿Tiene (calefacción/aire acondicionado)?
Where can I buy a cell-phone?	¿Dónde puedo comprar un teléfono celular?	Where can I check email?	¿Dónde se puede chequear el email?
Could you tell me what time it is?	¿Podría decirme qué hora es?	Are there student dis-counts available?	¿Hay descuentos para estudiantes?
Can you take me to (the train station)?	¿Podría llevarme a (la estación de tren)?	How much does it cost per day/week?	¿Cuanto cuesta por día/semana?
Can you let me know when we get to...?	¿Me podría avisar cuando lleguemos a...?	Round-trip/one-way	Ida y vuelta/ida

ACCOMMODATIONS

ENGLISH	SPANISH	ENGLISH	SPANISH
Is there a cheap hotel around here?	¿Hay un hotel económico por aquí?	Are there rooms with windows?	¿Hay habitaciones con ventanas?
Do you have rooms available?	¿Tiene habitaciones libres?	I am going to stay for (four) days.	Me voy a quedar (cuatro) días.
I would like to reserve a room.	Quisiera reservar una habitación.	Are there cheaper rooms?	¿Hay habitaciones más baratas?
Can I see a room?	¿Podría ver una habit-ación?	Do they come with private baths?	¿Vienen con baño privado?
Do you have any singles/doubles?	¿Tiene habitaciones sencillas/dobles?	Is there hot water?	¿Hay agua caliente?
Does it have (heating/A/C)?	¿Tiene (calefacción/aire acondicionado)?	Who's there?	¿Quién es?
I need another key/towel/pillow.	Necesito otra llave/toalla/almohada.	My bedsheets are dirty.	Mis sábanas están sucias.
The shower/sink/toilet is broken.	La ducha/pila/el servicio no funciona.	I'll take it.	Lo tomo.
There are cockroaches in my room.	Hay cucarachas en mi habitación.	Dance, cockroaches, dance!	Bailen, cucarachas, bailen!

EMERGENCY

ENGLISH	SPANISH	ENGLISH	SPANISH
Help!	¡Socorro! ¡Ayúdeme!	Call the police!	¡Llame a la policía!
I am hurt.	Estoy herido(a).	Leave me alone!	¡Déjame en paz!

ENGLISH	SPANISH	ENGLISH	SPANISH
It's an emergency!	¡Es una emergencia!	They robbed me!	¡Me han robado!
Fire!	¡Fuego!/¡Incendio!	They went that way!	¡Fueron en esa dirección!
Call a clinic/ambulance/doctor/priest!	¡Llame a una clínica/una ambulancia/un médico/un padre!	I will only speak in the presence of a lawyer.	Sólo hablaré en presencia de un abogado(a).
I need to contact my embassy.	Necesito contactar mi embajada.	Don't touch me!	¡No me toque!

MEDICAL

ENGLISH	SPANISH	ENGLISH	SPANISH
I feel bad/better/fine/worse.	Me siento mal/mejor/bien/peor.	What is this medicine for?	¿Para qué es esta medicina?
I have a headache.	Tengo un dolor de cabeza.	Where is the nearest hospital/doctor?	¿Dónde está el hospital/doctor más cercano?
I'm sick/ill.	Estoy enfermo(a).	I have a stomach ache.	Me duele el estómago.
I'm allergic to...	Soy alérgico(a) a...	Here is my prescription.	Aquí está la receta médica.
I think I'm going to vomit.	Pienso que voy a vomitar.	I haven't been able to go to the bathroom in (four) days.	No he podido ir al baño en (cuatro) días.
I have a cold/a fever/diarrhea/nausea.	Tengo gripe/una calentura/diarrea/náusea.	Call a doctor, please.	Llame a un médico, por favor

INTERPERSONAL INTERACTIONS

ENGLISH	SPANISH	ENGLISH	SPANISH
What is your name?	¿Cómo se llama?	Do you come here often?	¿Viene aquí a menudo?
Pleased to meet you.	Encantado(a)/Mucho gusto.	How do you say...in Spanish/English?	¿Comó se dice...en español/inglés?
Where are you from?	¿De dónde es?	I'm (twenty) years old.	Tengo (veinte) años.
This is my first time in Costa Rica.	Esta es mi primera vez en Costa Rica.	I have a boyfriend/girlfriend/spouse.	Tengo novio/novia/esposo(a).
What a shame: you bought Lonely Planet!	¡Qué lástima: compraste Lonely Planet!	What does...mean?	¿Qué significa...?

OUTDOORS/RECREATION

ENGLISH	SPANISH	ENGLISH	SPANISH
Is it safe to swim here?	¿Es seguro nadar aquí?	Do you have sunscreen?	¿Tiene crema solar?
What time is high/low tide?	¿A qué hora es marea alta/baja?	Is there a strong current?	¿Hay una corriente fuerte?
A bee stung me.	Una abeja me picada.	Where can I rent a surfboard/snorkel/bike/tent?	¿Dónde puedo alquilar un planeador de mar/esnórkel/bicicleta/tienda de campaño.
Where is the trail?	¿Dónde está el rastro?	A snake bit me.	Una serpiente me mordió.
Do I need a guide?	¿Necesito una guí?	Can I camp here?	¿Puedo acampar aquí?

NUMBERS, DAYS, AND MONTHS

ENGLISH	SPANISH	ENGLISH	SPANISH	ENGLISH	SPANISH
0	cero	20	veinte	day before	anteayer
1	uno	21	veintiuno	weekend	fin de semana
2	dos	22	veintidos	morning	mañana
3	tres	30	treinta	afternoon	tarde
4	cuatro	40	cuarenta	night	noche
5	cinco	50	cincuenta	month	mes
6	seis	100	cien	year	año

APPENDIX

ENGLISH	SPANISH	ENGLISH	SPANISH	ENGLISH	SPANISH
7	siete	1000	un mil	early/late	temprano/tarde
8	ocho	1 million	un millón	January	enero
9	nueve	Sunday	domingo	February	febrero
10	diez	Monday	lunes	March	marzo
11	once	Tuesday	martes	April	abril
12	doce	Wednesday	miércoles	May	mayo
13	trece	Thursday	jueves	June	junio
14	catorce	Friday	viernes	July	julio
15	quince	Saturday	sábado	August	agosto
16	dieciseis	today	hoy	September	septiembre
17	diecisiete	tomorrow	mañana	October	octubre
18	dieciocho	day after tomorrow	pasado mañana	November	noviembre
19	ciecinueve	yesterday	ayer	December	diciembre

EATING OUT

ENGLISH	SPANISH	ENGLISH	SPANISH
breakfast	desayuno	Do you have anything vegetarian/without meat?	¿Hay algún plato vegetariano/sin carne?
lunch	almuerzo	I would like to order (the eel).	Quisiera (el congrio).
dinner	comida/cena	This is too spicy.	Es demasiado pica.
dessert	postre	Can I see the menu?	¿Podría ver la carta/el menú?
drink (alcoholic)	bebida (trago)	Where is a good restaurant?	¿Dónde está un restaurante bueno?
spoon	cuchara	Do you have hot sauce?	¿Tiene salsa picante?
cup	copa/taza	Table for (one), please.	Mesa para (uno), por favor.
knife	cuchillo	Do you take credit cards?	¿Aceptan tarjetas de crédito?
fork	tenedor	Disgusting!	¡Guácala!/¡Que asco!
napkin	servilleta	Delicious!	¡Qué rico!
bon appétit	buen provecho	Check, please.	¡La cuenta, por favor!

MENU READER

SPANISH	ENGLISH	SPANISH	ENGLISH
a la plancha	grilled	legumbres	vegetables/legumes
al vapor	steamed	lima	lime
aceite	oil	limón	lemon
aceituna	olive	limonada	lemonade
agua (purificada)	water (purified)	locos	abalone (white fish)
ajo	garlic	lomo	steak or chop
almeja	clam	macedonia	syrupy dessert
arroz	rice	maíz	corn
bistec	beefsteak	mariscos	seafood
café	coffee	miel	honey
caliente	hot	naranja	orange
camarones	shrimp	nata	cream
carne	meat	pan	bread
cebolla	onion	paps	potatoes
cerveza	beer	papas fritas	french fries
chorizo	spicy sausage	parrillas	various grilled meats
coco	coconut	pasteles	desserts/pies
congrio	eel	pescado	fish

SPANISH	ENGLISH	SPANISH	ENGLISH
cordero	lamb	pimienta	pepper
dulces	sweets	plato	plate
dulce de leche	caramelized milk	pollo	chicken
gallo pinto	fried rice and beans cooked with spices	puerco	pork
ensalada	salad	queso	cheese
entrada	appetizer	sal	salt
gaseosa	soda	sopa	soup
kuchen	pastry with fruit	tragos	mixed drinks/liquor
leche	milk	wino tinto/blanco	red wine/white

SPANISH GLOSSARY

aduana: customs

agencia de viaje: travel agency

aguardiente: strong liquor

aguas termales: hot springs

ahora: now

ahorita: "now in just a little bit," which can mean anything from 5min. to 5hr.

aire acondicionado: air-conditioned (A/C)

al gusto: as you wish

alemán: German

almacén: (grocery) store

almuerzo: lunch, midday meal

alpaca: shaggy-haired, long-necked animal in the cameloid family

altiplano: highland

amigo/a: friend

andén: platform

anexo: neighborhood

arroz: rice

arroz chaufa: Chinese-style fried rice

artesanía: arts and crafts

avenida: avenue

bahía: bay

bandido: bandit

baño: bathroom or natural spa

barato/a: cheap

barranca: canyon

barro: mud

barrio: neighborhood

biblioteca: library

bistec/bistek: beefsteak

bocaditos: bar appetizers

bodega: convenience store or winery

boletería: ticket counter

bonito/a: pretty/beautiful

borracho/a: drunk

bosque: forest

botica: drugstore

bueno/a: good

buena suerte: good luck

buen provecho: bon appétit

burro: donkey

caballero: gentleman

caballo: horse

cabiñas: cabins

cajeros: cashiers

cajeros automáticos: ATMs

caldera: coffee or tea pot

caldo: soup, broth, or stew

calle: street

cama: bed

cambio: change

caminata: hike

camino: path, track, road

camión: truck

camioneta: small, pickup-sized truck

campamento: campground

campesino/a: person from a rural area, peasant

campo: countryside

canotaje: rafting

cantina: drinking establishment, usually male-dominated

capilla: chapel

caro/a: expensive

carretera: highway

carro: car, or sometimes a train car

casa: house

casa de cambio: currency exchange establishment

casado/a: married

cascadas: waterfalls

casona: mansion

catedral: cathedral

centro: city center

cerca: near/nearby

cerro: hill

cerveza: beer

ceviche: raw fish marinated in lemon juice, herbs, and veggies

chico/a: boy/girl, little

chicharrón: bite-sized pieces of fried meat, usually pork

cigarillo: cigarette

cine: cinema

ciudad: city

ciudadela: neighborhood in a large city

coche: car

colectivo: shared taxi

coliseo: coliseum/stadium

comedor: dining room

comida típica: typical/traditional dishes

con: with

consulado: consulate

correo: post office

cordillera: mountain range

crucero: crossroads

Cruz Roja: Red Cross

cuadra: street block

cuarto: room

cuenta: bill/check

cuento: story/account

cueva: cave

curandero: healer
damas: ladies
desayuno: breakfast
descompuesto: broken, out of order; spoiled/rotten food
desierto: desert
despacio: slow
de turno: 24hr. rotating schedule for pharmacies
dinero: money
discoteca: dance club
dueño/a: owner
edificio: building
embajada: embassy
embarcadero: dock
emergencia: emergency
encomiendas: estates granted to Spanish settlers in Latin America
entrada: entrance
estadio: stadium
este: east
estrella: star
extranjero: foreign/foreigner
farmacia en turno: 24hr. pharmacy
feliz: happy
ferrocarril: railroad
fiesta: party, holiday
finca: plantation-like agricultural enterprise or a ranch
friajes: sudden cold winds
frijoles: beans
frontera: border
fumar: to smoke
fumaroles: hole in a volcanic region which emits hot vapors
fundo: large estate or tract of land
fútbol: soccer
ganga: bargain
gobierno: government
gordo/a: fat
gorra: cap
gratis: free
gringo/a: North American
guanaco: animal in the cameloid family
habitación: a room
hacer una caminata: take a hike

hacienda: ranch
helado: ice cream
hermano/a: brother/sister
hervido/a: boiled
hielo: ice
hijo/a: son/daughter
hombre: man
iglesia: church
impuestos: taxes
impuesto valor añadido (IVA): value added tax (VAT)
indígena: indigenous, refers to the native population
isla: island
jarra: 1L pitcher of beer
jirón: street
jugo: juice
ladrón: thief
lago/laguna: lake
lancha: small boat
langosta: lobster
larga distancia: long distance
lavandería: laundromat
lejos: far
lente: slow
librería: bookstore
loma: hill
madre: mother
malo/a: bad
malecón: pier or seaside thoroughfare
maletas: luggage, suitcases
maneje despacio: drive slowly
manjar blanco: a whole-milk caramel spread
mar: sea
matas: shrubs, jungle brush
matrimonial: double bed
menestras: lentils/beans, or bean stew
mercado: market
merienda: snack
mestizaje: crossing of races
mestizo/a: person of mixed European and indigenous descent
microbus: local bus
mirador: observatory or look-out point
muelle: wharf

muerte: death
museo: museum
música folklórica: folk music
nada: nothing
niño/a: child
norte: north
obra: work of art/play
obraje: primitive textile workshop
oeste: west
oficina de turismo: tourist office
padre: father
pampa: a plain (geographical)
pan: bread
panadería: bakery
panga: motorboat
parada: stop (on a bus or train)
parilla: various cuts of meat, grilled
paro: labor strike
parroquia: parish
paseo turístico: tour covering a series of sites
payaso: clown
pelea de gallos: cockfighting
peligroso/a: dangerous
peninsulares: Spanish-born colonists
peña: folkl music club
pescado: fish
picante: spicy
pisa de uvas: grape-stomping
playa: beach
población: population, settlement
policía: police
pollo a la brasa: roasted chicken
pueblito: small town
pueblo: town
puente: bridge
puerta: door
puerto: port
rana: frog
recreo: place of amusement, restaurant/bar on the outskirts of a city
refrescos: refreshments, soft drinks
reloj: watch, clock
río: river

ropa: clothes
sábanas: bedsheets
sabor: flavor
sala: living room
salida: exit
salto: waterfall
salsa: sauce (can be of many varieties)
seguro/a: lock, insurance; adj.: safe
semáforo: traffic light
semana: week
Semana Santa: Holy Week
sexo: sex

shaman/chaman: spiritual healer
SIDA: Spanish acronym for AIDS
siesta: mid-afternoon nap; businesses often close at this time
sol: sun
solito/a: alone
solo/a: alone
solo carril: one-lane road or bridge
soltero/a: single (unmarried)
supermercado: supermarket
sur: south

tarifa: fee
telenovela: soap opera
termas: hot mineral springs
terminal terrestre: bus station
tienda: store
tipo de cambio: exchange rate
trago: mixed drink/shot of alcohol
triste: sad
trucha: trout
turismo: tourism
turista: tourist
valle: valley
volcán: volcano
zona: zone

TICO TALK: COSTA RICAN LANGUAGE QUIRKS

¡OJO! Recognizing, and in some cases, using local colloquialisms are often great ways to build a cultural bridge and befriend the *ticos* you encounter on the road. A few warnings: Politeness is important in Costa Rican culture, so refrain from using any of this slang in formal or business settings, or when interacting with people of authority or respect (including elders). Practice discretion and caution when using certain negative words; they are more for understanding situations and surroundings rather than for actual usage.

agüevarse: to become sad, bored
al dele: upright
almadiada: slightly drunk
anticos: before
apretaera: black ant
armarse la gorda:, brawl
bañazo: something or someone ridiculous or embarrassing
birra: beer
bostezo: something or someone that is boring
buena nota: someone who is nice, pleasant
buseta: a bus used for public transportation
cabanga: sadness from missing someone; sometimes used to describe homesickness
cachos: shoes
cálamo: smart
cañas: *colónes* (Costa Rican currency)

casado: Costa Rican lunch that usually includes rice and beans, a steak, two eggs, and plantains
chao: goodbye (from Italian "ciao")
chapón: simpleton
chapulín: young thief
chavalo: young boy, guy
Chepe: Costa Rica's capital, San José
chiva, chivísima: expression used among youths that denotes liking
ponerse chiva: to get mad
con toda la pata: 1) satisfied, 2) very good, 3) in a good state of health
corrongo: funny, pretty
dicha: luck
diez con hueco: deception (allusion to a perforated coin with no value)
dolor de huevos: 1) someone who is vain

or presumptuous, 2) a tedious chore or activity
echar(le) un ojo (a algo): to observe, guard
filo: hunger
fregar: to bother, annoy
gato: 1) person with green or blue eyes, 2) someone who's talented at something
guachimán: guardian, generally the person who takes care of cars parked on the street
guacho: watch
guachos: eyes
lo estoy guachando: I am watching/supervising it
guaro: liquor made from sugar cane (Costa Rican national drink); by extension, any alcoholic beverage, liquor

güeiso: 1) something ugly, bad, 2) when you are left alone

güila: young boy/girl

hablar paja: to speak trivialities, say nothing of importance

hablar (hasta) por los codos: to speak too much, to chatter

harina: money, "dough"

jacha: face

jalar: to be boyfriend and girlfriend

joder: to bother, annoy, drive someone crazy

jupa: head

jupón: stubborn person

lata: bus

lavado: without money

ligar: to flirt, to seek someone's company with romantic/emotional intentions

limpio: with no money

macho, machito: someone with light-colored skin and hair

mae/maje: used among young people to address each other

mariconera: man purse

media teja: 50 *colón* bill

mejenga: pick-up or neighborhood soccer match; depreciative when a professional team does not show much talent on the field

menear: to "shake it," dance

menudo: bunch of coins

montado: self seeking, a person who takes advantage of others (v.: montarse)

mosca/mosquita muerta: person that feigns innocence or weakness

mota: marijuana

ni papa: nothing

¡ojo!: Watch out!

pa'l tigre: to feel or be bad for some reason; opposite of "pura vida"

pachanga: celebration

pacho: comical situation

paja: trivialities

palmar: to die

pelada: embarrassing, to do something wrong

pendejo: strong term for fearful, dumb, or incompetent at certain things

pinche: greedy, stingy, avaricious

plata: money

playo: homosexual

ponerse las pilas: 1) to hurry, do something with more effort or will, 2) to become ready, attentive

porfa: please (abbreviated form of "por favor")

pringa pie: diarrhea

¡pura vida!: expression of satisfaction

quitarse: to go back on something previously said or agreed upon

rajón: presumptuous (v.: rajar)

rata: thief

un rico: good-looking, attractive man

una rica: good-looking, attractive, sexy woman.

rojo, rojito: 1) 1000 *colón* bill, 2) taxi

rulear: to sleep

salado: without luck

sobre: bed

soplado: very quick

¡suave!: expression used to ask someone to wait or stop

tanate: a lot

tatas: parents

teja: 100 *colón* bill

teresa: euphemistic word for breast

tigra: bored

tombo: policeman

torta: problem

tortillera: lesbian

troliar: to walk

tuanis: good, wonderful

tucán: 5000 *colón* bill

turno: party, specific fair of some community

la U: the University

¡upe!: expression used in place of knocking at the door

vacilón: fun, comical, entertaining

verde: someone who studies a lot or is very responsible with his/her studie

volado: crazy

vuelto: change (of money) when buying something

wuata (güater): water

¿Y diay?: What's up? What happened? How have you been? What's wrong?

INDEX

Index

INDEX

READY. SET.

LET'S GO

www.letsgo.com

THE STUDENT TRAVEL GUIDE

MAP INDEX

MAP LEGEND

■ Point of Interest	➕ Hospital/Clinic	Building	⌢ Picnic Area	**ABBREVIATIONS:**
🏨 Hotel/Hostel	Police	Park: city, other	🏊 Beach	Lg. Laguna, Lago
🏕 Camping	✉ Post Office	Plaza/other area	⊙ Thermal Bath	M.N. Monumento Nacional
🍴 Food	ⓘ Tourist Information	Beach	◠ Cave	PL. Plaza
🍸 Nightlife	℞ Pharmacy	Water	∫ Waterfall	Pq. Parque
🏛 Museum	Embassy/Consulate	Mangroves	▲ Peak	P.I. Parque Internacional
✝ Church	☎ Telephone Office	Swamp	Mountain Range	P.N. Parque Nacional
✡ Synagogue	✈ Airport	Pedestrian Zone	▲ Ranger Station	Q. Quebrada
🎭 Theater	🚌 Bus Station	Steps	▲ Archaeological Site	R. Río
💻 Internet Café	🚂 Train Station	Trail	✝ Monastery	R.B. Reserva Biológica
$ Bank	⚓ Ferry Landing	Ferry Route	Border Crossing	R.E. Reserva Ecológica

ABBREVIATIONS:
Lg. Laguna, Lago
M.N. Monumento Nacional
PL. Plaza
Pq. Parque
P.I. Parque Internacional
P.N. Parque Nacional
Q. Quebrada
R. Río
R.B. Reserva Biológica
R.E. Reserva Ecológica
R.F. Reserva Forestal
R.F.S. Refugio de Fauna Silvestre
R.I. Reserva Internacional
R.S. Refugio Silvestre
R.V.S. Refugio de Vida Silvestre

The Let's Go compass always points NORTH.

Maps by Let's Go copyright © 2010 by Let's Go, Inc.

Distributed by Publishers Group West.
Printed in Canada by Friesens Corp.

ISBN-13: 978-1-59880-315-0
ISBN-10:1-59880-315-8
Fifth edition
10 9 8 7 6 5 4 3 2 1

Let's Go Costa Rica is written by Let's Go Publications, 67 Mount Auburn St., Cambridge, MA 02138, USA.

Let's Go® and the LG logo are trademarks of Let's Go, Inc.